*Oracle Press*™

Oracle Database 11*g* SQL

Oracle Database 11g SQL

Jason Price

New York   Chicago   San Francisco
Lisbon   London   Madrid   Mexico City   Milan
New Delhi   San Juan   Seoul   Singapore   Sydney   Toronto

The McGraw·Hill Companies

Library of Congress Cataloging-in-Publication Data

Price, Jason.
  Oracle database 11g SQL/Jason Price.
      p. cm.
  ISBN 0-07-149850-8 (alk. paper)
  1. Oracle (Computer file) 2. SQL (Computer program language) I.
Title.
QA76.9.D3P729674 2007
005.13'3--dc22

2007044728

McGraw-Hill books are available at special quantity discounts to use as premiums and sales promotions, or for use in corporate training programs. For more information, please write to the Director of Special Sales, Professional Publishing, McGraw-Hill, Two Penn Plaza, New York, NY 10121-2298. Or contact your local bookstore.

Oracle Database 11*g* SQL

   34567890 FGR FGR 019

ISBN 978-0-07-149850-0
MHID   0-07-149850-8

Sponsoring Editor	**Proofreader**
Lisa McClain	Paul Tyler
Editorial Supervisor	**Indexer**
Patty Mon	Jack Lewis
Project Editor	**Production Supervisor**
Laura Stone	James Kussow
Acquisitions Coordinator	**Composition**
Mandy Canales	Apollo Publishing Services
Technical Editor	**Art Director, Cover**
Scott Mikolaitis	Jeff Weeks
Copy Editor	**Cover Designer**
Carl Wikander	Pattie Lee

**This book is dedicated to my family.
Even though you're far away, you are still in my heart.**

About the Author

Jason Price is a freelance consultant and former product manager of Oracle Corporation. He has contributed to many of Oracle's products, including the database, the application server, and several of the CRM applications. Jason is an Oracle Certified Database Administrator and Application Developer, and has more than 15 years of experience in the software industry. Jason has written many books on Oracle, Java, and .NET. Jason holds a Bachelor of Science degree (with honors) in physics from the University of Bristol, England.

About the Technical Editor

Scott Mikolaitis is an applications architect at Oracle Corporation and has worked at Oracle for over ten years. He performs prototyping and standards development for the SOA technology in Oracle Fusion. Scott also enjoys working with web services in Java as well as Jabber for human and system interaction patterns. He spends his spare time on DIY home improvement and gas-fueled RC cars.

Contents at a Glance

Contents

Acknowledgments

Thanks to the wonderful people at McGraw-Hill, including Lisa McClain, Mandy Canales, Carl Wikander, and Laura Stone. Thanks also to Scott Mikolaitis for his thorough technical review.

Introduction

oday's database management systems are accessed using a standard language known as *Structured Query Language*, or SQL. Among other things, SQL allows you to retrieve, add, update, and delete information in a database. In this book, you'll learn how to master SQL, and you'll find a wealth of practical examples. You can also get all the scripts and programs featured in this book online (see the last section, "Retrieving the Examples," for details).

With this book, you will

- Master standard SQL, as well as the extensions developed by Oracle Corporation for use with the specific features of the Oracle database.

- Explore PL/SQL (Procedural Language/SQL), which is built on top of SQL and enables you to write programs that contain SQL statements.

- Use SQL*Plus to execute SQL statements, scripts, and reports; SQL*Plus is a tool that allows you to interact with the database.

- Execute queries, inserts, updates, and deletes against a database.

- Create database tables, sequences, indexes, views, and users.

- Perform transactions containing multiple SQL statements.

- Define database object types and create object tables to handle advanced data.

- Use large objects to handle multimedia files containing images, music, and movies.

- Perform complex calculations using analytic functions.

- Use all the very latest Oracle Database 11*g* features such as PIVOT and UNPIVOT, flashback archives, and much more.

- Implement high-performance tuning techniques to make your SQL statements really fly.

- Write Java programs to access an Oracle database using JDBC.
- Explore the XML capabilities of the Oracle database.

This book contains 17 chapters and one appendix.

Chapter 1: Introduction

In this chapter, you'll learn about relational databases, be introduced to SQL, see a few simple queries, use SQL*Plus and SQL Developer to execute queries, and briefly see PL/SQL.

Chapter 2: Retrieving Information from Database Tables

You'll explore how to retrieve information from one or more database tables using SELECT statements, use arithmetic expressions to perform calculations, filter rows using a WHERE clause, and sort the rows retrieved from a table.

Chapter 3: Using SQL*Plus

In this chapter, you'll use SQL*Plus to view a table's structure, edit a SQL statement, save and run scripts, format column output, define and use variables, and create reports.

Chapter 4: Using Simple Functions

In this chapter, you'll learn about some of the Oracle database's built-in functions. A function can accept input parameters and returns an output parameter. Functions allow you to perform tasks such as computing averages and square roots of numbers.

Chapter 5: Storing and Processing Dates and Times

You'll learn how the Oracle database processes and stores dates and times, collectively known as datetimes. You'll also learn about timestamps that allow you to store a specific date and time, and time intervals that allow you to store a length of time.

Chapter 6: Subqueries

You'll learn how to place a SELECT statement within an outer SQL statement. The inner SELECT statement is known as a subquery. You'll learn about the different types of subqueries and see how subqueries allow you to build up very complex statements from simple components.

Chapter 7: Advanced Queries

In this chapter, you'll learn how to perform queries containing advanced operators and functions such as: set operators that combine rows returned by multiple queries, the TRANSLATE() function to convert characters in one string to characters in another string, the DECODE() function to search a set of values for a certain value, the CASE expression to perform if-then-else logic, and the ROLLUP and CUBE clauses to return rows containing subtotals. You'll learn about the analytic functions that enable you to perform complex calculations such as finding the top-selling product type for each month, the top salespersons, and so on. You'll see how to perform queries against data that is organized into a hierarchy. You'll also explore the MODEL clause, which performs inter-row calculations. Finally, you'll see the new Oracle Database 11*g* PIVOT and UNPIVOT clauses, which are useful for seeing overall trends in large amounts of data.

Chapter 8: Changing Table Contents

You'll learn how to add, modify, and remove rows using the INSERT, UPDATE, and DELETE statements, and how to make the results of your transactions permanent using the COMMIT statement or undo their results entirely using the ROLLBACK statement. You'll also learn how an Oracle database can process multiple transactions at the same time.

Chapter 9: Users, Privileges, and Roles

In this chapter, you'll learn about database users and see how privileges and roles are used to enable users to perform specific tasks in the database.

Chapter 10: Creating Tables, Sequences, Indexes, and Views

You'll learn about tables and sequences, which generate a series of numbers, and indexes, which act like an index in a book and allow you quick access to rows. You'll also learn about views, which are predefined queries on one or more tables; among other benefits, views allow you to hide complexity from a user, and implement another layer of security by only allowing a view to access a limited set of data in the tables. You'll also examine flashback data archives, which are new for Oracle Database 11*g*. A flashback data archive stores changes made to a table over a period of time.

Chapter 11: Introducing PL/SQL Programming

In this chapter, you'll explore PL/SQL, which is built on top of SQL and enables you to write stored programs in the database that contain SQL statements. PL/SQL contains standard programming constructs.

Chapter 12: Database Objects

You'll learn how to create database object types, which may contain attributes and methods. You'll use object types to define column objects and object tables, and see how to manipulate objects using SQL and PL/SQL.

Chapter 13: Collections

In this chapter, you'll learn how to create collection types, which may contain multiple elements. You'll use collection types to define columns in tables. You'll see how to manipulate collections using SQL and PL/SQL.

Chapter 14: Large Objects

You'll learn about large objects, which can be used to store up to 128 terabytes of character and binary data or point to an external file. You'll also learn about the older LONG types, which are still supported in Oracle Database 11*g* for backward compatibility.

Chapter 15: Running SQL Using Java

In this chapter, you'll learn the basics of running SQL using Java through the Java Database Connectivity (JDBC) applications programming interface, which is the glue that allows a Java program to access a database.

Chapter 16: SQL Tuning

You'll see SQL tuning tips that you can use to shorten the length of time your queries take to execute. You'll also learn about the Oracle optimizer and examine how to pass hints to the optimizer.

Chapter 17: XML and the Oracle Database

The Extensible Markup Language (XML) is a general-purpose markup language. XML enables you to share structured data across the Internet, and can be used to encode data and other documents. In this chapter, you'll see how to generate XML from relational data and how to save XML in the database.

Appendix: Oracle Data Types

This appendix shows the data types available in Oracle SQL and PL/SQL.

Intended Audience

This book is suitable for the following readers:

- Developers who need to write SQL and PL/SQL.

- Database administrators who need in-depth knowledge of SQL.

- Business users who need to write SQL queries to get information from their organization's database.

- Technical managers or consultants who need an introduction to SQL and PL/SQL.

No prior knowledge of the Oracle database, SQL, or PL/SQL is assumed; you can find everything you need to know to become a master in this book.

Retrieving the Examples

All the SQL scripts, programs, and other files used in this book can be downloaded from the Oracle Press website at www.OraclePressBooks.com. The files are contained in a Zip file. Once you've downloaded the Zip file, you need to extract its contents. This will create a directory named `sql_book` that contains the following subdirectories:

- **`Java`**   Contains the Java programs used in Chapter 15

- **`sample_files`**   Contains the sample files used in Chapter 14

- **`SQL`**   Contains the SQL scripts used throughout the book, including scripts to create and populate the example database tables

- **`xml_files`**   Contains the XML used in Chapter 17

I hope you enjoy this book!

CHAPTER

1

Introduction

n this chapter, you will learn about the following:

- Relational databases.

- The Structured Query Language (SQL), which is used to access a database.

- SQL*Plus, Oracle's interactive text-based tool for running SQL statements.

- SQL Developer, which is a graphical tool for database development.

- PL/SQL, Oracle's procedural programming language. PL/SQL allows you to develop programs that are stored in the database.

Let's plunge in and consider what a relational database is.

What Is a Relational Database?

The concept of a relational database was originally developed back in 1970 by Dr. E.F. Codd. He laid down the theory of relational databases in his seminal paper entitled "A Relational Model of Data for Large Shared Data Banks," published in *Communications of the ACM* (Association for Computing Machinery), Vol. 13, No. 6, June 1970.

The basic concepts of a relational database are fairly easy to understand. A *relational database* is a collection of related information that has been organized into *tables*. Each table stores data in *rows*; the data is arranged into *columns*. The tables are stored in database *schemas*, which are areas where users may store their own tables. A user may grant *permissions* to other users so they can access their tables.

Most of us are familiar with data being stored in tables—stock prices and train timetables are sometimes organized into tables. One example table used in this book records customer information for an imaginary store; the table stores the customer first names, last names, dates of birth (dobs), and phone numbers:

```
first_name last_name  dob         phone
---------- ---------- ----------- ------------
John       Brown      01-JAN-1965 800-555-1211
Cynthia    Green      05-FEB-1968 800-555-1212
Steve      White      16-MAR-1971 800-555-1213
Gail       Black                  800-555-1214
Doreen     Blue       20-MAY-1970
```

This table could be stored in a variety of forms:

- A card in a box

- An HTML file on a web page

- A table in a database

An important point to remember is that the information that makes up a database is different from the system used to access that information. The software used to access a database is known as a *database management system*. The Oracle database is one such piece of software; other examples include SQL Server, DB2, and MySQL.

Of course, every database must have some way to get data in and out of it, preferably using a common language understood by all databases. Database management systems implement a standard language known as *Structured Query Language*, or SQL. Among other things, SQL allows you to retrieve, add, modify, and delete information in a database.

Introducing the Structured Query Language (SQL)

Structured Query Language (SQL) is the standard language designed to access relational databases. SQL should be pronounced as the letters "S-Q-L."

NOTE
"S-Q-L" is the correct way to pronounce SQL according to the American National Standards Institute. However, the single word "sequel" is frequently used instead.

SQL is based on the groundbreaking work of Dr. E.F. Codd, with the first implementation of SQL being developed by IBM in the mid-1970s. IBM was conducting a research project known as System R, and SQL was born from that project. Later, in 1979, a company then known as Relational Software Inc. (known today as Oracle Corporation) released the first commercial version of SQL. SQL is now fully standardized and recognized by the American National Standards Institute.

SQL uses a simple syntax that is easy to learn and use. You'll see some simple examples of its use in this chapter. There are five types of SQL statements, outlined in the following list:

- **Query statements** retrieve rows stored in database tables. You write a query using the SQL SELECT statement.

- **Data Manipulation Language (DML) statements** modify the contents of tables. There are three DML statements:

  - **INSERT** adds rows to a table.

  - **UPDATE** changes rows.

  - **DELETE** removes rows.

- **Data Definition Language (DDL) statements** define the data structures, such as tables, that make up a database. There are five basic types of DDL statements:

  - **CREATE** creates a database structure. For example, CREATE TABLE is used to create a table; another example is CREATE USER, which is used to create a database user.

  - **ALTER** modifies a database structure. For example, ALTER TABLE is used to modify a table.

  - **DROP** removes a database structure. For example, DROP TABLE is used to remove a table.

  - **RENAME** changes the name of a table.

  - **TRUNCATE** deletes all the rows from a table.

- **Transaction Control (TC) statements** either permanently record any changes made to rows, or undo those changes. There are three TC statements:

  - **COMMIT** permanently records changes made to rows.

  - **ROLLBACK** undoes changes made to rows.

  - **SAVEPOINT** sets a "save point" to which you can roll back changes.

- **Data Control Language (DCL) statements** change the permissions on database structures. There are two DCL statements:

  - **GRANT** gives another user access to your database structures.

  - **REVOKE** prevents another user from accessing your database structures.

There are many ways to run SQL statements and get results back from the database, some of which include programs written using Oracle Forms and Reports. SQL statements may also be embedded within programs written in other languages, such as Oracle's Pro*C++, which allows you to add SQL statements to a C++ program. You can also add SQL statements to a Java program using JDBC; for more details, see my book *Oracle9i JDBC Programming* (Oracle Press, 2002).

Oracle also has a tool called SQL*Plus that allows you to enter SQL statements using the keyboard or to run a script containing SQL statements. SQL*Plus enables you to conduct a "conversation" with the database; you enter SQL statements and view the results returned by the database. You'll be introduced to SQL*Plus next.

Using SQL*Plus

If you're at all familiar with the Oracle database, chances are that you're already familiar with SQL*Plus. If you're not, don't worry: you'll learn how to use SQL*Plus in this book.

In the following sections, you'll learn how to start SQL*Plus and run a query.

Starting SQL*Plus

If you're using Windows XP Professional Edition and Oracle Database 11*g*, you can start SQL*Plus by clicking start and selecting All Programs | Oracle | Application Development | SQL Plus.

Figure 1-1 shows SQL*Plus running on Windows XP. SQL*Plus asks you for a username. Figure 1-1 shows the scott user connecting to the database (scott is an example user that is contained in many Oracle databases; scott has a default password of tiger). The host string after the @ character tells SQL*Plus where the database is running. If you are running the database on your own computer, you'll typically omit the host string (that is, you enter scott/tiger)—doing this causes SQL*Plus to attempt to connect to a database on the same machine on which SQL*Plus is running. If the database isn't running on your machine, you should speak with your database administrator (DBA) to get the host string. If the scott user doesn't exist or is locked, ask your DBA for an alternative user and password (for the examples in the first part of this chapter, you can use any user; you don't absolutely have to use the scott user).

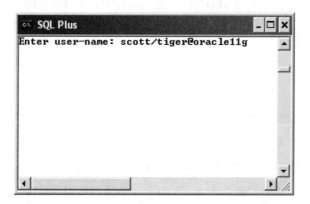

FIGURE 1-1   *Oracle Database 11g SQL*Plus Running on Windows XP*

If you're using Windows XP and Oracle Database 10g or below, you can run a special Windows-only version of SQL*Plus. You start this version of SQL*Plus by clicking Start and selecting All Programs | Oracle | Application Development | SQL Plus. The Windows-only version of SQL*Plus is deprecated in Oracle Database 11g (that is, it doesn't ship with 11g), but it will still connect to an 11g database. Figure 1-2 shows the Windows-only version of Oracle Database 10g SQL*Plus running on Windows XP.

NOTE
The Oracle Database 11g version of SQL*Plus is slightly nicer than the Windows-only version. In the 11g version, you can scroll through previous commands you've run by pressing the UP and DOWN ARROW keys on the keyboard.

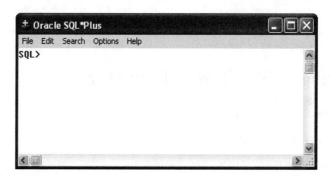

FIGURE 1-2   *Oracle Database 10g SQL*Plus Running on Windows XP*

Starting SQL*Plus from the Command Line

You can also start SQL*Plus from the command line. To do this, you use the `sqlplus` command. The full syntax for the `sqlplus` command is

```
sqlplus [user_name[/password[@host_string]]]
```

where

- *user_name* is the name of the database user.

- *password* is the password for the database user.

- *host_string* is the database you want to connect to.

The following examples show `sqlplus` commands:

```
sqlplus scott/tiger
sqlplus scott/tiger@orcl
```

If you're using SQL*Plus with a Windows operating system, the Oracle installer automatically adds the directory for SQL*Plus to your path. If you're using a non-Windows operating system (for example, Unix or Linux), either you must be in the same directory as the SQL*Plus program to run it or, better still, you should add the directory to your path. If you need help with that, talk to your system administrator.

For security, you can hide the password when connecting to the database. For example, you can enter

```
sqlplus scott@orcl
```

SQL*Plus then prompts you to enter the password. As you type in the password, it is hidden from prying eyes. This also works when starting SQL*Plus in Windows.

You can also just enter

```
sqlplus
```

SQL*Plus then prompts you for the user name and password. You can specify the host string by adding it to the user name (for example, `scott@orcl`).

Performing a SELECT Statement Using SQL*Plus

Once you're logged onto the database using SQL*Plus, go ahead and run the following SELECT statement (it returns the current date):

```
SELECT SYSDATE FROM dual;
```

SYSDATE is a built-in database function that returns the current date, and the `dual` table is a table that contains a single row. The `dual` table is useful when you need the database to evaluate an expression (e.g., 2 * 15 / 5), or when you want to get the current date.

NOTE
*SQL statements directly entered into SQL*Plus are terminated using a semicolon character (;).*

This illustration shows the results of this SELECT statement in SQL*Plus running on Windows. As you can see, the query displays the current date from the database.

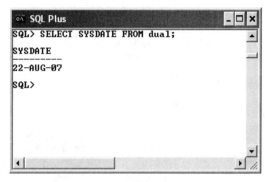

You can edit your last SQL statement in SQL*Plus by entering EDIT. Doing this is useful when you make a mistake or you want to make a change to your SQL statement. On Windows, when you enter EDIT you are taken to the Notepad application; you then use Notepad to edit your SQL statement. When you exit Notepad and save your statement, the new statement is passed back to SQL*Plus, where you can re-execute it by entering a forward slash (/). On Linux or Unix, the default editor is typically set to vi or emacs.

NOTE
*You'll learn more about editing SQL statements using SQL*Plus in Chapter 3.*

SQL Developer

You can also enter SQL statements using SQL Developer. SQL Developer uses a very nice graphical user interface through which you can enter SQL statements, examine database tables, run scripts, edit and debug PL/SQL code, and much more. SQL Developer can connect to any Oracle Database, version 9.2.0.1 and higher, and runs on Windows, Linux, and Mac OSX. The following illustration shows SQL Developer running.

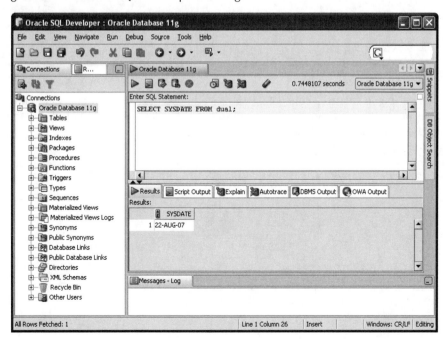

You need to have Java installed on your computer before you can run SQL Developer. If you're using Windows XP Professional Edition and Oracle Database 11*g*, you start SQL Developer by clicking Start and selecting All Programs | Oracle | Application Development | SQL Developer. SQL Developer will prompt you to select the Java executable. You then browse to the location where you have installed it and select the executable. Next, you need to create a connection by right-clicking Connections and selecting New Connection, as shown in the following illustration.

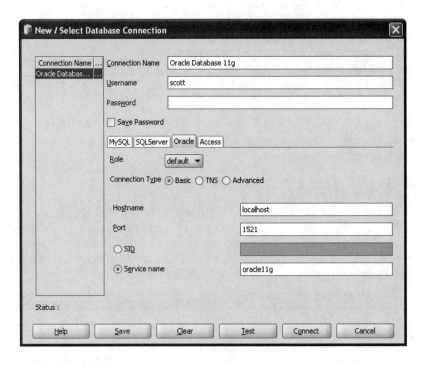

Once you've created a connection and tested it, you can use it to connect to the database and run queries, examine database tables, and so on. The following illustration shows the details for a database table named `customers`.

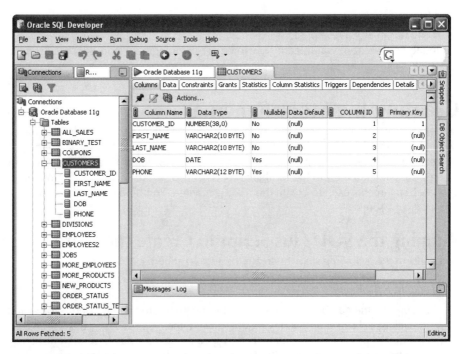

You can also view the data stored in a table, as shown in the following illustration.

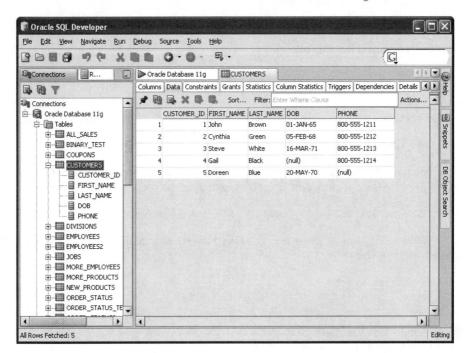

You can see full details on using SQL Developer by selecting Help | Table of Contents from the menu bar in SQL Developer.

In the next section, you'll learn how to create the imaginary store schema used throughout this book.

Creating the Store Schema

The imaginary store sells items such as books, videos, DVDs, and CDs. The database for the store will hold information about the customers, employees, products, and sales. The SQL*Plus script to create the database is named `store_schema.sql`, which is located in the `SQL` directory where you extracted the Zip file for this book. The `store_schema.sql` script contains the DDL and DML statements used to create the `store` schema. You'll now learn how to run the `store_schema.sql` script.

Running the SQL*Plus Script to Create the Store Schema

You perform the following steps to create the `store` schema:

1. Start SQL*Plus.

2. Log into the database as a user with privileges to create new users, tables, and PL/SQL packages. I run scripts in my database using the `system` user; this user has all the required privileges. You may need to speak with your database administrator about setting up a user for you with the required privileges (they might also run the `store_schema.sql` script for you).

3. Run the `store_schema.sql` script from within SQL*Plus using the @ command.

The @ command has the following syntax:

```
@ directory\store_schema.sql
```

where `directory` is the directory where your `store_schema.sql` script is located.
For example, if the script is stored in `E:\sql_book\SQL`, then you enter

```
@ E:\sql_book\SQL\store_schema.sql
```

If you have placed the `store_schema.sql` script in a directory that contains spaces, then you must place the directory and script in quotes after the @ command. For example:

```
@ "E:\Oracle SQL book\sql_book\SQL\store_schema.sql"
```

If you're using Unix or Linux and you saved the script in a directory named `SQL` in the `tmp` file system, then you enter

```
@ /tmp/SQL/store_schema.sql
```

NOTE
Windows uses backslash characters (\) in directory paths, whereas Unix and Linux use forward slash characters (/).

The first executable line in the `store_schema.sql` script attempts to drop the `store` user, generating an error because the user doesn't exist yet. Don't worry about the error: the line is there so you don't have to manually drop the `store` user when recreating the schema later in the book.

When the `store_schema.sql` script has finished running, you'll be connected as the `store` user. If you want to, open the `store_schema.sql` script using a text editor like Windows Notepad and examine the statements contained in it. Don't worry about the details of the statements contained in the script—you'll learn the details as you progress through this book.

NOTE
To end SQL*Plus, you enter `EXIT`. *To reconnect to the* `store` *schema in SQL*Plus, you enter* `store` *as the user name with a password of* `store_password`. *While you're connected to the database, SQL*Plus maintains a database session for you. When you disconnect from the database, your session is ended. You can disconnect from the database and keep SQL*Plus running by entering* `DISCONNECT`. *You can then reconnect to a database by entering* `CONNECT`.

Data Definition Language (DDL) Statements Used to Create the Store Schema

As mentioned earlier, Data Definition Language (DDL) statements are used to create users and tables, plus many other types of structures in the database. In this section, you'll see the DDL statements used to create the `store` user and some of the tables.

NOTE
The SQL statements you'll see in the rest of this chapter are the same as those contained in the `store_schema.sql` *script. You don't have to type the statements in yourself: you just run the* `store_schema` `.sql` *script.*

The next sections describe the following:

- How to create a database user

- The commonly used data types used in an Oracle database

- Some of the tables in the imaginary store

Creating a Database User

To create a user in the database, you use the `CREATE USER` statement. The simplified syntax for the `CREATE USER` statement is as follows:

```
CREATE USER user_name IDENTIFIED BY password;
```

where

- *`user_name`* is the user name

- *`password`* is the password for the user

For example, the following CREATE USER statement creates the store user with a password of store_password:

```
CREATE USER store IDENTIFIED BY store_password;
```

If you want the user to be able to work in the database, the user must be granted the necessary *permissions* to do that work. In the case of store, this user must be able to log onto the database (which requires the connect permission) and create items like database tables (which requires the resource permission). Permissions are granted by a privileged user (for example, the system user) using the GRANT statement.

The following example grants the connect and resource permissions to store:

```
GRANT connect, resource TO store;
```

Once a user has been created, the database tables and other database objects can be created in the associated schema for that user. Many of the examples in this book use the store schema. Before I get into the details of the store tables, you need to know about the commonly used Oracle database types.

The Common Oracle Database Types

There are many types that may be used to handle data in an Oracle database. Some of the commonly used types are shown in Table 1-1.

You can see all the data types in the appendix. The following table illustrates a few examples of how numbers of type NUMBER are stored in the database.

Format	Number Supplied	Number Stored
NUMBER	1234.567	1234.567
NUMBER(6, 2)	123.4567	123.46
NUMBER(6, 2)	12345.67	Number exceeds the specified precision and is therefore rejected by the database.

Examining the Store Tables

In this section, you'll learn how the tables for the store schema are created. Some of the information held in the store schema includes

- Customer details

- Types of products sold

- Product details

- A history of the products purchased by the customers

- Employees of the store

- Salary grades

The following tables are used to hold the information:

- **customers** holds the customer details.

- **product_types** holds the types of products sold by the store.

- **products** holds the product details.

- **purchases** holds which products were purchased by which customers.

- **employees** holds the employee details.

- **salary_grades** holds the salary grade details.

Oracle Type	Meaning
CHAR(*length*)	Stores strings of a fixed length. The *length* parameter specifies the length of the string. If a string of a smaller length is stored, it is padded with spaces at the end. For example, CHAR(2) may be used to store a fixed-length string of two characters; if 'C' is stored in a CHAR(2), then a single space is added at the end; 'CA' is stored as is, with no padding.
VARCHAR2(*length*)	Stores strings of a variable length. The *length* parameter specifies the maximum length of the string. For example, VARCHAR2(20) may be used to store a string of up to 20 characters in length. No padding is used at the end of a smaller string.
DATE	Stores dates and times. The DATE type stores the century, all four digits of a year, the month, the day, the hour (in 24-hour format), the minute, and the second. The DATE type may be used to store dates and times between January 1, 4712 B.C. and December 31, 4712 A.D.
INTEGER	Stores integers. An integer doesn't contain a floating point: it is a whole number, such as 1, 10, and 115.
NUMBER(*precision, scale*)	Stores floating point numbers, but may also be used to store integers. The *precision* is the maximum number of digits (left and right of a decimal point, if used) that may be used for the number. The maximum precision supported by the Oracle database is 38. The *scale* is the maximum number of digits to the right of a decimal point (if used). If neither *precision* nor *scale* is specified, any number may be stored up to a precision of 38 digits. Any attempt to store a number that exceeds the *precision* is rejected by the database.
BINARY_FLOAT	Introduced in Oracle Database 10g, stores a single precision 32-bit floating point number. You'll learn more about BINARY_ FLOAT later in the section "The BINARY_FLOAT and BINARY_ DOUBLE Types."
BINARY_DOUBLE	Introduced in Oracle Database 10g, stores a double precision 64-bit floating point number. You'll learn more about BINARY_ DOUBLE later in the section "The BINARY_FLOAT and BINARY_ DOUBLE Types."

TABLE 1-1   *Commonly Used Oracle Data Types*

NOTE
The `store_schema.sql` *script creates other tables and database
items not mentioned in the previous list. You'll learn about these items
in later chapters.*

In the following sections, you'll see the details of some of the tables, and you'll see the
`CREATE TABLE` statements included in the `store_schema.sql` script that create the tables.

The customers Table   The `customers` table holds the details of the customers. The
following items are held in this table:

- First name

- Last name

- Date of birth (dob)

- Phone number

Each of these items requires a column in the `customers` table. The `customers` table is
created by the `store_schema.sql` script using the following `CREATE TABLE` statement:

```
CREATE TABLE customers (
  customer_id INTEGER CONSTRAINT customers_pk PRIMARY KEY,
  first_name VARCHAR2(10) NOT NULL,
  last_name VARCHAR2(10) NOT NULL,
  dob DATE,
  phone VARCHAR2(12)
);
```

As you can see, the `customers` table contains five columns, one for each item in the
previous list, and an extra column named `customer_id`. The columns are

- **`customer_id`**   Contains a unique integer for each row in the table. Each table should
  have one or more columns that uniquely identifies each row; the column(s) are known as
  the *primary key*. The `CONSTRAINT` clause indicates that the `customer_id` column is the
  primary key. A `CONSTRAINT` clause restricts the values stored in a column, and, for the
  `customer_id` column, the `PRIMARY KEY` keywords indicate that the `customer_id`
  column must contain a unique value for each row. You can also attach an optional
  name to a constraint, which must immediately follow the `CONSTRAINT` keyword—for
  example, `customers_pk`. You should always name your primary key constraints, so
  that when a constraint error occurs it is easy to spot where it happened.

- **`first_name`**   Contains the first name of the customer. You'll notice the use of the `NOT`
  `NULL` constraint for this column—this means that a value must be supplied for `first_`
  `name` when adding or modifying a row. If a `NOT NULL` constraint is omitted, a user
  doesn't need to supply a value and the column can remain empty.

- **last_name** Contains the last name of the customer. This column is NOT NULL, and therefore a value must be supplied when adding or modifying a row.

- **dob** Contains the date of birth for the customer. Notice that no NOT NULL constraint is specified for this column; therefore, the default NULL is assumed, and a value is optional when adding or modifying a row.

- **phone** Contains the phone number of the customer. This is an optional value.

The store_schema.sql script populates the customers table with the following rows:

```
customer_id first_name last_name  dob       phone
----------- ---------- ---------- --------- ------------
          1 John       Brown      01-JAN-65 800-555-1211
          2 Cynthia    Green      05-FEB-68 800-555-1212
          3 Steve      White      16-MAR-71 800-555-1213
          4 Gail       Black                800-555-1214
          5 Doreen     Blue       20-MAY-70
```

Notice that customer #4's date of birth is null, as is customer #5's phone number.

You can see the rows in the customers table for yourself by executing the following SELECT statement using SQL*Plus:

SELECT * FROM customers;

The asterisk (*) indicates that you want to retrieve all the columns from the customers table.

> **NOTE**
> *In this book, SQL statements shown in* **bold** *are statements you should type in and run if you want to follow along with the examples. Non-bold statements are statements you don't need to type in.*

The product_types Table The product_types table holds the names of the product types sold by the store. This table is created by the store_schema.sql script using the following CREATE TABLE statement:

```
CREATE TABLE product_types (
  product_type_id INTEGER CONSTRAINT product_types_pk PRIMARY KEY,
  name VARCHAR2(10) NOT NULL
);
```

The product_types table contains the following two columns:

- **product_type_id** uniquely identifies each row in the table; the product_type_id column is the primary key for this table. Each row in the product_types table must have a unique integer value for the product_type_id column.

- **name** contains the product type name. It is a NOT NULL column, and therefore a value must be supplied when adding or modifying a row.

The `store_schema.sql` script populates the `product_types` table with the following rows:

```
product_type_id name
--------------- -----------
              1 Book
              2 Video
              3 DVD
              4 CD
              5 Magazine
```

The `product_types` table contains the product types for the store. Each product sold by the store must be one of these types.

You can see the rows in the `product_types` table for yourself by executing the following `SELECT` statement using SQL*Plus:

```
SELECT * FROM product_types;
```

The products Table   The `products` table holds the products sold by the store. The following pieces of information are held for each product:

- Product type

- Name

- Description

- Price

The `store_schema.sql` script creates the `products` table using the following CREATE TABLE statement:

```
CREATE TABLE products (
  product_id INTEGER CONSTRAINT products_pk PRIMARY KEY,
  product_type_id INTEGER
    CONSTRAINT products_fk_product_types
    REFERENCES product_types(product_type_id),
  name VARCHAR2(30) NOT NULL,
  description VARCHAR2(50),
  price NUMBER(5, 2)
);
```

The columns in this table are as follows:

- **product_id** uniquely identifies each row in the table. This column is the primary key of the table.

- **product_type_id** associates each product with a product type. This column is a reference to the `product_type_id` column in the `product_types` table; it is known as a *foreign key* because it references a column in another table. The table containing the foreign key (the `products` table) is known as the *detail* or *child* table, and the table that is referenced (the `product_types` table) is known as the *master* or *parent* table.

This type of relationship is known as a *master-detail* or *parent-child* relationship. When you add a new product, you associate that product with a type by supplying a matching `product_types.product_type_id` value in the `products.product_type_id` column (you'll see an example later).

- **name** contains the product name, which must be specified, as the name column is NOT NULL.

- **description** contains an optional description of the product.

- **price** contains an optional price for a product. This column is defined as NUMBER(5, 2)—the precision is 5, and therefore a maximum of 5 digits may be supplied for this number. The scale is 2; therefore 2 of those maximum 5 digits may be to the right of the decimal point.

The following is a subset of the rows stored in the `products` table:

```
product_id    product_type_id name          description     price
----------    --------------- ------------  ------------    ----------
         1                  1 Modern        A               19.95
                             Science        description
                                            of modern
                                            science

         2                  1 Chemistry     Introduction       30
                                            to Chemistry

         3                  2 Supernova     A star          25.99
                                            explodes

         4                  2 Tank War      Action movie    13.95
                                            about a
                                            future war
```

The first row in the `products` table has a `product_type_id` of 1, which means the product is a book (this `product_type_id` matches the "book" product type in the `product_types` table). The second product is also a book, but the third and fourth products are videos (their `product_type_id` is 2, which matches the "video" product type in the `product_types` table).

You can see all the rows in the `products` table for yourself by executing the following SELECT statement using SQL*Plus:

```
SELECT * FROM products;
```

The purchases Table   The `purchases` table holds the purchases made by a customer. For each purchase made by a customer, the following information is held:

- Product ID

- Customer ID

- Number of units of the product that were purchased by the customer

The store_schema.sql script uses the following CREATE TABLE statement to create the purchases table:

```
CREATE TABLE purchases (
  product_id INTEGER
    CONSTRAINT purchases_fk_products
    REFERENCES products(product_id),
  customer_id INTEGER
    CONSTRAINT purchases_fk_customers
    REFERENCES customers(customer_id),
  quantity INTEGER NOT NULL,
  CONSTRAINT purchases_pk PRIMARY KEY (product_id, customer_id)
);
```

The columns in this table are as follows:

- **product_id** contains the ID of the product that was purchased. This must match a product_id column value in the products table.

- **customer_id** contains the ID of a customer who made the purchase. This must match a customer_id column value in the customers table.

- **quantity** contains the number of units of the product that were purchased by the customer.

The purchases table has a primary key constraint named purchases_pk that spans two columns: product_id and customer_id. The combination of the two column values must be unique for each row. When a primary key consists of multiple columns, it is known as a *composite* primary key.

The following is a subset of the rows that are stored in the purchases table:

```
product_id customer_id    quantity
---------- -----------  ----------
         1           1           1
         2           1           3
         1           4           1
         2           2           1
         1           3           1
```

As you can see, the combination of the values in the product_id and customer_id columns is unique for each row.

You can see all the rows in the purchases table for yourself by executing the following SELECT statement using SQL*Plus:

```
SELECT * FROM purchases;
```

The employees Table   The employees table holds the details of the employees. The following information is held in the table:

- Employee ID

- The ID of the employee's manager (if applicable)

- First name

- Last name

- Title

- Salary

The store_schema.sql script uses the following CREATE TABLE statement to create the employees table:

```
CREATE TABLE employees (
  employee_id INTEGER CONSTRAINT employees_pk PRIMARY KEY,
  manager_id INTEGER,
  first_name VARCHAR2(10) NOT NULL,
  last_name VARCHAR2(10) NOT NULL,
  title VARCHAR2(20),
  salary NUMBER(6, 0)
);
```

The store_schema.sql script populates the employees table with the following rows:

employee_id	manager_id	first_name	last_name	title	salary
1		James	Smith	CEO	800000
2	1	Ron	Johnson	Sales Manager	600000
3	2	Fred	Hobbs	Salesperson	150000
4	2	Susan	Jones	Salesperson	500000

As you can see, James Smith doesn't have a manager. That's because he is the CEO of the store.

The salary_grades Table The salary_grades table holds the different salary grades available to employees. The following information is held:

- Salary grade ID

- Low salary boundary for the grade

- High salary boundary for the grade

The store_schema.sql script uses the following CREATE TABLE statement to create the salary_grades table:

```
CREATE TABLE salary_grades (
  salary_grade_id INTEGER CONSTRAINT salary_grade_pk PRIMARY KEY,
  low_salary  NUMBER(6, 0),
  high_salary NUMBER(6, 0)
);
```

The `store_schema.sql` script populates the `salary_grades` table with the following rows:

```
salary_grade_id low_salary high_salary
--------------- ---------- -----------
              1          1      250000
              2     250001      500000
              3     500001      750000
              4     750001      999999
```

Adding, Modifying, and Removing Rows

In this section, you'll learn how to add, modify, and remove rows in database tables by using the SQL `INSERT`, `UPDATE`, and `DELETE` statements. You can make your row changes permanent in the database using the `COMMIT` statement, or you can undo them using the `ROLLBACK` statement. This section doesn't exhaustively cover all the details of using these statements; you'll learn more about them in Chapter 8.

Adding a Row to a Table

You use the `INSERT` statement to add new rows to a table. You can specify the following information in an `INSERT` statement:

- The table into which the row is to be inserted

- A list of columns for which you want to specify column values

- A list of values to store in the specified columns

When inserting a row, you need to supply a value for the primary key and all other columns that are defined as `NOT NULL`. You don't have to specify values for the other columns if you don't want to; those columns will be automatically set to null if you omit values for them.

You can tell which columns are defined as `NOT NULL` using the SQL*Plus `DESCRIBE` command. The following example `DESCRIBE`s the `customers` table:

```
SQL> DESCRIBE customers
 Name                                      Null?    Type
 ----------------------------------------- -------- ------------
 CUSTOMER_ID                               NOT NULL NUMBER(38)
 FIRST_NAME                                NOT NULL VARCHAR2(10)
 LAST_NAME                                 NOT NULL VARCHAR2(10)
 DOB                                                DATE
 PHONE                                              VARCHAR2(12)
```

As you can see, the `customer_id`, `first_name`, and `last_name` columns are `NOT NULL`, meaning that you must supply a value for these columns. The `dob` and `phone` columns don't require a value; you could omit the values if you wanted, and they would be automatically set to null.

Go ahead and run the following `INSERT` statement, which adds a row to the `customers` table; notice that the order of values in the `VALUES` list matches the order in which the columns are specified in the column list:

```
SQL> INSERT INTO customers (
  2    customer_id, first_name, last_name, dob, phone
```

```
3  ) VALUES (
4     6, 'Fred', 'Brown', '01-JAN-1970', '800-555-1215'
5  );
```

```
1 row created.
```

NOTE
SQL*Plus automatically numbers lines after you hit ENTER at the end of each line.

In the previous example, SQL*Plus responds that one row has been created after the INSERT statement is executed. You can verify this by running the following SELECT statement:

```
SELECT *
FROM customers;
```

```
CUSTOMER_ID FIRST_NAME LAST_NAME  DOB        PHONE
----------- ---------- ---------- --------- ------------
          1 John       Brown      01-JAN-65 800-555-1211
          2 Cynthia    Green      05-FEB-68 800-555-1212
          3 Steve      White      16-MAR-71 800-555-1213
          4 Gail       Black                800-555-1214
          5 Doreen     Blue       20-MAY-70
          6 Fred       Brown      01-JAN-70 800-555-1215
```

Notice the new row that has been added to the end of the table.

By default, the Oracle database displays dates in the format DD-MON-YY, where DD is the day number, MON is the first three characters of the month (in uppercase), and YY is the last two digits of the year. The database actually stores all four digits for the year, but by default it only displays the last two digits.

When a row is added to the customers table, a unique value for the customer_id column must be given. The Oracle database will prevent you from adding a row with a primary key value that already exists in the table; for example, the following INSERT statement causes an error because a row with a customer_id of 1 already exists:

```
SQL> INSERT INTO customers (
  2     customer_id, first_name, last_name, dob, phone
  3  ) VALUES (
  4     1, 'Lisa', 'Jones', '02-JAN-1971', '800-555-1225'
  5  );
```

```
INSERT INTO customers (
*
ERROR at line 1:
ORA-00001: unique constraint (STORE.CUSTOMERS_PK) violated
```

Notice that the name of the constraint is shown in the error (CUSTOMERS_PK). That's why you should always name your primary key constraints; otherwise, the Oracle database assigns an unfriendly system-generated name to a constraint (for example, SYS_C0011277).

Modifying an Existing Row in a Table

You use the UPDATE statement to change rows in a table. Normally, when you use the UPDATE statement, you specify the following information:

- The table containing the rows that are to be changed

- A WHERE clause that specifies the rows that are to be changed

- A list of column names, along with their new values, specified using the SET clause

You can change one or more rows using the same UPDATE statement. If more than one row is specified, the same change will be made for all the rows. The following example updates customer #2's last_name to Orange:

```
UPDATE customers
SET last_name = 'Orange'
WHERE customer_id = 2;
```

```
1 row updated.
```

SQL*Plus confirms that one row was updated.

CAUTION
If you forget to add a WHERE *clause, then all the rows will be updated.*

The following query confirms the update worked:

```
SELECT *
FROM customers
WHERE customer_id = 2;
```

```
CUSTOMER_ID FIRST_NAME LAST_NAME  DOB        PHONE
----------- ---------- ---------- ---------- ------------
          2 Cynthia    Orange     05-FEB-68  800-555-1212
```

Removing a Row from a Table

You use the DELETE statement to remove rows from a table. You typically use a WHERE clause to limit the rows you wish to delete; if you don't, *all* the rows will be deleted from the table.
The following DELETE statement removes customer #2:

```
DELETE FROM customers
WHERE customer_id = 2;
```

```
1 row deleted.
```

To undo the changes you've made to the rows, you use ROLLBACK:

```
ROLLBACK;
```

```
Rollback complete.
```

Go ahead and run the ROLLBACK to undo any changes you've made so far. That way, your results will match those shown in subsequent chapters.

NOTE
You can make changes to rows permanent using COMMIT. *You'll see how to do that in Chapter 8.*

The BINARY_FLOAT and BINARY_DOUBLE Types

Oracle Database 10*g* introduced two new data types: BINARY_FLOAT and BINARY_DOUBLE. BINARY_FLOAT stores a single precision 32-bit floating point number; BINARY_DOUBLE stores a double precision 64-bit floating point number. These new data types are based on the IEEE (Institute of Electrical and Electronics Engineers) standard for binary floating-point arithmetic.

Benefits of BINARY_FLOAT and BINARY_DOUBLE

BINARY_FLOAT and BINARY_DOUBLE are intended to complement the existing NUMBER type. BINARY_FLOAT and BINARY_DOUBLE offer the following benefits over NUMBER:

- **Smaller storage required**   BINARY_FLOAT and BINARY_DOUBLE require 5 and 9 bytes of storage space, whereas NUMBER might use up to 22 bytes.

- **Greater range of numbers represented**   BINARY_FLOAT and BINARY_DOUBLE support numbers much larger and smaller than can be stored in a NUMBER.

- **Faster performance of operations**   Operations involving BINARY_FLOAT and BINARY_DOUBLE are typically performed faster than NUMBER operations. This is because BINARY_FLOAT and BINARY_DOUBLE operations are typically performed in the hardware, whereas NUMBERs must first be converted using software before operations can be performed.

- **Closed operations**   Arithmetic operations involving BINARY_FLOAT and BINARY_DOUBLE are closed, which means that either a number or a special value is returned. For example, if you divide a BINARY_FLOAT by another BINARY_FLOAT, a BINARY_FLOAT is returned.

- **Transparent rounding**   BINARY_FLOAT and BINARY_DOUBLE use binary (base 2) to represent a number, whereas NUMBER uses decimal (base 10). The base used to represent a number affects how rounding occurs for that number. For example, a decimal floating-point number is rounded to the nearest decimal place, but a binary floating-point number is rounded to the nearest binary place.

TIP
If you are developing a system that involves a lot of numerical computations, you should use BINARY_FLOAT *and* BINARY_DOUBLE *to represent numbers. Of course, you must be using Oracle Database 10g or higher.*

Using BINARY_FLOAT and BINARY_DOUBLE in a Table

The following statement creates a table named `binary_test` that contains a `BINARY_FLOAT` and a `BINARY_DOUBLE` column:

```
CREATE TABLE binary_test (
  bin_float BINARY_FLOAT,
  bin_double BINARY_DOUBLE
);
```

NOTE
You'll find a script named `oracle_10g_examples.sql` *in the* SQL *directory that creates the* `binary_test` *table in the* store *schema. The script also performs the* INSERT *statements you'll see in this section. You can run this script if you are using Oracle Database 10*g *or higher.*

The following example adds a row to the `binary_test` table:

```
INSERT INTO binary_test (
  bin_float, bin_double
) VALUES (
  39.5f, 15.7d
);
```

Notice that f indicates a number is a `BINARY_FLOAT`, and d indicates a number is a `BINARY_DOUBLE`.

Special Values

You can also use the special values shown in Table 1-2 with a `BINARY_FLOAT` or `BINARY_DOUBLE`.
The following example inserts `BINARY_FLOAT_INFINITY` and `BINARY_DOUBLE_INFINITY` into the `binary_test` table:

```
INSERT INTO binary_test (
  bin_float, bin_double
) VALUES (
  BINARY_FLOAT_INFINITY, BINARY_DOUBLE_INFINITY
);
```

Special Value	Description
BINARY_FLOAT_NAN	Not a number (NaN) for the BINARY_FLOAT type
BINARY_FLOAT_INFINITY	Infinity (INF) for the BINARY_FLOAT type
BINARY_DOUBLE_NAN	Not a number (NaN) for the BINARY_DOUBLE type
BINARY_DOUBLE_INFINITY	Infinity (INF) for the BINARY_DOUBLE type

TABLE 1-2 *Special Values*

The following query retrieves the rows from `binary_test`:

```
SELECT *
FROM binary_test;

BIN_FLOAT BIN_DOUBLE
---------- ----------
 3.95E+001  1.57E+001
       Inf        Inf
```

Quitting SQL*Plus

You use the EXIT command to quit from SQL*Plus. The following example quits SQL*Plus using the EXIT command:

```
EXIT
```

NOTE
*When you exit SQL*Plus in this way, it automatically performs a COMMIT for you. If SQL*Plus terminates abnormally—for example, if the computer on which SQL*Plus is running crashes—a ROLLBACK is automatically performed. You'll learn more about this in Chapter 8.*

Introducing Oracle PL/SQL

PL/SQL is Oracle's procedural language that allows you to add programming constructs around SQL statements. PL/SQL is primarily used for creating procedures and functions in a database that contain business logic. PL/SQL contains standard programming constructs such as

- Variable declarations
- Conditional logic (if-then-else, and so on)
- Loops
- Procedures and functions

The following CREATE PROCEDURE statement creates a procedure named `update_product_price()`. The procedure multiplies the price of a product by a factor—the product ID and the factor are passed as parameters to the procedure. If the specified product doesn't exist, the procedure takes no action; otherwise, it updates the product price.

NOTE
Don't worry about the details of the PL/SQL shown in the following listing—you'll learn all about PL/SQL in Chapter 11. I just want you to get a feel for PL/SQL at this stage.

```
CREATE PROCEDURE update_product_price (
  p_product_id IN products.product_id%TYPE,
  p_factor     IN NUMBER
) AS
  product_count INTEGER;
```

```
BEGIN
  -- count the number of products with the
  -- supplied product_id (will be 1 if the product exists)
  SELECT COUNT(*)
  INTO product_count
  FROM products
  WHERE product_id = p_product_id;

  -- if the product exists (i.e. product_count = 1) then
  -- update that product's price
  IF product_count = 1 THEN
    UPDATE products
    SET price = price * p_factor
    WHERE product_id = p_product_id;
    COMMIT;
  END IF;
EXCEPTION
  WHEN OTHERS THEN
    ROLLBACK;
END update_product_price;
/
```

Exceptions are used to handle errors that occur in PL/SQL code. The EXCEPTION block in the previous example performs a ROLLBACK if an exception is thrown in the code.

Summary

In this chapter, you have learned the following:

- A relational database is a collection of related information that has been organized into structures known as tables. Each table contains rows that are further organized into columns. These tables are stored in the database in structures known as schemas, which are areas where database users may store their objects (such as tables and PL/SQL procedures).

- Structured Query Language (SQL) is the standard language designed to access relational databases.

- SQL*Plus allows you to run SQL statements and SQL*Plus commands.

- SQL Developer is a graphical tool for database development.

- How to run SELECT, INSERT, UPDATE, and DELETE statements.

- PL/SQL is Oracle's procedural language that contains programming statements.

In the next chapter, you'll learn more about retrieving information from database tables.

CHAPTER
2

Retrieving Information
from Database Tables

n this chapter, you will see how to

- Retrieve information from one or more database tables using SELECT statements

- Use arithmetic expressions to perform calculations

- Limit the retrieval of rows to just those you are interested in using a WHERE clause

- Sort the rows retrieved from a table

The examples in this section use the store schema. If you want to follow along with the examples, you should start SQL*Plus and log in as the store user.

Performing Single Table SELECT Statements

You use the SELECT statement to retrieve information from database tables. In the statement's simplest form, you specify the table and columns from which you want to retrieve data. The following SELECT statement retrieves the customer_id, first_name, last_name, dob, and phone columns from the customers table:

```
SELECT customer_id, first_name, last_name, dob, phone
FROM customers;
```

Immediately after the SELECT keyword, you supply the column names that you want to retrieve; after the FROM keyword, you supply the table name. The SQL statement is ended using a semicolon (;). SELECT statements are also known as *queries*.

You don't tell the database management system software exactly how to access the information you want. You just tell it what you want and let the software worry about how to actually get it. The items that immediately follow the SELECT keyword needn't always be columns from a table: They can be any valid expression. You'll see examples of expressions later in this chapter.

After you press ENTER at the end of the SQL statement, the statement is executed and the results are returned to SQL*Plus for display on the screen:

```
CUSTOMER_ID FIRST_NAME LAST_NAME  DOB       PHONE
----------- ---------- ---------- --------- ------------
          1 John       Brown      01-JAN-65 800-555-1211
          2 Cynthia    Green      05-FEB-68 800-555-1212
          3 Steve      White      16-MAR-71 800-555-1213
          4 Gail       Black                800-555-1214
          5 Doreen     Blue       20-MAY-70
```

The rows returned by the database are known as a *result set*. As you can see from the example, the Oracle database converts the column names into their uppercase equivalents. Character and date columns are left-justified; number columns are right-justified. By default, the Oracle database displays dates in the format DD-MON-YY, where DD is the day number, MON is the first three characters of the month (in uppercase), and YY is the last two digits of the year. The database actually stores all four digits for the year, but by default it displays only the last two digits.

NOTE
A database administrator can change the default display format for dates by setting an Oracle database parameter called NLS_DATE_ FORMAT. *You'll learn more about dates in Chapter 5.*

Although you can specify column names and table names using either lowercase or uppercase text, it is better to stick with one style. The examples in this book use uppercase for SQL and Oracle keywords, and lowercase for everything else.

Retrieving All Columns from a Table

If you want to retrieve all columns in a table, you can use the asterisk character (*) in place of a list of columns. In the following query, the asterisk is used to retrieve all columns from the customers table:

```
SELECT *
FROM customers;

CUSTOMER_ID FIRST_NAME LAST_NAME  DOB       PHONE
----------- ---------- ---------- --------- ------------
          1 John       Brown      01-JAN-65 800-555-1211
          2 Cynthia    Green      05-FEB-68 800-555-1212
          3 Steve      White      16-MAR-71 800-555-1213
          4 Gail       Black                800-555-1214
          5 Doreen     Blue       20-MAY-70
```

As you can see, all the columns in the customers table are retrieved.

Specifying Rows to Retrieve Using the WHERE Clause

You use the WHERE clause in a query to specify the rows you want to retrieve. This is very important, as Oracle has the capacity to store large numbers of rows in a table, and you may be interested in only a very small subset of those rows. You place the WHERE clause after the FROM clause:

```
SELECT list of items
FROM list of tables
WHERE list of conditions;
```

In the following query, the WHERE clause is used to retrieve the row from the customers table where the customer_id column is equal to 2:

```
SELECT *
FROM customers
WHERE customer_id = 2;

CUSTOMER_ID FIRST_NAME LAST_NAME  DOB       PHONE
----------- ---------- ---------- --------- ------------
          2 Cynthia    Green      05-FEB-68 800-555-1212
```

Row Identifiers

Each row in an Oracle database has a unique row identifier, or *rowid,* which is used internally by the Oracle database to store the physical location of the row. A rowid is an 18-digit number that is represented as a base-64 number. You can view the rowid for rows in a table by retrieving the ROWID column in a query. For example, the following query retrieves the ROWID and customer_id columns from the customers table; notice the base-64 number in the output:

```
SELECT ROWID, customer_id
FROM customers;

ROWID              CUSTOMER_ID
------------------ -----------
AAAF4yAABAAAHeKAAA           1
AAAF4yAABAAAHeKAAB           2
AAAF4yAABAAAHeKAAC           3
AAAF4yAABAAAHeKAAD           4
AAAF4yAABAAAHeKAAE           5
```

When you describe a table using the SQL*Plus DESCRIBE command, ROWID doesn't appear in the output from the command because it is only used internally by the database. ROWID is known as a *pseudo* column. The following example describes the customers table; notice ROWID doesn't appear in the output:

```
DESCRIBE customers
 Name                                      Null?    Type
 ----------------------------------------- -------- ------------
 CUSTOMER_ID                               NOT NULL NUMBER(38)
 FIRST_NAME                                NOT NULL VARCHAR2(10)
 LAST_NAME                                 NOT NULL VARCHAR2(10)
 DOB                                                DATE
 PHONE                                              VARCHAR2(12)
```

Row Numbers

Another pseudo column is ROWNUM, which returns the row number in a result set. The first row returned by a query has a row number of 1, the second has a row number of 2, and so on. For example, the following query includes ROWNUM when retrieving the rows from the customers table:

```
SELECT ROWNUM, customer_id, first_name, last_name
FROM customers;

    ROWNUM CUSTOMER_ID FIRST_NAME LAST_NAME
---------- ----------- ---------- ----------
         1           1 John       Brown
         2           2 Cynthia    Green
         3           3 Steve      White
         4           4 Gail       Black
         5           5 Doreen     Blue
```

Here's another example:

```
SELECT ROWNUM, customer_id, first_name, last_name
FROM customers
WHERE customer_id = 3;

   ROWNUM CUSTOMER_ID FIRST_NAME LAST_NAME
---------- ----------- ---------- ----------
        1           3 Steve      White
```

Performing Arithmetic

Oracle allows you to perform arithmetic in SQL statements using arithmetic expressions, consisting of addition, subtraction, multiplication, and division. Arithmetic expressions consist of two *operands*—numbers or dates—and an arithmetic *operator*. The four arithmetic operators are shown in the following table:

Operator	Description
+	Addition
−	Subtraction
*	Multiplication
/	Division

The following query shows how to use the multiplication operator (*) to calculate 2 multiplied by 6 (the numbers 2 and 6 are the operands):

```
SELECT 2*6
FROM dual;

       2*6
----------
        12
```

As you can see from this query, the correct result of 12 is displayed. The use of 2*6 in the query is an example of an *expression*. An expression may contain a combination of columns, literal values, and operators.

Performing Date Arithmetic

You can use the addition and subtraction operators with dates. You can add a number—representing a number of days—to a date. The following example adds two days to July 25, 2007, and displays the resulting date:

```
SELECT TO_DATE('25-JUL-2007') + 2
FROM dual;

TO_DATE(
---------
27-JUL-07
```

The dual Table

You'll notice the use of the `dual` table in the previous example. I mentioned the `dual` table in the previous chapter—`dual` is a table that contains a single row. The following output from the `DESCRIBE` command shows the structure of the `dual` table, along with a query that retrieves the row from the `dual` table:

```
DESCRIBE dual
 Name                                      Null?    Type
 ----------------------------------------- -------- -----------
 DUMMY                                               VARCHAR2(1)

SELECT *
FROM dual;

D
-
X
```

Notice the `dual` table has one `VARCHAR2` column named `dummy` and contains a single row with the value `X`.

NOTE
`TO_DATE()` is a function that converts a string to a date. You'll learn more about `TO_DATE()` in Chapter 5.

The next example subtracts three days from August 2, 2007:

```
SELECT TO_DATE('02-AUG-2007') - 3
FROM dual;

TO_DATE('
---------
30-JUL-07
```

You can also subtract one date from another, yielding the number of days between the two dates. The following example subtracts July 25, 2007, from August 2, 2007:

```
SELECT TO_DATE('02-AUG-2007') - TO_DATE('25-JUL-2007')
FROM dual;

TO_DATE('02-AUG-2007')-TO_DATE('25-JUL-2007')
---------------------------------------------
                                            8
```

Using Columns in Arithmetic

Operands do not have to be literal numbers or dates; they may also be columns from a table. In the following query, the `name` and `price` columns are retrieved from the `products` table; notice that 2 is added to the value in the `price` column using the addition operator (+) to form the expression `price + 2`:

```
SELECT name, price + 2
FROM products;
```

```
NAME                            PRICE+2
------------------------------ ----------
Modern Science                    21.95
Chemistry                            32
Supernova                         27.99
Tank War                          15.95
Z Files                           51.99
2412: The Return                  16.95
Space Force 9                     15.49
From Another Planet               14.99
Classical Music                   12.99
Pop 3                             17.99
Creative Yell                     16.99
My Front Line                     15.49
```

You can also combine more than one operator in an expression. In the following query, the price column is multiplied by 3, and then 1 is added to the resulting value:

```
SELECT name, price * 3 + 1
FROM products;
```

```
NAME                            PRICE*3+1
------------------------------ ----------
Modern Science                    60.85
Chemistry                            91
Supernova                         78.97
Tank War                          42.85
Z Files                          150.97
2412: The Return                  45.85
Space Force 9                     41.47
From Another Planet               39.97
Classical Music                   33.97
Pop 3                             48.97
Creative Yell                     45.97
My Front Line                     41.47
```

The normal rules of arithmetic operator precedence apply in SQL: multiplication and division are performed first, followed by addition and subtraction. If operators of the same precedence are used, they are performed from left to right. For example, in the expression $10*12/3-1$, the first calculation would be 10 multiplied by 12, yielding a result of 120; then 120 would be divided by 3, yielding 40; finally, 1 would be subtracted from 40, yielding 39:

```
SELECT 10 * 12 / 3 - 1
FROM dual;
```

```
10*12/3-1
----------
    39
```

You can also use parentheses () to specify the order of execution for the operators, as in the following:

```
SELECT 10 * (12 / 3 - 1)
FROM dual;

10*(12/3-1)
-----------
         30
```

In this example, the parentheses are used to force calculation of 12/3-1 first, the result of which is then multiplied by 10, yielding 30 as the final answer.

Using Column Aliases

As you've seen, when you select a column from a table, Oracle uses the uppercase version of the column name as the header for the column in the output. For example, when you select the price column, the header in the resulting output is PRICE. When you use an expression, Oracle strips out the spaces and uses the expression as the header. You aren't limited to using the header generated by Oracle; you can provide your own using an *alias*. In the following query, the expression price * 2 is given the alias DOUBLE_PRICE:

```
SELECT price * 2 DOUBLE_PRICE
FROM products;

DOUBLE_PRICE
------------
        39.9
          60
       51.98
        27.9
       99.98
        29.9
       26.98
       25.98
       21.98
       31.98
       29.98
       26.98
```

If you want to use spaces and preserve the case of your alias text, you must place the text within double quotation marks (""):

```
SELECT price * 2 "Double Price"
FROM products;

Double Price
------------
        39.9
...
```

You can also use the optional AS keyword before the alias, as shown in the following query:

```
SELECT 10 * (12 / 3 - 1) AS "Computation"
FROM dual;

Computation
-----------
         30
```

Combining Column Output Using Concatenation

You can combine the column values retrieved by a query using concatenation, which allows you to create more friendly and meaningful output. For example, in the `customers` table, the `first_name` and `last_name` columns contain the customer name, and in the previous queries the column values were displayed independently. But wouldn't it be nice to combine the `first_name` and `last_name` columns? You can do this using the concatenation operator (||), as shown in the following query; notice that a space character is added after the `first_name` column, and then the `last_name` column is added:

```
SELECT first_name || ' ' || last_name AS "Customer Name"
FROM customers;

Customer Name
-------------------
John Brown
Cynthia Green
Steve White
Gail Black
Doreen Blue
```

The `first_name` and `last_name` column values are combined together in the output under the `"Customer Name"` alias.

Null Values

How does a database represent a value that is unknown? It uses a special value called a *null value*. A null value is not a blank string—it is a distinct value. A null value means the value for the column is unknown.

When you retrieve a column that contains a null value, you see nothing in the output for that column. You saw this (or rather, didn't see it!) in the earlier examples that retrieved rows from the `customers` table: customer #4 has a null value in the `dob` column, and customer #5 has a null value in the `phone` column. In case you missed it, here's the query again:

```
SELECT *
FROM customers;

CUSTOMER_ID FIRST_NAME LAST_NAME  DOB       PHONE
----------- ---------- ---------- --------- ------------
          1 John       Brown      01-JAN-65 800-555-1211
          2 Cynthia    Green      05-FEB-68 800-555-1212
          3 Steve      White      16-MAR-71 800-555-1213
          4 Gail       Black                800-555-1214
          5 Doreen     Blue       20-MAY-70
```

You can also check for null values using IS NULL in a query. In the following example, customer #4 is retrieved because its dob value is null:

```
SELECT customer_id, first_name, last_name, dob
FROM customers
WHERE dob IS NULL;

CUSTOMER_ID FIRST_NAME LAST_NAME  DOB
----------- ---------- ---------- ---------
          4 Gail       Black
```

In the next example, customer #5 is retrieved because its phone value is null:

```
SELECT customer_id, first_name, last_name, phone
FROM customers
WHERE phone IS NULL;

CUSTOMER_ID FIRST_NAME LAST_NAME  PHONE
----------- ---------- ---------- ------------
          5 Doreen     Blue
```

Since null values don't display anything, how do you tell the difference between a null value and a blank string? The answer is to use the Oracle NVL() built-in function. NVL() returns another value in place of a null. NVL() accepts two parameters: a column (or, more generally, any expression that results in a value) and the value to be returned if the first parameter is null. In the following query, NVL() returns string 'Unknown phone number' when the phone column contains a null value:

```
SELECT customer_id, first_name, last_name,
  NVL(phone, 'Unknown phone number') AS PHONE_NUMBER
FROM customers;

CUSTOMER_ID FIRST_NAME LAST_NAME  PHONE_NUMBER
----------- ---------- ---------- --------------------
          1 John       Brown      800-555-1211
          2 Cynthia    Green      800-555-1212
          3 Steve      White      800-555-1213
          4 Gail       Black      800-555-1214
          5 Doreen     Blue       Unknown phone number
```

You can also use NVL() to convert null numbers and dates. In the following query, NVL() returns the date 01-JAN-2000 when the dob column contains a null value:

```
SELECT customer_id, first_name, last_name, NVL(dob, '01-JAN-2000') AS DOB
FROM customers;

CUSTOMER_ID FIRST_NAME LAST_NAME  DOB
----------- ---------- ---------- ---------
          1 John       Brown      01-JAN-65
          2 Cynthia    Green      05-FEB-68
```

```
3 Steve      White      16-MAR-71
4 Gail       Black      01-JAN-00
5 Doreen     Blue       20-MAY-70
```

Notice that customer #4's dob is now displayed as 01-JAN-00.

Displaying Distinct Rows

Suppose you wanted to get the list of customers who purchased products from our imaginary store. You can get that list using the following query, which retrieves the customer_id column from the purchases table:

```
SELECT customer_id
FROM purchases;
```

```
CUSTOMER_ID
-----------
          1
          2
          3
          4
          1
          2
          3
          4
          3
```

The customer_id column contains the IDs of customers who purchased a product. As you can see from the output returned by the query, some customers made more than one purchase and therefore appear twice. Wouldn't it be great if you could throw out the duplicate rows that contain the same customer ID? You do this using the DISTINCT keyword. In the following query, DISTINCT is used to suppress the duplicate rows:

```
SELECT DISTINCT customer_id
FROM purchases;
```

```
CUSTOMER_ID
-----------
          1
          2
          4
          3
```

From this list, it's easy to see that customers #1, #2, #3, and #4 made purchases; the duplicate rows are suppressed.

Comparing Values

The following table lists the operators you can use to compare values:

Operator	Description
=	Equal
<> or !=	Not equal
<	Less than
>	Greater than
<=	Less than or equal to
>=	Greater than or equal to
ANY	Compares one value with any value in a list
SOME	Identical to the ANY operator; you should use ANY rather than SOME because ANY is more widely used and readable.
ALL	Compares one value with all values in a list

The following query uses the not equal (<>) operator in the WHERE clause to retrieve the rows from the customers table whose customer_id is not equal to 2:

```
SELECT *
FROM customers
WHERE customer_id <> 2;

CUSTOMER_ID FIRST_NAME LAST_NAME  DOB       PHONE
----------- ---------- ---------- --------- ------------
          1 John       Brown      01-JAN-65 800-555-1211
          3 Steve      White      16-MAR-71 800-555-1213
          4 Gail       Black                800-555-1214
          5 Doreen     Blue       20-MAY-70
```

The next query uses the > operator to retrieve the product_id and name columns from the products table where the product_id column is greater than 8:

```
SELECT product_id, name
FROM products
WHERE product_id > 8;

PRODUCT_ID  NAME
----------- ----------------
          9 Classical Music
         10 Pop 3
         11 Creative Yell
         12 My Front Line
```

The following query uses the ROWNUM pseudo column and the <= operator to retrieve the first 3 rows from the products table:

```
SELECT ROWNUM, product_id, name
FROM products
WHERE ROWNUM <= 3;
```

```
ROWNUM PRODUCT_ID NAME
---------- ---------- --------------
         1          1 Modern Science
         2          2 Chemistry
         3          3 Supernova
```

You use the ANY operator in a WHERE clause to compare a value with *any* of the values in a list. You must place an =, <>, <, >, <=, or >= operator before ANY. The following query uses ANY to retrieve rows from the customers table where the value in the customer_id column is greater than any of the values 2, 3, or 4:

```
SELECT *
FROM customers
WHERE customer_id > ANY (2, 3, 4);
```

```
CUSTOMER_ID FIRST_NAME LAST_NAME  DOB       PHONE
----------- ---------- ---------- --------- ------------
          3 Steve      White      16-MAR-71 800-555-1213
          4 Gail       Black                800-555-1214
          5 Doreen     Blue       20-MAY-70
```

You use the ALL operator in a WHERE clause to compare a value with *all* of the values in a list. You must place an =, <>, <, >, <=, or >= operator before ALL. The following query uses ALL to retrieve rows from the customers table where the value in the customer_id column is greater than all of the values 2, 3, and 4:

```
SELECT *
FROM customers
WHERE customer_id > ALL (2, 3, 4);
```

```
CUSTOMER_ID FIRST_NAME LAST_NAME  DOB       PHONE
----------- ---------- ---------- --------- ------------
          5 Doreen     Blue       20-MAY-70
```

Only customer #5 is returned because 5 is greater than 2, 3, and 4.

Using the SQL Operators

The SQL operators allow you to limit rows based on pattern matching of strings, lists of values, ranges of values, and null values. The SQL operators are listed in the following table:

Operator	Description
LIKE	Matches patterns in strings
IN	Matches lists of values
BETWEEN	Matches a range of values
IS NULL	Matches null values
IS NAN	Matches the NAN special value, which means "not a number" (introduced in Oracle Database 10*g*)
IS INFINITE	Matches infinite BINARY_FLOAT and BINARY_DOUBLE values (introduced in Oracle Database 10*g*)

You can also use NOT to reverse the meaning of an operator:

- NOT LIKE
- NOT IN
- NOT BETWEEN
- IS NOT NULL
- IS NOT NAN
- IS NOT INFINITE

You'll learn about the LIKE, IN, and BETWEEN operators in the following sections.

Using the LIKE Operator

You use the LIKE operator in a WHERE clause to search a string for a pattern. You specify patterns using a combination of normal characters and the following two wildcard characters:

- **Underscore (_)**   Matches one character in a specified position
- **Percent (%)**   Matches any number of characters beginning at the specified position

For example, consider the following pattern:

```
'_o%'
```

The underscore (_) matches any one character in the first position, the o matches an *o* character in the second position, and the percent (%) matches any characters following the *o* character. The following query uses the LIKE operator to search the first_name column of the customers table for the pattern '_o%':

```
SELECT *
FROM customers
WHERE first_name LIKE '_o%';

CUSTOMER_ID FIRST_NAME LAST_NAME  DOB       PHONE
----------- ---------- ---------- --------- ------------
          1 John       Brown      01-JAN-65 800-555-1211
          5 Doreen     Blue       20-MAY-70
```

As you can see from the results, two rows are returned, because the strings John and Doreen both have o as the second character.

The next query uses NOT LIKE to get the rows not retrieved by the previous query:

```
SELECT *
FROM customers
WHERE first_name NOT LIKE '_o%';
```

```
CUSTOMER_ID FIRST_NAME LAST_NAME  DOB        PHONE
----------- ---------- ---------- ---------  ------------
          2 Cynthia    Green      05-FEB-68  800-555-1212
          3 Steve      White      16-MAR-71  800-555-1213
          4 Gail       Black                 800-555-1214
```

If you need to search for actual underscore or percent characters in a string, you can use the ESCAPE option to identify those characters. For example, consider the following pattern:

```
'%\%%' ESCAPE '\'
```

The character after the ESCAPE tells the database how to differentiate between characters to search for and wildcards, and in the example the backslash character (\) is used. The first % is treated as a wildcard and matches any number of characters; the second % is treated as an actual character to search for; the third % is treated as a wildcard and matches any number of characters. The following query uses the promotions table, which contains the details for products being discounted by the store (you'll learn more about this table later in this book). The query uses the LIKE operator to search the name column of the promotions table for the pattern '%\%%' ESCAPE '\':

```
SELECT name
FROM promotions
WHERE name LIKE '%\%%' ESCAPE '\';

NAME
------------------------------
10% off Z Files
20% off Pop 3
30% off Modern Science
20% off Tank War
10% off Chemistry
20% off Creative Yell
15% off My Front Line
```

As you can see from the results, the query returns the rows whose names contain a percentage character.

Using the IN Operator

You may use the IN operator in a WHERE clause to retrieve the rows whose column value is in a list. The following query uses IN to retrieve rows from the customers table where the customer_id is 2, 3, or 5:

```
SELECT *
FROM customers
WHERE customer_id IN (2, 3, 5);

CUSTOMER_ID FIRST_NAME LAST_NAME  DOB        PHONE
----------- ---------- ---------- ---------  ------------
          2 Cynthia    Green      05-FEB-68  800-555-1212
          3 Steve      White      16-MAR-71  800-555-1213
          5 Doreen     Blue       20-MAY-70
```

NOT IN retrieves the rows not retrieved by IN:

```
SELECT *
FROM customers
WHERE customer_id NOT IN (2, 3, 5);
```

```
CUSTOMER_ID FIRST_NAME LAST_NAME  DOB        PHONE
----------- ---------- ---------- ---------- ------------
          1 John       Brown      01-JAN-65  800-555-1211
          4 Gail       Black                 800-555-1214
```

One important point to be aware of is that NOT IN returns false if a value in the list is null. This is illustrated by the following query, which doesn't return any rows because null is included in the list:

```
SELECT *
FROM customers
WHERE customer_id NOT IN (2, 3, 5, NULL);
```

```
no rows selected
```

CAUTION
NOT IN *returns false if a value in the list is null. This is important because, since you can use any expression in the list and not just literal values, it can be difficult to spot when a null value occurs. Consider using* NVL() *with expressions that might return a null value.*

Using the BETWEEN Operator

You may use the BETWEEN operator in a WHERE clause to retrieve the rows whose column value is in a specified range. The range is *inclusive*, which means the values at both ends of the range are included. The following query uses BETWEEN to retrieve the rows from the customers table where the customer_id is between 1 and 3:

```
SELECT *
FROM customers
WHERE customer_id BETWEEN 1 AND 3;
```

```
CUSTOMER_ID FIRST_NAME LAST_NAME  DOB        PHONE
----------- ---------- ---------- ---------- ------------
          1 John       Brown      01-JAN-65  800-555-1211
          2 Cynthia    Green      05-FEB-68  800-555-1212
          3 Steve      White      16-MAR-71  800-555-1213
```

NOT BETWEEN retrieves the rows not retrieved by BETWEEN:

```
SELECT *
FROM customers
WHERE customer_id NOT BETWEEN 1 AND 3;
```

```
CUSTOMER_ID FIRST_NAME LAST_NAME  DOB        PHONE
----------- ---------- ---------- --------- ------------
          4 Gail       Black                 800-555-1214
          5 Doreen     Blue       20-MAY-70
```

Using the Logical Operators

The logical operators allow you to limit rows based on logical conditions. The logical operators are listed in the following table:

Operator	Description
x AND y	Returns true when both x and y are true
x OR y	Returns true when either x or y is true
NOT x	Returns true if x is false, and returns false if x is true

The following query illustrates the use of the AND operator to retrieve the rows from the customers table where *both* of the following conditions are true:

- The dob column is greater than January 1, 1970.

- The customer_id column is greater than 3.

```
SELECT *
FROM customers
WHERE dob > '01-JAN-1970'
AND customer_id > 3;
```

```
CUSTOMER_ID FIRST_NAME LAST_NAME  DOB        PHONE
----------- ---------- ---------- --------- ------------
          5 Doreen     Blue       20-MAY-70
```

The next query illustrates the use of the OR operator to retrieve rows from the customers table where *either* of the following conditions is true:

- The dob column is greater than January 1, 1970.

- The customer_id column is greater than 3.

```
SELECT *
FROM customers
WHERE dob > '01-JAN-1970'
OR customer_id > 3;
```

```
CUSTOMER_ID FIRST_NAME LAST_NAME  DOB        PHONE
----------- ---------- ---------- --------- ------------
          3 Steve      White      16-MAR-71 800-555-1213
          4 Gail       Black                 800-555-1214
          5 Doreen     Blue       20-MAY-70
```

You can also use AND and OR to combine expressions in a WHERE clause, as you'll see in the following section.

Operator Precedence

If you combine AND and OR in the same expression, the AND operator takes precedence over the OR operator ("takes precedence over" means it's executed first). The comparison operators take precedence over AND. Of course, you can override the default precedence by using parentheses to indicate the order in which you want to execute the expressions.

The following example retrieves the rows from the customers table where *either* of the following two conditions is true:

■ The dob column is greater than January 1, 1970.

■ The customer_id column is less than 2 *and* the phone column has 1211 at the end.

```
SELECT *
FROM customers
WHERE dob > '01-JAN-1970'
OR customer_id < 2
AND phone LIKE '%1211';
```

```
CUSTOMER_ID FIRST_NAME LAST_NAME  DOB       PHONE
----------- ---------- ---------- --------- ------------
          1 John       Brown      01-JAN-65 800-555-1211
          3 Steve      White      16-MAR-71 800-555-1213
          5 Doreen     Blue       20-MAY-70
```

As mentioned earlier, AND takes precedence over OR, so you can think of the WHERE clause in the previous query as follows:

```
dob > '01-JAN-1970' OR (customer_id < 2 AND phone LIKE '%1211')
```

Therefore, customers #1, #3, and #5 are returned by the query.

Sorting Rows Using the ORDER BY Clause

You use the ORDER BY clause to sort the rows retrieved by a query. The ORDER BY clause may specify one or more columns on which to sort the data; also, the ORDER BY clause must follow the FROM clause or the WHERE clause (if a WHERE clause is supplied).

The following query uses ORDER BY to sort the rows retrieved from the customers table by the last_name:

```
SELECT *
FROM customers
ORDER BY last_name;
```

```
CUSTOMER_ID FIRST_NAME LAST_NAME  DOB       PHONE
----------- ---------- ---------- --------- ------------
          4 Gail       Black                800-555-1214
          5 Doreen     Blue       20-MAY-70
          1 John       Brown      01-JAN-65 800-555-1211
          2 Cynthia    Green      05-FEB-68 800-555-1212
          3 Steve      White      16-MAR-71 800-555-1213
```

By default, ORDER BY sorts the columns in ascending order (lower values appear first). You can use the DESC keyword to sort the columns in descending order (higher values appear first). You can also use the ASC keyword to explicitly specify an ascending sort—as I mentioned, ascending order is the default, but you can still specify it if you want to make it clear what the order is for the sort.

The next query uses ORDER BY to sort the rows retrieved from the customers table by ascending first_name and descending last_name:

```
SELECT *
FROM customers
ORDER BY first_name ASC, last_name DESC;

CUSTOMER_ID FIRST_NAME LAST_NAME  DOB        PHONE
----------- ---------- ---------- ---------- ------------
          2 Cynthia    Green      05-FEB-68 800-555-1212
          5 Doreen     Blue       20-MAY-70
          4 Gail       Black                 800-555-1214
          1 John       Brown      01-JAN-65 800-555-1211
          3 Steve      White      16-MAR-71 800-555-1213
```

You can also use a column position number in the ORDER BY clause to indicate which column to sort: Use 1 to sort by the first column selected, 2 to sort by the second column selected, and so on. In the following query, column 1 (the customer_id column) is used to sort the rows:

```
SELECT customer_id, first_name, last_name
FROM customers
ORDER BY 1;

CUSTOMER_ID FIRST_NAME LAST_NAME
----------- ---------- ----------
          1 John       Brown
          2 Cynthia    Green
          3 Steve      White
          4 Gail       Black
          5 Doreen     Blue
```

Because the customer_id column is in position 1 after the SELECT keyword, it is the column used in the sort.

Performing SELECT Statements That Use Two Tables

Database schemas have more than one table, with those tables storing different data. For example, the store schema has tables that store information on customers, products, employees, and so on. Up to now, all the queries shown in this book retrieve rows from only one table. In the real world, you will often need to get information from multiple tables; for example, you might need to get the name of a product and the name of its product type. In this section, you'll learn how to perform queries that use two tables; later, you'll see queries that use more than two tables.

Let's return to the example where you want to get the name of product #3 and its product type. The name of the product is stored in the name column of the products table, and the name of the product type is stored in the name column of the product_types table. The products and product_types tables are related to each other via the foreign key column product_type_id; the product_type_id column (the foreign key) of the products table points to the product_type_id column (the primary key) of the product_types table.

The following query retrieves the name and product_type_id columns from the products table for product #3:

```
SELECT name, product_type_id
FROM products
WHERE product_id = 3;
```

```
NAME                                   PRODUCT_TYPE_ID
------------------------------         ---------------
Supernova                                            2
```

The next query retrieves the name column from the product_types table for the product_type_id of 2:

```
SELECT name
FROM product_types
WHERE product_type_id = 2;
```

```
NAME
----------
Video
```

From this, you know that product #3 is a video. Nothing new so far, but what you really want is to retrieve the product name and its product type name using one query. You do this using a *table join* in the query. To join two tables in a query, you include both tables in the query's FROM clause and include the related columns from each table in the WHERE clause.

For our example query, the FROM clause becomes

```
FROM products, product_types
```

And the WHERE clause is

```
WHERE products.product_type_id = product_types.product_type_id
AND products.product_id = 3;
```

The join is the first condition in the WHERE clause (products.product_type_id = product_types.product_type_id); typically, the columns used in the join are a primary key from one table and a foreign key from the other table. Because the equality operator (=) is used in the join condition, the join is known as an *equijoin*. The second condition in the WHERE clause (products.product_id = 3) gets product #3, the product we are interested in viewing.

You'll notice the tables as well as their columns are included in the WHERE clause. This is because there is a product_type_id column in both the products and product_types tables, and you need to tell the database which table the column you want to use is in. If the columns had different names you could omit the table names, but you should always include them to make it clear where the columns come from.

The SELECT clause for the query is

```
SELECT products.name, product_types.name
```

Notice the tables and their columns are specified again.

Putting everything together, the completed query is

```
SELECT products.name, product_types.name
FROM products, product_types
WHERE products.product_type_id = product_types.product_type_id
AND products.product_id = 3;

NAME                                   NAME
------------------------------------   ----------
Supernova                              Video
```

Perfect! This is exactly what we wanted: the name of the product and the name of the product type. The next query gets all the products and orders them by the products.name column:

```
SELECT products.name, product_types.name
FROM products, product_types
WHERE products.product_type_id = product_types.product_type_id
ORDER BY products.name;

NAME                                   NAME
------------------------------------   ----------
2412: The Return                       Video
Chemistry                              Book
Classical Music                        CD
Creative Yell                          CD
From Another Planet                    DVD
Modern Science                         Book
Pop 3                                  CD
Space Force 9                          DVD
Supernova                              Video
Tank War                               Video
Z Files                                Video
```

Notice the product with the name "My Front Line" is missing from the results. The product_type_id for this product row is null, and the join condition does not return the row. You'll see how to include this row later in the section "Outer Joins."

The join syntax you've seen in this section uses Oracle's syntax for joins, which is based on the American National Standards Institute (ANSI) SQL/86 standard. With the introduction of Oracle Database 9*i*, the database also implements the ANSI SQL/92 standard syntax for joins; you'll see this new syntax later in the section "Performing Joins Using the SQL/92 Syntax." You should use the SQL/92 standard in your queries when working with Oracle Database 9*i* and above, and you should use SQL/86 queries only when you're using Oracle Database 8*i* and below.

Using Table Aliases

In the previous section you saw the following query:

```
SELECT products.name, product_types.name
FROM products, product_types
WHERE products.product_type_id = product_types.product_type_id
ORDER BY products.name;
```

Notice that the `products` and `product_types` table names are used in the `SELECT` and `WHERE` clauses. Repeating the table names is redundant typing. A better way is to define table aliases in the `FROM` clause and then use the aliases when referencing the tables elsewhere in the query. For example, the following query uses the alias `p` for the `products` table and `pt` for the `product_types` table; notice the table aliases are specified in the `FROM` clause, and the aliases are placed before the columns in the rest of the query:

```
SELECT p.name, pt.name
FROM products p, product_types pt
WHERE p.product_type_id = pt.product_type_id
ORDER BY p.name;
```

TIP
Table aliases also make your queries more readable, especially when you start writing longer queries that use many tables.

Cartesian Products

If a join condition is missing, you will end up joining all rows from one table with all the rows from the other table; this result set is known as a *Cartesian product*. When this occurs, you will end up with a lot of rows being returned by the query. For example, assume you had one table containing 50 rows and a second table containing 100 rows. If you select columns from those two tables without a join, you would get 5,000 rows returned. This result happens because each row from table 1 would be joined to each row in table 2, which would yield a total of 50 rows multiplied by 100 rows, or 5,000 rows.

The following example shows a subset of the rows for a Cartesian product between the `product_types` and `products` tables:

```
SELECT pt.product_type_id, p.product_id
FROM product_types pt, products p;

PRODUCT_TYPE_ID PRODUCT_ID
--------------- ----------
              1          1
              1          2
              1          3
              1          4
              1          5
...
              5          8
              5          9
              5         10
              5         11
              5         12

60 rows selected.
```

A total of 60 rows are selected because the `product_types` and `products` tables contain 5 and 12 rows, respectively, and 5*12 = 60.

Performing SELECT Statements That Use More than Two Tables

Joins can be used to connect any number of tables. You use the following formula to calculate the number of joins you will need in your WHERE clause:

Number of joins = the number of tables used in the query – 1

For example, the following query uses two tables and one join:

```
SELECT p.name, pt.name
FROM products p, product_types pt
WHERE p.product_type_id = pt.product_type_id
ORDER BY p.name;
```

Let's consider a more complicated example that uses four tables—and therefore requires three joins. Let's say you want to see the following information:

■ The purchases each customer has made (comes from the `purchases` table)

■ The customer's first and last name (comes from the `customers` table)

■ The name of the product they purchased (comes from the `products` table)

■ The name of the product type (comes from the `product_types` table)

In order to view this information, you need to query the `customers`, `purchases`, `products`, and `product_types` tables, and the joins use the foreign key relationships between these tables. The following list shows the required joins:

1. To get the customer who made the purchase, join the `customers` and `purchases` tables using the `customer_id` columns (`customers.customer_id` = `purchases.customer_id`).

2. To get the product purchased, join the `products` and `purchases` tables using the `product_id` columns (`products.product_id` = `purchases.product_id`).

3. To get the product type name for the product, join the `products` and `product_types` tables using the `product_type_id` columns (`products.product_type_id` = `product_types.product_type_id`).

The following query uses these joins; notice I've used table aliases and renamed the headings for the product name to PRODUCT and the product type name to TYPE:

```
SELECT c.first_name, c.last_name, p.name AS PRODUCT, pt.name AS TYPE
FROM customers c, purchases pr, products p, product_types pt
WHERE c.customer_id = pr.customer_id
AND p.product_id = pr.product_id
AND p.product_type_id = pt.product_type_id
ORDER BY p.name;
```

```
FIRST_NAME LAST_NAME  PRODUCT                         TYPE
---------- ---------- ------------------------------- ----------
John       Brown      Chemistry                       Book
Cynthia    Green      Chemistry                       Book
Steve      White      Chemistry                       Book
Gail       Black      Chemistry                       Book
John       Brown      Modern Science                  Book
Cynthia    Green      Modern Science                  Book
Steve      White      Modern Science                  Book
Gail       Black      Modern Science                  Book
Steve      White      Supernova                       Video
```

The multi-table queries you've seen so far use the equality operator (=) in the join conditions; these joins are known as *equijoins*. As you'll see in the next section, the equijoin is not the only join you can use.

Join Conditions and Join Types

In this section, you'll explore join conditions and join types that allow you to create more advanced queries.

There are two types of join conditions, which are based on the operator you use in your join:

■ **Equijoins** use the equality operator (=). You've already seen examples of equijoins.

■ **Non-equijoins** use an operator other than the equality operator, such as <, >, BETWEEN, and so on. You'll see an example of a non-equijoin shortly.

There are also three different types of joins:

■ **Inner joins** return a row *only* when the columns in the join contain values that satisfy the join condition. This means that if a row has a null value in one of the columns in the join condition, that row isn't returned. The examples you've seen so far have been inner joins.

■ **Outer joins** return a row *even when* one of the columns in the join condition contains a null value.

■ **Self joins** return rows joined on the same table.

You'll learn about non-equijoins, outer joins, and self joins next.

Non-equijoins

A non-equijoin uses an operator other than the equality operator (=) in the join. These operators are not-equal (<>), less than (<), greater than (>), less than or equal to (<=), greater than or equal to (>=), LIKE, IN, and BETWEEN. It's pretty rare to encounter situations where you need to use a non-equijoin, but I have come across a few occasions when I've needed to use one; on those occasions I've had to use the BETWEEN operator.

For example, let's say you want to get the salary grades for the employees. First, the following query retrieves the salary grades from the salary_grades table:

```
SELECT *
FROM salary_grades;
```

```
SALARY_GRADE_ID LOW_SALARY HIGH_SALARY
--------------- ---------- -----------
              1          1      250000
              2     250001      500000
              3     500001      750000
              4     750001      999999
```

The next query uses a non-equijoin to retrieve the salary and salary grades for the employees; the salary grade is determined using the BETWEEN operator:

```
SELECT e.first_name, e.last_name, e.title, e.salary, sg.salary_grade_id
FROM employees e, salary_grades sg
WHERE e.salary BETWEEN sg.low_salary AND sg.high_salary
ORDER BY salary_grade_id;
```

```
FIRST_NAME LAST_NAME  TITLE                   SALARY SALARY_GRADE_ID
---------- ---------- ------------------- ---------- ---------------
Fred       Hobbs      Salesperson             150000               1
Susan      Jones      Salesperson             500000               2
Ron        Johnson    Sales Manager           600000               3
James      Smith      CEO                     800000               4
```

In this query, the BETWEEN operator returns true if the employee's salary is between the low salary and high salary for the salary grade; when true is returned, the salary grade found is the salary grade for the employee. For example, Fred Hobbs' salary is $150,000; this is between the low salary of $1 and the high salary of $250,000 in the salary_grades table for the salary_grade_id of 1; therefore, Fred Hobbs' salary grade is 1. Similarly, Susan Jones' salary is $500,000; this is between the low salary of $250,001 and the high salary of $500,000 for the salary grade ID of 2; therefore, Susan Jones' salary grade is 2. Ron Johnson and James Smith have salary grades of 3 and 4 respectively.

Outer Joins

An outer join retrieves a row even when one of the columns in the join contains a null value. You perform an outer join by supplying the outer join operator in the join condition; the Oracle proprietary outer join operator is a plus character in parentheses (+).

Let's take a look at an example. Remember the query earlier that didn't show the "My Front Line" product because its product_type_id is null? You can use an outer join to get that row. In the following query, notice that the Oracle outer join operator (+) is on the opposite side of the product_type_id column in the product table (this is the column that contains the null value):

```
SELECT p.name, pt.name
FROM products p, product_types pt
WHERE p.product_type_id = pt.product_type_id (+)
ORDER BY p.name;
```

```
NAME                                NAME
----------------------------------  ----------
2412: The Return                    Video
Chemistry                           Book
Classical Music                     CD
Creative Yell                       CD
From Another Planet                 DVD
Modern Science                      Book
My Front Line
Pop 3                               CD
Space Force 9                       DVD
Supernova                           Video
Tank War                            Video
Z Files                             Video
```

Notice that "My Front Line"—the product with the null `product_type_id`—is now retrieved, even though its `product_type_id` is null.

NOTE
You can place the outer join operator on either side of the join operator, but you always place it on the opposite side of the column that contains the null value.

The following query returns the same results as the previous one, but notice that the column with the null value (`pt.product_type_id`) and the Oracle outer join operator are on the left of the equality operator:

```
SELECT p.name, pt.name
FROM products p, product_types pt
WHERE pt.product_type_id (+) = p.product_type_id
ORDER BY p.name;
```

Left and Right Outer Joins

Outer joins can be split into two types:

- Left outer joins

- Right outer joins

To understand the difference between left and right outer joins, consider the following syntax:

```
SELECT ...
FROM table1, table2
...
```

Assume the tables are to be joined on `table1.column1` and `table2.column2`. Also, assume `table1` contains a row with a null value in `column1`. To perform a left outer join, the WHERE clause is

```
WHERE table1.column1 = table2.column2 (+);
```

NOTE
In a left outer join, the outer join operator is actually on the right of the equality operator.

Next, assume `table2` contains a row with a null value in `column2`. To perform a right outer join, you switch the position of the Oracle outer join operator to the *left* of the equality operator, and the `WHERE` clause becomes

```
WHERE table1.column1 (+) = table2.column2;
```

NOTE
As you'll see, if `table1` and `table2` both contain rows with null values, you get different results depending on whether you use a left or right outer join.

Let's take a look at some concrete examples to make left and right outer joins clearer.

An Example of a Left Outer Join   The following query uses a left outer join; notice that the Oracle outer join operator appears on the *right* of the equality operator:

```
SELECT p.name, pt.name
FROM products p, product_types pt
WHERE p.product_type_id = pt.product_type_id (+)
ORDER BY p.name;
```

```
NAME                            NAME
------------------------------  ----------
2412: The Return                Video
Chemistry                       Book
Classical Music                 CD
Creative Yell                   CD
From Another Planet             DVD
Modern Science                  Book
My Front Line
Pop 3                           CD
Space Force 9                   DVD
Supernova                       Video
Tank War                        Video
Z Files                         Video
```

Notice all the rows from the `products` table are retrieved, including the "My Front Line" row, which has a null value in the `product_type_id` column.

An Example of a Right Outer Join   The `product_types` table contains a type of product not referenced in the `products` table (there are no magazines in the `products` table); the magazine product type appears at the end of the following example:

```
SELECT *
FROM product_types;
```

```
PRODUCT_TYPE_ID NAME
--------------- ----------
              1 Book
              2 Video
              3 DVD
              4 CD
              5 Magazine
```

You can retrieve the magazine in a join on the `products` and `product_types` tables by using a right outer join, as shown in the following query; notice that the Oracle outer join operator appears on the *left* of the equality operator:

```
SELECT p.name, pt.name
FROM products p, product_types pt
WHERE p.product_type_id (+) = pt.product_type_id
ORDER BY p.name;
```

```
NAME                            NAME
------------------------------  ----------
2412: The Return                Video
Chemistry                       Book
Classical Music                 CD
Creative Yell                   CD
From Another Planet             DVD
Modern Science                  Book
Pop 3                           CD
Space Force 9                   DVD
Supernova                       Video
Tank War                        Video
Z Files                         Video
                                Magazine
```

Limitations on Outer Joins

There are limitations when using outer joins, and you will learn about some of them in this section.

You may only place the outer join operator on one side of the join (not both). If you try to place the Oracle outer join operator on both sides, you get an error, as shown in the following example:

```
SQL> SELECT p.name, pt.name
  2  FROM products p, product_types pt
  3  WHERE p.product_type_id (+) = pt.product_type_id (+);
WHERE p.product_type_id (+) = pt.product_type_id (+)
                                *
ERROR at line 3:
ORA-01468: a predicate may reference only one outer-joined table
```

You cannot use an outer join condition with the `IN` operator:

```
SQL> SELECT p.name, pt.name
  2  FROM products p, product_types pt
  3  WHERE p.product_type_id (+) IN (1, 2, 3, 4);
WHERE p.product_type_id (+) IN (1, 2, 3, 4)
                                *
ERROR at line 3:
ORA-01719: outer join operator (+) not allowed in operand of OR or IN
```

You cannot use an outer join condition with another join using the OR operator:

```
SQL> SELECT p.name, pt.name
  2  FROM products p, product_types pt
  3  WHERE p.product_type_id (+) = pt.product_type_id
  4  OR p.product_type_id = 1;
WHERE p.product_type_id (+) = pt.product_type_id
                                  *
ERROR at line 3:
ORA-01719: outer join operator (+) not allowed in operand of OR or IN
```

NOTE
*These are the commonly encountered limitations when using the
outer join operator. For all the limitations, read the Oracle Database
SQL Reference manual from Oracle Corporation.*

Self Joins

A self join is a join made on the same table. To perform a self join, you must use a different table
alias to identify each reference to the table in the query. Let's consider an example. The employees
table has a manager_id column that contains the employee_id of the manager for each
employee; if the employee has no manager, then the manager_id is null. The employees table
contains the following rows:

```
EMPLOYEE_ID MANAGER_ID FIRST_NAME LAST_NAME  TITLE          SALARY
----------- ---------- ---------- ---------- -----------   --------
          1            James      Smith      CEO            800000
          2          1 Ron        Johnson    Sales Manager  600000
          3          2 Fred       Hobbs      Salesperson    150000
          4          2 Susan      Jones      Salesperson    500000
```

James Smith—the CEO—has a null value for the manager_id, meaning that he doesn't have a
manager. Susan Jones and Fred Hobbs are managed by Ron Johnson, and Ron Johnson is managed
by James Smith.

You can use a self join to display the names of each employee and their manager. In the
following query, the employees table is referenced twice, using two aliases w and m. The w alias
is used to get the worker name, and the m alias is used to get the manager name. The self join is
made between w.manager_id and m.employee_id:

```
SELECT w.first_name || ' ' || w.last_name || ' works for '||
    m.first_name || ' ' || m.last_name
FROM employees w, employees m
WHERE w.manager_id = m.employee_id
ORDER BY w.first_name;

W.FIRST_NAME||''||W.LAST_NAME||'WORKSFOR'||M.FIRST_NA
----------------------------------------------------
Fred Hobbs works for Ron Johnson
Ron Johnson works for James Smith
Susan Jones works for Ron Johnson
```

Because James Smith's manager_id is null, the join condition does not return the row.

You can perform outer joins in combination with self joins. In the following query, an outer join is used with the self join shown in the previous example to retrieve the row for James Smith. You'll notice the use of the NVL() function to provide a string indicating that James Smith works for the shareholders (he's the CEO, so he reports to the store's shareholders):

```
SELECT w.last_name || ' works for ' ||
 NVL(m.last_name, 'the shareholders')
FROM employees w, employees m
WHERE w.manager_id = m.employee_id (+)
ORDER BY w.last_name;

W.LAST_NAME||'WORKSFOR'||NVL(M.LAST_N
-------------------------------------
Hobbs works for Johnson
Johnson works for Smith
Jones works for Johnson
Smith works for the shareholders
```

Performing Joins Using the SQL/92 Syntax

The joins you've seen so far use Oracle's syntax for joins, which is based on the ANSI SQL/86 standard. With the introduction of Oracle Database 9*i*, the database implements the ANSI SQL/92 standard syntax for joins, and you should use SQL/92 in your queries. You'll see how to use SQL/92 in this section, including its use in avoiding unwanted Cartesian products.

NOTE
You can visit the ANSI website at www.ansi.org.

Performing Inner Joins on Two Tables Using SQL/92

Earlier, you saw the following query, which uses the SQL/86 standard for performing an inner join:

```
SELECT p.name, pt.name
FROM products p, product_types pt
WHERE p.product_type_id = pt.product_type_id
ORDER BY p.name;
```

SQL/92 introduces the INNER JOIN and ON clauses for performing an inner join. The following example rewrites the previous query using the INNER JOIN and ON clauses:

```
SELECT p.name, pt.name
FROM products p INNER JOIN product_types pt
ON p.product_type_id = pt.product_type_id
ORDER BY p.name;
```

You can also use non-equijoin operators with the ON clause. Earlier, you saw the following query, which uses the SQL/86 standard for performing a non-equijoin:

```
SELECT e.first_name, e.last_name, e.title, e.salary, sg.salary_grade_id
FROM employees e, salary_grades sg
WHERE e.salary BETWEEN sg.low_salary AND sg.high_salary
ORDER BY salary_grade_id;
```

The following example rewrites this query to use the SQL/92 standard:

```
SELECT e.first_name, e.last_name, e.title, e.salary, sg.salary_grade_id
FROM employees e INNER JOIN salary_grades sg
ON e.salary BETWEEN sg.low_salary AND sg.high_salary
ORDER BY salary_grade_id;
```

Simplifying Joins with the USING Keyword

SQL/92 allows you to further simplify the join condition with the USING clause, but with the following limitations:

- The query must use an equijoin.

- The columns in the equijoin must have the same name.

Most of the joins you'll perform will be equijoins, and if you always use the same name as the primary key for your foreign keys, you'll satisfy these limitations.

The following query uses the USING clause instead of ON:

```
SELECT p.name, pt.name
FROM products p INNER JOIN product_types pt
USING (product_type_id);
```

If you wanted to retrieve the product_type_id, you must provide only this column name on its own without a table name or alias in the SELECT clause, as for example:

```
SELECT p.name, pt.name, product_type_id
FROM products p INNER JOIN product_types pt
USING (product_type_id);
```

If you try to provide a table alias with the column, such as p.product_type_id for example, you'll get an error:

```
SQL> SELECT p.name, pt.name, p.product_type_id
  2  FROM products p INNER JOIN product_types pt
  3  USING (product_type_id);
SELECT p.name, pt.name, p.product_type_id
                          *
ERROR at line 1:
ORA-25154: column part of USING clause cannot have qualifier
```

Also, you only use the column name on its own within the USING clause. For example, if you specify USING (p.product_type_id) in the previous query instead of USING (product_type_id), you'll get an error:

```
SQL> SELECT p.name, pt.name, p.product_type_id
  2  FROM products p INNER JOIN product_types pt
  3  USING (p.product_type_id);
USING (p.product_type_id)
         *
ERROR at line 3:
ORA-01748: only simple column names allowed here
```

CAUTION
Don't use a table name or alias when referencing columns used in a
USING *clause. You'll get an error if you do.*

Performing Inner Joins on More than Two Tables Using SQL/92

Earlier you saw the following SQL/86 query, which retrieves rows from the customers, purchases, products, and product_types tables:

```
SELECT c.first_name, c.last_name, p.name AS PRODUCT, pt.name AS TYPE
FROM customers c, purchases pr, products p, product_types pt
WHERE c.customer_id = pr.customer_id
AND p.product_id = pr.product_id
AND p.product_type_id = pt.product_type_id
ORDER BY p.name;
```

The following example rewrites this query using SQL/92; notice how the foreign key relationships are navigated using multiple INNER JOIN and USING clauses:

```
SELECT c.first_name, c.last_name, p.name AS PRODUCT, pt.name AS TYPE
FROM customers c INNER JOIN purchases pr
USING (customer_id)
INNER JOIN products p
USING (product_id)
INNER JOIN product_types pt
USING (product_type_id)
ORDER BY p.name;
```

Performing Inner Joins on Multiple Columns Using SQL/92

If your join uses more than one column from the two tables, you provide those columns in your ON clause and use the AND operator. For example, let's say you have two tables named table1 and table2 and you want to join these tables using columns named column1 and column2 in both tables. Your query would be

```
SELECT ...
FROM table1 INNER JOIN table2
ON table1.column1 = table2.column1
AND table1.column2 = table2.column2;
```

You can further simplify your query with the USING clause, but only if you're performing an equijoin and the column names are identical. For example, the following query rewrites the previous example with the USING clause:

```
SELECT ...
FROM table1 INNER JOIN table2
USING (column1, column2);
```

Performing Outer Joins Using SQL/92

Earlier you saw how to perform outer joins using the outer join operator (+), which is Oracle proprietary syntax. SQL/92 uses a different syntax for performing outer joins. Instead of using (+), you specify the type of join in the FROM clause using the following syntax:

```
FROM table1 { LEFT | RIGHT | FULL } OUTER JOIN table2
```

where

- *table1* and *table2* are the tables you want to join.

- LEFT means you want to perform a left outer join.

- RIGHT means you want to perform a right outer join.

- FULL means you want to perform a full outer join. A full outer join uses all rows in *table1* and *table2*, including those that have null values in the columns used in the join. You cannot directly perform a full outer join using the (+) operator.

You'll see how to perform left, right, and full outer joins using the SQL/92 syntax in the following sections.

Performing Left Outer Joins Using SQL/92

Earlier you saw the following query, which performed a left outer join using the Oracle proprietary (+) operator:

```
SELECT p.name, pt.name
FROM products p, product_types pt
WHERE p.product_type_id = pt.product_type_id (+)
ORDER BY p.name;
```

The next example rewrites this query using the SQL/92 LEFT OUTER JOIN keywords:

```
SELECT p.name, pt.name
FROM products p LEFT OUTER JOIN product_types pt
USING (product_type_id)
ORDER BY p.name;
```

Performing Right Outer Joins Using SQL/92

Earlier you saw the following query, which performed a right outer join using the Oracle proprietary (+) operator:

```
SELECT p.name, pt.name
FROM products p, product_types pt
WHERE p.product_type_id (+) = pt.product_type_id
ORDER BY p.name;
```

The next example rewrites this query using the SQL/92 RIGHT OUTER JOIN keywords:

```
SELECT p.name, pt.name
FROM products p RIGHT OUTER JOIN product_types pt
USING (product_type_id)
ORDER BY p.name;
```

Performing Full Outer Joins Using SQL/92

A full outer join uses all rows in the joined tables, including those that have null values in either of the columns used in the join. The following example shows a query that uses the SQL/92 FULL OUTER JOIN keywords:

```
SELECT p.name, pt.name
FROM products p FULL OUTER JOIN product_types pt
USING (product_type_id)
ORDER BY p.name;
```

```
NAME                             NAME
-------------------------------  ----------
2412: The Return                 Video
Chemistry                        Book
Classical Music                  CD
Creative Yell                    CD
From Another Planet              DVD
Modern Science                   Book
My Front Line
Pop 3                            CD
Space Force 9                    DVD
Supernova                        Video
Tank War                         Video
Z Files                          Video
                                 Magazine
```

Notice that both "My Front Line" from the products table and "Magazine" from the product_types table are returned.

Performing Self Joins Using SQL/92

The following example uses SQL/86 to perform a self join on the employees table:

```
SELECT w.last_name || ' works for ' || m.last_name
FROM employees w, employees m
WHERE w.manager_id = m.employee_id;
```

The next example rewrites this query to use the SQL/92 INNER JOIN and ON keywords:

```
SELECT w.last_name || ' works for ' || m.last_name
FROM employees w INNER JOIN employees m
ON w.manager_id = m.employee_id;
```

Performing Cross Joins Using SQL/92

Earlier you saw how omitting a join condition between two tables leads to a Cartesian product. By using the SQL/92 join syntax, you avoid inadvertently producing a Cartesian product because you must always provide an ON or USING clause to join the tables—this is a good thing because you usually don't want a Cartesian product.

If you really want a Cartesian product, the SQL/92 standard requires that you explicitly state this in your query using the CROSS JOIN keywords. In the following query, a Cartesian product between the product_types and products tables is generated using the CROSS JOIN keywords:

```
SELECT *
FROM product_types CROSS JOIN products;
```

Summary

In this chapter, you have learned the following:

- How to perform single and multiple table queries

- How to select all columns from a table using an asterisk (*) in a query

- How a row identifier (rowid) is used internally by the Oracle database to store the location of a row

- How to perform arithmetic in SQL

- How to use addition and subtraction operators with dates

- How to reference tables and columns using aliases

- How to merge column output using the concatenation operator (||)

- How nulls are used to represent unknown values

- How to display distinct rows using the DISTINCT operator

- How to limit the retrieval of rows using the WHERE clause

- How to sort rows using the ORDER BY clause

- How to perform inner, outer, and self joins using the SQL/86 and SQL/92 syntax

In the next chapter, you'll learn about SQL*Plus.

CHAPTER
3

Using SQL*Plus

n this chapter, you will see how to do the following:

- View the structure of a table.

- Edit an SQL statement.

- Save and run scripts containing SQL statements and SQL*Plus commands.

- Format the results returned by SQL*Plus.

- Use variables in SQL*Plus.

- Create simple reports.

- Get help from SQL*Plus.

- Automatically generate SQL statements.

- Disconnect from a database and exit SQL*Plus.

Let's plunge in and examine how you view the structure of a table.

Viewing the Structure of a Table

Knowing the structure of a table is useful because you can use the information to formulate an SQL statement. For example, you can figure out the columns you want to retrieve in a query. You use the DESCRIBE command to view the structure of a table.

The following example uses DESCRIBE to view the structure of the customers table; notice that the semicolon character (;) is omitted from the end of the command:

```
SQL> DESCRIBE customers
 Name                      Null?    Type
 ------------------------- -------- --------------
 CUSTOMER_ID               NOT NULL NUMBER(38)
 FIRST_NAME                NOT NULL VARCHAR2(10)
 LAST_NAME                 NOT NULL VARCHAR2(10)
 DOB                                DATE
 PHONE                              VARCHAR2(12)
```

The output from DESCRIBE has three columns that show the structure of the table. These columns are as follows:

- **Name** lists the names of the columns contained in the table. In the example, you can see the customers table has five columns: customer_id, first_name, last_name, dob, and phone.

- **Null?** indicates whether the column can store null values. If set to NOT NULL, the column cannot store a null value; if blank, the column can store a null value. In the preceding example, you can see that the customer_id, first_name, and last_name columns cannot store null values, but the dob and phone columns can.

■   **Type** indicates the type of the column. In the preceding example, you can see that the type of the `customer_id` column is NUMBER(38) and that the type of the `first_name` is VARCHAR2(10).

You can save some typing by shortening the DESCRIBE command to DESC (DESC[RIBE]). The following command uses DESC to view the structure of the `products` table:

```
SQL> DESC products
 Name                     Null?     Type
 ---------------------    --------  --------------
 PRODUCT_ID               NOT NULL  NUMBER(38)
 PRODUCT_TYPE_ID                    NUMBER(38)
 NAME                     NOT NULL  VARCHAR2(30)
 DESCRIPTION                        VARCHAR2(50)
 PRICE                              NUMBER(5,2)
```

Editing SQL Statements

As you may have noticed, it becomes tedious to have to repeatedly type similar SQL statements into SQL*Plus. You will be pleased to know SQL*Plus stores your previous SQL statement in a buffer. You can then edit the lines that make up your SQL statement stored in the buffer.

Some of the editing commands are listed in the following table; notice the optional part of each command in square brackets (for example, you can abbreviate the APPEND command to A).

Command	Description
A[PPEND] *text*	Appends *text* to the current line.
C[HANGE] /*old*/*new*	Changes the text specified by *old* to *new* in the current line.
CL[EAR] BUFF[ER]	Clears all lines from the buffer.
DEL	Deletes the current line.
DEL *x*	Deletes the line specified by the line number *x* (line numbers start with 1).
L[IST]	Lists all the lines in the buffer.
L[IST] *x*	Lists line number *x*.
R[UN] or /	Runs the statement stored in the buffer. You can also use / to run the statement.
x	Makes the line specified by the line number *x* the current line.

Let's take a look at some examples of using the SQL*Plus editing commands. The following example shows a query in SQL*Plus:

```
SQL> SELECT customer_id, first_name, last_name
  2  FROM customers
  3  WHERE customer_id = 1;
```

SQL*Plus automatically increments the line number when you press ENTER. You can make line 1 the current line by entering 1 at the prompt:

```
SQL> 1
  1* SELECT customer_id, first_name, last_name
```

Notice that SQL*Plus displays the current line and the line number. The following example uses APPEND to add ", dob" to the end of the line:

```
SQL> APPEND , dob
  1* SELECT customer_id, first_name, last_name, dob
```

The next example uses LIST to show all the lines in the buffer:

```
SQL> LIST
  1  SELECT customer_id, first_name, last_name, dob
  2  FROM customers
  3* WHERE customer_id = 1
```

Notice that the current line has been changed to the last line, as indicated by the asterisk character (*). The following example uses CHANGE to replace "customer_id = 1" with "customer_id = 2" in this last line:

```
SQL> CHANGE /customer_id = 1/customer_id = 2
  3* WHERE customer_id = 2
```

The next example uses RUN to execute the query:

```
SQL> RUN
  1  SELECT customer_id, first_name, last_name, dob
  2  FROM customers
  3* WHERE customer_id = 2

CUSTOMER_ID FIRST_NAME LAST_NAME  DOB
----------- ---------- ---------- ---------
          2 Cynthia    Green      05-FEB-68
```

You can also use a forward slash character (/) to run the SQL statement; for example:

```
SQL> /

CUSTOMER_ID FIRST_NAME LAST_NAME  DOB
----------- ---------- ---------- ---------
          2 Cynthia    Green      05-FEB-68
```

Saving, Retrieving, and Running Files

SQL*Plus allows you to save, retrieve, and run scripts containing SQL*Plus commands and SQL statements. You've already seen one example of running an SQL*Plus script: the store_schema.sql script file that was run in Chapter 1.

Some of the file commands are listed in the following table.

Command	Description
SAV[E] *filename* [{ REPLACE | APPEND }]	Saves the contents of the SQL*Plus buffer to a file specified by *filename*. You append the content of the buffer to an existing file using the APPEND option. You overwrite an existing file using the REPLACE option.
GET *filename*	Retrieves the contents of the file specified by *filename* into the SQL*Plus buffer.
STA[RT] *filename*	Retrieves the contents of the file specified by *filename* into the SQL*Plus buffer and then attempts to run the contents of the buffer.
@ *filename*	Same as the START command.
ED[IT]	Copies the contents of the SQL*Plus buffer to a file named afiedt.buf and then starts the default editor for the operating system. When you exit the editor, the contents of the edited file are copied to the SQL*Plus buffer.
ED[IT] *filename*	Same as the EDIT command, but you can specify a file to start editing. You specify the file to edit using the *filename* parameter.
SPO[OL] *filename*	Copies the output from SQL*Plus to the file specified by *filename*.
SPO[OL] OFF	Stops the copying of output from SQL*Plus to the file, then closes that file.

Let's take a look at some examples of using these SQL*Plus commands. If you want to follow along with the examples, go ahead and enter the following query into SQL*Plus:

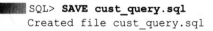
SQL> **SELECT customer_id, first_name, last_name**
  2 **FROM customers**
  3 **WHERE customer_id = 1;**

The following example uses SAVE to save the contents of the SQL*Plus buffer to a file named cust_query.sql:

SQL> **SAVE cust_query.sql**
Created file cust_query.sql

NOTE
On my computer, the cust_query.sql *file is saved in the* E:\ oracle_11g\product\11.1.0\db_1\BIN *directory.*

The next example uses GET to retrieve the contents of the cust_query.sql file:

SQL> **GET cust_query.sql**
  1 SELECT customer_id, first_name, last_name
  2 FROM customers
  3* WHERE customer_id = 1

The following example runs the query using /:

```
SQL> /

CUSTOMER_ID FIRST_NAME LAST_NAME
----------- ---------- ----------
          1 John       Brown
```

The next example uses START to load and run the contents of the cust_query.sql file in one step:

```
SQL> START cust_query.sql

CUSTOMER_ID FIRST_NAME LAST_NAME
----------- ---------- ----------
          1 John       Brown
```

You can edit the contents of the SQL*Plus buffer using the EDIT command:

```
SQL> EDIT
```

The EDIT command starts the default editor for your operating system. On Windows the default editor is Notepad. On Unix and Linux the default editors are vi or emacs, respectively.

Figure 3-1 shows the contents of the SQL*Plus buffer in Notepad. Notice the SQL statement is terminated using a slash character (/) rather than a semicolon.

In your editor, change the WHERE clause to WHERE customer_id = 2, then save and exit the editor (in Notepad, you select File | Exit, then click Yes to save your query). SQL*Plus displays the following output containing your modified query; notice that the WHERE clause has been changed:

```
1  SELECT customer_id, first_name, last_name
2  FROM customers
3* WHERE customer_id = 2
```

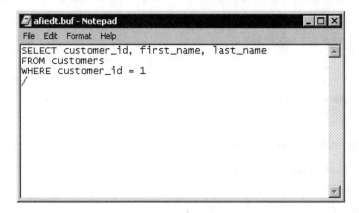

FIGURE 3-1 *Editing the SQL*Plus buffer contents using Notepad*

Changing the Default Editor

You can change the default editor using the SQL*Plus DEFINE command:

```
DEFINE _EDITOR = 'editor'
```

where *editor* is the name of your preferred editor.

For example, the following command sets the default editor to vi:

```
DEFINE _EDITOR = 'vi'
```

You can also change the default editor SQL*Plus uses by adding the line DEFINE _ EDITOR = '*editor*' to a new file named login.sql, where *editor* is the name of your preferred editor. You can add any SQL*Plus commands you want to this file. SQL*Plus will check the current directory for a login.sql file and execute it when SQL*Plus starts. If there is no login.sql file in the current directory, then SQL*Plus will check all directories (and their subdirectories) in the SQLPATH environment variable for a login.sql file. On Windows, SQLPATH is defined as a registry entry in HKEY_LOCAL_MACHINE\SOFTWARE\ ORACLE*oracle_home_key* (where *oracle_home_key* is the key for the associated installation of the Oracle database). On my Windows XP computer running Oracle Database 11*g*, SQLPATH is set to E:\oracle_11g\product\11.1.0\db_1\dbs. On Unix or Linux, there is no default SQLPATH defined, and you will need to add it as an environment variable. For further details on setting up a login.sql file, you can read the *SQL*Plus User's Guide and Reference*, published by Oracle Corporation.

You run your modified query using the slash character (/):

```
SQL> /

CUSTOMER_ID FIRST_NAME LAST_NAME
----------- ---------- ----------
          2 Cynthia    Green
```

TIP
*In the Oracle Database 11g version of SQL*Plus, you can also scroll through your previously executed statements using the UP and DOWN ARROW keys on the keyboard. Once you've selected a statement, you can use the LEFT and RIGHT ARROW keys to move the cursor to a specific point in the statement.*

You use the SPOOL command to copy the output from SQL*Plus to a file. The following example spools the output to a file named cust_results.txt, runs the query again, and then turns spooling off by executing SPOOL OFF:

```
SQL> SPOOL cust_results.txt
SQL> /

CUSTOMER_ID FIRST_NAME LAST_NAME
----------- ---------- ----------
          2 Cynthia    Green

SQL> SPOOL OFF
```

Feel free to examine the `cust_results.txt` file; it will contain the previous output between the slash (/) and `SPOOL OFF`. On my Windows XP computer, the file is stored in `E:\oracle_11g\product\11.1.0\db_1\BIN`; the directory used is the current directory you are in when you start SQL*Plus.

You can also specify the full directory path where you want the spool file to be written; for example:

```
SPOOL C:\my_files\spools\cust_results.txt
```

Formatting Columns

You use the `COLUMN` command to format the display of column headings and column data. The simplified syntax for the `COLUMN` command is as follows:

```
COL[UMN] {column | alias} [options]
```

where

- *column* is the column name.

- *alias* is the column alias to be formatted. In Chapter 2, you saw that you can "rename" a column using a column alias; you can reference an alias in the `COLUMN` command.

- *options* are one or more options to be used to format the column or alias.

There are a number of options you can use with the `COLUMN` command. The following table shows some of these options.

Option	Description
FOR[MAT] *format*	Sets the format for the display of the column or alias to the *format* string.
HEA[DING] *heading*	Sets the heading of the column or alias to the *heading* string.
JUS[TIFY] [{ LEFT | CENTER | RIGHT }]	Places the column output to the left, center, or right.
WRA[PPED]	Wraps the end of a string onto the next line of output. This option may cause individual words to be split across multiple lines.
WOR[D_WRAPPED]	Similar to the `WRAPPED` option, except individual words are not split across two lines.
CLE[AR]	Clears any formatting of columns (that is, sets the formatting back to the default).

The *format* string in the previous table may take a number of formatting parameters. The parameters you specify depend on the data stored in your column:

- If your column contains characters, you use A*x* to format the characters, where *x* specifies the width for the characters. For example, A12 sets the width to 12 characters.

■   If your column contains numbers, you can use any of a variety of number formats, which are shown later in Table 4-4 of Chapter 4. For example, `$99.99` sets the format to a dollar sign, followed by two digits, the decimal point, plus another two digits.

■   If your column contains a date, you can use any of the date formats shown later in Table 5-2 of Chapter 5. For example, `MM-DD-YYYY` sets the format to a two-digit month (`MM`), a two-digit day (`DD`), and a four-digit year (`YYYY`).

Let's take a look at an example. You'll see how to format the output of a query that retrieves the `product_id`, `name`, `description`, and `price` columns from the `products` table. The display requirements, format strings, and `COLUMN` commands are shown in the following table:

Column	Display As...	Format	COLUMN Command
product_id	Two digits	99	COLUMN product_id FORMAT 99
name	Thirteen-character word-wrapped strings and set the column heading to PRODUCT_NAME	A13	COLUMN name HEADING PRODUCT_NAME FORMAT A13 WORD_WRAPPED
description	Thirteen-character word-wrapped strings	A13	COLUMN description FORMAT A13 WORD_WRAPPED
price	Dollar symbol, with two digits before and after the decimal point	$99.99	COLUMN price FORMAT $99.99

The following example shows the `COLUMN` commands in SQL*Plus:

```
SQL> COLUMN product_id FORMAT 99
SQL> COLUMN name HEADING PRODUCT_NAME FORMAT A13 WORD_WRAPPED
SQL> COLUMN description FORMAT A13 WORD_WRAPPED
SQL> COLUMN price FORMAT $99.99
```

The next example runs a query to retrieve some rows from the `products` table; notice the formatting of the columns in the output:

```
SQL> SELECT product_id, name, description, price
  2  FROM products
  3  WHERE product_id < 6;

PRODUCT_ID PRODUCT_NAME  DESCRIPTION     PRICE
---------- ------------- ------------- --------
         1 Modern        A description  $19.95
           Science       of modern
                         science

         2 Chemistry     Introduction   $30.00
                         to Chemistry
```

```
             3 Supernova       A star          $25.99
                               explodes

             4 Tank War        Action movie    $13.95

PRODUCT_ID PRODUCT_NAME    DESCRIPTION        PRICE
---------- ------------    ------------    --------
                               about a
                               future war

             5 Z Files         Series on       $49.99
                               mysterious
                               activities
```

This output is readable, but wouldn't it be nice if you could display the headings just once at the top? You do that by setting the page size, as you'll see next.

Setting the Page Size

You set the number of lines in a page using the SET PAGESIZE command. This command sets the number of lines that SQL*Plus considers one "page" of output, after which SQL*Plus will display the headings again.

The following example sets the page size to 100 lines using the SET PAGESIZE command and runs the query again using /:

```
SQL> SET PAGESIZE 100
SQL> /

PRODUCT_ID PRODUCT_NAME    DESCRIPTION        PRICE
---------- ------------    ------------    --------
             1 Modern          A description   $19.95
               Science         of modern
                               science

             2 Chemistry       Introduction    $30.00
                               to Chemistry

             3 Supernova       A star          $25.99
                               explodes

             4 Tank War        Action movie    $13.95
                               about a
                               future war

             5 Z Files         Series on       $49.99
                               mysterious
                               activities
```

Notice that the headings are shown only once, at the top, and the resulting output looks better.

NOTE
The maximum number for the page size is 50,000.

Setting the Line Size

You set the number of characters in a line using the SET LINESIZE command. The following example sets the line size to 50 lines and runs another query:

```
SQL> SET LINESIZE 50
SQL> SELECT * FROM customers;

CUSTOMER_ID FIRST_NAME LAST_NAME  DOB
----------- ---------- ---------- ---------
PHONE
------------
          1 John       Brown      01-JAN-65
800-555-1211

          2 Cynthia    Green      05-FEB-68
800-555-1212

          3 Steve      White      16-MAR-71
800-555-1213

          4 Gail       Black
800-555-1214

          5 Doreen     Blue       20-MAY-70
```

The lines don't span more than 50 characters.

NOTE
The maximum number for the line size is 32,767.

Clearing Column Formatting

You clear the formatting for a column using the CLEAR option of the COLUMN command. For example, the following COLUMN command clears the formatting for the product_id column:

```
SQL> COLUMN product_id CLEAR
```

You can clear the formatting for all columns using CLEAR COLUMNS. For example:

```
SQL> CLEAR COLUMNS
```

Once you've cleared the columns, the output from the queries will use the default format.

Using Variables

In this section, you'll see how to create variables that may be used in place of actual values in SQL statements. These variables are known as *substitution variables* because they are used as substitutes for values. When you run an SQL statement, you enter values for the variables; the values are then "substituted" into the SQL statement.

There are two types of substitution variables:

■ **Temporary variables**   A temporary variable is valid only for the SQL statement in which it is used—it doesn't persist.

■ **Defined variables**   A defined variable persists until you explicitly remove it, redefine it, or exit SQL*Plus.

You'll learn how to use these types of variables in this section.

Temporary Variables

You define a temporary variable using the ampersand character (&) in an SQL statement, followed by the name you want to call your variable. For example, &v_product_id defines a variable named v_product_id.

When you run the following query, SQL*Plus prompts you to enter a value for v_product_id and then uses that value in the WHERE clause. If you enter the value 2 for v_product_id, the details for product #2 will be displayed.

```
SQL> SELECT product_id, name, price
  2  FROM products
  3  WHERE product_id = &v_product_id;
Enter value for v_product_id: 2
old   3: WHERE product_id = &v_product_id
new   3: WHERE product_id = 2

PRODUCT_ID NAME                                 PRICE
---------- ------------------------------- ----------
         2 Chemistry                               30
```

Notice that SQL*Plus does the following:

■ Prompts you to enter a value for v_product_id.

■ Substitutes the value you entered for v_product_id in the WHERE clause.

SQL*Plus shows you the substitution in the old and new lines in the output, along with the line number in the query where the substitution was performed. In the previous example, you can see that the old and new lines indicate that v_product_id is set to 2 in the WHERE clause.

Why Are Variables Useful?

Variables are useful because they allow you to create scripts that a user who doesn't know SQL can run. Your script would prompt the user to enter the value for a variable and use that value in an SQL statement. Let's take a look at an example.

Suppose you wanted to create a script for a user who doesn't know SQL, but who wants to see the details of a single specified product in the store. To do this, you could hard code the `product_id` value in the `WHERE` clause of a query and place it in an SQL*Plus script. For example, the following query retrieves product #1:

```
SELECT product_id, name, price
FROM products
WHERE product_id = 1;
```

This query works, but it only retrieves product #1. What if you wanted to change the `product_id` value to retrieve a different row? You could modify the script, but this would be tedious. Wouldn't it be great if you could supply a variable for the `product_id`? You can do that using a substitution variable.

If you rerun the query using the slash character (/), SQL*Plus will ask you to enter a new value for `v_product_id`. For example:

```
SQL> /
Enter value for v_product_id: 3
old   3: WHERE product_id = &v_product_id
new   3: WHERE product_id = 3

PRODUCT_ID NAME                                    PRICE
---------- ------------------------------ ----------
         3 Supernova                              25.99
```

Once again, SQL*Plus echoes the old line of the SQL statement (`old 3: WHERE product_id = &v_product_id`), followed by the new line containing the variable value you entered (`new 3: WHERE product_id = 3`).

Controlling Output Lines

You may control the output of the old and new lines using the `SET VERIFY` command. If you enter `SET VERIFY OFF`, the old and new lines are suppressed. For example:

```
SQL> SET VERIFY OFF
SQL> /
Enter value for v_product_id: 4

PRODUCT_ID NAME                                    PRICE
---------- ------------------------------ ----------
         4 Tank War                               13.95
```

To turn the echoing of the lines back on, you enter SET VERIFY ON. For example:

```
SQL> SET VERIFY ON
```

Changing the Variable Definition Character

You can use the SET DEFINE command to specify a character other than an ampersand (&) for defining a variable. The following example shows how to set the variable character to the pound character (#) and shows a new query:

```
SQL> SET DEFINE '#'
SQL> SELECT product_id, name, price
  2  FROM products
  3  WHERE product_id = #v_product_id;
Enter value for v_product_id: 5
old   3: WHERE product_id = #v_product_id
new   3: WHERE product_id = 5

PRODUCT_ID NAME                                 PRICE
---------- ------------------------------  ----------
         5 Z Files                              49.99
```

The next example uses SET DEFINE to change the character back to an ampersand:

```
SQL> SET DEFINE '&'
```

Substituting Table and Column Names Using Variables

You can also use variables to substitute the names of tables and columns. For example, the following query defines variables for a column name (v_col), a table name (v_table), and a column value (v_val):

```
SQL> SELECT name, &v_col
  2  FROM &v_table
  3  WHERE &v_col = &v_val;
Enter value for v_col: product_type_id
old   1: SELECT name, &v_col
new   1: SELECT name, product_type_id
Enter value for v_table: products
old   2: FROM &v_table
new   2: FROM products
Enter value for v_col: product_type_id
Enter value for v_val: 1
old   3: WHERE &v_col = &v_val
new   3: WHERE product_type_id = 1

NAME                             PRODUCT_TYPE_ID
------------------------------   ---------------
Modern Science                                 1
Chemistry                                      1
```

You can avoid having to repeatedly enter a variable by using &&. For example:

```
SQL> SELECT name, &&v_col
  2  FROM &v_table
  3  WHERE &&v_col = &v_val;
Enter value for v_col: product_type_id
old    1: SELECT name, &&v_col
new    1: SELECT name, product_type_id
Enter value for v_table: products
old    2: FROM &v_table
new    2: FROM products
Enter value for v_val: 1
old    3: WHERE &&v_col = &v_val
new    3: WHERE product_type_id = 1

NAME                             PRODUCT_TYPE_ID
-------------------------------- ---------------
Modern Science                                 1
Chemistry                                      1
```

Variables give you a lot of flexibility in writing queries that another user may run. You can give the user a script and have them enter the variable values.

Defined Variables

You can define a variable prior to using it in an SQL statement. You may use these variables multiple times within an SQL statement. A defined variable persists until you explicitly remove it, redefine it, or exit SQL*Plus.

You define a variable using the DEFINE command. When you're finished with your variable, you remove it using UNDEFINE. You'll learn about these commands in this section. You'll also learn about the ACCEPT command, which allows you to define a variable and set its data type.

You can also define variables in an SQL*Plus script and pass values to those variables when the script is run. This feature enables you to write generic reports that any user can run—even if they're unfamiliar with SQL. You'll learn how to create simple reports later in the section "Creating Simple Reports."

Defining and Listing Variables Using the DEFINE Command

You use the DEFINE command to both define a new variable and list the currently defined variables. The following example defines a variable named v_product_id and sets its value to 7:

```
SQL> DEFINE v_product_id = 7
```

You can view the definition of a variable using the DEFINE command followed by the name of the variable. The following example displays the definition of v_product_id:

```
SQL> DEFINE v_product_id
DEFINE V_PRODUCT_ID           = "7" (CHAR)
```

Notice that v_product_id is defined as a CHAR variable.

You can see all your session variables by entering DEFINE on its own. For example:

```
SQL> DEFINE
DEFINE _DATE              = "12-AUG-07" (CHAR)
DEFINE _CONNECT_IDENTIFIER = "Oracle11g" (CHAR)
DEFINE _USER              = "STORE" (CHAR)
DEFINE _PRIVILEGE         = "" (CHAR)
DEFINE _SQLPLUS_RELEASE   = "1101000400" (CHAR)
DEFINE _EDITOR            = "Notepad" (CHAR)
DEFINE _O_VERSION         = "Oracle Database 11g ..." (CHAR)
DEFINE _O_RELEASE         = "1101000500" (CHAR)
DEFINE _RC                = "0" (CHAR)
DEFINE V_PRODUCT_ID       = "7" (CHAR)
```

You can use a defined variable to specify an element such as a column value in an SQL statement. For example, the following query uses references v_product_id in the WHERE clause:

```
SQL> SELECT product_id, name, price
  2  FROM products
  3  WHERE product_id = &v_product_id;
old   3: WHERE product_id = &v_product_id
new   3: WHERE product_id = 7

PRODUCT_ID NAME                                     PRICE
---------- ------------------------------ ----------
         7 Space Force 9                            13.49
```

You're not prompted for the value of v_product_id; that's because v_product_id was set to 7 when the variable was defined earlier.

Defining and Setting Variables Using the ACCEPT Command

The ACCEPT command waits for a user to enter a value for a variable. You can use the ACCEPT command to set an existing variable to a new value or to define a new variable and initialize it with a value. The ACCEPT command also allows you to specify the data type for the variable. The simplified syntax for the ACCEPT command is as follows:

```
ACCEPT variable_name [type] [FORMAT format] [PROMPT prompt] [HIDE]
```

where

- *variable_name* is the variable name.

- *type* is the data type for the variable. You can use the CHAR, NUMBER, and DATE types. By default, variables are defined using the CHAR type. DATE variables are actually stored as CHAR variables.

- *format* is the format used for the variable. Some examples include A15 (15 characters), 9999 (a four-digit number), and DD-MON-YYYY (a date). You can view the number formats in Table 4-4 of Chapter 4; you can view the date formats in Table 5-2 of Chapter 5.

- *prompt* is the text displayed by SQL*Plus as a prompt to the user to enter the variable's value.

■ HIDE means hide the value as it is entered. For example, you might want to hide passwords or other sensitive information.

Let's take a look at some examples of the ACCEPT command. The following example defines a variable named v_customer_id as a two-digit number:

```
SQL> ACCEPT v_customer_id NUMBER FORMAT 99 PROMPT 'Customer id: '
Customer id: 5
```

The next example defines a DATE variable named v_date; the format is DD-MON-YYYY:

```
SQL> ACCEPT v_date DATE FORMAT 'DD-MON-YYYY' PROMPT 'Date: '
Date: 12-DEC-2006
```

The next example defines a CHAR variable named v_password; the value entered is hidden using HIDE:

```
SQL> ACCEPT v_password CHAR PROMPT 'Password: ' HIDE
Password:
```

In Oracle Database 9*i* and below, the value appears as a string of asterisk characters (*) to hide the value as you enter it. In Oracle Database 10*g* and above, nothing is displayed as you type the value.

You can view your variables using the DEFINE command. For example:

```
SQL> DEFINE
...
DEFINE V_CUSTOMER_ID =          5 (NUMBER)
DEFINE V_DATE        = "12-DEC-2006" (CHAR)
DEFINE V_PASSWORD    = "1234567" (CHAR)
DEFINE V_PRODUCT_ID  = "7" (CHAR)
```

Notice that v_date is stored as a CHAR.

Removing Variables Using the UNDEFINE Command

You remove variables using the UNDEFINE command. The following example uses UNDEFINE to remove v_customer_id, v_date, v_password, and v_product_id:

```
SQL> UNDEFINE v_customer_id
SQL> UNDEFINE v_date
SQL> UNDEFINE v_password
SQL> UNDEFINE v_product_id
```

NOTE
*All your variables are removed when you exit SQL*Plus, even if you don't explicitly remove them using the UNDEFINE command.*

Creating Simple Reports

You can use variables in an SQL*Plus script to create reports that a user can run. You'll find the SQL*Plus scripts referenced in this section in the SQL directory.

TIP
SQL*Plus was not specifically designed as a full-fledged reporting tool. If you have complex reporting requirements, you should use software like Oracle Reports.

Using Temporary Variables in a Script

The following `report1.sql` script uses a temporary variable named `v_product_id` in the WHERE clause of a query:

```
-- suppress display of the statements and verification messages
SET ECHO OFF
SET VERIFY OFF

SELECT product_id, name, price
FROM products
WHERE product_id = &v_product_id;
```

The SET ECHO OFF command stops SQL*Plus from displaying the SQL statements and commands in the script. SET VERIFY OFF suppresses display of the verification messages. I put these two commands in to minimize the number of extra lines displayed by SQL*Plus when you run the script.

You can run `report1.sql` in SQL*Plus using the @ command. For example:

```
SQL> @ C:\sql_book\SQL\report1.sql
Enter value for v_product_id: 2

PRODUCT_ID NAME                                          PRICE
---------- ------------------------------ ----------
         2 Chemistry                                        30
```

You'll need to replace the directory in the example with the directory where you saved the files for this book. Also, if you have spaces in the directory, you'll need to put everything after the @ command in quotes; for example:

```
@ "C:\my directory\sql book\SQL\report1.sql"
```

Using Defined Variables in a Script

The following `report2.sql` script uses the ACCEPT command to define a variable named `v_product_id`:

```
SET ECHO OFF
SET VERIFY OFF

ACCEPT v_product_id NUMBER FORMAT 99 PROMPT 'Enter product id: '

SELECT product_id, name, price
FROM products
WHERE product_id = &v_product_id;
```

```
-- clean up
UNDEFINE v_product_id
```

Notice that a user-friendly prompt is specified for the entry of `v_product_id` and that `v_product_id` is removed at the end of the script—doing this makes the script cleaner.

You can run the `report2.sql` script using SQL*Plus:

```
SQL> @ C:\sql_book\SQL\report2.sql
Enter product id: 4

PRODUCT_ID NAME                                     PRICE
---------- ------------------------------ ----------
         4 Tank War                                 13.95
```

Passing a Value to a Variable in a Script

You can pass a value to a variable when you run your script. When you do this, you reference the variable in the script using a number. The following script `report3.sql` shows an example of this; notice that the variable is identified using `&1`:

```
SET ECHO OFF
SET VERIFY OFF

SELECT product_id, name, price
FROM products
WHERE product_id = &1;
```

When you run `report3.sql`, you supply the variable's value after the script name. The following example passes the value 3 to `report3.sql`:

```
SQL> @ C:\sql_book\SQL\report3.sql 3
PRODUCT_ID NAME                                     PRICE
---------- ------------------------------ ----------
         3 Supernova                                25.99
```

If you have spaces in the directory where you saved the scripts, you'll need to put the directory and script name in quotes; for example:

```
@ "C:\my directory\sql book\SQL\report3.sql" 3
```

You can pass any number of parameters to a script, with each value corresponding to the matching number in the script. The first parameter corresponds to `&1`, the second to `&2`, and so on. The following `report4.sql` script shows an example with two parameters:

```
SET ECHO OFF
SET VERIFY OFF

SELECT product_id, product_type_id, name, price
FROM products
WHERE product_type_id = &1
AND price > &2;
```

The following example run of `report4.sql` shows the addition of two values for &1 and &2, which are set to 1 and 9.99, respectively:

```
SQL> @ C:\sql_book\SQL\report4.sql 1 9.99

PRODUCT_ID PRODUCT_TYPE_ID NAME                                          PRICE
---------- --------------- --------------------------------------- ----------
         1               1 Modern Science                               19.95
         2               1 Chemistry                                       30
```

Because &1 is set to 1, the `product_type_id` column in the `WHERE` clause is set to 1. Also, because &2 is set to 9.99, the `price` column in the `WHERE` clause is set to 9.99. Therefore, rows with a `product_type_id` of 1 and a `price` greater than 9.99 are displayed.

Adding a Header and Footer

You add a header and footer to your report using the `TTITLE` and `BTITLE` commands. The following is an example `TTITLE` command:

```
TTITLE LEFT 'Run date: ' _DATE CENTER 'Run by the ' SQL.USER ' user'
RIGHT 'Page: ' FORMAT 999 SQL.PNO SKIP 2
```

The following list explains the contents of this command:

- `_DATE` displays the current date.

- `SQL.USER` displays the current user.

- `SQL.PNO` displays the current page (`FORMAT` is used to format the number).

- `LEFT`, `CENTER`, and `RIGHT` justify the text.

- `SKIP 2` skips two lines.

If the example is run on August 12, 2007 by the `store` user, it displays

```
Run date: 12-AUG-07       Run by the STORE user                  Page:    1
```

The next example shows a `BTITLE` command:

```
BTITLE CENTER 'Thanks for running the report' RIGHT 'Page: ' FORMAT 999 SQL.PNO
```

This command displays

```
                    Thanks for running the report           Page:    1
```

The following `report5.sql` script contains the `TTITLE` and `BTITLE` commands:

```
TTITLE LEFT 'Run date: ' _DATE CENTER 'Run by the ' SQL.USER ' user'
RIGHT 'Page: ' FORMAT 999 SQL.PNO SKIP 2

BTITLE CENTER 'Thanks for running the report' RIGHT 'Page: '
FORMAT 999 SQL.PNO

SET ECHO OFF
```

```
SET VERIFY OFF
SET PAGESIZE 30
SET LINESIZE 70
CLEAR COLUMNS
COLUMN product_id HEADING ID FORMAT 99
COLUMN name HEADING 'Product Name' FORMAT A20 WORD_WRAPPED
COLUMN description HEADING Description FORMAT A30 WORD_WRAPPED
COLUMN price HEADING Price FORMAT $99.99

SELECT product_id, name, description, price
FROM products;

CLEAR COLUMNS
TTITLE OFF
BTITLE OFF
```

The last two lines switch off the header and footer set by the TTITLE and BTITLE commands. The following example shows a run of report5.sql:

SQL> @ **C:\sql_book\SQL\report5.sql**

```
Run date: 12-AUG-07    Run by the STORE user         Page:    1

ID Product Name        Description                  Price
--- -------------------- ------------------------------ -------
  1 Modern Science      A description of modern      $19.95
                        science

  2 Chemistry           Introduction to Chemistry    $30.00
  3 Supernova           A star explodes              $25.99
  4 Tank War            Action movie about a future  $13.95
                        war

  5 Z Files             Series on mysterious         $49.99
                        activities

  6 2412: The Return    Aliens return                $14.95
  7 Space Force 9       Adventures of heroes         $13.49
  8 From Another Planet Alien from another planet    $12.99
                        lands on Earth

  9 Classical Music     The best classical music     $10.99
 10 Pop 3               The best popular music       $15.99
 11 Creative Yell       Debut album                  $14.99
 12 My Front Line       Their greatest hits          $13.49

              Thanks for running the report         Page:    1
```

Computing Subtotals

You can add a subtotal for a column using a combination of the BREAK ON and COMPUTE commands. BREAK ON causes SQL*Plus to break up output based on a change in a column value, and COMPUTE causes SQL*Plus to compute a value for a column.

The following `report6.sql` script shows how to compute a subtotal for products of the same type:

```
BREAK ON product_type_id
COMPUTE SUM OF price ON product_type_id

SET ECHO OFF
SET VERIFY OFF
SET PAGESIZE 50
SET LINESIZE 70

CLEAR COLUMNS
COLUMN price HEADING Price FORMAT $999.99

SELECT product_type_id, name, price
FROM products
ORDER BY product_type_id;

CLEAR COLUMNS
```

The following example shows a run of `report6.sql`:

```
SQL> @ C:\sql_book\SQL\report6.sql

PRODUCT_TYPE_ID NAME                                 Price
--------------- -------------------------------- --------
              1 Modern Science                     $19.95
                Chemistry                          $30.00
***************                                  --------
sum                                                $49.95
              2 Supernova                          $25.99
                Tank War                           $13.95
                Z Files                            $49.99
                2412: The Return                   $14.95
***************                                  --------
sum                                               $104.88
              3 Space Force 9                      $13.49
                From Another Planet                $12.99
***************                                  --------
sum                                                $26.48
              4 Classical Music                    $10.99
                Pop 3                              $15.99
                Creative Yell                      $14.99
***************                                  --------
sum                                                $41.97
                My Front Line                      $13.49
***************                                  --------
sum                                                $13.49
```

Notice that whenever a new value for `product_type_id` is encountered, SQL*Plus breaks up the output and computes a sum for the `price` columns for the rows with the same `product_type_id`. The `product_type_id` value is shown only once for rows with the same `product_type_id`. For example, "Modern Science" and "Chemistry" are both books and have a `product_type_id` of 1, and 1 is shown once for "Modern Science." The sum of the prices for these two books is $49.95. The other sections of the report contain the sum of the prices for products with different `product_type_id` values.

Getting Help from SQL*Plus

You can get help from SQL*Plus using the HELP command. The following example runs HELP:

```
SQL> HELP
```

```
HELP
----


Accesses this command line help system. Enter HELP INDEX or ? INDEX
for a list of topics. In iSQL*Plus, click the Help button to display
iSQL*Plus online help.
You can view SQL*Plus resources at http://otn.oracle.com/tech/sql_plus/
and the Oracle Database Library at http://otn.oracle.com/documentation/


HELP|? [topic]
```

The next example runs HELP INDEX:

```
SQL> HELP INDEX
```

```
Enter Help [topic] for help.

 @                  COPY            PAUSE                    SHUTDOWN
 @@                 DEFINE          PRINT                    SPOOL
 /                  DEL             PROMPT                   SQLPLUS
 ACCEPT             DESCRIBE        QUIT                     START
 APPEND             DISCONNECT      RECOVER                  STARTUP
 ARCHIVE LOG        EDIT            REMARK                   STORE
 ATTRIBUTE          EXECUTE         REPFOOTER                TIMING
 BREAK              EXIT            REPHEADER                TTITLE
 BTITLE             GET             RESERVED WORDS (SQL)     UNDEFINE
 CHANGE             HELP            RESERVED WORDS (PL/SQL)  VARIABLE
 CLEAR              HOST            RUN                      WHENEVER OSERROR
 COLUMN             INPUT           SAVE                     WHENEVER SQLERROR
 COMPUTE            LIST            SET
 CONNECT            PASSWORD        SHOW
```

The following example runs HELP EDIT:

```
SQL> HELP EDIT
```

```
EDIT
----
```

```
Invokes an operating system text editor on the contents of the
specified file or on the contents of the SQL buffer. The buffer
has no command history list and does not record SQL*Plus commands.

ED[IT] [file_name[.ext]]

Not available in iSQL*Plus
```

Automatically Generating SQL Statements

In this section, I'll briefly show you a technique of writing SQL statements that produce other SQL statements. This capability is very useful and can save you a lot of typing when writing SQL statements that are similar. One simple example is an SQL statement that produces DROP TABLE statements, which remove tables from a database. The following query produces a series of DROP TABLE statements that drop the tables from the store schema:

```
SELECT 'DROP TABLE ' || table_name || ';'
FROM user_tables;

'DROPTABLE'||TABLE_NAME||';'
-----------------------------------------
DROP TABLE COUPONS;
DROP TABLE CUSTOMERS;
DROP TABLE EMPLOYEES;
DROP TABLE PRODUCTS;
DROP TABLE PRODUCT_TYPES;
DROP TABLE PROMOTIONS;
DROP TABLE PURCHASES;
DROP TABLE PURCHASES_TIMESTAMP_WITH_TZ;
DROP TABLE PURCHASES_WITH_LOCAL_TZ;
DROP TABLE PURCHASES_WITH_TIMESTAMP;
DROP TABLE SALARY_GRADES;
```

NOTE
user_tables *contains the details of the tables in the user's schema.*
The table_name *column contains names of the tables.*

You can spool the generated SQL statements to a file and run them later.

Disconnecting from the Database and Exiting SQL*Plus

You can disconnect from the database and keep SQL*Plus running by entering DISCONNECT (SQL*Plus also automatically performs a COMMIT for you). While you're connected to the database, SQL*Plus maintains a database session for you. When you disconnect from the database, your session is ended. You can reconnect to a database by entering CONNECT.

To end SQL*Plus, you enter EXIT (SQL*Plus also automatically performs a COMMIT for you).

Summary

In this chapter, you learned how to do the following:

- View the structure of a table
- Edit an SQL statement
- Save, retrieve, and run files containing SQL and SQL*Plus commands
- Format the results returned by SQL*Plus
- Set the page and line size for SQL*Plus output
- Use variables in SQL*Plus
- Create simple reports
- Get help from SQL*Plus
- Write SQL statements that generate other SQL statements
- Disconnect from the database and exit SQL*Plus

For further details on SQL*Plus, you can read the *SQL*Plus User's Guide and Reference,* published by Oracle Corporation.

In the next chapter, you'll learn how to use functions.

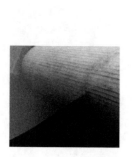

CHAPTER
4

Using Simple Functions

n this chapter, you'll learn about some of the Oracle database's built-in functions. A function accepts zero or more input parameters and returns an output parameter. There are two main types of functions you can use in an Oracle database:

- **Single-row functions** operate on one row at a time and return one row of output for each input row. An example single-row function is CONCAT(*x*, *y*), which appends *y* to *x* and returns the resulting string.

- **Aggregate functions** operate on multiple rows at the same time and return one row of output. An example aggregate function is AVG(*x*), which returns the average of *x* where *x* may be a column or, more generally, any expression.

You'll learn about single-row functions first, followed by aggregate functions. You'll see more advanced functions as you progress through this book.

Using Single-Row Functions

A single-row function operates on one row at a time and returns one row of output for each row. There are five main types of single-row functions:

- **Character functions** manipulate strings of characters.

- **Numeric functions** perform calculations.

- **Conversion functions** convert a value from one database type to another.

- **Date functions** process dates and times.

- **Regular expression functions** use regular expressions to search data. These functions were introduced in Oracle Database 10*g* and are expanded in 11*g*.

You'll learn about character functions first, followed by numeric functions, conversion functions, and regular expression functions. You'll learn about date functions in the next chapter.

Character Functions

Character functions accept character input, which may come from a column in a table or, more generally, from any expression. This input is processed and a result returned. An example character function is UPPER(), which converts the letters in an input string to uppercase and returns the new string. Another example is NVL(), which converts a null value to another value. In Table 4-1, which shows some of the character functions, and in all the syntax definitions that follow, *x* and *y* may represent columns from a table or, more generally, any valid expressions.

You'll learn more about some of the functions shown in Table 4-1 in the following sections.

Function	Description
ASCII(*x*)	Returns the ASCII value for the character *x*.
CHR(*x*)	Returns the character with the ASCII value of *x*.
CONCAT(*x*, *y*)	Appends *y* to *x* and then returns the new string.
INITCAP(*x*)	Converts the initial letter of each word in *x* to uppercase and returns the new string.
INSTR(x, *find_string* [, *start*] [, *occurrence*])	Searches for *find_string* in *x* and returns the position at which *find_string* occurs. You can supply an optional *start* position to begin the search. You can also supply an optional *occurrence* that indicates which occurrence of *find_string* should be returned.
LENGTH(*x*)	Returns the number of characters in *x*.
LOWER(*x*)	Converts the letters in *x* to lowercase and returns the new string.
LPAD(*x*, *width* [, *pad_string*])	Pads *x* with spaces to left to bring the total length of the string up to *width* characters. You can supply an optional *pad_string*, which specifies a string to be repeated to the left of *x* to fill up the padded space. The resulting padded string is returned.
LTRIM(*x* [, *trim_string*])	Trims characters from the left of *x*. You can supply an optional *trim_string*, which specifies the characters to trim; if no *trim_string* is supplied, then spaces are trimmed by default.
NANVL(*x*, *value*)	Returns *value* if *x* matches the NAN (not a number) special value; otherwise *x* is returned. (This function was introduced in Oracle Database 10*g*.)
NVL(*x*, *value*)	Returns *value* if *x* is null; otherwise *x* is returned.
NVL2(*x*, *value1*, *value2*)	Returns *value1* if *x* is not null; otherwise *value2* is returned.
REPLACE(*x*, *search_string*, *replace_string*)	Searches *x* for *search_string* and replaces it with *replace_string*.
RPAD(*x*, *width* [, *pad_string*])	Same as LPAD(), but *x* is padded to the right.
RTRIM(*x* [, *trim_string*])	Same as LTRIM(), but *x* is trimmed from the right.
SOUNDEX(*x*)	Returns a string containing the phonetic representation of *x*. This lets you compare words that sound alike in English but are spelled differently.
SUBSTR(*x*, *start* [, *length*])	Returns a substring of *x* that begins at the position specified by *start*. You can supply an optional *length* for the substring.
TRIM([*trim_char* FROM) *x*)	Trims characters from the left and right of *x*. You can supply an optional *trim_char*, which specifies the characters to trim; if no *trim_char* is supplied, spaces are trimmed by default.
UPPER(*x*)	Converts the letters in *x* to uppercase and returns the new string.

TABLE 4-1   *Character Functions*

ASCII() and CHR()

You use ASCII (*x*) to get the ASCII value for the character *x*. You use CHR (*x*) to get the character with the ASCII value of *x*.

The following query gets the ASCII value of a, A, z, Z, 0, and 9 using ASCII ():

```
SELECT ASCII('a'), ASCII('A'), ASCII('z'), ASCII('Z'), ASCII(0), ASCII(9)
FROM dual;
```

ASCII('A')	ASCII('A')	ASCII('Z')	ASCII('Z')	ASCII(0)	ASCII(9)
97	65	122	90	48	57

NOTE
The dual *table is used in this query. As you saw in Chapter 2, the* dual *table contains a single row through which you may perform queries that don't go against a particular table.*

The following query gets the characters with the ASCII values of 97, 65, 122, 90, 48, and 57 using CHR ():

```
SELECT CHR(97), CHR(65), CHR(122), CHR(90), CHR(48), CHR(57)
FROM dual;
```

```
C C C C C C
- - - - - -
a A z Z 0 9
```

Notice the characters returned from CHR () in this query are the same as those passed to ASCII () in the previous query. This shows that CHR () and ASCII () have the opposite effect.

CONCAT()

You use CONCAT (*x*, *y*) to append *y* to *x* and then return the new string.

The following query appends last_name to first_name using CONCAT ():

```
SELECT CONCAT(first_name, last_name)
FROM customers;
```

```
CONCAT(FIRST_NAME,LA
--------------------
JohnBrown
CynthiaGreen
SteveWhite
GailBlack
DoreenBlue
```

NOTE
CONCAT () *is the same as the* || *operator you saw in Chapter 2.*

INITCAP()

You use INITCAP (*x*) to convert the initial letter of each word in *x* to uppercase.

The following query retrieves the product_id and description columns from the products table, then uses INITCAP() to convert the first letter of each word in description to uppercase:

```
SELECT product_id, INITCAP(description)
FROM products
WHERE product_id < 4;

PRODUCT_ID INITCAP(DESCRIPTION)
---------- -----------------------------
         1 A Description Of Modern Science
         2 Introduction To Chemistry
         3 A Star Explodes
```

INSTR()

You use INSTR(*x, find_string* [, *start*] [, *occurrence*]) to search for *find_string* in *x*. INSTR() returns the position at which *find_string* occurs. You can supply an optional *start* position to begin the search. You can also supply an optional *occurrence* that indicates which occurrence of *find_string* should be returned.

The following query gets the position where the string Science occurs in the name column for product #1:

```
SELECT name, INSTR(name, 'Science')
FROM products
WHERE product_id = 1;

NAME                            INSTR(NAME,'SCIENCE')
------------------------------- ---------------------
Modern Science                                      8
```

The next query displays the position where the second occurrence of the e character occurs, starting from the beginning of the product name:

```
SELECT name, INSTR(name, 'e', 1, 2)
FROM products
WHERE product_id = 1;

NAME                            INSTR(NAME,'E',1,2)
------------------------------- -------------------
Modern Science                                   11
```

Notice the second e in Modern Science is the eleventh character.

You can also use dates with character functions. The following query gets the position where the string JAN occurs in the dob column for customer #1:

```
SELECT customer_id, dob, INSTR(dob, 'JAN')
FROM customers
WHERE customer_id = 1;

CUSTOMER_ID DOB       INSTR(DOB,'JAN')
----------- --------- ----------------
          1 01-JAN-65                4
```

LENGTH()

You use LENGTH(*x*) to get the number of characters in *x*. The following query gets the length of the strings in the name column of the products table using LENGTH():

```
SELECT name, LENGTH(name)
FROM products;
```

```
NAME                            LENGTH(NAME)
------------------------------- ------------
Modern Science                            14
Chemistry                                  9
Supernova                                  9
Tank War                                   8
Z Files                                    7
2412: The Return                          16
Space Force 9                             13
From Another Planet                       19
Classical Music                           15
Pop 3                                      5
Creative Yell                             13
My Front Line                             13
```

The next query gets the total number of characters that make up the product price; notice that the decimal point (.) is counted in the number of price characters:

```
SELECT price, LENGTH(price)
FROM products
WHERE product_id < 3;
```

```
     PRICE LENGTH(PRICE)
---------- -------------
     19.95             5
        30             2
```

LOWER() and UPPER()

You use LOWER(*x*) to convert the letters in *x* to lowercase. Similarly, you use UPPER(*x*) to convert the letters in *x* to uppercase.

The following query converts the strings in the first_name column to uppercase using the UPPER() function and the strings in the last_name column to lowercase using the LOWER() function:

```
SELECT UPPER(first_name), LOWER(last_name)
FROM customers;
```

```
UPPER(FIRS LOWER(LAST
---------- ----------
JOHN       brown
CYNTHIA    green
```

```
STEVE      white
GAIL       black
DOREEN     blue
```

LPAD() and RPAD()

You use LPAD(*x*, *width* [, *pad_string*]) to pad *x* with spaces to the left to bring the total length of the string up to *width* characters. You can supply an optional *pad_string*, which specifies a string to be repeated to the left of *x* to fill up the padded space. The resulting padded string is then returned. Similarly, you use RPAD(*x*, *width* [, *pad_string*]) to pad *x* with strings to the right.

The following query retrieves the name and price columns from the products table. The name column is right-padded using RPAD() to a length of 30 characters, with periods filling up the padded space. The price column is left-padded using LPAD() to a length of 8, with the string *+ filling up the padded space.

```
SELECT RPAD(name, 30, '.'), LPAD(price, 8, '*+')
FROM products
WHERE product_id < 4;

RPAD(NAME,30,'.')                LPAD(PRI
------------------------------   --------
Modern Science...............    *+*19.95
Chemistry....................    *+*+*+30
Supernova....................    *+*25.99
```

> **NOTE**
> *This example shows that character functions can use numbers.*
> *Specifically, the* price *column in the example contains a number*
> *that was left-padded by* LPAD().

LTRIM(), RTRIM(), and TRIM()

You use LTRIM(*x* [, *trim_string*]) to trim characters from the left of *x*. You can supply an optional *trim_string*, which specifies the characters to trim; if no *trim_string* is supplied; spaces are trimmed by default. Similarly, you use RTRIM() to trim characters from the right of *x*. You use TRIM() to trim characters from the left and right of *x*. The following query uses these three functions:

```
SELECT
  LTRIM('  Hello Gail Seymour!'),
  RTRIM('Hi Doreen Oakley!abcabc', 'abc'),
  TRIM('0' FROM '000Hey Steve Button!00000')
FROM dual;

LTRIM('HELLOGAILSEY RTRIM('HIDOREENOA TRIM('0'FROM'000H
-------------------- ------------------ -----------------
Hello Gail Seymour! Hi Doreen Oakley! Hey Steve Button!
```

NVL()

You use NVL() to convert a null value to another value. NVL(*x*, *value*) returns *value* if *x* is null; otherwise *x* is returned.

The following query retrieves the customer_id and phone columns from the customers table. Null values in the phone column are converted to the string Unknown Phone Number by NVL():

```
SELECT customer_id, NVL(phone, 'Unknown Phone Number')
FROM customers;
```

```
CUSTOMER_ID NVL(PHONE,'UNKNOWNPH
----------- --------------------
          1 800-555-1211
          2 800-555-1212
          3 800-555-1213
          4 800-555-1214
          5 Unknown Phone Number
```

The phone column for customer #5 is converted to Unknown Phone Number because the phone column is null for that row.

NVL2()

NVL2(*x*, *value1*, *value2*) returns *value1* if *x* is not null; otherwise *value2* is returned.

The following query retrieves the customer_id and phone columns from the customers table. Non-null values in the phone column are converted to the string Known, and null values are converted to Unknown:

```
SELECT customer_id, NVL2(phone, 'Known', 'Unknown')
FROM customers;
```

```
CUSTOMER_ID NVL2(PH
----------- -------
          1 Known
          2 Known
          3 Known
          4 Known
          5 Unknown
```

Notice that the phone column values are converted to Known for customers #1 through #4 because the phone column values for those rows are not null. For customer #5 the phone column value is converted to Unknown because the phone column is null for that row.

REPLACE()

You use REPLACE(*x*, *search_string*, *replace_string*) to search *x* for *search_string* and replace it with *replace_string*.

The following example retrieves the name column from the products table for product #1 (whose name is Modern Science) and replaces the string Science with Physics using REPLACE():

```
SELECT REPLACE(name, 'Science', 'Physics')
FROM products
WHERE product_id = 1;

REPLACE(NAME,'SCIENCE','PHYSICS')
--------------------------------
Modern Physics
```

NOTE
REPLACE() *doesn't modify the actual row in the database; only the row returned by the function is modified.*

SOUNDEX()

You use SOUNDEX(*x*) to get a string containing the phonetic representation of *x*. This lets you compare words that sound alike in English but are spelled differently.

The following query retrieves the last_name column from the customers table where last_name sounds like "whyte":

```
SELECT last_name
FROM customers
WHERE SOUNDEX(last_name) = SOUNDEX('whyte');

LAST_NAME
----------
White
```

The next query gets last names that sound like "bloo":

```
SELECT last_name
FROM customers
WHERE SOUNDEX(last_name) = SOUNDEX('bloo');

LAST_NAME
----------
Blue
```

SUBSTR()

You use SUBSTR(*x*, *start* [, *length*]) to return a substring of *x* that begins at the position specified by *start*. You can also provide an optional *length* for the substring.

The following query uses SUBSTR() to get the 7-character substring starting at position 2 from the name column of the products table:

```
SELECT SUBSTR(name, 2, 7)
FROM products
WHERE product_id < 4;

SUBSTR(
-------
odern S
hemistr
upernov
```

Using Expressions with Functions

You're not limited to using columns in functions: you can supply any valid expression that evaluates to a string. The following query uses the SUBSTR() function to get the substring little from the string Mary had a little lamb:

```
SELECT SUBSTR('Mary had a little lamb', 12, 6)
FROM dual;

SUBSTR
------
little
```

Combining Functions

You can use any valid combination of functions in an SQL statement. The following query combines the UPPER() and SUBSTR() functions; notice that the output from SUBSTR() is passed to UPPER():

```
SELECT name, UPPER(SUBSTR(name, 2, 8))
FROM products
WHERE product_id < 4;

NAME                              UPPER(SU
-------------------------------   --------
Modern Science                    ODERN SC
Chemistry                         HEMISTRY
Supernova                         UPERNOVA
```

NOTE
This ability to combine functions is not limited to character functions. Any valid combination of functions will work.

Numeric Functions

You use the numeric functions to perform calculations. These functions accept an input number, which may come from a numeric column or any expression that evaluates to a number. A calculation is then performed and a number returned. An example of a numeric function is SQRT(*x*), which returns the square root of *x*.

Table 4-2 shows some of the numeric functions.

You'll learn more about some of the functions shown in Table 4-2 in the following sections.

Function	Description	Examples
ABS(x)	Returns the absolute value of x.	ABS(10) = 10 ABS(-10) = 10
ACOS(x)	Returns the arccosine of x.	ACOS(1) = 0 ACOS(-1) = 3.14159265
ASIN(x)	Returns the arcsine of x.	ASIN(1) = 1.57079633 ASIN(-1) = -1.5707963
ATAN(x)	Returns the arctangent of x.	ATAN(1) = .785398163 ATAN(-1) = -.78539816

TABLE 4-2 *Numeric Functions*

Function	Description	Examples
ATAN2 (*x*, *y*)	Returns the arctangent of *x* and *y*.	ATAN2 (1, -1) = 2.35619449
BITAND (*x*, *y*)	Returns the result of performing a bitwise AND on *x* and *y*.	BITAND (0, 0) = 0 BITAND (0, 1) = 0 BITAND (1, 0) = 0 BITAND (1, 1) = 1 BITAND (1010, 1100) = 64
COS (*x*)	Returns the cosine of *x*, where *x* is an angle in radians.	COS (90 * 3.1415926) = 1 COS (45 * 3.1415926) = -1
COSH (*x*)	Returns the hyperbolic cosine of *x*.	COSH (3.1415926) = 11.5919527
CEIL (*x*)	Returns the smallest integer greater than or equal to *x*.	CEIL (5.8) = 6 CEIL (-5.2) = -5
EXP (*x*)	Returns the result of the number *e* raised to the power *x*, where *e* is approximately 2.71828183.	EXP (1) = 2.71828183 EXP (2) = 7.3890561
FLOOR (*x*)	Returns the largest integer less than or equal to *x*.	FLOOR (5.8) = 5 FLOOR (-5.2) = -6
LOG (*x*, *y*)	Returns the logarithm, base *x*, of *y*.	LOG (2, 4) = 2 LOG (2, 5) = 2.32192809
LN (*x*)	Returns the natural logarithm of *x*.	LN (2.71828183) = 1
MOD (*x*, *y*)	Returns the remainder when *x* is divided by *y*.	MOD (8, 3) = 2 MOD (8, 4) = 0
POWER (*x*, *y*)	Returns the result of *x* raised to the power *y*.	POWER (2, 1) = 2 POWER (2, 3) = 8
ROUND (*x* [, *y*])	Returns the result of rounding *x* to an optional *y* decimal places. If *y* is omitted, *x* is rounded to zero decimal places. If *y* is negative, *x* is rounded to the left of the decimal point.	ROUND (5.75) = 6 ROUND (5.75, 1) = 5.8 ROUND (5.75, -1) = 10
SIGN (*x*)	Returns -1 if *x* is negative, 1 if *x* is positive, or 0 if *x* is zero.	SIGN (-5) = -1 SIGN (5) = 1 SIGN (0) = 0
SIN (*x*)	Returns the sine of *x*.	SIN (0) = 0
SINH (*x*)	Returns the hyperbolic sine of *x*.	SINH (1) = 1.17520119
SQRT (*x*)	Returns the square root of *x*.	SQRT (25) = 5 SQRT (5) = 2.23606798
TAN (*x*)	Returns the tangent of *x*.	TAN (0) = 0
TANH (*x*)	Returns the hyperbolic tangent of *x*.	TANH (1) = .761594156
TRUNC (*x* [, *y*])	Returns the result of truncating *x* to an optional *y* decimal places. If *y* is omitted, *x* is truncated to zero decimal places. If *y* is negative, *x* is truncated to the left of the decimal point.	TRUNC (5.75) = 5 TRUNC (5.75, 1) = 5.7 TRUNC (5.75, -1) = 0

TABLE 4-2   *Numeric Functions* (continued)

ABS()

You use ABS (*x*) to get the absolute value of *x*. The absolute value of a number is that number without any positive or negative sign. The following query gets the absolute value of 10 and –10:

```
SELECT ABS(10), ABS(-10)
FROM dual;
```

```
  ABS(10)   ABS(-10)
---------- ----------
       10         10
```

The absolute value of 10 is 10. The absolute value of –10 is 10.

Of course, the parameters that are input to any of the number functions don't have to be literal numbers. The input may also be a numeric column from a table or, more generally, any valid expression. The following query gets the absolute value of subtracting 30 from the price column from the products table for the first three products:

```
SELECT product_id, price, price - 30, ABS(price - 30)
FROM products
WHERE product_id < 4;
```

```
PRODUCT_ID      PRICE   PRICE-30 ABS(PRICE-30)
---------- ---------- ---------- -------------
         1      19.95     -10.05         10.05
         2         30          0             0
         3      25.99      -4.01          4.01
```

CEIL()

You use CEIL (*x*) to get the smallest integer greater than or equal to *x*. The following query uses CEIL () to get the absolute values of 5.8 and –5.2:

```
SELECT CEIL(5.8), CEIL(-5.2)
FROM dual;
```

```
 CEIL(5.8) CEIL(-5.2)
---------- ----------
         6         -5
```

The ceiling for 5.8 is 6, because 6 is the smallest integer greater than 5.8. The ceiling for –5.2 is –5, because –5.2 is negative, and the smallest integer greater than this is –5.

FLOOR()

You use FLOOR (*x*) to get the largest integer less than or equal to *x*. The following query uses FLOOR () to get the absolute value of 5.8 and –5.2:

```
SELECT FLOOR(5.8), FLOOR(-5.2)
FROM dual;
```

```
FLOOR(5.8) FLOOR(-5.2)
---------- -----------
         5          -6
```

The floor for 5.8 is 5; because 5 is the largest integer less than 5.8. The floor for –5.2 is –6, because –5.2 is negative, and the largest integer less than this is –6.

MOD()

You use MOD(x, y) to get the remainder when x is divided by y. The following query uses MOD() to get the remainder when 8 is divided by 3 and 4:

```
SELECT MOD(8, 3), MOD(8, 4)
FROM dual;
```

```
 MOD(8,3)    MOD(8,4)
---------- ----------
         2           0
```

The remainder when 8 is divided by 3 is 2: 3 goes into 8 twice, leaving 2 left over—the remainder. The remainder when 8 is divided by 4 is 0: 4 goes into 8 twice, leaving nothing left over.

POWER()

You use POWER(x, y) to get the result of x raised to the power y. The following query uses POWER() to get 2 raised to the power 1 and 3:

```
SELECT POWER(2, 1), POWER(2, 3)
FROM dual;
```

```
POWER(2,1) POWER(2,3)
---------- ----------
         2          8
```

When 2 is raised to the power 1, which is equivalent to 2*1, the result is 2; 2 raised to the power 3 is equivalent to 2*2*2, the result of which is 8.

ROUND()

You use ROUND(x, [y]) to get the result of rounding x to an optional y decimal places. If y is omitted, x is rounded to zero decimal places. If y is negative, x is rounded to the left of the decimal point.

The following query uses ROUND() to get the result of rounding 5.75 to zero, 1, and –1 decimal places:

```
SELECT ROUND(5.75), ROUND(5.75, 1), ROUND(5.75, -1)
FROM dual;
```

```
ROUND(5.75) ROUND(5.75,1) ROUND(5.75,-1)
----------- ------------- --------------
          6           5.8             10
```

5.75 rounded to zero decimal places is 6; 5.75 rounded to one decimal place (to the right of the decimal point) is 5.8; and 5.75 rounded to one decimal place to the left of the decimal point (as indicated using a negative sign) is 10.

SIGN()

You use SIGN(*x*) to get the sign of *x*. SIGN() returns –1 if *x* is negative, 1 if *x* is positive, or 0 if *x* is zero. The following query gets the sign of –5, 5, and 0:

```
SELECT SIGN(-5), SIGN(5), SIGN(0)
FROM dual;
```

```
 SIGN(-5)   SIGN(5)   SIGN(0)
---------- ---------- ----------
       -1         1         0
```

The sign of –5 is –1; the sign of 5 is 1; the sign of 0 is 0.

SQRT()

You use SQRT(*x*) to get the square root of *x*. The following query gets the square root of 25 and 5:

```
SELECT SQRT(25), SQRT(5)
FROM dual;
```

```
 SQRT(25)    SQRT(5)
---------- ----------
        5  2.23606798
```

The square root of 25 is 5; the square root of 5 is approximately 2.236.

TRUNC()

You use TRUNC(*x*, [*y*]) to get the result of truncating the number *x* to an optional *y* decimal places. If *y* is omitted, *x* is truncated to zero decimal places. If *y* is negative, *x* is truncated to the left of the decimal point. The following query truncates 5.75 to zero, 1, and –1 decimal places:

```
SELECT TRUNC(5.75), TRUNC(5.75, 1), TRUNC(5.75, -1)
FROM dual;
```

```
TRUNC(5.75) TRUNC(5.75,1) TRUNC(5.75,-1)
----------- ------------- --------------
          5           5.7              0
```

In the above, 5.75 truncated to zero decimal places is 5; 5.75 truncated to one decimal place (to the right of the decimal point) is 5.7; and 5.75 truncated to one decimal place to the left of the decimal point (as indicated using a negative sign) is 0.

Conversion Functions

Sometimes you need to convert a value from one data type to another. For example, you might want to reformat the price of a product that is stored as a number (e.g., 1346.95) to a string containing dollar signs and commas (e.g., $1,346.95). For this purpose, you use a conversion function to convert a value from one data type to another.

Table 4-3 shows some of the conversion functions.

You'll learn more about the TO_CHAR() and TO_NUMBER() functions in the following sections. You'll learn about some of the other functions in Table 4-3 as you progress through this book. You can find out more about national language character sets and Unicode in the *Oracle Database Globalization Support Guide* from Oracle Corporation.

Function	Description
ASCIISTR(*x*)	Converts *x* to an ASCII string, where *x* may be a string in any character set.
BIN_TO_NUM(*x*)	Converts a binary number *x* to a NUMBER.
CAST(*x* AS *type*)	Converts *x* to a compatible database type specified in *type*.
CHARTOROWID(*x*)	Converts *x* to a ROWID.
COMPOSE(*x*)	Converts *x* to a Unicode string in its fully normalized form in the same character set as *x*. Unicode uses a 2-byte character set and can represent over 65,000 characters; it may also be used to represent non-English characters.
CONVERT(*x*, *source_char_set*, *dest_char_set*)	Converts *x* from *source_char_set* to *dest_char_set*.
DECODE(*x*, *search*, *result*, *default*)	Compares *x* with the value in *search*; if equal, DECODE() returns the value in *result*; otherwise the value in *default* is returned.
DECOMPOSE(*x*)	Converts *x* to a Unicode string after decomposition of the string into the same character set as *x*.
HEXTORAW(*x*)	Converts the character *x* containing hexadecimal digits (base-16) to a binary number (RAW). This function then returns the RAW number.
NUMTODSINTERVAL(*x*)	Converts the number *x* to an INTERVAL DAY TO SECOND. You'll learn about date and time interval–related functions in the next chapter.
NUMTOYMINTERVAL(*x*)	Converts the number *x* to an INTERVAL YEAR TO MONTH.
RAWTOHEX(*x*)	Converts the binary number (RAW) *x* to a VARCHAR2 string containing the equivalent hexadecimal number.
RAWTONHEX(*x*)	Converts the binary number (RAW) *x* to an NVARCHAR2 string containing the equivalent hexadecimal number. (NVARCHAR2 stores a string using the national character set.)
ROWIDTOCHAR(*x*)	Converts the ROWID *x* to a VARCHAR2 string.
ROWIDTONCHAR(*x*)	Converts the ROWID *x* to an NVARCHAR2 string.
TO_BINARY_DOUBLE(*x*)	Converts *x* to a BINARY_DOUBLE. (This function was introduced in Oracle Database 10*g*.)
TO_BINARY_FLOAT(*x*)	Converts *x* to a BINARY_FLOAT. (This function was introduced in Oracle Database 10*g*.)
TO_BLOB(*x*)	Converts *x* to a binary large object (BLOB). A BLOB is used to store large amounts of binary data. You'll learn about large objects in Chapter 14.

TABLE 4-3 *Conversion Functions*

Function	Description
TO_CHAR(*x* [, *format*])	Converts *x* to a VARCHAR2 string. You can supply an optional *format* that indicates the format of *x*.
TO_CLOB(*x*)	Converts *x* to a character large object (CLOB). A CLOB is used to store large amounts of character data.
TO_DATE(*x* [, *format*])	Converts *x* to a DATE.
TO_DSINTERVAL(*x*)	Converts the string *x* to an INTERVAL DAY TO SECOND.
TO_MULTI_BYTE(*x*)	Converts the single-byte characters in *x* to their corresponding multi-byte characters. The return type is the same as the type for *x*.
TO_NCHAR(*x*)	Converts *x* in the database character set to an NVARCHAR2 string.
TO_NCLOB(*x*)	Converts *x* to a large object NCLOB. An NCLOB is used to store large amounts of national language character data.
TO_NUMBER(*x* [, *format*])	Converts *x* to a NUMBER.
TO_SINGLE_BYTE(*x*)	Converts the multi-byte characters in *x* to their corresponding single-byte characters. The return type is the same as the type for *x*.
TO_TIMESTAMP(*x*)	Converts the string *x* to a TIMESTAMP.
TO_TIMESTAMP_TZ(*x*)	Converts the string *x* to a TIMESTAMP WITH TIME ZONE.
TO_YMINTERVAL(*x*)	Converts the string *x* to an INTERVAL YEAR TO MONTH.
TRANSLATE(*x*, *from_string*, *to_string*)	Converts all occurrences of *from_string* in *x* to *to_string*.
UNISTR(*x*)	Converts the characters in *x* to an NCHAR character. (NCHAR stores a character using the national language character set.)

TABLE 4-3 *Conversion Functions* (continued)

TO_CHAR()

You use TO_CHAR(*x* [, *format*]) to convert *x* to a string. You can also provide an optional *format* that indicates the format of *x*. The structure *format* depends on whether *x* is a number or date. You'll learn how to use TO_CHAR() to convert a number to a string in this section, and you'll see how to convert a date to a string in the next chapter.

Let's take a look at a couple of simple queries that use TO_CHAR() to convert a number to a string. The following query converts 12345.67 to a string:

```
SELECT TO_CHAR(12345.67)
FROM dual;

TO_CHAR(1
---------
12345.67
```

The next query uses TO_CHAR() to convert 12345678.90 to a string and specifies this number is to be converted using the format 99,999.99. This results in the string returned by TO_CHAR() having a comma to delimit the thousands:

```
SELECT TO_CHAR(12345.67, '99,999.99')
FROM dual;

TO_CHAR(12
----------
 12,345.67
```

The optional *format* string you may pass to TO_CHAR() has a number of parameters that affect the string returned by TO_CHAR(). Some of these parameters are listed in Table 4-4.

Parameter	Format Examples	Description
9	999	Returns digits in specified positions, with a leading negative sign if the number is negative.
0	0999 9990	0999: Returns a number with leading zeros. 9990: Returns a number with trailing zeros.
.	999.99	Returns a decimal point in the specified position.
,	9,999	Returns a comma in the specified position.
$	$999	Returns a leading dollar sign.
B	B9.99	If the integer part of a fixed point number is zero, returns spaces for the zeros.
C	C999	Returns the ISO currency symbol in the specified position. The symbol comes from the NLS_ISO_CURRENCY database parameter set by a DBA.
D	9D99	Returns the decimal point symbol in the specified position. The symbol comes from the NLS_NUMERIC_CHARACTER database parameter (the default is a period character).
EEEE	9.99EEEE	Returns the number using the scientific notation.
FM	FM90.9	Removes leading and trailing spaces from the number.
G	9G999	Returns the group separator symbol in the specified position. The symbol comes from the NLS_NUMERIC_CHARACTER database parameter.
L	L999	Returns the local currency symbol in the specified position. The symbol comes from the NLS_CURRENCY database parameter.

TABLE 4-4 *Numeric Formatting Parameters*

Parameter	Format Examples	Description
MI	999MI	Returns a negative number with a trailing minus sign. Returns a positive number with a trailing space.
PR	999PR	Returns a negative number in angle brackets (< >). Returns a positive number with leading and trailing spaces.
RN rn	RN rn	Returns the number as Roman numerals. RN returns uppercase numerals; rn returns lowercase numerals. The number must be an integer between 1 and 3999.
S	S999 999S	S999: Returns a negative number with a leading negative sign; returns a positive number with a leading positive sign. 999S: Returns a negative number with a trailing negative sign; returns a positive number with a trailing positive sign.
TM	TM	Returns the number using the minimum number of characters. The default is TM9, which returns the number using fixed notation unless the number of characters is greater than 64. If greater than 64, the number is returned using scientific notation.
U	U999	Returns the dual currency symbol (Euro, for example) in the specified position. The symbol comes from the NLS_DUAL_CURRENCY database parameter.
V	99V99	Returns the number multiplied by 10^x where x is the number of 9 characters after the V. If necessary, the number is rounded.
X	XXXX	Returns the number in hexadecimal. If the number is not an integer, the number is rounded to an integer.

TABLE 4-4 *Numeric Formatting Parameters* (continued)

Let's look at some more examples that convert numbers to strings using TO_CHAR(). The following table shows examples of calling TO_CHAR(), along with the output returned.

TO_CHAR() Function Call	Output
TO_CHAR(12345.67, '99999.99')	12345.67
TO_CHAR(12345.67, '99,999.99')	12,345.67
TO_CHAR(-12345.67, '99,999.99')	-12,345.67
TO_CHAR(12345.67, '099,999.99')	012,345.67
TO_CHAR(12345.67, '99,999.9900')	12,345.6700
TO_CHAR(12345.67, '$99,999.99')	$12,345.67
TO_CHAR(0.67, 'B9.99')	.67

TO_CHAR() Function Call	Output
`TO_CHAR(12345.67, 'C99,999.99')`	USD12,345.67
`TO_CHAR(12345.67, '99999D99')`	12345.67
`TO_CHAR(12345.67, '99999.99EEEE')`	1.23E+04
`TO_CHAR(0012345.6700, 'FM99999.99')`	12345.67
`TO_CHAR(12345.67, '99999G99')`	123,46
`TO_CHAR(12345.67, 'L99,999.99')`	$12,345.67
`TO_CHAR(-12345.67, '99,999.99MI')`	12,345.67
`TO_CHAR(-12345.67, '99,999.99PR')`	12,345.67
`TO_CHAR(2007, 'RN')`	MMVII
`TO_CHAR(12345.67, 'TM')`	12345.67
`TO_CHAR(12345.67, 'U99,999.99')`	$12,345.67
`TO_CHAR(12345.67, '99999V99')`	1234567

TO_CHAR() will return a string of pound characters (#) if you try to format a number that contains too many digits for the format. For example:

```
SELECT TO_CHAR(12345678.90, '99,999.99')
FROM dual;

TO_CHAR(12
----------
##########
```

Pound characters are returned by TO_CHAR() because the number 12345678.90 has more digits than those allowed in the format 99,999.99.

You can also use TO_CHAR() to convert columns containing numbers to strings. For example, the following query uses TO_CHAR() to convert the price column of the products table to a string:

```
SELECT product_id, 'The price of the product is' || TO_CHAR(price, '$99.99')
FROM products
WHERE product_id < 5;

PRODUCT_ID 'THEPRICEOFTHEPRODUCTIS'||TO_CHAR(
---------- --------------------------------
         1 The price of the product is $19.95
         2 The price of the product is $30.00
         3 The price of the product is $25.99
         4 The price of the product is $13.95
```

TO_NUMBER()

You use TO_NUMBER(x [, $format$]) to convert x to a number. You can provide an optional $format$ string to indicate the format of x. Your $format$ string may use the same parameters as those listed earlier in Table 4-4.

The following query converts the string 970.13 to a number using TO_NUMBER():

```
SELECT TO_NUMBER('970.13')
FROM dual;

TO_NUMBER('970.13')
-------------------
             970.13
```

The next query converts the string 970.13 to a number using TO_NUMBER() and then adds 25.5 to that number:

```
SELECT TO_NUMBER('970.13') + 25.5
FROM dual;

TO_NUMBER('970.13')+25.5
------------------------
                  995.63
```

The next query converts the string -$12,345.67 to a number, passing the format string $99,999.99 to TO_NUMBER():

```
SELECT TO_NUMBER('-$12,345.67', '$99,999.99')
FROM dual;

TO_NUMBER('-$12,345.67','$99,999.99')
-------------------------------------
                           -12345.67
```

CAST()

You use CAST(*x* AS *type*) to convert *x* to a compatible database type specified by *type*. The following table shows the valid type conversions (valid conversions are marked with an X):

	From						
To	BINARY_FLOAT BINARY_DOUBLE	CHAR VARCHAR2	NUMBER	DATE TIMESTAMP INTERVAL	RAW	ROWID UROWID	NCHAR NVARCHAR2
BINARY_FLOAT BINARY_DOUBLE	X	X	X				X
CHAR VARCHAR2	X	X	X	X	X	X	
NUMBER	X	X	X				X
DATE TIMESTAMP INTERVAL		X		X			
RAW		X			X		
ROWID UROWID		X				X	
NCHAR NVARCHAR2	X		X	X	X	X	X

The following query shows the use of CAST() to convert literal values to specific types:

```
SELECT
  CAST(12345.67 AS VARCHAR2(10)),
  CAST('9A4F' AS RAW(2)),
  CAST('05-JUL-07' AS DATE),
  CAST(12345.678 AS NUMBER(10,2))
FROM dual;


CAST(12345 CAST CAST('05- CAST(12345.678ASNUMBER(10,2))
---------- ---- --------- ------------------------------
12345.67   9A4F 05-JUL-07                     12345.68
```

You can also convert column values from one type to another, as shown in the following query:

```
SELECT
  CAST(price AS VARCHAR2(10)),
  CAST(price + 2 AS NUMBER(7,2)),
  CAST(price AS BINARY_DOUBLE)
FROM products
WHERE product_id = 1;


CAST(PRICE CAST(PRICE+2ASNUMBER(7,2)) CAST(PRICEASBINARY_DOUBLE)
---------- -------------------------- --------------------------
19.95                           21.95                  1.995E+001
```

You'll see additional examples in Chapter 5 that show how to use CAST() to convert dates, times, and intervals. Also, Chapter 13 shows how you use CAST() to convert collections.

Regular Expression Functions

In this section, you'll learn about regular expressions and their associated Oracle database functions. These functions allow you to search for a pattern of characters in a string. For example, let's say you have the following list of years,

```
1965
1968
1971
1970
```

and want to get the years 1965 through to 1968. You can do this using the following regular expression:

```
^196[5-8]$
```

The regular expression contains a number of *metacharacters*. In this example, ^, [5-8], and $ are the metacharacters; ^ matches the beginning position of a string; [5-8] matches characters between 5 and 8; $ matches the end position of a string. Therefore ^196 matches a string that begins with 196, and [5-8]$ matches a string that ends with 5, 6, 7, or 8. So ^196[5-8]$ matches 1965, 1966, 1967, and 1968, which are the years you wanted to get from the list.

The next example uses the following string, which contains a quote from Shakespeare's *Romeo and Juliet:*

```
But, soft! What light through yonder window breaks?
```

Let's say you want to get the substring `light`. You do this using the following regular expression:

```
l[[:alpha:]]{4}
```

In this regular expression, `[[:alpha:]]` and `{4}` are the metacharacters. `[[:alpha:]]` matches an alphanumeric character A-Z and a-z; `{4}` repeats the previous match four times. When `l`, `[[:alpha:]]`, and `{4}` are combined, they match a sequence of five letters starting with `l`. Therefore, the regular expression `l[[:alpha:]]{4}` matches `light` in the string.

Table 4-5 lists some the metacharacters you can use in a regular expression, along with their meaning and an example of their use.

Metacharacters	Meaning	Examples
\	Matches a special character or a literal or performs a backreference. (A backreference repeats the previous match.)	\n matches the newline character \\ matches \ \(matches (\) matches)
^	Matches the position at the start of the string.	^A matches A if A is the first character in the string.
$	Matches the position at the end of the string.	$B matches B if B is the last character in the string.
*	Matches the preceding character zero or more times.	ba*rk matches brk, bark, baark, and so on.
+	Matches the preceding character one or more times.	ba+rk matches bark, baark, and so on, but not brk.
?	Matches the preceding character zero or one time.	ba?rk matches brk and bark only.
{n}	Matches a character exactly *n* times, where *n* is an integer.	hob{2}it matches hobbit.
{n,m}	Matches a character at least *n* times and at most *m* times, where *n* and *m* are both integers.	hob{2,3}it matches hobbit and hobbbit only.
.	Matches any single character except null.	hob.it matches hobait, hobbit, and so on.

TABLE 4-5 *Regular Expression Metacharacters*

Metacharacters	Meaning	Examples
(pattern)	A subexpression that matches the specified pattern. You use subexpressions to build up complex regular expressions. You can access the individual matches, known as captures, from this type of subexpression.	anatom(y|ies) matches anatomy and anatomies.
x|y	Matches x or y, where x and y are one or more characters.	war|peace matches war or peace.
[abc]	Matches any of the enclosed characters.	[ab]bc matches abc and bbc.
[a-z]	Matches any character in the specified range.	[a-c]bc matches abc, bbc, and cbc.
[: :]	Specifies a character class and matches any character in that class.	[:alphanum:] matches alphanumeric characters 0–9, A–Z, and a–z. [:alpha:] matches alphabetic characters A–Z and a–z. [:blank:] matches space or tab. [:digit:] matches digits 0–9. [:graph:] matches non-blank characters. [:lower:] matches lowercase alphabetic characters a–z. [:print:] is similar to [:graph:] except [:print:] includes the space character. [:punct:] matches punctuation characters .,"' , and so on. [:space:] matches all whitespace characters. [:upper:] matches all uppercase alphabetic characters A–Z. [:xdigit:] matches characters permissible in a hexadecimal number 0–9, A–F, and a–f.
[..]	Matches one collation element, like a multicharacter element.	No example.
[==]	Specifies equivalence classes.	No example.

TABLE 4-5   *Regular Expression Metacharacters* (continued)

Metacharacters	Meaning	Examples
\n	This is a backreference to an earlier capture, where n is a positive integer.	(.)\1 matches two consecutive identical characters. The (.) captures any single character except null, and the \1 repeats the capture, matching the same character again, therefore matching two consecutive identical characters.

TABLE 4-5   *Regular Expression Metacharacters* (continued)

Oracle Database 10g Release 2 introduced a number of Perl-influenced metacharacters, which are shown in Table 4-6.

Table 4-7 shows the regular expression functions. Regular expression functions were introduced in Oracle Database 10g, and additional items have been added to 11g, as shown in the table.

Metacharacters	Meaning
\d	Digit character
\D	Non-digit character
\w	Word character
\W	Non-word character
\s	Whitespace character
\S	Non-whitespace character
\A	Matches only at the beginning of a string or before a newline character at the end of a string
\Z	Matches only at the end of a string
*?	Matches the preceding pattern element 0 or more times
+?	Matches the preceding pattern element 1 or more times
??	Matches the preceding pattern element 0 or 1 time
{n}	Matches the preceding pattern element exactly n times
{n,}	Matches the preceding pattern element at least n times
{n,m}	Matches the preceding pattern element at least n but not more than m times

TABLE 4-6   *Perl-Influenced Metacharacters*

Function	Description
`REGEXP_LIKE(x, pattern [, match_option])`	Searches x for the regular expression defined in the `pattern` parameter. You can also provide an optional `match_option`, which may be set to one of the following characters: ■ `'c'`, which specifies case-sensitive matching (this is the default) ■ `'I'`, which specifies case-insensitive matching ■ `'n'`, which allows you to use the match-any-character operator ■ `'m'`, which treats x as a multiple line
`REGEXP_INSTR(x, pattern [, start [, occurrence [, return_option [, match_option [, subexp_option]]]]])`	Searches x for the `pattern` and returns the position at which the `pattern` occurs. You can supply an optional: ■ `start` position to begin the search. The default is 1, which is the first character in x. ■ `occurrence` that indicates which occurrence of `pattern` should be returned. The default is 1, which means the function returns the position of the first occurrence of `pattern` in x. ■ `return_option` that indicates what integer to return. 0 specifies the integer to return is the position of the first character in x; 1 specifies the integer to return is the position of the character in x after the occurrence. ■ `match_option` to change the default matching. Works in the same way as specified in `REGEXP_LIKE()`. ■ `subexp_option` (new for Oracle Database 11*g*) works as follows: for a pattern with subexpressions, `subexp_option` is a nonnegative integer from 0 to 9 indicating which subexpression in `pattern` is the target of the function. For example, consider the following expression: `0123(((abc)(de)f)ghi)45(678)` This expression has five subexpressions in the following order: `"abcdefghi"`, `"abcdef"`, `"abc"`, `"de"`, and `"678"`. If `subexp_option` is 0, the position of `pattern` is returned. If `pattern` does not have the correct number of subexpressions, then the function returns 0. A null `subexp_option` value returns null. The default value for `subexp_option` is 0.

TABLE 4-7   *Regular Expression Functions*

Function	Description
REGEXP_REPLACE(*x*, *pattern* [, *replace_string* [, *start* [, *occurrence* [, *match_option*]]]])	Searches *x* for the *pattern* and replaces it with *replace_string*. The other options have the same meaning as those shown earlier.
REGEXP_SUBSTR(*x*, *pattern* [, *start* [, *occurrence* [, *match_option* [, *subexp_option*]]]])	Returns a substring of *x* that matches *pattern*; the search begins at the position specified by *start*. The other options have the same meaning as those shown earlier. The *subexp_option* (new for Oracle Database 11*g*) works in the same way as shown for REGEXP_INSTR().
REGEXP_COUNT(*x*, *pattern* [, *start* [, *match_option*]])	New for Oracle Database 11*g*. Searches in *x* for the *pattern* and returns the number of times the *pattern* is found in *x*. You can supply an optional: <ul><li>*start* position to begin the search. The default is 1, which is the first character in *x*.</li><li>*match_option* to change the default matching. Works in the same way as shown for REGEXP_LIKE().</li></ul>

TABLE 4-7 *Regular Expression Functions* (continued)

You'll learn more about the regular expression functions in the following sections.

REGEXP_LIKE()

You use REGEXP_LIKE(*x*, *pattern* [, *match_option*]) to search *x* for the regular expression defined in the *pattern* parameter. You can also provide an optional *match_option*, which may be set to one of the following characters:

■ 'c', which specifies case-sensitive matching (this is the default)

■ 'I', which specifies case-insensitive matching

■ 'n', which allows you to use the match-any-character operator

■ 'm', which treats *x* as a multiple line

The following query retrieves customers whose date of birth is between 1965 and 1968 using REGEXP_LIKE():

```
SELECT customer_id, first_name, last_name, dob
FROM customers
WHERE REGEXP_LIKE(TO_CHAR(dob, 'YYYY'), '^196[5-8]$');

CUSTOMER_ID FIRST_NAME LAST_NAME  DOB
----------- ---------- ---------- ---------
          1 John       Brown      01-JAN-65
          2 Cynthia    Green      05-FEB-68
```

The next query retrieves customers whose first name starts with J or j. Notice the regular expression passed to REGEXP_LIKE() is ^j and the match option is i (i indicates case-insensitive matching and so in this example ^j matches J or j).

```
SELECT customer_id, first_name, last_name, dob
FROM customers
WHERE REGEXP_LIKE(first_name, '^j', 'i');
```

```
CUSTOMER_ID FIRST_NAME LAST_NAME  DOB
----------- ---------- ---------- ---------
          1 John       Brown      01-JAN-65
```

REGEXP_INSTR()

You use REGEXP_INSTR(x, pattern [, start [, occurrence [, return_option [, match_option]]]]) to search x for the pattern ;. This function returns the position at which pattern occurs (positions start at number 1).

The following query returns the position that matches the regular expression l[[: alpha:]]{4} using REGEXP_INSTR():

```
SELECT
  REGEXP_INSTR('But, soft! What light through yonder window breaks?',
  'l[[:alpha:]]{4}') AS result
FROM dual;
```

```
    RESULT
----------
        17
```

Notice that 17 is returned, which is the position of the l in light.

The next query returns the position of the second occurrence that matches the regular expression s[[:alpha:]]{3} starting at position 1:

```
SELECT
  REGEXP_INSTR('But, soft! What light through yonder window softly breaks?',
  's[[:alpha:]]{3}', 1, 2) AS result
FROM dual;
```

```
    RESULT
----------
        45
```

The next query returns the position of the second occurrence that matches the letter o starting the search at position 10:

```
SELECT
  REGEXP_INSTR('But, soft! What light through yonder window breaks?',
  'o', 10, 2) AS result
FROM dual;
```

```
    RESULT
----------
        32
```

REGEXP_REPLACE()

You use REGEXP_REPLACE(*x, pattern* [, *replace_string* [, *start* [, *occurrence* [, *match_option*]]]]) to search *x* for the *pattern* and replace it with *replace_string*.

The following query replaces the substring that matches the regular expression 1[[:alpha:]]{4} with the string 'sound' using REGEXP_REPLACE():

```
SELECT
 REGEXP_REPLACE('But, soft! What light through yonder window breaks?',
  'l[[:alpha:]]{4}', 'sound') AS result
FROM dual;

RESULT
--------------------------------------------------
But, soft! What sound through yonder window breaks?
```

Notice that light has been replaced by sound.

REGEXP_SUBSTR()

You use REGEXP_SUBSTR(*x, pattern* [, *start* [, *occurrence* [, *match_option*]]]) to get a substring of *x* that matches *pattern*; the search begins at the position specified by *start*.

The following query returns the substring that matches the regular expression 1[[:alpha:]]{4} using REGEXP_SUBSTR():

```
SELECT
 REGEXP_SUBSTR('But, soft! What light through yonder window breaks?',
  'l[[:alpha:]]{4}') AS result
FROM dual;

RESUL
-----
light
```

REGEXP_COUNT()

REGEXP_COUNT() is new for Oracle Database 11*g*. You use REGEXP_COUNT(*x, pattern* [, *start* [, *match_option*]]) to search in *x* for the *pattern* and get the number of times *pattern* is found in *x*. You can provide an optional *start* number to indicate the character in *x* to begin searching for *pattern* and an optional *match_option* string to indicate the match option.

The following query returns the number of times the regular expression s[[:alpha:]]{3} occurs in a string using REGEXP_COUNT():

```
SELECT
 REGEXP_COUNT('But, soft! What light through yonder window softly breaks?',
  's[[:alpha:]]{3}') AS result
FROM dual;

    RESULT
----------
         2
```

Notice that 2 is returned, which means the regular expression has two matches in the supplied string.

Using Aggregate Functions

The functions you've seen so far operate on a single row at a time and return one row of output for each input row. In this section, you'll learn about aggregate functions, which operate on a group of rows and return one row of output.

NOTE
Aggregate functions are also known as group functions because they operate on groups of rows.

Table 4-8 lists some of the aggregate functions, all of which return a NUMBER. Here are some points to remember when using aggregate functions:

■ You can use the aggregate functions with any valid expression. For example, you can use the COUNT(), MAX(), and MIN() functions with numbers, strings, and datetimes.

■ Null values are ignored by aggregate functions, because a null value indicates the value is unknown and therefore cannot be used in the aggregate function's calculation.

■ You can use the DISTINCT keyword with an aggregate function to exclude duplicate entries from the aggregate function's calculation.

You'll learn more about some of the aggregate functions shown in Table 4-8 in the following sections. In Chapters 7 and 8, you'll see how to use these functions in conjunction with the SELECT statement's ROLLUP and RETURNING clauses. As you'll see, ROLLUP allows you to get a subtotal for a group of rows, where the subtotal is calculated using one of the aggregate functions; RETURNING allows you to store the value returned by an aggregate function in a variable.

Function	Description
AVG(x)	Returns the average value of x
COUNT(x)	Returns the number of rows returned by a query involving x
MAX(x)	Returns the maximum value of x
MEDIAN(x)	Returns the median value of x
MIN(x)	Returns the minimum value of x
STDDEV(x)	Returns the standard deviation of x
SUM(x)	Returns the sum of x
VARIANCE(x)	Returns the variance of x

TABLE 4-8 *Aggregate Functions*

AVG()

You use AVG (*x*) to get the average value of *x*. The following query gets the average price of the products; notice that the price column from the products table is passed to the AVG () function:

```
SELECT AVG(price)
FROM products;

AVG(PRICE)
----------
19.7308333
```

You can use the aggregate functions with any valid expression. For example, the following query passes the expression price + 2 to AVG (); this adds 2 to each row's price and then returns the average of those values.

```
SELECT AVG(price + 2)
FROM products;

AVG(PRICE)
----------
21.7308333
```

You can use the DISTINCT keyword to exclude identical values from a computation. For example, the following query uses the DISTINCT keyword to exclude identical values in the price column when computing the average using AVG ():

```
SELECT AVG(DISTINCT price)
FROM products;

AVG(DISTINCTPRICE)
------------------
        20.2981818
```

Notice that the average in this example is slightly higher than the average returned by the first query in this section. This is because the value for product #12 (13.49) in the price column is the same as the value for product #7; it is considered a duplicate and excluded from the computation performed by AVG (). Therefore, the average is slightly higher in this example.

COUNT()

You use COUNT (*x*) to get the number of rows returned by a query. The following query gets the number of rows in the products table using COUNT ():

```
SELECT COUNT(product_id)
FROM products;

COUNT(PRODUCT_ID)
-----------------
               12
```

TIP
You should avoid using the asterisk (*) with the COUNT() *function,*
as it may take longer for COUNT() *to return the result. Instead, you*
should use a column in the table or use the ROWID *pseudo column.*
(As you saw in Chapter 2, the ROWID *column contains the internal*
location of the row in the Oracle database.)

The following example passes ROWID to COUNT() and gets the number of rows in the
products table:

```
SELECT COUNT(ROWID)
FROM products;

COUNT(ROWID)
------------
          12
```

MAX() and MIN()

You use MAX(*x*) and MIN(*x*) to get the maximum and minimum values for *x*. The following
query gets the maximum and minimum values of the price column from the products table
using MAX() and MIN():

```
SELECT MAX(price), MIN(price)
FROM products;

MAX(PRICE) MIN(PRICE)
---------- ----------
     49.99      10.99
```

You may use MAX() and MIN() with any type, including strings and dates. When you use
MAX() with strings, the strings are ordered alphabetically with the "maximum" string being at
the bottom of a list and the "minimum" string being at the top of the list. For example, the string
Albert would appear before Zeb in such a list. The following example gets the maximum and
minimum name strings from the products table using MAX() and MIN():

```
SELECT MAX(name), MIN(name)
FROM products;

MAX(NAME)                           MIN(NAME)
----------------------------------  ------------------------------
Z Files                             2412: The Return
```

In the case of dates, the "maximum" date occurs at the latest point in time, and the
"minimum" date at the earliest point in time. The following query gets the maximum and
minimum dob from the customers table using MAX() and MIN():

```
SELECT MAX(dob), MIN(dob)
FROM customers;

MAX(DOB)   MIN(DOB)
---------  ---------
16-MAR-71 01-JAN-65
```

STDDEV()

You use STDDEV (*x*) to get the standard deviation of *x*. Standard deviation is a statistical function and is defined as the square root of the variance (you'll learn about variance shortly).

The following query gets the standard deviation of the price column values from the products table using STDDEV ():

```
SELECT STDDEV(price)
FROM products;

STDDEV(PRICE)
-------------
   11.0896303
```

SUM()

SUM (*x*) adds all the values in *x* and returns the total. The following query gets the sum of the price column from the products table using SUM ():

```
SELECT SUM(price)
FROM products;

SUM(PRICE)
----------
    236.77
```

VARIANCE()

You use VARIANCE (*x*) to get the variance of *x*. Variance is a statistical function and is defined as the spread or variation of a group of numbers in a sample. Variance is equal to the square of the standard deviation.

The following example gets the variance of the price column values from the products table using VARIANCE ():

```
SELECT VARIANCE(price)
FROM products;

VARIANCE(PRICE)
---------------
    122.979899
```

Grouping Rows

Sometimes you need to group blocks of rows in a table and get some information on those groups of rows. For example, you might want to get the average price for the different types of products in the products table. You'll see how to do this the hard way first, then you'll see the easy way, which involves using the GROUP BY clause to group similar rows together.

To do it the hard way, you limit the rows passed to the AVG () function using a WHERE clause. For example, the following query gets the average price for books from the products table (books have a product_type_id of 1):

```
SELECT AVG(price)
FROM products
WHERE product_type_id = 1;
```

```
AVG(PRICE)
----------
    24.975
```

To get the average price for the other types of products, you would need to perform additional queries with different values for the product_type_id in the WHERE clause. As you can imagine, this is very labor intensive. You'll be glad to know there's an easier way to do this through the use of the GROUP BY clause.

Using the GROUP BY Clause to Group Rows

You use the GROUP BY clause to group rows into blocks with a common column value. For example, the following query groups the rows from the products table into blocks with the same product_type_id:

```
SELECT product_type_id
FROM products
GROUP BY product_type_id;
```

```
PRODUCT_TYPE_ID
---------------
              1

              2
              3
              4
```

Notice that there's one row in the result set for each block of rows with the same product_type_id and that there's a gap between 1 and 2 (you'll see why this gap occurs shortly). In the result set, there's one row for products with a product_type_id of 1, another for products with a product_type_id of 2, and so on. There are actually two rows in the products table with a product_type_id of 1, four rows with a product_type_id of 2, and so on for the other rows in the table. These rows are grouped together into separate blocks by the GROUP BY clause, one block for each product_type_id. The first block contains two rows, the second contains four rows, and so on.

The gap between 1 and 2 is caused by a row whose product_type_id is null. This row is shown in the following example:

```
SELECT product_id, name, price
FROM products
WHERE product_type_id IS NULL;
```

```
PRODUCT_ID NAME                               PRICE
---------- ------------------------------ ----------
        12 My Front Line                      13.49
```

Because this row's `product_type_id` is null, the GROUP BY clause in the earlier query groups this row into a single block. The row in the result set is blank because the `product_type_id` is null for the block, so there's a gap between 1 and 2.

Using Multiple Columns in a Group

You can specify multiple columns in a GROUP BY clause. For example, the following query includes the `product_id` and `customer_id` columns from the `purchases` table in a GROUP BY clause:

```
SELECT product_id, customer_id
FROM purchases
GROUP BY product_id, customer_id;

PRODUCT_ID CUSTOMER_ID
---------- -----------
         1           1
         1           2
         1           3
         1           4
         2           1
         2           2
         2           3
         2           4
         3           3
```

Using Groups of Rows with Aggregate Functions

You can pass blocks of rows to an aggregate function. The aggregate function performs its computation on the group of rows in each block and returns one value per block. For example, to get the number of rows with the same `product_type_id` from the `products` table, you do the following:

- Use the GROUP BY clause to group rows into blocks with the same `product_type_id`.

- Use COUNT(ROWID) to get the number of rows in each block.

The following query shows this:

```
SELECT product_type_id, COUNT(ROWID)
FROM products
GROUP BY product_type_id
ORDER BY product_type_id;

PRODUCT_TYPE_ID COUNT(ROWID)
--------------- ------------
              1            2
              2            4
              3            2
              4            3
                           1
```

Notice that there are five rows in the result set, with each row corresponding to one or more rows in the products table grouped together with the same product_type_id. From the result set, you can see there are two rows with a product_type_id of 1, four rows with a product_type_id of 2, and so on. The last line in the result set shows there is one row with a null product_type_id (this is caused by the "My Front Line" product mentioned earlier).

Let's take a look at another example. To get the average price for the different types of products in the products table, you do the following:

■ Use the GROUP BY clause to group rows into blocks with the same product_type_id.

■ Use AVG(price) to get the average price for each block of rows.

The following query shows this:

```
SELECT product_type_id, AVG(price)
FROM products
GROUP BY product_type_id
ORDER BY product_type_id;

PRODUCT_TYPE_ID AVG(PRICE)
--------------- ----------
              1     24.975
              2      26.22
              3      13.24
              4      13.99
                    13.49
```

Each group of rows with the same product_type_id is passed to the AVG() function. AVG() then computes the average price for each group. As you can see from the result set, the average price for the group of products with a product_type_id of 1 is 24.975. Similarly, the average price of the products with a product_type_id of 2 is 26.22. Notice that the last row in the result set shows an average price of 13.49; this is simply the price of the "My Front Line" product, the only row with a null product_type_id.

You can use any of the aggregate functions with the GROUP BY clause. For example, the next query gets the variance of product prices for each product_type_id:

```
SELECT product_type_id, VARIANCE(price)
FROM products
GROUP BY product_type_id
ORDER BY product_type_id;

PRODUCT_TYPE_ID VARIANCE(PRICE)
--------------- ---------------
              1        50.50125
              2        280.8772
              3            .125
              4               7
                              0
```

One point to remember is that you don't have to include the columns used in the GROUP BY in the list of columns immediately after the SELECT. For example, the following query is the same as the previous one except product_type_id is omitted from the SELECT clause:

```
SELECT VARIANCE(price)
FROM products
GROUP BY product_type_id
ORDER BY product_type_id;

VARIANCE(PRICE)
---------------
       50.50125
       280.8772
           .125
              7
              0
```

You can also include an aggregate function call in the ORDER BY, as shown in the following query:

```
SELECT VARIANCE(price)
FROM products
GROUP BY product_type_id
ORDER BY VARIANCE(price);

VARIANCE(PRICE)
---------------
              0
           .125
              7
       50.50125
       280.8772
```

Incorrect Usage of Aggregate Function Calls

When your query contains an aggregate function—and retrieves columns not placed within an aggregate function—those columns must be placed in a GROUP BY clause. If you forget to do this, you'll get the following error: ORA-00937: not a single-group group function. For example, the following query attempts to retrieve the product_type_id column and AVG(price) but omits a GROUP BY clause for product_type_id:

```
SQL> SELECT product_type_id, AVG(price)
  2  FROM products;
SELECT product_type_id, AVG(price)
       *
ERROR at line 1:
ORA-00937: not a single-group group function
```

The error occurs because the database doesn't know what to do with the product_type_id column. Think about it: the query attempts to use the AVG() aggregate function, which operates on multiple rows, but also attempts to get the `product_type_id` column values for each individual row. You can't do both at the same time. You must provide a GROUP BY clause to tell the database to group multiple rows with the same `product_type_id` together; then the database passes those groups of rows to the AVG() function.

CAUTION
When a query contains an aggregate function—and retrieves columns not placed within an aggregate function—then those columns must be placed in a GROUP BY clause.

Also, you cannot use an aggregate function to limit rows in a WHERE clause. If you try to do so, you will get the following error: `ORA-00934: group function is not allowed here`. For example:

```
SQL> SELECT product_type_id, AVG(price)
  2  FROM products
  3  WHERE AVG(price) > 20
  4  GROUP BY product_type_id;
WHERE AVG(price) > 20
      *
ERROR at line 3:
ORA-00934: group function is not allowed here
```

The error occurs because you may only use the WHERE clause to filter *individual* rows, not *groups* of rows. To filter groups of rows, you use the HAVING clause, which you'll learn about next.

Using the HAVING Clause to Filter Groups of Rows

You use the HAVING clause to filter groups of rows. You place the HAVING clause after the GROUP BY clause:

```
SELECT ...
FROM ...
WHERE
GROUP BY ...
HAVING ...
ORDER BY ...;
```

NOTE
GROUP BY can be used without HAVING, but HAVING must be used in conjunction with GROUP BY.

Let's take a look at an example. Say you want to view the types of products that have an average price greater than $20. To do this, you do the following:

■ Use the GROUP BY clause to group rows into blocks with the same `product_type_id`.

■ Use the HAVING clause to limit the returned results to those groups that have an average price greater than $20.

The following query shows this:

```
SELECT product_type_id, AVG(price)
FROM products
GROUP BY product_type_id
HAVING AVG(price) > 20;

PRODUCT_TYPE_ID AVG(PRICE)
--------------- ----------
              1     24.975
              2      26.22
```

As you can see, only the groups of rows having an average price greater than $20 are displayed.

Using the WHERE and GROUP BY Clauses Together

You can use the WHERE and GROUP BY clauses together in the same query. When you do this, first the WHERE clause filters the rows returned, then the GROUP BY clause groups the remaining rows into blocks. For example, the following query uses

- A WHERE clause to filter the rows from the products table to select those whose price is less than $15.

- A GROUP BY clause to group the remaining rows by the product_type_id column.

```
SELECT product_type_id, AVG(price)
FROM products
WHERE price < 15
GROUP BY product_type_id
ORDER BY product_type_id;

PRODUCT_TYPE_ID AVG(PRICE)
--------------- ----------
              2      14.45
              3      13.24
              4      12.99
                     13.49
```

Using the WHERE, GROUP BY, and HAVING Clauses Together

You can use the WHERE, GROUP BY, and HAVING clauses together in the same query. When you do this, the WHERE clause first filters the rows, the GROUP BY clause then groups the remaining rows into blocks, and finally the HAVING clause filters the row groups. For example, the following query uses

- A WHERE clause to filter the rows from the products table to select those whose price is less than $15.

- A GROUP BY clause to group the remaining rows by the product_type_id column.

- A HAVING clause to filter the row groups to select those whose average price is greater than $13.

```
SELECT product_type_id, AVG(price)
FROM products
WHERE price < 15
GROUP BY product_type_id
HAVING AVG(price) > 13
ORDER BY product_type_id;
```

```
PRODUCT_TYPE_ID AVG(PRICE)
--------------- ----------
              2      14.45
              3      13.24
                     13.49
```

Compare these results with the previous example. Notice that the group of rows with the `product_type_id` of 4 is filtered out. That's because the group of rows has an average price less than $13.

The final query uses `ORDER BY AVG(price)` to re-order the results by the average price:

```
SELECT product_type_id, AVG(price)
FROM products
WHERE price < 15
GROUP BY product_type_id
HAVING AVG(price) > 13
ORDER BY AVG(price);
```

```
PRODUCT_TYPE_ID AVG(PRICE)
--------------- ----------
              3      13.24
                     13.49
              2      14.45
```

Summary

In this chapter, you have learned the following:

- The Oracle database has two main groups of functions: single-row functions and aggregate functions.

- Single-row functions operate on one row at a time and return one row of output for each input row. There are five main types of single-row functions: character functions, numeric functions, conversion functions, date functions, and regular expression functions.

- Aggregate functions operate on multiple rows and return one row of output.

- Blocks of rows may be grouped together using the GROUP BY clause.

- Groups of rows may be filtered using the HAVING clause.

In the next chapter, you'll learn about dates and times.

CHAPTER
5

Storing and Processing
Dates and Times

n this chapter, you will see how to

- Process and store a specific date and time, collectively known as a datetime. An example of a datetime is 7:15:30 p.m. on October 10, 2007. You store a datetime using the DATE type. The DATE type stores the century, all four digits of a year, the month, the day, the hour (in 24-hour format), the minute, and the second.

- Use *timestamps* to store a specific date and time. A timestamp stores the century, all four digits of a year, the month, the day, the hour (in 24-hour format), the minute, and the second. The advantages of a timestamp over a DATE are that a timestamp can store a fractional second and a time zone.

- Use time *intervals* to store a length of time. An example of a time interval is 1 year 3 months.

Let's plunge in and see some simple examples of storing and retrieving dates.

Simple Examples of Storing and Retrieving Dates

By default the database uses the format DD-MON-YYYY to represent a date, where

- DD is a two-digit day, e.g., 05

- MON is the first three letters of the month, e.g., FEB

- YYYY is a four-digit year, e.g., 1968

Let's take a look at an example of adding a row to the customers table, which contains a DATE column named dob. The following INSERT adds a row to the customers table, setting the dob column to 05-FEB-1968:

```
INSERT INTO customers (
  customer_id, first_name, last_name, dob, phone
) VALUES (
  6, 'Fred', 'Brown', '05-FEB-1968', '800-555-1215'
);
```

You can also use the DATE keyword to supply a date literal to the database. The date must use the ANSI standard date format YYYY-MM-DD, where

- YYYY is a four-digit year.

- MM is a two-digit month from 1 to 12.

- DD is a two-digit day.

TIP
Using ANSI standard dates in SQL statements has the advantage that those statements could potentially run against non-Oracle databases.

For example, to specify a date of October 25, 1972, you use DATE '1972-10-25'. The following INSERT adds a row to the customers table, specifying DATE '1972-10-25' for the dob column:

```
INSERT INTO customers (
  customer_id, first_name, last_name, dob, phone
) VALUES (
  7, 'Steve', 'Purple', DATE '1972-10-25', '800-555-1215'
);
```

By default, the database returns dates in the format DD-MON-YY, where YY are the last two digits of the year. For example, the following example retrieves rows from the customers table and then performs a ROLLBACK to undo the results of the previous two INSERT statements; notice the two-digit years in the dob column returned by the query:

```
SELECT *
FROM customers;
```

```
CUSTOMER_ID FIRST_NAME LAST_NAME  DOB        PHONE
----------- ---------- ---------- ---------  ------------
          1 John       Brown      01-JAN-65  800-555-1211
          2 Cynthia    Green      05-FEB-68  800-555-1212
          3 Steve      White      16-MAR-71  800-555-1213
          4 Gail       Black                 800-555-1214
          5 Doreen     Blue       20-MAY-70
          6 Fred       Brown      05-FEB-68  800-555-1215
          7 Steve      Purple     25-OCT-72  800-555-1215
```

```
ROLLBACK;
```

Customer #4's dob is null and is therefore blank in the previous result set.

NOTE
If you actually ran the two INSERT statements, make sure you undo the changes by executing the ROLLBACK. That way, you'll keep the database in its initial state, and the results from your queries will match those in this chapter.

In this section, you saw some simple examples of using dates that use default formats. You'll learn how to provide your own date formats in the following section and see how to convert a datetime to another database type.

Converting Datetimes Using TO_CHAR() and TO_DATE()

The Oracle database has functions that enable you to convert a value in one data type to another. You saw some of these functions in the previous chapter. In this section, you'll see how to use the TO_CHAR() and TO_DATE() functions to convert a datetime to a string and vice versa. Table 5-1 summarizes the TO_CHAR() and TO_DATE() functions.

Function	Description
TO_CHAR(*x* [, *format*])	Converts *x* to a string. You can also supply an optional *format* for *x*. You saw how to use TO_CHAR() to convert a number to a string in the previous chapter. In this chapter, you'll see how to convert a datetime to a string.
TO_DATE(*x* [, *format*])	Converts the string *x* to a DATE.

TABLE 5-1   *TO_CHAR() and TO_DATE() Conversion Functions*

Let's start off by examining how you use TO_CHAR() to convert a datetime to a string. Later, you'll see how to use TO_DATE() to convert a string to a DATE.

Using TO_CHAR() to Convert a Datetime to a String

You can use TO_CHAR(*x* [, *format*]) to convert the datetime *x* to a string. You can also provide an optional *format* for *x*. An example format is MONTH DD, YYYY, where

- MONTH is the full name of the month in uppercase, e.g., JANUARY.

- DD is the two-digit day.

- YYYY is the four-digit year.

The following query uses TO_CHAR() to convert the dob column from the customers table to a string with the format MONTH DD, YYYY:

```
SELECT customer_id, TO_CHAR(dob, 'MONTH DD, YYYY')
FROM customers;

CUSTOMER_ID TO_CHAR(DOB,'MONTH
----------- ------------------
          1 JANUARY   01, 1965
          2 FEBRUARY  05, 1968
          3 MARCH     16, 1971
          4
          5 MAY       20, 1970
```

The next query gets the current date and time from the database using the SYSDATE function, then converts the date and time to a string using TO_CHAR() with the format MONTH DD, YYYY, HH24:MI:SS. The time portion of this format indicates that the hours are in 24-hour format and that the minutes and seconds are also to be included in the string.

```
SELECT TO_CHAR(SYSDATE, 'MONTH DD, YYYY, HH24:MI:SS')
FROM dual;

TO_CHAR(SYSDATE,'MONTHDD,YYY
---------------------------
NOVEMBER  05, 2007, 12:34:36
```

When you use TO_CHAR() to convert a datetime to a string, the format has a number of parameters that affect the returned string. Some of these parameters are listed in Table 5-2.

Aspect	Parameter	Description	Example
Century	CC	Two-digit century.	21
	SCC	Two-digit century with a negative sign (–) for B.C.	–10
Quarter	Q	One-digit quarter of the year.	1
Year	YYYY	All four digits of the year.	2008
	IYYY	All four digits of the ISO year.	2008
	RRRR	All four digits of the rounded year (governed by the present year). See the section "How Oracle Interprets Two-Digit Years" later in this chapter for details.	2008
	SYYYY	All four digits of the year with a negative sign (–) for B.C.	–1001
	Y,YYY	All four digits of the year, with a comma after the first digit.	2,008
	YYY	Last three digits of the year.	008
	IYY	Last three digits of the ISO year.	008
	YY	Last two digits of the year.	08
	IY	Last two digits of the ISO year.	06
	RR	Last two digits of the rounded year, which depend on the present year. See the section "How Oracle Interprets Two-Digit Years" later in this chapter for details.	08
	Y	Last digit of the year.	8
	I	Last digit of the ISO year.	8
	YEAR	Name of the year in uppercase.	TWO THOUSAND-EIGHT
	Year	Name of the year with the first letter in uppercase.	Two Thousand-Eight
Month	MM	Two-digit month of the year.	01
	MONTH	Full name of the month in uppercase, right-padded with spaces to a total length of nine characters.	JANUARY
	Month	Full name of the month with first letter in uppercase, right-padded with spaces to a total length of nine characters.	January
	MON	First three letters of the name of the month in uppercase.	JAN
	Mon	First three letters of the name of the month with the first letter in uppercase.	Jan

TABLE 5-2 *Datetime Formatting Parameters*

Aspect	Parameter	Description	Example
	RM	Roman numeral month.	The Roman numeral month for the fourth month (April) is IV.
Week	WW	Two-digit week of the year.	02
	IW	Two-digit ISO week of the year.	02
	W	One-digit week of the month.	2
Day	DDD	Three-digit day of the year.	103
	DD	Two-digit day of the month.	31
	D	One-digit day of the week.	5
	DAY	Full name of the day in uppercase.	SATURDAY
	Day	Full name of the day with the first letter in uppercase.	Saturday
	DY	First three letters of the name of the day in uppercase.	SAT
	Dy	First three letters of the name of the day with the first letter in uppercase.	Sat
	J	Julian day—the number of days that have passed since January 1, 4713 B.C.	2439892
Hour	HH24	Two-digit hour in 24-hour format.	23
	HH	Two-digit hour in 12-hour format.	11
Minute	MI	Two-digit minute.	57
Second	SS	Two-digit second.	45
	FF[1..9]	Fractional seconds with an optional number of digits to the right of the decimal point. Only applies timestamps, which you'll learn about in the section "Using Timestamps" later in this chapter.	When dealing with 0.123456789 seconds, FF3 would round the seconds to 0.123.
	SSSSS	Number of seconds past 12 A.M.	46748
	MS	Millisecond (millionths of a second).	100
	CS	Centisecond (hundredths of a second).	10
Separators	-/,.;: "text"	Characters that allow you to separate the aspects of a date and time. You can supply freeform text in quotes as a separator.	For the date December 13, 1969, DD-MM-YYYY would produce 12-13-1969, and DD/MM/YYYY would produce 12/13/1969.
Suffixes	AM or PM	AM or PM as appropriate.	AM
	A.M. or P.M.	A.M. or P.M. as appropriate.	P.M.
	AD or BC	AD or BC as appropriate.	AD

TABLE 5-2   *Datetime Formatting Parameters* (continued)

Aspect	Parameter	Description	Example
	A.D. or B.C.	A.D. or B.C. as appropriate.	B.C.
	TH	Suffix to a number. You can make the suffix uppercase by specifying the numeric format in uppercase and vice versa for lowercase.	For a day number of 28, ddTH would produce 28th, and DDTH would produce 28TH.
	SP	Number is spelled out.	For a day number of 28, DDSP would produce TWENTY-EIGHT, and ddSP would produce twenty-eight.
	SPTH	Combination of TH and SP.	For a day number of 28, DDSPTH would produce TWENTY-EIGHTH, and ddSPTH would produce twenty-eighth.
Era	EE	Full era name for Japanese Imperial, ROC Official, and Thai Buddha calendars.	No example
	E	Abbreviated era name.	No example
Time zones	TZH	Time zone hour. You'll learn about time zones later in the section "Using Time Zones."	12
	TZM	Time zone minute.	30
	TZR	Time zone region.	PST
	TZD	Time zone with daylight savings information.	No example

TABLE 5-2 *Datetime Formatting Parameters* (continued)

The following table shows examples of strings to format the date February 5, 1968, along with the string returned from a call to TO_CHAR().

Format String	Returned String
MONTH DD, YYYY	FEBRUARY 05, 1968
MM/DD/YYYY	02/05/1968
MM-DD-YYYY	02-05-1968
DD/MM/YYYY	05/02/1968
DAY MON, YY AD	MONDAY FEB, 68 AD
DDSPTH "of" MONTH, YEAR A.D.	FIFTH of FEBRUARY, NINETEEN SIXTY-EIGHT A.D.
CC, SCC	20, 20
Q	1

Format String	Returned String
YYYY, IYYY, RRRR, SYYYY, Y,YYY, YYY, IYY, YY, IY, RR, Y, I, YEAR, Year	1968, 1968, 1968, 1968, 1,968, 968, 968, 68, 68, 68, 8, 8, NINETEEN SIXTY-EIGHT, Nineteen Sixty-Eight
MM, MONTH, Month, MON, Mon, RM	02, FEBRUARY, February, FEB, Feb, II
WW, IW, W	06, 06, 1
DDD, DD, DAY, Day, DY, Dy, J	036, 05, MONDAY, Monday, MON, Mon, 2439892
ddTH, DDTH, ddSP, DDSP, DDSPTH	05th, 05TH, five, FIVE, FIFTH

You can see the results shown in this table by calling `TO_CHAR()` in a query. For example, the following query converts February 5, 1968, to a string with the format `MONTH DD, YYYY`:

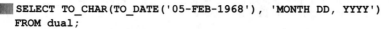

```
SELECT TO_CHAR(TO_DATE('05-FEB-1968'), 'MONTH DD, YYYY')
FROM dual;

TO_CHAR(TO_DATE('0
------------------
FEBRUARY  05, 1968
```

> **NOTE**
> *The* `TO_DATE()` *function converts a string to a datetime. You'll learn more about the* `TO_DATE()` *function shortly.*

The following table shows examples of strings to format the time 19:32:36 (32 minutes and 36 seconds past 7 P.M.)—along with the output that would be returned from a call to `TO_CHAR()` with that time and format string.

Format String	Returned String
HH24:MI:SS	19:32:36
HH.MI.SS AM	7.32.36 PM

Using TO_DATE() to Convert a String to a Datetime

You use `TO_DATE(x [, format])` to convert the *x* string to a datetime. You can provide an optional *format* string to indicate the format of *x*. If you omit *format*, the date must be in the default database format (usually `DD-MON-YYYY` or `DD-MON-YY`).

> **NOTE**
> *The* `NLS_DATE_FORMAT` *database parameter specifies the default date format for the database. As you'll learn later in the section "Setting the Default Date Format," you can change the setting of* `NLS_DATE_FORMAT`.

The following query uses `TO_DATE()` to convert the strings `04-JUL-2007` and `04-JUL-07` to the date July 4, 2007; notice that the final date is displayed in the default format of `DD-MON-YY`:

```
SELECT TO_DATE('04-JUL-2007'), TO_DATE('04-JUL-07')
FROM dual;

TO_DATE(' TO_DATE('
--------- ---------
04-JUL-07 04-JUL-07
```

Specifying a Datetime Format

As mentioned earlier, you can supply an optional format for a datetime to `TO_DATE()`. You use the same format parameters as those defined previously in Table 5-2. The following query uses `TO_DATE()` to convert the string `July 4, 2007` to a date, passing the format string `MONTH DD, YYYY` to `TO_DATE()`:

```
SELECT TO_DATE('July 4, 2007', 'MONTH DD, YYYY')
FROM dual;

TO_DATE('
---------
04-JUL-07
```

The next query passes the format string `MM.DD.YY` to `TO_DATE()` and converts the string `7.4.07` to the date July 4, 2007; again, the final date is displayed in the default format `DD-MON-YY`:

```
SELECT TO_DATE('7.4.07', 'MM.DD.YY')
FROM dual;

TO_DATE('
---------
04-JUL-07
```

Specifying Times

You can also specify a time with a datetime. If you don't supply a time with a datetime, the time part of your datetime defaults to 12:00:00 A.M. You can supply the format for a time using the various formats shown earlier in Table 5-3. One example time format is `HH24:MI:SS`, where

- `HH24` is a two-digit hour in 24-hour format from 00 to 23.

- `MI` is a two-digit minute from 00 to 59.

- `SS` is a two-digit second from 00 to 59.

An example of a time that uses the `HH24:MI:SS` format is 19:32:36. A full example of a datetime that uses this time is

```
05-FEB-1968 19:32:36
```

with the format for this datetime being

```
DD-MON-YYYY HH24:MI:SS
```

The following TO_DATE() call shows the use of this datetime format and value:

```
TO_DATE('05-FEB-1968 19:32:36', 'DD-MON-YYYY HH24:MI:SS')
```

The datetime returned by TO_DATE() in the previous example is used in the following INSERT that adds a row to the customers table; notice that the dob column for the new row is set to the datetime returned by TO_DATE():

```
INSERT INTO customers (
  customer_id, first_name, last_name,
  dob,
  phone
) VALUES (
  6, 'Fred', 'Brown',
  TO_DATE('05-FEB-1968 19:32:36', 'DD-MON-YYYY HH24:MI:SS'),
  '800-555-1215'
);
```

You use TO_CHAR() to view the time part of a datetime. For example, the following query retrieves the rows from the customers table and uses TO_CHAR() to convert the dob column values; notice that customer #6 has the time previously set in the INSERT:

```
SELECT customer_id, TO_CHAR(dob, 'DD-MON-YYYY HH24:MI:SS')
FROM customers;

CUSTOMER_ID TO_CHAR(DOB,'DD-MON-
----------- --------------------
          1 01-JAN-1965 00:00:00
          2 05-FEB-1968 00:00:00
          3 16-MAR-1971 00:00:00
          4
          5 20-MAY-1970 00:00:00
          6 05-FEB-1968 19:32:36
```

Notice the time for the dob column for customers #1, #2, #3, and #5 is set to 00:00:00 (12 a.m.). This is the default time substituted by the database when you don't provide a time in a datetime.

The next statement rolls back the addition of the new row:

```
ROLLBACK;
```

NOTE
If you actually ran the earlier INSERT *statement, make sure you undo the change using* ROLLBACK.

Combining TO_CHAR() and TO_DATE() Calls

You can combine TO_CHAR() and TO_DATE() calls; doing this allows you to use datetimes in different formats. For example, the following query combines TO_CHAR() and TO_DATE() in order to view just the time part of a datetime; notice that the output from TO_DATE() is passed to TO_CHAR():

```
SELECT TO_CHAR(TO_DATE('05-FEB-1968 19:32:36',
  'DD-MON-YYYY HH24:MI:SS'), 'HH24:MI:SS')
FROM dual;

TO_CHAR(
--------
19:32:36
```

Setting the Default Date Format

The default date format is specified in the NLS_DATE_FORMAT database parameter. A DBA can change the setting of NLS_DATE_FORMAT by setting this parameter's value in the database's init.ora or spfile.ora file, both of which are read when the database is started. A DBA can also set NLS_DATE_FORMAT using the ALTER SYSTEM command. You can also set the NLS_DATE_FORMAT parameter for your own session using SQL*Plus, which you do by using the ALTER SESSION command. For example, the following ALTER SESSION statement sets NLS_DATE_FORMAT to MONTH-DD-YYYY:

```
ALTER SESSION SET NLS_DATE_FORMAT = 'MONTH-DD-YYYY';

Session altered
```

NOTE
A session is started when you connect to a database and is ended when you disconnect.

You can see the use of this new date format in the results from the following query that retrieves the dob column for customer #1:

```
SELECT dob
FROM customers
WHERE customer_id = 1;

DOB
-----------------
JANUARY   -01-1965
```

You may also use the new date format when inserting a row in the database. For example, the following INSERT adds a new row to the customers table; notice the use of the format MONTH-DD-YYYY when supplying the dob column's value:

```
INSERT INTO customers (
  customer_id, first_name, last_name, dob, phone
) VALUES (
  6, 'Fred', 'Brown', 'MARCH-15-1970', '800-555-1215'
);
```

Go ahead and disconnect from the database and connect again as the store user; you'll find that the date format is back to the default. That's because any changes you make using the ALTER SESSION statement last only for that particular session—when you disconnect, you lose the change.

NOTE
If you ran the previous INSERT *statement, go ahead and delete the row using* DELETE FROM customers WHERE customer_id = 6.

How Oracle Interprets Two-Digit Years

The Oracle database stores all four digits of the year, but if you supply only two digits, the database will interpret the century according to whether the YY or RR format is used.

TIP
You should always specify all four digits of the year. That way, you won't get confused as to which year you mean.

Let's take a look at the YY format first, followed by the RR format.

Using the YY Format

If your date format uses YY for the year and you supply only two digits of a year, then the century for your year is assumed to be the same as the present century currently set on the database server. Therefore, *the first two digits of your supplied year are set to the first two digits of the present year.* For example, if your supplied year is 15 and the present year is 2007, your supplied year is set to 2015; similarly, a supplied year of 75 is set to 2075.

NOTE
If you use the YYYY *format but only supply a two-digit year, then your year is interpreted using the* YY *format.*

Let's take a look at a query that uses the YY format for interpreting the years 15 and 75. In the following query, notice that the input dates 15 and 75 are passed to TO_DATE(), whose output is passed to TO_CHAR(), which converts the dates to a string with the format DD-MON-YYYY. (The YYYY format is used here, so you can see that all four digits of the year returned by TO_DATE().)

```
SELECT
    TO_CHAR(TO_DATE('04-JUL-15', 'DD-MON-YY'), 'DD-MON-YYYY'),
    TO_CHAR(TO_DATE('04-JUL-75', 'DD-MON-YY'), 'DD-MON-YYYY')
FROM dual;

TO_CHAR(TO_ TO_CHAR(TO_
----------- -----------
04-JUL-2015 04-JUL-2075
```

As expected, the years 15 and 75 are interpreted as 2015 and 2075.

Using the RR Format

If your date format is RR and you supply the last two digits of a year, the first two digits of your year are determined using the two-digit year you supply (your *supplied year*) and the last two digits of the present date on the database server (the *present year*). The rules used to determine the century of your supplied year are as follows:

■ **Rule 1**   If your supplied year is between 00 and 49 and the present year is between 00 and 49, the century is the same as the present century. Therefore, *the first two digits of your supplied year are set to the first two digits of the present year*. For example, if your supplied year is 15 and the present year is 2007, your supplied year is set to 2015.

■ **Rule 2**   If your supplied year is between 50 and 99 and the present year is between 00 and 49, the century is the present century minus 1. Therefore, *the first two digits of your supplied year are set to the present year's first two digits minus 1*. For example, if your supplied year is 75 and the present year is 2007, your supplied year is set to 1975.

■ **Rule 3**   If your supplied year is between 00 and 49 and the present year is between 50 and 99, the century is the present century plus 1. Therefore, *the first two digits of your supplied year are set to the present year's first two digits plus 1*. For example, if your supplied year is 15 and the present year is 2075, your supplied year is set to 2115.

■ **Rule 4**   If your supplied year is between 50 and 99 and the present year is between 50 and 99, the century is the same as the present century. Therefore, *the first two digits of your supplied year are set to the first two digits of the present year*. For example, if your supplied year is 55 and the present year is 2075, your supplied year is set to 2055.

Table 5-3 summarizes these results.

NOTE
If you use the RRRR *format but supply only a two-digit year, then your year is interpreted using the* RR *format.*

		Two-Digit Supplied Year	
		00–49	**50–99**
Last Two Digits of Present Year	**00–49**	Rule 1: First two digits of supplied year are set to first two digits of present year.	Rule 2: First two digits of supplied year are set to present year's first two digits minus 1.
	50–99	Rule 3: First two digits of supplied year are set to present year's first two digits plus 1.	Rule 4: First two digits of supplied year are set to first two digits of present year.

TABLE 5-3   *How Two-Digit Years Are Interpreted*

Let's take a look at a query that uses the RR format for interpreting the years 15 and 75. (In the following query, you should assume the present year is 2007.)

```
SELECT
    TO_CHAR(TO_DATE('04-JUL-15', 'DD-MON-RR'), 'DD-MON-YYYY'),
    TO_CHAR(TO_DATE('04-JUL-75', 'DD-MON-RR'), 'DD-MON-YYYY')
FROM dual;

TO_CHAR(TO_ TO_CHAR(TO_
----------- -----------
04-JUL-2015 04-JUL-1975
```

As expected from rules 1 and 2, the years 15 and 75 are interpreted as 2015 and 1975.
In the next query, you should assume the present year is 2075.

```
SELECT
    TO_CHAR(TO_DATE('04-JUL-15', 'DD-MON-RR'), 'DD-MON-YYYY'),
    TO_CHAR(TO_DATE('04-JUL-55', 'DD-MON-RR'), 'DD-MON-YYYY')
FROM dual;

TO_CHAR(TO_ TO_CHAR(TO_
----------- -----------
04-JUL-2115 04-JUL-2055
```

As expected from rules 3 and 4, the years 15 and 75 are interpreted as 2115 and 2055.

Using Datetime Functions

You use the datetime functions to get or process datetimes and timestamps (you'll learn about timestamps later in this chapter). Table 5-4 shows some of the datetime functions. In this table, *x* represents a datetime or a timestamp.

You'll learn more about the functions shown in Table 5-4 in the following sections.

ADD_MONTHS()

ADD_MONTHS(*x*, *y*) returns the result of adding *y* months to *x*. If *y* is negative, then *y* months are subtracted from *x*. The following example adds 13 months to January 1, 2007:

```
SELECT ADD_MONTHS('01-JAN-2007', 13)
FROM dual;

ADD_MONTH
---------
01-FEB-08
```

The next example subtracts 13 months from the January 1, 2008; notice that –13 months are "added" to this date using ADD_MONTHS():

```
SELECT ADD_MONTHS('01-JAN-2008', -13)
FROM dual;

ADD_MONTH
---------
01-DEC-06
```

Function	Description
ADD_MONTHS(*x*, y)	Returns the result of adding y months to *x*. If y is negative, y months are subtracted from *x*.
LAST_DAY(*x*)	Returns the last day of the month part of *x*.
MONTHS_BETWEEN(*x*, y)	Returns the number of months between *x* and y. If *x* appears before y on the calendar, the number returned is positive; otherwise the number is negative.
NEXT_DAY(*x*, *day*)	Returns the datetime of the next day following *x*; *day* is specified as a literal string (SATURDAY, for example).
ROUND(*x* [, *unit*])	Rounds *x*. By default, *x* is rounded to the beginning of the nearest day. You may supply an optional *unit* string that indicates the rounding unit; for example, YYYY rounds *x* to the first day of the nearest year.
SYSDATE	Returns the current datetime set in the database server's operating system.
TRUNC(*x* [, *unit*])	Truncates *x*. By default, *x* is truncated to the beginning of the day. You may supply an optional *unit* string that indicates the truncating unit; for example, MM truncates *x* to the first day of the month.

TABLE 5-4   *Datetime Functions*

You can provide a time and date to the ADD_MONTHS() function. For example, the following query adds two months to the datetime 7:15:26 P.M. on January 1, 2007:

```
SELECT ADD_MONTHS(TO_DATE('01-JAN-2007 19:15:26',
  'DD-MON-YYYY HH24:MI:SS'), 2)
FROM dual;

ADD_MONTH
---------
01-MAR-07
```

The next query rewrites the previous example to convert the returned datetime from ADD_MONTHS() to a string using TO_CHAR() with the format DD-MON-YYYY HH24:MI:SS:

```
SELECT TO_CHAR(ADD_MONTHS(TO_DATE('01-JAN-2007 19:15:26',
  'DD-MON-YYYY HH24:MI:SS'), 2), 'DD-MON-YYYY HH24:MI:SS')
FROM dual;

TO_CHAR(ADD_MONTHS(T
--------------------
01-MAR-2007 19:15:26
```

NOTE
You can provide a date and time to any of the functions shown earlier in Table 5-4.

LAST_DAY()

LAST_DAY (*x*) returns the date of the last day of the month part of *x*. The following example displays the last date in January 2008:

```
SELECT LAST_DAY('01-JAN-2008')
FROM dual;

LAST_DAY(
---------
31-JAN-08
```

MONTHS_BETWEEN()

MONTHS_BETWEEN (*x*, *y*) returns the number of months between *x* and *y*. If *x* occurs before *y* in the calendar, then the number returned by MONTHS_BETWEEN() is negative.

NOTE
The ordering of the dates in your call to the MONTHS_BETWEEN() *function is important: the* later date *must appear* first *if you want the result as a positive number.*

The following example displays the number of months between May 25, 2008, and January 15, 2008. Notice that since the later date (May 25, 2008) appears first, the result returned is a positive number:

```
SELECT MONTHS_BETWEEN('25-MAY-2008', '15-JAN-2008')
FROM dual;

MONTHS_BETWEEN('25-MAY-2008','15-JAN-2008')
-------------------------------------------
                                 4.32258065
```

The next example reverses the same dates in the call to the MONTHS_BETWEEN() function, and therefore the returned result is a negative number of months:

```
SELECT MONTHS_BETWEEN('15-JAN-2008', '25-MAY-2008')
FROM dual;

MONTHS_BETWEEN('15-JAN-2008','25-MAY-2008')
-------------------------------------------
                                 -4.3225806
```

NEXT_DAY()

NEXT_DAY (*x*, *day*) returns the date of the next day following *x*; you specify *day* as a literal string (SATURDAY, for example).

The following example displays the date of the next Saturday after January 1, 2008:

```
SELECT NEXT_DAY('01-JAN-2008', 'SATURDAY')
FROM dual;
```

```
NEXT_DAY(
---------
05-JAN-08
```

ROUND()

ROUND(*x* [, *unit*]) rounds *x*, by default, to the beginning of the nearest day. If you supply an optional *unit* string, *x* is rounded to that unit; for example, YYYY rounds *x* to the first day of the nearest year. You can use many of the parameters shown earlier in Table 5-2 to round a datetime.

The following example uses ROUND() to round October 25, 2008, up to the first day in the nearest year, which is January 1, 2009. Notice that the date is specified as 25-OCT-2008 and is contained within a call to the TO_DATE() function:

```
SELECT ROUND(TO_DATE('25-OCT-2008'), 'YYYY')
FROM dual;

ROUND(TO_
---------
01-JAN-09
```

The next example rounds May 25, 2008, to the first day in the nearest month, which is June 1, 2008, because May 25 is closer to the beginning of June than it is to the beginning of May:

```
SELECT ROUND(TO_DATE('25-MAY-2008'), 'MM')
FROM dual;

ROUND(TO_
---------
01-JUN-08
```

The next example rounds 7:45:26 P.M. on May 25, 2008, to the nearest hour, which is 8:00 P.M.:

```
SELECT TO_CHAR(ROUND(TO_DATE('25-MAY-2008 19:45:26',
  'DD-MON-YYYY HH24:MI:SS'), 'HH24'), 'DD-MON-YYYY HH24:MI:SS')
FROM dual;

TO_CHAR(ROUND(TO_DAT
--------------------
25-MAY-2008 20:00:00
```

SYSDATE

SYSDATE returns the current datetime set in the database server's operating system. The following example gets the current date:

```
SELECT SYSDATE
FROM dual;

SYSDATE
---------
05-NOV-07
```

TRUNC()

TRUNC(*x* [, *unit*]) truncates *x*. By default, *x* is truncated to the beginning of the day. If you supply an optional *unit* string, *x* is truncated to that unit; for example, MM truncates *x* to the first day in the month. You can use many of the parameters shown earlier in Table 5-2 to truncate a datetime.

The following example uses TRUNC() to truncate May 25, 2008, to the first day in the year, which is January 1, 2008:

```
SELECT TRUNC(TO_DATE('25-MAY-2008'), 'YYYY')
FROM dual;

TRUNC(TO_
---------
01-JAN-08
```

The next example truncates May 25, 2008, to the first day in the month, which is May 1, 2008:

```
SELECT TRUNC(TO_DATE('25-MAY-2008'), 'MM')
FROM dual;

TRUNC(TO_
---------
01-MAY-08
```

The next example truncates 7:45:26 P.M. on May 25, 2008, to the hour, which is 7:00 P.M.:

```
SELECT TO_CHAR(TRUNC(TO_DATE('25-MAY-2008 19:45:26',
  'DD-MON-YYYY HH24:MI:SS'), 'HH24'), 'DD-MON-YYYY HH24:MI:SS')
FROM dual;

TO_CHAR(TRUNC(TO_DAT
--------------------
25-MAY-2008 19:00:00
```

Using Time Zones

Oracle Database 9*i* introduced the ability to use different time zones. A time zone is an offset from the time in Greenwich, England. The time in Greenwich was once known as Greenwich Mean Time (GMT), but is now known as Coordinated Universal Time (UTC, which comes from the initials of the French wording).

You specify a time zone using either an offset from UTC or a geographic region (e.g., PST). When you specify an offset, you use HH:MI prefixed with a plus or minus sign:

```
+|-HH:MI
```

where

- + or − indicates an increase or decrease for the offset from UTC.

- HH:MI specifies the offset in hours and minutes for the time zone.

NOTE
The time zone hour and minute use the format parameters TZH *and*
TZR, *shown earlier in Table 5-2.*

The following example shows offsets of 8 hours behind UTC and 2 hours 15 minutes ahead
of UTC:

```
-08:00
+02:15
```

You may also specify a time zone using the geographical region. For example, PST indicates
Pacific Standard Time, which is 8 hours behind UTC. EST indicates Eastern Standard Time, which
is 5 hours behind UTC.

NOTE
The time zone region uses the format parameter TZR, *shown earlier in
Table 5-2.*

Time Zone Functions

There are a number of functions that are related to time zones; these functions are shown in
Table 5-5.
You'll learn more about these functions in the following sections.

The Database Time Zone and Session Time Zone

If you're working for a large worldwide organization, the database you access may be located in
a different time zone than your local time zone. The time zone for the database is known as the
database time zone, and the time zone set for your database session is known as the *session time
zone.* You'll learn about the database and session time zones in the following sections.

Function	Description
CURRENT_DATE	Returns the current date in the local time zone set for the database session
DBTIMEZONE	Returns the time zone for the database
NEW_TIME(x, time_zone1, time_zone2)	Converts x from time_zone1 to time_zone2 and returns the new datetime
SESSIONTIMEZONE	Returns the time zone for the database session
TZ_OFFSET(time_zone)	Returns the offset for time_zone in hours and minutes

TABLE 5-5 *Time Zone Functions*

The Database Time Zone

The database time zone is controlled using the TIME_ZONE database parameter. Your database administrator can change the setting of the TIME_ZONE parameter in the database's init.ora or spfile.ora file, or by using ALTER DATABASE SET TIME_ZONE = *offset | region* (e.g., ALTER DATABASE SET TIME_ZONE = '-8:00' or ALTER DATABASE SET TIME_ ZONE = 'PST').

You can get the database time zone using the DBTIMEZONE function. For example, the following query gets the time zone for my database:

```
SELECT DBTIMEZONE
FROM dual;

DBTIME
------
+00:00
```

As you can see, +00:00 is returned. This means my database uses the time zone set in the operating system, which is set to PST on my computer.

> **NOTE**
> *The Windows operating system is typically set up to adjust the clock for daylight savings. For California, this means that in the summer the clock is only 7 hours behind UTC, rather than 8 hours. When I wrote this chapter, I set the date to November 5, 2007, which means my clock is 8 hours behind UTC (I'm located in California).*

The Session Time Zone

The session time zone is the time zone for a particular session. By default, the session time zone is the same as the operating system time zone. You can change your session time zone using the ALTER SESSION statement to set the session TIME_ZONE parameter (e.g., ALTER SESSION SET TIME_ZONE = 'PST' sets the local time zone to Pacific Standard Time). You can also set the session TIME_ZONE to LOCAL, which sets the time zone to the one used by the operating system of the computer on which the ALTER SESSION statement was run. You can also set the session TIME_ZONE to DBTIMEZONE, which sets the time zone to the one used by the database.

You can get the session time zone using the SESSIONTIMEZONE function. For example, the following query gets the time zone for my session:

```
SELECT SESSIONTIMEZONE
FROM dual;

SESSIONTIMEZONE
---------------
-08:00
```

As you can see, my session time zone is 8 hours behind UTC.

Getting the Current Date in the Session Time Zone

The SYSDATE function gets the date from the database. This gives you the date in the database time zone. You can get the date in your session time zone using the CURRENT_DATE function. For example:

```
SELECT CURRENT_DATE
FROM dual;

CURRENT_D
---------
05-NOV-07
```

Obtaining Time Zone Offsets

You can get the time zone offset hours using the TZ_OFFSET() function, passing the time zone region name to TZ_OFFSET(). For example, the following query uses TZ_OFFSET() to get the time zone offset hours for PST, which is 8 hours behind UTC:

```
SELECT TZ_OFFSET('PST')
FROM dual;

TZ_OFFS
-------
-08:00
```

NOTE
In the summer, this will be –7:00 when using Windows, which sets the clock automatically to adjust for daylight savings.

Obtaining Time Zone Names

You can obtain all the time zone names by selecting all the rows from v$timezone_names. To query v$timezone_names, you should first connect to the database as the system user. The following query shows the first five rows from v$timezone_names:

```
SELECT *
FROM v$timezone_names
WHERE ROWNUM <= 5
ORDER BY tzabbrev;

TZNAME                 TZABBREV
-------------------    --------
Africa/Algiers         CET
Africa/Algiers         LMT
Africa/Algiers         PMT
Africa/Algiers         WEST
Africa/Algiers         WET
```

You may use any of the tzname or tzabbrev values for your time zone setting.

NOTE
The ROWNUM pseudo column contains the row number. For example, the first row returned by a query has a row number of 1, the second has a row number of 2, and so on. Therefore, the WHERE clause in the previous query causes the query to return the first five rows.

Converting a Datetime from One Time Zone to Another

You use the NEW_TIME() function to convert a datetime from one time zone to another. For example, the following query uses NEW_TIME() to convert 7:45 P.M. on May 13, 2008, from PST to EST:

```
SELECT TO_CHAR(NEW_TIME(TO_DATE('25-MAY-2008 19:45',
 'DD-MON-YYYY HH24:MI'), 'PST', 'EST'), 'DD-MON-YYYY HH24:MI')
FROM dual;

TO_CHAR(NEW_TIME(
-----------------
25-MAY-2008 22:45
```

EST is 3 hours ahead of PST: therefore, 3 hours are added to 7:45 P.M. to give 10:45 P.M. (or 22:45 in 24-hour format).

Using Timestamps

Oracle Database 9*i* introduced the ability to store timestamps. A timestamp stores the century, all four digits of a year, the month, the day, the hour (in 24-hour format), the minute, and the second. The advantages of a timestamp over a DATE are

- A timestamp can store a fractional second.

- A timestamp can store a time zone.

Let's examine the timestamp types.

Using the Timestamp Types

There are three timestamp types, which are shown in Table 5-6.

Type	Description
TIMESTAMP[(seconds_precision)]	Stores the century, all four digits of a year, the month, the day, the hour (in 24-hour format), the minute, and the second. You can specify an optional precision for the seconds using seconds_precision, which can be an integer from 0 to 9; the default is 9, which means you can store up to 9 digits to the right of the decimal point for your second. If you try to add a row with more digits in the fractional second than the TIMESTAMP can store, then your fractional amount is rounded.
TIMESTAMP[(seconds_precision)] WITH TIME ZONE	Extends TIMESTAMP to store a time zone.
TIMESTAMP[(seconds_precision)] WITH LOCAL TIME ZONE	Extends TIMESTAMP to convert a supplied datetime to the local time zone set for the database. The process of conversion is known as *normalizing* the datetime.

TABLE 5-6 *Timestamp Types*

You'll learn how to use these timestamp types in the following sections.

Using the TIMESTAMP Type

As with the other types, you can use the TIMESTAMP type to define a column in a table. The following statement creates a table named purchases_with_timestamp that stores customer purchases. This table contains a TIMESTAMP column named made_on to record when a purchase was made; notice a precision of 4 is set for the TIMESTAMP (this means up to four digits may be stored to the right of the decimal point for the second):

```
CREATE TABLE purchases_with_timestamp (
    product_id INTEGER REFERENCES products(product_id),
    customer_id INTEGER REFERENCES customers(customer_id),
    made_on TIMESTAMP(4)
);
```

NOTE
The purchases_with_timestamp *table is created and populated with rows by the* store_schema.sql *script. You'll see other tables in the rest of this chapter that are also created by the script, so you don't need to type in the* CREATE TABLE *or any of the* INSERT *statements shown in this chapter.*

To supply a TIMESTAMP literal value to the database, you use the TIMESTAMP keyword along with a datetime in the following format:

```
TIMESTAMP 'YYYY-MM-DD HH24:MI:SS.SSSSSSSSS'
```

Notice there are nine S characters after the decimal point, which means you can supply up to nine digits for the fractional second in your literal string. The number of digits you can actually store in a TIMESTAMP column depends on how many digits were set for storage of fractional seconds when the column was defined. For example, up to four digits can be stored in the made_ on column of the purchases_with_timestamp table. If you try to add a row with more than four fractional second digits, your fractional amount is rounded. For example,

```
2005-05-13 07:15:31.123456789
```

would be rounded to

```
2005-05-13 07:15:31.1235
```

The following INSERT statement adds a row to the purchases_with_timestamp table; notice the use of the TIMESTAMP keyword to supply a datetime literal:

```
INSERT INTO purchases_with_timestamp (
    product_id, customer_id, made_on
) VALUES (
    1, 1, TIMESTAMP '2005-05-13 07:15:31.1234'
);
```

The following query retrieves the row:

```
SELECT *
FROM purchases_with_timestamp;

PRODUCT_ID CUSTOMER_ID MADE_ON
---------- ----------- -------------------------
         1           1 13-MAY-05 07.15.31.1234 AM
```

Using the TIMESTAMP WITH TIME ZONE Type

The TIMESTAMP WITH TIME ZONE type extends TIMESTAMP to store a time zone. The following statement creates a table named purchases_timestamp_with_tz that stores customer purchases; this table contains a TIMESTAMP WITH TIME ZONE column named made_on to record when a purchase was made:

```
CREATE TABLE purchases_timestamp_with_tz (
  product_id INTEGER REFERENCES products(product_id),
  customer_id INTEGER REFERENCES customers(customer_id),
  made_on TIMESTAMP(4) WITH TIME ZONE
);
```

To supply a timestamp literal with a time zone to the database, you simply add the time zone to your TIMESTAMP. For example, the following TIMESTAMP includes a time zone offset of –07:00:

```
TIMESTAMP '2005-05-13 07:15:31.1234 -07:00'
```

You may also supply a time zone region, as shown in the following example that specifies PST as the time zone:

```
TIMESTAMP '2005-05-13 07:15:31.1234 PST'
```

The following example adds two rows to the purchases_timestamp_with_tz table:

```
INSERT INTO purchases_timestamp_with_tz (
  product_id, customer_id, made_on
) VALUES (
  1, 1, TIMESTAMP '2005-05-13 07:15:31.1234 -07:00'
);

INSERT INTO purchases_timestamp_with_tz (
  product_id, customer_id, made_on
) VALUES (
  1, 2, TIMESTAMP '2005-05-13 07:15:31.1234 PST'
);
```

The following query retrieves the rows:

```
SELECT *
FROM purchases_timestamp_with_tz;
```

```
PRODUCT_ID CUSTOMER_ID MADE_ON
---------- ----------- --------------------------------
         1           1 13-MAY-05 07.15.31.1234 AM -07:00
         1           2 13-MAY-05 07.15.31.1234 AM PST
```

Using the TIMESTAMP WITH LOCAL TIME ZONE Type

The TIMESTAMP WITH LOCAL TIME ZONE type extends TIMESTAMP to store a timestamp with the local time zone set for your database. When you supply a timestamp for storage in a TIMESTAMP WITH LOCAL TIME ZONE column, your timestamp is converted—or *normalized*—to the time zone set for the database. When you retrieve the timestamp, it is normalized to the time zone set for your session.

TIP

You should use TIMESTAMP WITH LOCAL TIME ZONE *to store timestamps when your organization has a global system accessed throughout the world. This is because* TIMESTAMP WITH LOCAL TIME ZONE *stores a timestamp using the local time where the database is located, but users see the timestamp normalized to their own time zone.*

My database time zone is PST (PST is 8 hours behind UTC), and I want to store the following timestamp in my database:

```
2005-05-13 07:15:30 EST
```

EST is 5 hours behind UTC, and the difference between PST and EST is 3 hours (8 − 5 = 3). Therefore, to normalize the previous timestamp for PST, 3 hours must be subtracted from it to give the following normalized timestamp:

```
2005-05-13 04:15:30
```

This is the timestamp that would be stored in a TIMESTAMP WITH LOCAL TIME ZONE column in my database.

The following statement creates a table named purchases_with_local_tz that stores customer purchases; this table contains a TIMESTAMP WITH LOCAL TIME ZONE column named made_on to record when a purchase was made:

```
CREATE TABLE purchases_with_local_tz (
  product_id INTEGER REFERENCES products(product_id),
  customer_id INTEGER REFERENCES customers(customer_id),
  made_on TIMESTAMP(4) WITH LOCAL TIME ZONE
);
```

The following INSERT adds a row to the purchases_with_local_tz table with the made_on column set to 2005-05-13 07:15:30 EST:

```
INSERT INTO purchases_with_local_tz (
  product_id, customer_id, made_on
) VALUES (
  1, 1, TIMESTAMP '2005-05-13 07:15:30 EST'
);
```

Although the timestamp for the `made_on` column is set to `2005-05-13 07:15:30 EST`, the actual timestamp stored in my database is `2005-05-13 04:15:30` (the timestamp normalized for PST).

The following query retrieves the row:

```
SELECT *
FROM purchases_with_local_tz;

PRODUCT_ID CUSTOMER_ID MADE_ON
---------- ----------- -------------------------
         1           1 13-MAY-05 04.15.30.0000 AM
```

Because my database time zone and session time zone are both PST, the timestamp returned by the query is for PST.

CAUTION
The timestamp returned by the previous query is normalized for PST. If your database time zone or session time zone are not PST, the timestamp returned when you run the query will be different (it will be normalized for your time zone).

If I set the local time zone for my session to EST and repeat the previous query, I get the timestamp normalized for EST:

```
ALTER SESSION SET TIME_ZONE = 'EST';

Session altered.

SELECT *
FROM purchases_with_local_tz;

PRODUCT_ID CUSTOMER_ID MADE_ON
---------- ----------- -------------------------
         1           1 13-MAY-05 07.15.30.0000 AM
```

As you can see, the timestamp returned by the query is `13-MAY-05 07.15.30.0000 AM`, which is the timestamp normalized for the session time zone of EST. Because EST is three hours ahead of PST, three hours must be added to `13-MAY-05 04:15:30` (the timestamp stored in the database) to give `13-MAY-05 07.15.30 AM` (the timestamp returned by the query).

The following statement sets my session time zone back to PST:

```
ALTER SESSION SET TIME_ZONE = 'PST';

Session altered.
```

Timestamp Functions

There are a number of functions that allow you to get and process timestamps. These functions are shown in Table 5-7.

You'll learn more about the functions shown in Table 5-7 in the following sections.

Function	Description
CURRENT_TIMESTAMP	Returns a TIMESTAMP WITH TIME ZONE containing the current date and time for the session, plus the session time zone.
EXISTRACT({ YEAR | MONTH | DAY | HOUR | MINUTE | SECOND } | { TIMEZONE_HOUR | TIMEZONE_MINUTE } | { TIMEZONE_REGION | } TIMEZONE_ABBR } FROM x)	Extracts and returns the year, month, day, hour, minute, second, or time zone from x; x may be a timestamp or a DATE.
FROM_TZ(x, time_zone)	Converts the TIMESTAMP x to the time zone specified by time_zone and returns a TIMESTAMP WITH TIMEZONE; time_zone must be specified as a string of the form +|- HH:MI. The function basically merges x and time_zone into one value.
LOCALTIMESTAMP	Returns a TIMESTAMP containing the current date and time for the session.
SYSTIMESTAMP	Returns a TIMESTAMP WITH TIME ZONE containing the current date and time for the database, plus the database time zone.
SYS_EXTRACT_UTC(x)	Converts the TIMESTAMP WITH TIMEZONE x to a TIMESTAMP containing the date and time in UTC.
TO_TIMESTAMP(x, [format])	Converts the string x to a TIMESTAMP. You may also specify an optional format for x.
TO_TIMESTAMP_TZ(x, [format])	Converts the string x to a TIMESTAMP WITH TIMEZONE. You may also specify an optional format for x.

TABLE 5-7 *Timestamp Functions*

CURRENT_TIMESTAMP, LOCALTIMESTAMP, and SYSTIMESTAMP

The following query calls the CURRENT_TIMESTAMP, LOCALTIMESTAMP, and SYSTIMESTAMP functions (my session time zone and database time zone are both PST, which is 8 hours behind UTC):

```
SELECT CURRENT_TIMESTAMP, LOCALTIMESTAMP, SYSTIMESTAMP
FROM dual;

CURRENT_TIMESTAMP
---------------------------------
LOCALTIMESTAMP
---------------------------------
SYSTIMESTAMP
---------------------------------
05-NOV-07 12.15.32.734000 PM PST
05-NOV-07 12.15.32.734000 PM
05-NOV-07 12.15.32.734000 PM -08:00
```

If I change my session `TIME_ZONE` to EST and repeat the previous query, I get the following results:

```
ALTER SESSION SET TIME_ZONE = 'EST';

Session altered.
```

```
SELECT CURRENT_TIMESTAMP, LOCALTIMESTAMP, SYSTIMESTAMP
FROM dual;

CURRENT_TIMESTAMP
-----------------------------------------------------------
LOCALTIMESTAMP
-----------------------------------------------------------
SYSTIMESTAMP
-----------------------------------------------------------
05-NOV-07 03.19.57.562000 PM EST
05-NOV-07 03.19.57.562000 PM
05-NOV-07 12.19.57.562000 PM -08:00
```

The following statement sets my session time zone back to PST:

```
ALTER SESSION SET TIME_ZONE = 'PST';

Session altered.
```

EXTRACT()

`EXTRACT()` extracts and returns the year, month, day, hour, minute, second, or time zone from *x*; *x* may be a timestamp or a `DATE`. The following query uses `EXTRACT()` to get the year, month, and day from a `DATE` returned by `TO_DATE()`:

```
SELECT
    EXTRACT(YEAR FROM TO_DATE('01-JAN-2008 19:15:26',
        'DD-MON-YYYY HH24:MI:SS')) AS YEAR,
    EXTRACT(MONTH FROM TO_DATE('01-JAN-2008 19:15:26',
        'DD-MON-YYYY HH24:MI:SS')) AS MONTH,
    EXTRACT(DAY FROM TO_DATE('01-JAN-2008 19:15:26',
        'DD-MON-YYYY HH24:MI:SS')) AS DAY
FROM dual;

      YEAR      MONTH        DAY
---------- ---------- ----------
      2008          1          1
```

The next query uses `EXTRACT()` to get the hour, minute, and second from a `TIMESTAMP` returned by `TO_TIMESTAMP()`:

```
SELECT
    EXTRACT(HOUR FROM TO_TIMESTAMP('01-JAN-2008 19:15:26',
        'DD-MON-YYYY HH24:MI:SS')) AS HOUR,
    EXTRACT(MINUTE FROM TO_TIMESTAMP('01-JAN-2008 19:15:26',
        'DD-MON-YYYY HH24:MI:SS')) AS MINUTE,
    EXTRACT(SECOND FROM TO_TIMESTAMP('01-JAN-2008 19:15:26',
        'DD-MON-YYYY HH24:MI:SS')) AS SECOND
```

```
FROM dual;

      HOUR      MINUTE     SECOND
---------- ---------- ----------
        19         15         26
```

The following query uses EXTRACT() to get the time zone hour, minute, second, region, and region abbreviation from a TIMESTAMP WITH TIMEZONE returned by TO_TIMESTAMP_TZ():

```
SELECT
  EXTRACT(TIMEZONE_HOUR FROM TO_TIMESTAMP_TZ(
    '01-JAN-2008 19:15:26 -7:15', 'DD-MON-YYYY HH24:MI:SS TZH:TZM'))
    AS TZH,
  EXTRACT(TIMEZONE_MINUTE FROM TO_TIMESTAMP_TZ(
    '01-JAN-2008 19:15:26 -7:15', 'DD-MON-YYYY HH24:MI:SS TZH:TZM'))
    AS TZM,
  EXTRACT(TIMEZONE_REGION FROM TO_TIMESTAMP_TZ(
    '01-JAN-2008 19:15:26 PST', 'DD-MON-YYYY HH24:MI:SS TZR'))
    AS TZR,
  EXTRACT(TIMEZONE_ABBR FROM TO_TIMESTAMP_TZ(
    '01-JAN-2008 19:15:26 PST', 'DD-MON-YYYY HH24:MI:SS TZR'))
    AS TZA
FROM dual;

       TZH        TZM TZR         TZA
---------- ---------- ----------- ----------
        -7        -15 PST         PST
```

FROM_TZ()

FROM_TZ(x, time_zone) converts the TIMESTAMP x to the time zone specified by time_zone and returns a TIMESTAMP WITH TIMEZONE; time_zone must be specified as a string of the form +|- HH:MI. The function basically merges x and time_zone into one value.

For example, the following query merges the timestamp 2008-05-13 07:15:31.1234 and the time zone offset of -7:00 from UTC:

```
SELECT FROM_TZ(TIMESTAMP '2008-05-13 07:15:31.1234', '-7:00')
FROM dual;

FROM_TZ(TIMESTAMP'2008-05-1307:15:31.1234','-7:00')
-------------------------------------------------
13-MAY-08 07.15.31.123400000 AM -07:00
```

SYS_EXTRACT_UTC()

SYS_EXTRACT_UTC(x) converts the TIMESTAMP WITH TIMEZONE x to a TIMESTAMP containing the date and time in UTC.

The following query converts 2008-11-17 19:15:26 PST to UTC:

```
SELECT SYS_EXTRACT_UTC(TIMESTAMP '2008-11-17 19:15:26 PST')
FROM dual;

SYS_EXTRACT_UTC(TIMESTAMP'2008-11-1719:15:26PST')
-------------------------------------------------
18-NOV-08 03.15.26.000000000 AM
```

Because PST is 8 hours behind UTC in the winter, the query returns a `TIMESTAMP` 8 hours ahead of `2008-11-17 19:15:26 PST`, which is `18-NOV-08 03.15.26 AM`.

For a date in the summer, the returned `TIMESTAMP` is only 7 hours ahead of UTC:

```
SELECT SYS_EXTRACT_UTC(TIMESTAMP '2008-05-17 19:15:26 PST')
FROM dual;

SYS_EXTRACT_UTC(TIMESTAMP'2008-05-1719:15:26PST')
-------------------------------------------------
18-MAY-08 02.15.26.000000000 AM
```

TO_TIMESTAMP()

`TO_TIMESTAMP(x, format)` converts the string *x* (which may be a `CHAR`, `VARCHAR2`, `NCHAR`, or `NVARCHAR2`) to a `TIMESTAMP`. You may also specify an optional *format* for *x*.

The following query converts the string `2005-05-13 07:15:31.1234` with the format `YYYY-MM-DD HH24:MI:SS.FF` to a `TIMESTAMP`:

```
SELECT TO_TIMESTAMP('2008-05-13 07:15:31.1234', 'YYYY-MM-DD HH24:MI:SS.FF')
FROM dual;

TO_TIMESTAMP('2008-05-1307:15:31.1234','YYYY-MM-DDHH24:MI:SS.FF')
----------------------------------------------------------------
13-MAY-08 07.15.31.123400000 AM
```

TO_TIMESTAMP_TZ()

`TO_TIMESTAMP_TZ(x, [format])` converts *x* to a `TIMESTAMP WITH TIMEZONE`. You may specify an optional *format* for *x*.

The following query passes the PST time zone (identified using `TZR` in the format string) to `TO_TIMESTAMP_TZ()`:

```
SELECT TO_TIMESTAMP_TZ('2008-05-13 07:15:31.1234 PST',
  'YYYY-MM-DD HH24:MI:SS.FF TZR')
FROM dual;

TO_TIMESTAMP_TZ('2008-05-1307:15:31.1234PST','YYYY-MM-DDHH24:MI:SS.FFTZR')
-------------------------------------------------------------------------
13-MAY-08 07.15.31.123400000 AM PST
```

The next query uses a time zone offset of –7:00 from UTC (–7:00 is identified using `TZR` and `TZM` in the format string):

```
SELECT TO_TIMESTAMP_TZ('2008-05-13 07:15:31.1234 -7:00',
  'YYYY-MM-DD HH24:MI:SS.FF TZH:TZM')
FROM dual;

TO_TIMESTAMP_TZ('2008-05-1307:15:31.1234-7:00','YYYY-MM-DDHH24:MI:SS.FFTZH
-------------------------------------------------------------------------
13-MAY-08 07.15.31.123400000 AM -07:00
```

Converting a String to a TIMESTAMP WITH LOCAL TIME ZONE

You can use the CAST() function to convert a string to a TIMESTAMP WITH LOCAL TIME ZONE. You were introduced to CAST() in the previous chapter. As a reminder, CAST(*x* AS *type*) converts *x* to a compatible database type specified by *type*.

The following query uses CAST() to convert the string 13-JUN-08 to a TIMESTAMP WITH LOCAL TIME ZONE:

```
SELECT CAST('13-JUN-08' AS TIMESTAMP WITH LOCAL TIME ZONE)
FROM dual;

CAST('13-JUN-08'ASTIMESTAMPWITHLOCALTIMEZONE)
---------------------------------------------
13-JUN-08 12.00.00.000000 AM
```

The timestamp returned by this query contains the date June 13, 2008 and the time of 12 A.M.

The next query uses CAST() to convert a more complex string to a TIMESTAMP WITH LOCAL TIME ZONE:

```
SELECT CAST(TO_TIMESTAMP_TZ('2008-05-13 07:15:31.1234 PST',
 'YYYY-MM-DD HH24:MI:SS.FF TZR') AS TIMESTAMP WITH LOCAL TIME ZONE)
FROM dual;

CAST(TO_TIMESTAMP_TZ('2008-05-1307:15:31.1234PST','YYYY-MM-DDHH24:MI:SS.FF
---------------------------------------------------------------------------
13-MAY-08 06.15.31.123400 AM
```

The timestamp returned by this query contains the date May 13, 2008 and the time of 6:15:31.1234 AM PST (PST is the time zone for both my database and session).

The following query does the same thing as the previous one, except this time EST is the time zone:

```
SELECT CAST(TO_TIMESTAMP_TZ('2008-05-13 07:15:31.1234 EST',
 'YYYY-MM-DD HH24:MI:SS.FF TZR') AS TIMESTAMP WITH LOCAL TIME ZONE)
FROM dual;

CAST(TO_TIMESTAMP_TZ('2008-05-1307:15:31.1234EST','YYYY-MM-DDHH24:MI:SS.FF
---------------------------------------------------------------------------
13-MAY-08 04.15.31.123400 AM
```

The timestamp returned by this query contains the date May 13, 2008 and the time of 4:15:31.1234 AM PST (because PST is 3 hours behind EST, the time returned in the timestamp is 3 hours earlier than the time in the actual query).

Using Time Intervals

Oracle Database 9*i* introduced data types that allow you to store time *intervals*. Examples of time intervals include

- 1 year 3 months

- 25 months

- −3 days 5 hours 16 minutes

- 1 day 7 hours

- −56 hours

NOTE
Do not confuse time intervals with datetimes or timestamps. A time interval records a length of time (e.g., 1 year 3 months), whereas a datetime or timestamp records a specific date and time (e.g., 7:32:16 P.M. on October 28, 2006).

In our imaginary online store, you might want to offer limited time discounts on products. For example, you could give customers a coupon that is valid for a few months, or you could run a special promotion for a few days. You'll see examples that feature coupons and promotions later in this section.

Table 5-8 shows the interval types.

You'll learn how to use the time interval types in the following sections.

Using the INTERVAL YEAR TO MONTH Type

INTERVAL YEAR TO MONTH stores a time interval measured in years and months. The following statement creates a table named coupons that stores coupon information. The coupons table contains an INTERVAL YEAR TO MONTH column named duration to record the interval of

Type	Description
INTERVAL YEAR[(*years_precision*)] TO MONTH	Stores a time interval measured in years and months. You can specify an optional precision for the years using *years_precision*, which may be an integer from 0 to 9. The default precision is 2, which means you can store two digits for the years in your interval. If you try to add a row with more year digits than your INTERVAL YEAR TO MONTH column can store, you'll get an error. You can store a positive or negative time interval.

INTERVAL DAY[
  (*days_precision*)
]
TO SECOND[
  (*seconds_precision*)
]
	Stores a time interval measured in days and seconds. You can specify an optional precision for the days using *days_precision* (an integer from 0 to 9; the default is 2). In addition, you can also specify an optional precision for the fractional seconds using *seconds_precision* (an integer from 0 to 9; the default is 6). You can store a positive or negative time interval.

TABLE 5-8 *Time Interval Types*

time for which the coupon is valid; notice that I've provided a precision of 3 for the `duration` column, which means that up to three digits may be stored for the year:

```
CREATE TABLE coupons (
  coupon_id INTEGER CONSTRAINT coupons_pk PRIMARY KEY,
  name VARCHAR2(30) NOT NULL,
  duration INTERVAL YEAR(3) TO MONTH
);
```

To supply an `INTERVAL YEAR TO MONTH` literal value to the database, you use the following simplified syntax:

```
INTERVAL '[+|-][y][-m]' [YEAR[(years_precision)])] [TO MONTH]
```

where

- + or − is an optional indicator that specifies whether the time interval is positive or negative (the default is positive).

- *y* is the optional number of years for the interval.

- *m* is the optional number of months for the interval. If you supply years *and* months, you must include `TO MONTH` in your literal.

- *years_precision* is the optional precision for the years (the default is 2).

The following table shows some examples of year-to-month interval literals.

Literal	Description
`INTERVAL '1' YEAR`	Interval of 1 year.
`INTERVAL '11' MONTH`	Interval of 11 months.
`INTERVAL '14' MONTH`	Interval of 14 months (equivalent to 1 year 2 months).
`INTERVAL '1-3' YEAR TO MONTH`	Interval of 1 year 3 months.
`INTERVAL '0-5' YEAR TO MONTH`	Interval of 0 years 5 months.
`INTERVAL '123' YEAR(3) TO MONTH`	Interval of 123 years with a precision of 3 digits.
`INTERVAL '-1-5' YEAR TO MONTH`	A negative interval of 1 year 5 months.
`INTERVAL '1234' YEAR(3)`	Invalid interval: 1234 contains four digits and therefore contains one too many digits allowed by the precision of 3 (three digits maximum).

The following `INSERT` statements add rows to the `coupons` table with the `duration` column set to some of the intervals shown in the previous table:

```
INSERT INTO coupons (coupon_id, name, duration)
VALUES (1, '$1 off Z Files', INTERVAL '1' YEAR);

INSERT INTO coupons (coupon_id, name, duration)
VALUES (2, '$2 off Pop 3', INTERVAL '11' MONTH);
```

```
INSERT INTO coupons (coupon_id, name, duration)
VALUES (3, '$3 off Modern Science', INTERVAL '14' MONTH);

INSERT INTO coupons (coupon_id, name, duration)
VALUES (4, '$2 off Tank War', INTERVAL '1-3' YEAR TO MONTH);

INSERT INTO coupons (coupon_id, name, duration)
VALUES (5, '$1 off Chemistry', INTERVAL '0-5' YEAR TO MONTH);

INSERT INTO coupons (coupon_id, name, duration)
VALUES (6, '$2 off Creative Yell', INTERVAL '123' YEAR(3));
```

If you try to add a row with the `duration` column set to the invalid interval of `INTERVAL '1234' YEAR(3)`, you'll get an error because the precision of the `duration` column is 3 and is therefore too small to accommodate the number 1234. The following `INSERT` shows the error:

```
SQL> INSERT INTO coupons (coupon_id, name, duration)
  2 VALUES (7, '$1 off Z Files', INTERVAL '1234' YEAR(3));
VALUES (7, '$1 off Z Files', INTERVAL '1234' YEAR(3))
                                        *
ERROR at line 2:
ORA-01873: the leading precision of the interval is too small
```

The following query retrieves the rows from the `coupons` table; notice the formatting of the `duration` values:

```
SELECT *
FROM coupons;

COUPON_ID NAME                           DURATION
---------- ------------------------------ --------
        1 $1 off Z Files                 +001-00
        2 $2 off Pop 3                   +000-11
        3 $3 off Modern Science          +001-02
        4 $2 off Tank War                +001-03
        5 $1 off Chemistry               +000-05
        6 $2 off Creative Yell           +123-00
```

Using the INTERVAL DAY TO SECOND Type

`INTERVAL DAY TO SECOND` stores time intervals measured in days and seconds. The following statement creates a table named `promotions` that stores promotion information. The promotions table contains an `INTERVAL DAY TO SECOND` column named `duration` to record the interval of time for which the promotion is valid:

```
CREATE TABLE promotions (
  promotion_id INTEGER CONSTRAINT promotions_pk PRIMARY KEY,
  name VARCHAR2(30) NOT NULL,
  duration INTERVAL DAY(3) TO SECOND (4)
);
```

Notice I've provided a precision of 3 for the day and a precision of 4 for the fractional seconds of the `duration` column. This means that up to three digits may be stored for the day of the interval and up to four digits to the right of the decimal point for the fractional seconds.

To supply an INTERVAL DAY TO SECOND literal value to the database, you use the following simplified syntax:

```
INTERVAL '[+|-][d] [h[:m[:s]]]' [DAY[(days_precision)]])
[TO HOUR | MINUTE | SECOND[(seconds_precision)]]
```

where

- + or – is an optional indicator that specifies whether the time interval is positive or negative (the default is positive).

- d is the number of days for the interval.

- h is the optional number of hours for the interval; if you supply days and hours, you must include TO HOUR in your literal.

- m is the optional number of minutes for the interval; if you supply days and minutes, you must include TO MINUTES in your literal.

- s is the optional number of seconds for the interval; if you supply days and seconds, you must include TO SECOND in your literal.

- days_precision is the optional precision for the days (the default is 2).

- seconds_precision is the optional precision for the fractional seconds (the default is 6).

The following table shows some examples of day-to-second interval literals.

Literal	Description
INTERVAL '3' DAY	Interval of 3 days.
INTERVAL '2' HOUR	Interval of 2 hours.
INTERVAL '25' MINUTE	Interval of 25 minutes.
INTERVAL '45' SECOND	Interval of 45 seconds.
INTERVAL '3 2' DAY TO HOUR	Interval of 3 days 2 hours.
INTERVAL '3 2:25' DAY TO MINUTE	Interval of 3 days 2 hours 25 minutes.
INTERVAL '3 2:25:45' DAY TO SECOND	Interval of 3 days 2 hours 25 minutes 45 seconds.
INTERVAL '123 2:25:45.12' DAY(3) TO SECOND(2)	Interval of 123 days 2 hours 25 minutes 45.12 seconds; the precision for days is 3 digits, and the precision for the fractional seconds is 2 digits.
INTERVAL '3 2:00:45' DAY TO SECOND	Interval of 3 days 2 hours 0 minutes 45 seconds.
INTERVAL '-3 2:25:45' DAY TO SECOND	Negative interval of 3 days 2 hours 25 minutes 45 seconds.
INTERVAL '1234 2:25:45' DAY(3) TO SECOND	Invalid interval because the number of digits in the days exceeds the specified precision of 3.
INTERVAL '123 2:25:45.123' DAY TO SECOND(2)	Invalid interval because the number of digits in the fractional seconds exceeds the specified precision of 2.

The following INSERT statements add rows to the promotions table:

```
INSERT INTO promotions (promotion_id, name, duration)
VALUES (1, '10% off Z Files', INTERVAL '3' DAY);

INSERT INTO promotions (promotion_id, name, duration)
VALUES (2, '20% off Pop 3', INTERVAL '2' HOUR);

INSERT INTO promotions (promotion_id, name, duration)
VALUES (3, '30% off Modern Science', INTERVAL '25' MINUTE);

INSERT INTO promotions (promotion_id, name, duration)
VALUES (4, '20% off Tank War', INTERVAL '45' SECOND);

INSERT INTO promotions (promotion_id, name, duration)
VALUES (5, '10% off Chemistry', INTERVAL '3 2:25' DAY TO MINUTE);

INSERT INTO promotions (promotion_id, name, duration)
VALUES (6, '20% off Creative Yell', INTERVAL '3 2:25:45' DAY TO SECOND);

INSERT INTO promotions (promotion_id, name, duration)
VALUES (7, '15% off My Front Line',
 INTERVAL '123 2:25:45.12' DAY(3) TO SECOND(2));
```

The following query retrieves the rows from the promotions table; notice the formatting of the duration values:

```
SELECT *
FROM promotions;

PROMOTION_ID NAME                           DURATION
------------ ------------------------------ -------------------
           1 10% off Z Files                +003 00:00:00.0000
           2 20% off Pop 3                  +000 02:00:00.0000
           3 30% off Modern Science         +000 00:25:00.0000
           4 20% off Tank War               +000 00:00:45.0000
           5 10% off Chemistry              +003 02:25:00.0000
           6 20% off Creative Yell          +003 02:25:45.0000
           7 15% off My Front Line          +123 02:25:45.1200
```

Time Interval Functions

There are a number of functions that allow you to get and process time intervals; these functions are shown in Table 5-9.

You'll learn more about the functions shown in Table 5-9 in the following sections.

NUMTODSINTERVAL()

NUMTODSINTERVAL(x, *interval_unit*) converts the number x to an INTERVAL DAY TO SECOND. The interval for x is specified in *interval_unit*, which may be DAY, HOUR, MINUTE, or SECOND.

For example, the following query converts several numbers to time intervals using NUMTODSINTERVAL():

Function	Description
NUMTODSINTERVAL(x, *interval_unit*)	Converts the number x to an INTERVAL DAY TO SECOND. The interval for x is specified in *interval_unit*, which may be DAY, HOUR, MINUTE, or SECOND.
NUMTOYMINTERVAL(x, *interval_unit*)	Converts the number x to an INTERVAL YEAR TO MONTH. The interval for x is specified in *interval_unit*, which may be YEAR or MONTH.
TO_DSINTERVAL(x)	Converts the string x to an INTERVAL DAY TO SECOND.
TO_YMINTERVAL(x)	Converts the string x to an INTERVAL YEAR TO MONTH.

TABLE 5-9 *Time Interval Functions*

```
SELECT
  NUMTODSINTERVAL(1.5, 'DAY'),
  NUMTODSINTERVAL(3.25, 'HOUR'),
  NUMTODSINTERVAL(5, 'MINUTE'),
  NUMTODSINTERVAL(10.123456789, 'SECOND')
FROM dual;


NUMTODSINTERVAL(1.5,'DAY')
----------------------------------------------
NUMTODSINTERVAL(3.25,'HOUR')
----------------------------------------------
NUMTODSINTERVAL(5,'MINUTE')
----------------------------------------------
NUMTODSINTERVAL(10.123456789,'SECOND')
----------------------------------------------
+000000001 12:00:00.000000000
+000000000 03:15:00.000000000
+000000000 00:05:00.000000000
+000000000 00:00:10.123456789
```

NUMTOYMINTERVAL()

NUMTOYMINTERVAL(x, *interval_unit*) converts the number x to an INTERVAL YEAR TO MONTH. The interval for x is specified in *interval_unit*, which may be YEAR or MONTH.

For example, the following query converts two numbers to time intervals using NUMTOYMINTERVAL():

```
SELECT
  NUMTOYMINTERVAL(1.5, 'YEAR'),
  NUMTOYMINTERVAL(3.25, 'MONTH')
FROM dual;


NUMTOYMINTERVAL(1.5,'YEAR')
--------------------------
NUMTOYMINTERVAL(3.25,'MONTH')
--------------------------
+000000001-06
+000000000-03
```

Summary

In this chapter, you learned the following:

- You may store a datetime using the DATE type. The DATE type stores the century, all four digits of a year, the month, the day, the hour (in 24-hour format), the minute, and the second.

- You may use TO_CHAR() and TO_DATE() to convert between strings and dates and times.

- The Oracle database always stores all four digits of a year and interprets two-digit years using a set of rules. You should always specify all four digits of the year.

- There are a number of functions that process dates and times. An example is ADD_MONTHS(*x*, *y*), which returns the result of adding *y* months to *x*.

- Oracle Database 9*i* introduced the ability to use different time zones. A time zone is an offset from the time in Greenwich, England. The time in Greenwich was once known as Greenwich Mean Time (GMT), but it is now known as Coordinated Universal Time (UTC). You specify a time zone using either an offset from UTC or the name of the region (e.g., PST).

- Oracle Database 9*i* introduced the ability to store timestamps. A timestamp stores the century, all four digits of a year, the month, the day, the hour (in 24-hour format), the minute, and the second. The advantages of a timestamp over a DATE are a timestamp can store a fractional second and a time zone.

- Oracle Database 9*i* introduced the ability to handle time intervals, which allow you to store a length of time. An example time interval is 1 year 3 months.

In the next chapter, you'll learn how to nest one query within another.

CHAPTER
6

Subqueries

ll the queries you've seen so far in this book have contained just one SELECT statement. In this chapter, you will learn the following:

- How to place an inner SELECT statement within an outer SELECT, UPDATE, or DELETE statement. The inner SELECT is known as a *subquery*.

- The features of the different types of subqueries.

- How subqueries allow you to build up very complex statements from simple components.

Types of Subqueries

There are two basic types of subqueries:

- **Single-row subqueries** return zero rows or one row to the outer SQL statement. There is a special case of a single-row subquery that contains exactly one column; this type of subquery is called a *scalar subquery*.

- **Multiple-row subqueries** return one or more rows to the outer SQL statement.

In addition, there are three subtypes of subqueries that may return single or multiple rows:

- **Multiple-column subqueries** return more than one column to the outer SQL statement.

- **Correlated subqueries** reference one or more columns in the outer SQL statement. These are called "correlated" subqueries because they are related to the outer SQL statement through the same columns.

- **Nested subqueries** are placed within another subquery. You can nest subqueries to a depth of 255.

You'll learn about each of these types of subqueries and how to add them to SELECT, UPDATE, and DELETE statements. Let's plunge in and look at how to write single-row subqueries.

Writing Single-Row Subqueries

A single-row subquery is one that returns either zero rows or one row to the outer SQL statement. As you'll see in this section, you may place a subquery in a WHERE clause, a HAVING clause, or a FROM clause of a SELECT statement. You'll also see some errors you might encounter when running subqueries.

Subqueries in a WHERE Clause

You may place a subquery in the WHERE clause of another query. The following query contains a subquery placed in its WHERE clause; notice that the subquery is placed within parentheses (...):

```
SELECT first_name, last_name
FROM customers
WHERE customer_id =
  (SELECT customer_id
  FROM customers
```

```
WHERE last_name = 'Brown');
```

```
FIRST_NAME LAST_NAME
---------- ----------
John       Brown
```

This example retrieves the `first_name` and `last_name` of the row from the `customers` table whose `last_name` is Brown. Let's break this query down and analyze what's going on. The subquery in the `WHERE` clause is

```
SELECT customer_id
FROM customers
WHERE last_name = 'Brown';
```

This subquery is executed first (and only once) and returns the `customer_id` for the row whose `last_name` is Brown. The `customer_id` for this row is 1, which is passed to the `WHERE` clause of the outer query. Therefore, the outer query returns the same result as the following query:

```
SELECT first_name, last_name
FROM customers
WHERE customer_id = 1;
```

Using Other Single-Row Operators

The subquery example shown at the start of the previous section used the equality operator (=) in the `WHERE` clause. You may also use other comparison operators, such as <>, <, >, <=, and >=, with a single-row subquery. The following example uses > in the outer query's `WHERE` clause; the subquery uses the `AVG()` function to get the average price of the products, which is passed to the `WHERE` clause of the outer query. The entire query returns the `product_id`, `name`, and `price` of products whose price is greater than that average price.

```
SELECT product_id, name, price
FROM products
WHERE price >
  (SELECT AVG(price)
   FROM products);
```

```
PRODUCT_ID NAME                                   PRICE
---------- ------------------------------- ----------
         1 Modern Science                         19.95
         2 Chemistry                                 30
         3 Supernova                              25.99
         5 Z Files                                49.99
```

Let's break the example down to understand how it works. The following example shows the subquery run on its own:

```
SELECT AVG(price)
FROM products;
```

```
AVG(PRICE)
----------
19.7308333
```

NOTE
This subquery is an example of a scalar subquery, *because it returns exactly one row containing one column. The value returned by a scalar subquery is treated as a single scalar value.*

The value 19.7308333 returned by the subquery is used in the `WHERE` clause of the outer query, which is therefore equivalent to the following:

```
SELECT product_id, name, price
FROM products
WHERE price > 19.7308333;
```

Subqueries in a HAVING Clause

As you saw in Chapter 4, you use the `HAVING` clause to filter groups of rows. You may place a subquery in the `HAVING` clause of an outer query. Doing this allows you to filter groups of rows based on the result returned by your subquery.

The following example uses a subquery in the `HAVING` clause of the outer query. The example retrieves the `product_type_id` and the average price for products whose average price is less than the maximum of the average for the groups of the same product type:

```
SELECT product_type_id, AVG(price)
FROM products
GROUP BY product_type_id
HAVING AVG(price) <
  (SELECT MAX(AVG(price))
   FROM products
   GROUP BY product_type_id)
ORDER BY product_type_id;

PRODUCT_TYPE_ID AVG(PRICE)
--------------- ----------
              1     24.975
              3      13.24
              4      13.99
                     13.49
```

Notice the subquery uses `AVG()` to first compute the average price for each product type. The result returned by `AVG()` is then passed to `MAX()`, which returns the maximum of the averages.

Let's break the example down to understand how it works. The following example shows the output from the subquery when it is run on its own:

```
SELECT MAX(AVG(price))
FROM products
GROUP BY product_type_id;

MAX(AVG(PRICE))
---------------
          26.22
```

This value of 26.22 is used in the HAVING clause of the outer query to filter the group's rows to those having an average price less than 26.22. The following query shows a version of the outer query that retrieves the product_type_id and average price of the products grouped by product_type_id:

```
SELECT product_type_id, AVG(price)
FROM products
GROUP BY product_type_id
ORDER BY product_type_id;

PRODUCT_TYPE_ID AVG(PRICE)
--------------- ----------
              1     24.975
              2      26.22
              3      13.24
              4      13.99
                     13.49
```

The groups with a product_type_id of 1, 3, 4, and null have an average price less than 26.22. As expected, these are the same groups returned by the query at the start of this section.

Subqueries in a FROM Clause (Inline Views)

You may place a subquery in the FROM clause of an outer query. These types of subqueries are also known as *inline views*, because the subquery provides data in line with the FROM clause. The following simple example retrieves the products whose product_id is less than 3:

```
SELECT product_id
FROM
    (SELECT product_id
     FROM products
     WHERE product_id < 3);

PRODUCT_ID
----------
         1
         2
```

Notice that the subquery returns the rows from the products table whose product_id is less than 3 to the outer query, which then retrieves and displays those product_id values. As far as the FROM clause of the outer query is concerned, the output from the subquery is just another source of data.

The next example is more useful and retrieves the product_id and price from the products table in the outer query, and the subquery retrieves the number of times a product has been purchased:

```
SELECT prds.product_id, price, purchases_data.product_count
FROM products prds,
    (SELECT product_id, COUNT(product_id) product_count
```

```
   FROM purchases
   GROUP BY product_id) purchases_data
WHERE prds.product_id = purchases_data.product_id;

PRODUCT_ID      PRICE PRODUCT_COUNT
---------- ---------- -------------
         1      19.95             4
         2         30             4
         3      25.99             1
```

Notice that the subquery retrieves the product_id and COUNT(product_id) from the purchases table and returns them to the outer query. As you can see, the output from subquery is just another source of data to the FROM clause of the outer query.

Errors You Might Encounter

In this section, you'll see some errors you might encounter. Specifically, you'll see that a single-row subquery may return a maximum of one row and that a subquery may not contain an ORDER BY clause.

Single-Row Subqueries May Return a Maximum of One Row

If your subquery returns more than one row, you'll get the following error:

```
ORA-01427: single-row subquery returns more than one row.
```

For example, the subquery in the following statement attempts to pass multiple rows to the equality operator (=) in the outer query:

```
SQL> SELECT product_id, name
  2  FROM products
  3  WHERE product_id =
  4    (SELECT product_id
  5     FROM products
  6     WHERE name LIKE '%e%');

  (SELECT product_id
   *
ERROR at line 4:
ORA-01427: single-row subquery returns more than one row
```

There are nine rows in the products table whose names contain the letter e, and the subquery attempts to pass these rows to the equality operator in the outer query. Because the equality operator can handle only a single row, the query is invalid and an error is returned.

You'll learn how to return multiple rows from a subquery later in the section "Writing Multiple-Row Subqueries."

Subqueries May Not Contain an ORDER BY Clause

A subquery may not contain an ORDER BY clause. Instead, any ordering must be done in the outer query. For example, the following outer query has an ORDER BY clause at the end that sorts the product_id values in descending order:

```
SELECT product_id, name, price
FROM products
WHERE price >
  (SELECT AVG(price)
   FROM products)
ORDER BY product_id DESC;
```

```
PRODUCT_ID NAME                               PRICE
---------- ------------------------------ ----------
         5 Z Files                            49.99
         3 Supernova                          25.99
         2 Chemistry                             30
         1 Modern Science                     19.95
```

Writing Multiple-Row Subqueries

You use a multiple-row subquery to return one or more rows to an outer SQL statement. To handle a subquery that returns multiple rows, your outer query may use the IN, ANY, or ALL operator. As you saw in Chapter 2, you can use these operators to see if a column value is contained in a list of values; for example:

```
SELECT product_id, name
FROM products
WHERE product_id IN (1, 2, 3);
```

```
PRODUCT_ID NAME
---------- ------------------
         1 Modern Science
         2 Chemistry
         3 Supernova
```

As you'll see in this section, the list of values can come from a subquery.

NOTE
You can also use the EXISTS *operator to check if a value is in a list returned by a correlated subquery. You'll learn about this later, in the section "Writing Correlated Subqueries."*

Using IN with a Multiple-Row Subquery

As you saw in Chapter 2, you use IN to check if a value is in a specified list of values. The list of values may come from the results returned by a subquery. You can also use NOT IN to perform the logical opposite of IN: to check if a value is not in a specified list of values.

The following simple example uses IN to check if a product_id is in the list of values returned by the subquery; the subquery returns the product_id for products whose name contains the letter e:

```
SELECT product_id, name
FROM products
WHERE product_id IN
```

```
(SELECT product_id
 FROM products
 WHERE name LIKE '%e%');

PRODUCT_ID NAME
---------- -------------------
         1 Modern Science
         2 Chemistry
         3 Supernova
         5 Z Files
         6 2412: The Return
         7 Space Force 9
         8 From Another Planet
        11 Creative Yell
        12 My Front Line
```

The next example uses NOT IN to get the products that are not in the purchases table:

```
SELECT product_id, name
FROM products
WHERE product_id NOT IN
  (SELECT product_id
   FROM purchases);

PRODUCT_ID NAME
---------- -------------------
         4 Tank War
         5 Z Files
         6 2412: The Return
         7 Space Force 9
         8 From Another Planet
         9 Classical Music
        10 Pop 3
        11 Creative Yell
        12 My Front Line
```

Using ANY with a Multiple-Row Subquery

You use the ANY operator to compare a value with any value in a list. You must place an =, <>, <, >, <=, or >= operator before ANY in your query. The following example uses ANY to get the employees whose salary is less than any of the lowest salaries in the salary_grades table:

```
SELECT employee_id, last_name
FROM employees
WHERE salary < ANY
  (SELECT low_salary
   FROM salary_grades);

EMPLOYEE_ID LAST_NAME
----------- ----------
          2 Johnson
          3 Hobbs
          4 Jones
```

Using ALL with a Multiple-Row Subquery

You use the ALL operator to compare a value with any value in a list. You must place an =, <>, <, >, <=, or >= operator before ALL in your query. The following example uses ALL to get the employees whose salary is greater than all of the highest salaries in the salary_grades table:

```
SELECT employee_id, last_name
FROM employees
WHERE salary > ALL
  (SELECT high_salary
   FROM salary_grades);
```

```
no rows selected
```

As you can see, no employee has a salary greater than the highest salary.

Writing Multiple-Column Subqueries

The subqueries you've seen so far have returned rows containing one column. You're not limited to one column: you can write subqueries that return multiple columns. The following example retrieves the products with the lowest price for each product type group:

```
SELECT product_id, product_type_id, name, price
FROM products
WHERE (product_type_id, price) IN
  (SELECT product_type_id, MIN(price)
   FROM products
   GROUP BY product_type_id);
```

```
PRODUCT_ID PRODUCT_TYPE_ID NAME                                 PRICE
---------- --------------- ---------------------------- ----------
         1               1 Modern Science                       19.95
         4               2 Tank War                             13.95
         8               3 From Another Planet                  12.99
         9               4 Classical Music                      10.99
```

Notice that the subquery returns the product_type_id and the minimum price for each group of products, and these are compared in the outer query's WHERE clause with the product_type_id and price for each product.

Writing Correlated Subqueries

A correlated subquery references one or more columns in the outer SQL statement. These are called *correlated* subqueries, because they are related to the outer SQL statement through the same columns.

You typically use a correlated subquery when you need an answer to a question that depends on a value in each row contained in an outer query. For example, you might want to see whether there is a relationship between the data, but you don't care how many rows are returned by the subquery, that is, you just want to check whether *any* rows are returned, but you don't care how many.

A correlated subquery is run once for each row in the outer query; this is different from a non-correlated subquery, which is run once prior to running the outer query. In addition, a correlated subquery can resolve null values. You'll see examples in the following sections that illustrate these concepts.

A Correlated Subquery Example

The following correlated subquery retrieves the products that have a price greater than the average for their product type:

```
SELECT product_id, product_type_id, name, price
FROM products outer
WHERE price >
  (SELECT AVG(price)
   FROM products inner
   WHERE inner.product_type_id = outer.product_type_id);
```

```
PRODUCT_ID PRODUCT_TYPE_ID NAME                                PRICE
---------- --------------- ------------------------------ ----------
         2               1 Chemistry                              30
         5               2 Z Files                             49.99
         7               3 Space Force 9                       13.49
        10               4 Pop 3                               15.99
        11               4 Creative Yell                       14.99
```

Notice that I've used the alias `outer` to label the outer query and the alias `inner` for the inner subquery. The reference to the `product_type_id` column in both the inner and outer parts is what makes the inner subquery correlated with the outer query. Also, the subquery returns a single row containing the average price for the product.

In a correlated subquery, each row in the outer query is passed one at a time to the subquery. The subquery reads each row in turn from the outer query and applies it to the subquery until all the rows from the outer query have been processed. The results from the entire query are then returned.

In the previous example, the outer query retrieves each row from the `products` table and passes them to the inner query. Each row is read by the inner query, which calculates the average price for each product where the `product_type_id` in the inner query is equal to the `product_type_id` in the outer query.

Using EXISTS and NOT EXISTS with a Correlated Subquery

You use the `EXISTS` operator to check for the existence of rows returned by a subquery. Although you can use `EXISTS` with non-correlated subqueries, you'll typically use it with correlated subqueries. The `NOT EXISTS` operator does the logical opposite of `EXISTS`: it checks if rows do not exist in the results returned by a subquery.

Using EXISTS with a Correlated Subquery

The following example uses `EXISTS` to retrieve employees who manage other employees; notice that I don't care how many rows are returned by the subquery; I only care whether any rows are returned at all:

```
SELECT employee_id, last_name
FROM employees outer
WHERE EXISTS
  (SELECT employee_id
```

```
   FROM employees inner
   WHERE inner.manager_id = outer.employee_id);
```

```
EMPLOYEE_ID LAST_NAME
----------- ----------
          1 Smith
          2 Johnson
```

Because `EXISTS` just checks for the existence of rows returned by the subquery, a subquery doesn't have to return a column—it can just return a literal value. This feature can improve the performance of your query. For example, the following query rewrites the previous example with the subquery returning the literal value 1:

```
SELECT employee_id, last_name
FROM employees outer
WHERE EXISTS
  (SELECT 1
   FROM employees inner
   WHERE inner.manager_id = outer.employee_id);
```

```
EMPLOYEE_ID LAST_NAME
----------- ----------
          1 Smith
          2 Johnson
```

As long as the subquery returns one or more rows, `EXISTS` returns true; if the subquery returns no rows, `EXISTS` returns false. In the examples, I didn't care how many rows are returned by the subquery: All I cared about was whether any rows (or no rows) are returned, so that `EXISTS` returns true (or false). Because the outer query requires at least one column, the literal value 1 is returned by the subquery in the previous example.

Using NOT EXISTS with a Correlated Subquery

The following example uses `NOT EXISTS` to retrieve products that haven't been purchased:

```
SELECT product_id, name
FROM products outer
WHERE NOT EXISTS
  (SELECT 1
   FROM purchases inner
   WHERE inner.product_id = outer.product_id);
```

```
PRODUCT_ID NAME
---------- ------------------
         4 Tank War
         5 Z Files
         6 2412: The Return
         7 Space Force 9
         8 From Another Planet
         9 Classical Music
        10 Pop 3
        11 Creative Yell
        12 My Front Line
```

EXISTS and NOT EXISTS Versus IN and NOT IN

Earlier in the section "Using IN with a Multiple-Row Subquery," you saw how the IN operator is used to check if a value is contained in a list. EXISTS is different from IN: EXISTS checks just for the existence of rows, whereas IN checks for actual values.

TIP
EXISTS typically offers better performance than IN *with subqueries. Therefore, you should use* EXISTS *rather than IN wherever possible.*

You should be careful when writing queries that use NOT EXISTS or NOT IN. When a list of values contains a null value, NOT EXISTS returns true, but NOT IN returns false. Consider the following example that uses NOT EXISTS and retrieves the product types that don't have any products of that type in the products table:

```
SELECT product_type_id, name
FROM product_types outer
WHERE NOT EXISTS
  (SELECT 1
   FROM products inner
   WHERE inner.product_type_id = outer.product_type_id);


PRODUCT_TYPE_ID NAME
--------------- ----------
              5 Magazine
```

Notice one row is returned by this example. The next example rewrites the previous query to use NOT IN; notice that no rows are returned:

```
SELECT product_type_id, name
FROM product_types
WHERE product_type_id NOT IN
  (SELECT product_type_id
   FROM products);


no rows selected
```

No rows are returned because the subquery returns a list of product_id values, one of which is null (the product_type_id for product #12 is null). Because of this, NOT IN in the outer query returns false, and therefore no rows are returned. You can get around this by using the NVL() function to convert nulls to a value. In the following example, NVL() is used to convert null product_type_id values to 0:

```
SELECT product_type_id, name
FROM product_types
WHERE product_type_id NOT IN
  (SELECT NVL(product_type_id, 0)
   FROM products);


PRODUCT_TYPE_ID NAME
--------------- ----------
              5 Magazine
```

This time the row appears.

These examples illustrate another difference between correlated and non-correlated subqueries: a correlated query can resolve null values.

Writing Nested Subqueries

You can nest subqueries inside other subqueries to a depth of 255. You should use this technique sparingly—you may find your query performs better using table joins. The following example contains a nested subquery; notice that it is contained within a subquery, which is itself contained in an outer query:

```
SELECT product_type_id, AVG(price)
FROM products
GROUP BY product_type_id
HAVING AVG(price) <
  (SELECT MAX(AVG(price))
   FROM products
   WHERE product_type_id IN
     (SELECT product_id
      FROM purchases
      WHERE quantity > 1)
   GROUP BY product_type_id)
ORDER BY product_type_id;

PRODUCT_TYPE_ID AVG(PRICE)
--------------- ----------
              1     24.975
              3      13.24
              4      13.99
                     13.49
```

As you can see, this example is quite complex and contains three queries: a nested subquery, a subquery, and the outer query. These query parts are run in that order. Let's break the example down into the three parts and examine the results returned. The nested subquery is

```
SELECT product_id
FROM purchases
WHERE quantity > 1
```

This subquery returns the `product_id` for the products that have been purchased more than once. The rows returned by this subquery are

```
PRODUCT_ID
----------
         2
         1
```

The subquery that receives this output is

```
SELECT MAX(AVG(price))
FROM products
WHERE product_type_id IN
  (... output from the nested subquery ...)
GROUP BY product_type_id
```

This subquery returns the maximum average price for the products returned by the nested subquery. The row returned is

```
MAX(AVG(PRICE))
---------------
          26.22
```

This row is returned to the following outer query:

```
SELECT product_type_id, AVG(price)
FROM products
GROUP BY product_type_id
HAVING AVG(price) <
  (... output from the subquery ...)
ORDER BY product_type_id;
```

This query returns the `product_type_id` and average price of products that are less than average returned by the subquery. The rows returned are

```
PRODUCT_TYPE_ID AVG(PRICE)
--------------- ----------
              1     24.975
              3      13.24
              4      13.99
                     13.49
```

These are the rows returned by the complete query shown at the start of this section.

Writing UPDATE and DELETE Statements Containing Subqueries

So far, you've only seen subqueries contained in a SELECT statement. As you'll see in this section, you can also put subqueries inside UPDATE and DELETE statements.

Writing an UPDATE Statement Containing a Subquery

In an UPDATE statement, you can set a column to the result returned by a single-row subquery. For example, the following UPDATE statement sets employee #4's salary to the average of the high salary grades returned by a subquery:

```
UPDATE employees
SET salary =
  (SELECT AVG(high_salary)
   FROM salary_grades)
WHERE employee_id = 4;
```

```
1 row updated.
```

Doing this increases employee #4's salary from $500,000 to $625,000 (this is the average of the high salaries from the `salary_grades` table).

NOTE
If you execute the UPDATE *statement, remember to execute a*
ROLLBACK *to undo the change. That way, your results will match*
those shown later in this book.

Writing a DELETE Statement Containing a Subquery

You can use the rows returned by a subquery in the WHERE clause of a DELETE statement. For
example, the following DELETE statement removes the employee whose salary is greater than
the average of the high salary grades returned by a subquery:

```
DELETE FROM employees
WHERE salary >
  (SELECT AVG(high_salary)
  FROM salary_grades);
```

```
1 row deleted.
```

This DELETE statement removes employee #1.

NOTE
If you execute the DELETE *statement, remember to execute a*
ROLLBACK *to undo the removal of the row.*

Summary

In this chapter, you learned the following:

■   A subquery is a query placed within a SELECT, UPDATE, or DELETE statement.

■   Single-row subqueries return zero or one row.

■   Multiple-row subqueries return one or more rows.

■   Multiple-column subqueries return more than one column.

■   Correlated subqueries reference one or more columns in the outer SQL statement.

■   Nested subqueries are subqueries placed within another subquery.

In the next chapter, you'll learn about advanced queries.

CHAPTER
7

Advanced Queries

n this chapter, you will see how to

- Use the set operators, which allow you to combine rows returned by two or more queries.

- Use the TRANSLATE() function to translate characters in one string to characters in another string.

- Use the DECODE() function to search for a certain value in a set of values.

- Use the CASE expression to perform if-then-else logic in SQL.

- Perform queries on hierarchical data.

- Use the ROLLUP and CUBE clauses to get subtotals and totals for groups of rows.

- Take advantage of the analytic functions, which perform complex calculations, such as finding the top-selling product type for each month, the top salespersons, and so on.

- Perform inter-row calculations with the MODEL clause.

- Use the new Oracle Database 11*g* PIVOT and UNPIVOT clauses, which are useful for seeing overall trends in large amounts of data.

Let's plunge in and examine the set operators.

Using the Set Operators

The set operators allow you to combine rows returned by two or more queries. Table 7-1 shows the four set operators.

You must keep in mind the following restriction when using a set operator: *The number of columns and the column types returned by the queries must match, although the column names may be different.*

You'll learn how to use each of the set operators shown in Table 7-1 shortly, but first let's look at the example tables used in this section.

Operator	Description
UNION ALL	Returns all the rows retrieved by the queries, including duplicate rows.
UNION	Returns all non-duplicate rows retrieved by the queries.
INTERSECT	Returns rows that are retrieved by both queries.
MINUS	Returns the remaining rows when the rows retrieved by the second query are subtracted from the rows retrieved by the first query.

TABLE 7-1 *Set Operators*

The Example Tables

The products and more_products tables are created by the store_schema.sql script using the following statements:

```
CREATE TABLE products (
  product_id INTEGER
    CONSTRAINT products_pk PRIMARY KEY,
  product_type_id INTEGER
    CONSTRAINT products_fk_product_types
    REFERENCES product_types(product_type_id),
  name VARCHAR2(30) NOT NULL,
  description VARCHAR2(50),
  price NUMBER(5, 2)
);

CREATE TABLE more_products (
  prd_id INTEGER
    CONSTRAINT more_products_pk PRIMARY KEY,
  prd_type_id INTEGER
    CONSTRAINT more_products_fk_product_types
    REFERENCES product_types(product_type_id),
  name VARCHAR2(30) NOT NULL,
  available CHAR(1)
);
```

The following query retrieves the product_id, product_type_id, and name columns from the products table:

```
SELECT product_id, product_type_id, name
FROM products;
```

```
PRODUCT_ID PRODUCT_TYPE_ID NAME
---------- --------------- -------------------
         1               1 Modern Science
         2               1 Chemistry
         3               2 Supernova
         4               2 Tank War
         5               2 Z Files
         6               2 2412: The Return
         7               3 Space Force 9
         8               3 From Another Planet
         9               4 Classical Music
        10               4 Pop 3
        11               4 Creative Yell
        12                 My Front Line
```

The next query retrieves the prd_id, prd_type_id, and name columns from the more_products table:

```
SELECT prd_id, prd_type_id, name
FROM more_products;
```

```
    PRD_ID PRD_TYPE_ID NAME
---------- ----------- --------------
         1           1 Modern Science
         2           1 Chemistry
         3             Supernova
         4           2 Lunar Landing
         5           2 Submarine
```

Using the UNION ALL Operator

The UNION ALL operator returns all the rows retrieved by the queries, including duplicate rows. The following query uses UNION ALL; notice that all the rows from products and more_products are retrieved, including duplicates:

```
SELECT product_id, product_type_id, name
FROM products
UNION ALL
SELECT prd_id, prd_type_id, name
FROM more_products;
```

```
PRODUCT_ID PRODUCT_TYPE_ID NAME
---------- --------------- ------------------------------
         1               1 Modern Science
         2               1 Chemistry
         3               2 Supernova
         4               2 Tank War
         5               2 Z Files
         6               2 2412: The Return
         7               3 Space Force 9
         8               3 From Another Planet
         9               4 Classical Music
        10               4 Pop 3
        11               4 Creative Yell
        12                 My Front Line
         1               1 Modern Science
         2               1 Chemistry
         3                 Supernova
         4               2 Lunar Landing
         5               2 Submarine
```

```
17 rows selected.
```

You can sort the rows using the ORDER BY clause followed by the position of the column. The following example uses ORDER BY 1 to sort the rows by the first column retrieved by the two queries (product_id and prd_id):

```
SELECT product_id, product_type_id, name
FROM products
UNION ALL
SELECT prd_id, prd_type_id, name
FROM more_products
ORDER BY 1;
```

```
PRODUCT_ID PRODUCT_TYPE_ID NAME
---------- --------------- -------------------
         1               1 Modern Science
         1               1 Modern Science
         2               1 Chemistry
         2               1 Chemistry
         3               2 Supernova
         3                 Supernova
         4               2 Tank War
         4               2 Lunar Landing
         5               2 Z Files
         5               2 Submarine
         6               2 2412: The Return
         7               3 Space Force 9
         8               3 From Another Planet
         9               4 Classical Music
        10               4 Pop 3
        11               4 Creative Yell
        12                 My Front Line

17 rows selected.
```

Using the UNION Operator

The UNION operator returns only the non-duplicate rows retrieved by the queries. The following example uses UNION; notice the duplicate "Modern Science" and "Chemistry" rows are not retrieved, and so only 15 rows are returned:

```
SELECT product_id, product_type_id, name
FROM products
UNION
SELECT prd_id, prd_type_id, name
FROM more_products;

PRODUCT_ID PRODUCT_TYPE_ID NAME
---------- --------------- -------------------
         1               1 Modern Science
         2               1 Chemistry
         3               2 Supernova
         3                 Supernova
         4               2 Lunar Landing
         4               2 Tank War
         5               2 Submarine
         5               2 Z Files
         6               2 2412: The Return
         7               3 Space Force 9
         8               3 From Another Planet
         9               4 Classical Music
        10               4 Pop 3
        11               4 Creative Yell
        12                 My Front Line

15 rows selected.
```

Using the INTERSECT Operator

The INTERSECT operator returns only rows that are retrieved by both queries. The following example uses INTERSECT; notice that the "Modern Science" and "Chemistry" rows are returned:

```
SELECT product_id, product_type_id, name
FROM products
INTERSECT
SELECT prd_id, prd_type_id, name
FROM more_products;
```

```
PRODUCT_ID PRODUCT_TYPE_ID NAME
---------- --------------- --------------
         1               1 Modern Science
         2               1 Chemistry
```

Using the MINUS Operator

The MINUS operator returns the remaining rows when the rows retrieved by the second query are subtracted from the rows retrieved by the first query. The following example uses MINUS; notice that the rows from more_products are subtracted from products and the remaining rows are returned:

```
SELECT product_id, product_type_id, name
FROM products
MINUS
SELECT prd_id, prd_type_id, name
FROM more_products;
```

```
PRODUCT_ID PRODUCT_TYPE_ID NAME
---------- --------------- -------------------
         3               2 Supernova
         4               2 Tank War
         5               2 Z Files
         6               2 2412: The Return
         7               3 Space Force 9
         8               3 From Another Planet
         9               4 Classical Music
        10               4 Pop 3
        11               4 Creative Yell
        12                 My Front Line
```

```
10 rows selected.
```

Combining Set Operators

You can combine more than two queries with multiple set operators, with the returned results from one operator feeding into the next operator. By default, set operators are evaluated from top to bottom, but you should indicate the order using parentheses in case Oracle Corporation changes this default behavior in future software releases.

In the examples in this section, I'll use the following product_changes table (created by the store_schema.sql script):

```
CREATE TABLE product_changes (
  product_id INTEGER
    CONSTRAINT prod_changes_pk PRIMARY KEY,
  product_type_id INTEGER
    CONSTRAINT prod_changes_fk_product_types
    REFERENCES product_types(product_type_id),
  name VARCHAR2(30) NOT NULL,
  description VARCHAR2(50),
  price NUMBER(5, 2)
);
```

The following query returns the product_id, product_type_id, and name columns from the product_changes table:

```
SELECT product_id, product_type_id, name
FROM product_changes;

PRODUCT_ID PRODUCT_TYPE_ID NAME
---------- --------------- --------------
         1               1 Modern Science
         2               1 New Chemistry
         3               1 Supernova
        13               2 Lunar Landing
        14               2 Submarine
        15               2 Airplane
```

The next query does the following:

- Uses the UNION operator to combine the results from the products and more_products tables. (The UNION operator returns only the non-duplicate rows retrieved by the queries.)

- Uses the INTERSECT operator to combine the results from the previous UNION operator with the results from the product_changes table. (The INTERSECT operator only returns rows that are retrieved by both queries.)

- Uses parentheses to indicate the order of evaluation, which is: (1) the UNION between the products and more_products tables; (2) the INTERSECT.

```
(SELECT product_id, product_type_id, name
FROM products
UNION
SELECT prd_id, prd_type_id, name
FROM more_products)
INTERSECT
SELECT product_id, product_type_id, name
FROM product_changes;

PRODUCT_ID PRODUCT_TYPE_ID NAME
---------- --------------- --------------
         1               1 Modern Science
```

The following query has the parentheses set so that the INTERSECT is performed first; notice the different results returned by the query compared with the previous example:

```
SELECT product_id, product_type_id, name
FROM products
UNION
(SELECT prd_id, prd_type_id, name
FROM more_products
INTERSECT
SELECT product_id, product_type_id, name
FROM product_changes);
```

```
PRODUCT_ID PRODUCT_TYPE_ID NAME
---------- --------------- -------------------
         1               1 Modern Science
         2               1 Chemistry
         3               2 Supernova
         4               2 Tank War
         5               2 Z Files
         6               2 2412: The Return
         7               3 Space Force 9
         8               3 From Another Planet
         9               4 Classical Music
        10               4 Pop 3
        11               4 Creative Yell
        12                 My Front Line
```

This concludes the discussion of the set operators.

Using the TRANSLATE() Function

TRANSLATE(*x*, *from_string*, *to_string*) converts the occurrences of characters in *from_string* found in *x* to corresponding characters in *to_string*. The easiest way to understand how TRANSLATE() works is to see some examples.

The following example uses TRANSLATE() to shift each character in the string SECRET MESSAGE: MEET ME IN THE PARK by four places to the right: A becomes E, B becomes F, and so on:

```
SELECT TRANSLATE('SECRET MESSAGE: MEET ME IN THE PARK',
  'ABCDEFGHIJKLMNOPQRSTUVWXYZ',
  'EFGHIJKLMNOPQRSTUVWXYZABCD')
FROM dual;
```

```
TRANSLATE('SECRETMESSAGE:MEETMEINTH
------------------------------------
WIGVIX QIWWEKI: QIIX QI MR XLI TEVO
```

The next example takes the output of the previous example and shifts the characters four places to the left: E becomes A, F becomes B, and so on:

```
SELECT TRANSLATE('WIGVIX QIWWEKI: QIIX QI MR XLI TEVO',
  'EFGHIJKLMNOPQRSTUVWXYZABCD',
```

```
'ABCDEFGHIJKLMNOPQRSTUVWXYZ')
FROM dual;

TRANSLATE('WIGVIXQIWWEKI:QIIXQIMRXL
----------------------------------
SECRET MESSAGE: MEET ME IN THE PARK
```

You can of course pass column values to `TRANSLATE()`. The following example passes the `name` column from the `products` table to `TRANSLATE()`, which shifts the letters in the product name four places to the right:

```
SELECT product_id, TRANSLATE(name,
  'ABCDEFGHIJKLMNOPQRSTUVWXYZabcdefghijklmnopqrstuvwxyz',
  'EFGHIJKLMNOPQRSTUVWXYZABCDefghijklmnopqrstuvwxyzabcd')
FROM products;

PRODUCT_ID TRANSLATE(NAME,'ABCDEFGHIJKLMN
---------- -------------------------------
         1 Qshivr Wgmirgi
         2 Gliqmwxvc
         3 Wytivrsze
         4 Xero Aev
         5 D Jmpiw
         6 2412: Xli Vixyvr
         7 Wtegi Jsvgi 9
         8 Jvsq Ersxliv Tperix
         9 Gpewwmgep Qywmg
        10 Tst 3
        11 Gviexmzi Cipp
        12 Qc Jvsrx Pmri
```

You can also use `TRANSLATE()` to convert numbers. The following example takes the number 12345 and converts 5 to 6, 4 to 7, 3 to 8, 2 to 9, and 1 to 0:

```
SELECT TRANSLATE(12345,
  54321,
  67890)
FROM dual;

TRANS
-----
09876
```

Using the DECODE() Function

`DECODE(value, search_value, result, default_value)` compares `value` with `search_value`. If the values are equal, `DECODE()` returns `result`; otherwise, `default_value` is returned. `DECODE()` allows you to perform if-then-else logic in SQL without having to use PL/SQL. Each of the parameters to `DECODE()` can be a column, a literal value, a function, or a subquery.

NOTE
DECODE() *is an old Oracle proprietary function, and therefore you should use* CASE *expressions instead if you are using Oracle Database 9i and above (you will learn about* CASE *in the next section). The* DECODE() *function is mentioned here because you may encounter it when using older Oracle databases.*

The following example illustrates the use of DECODE() with literal values; DECODE() returns 2 (1 is compared with 1, and because they are equal 2 is returned):

```
SELECT DECODE(1, 1, 2, 3)
FROM dual;

DECODE(1,1,2,3)
---------------
              2
```

The next example uses DECODE() to compare 1 to 2, and because they are not equal 3 is returned:

```
SELECT DECODE(1, 2, 1, 3)
FROM dual;

DECODE(1,2,1,3)
---------------
              3
```

The next example compares the available column in the more_products table; if available equals Y, the string 'Product is available' is returned; otherwise, 'Product is not available' is returned:

```
SELECT prd_id, available,
  DECODE(available, 'Y', 'Product is available',
    'Product is not available')
FROM more_products;

    PRD_ID A DECODE(AVAILABLE,'Y','PR
---------- - ------------------------
         1 Y Product is available
         2 Y Product is available
         3 N Product is not available
         4 N Product is not available
         5 Y Product is available
```

You can pass multiple search and result parameters to DECODE(), as shown in the following example, which returns the product_type_id column as the name of the product type:

```
SELECT product_id, product_type_id,
  DECODE(product_type_id,
    1, 'Book',
    2, 'Video',
    3, 'DVD',
    4, 'CD',
    'Magazine')
```

```
FROM products;

PRODUCT_ID PRODUCT_TYPE_ID DECODE(P
---------- --------------- --------
         1               1 Book
         2               1 Book
         3               2 Video
         4               2 Video
         5               2 Video
         6               2 Video
         7               3 DVD
         8               3 DVD
         9               4 CD
        10               4 CD
        11               4 CD
        12                 Magazine
```

Notice that

- If product_type_id is 1, Book is returned.

- If product_type_id is 2, Video is returned.

- If product_type_id is 3, DVD is returned.

- If product_type_id is 4, CD is returned.

- If product_type_id is any other value, Magazine is returned.

Using the CASE Expression

The CASE expression performs if-then-else logic in SQL and is supported in Oracle Database 9*i* and above. The CASE expression works in a similar manner to DECODE(), but you should use CASE because it is ANSI-compliant and forms part of the SQL/92 standard. In addition, the CASE expression is easier to read.

There are two types of CASE expressions:

- Simple case expressions, which use expressions to determine the returned value

- Searched case expressions, which use conditions to determine the returned value

You'll learn about both of these types of CASE expressions next.

Using Simple CASE Expressions

Simple CASE expressions use embedded expressions to determine the value to return. Simple CASE expressions have the following syntax:

```
CASE search_expression
  WHEN expression1 THEN result1
  WHEN expression2 THEN result2
  ...
  WHEN expressionN THEN resultN
  ELSE default_result
END
```

where

- *search_expression* is the expression to be evaluated.

- *expression1, expression2, ..., expressionN* are the expressions to be evaluated against *search_expression*.

- *result1, result2, ..., resultN* are the returned results (one for each possible expression). If *expression1* evaluates to *search_expression*, *result1* is returned, and similarly for the other expressions.

- *default_result* is returned when no matching expression is found.

The following example shows a simple CASE expression that returns the product types as names:

```
SELECT product_id, product_type_id,
  CASE product_type_id
    WHEN 1 THEN 'Book'
    WHEN 2 THEN 'Video'
    WHEN 3 THEN 'DVD'
    WHEN 4 THEN 'CD'
    ELSE 'Magazine'
  END
FROM products;

PRODUCT_ID PRODUCT_TYPE_ID CASEPROD
---------- --------------- --------
         1               1 Book
         2               1 Book
         3               2 Video
         4               2 Video
         5               2 Video
         6               2 Video
         7               3 DVD
         8               3 DVD
         9               4 CD
        10               4 CD
        11               4 CD
        12                 Magazine
```

Using Searched CASE Expressions

Searched CASE expressions use conditions to determine the returned value. Searched CASE expressions have the following syntax:

```
CASE
  WHEN condition1 THEN result1
  WHEN condition2 THEN result2
  ...
  WHEN conditionN THEN resultN
  ELSE default_result
END
```

where

- *condition1, condition2, ..., conditionN* are the expressions to be evaluated.

- *result1, result2, ..., resultN* are the returned results (one for each possible condition). If *condition1* is true, *result1* is returned, and similarly for the other expressions.

- *default_result* is returned when there is no condition that returns true.

The following example illustrates the use of a searched CASE expression:

```
SELECT product_id, product_type_id,
  CASE
    WHEN product_type_id = 1 THEN 'Book'
    WHEN product_type_id = 2 THEN 'Video'
    WHEN product_type_id = 3 THEN 'DVD'
    WHEN product_type_id = 4 THEN 'CD'
    ELSE 'Magazine'
  END
FROM products;
```

```
PRODUCT_ID PRODUCT_TYPE_ID CASEPROD
---------- --------------- --------
         1               1 Book
         2               1 Book
         3               2 Video
         4               2 Video
         5               2 Video
         6               2 Video
         7               3 DVD
         8               3 DVD
         9               4 CD
        10               4 CD
        11               4 CD
        12                 Magazine
```

You can use operators in a searched CASE expression, as shown in the following example:

```
SELECT product_id, price,
  CASE
    WHEN price > 15 THEN 'Expensive'
    ELSE 'Cheap'
  END
FROM products;
```

```
PRODUCT_ID      PRICE CASEWHENP
---------- ---------- ---------
         1      19.95 Expensive
         2         30 Expensive
         3      25.99 Expensive
         4      13.95 Cheap
         5      49.99 Expensive
```

```
 6      14.95 Cheap
 7      13.49 Cheap
 8      12.99 Cheap
 9      10.99 Cheap
10      15.99 Expensive
11      14.99 Cheap
12      13.49 Cheap
```

You will see more advanced examples of CASE expressions later in this chapter and in Chapter 16.

Hierarchical Queries

You'll quite often encounter data that is organized in a hierarchical manner. Examples include the people who work in a company, a family tree, and the parts that make up an engine. In this section, you'll see queries that access a hierarchy of employees who work for our imaginary store.

The Example Data

You'll see the use of a table named more_employees, which is created by the store_schema.sql script as follows:

```
CREATE TABLE more_employees (
  employee_id INTEGER
    CONSTRAINT more_employees_pk PRIMARY KEY,
  manager_id INTEGER
    CONSTRAINT more_empl_fk_fk_more_empl
    REFERENCES more_employees(employee_id),
  first_name VARCHAR2(10) NOT NULL,
  last_name VARCHAR2(10) NOT NULL,
  title VARCHAR2(20),
  salary NUMBER(6, 0)
);
```

The manager_id column is a self-reference back to the employee_id column of the more_employees table; manager_id indicates the manager of an employee (if any). The following query returns the rows from more_employees:

```
SELECT *
FROM more_employees;
```

```
EMPLOYEE_ID MANAGER_ID FIRST_NAME LAST_NAME  TITLE            SALARY
----------- ---------- ---------- ---------- -------------- ----------
          1            James      Smith      CEO             800000
          2          1 Ron        Johnson    Sales Manager   600000
          3          2 Fred       Hobbs      Sales Person    200000
          4          1 Susan      Jones      Support Manager 500000
          5          2 Rob        Green      Sales Person     40000
          6          4 Jane       Brown      Support Person   45000
          7          4 John       Grey       Support Manager  30000
          8          7 Jean       Blue       Support Person   29000
```

9	6 Henry	Heyson	Support Person	30000
10	1 Kevin	Black	Ops Manager	100000
11	10 Keith	Long	Ops Person	50000
12	10 Frank	Howard	Ops Person	45000
13	10 Doreen	Penn	Ops Person	47000

As you can see, it's difficult to pick out the employee relationships from this data. Figure 7-1 shows the relationships in a graphical form.

As you can see from Figure 7-1, the elements—or *nodes*—form a tree. Trees of nodes have the following technical terms associated with them:

- **Root node** The root is the node at the top of the tree. In the example shown in Figure 7-1, the root node is James Smith, the CEO.

- **Parent node** A parent is a node that has one or more nodes beneath it. For example, James Smith is the parent to the following nodes: Ron Johnson, Susan Jones, and Kevin Black.

- **Child node** A child is a node that has one parent node above it. For example, Ron Johnson's parent is James Smith.

- **Leaf node** A leaf is a node that has no children. For example, Fred Hobbs and Rob Green are leaf nodes.

You use the CONNECT BY and START WITH clauses of a SELECT statement to perform hierarchical queries, as described next.

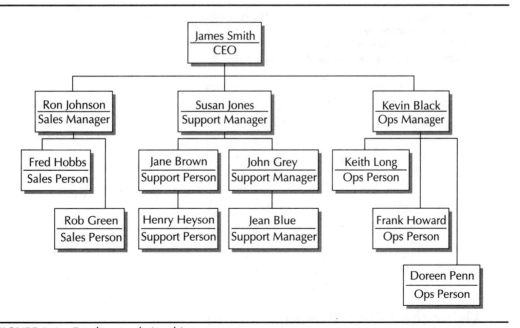

FIGURE 7-1 *Employee relationships*

Using the CONNECT BY and START WITH Clauses

The syntax for the CONNECT BY and START WITH clauses of a SELECT statement is

```
SELECT [LEVEL], column, expression, ...
FROM table
[WHERE where_clause]
[[START WITH start_condition] [CONNECT BY PRIOR prior_condition]];
```

where

- LEVEL is a pseudo column that tells you how far into a tree you are. LEVEL returns 1 for a root node, 2 for a child of the root, and so on.

- *start_condition* specifies where to start the hierarchical query. You must specify a START WITH clause when writing a hierarchical query. An example *start_condition* is employee_id = 1, which specifies the query starts from employee #1.

- *prior_condition* specifies the relationship between the parent and child rows. You must specify a CONNECT BY PRIOR clause when writing a hierarchical query. An example *prior_condition* is employee_id = manager_id, which specifies the relationship is between the parent employee_id and the child manager_id—that is, the child's manager_id points to the parent's employee_id.

The following query illustrates the use of the START WITH and CONNECT BY PRIOR clauses; notice that the first row contains the details of James Smith (employee #1), the second row contains the details of Ron Johnson, whose manager_id is 1, and so on:

```
SELECT employee_id, manager_id, first_name, last_name
FROM more_employees
START WITH employee_id = 1
CONNECT BY PRIOR employee_id = manager_id;
```

```
EMPLOYEE_ID MANAGER_ID FIRST_NAME LAST_NAME
----------- ---------- ---------- ---------
          1            James      Smith
          2          1 Ron        Johnson
          3          2 Fred       Hobbs
          5          2 Rob        Green
          4          1 Susan      Jones
          6          4 Jane       Brown
          9          6 Henry      Heyson
          7          4 John       Grey
          8          7 Jean       Blue
         10          1 Kevin      Black
         11         10 Keith      Long
         12         10 Frank      Howard
         13         10 Doreen     Penn
```

Using the LEVEL Pseudo Column

The next query illustrates the use of the LEVEL pseudo column to display the level in the tree:

```
SELECT LEVEL, employee_id, manager_id, first_name, last_name
FROM more_employees
START WITH employee_id = 1
CONNECT BY PRIOR employee_id = manager_id
ORDER BY LEVEL;
```

```
     LEVEL EMPLOYEE_ID MANAGER_ID FIRST_NAME LAST_NAME
---------- ----------- ---------- ---------- ---------
         1           1            James      Smith
         2           2          1 Ron        Johnson
         2           4          1 Susan      Jones
         2          10          1 Kevin      Black
         3           3          2 Fred       Hobbs
         3           7          4 John       Grey
         3          12         10 Frank      Howard
         3          13         10 Doreen     Penn
         3          11         10 Keith      Long
         3           5          2 Rob        Green
         3           6          4 Jane       Brown
         4           9          6 Henry      Heyson
         4           8          7 Jean       Blue
```

The next query uses the COUNT() function and LEVEL to get the number of levels in the tree:

```
SELECT COUNT(DISTINCT LEVEL)
FROM more_employees
START WITH employee_id = 1
CONNECT BY PRIOR employee_id = manager_id;
```

```
COUNT(DISTINCTLEVEL)
--------------------
                   4
```

Formatting the Results from a Hierarchical Query

You can format the results from a hierarchical query using LEVEL and the LPAD() function, which left-pads values with characters. The following query uses LPAD(' ', 2 * LEVEL - 1) to left-pad a total of 2 * LEVEL - 1 spaces; the result indents an employee's name with spaces based on their LEVEL (that is, LEVEL 1 isn't padded, LEVEL 2 is padded by two spaces, LEVEL 3 by four spaces, and so on):

```
SET PAGESIZE 999
COLUMN employee FORMAT A25
SELECT LEVEL,
  LPAD(' ', 2 * LEVEL - 1) || first_name || ' ' || last_name AS employee
FROM more_employees
START WITH employee_id = 1
CONNECT BY PRIOR employee_id = manager_id;
```

```
     LEVEL EMPLOYEE
---------- ------------------
         1 James Smith
         2   Ron Johnson
```

```
3        Fred Hobbs
3        Rob Green
2      Susan Jones
3        Jane Brown
4          Henry Heyson
3        John Grey
4          Jean Blue
2      Kevin Black
3        Keith Long
3        Frank Howard
3        Doreen Penn
```

The employee relationships are easy to pick out from these results.

Starting at a Node Other than the Root

You don't have to start at the root node when traversing a tree: you can start at any node using the START WITH clause. The following query starts with Susan Jones; notice that LEVEL returns 1 for Susan Jones, 2 for Jane Brown, and so on:

```sql
SELECT LEVEL,
  LPAD(' ', 2 * LEVEL - 1) || first_name || ' ' || last_name AS employee
FROM more_employees
START WITH last_name = 'Jones'
CONNECT BY PRIOR employee_id = manager_id;
```

```
    LEVEL EMPLOYEE
---------- -----------------
        1 Susan Jones
        2   Jane Brown
        3     Henry Heyson
        2   John Grey
        3     Jean Blue
```

If the store had more than one employee with the same name, you could simply use the employee_id in the query's START WITH clause. For example, the following query uses Susan Jones' employee_id of 4:

```sql
SELECT LEVEL,
  LPAD(' ', 2 * LEVEL - 1) || first_name || ' ' || last_name AS employee
FROM more_employees
START WITH employee_id = 4
CONNECT BY PRIOR employee_id = manager_id;
```

This query returns the same rows as the previous one.

Using a Subquery in a START WITH Clause

You can use a subquery in a START WITH clause. For example, the following query uses a subquery to select the employee_id whose name is Kevin Black; this employee_id is passed to the START WITH clause:

```sql
SELECT LEVEL,
  LPAD(' ', 2 * LEVEL - 1) || first_name || ' ' || last_name AS employee
```

```
FROM more_employees
START WITH employee_id = (
  SELECT employee_id
  FROM more_employees
  WHERE first_name = 'Kevin'
  AND last_name = 'Black'
)
CONNECT BY PRIOR employee_id = manager_id;

    LEVEL EMPLOYEE
---------- ---------------
         1  Kevin Black
         2    Keith Long
         2    Frank Howard
         2    Doreen Penn
```

Traversing Upward Through the Tree

You don't have to traverse a tree downward from parents to children: you can start at a child and traverse upward. You do this by switching child and parent columns in the CONNECT BY PRIOR clause. For example, CONNECT BY PRIOR manager_id = employee_id connects the child's manager_id to the parent's employee_id.

The following query starts with Jean Blue and traverses upward all the way to James Smith; notice that LEVEL returns 1 for Jean Blue, 2 for John Grey, and so on:

```
SELECT LEVEL,
  LPAD(' ', 2 * LEVEL - 1) || first_name || ' ' || last_name AS employee
FROM more_employees
START WITH last_name = 'Blue'
CONNECT BY PRIOR manager_id = employee_id;

    LEVEL EMPLOYEE
---------- -----------------
         1  Jean Blue
         2    John Grey
         3      Susan Jones
         4        James Smith
```

Eliminating Nodes and Branches from a Hierarchical Query

You can eliminate a particular node from a query tree using a WHERE clause. The following query eliminates Ron Johnson from the results using WHERE last_name != 'Johnson':

```
SELECT LEVEL,
  LPAD(' ', 2 * LEVEL - 1) || first_name || ' ' || last_name AS employee
FROM more_employees
WHERE last_name != 'Johnson'
START WITH employee_id = 1
CONNECT BY PRIOR employee_id = manager_id;

    LEVEL EMPLOYEE
---------- -----------------
         1 James Smith
         3     Fred Hobbs
```

```
3       Rob Green
2     Susan Jones
3       Jane Brown
4         Henry Heyson
3       John Grey
4         Jean Blue
2     Kevin Black
3       Keith Long
3       Frank Howard
3       Doreen Penn
```

You'll notice that although Ron Johnson is eliminated from the results, his employees Fred Hobbs and Rob Green are still included. To eliminate an entire branch of nodes from the results of a query, you add an AND clause to your CONNECT BY PRIOR clause. For example, the following query uses AND last_name != 'Johnson' to eliminate Ron Johnson and all his employees from the results:

```sql
SELECT LEVEL,
   LPAD(' ', 2 * LEVEL - 1) || first_name || ' ' || last_name AS employee
FROM more_employees
START WITH employee_id = 1
CONNECT BY PRIOR employee_id = manager_id
AND last_name != 'Johnson';
```

```
    LEVEL EMPLOYEE
---------- -------------------
        1  James Smith
        2    Susan Jones
        3      Jane Brown
        4        Henry Heyson
        3      John Grey
        4        Jean Blue
        2    Kevin Black
        3      Keith Long
        3      Frank Howard
        3      Doreen Penn
```

Including Other Conditions in a Hierarchical Query

You can include other conditions in a hierarchical query using a WHERE clause. The following example uses a WHERE clause to show only employees whose salaries are less than or equal to $50,000:

```sql
SELECT LEVEL,
   LPAD(' ', 2 * LEVEL - 1) || first_name || ' ' || last_name AS employee,
   salary
FROM more_employees
WHERE salary <= 50000
START WITH employee_id = 1
CONNECT BY PRIOR employee_id = manager_id;
```

LEVEL	EMPLOYEE	SALARY
3	Rob Green	40000
3	Jane Brown	45000
4	Henry Heyson	30000
3	John Grey	30000
4	Jean Blue	29000
3	Keith Long	50000
3	Frank Howard	45000
3	Doreen Penn	47000

This concludes the discussion of hierarchical queries. In the next section, you'll learn about advanced group clauses.

Using the Extended GROUP BY Clauses

In this section, you'll learn about

- ROLLUP, which extends the GROUP BY clause to return a row containing a subtotal for each group of rows, plus a row containing a grand total for all the groups.

- CUBE, which extends the GROUP BY clause to return rows containing a subtotal for all combinations of columns, plus a row containing the grand total.

First, let's look at the example tables used in this section.

The Example Tables

You'll see the use of the following tables that refine the representation of employees in our imaginary store:

- divisions, which stores the divisions within the company

- jobs, which stores the jobs within the company

- employees2, which stores the employees

These tables are created by the store_schema.sql script. The divisions table is created using the following statement:

```
CREATE TABLE divisions (
  division_id CHAR(3)
    CONSTRAINT divisions_pk PRIMARY KEY,
  name VARCHAR2(15) NOT NULL
);
```

The following query retrieves the rows from the divisions table:

```
SELECT *
FROM divisions;

DIV NAME
--- ----------
SAL Sales
```

```
OPE Operations
SUP Support
BUS Business
```

The `jobs` table is created using the following statement:

```
CREATE TABLE jobs (
  job_id CHAR(3)
    CONSTRAINT jobs_pk PRIMARY KEY,
  name VARCHAR2(20) NOT NULL
);
```

The next query retrieves the rows from the `jobs` table:

```
SELECT *
FROM jobs;

JOB NAME
--- ------------
WOR Worker
MGR Manager
ENG Engineer
TEC Technologist
PRE President
```

The `employees2` table is created using the following statement:

```
CREATE TABLE employees2 (
  employee_id INTEGER
    CONSTRAINT employees2_pk PRIMARY KEY,
  division_id CHAR(3)
    CONSTRAINT employees2_fk_divisions
    REFERENCES divisions(division_id),
  job_id CHAR(3) REFERENCES jobs(job_id),
  first_name VARCHAR2(10) NOT NULL,
  last_name VARCHAR2(10) NOT NULL,
  salary NUMBER(6, 0)
);
```

The following query retrieves the first five rows from the `employees2` table:

```
SELECT *
FROM employees2
WHERE ROWNUM <= 5;

EMPLOYEE_ID DIV JOB FIRST_NAME LAST_NAME    SALARY
----------- --- --- ---------- ---------- ----------
          1 BUS PRE James      Smith         800000
          2 SAL MGR Ron        Johnson       350000
          3 SAL WOR Fred       Hobbs         140000
          4 SUP MGR Susan      Jones         200000
          5 SAL WOR Rob        Green         350000
```

Using the ROLLUP Clause

The ROLLUP clause extends GROUP BY to return a row containing a subtotal for each group of rows, plus a row containing a total for all the groups.

As you saw in Chapter 4, you use GROUP BY to group rows into blocks with a common column value. For example, the following query uses GROUP BY to group the rows from the employees2 table by department_id and uses SUM() to get the sum of the salaries for each division_id:

```
SELECT division_id, SUM(salary)
FROM employees2
GROUP BY division_id
ORDER BY division_id;

DIV SUM(SALARY)
--- -----------
BUS     1610000
OPE     1320000
SAL     4936000
SUP     1015000
```

Passing a Single Column to ROLLUP

The following query rewrites the previous example to use ROLLUP; notice the additional row at the end, which contains the total salaries for all the groups:

```
SELECT division_id, SUM(salary)
FROM employees2
GROUP BY ROLLUP(division_id)
ORDER BY division_id;

DIV SUM(SALARY)
--- -----------
BUS     1610000
OPE     1320000
SAL     4936000
SUP     1015000
        8881000
```

NOTE
If you need the rows in a specific order, you should use an ORDER BY clause. You need to do this just in case Oracle Corporation decides to change the default order of rows returned by ROLLUP.

Passing Multiple Columns to ROLLUP

You can pass multiple columns to ROLLUP, which then groups the rows into blocks with the same column values. The following example passes the division_id and job_id columns of the employees2 table to ROLLUP, which groups the rows by those columns; in the output, notice that the salaries are summed by division_id and job_id, and that ROLLUP returns a row with the sum of the salaries in each `division_id`, plus a row at the end with the salary grand total:

```
SELECT division_id, job_id, SUM(salary)
FROM employees2
GROUP BY ROLLUP(division_id, job_id)
ORDER BY division_id, job_id;
```

```
DIV JOB SUM(SALARY)
--- --- -----------
BUS MGR      530000
BUS PRE      800000
BUS WOR      280000
BUS         1610000
OPE ENG      245000
OPE MGR      805000
OPE WOR      270000
OPE         1320000
SAL MGR     4446000
SAL WOR      490000
SAL         4936000
SUP MGR      465000
SUP TEC      115000
SUP WOR      435000
SUP         1015000
            8881000
```

Changing the Position of Columns Passed to ROLLUP

The next example switches `division_id` and `job_id`; this causes `ROLLUP` to calculate the sum of the salaries for each `job_id`:

```
SELECT job_id, division_id, SUM(salary)
FROM employees2
GROUP BY ROLLUP(job_id, division_id)
ORDER BY job_id, division_id;
```

```
JOB DIV SUM(SALARY)
--- --- -----------
ENG OPE      245000
ENG          245000
MGR BUS      530000
MGR OPE      805000
MGR SAL     4446000
MGR SUP      465000
MGR         6246000
PRE BUS      800000
PRE          800000
TEC SUP      115000
TEC          115000
WOR BUS      280000
WOR OPE      270000
```

```
WOR SAL     490000
WOR SUP     435000
WOR        1475000
           8881000
```

Using Other Aggregate Functions with ROLLUP

You can use any of the aggregate functions with ROLLUP (for a list of the main aggregate functions, see Table 4-8 in Chapter 4). The following example uses AVG() to calculate the average salaries:

```
SELECT division_id, job_id, AVG(salary)
FROM employees2
GROUP BY ROLLUP(division_id, job_id)
ORDER BY division_id, job_id;
```

```
DIV JOB AVG(SALARY)
--- --- -----------
BUS MGR  176666.667
BUS PRE     800000
BUS WOR     280000
BUS         322000
OPE ENG     245000
OPE MGR     201250
OPE WOR     135000
OPE      188571.429
SAL MGR  261529.412
SAL WOR     245000
SAL      259789.474
SUP MGR     232500
SUP TEC     115000
SUP WOR     145000
SUP      169166.667
         240027.027
```

Using the CUBE Clause

The CUBE clause extends GROUP BY to return rows containing a subtotal for all combinations of columns, plus a row containing the grand total. The following example passes division_id and job_id to CUBE, which groups the rows by those columns:

```
SELECT division_id, job_id, SUM(salary)
FROM employees2
GROUP BY CUBE(division_id, job_id)
ORDER BY division_id, job_id;
```

```
DIV JOB SUM(SALARY)
--- --- -----------
BUS MGR     530000
BUS PRE     800000
BUS WOR     280000
BUS        1610000
```

```
OPE  ENG      245000
OPE  MGR      805000
OPE  WOR      270000
OPE          1320000
SAL  MGR     4446000
SAL  WOR      490000
SAL          4936000
SUP  MGR      465000
SUP  TEC      115000
SUP  WOR      435000
SUP          1015000
     ENG      245000
     MGR     6246000
     PRE      800000
     TEC      115000
     WOR     1475000
             8881000
```

Notice that the salaries are summed by `division_id` and `job_id`. CUBE returns a row with the sum of the salaries for each `division_id`, along with the sum of all salaries for each `job_id` near the end. At the very end is a row with the grand total of the salaries.

The next example switches `division_id` and `job_id`:

```
SELECT job_id, division_id, SUM(salary)
FROM employees2
GROUP BY CUBE(job_id, division_id)
ORDER BY job_id, division_id;
```

```
JOB DIV SUM(SALARY)
--- --- -----------
ENG OPE      245000
ENG          245000
MGR BUS      530000
MGR OPE      805000
MGR SAL     4446000
MGR SUP      465000
MGR         6246000
PRE BUS      800000
PRE          800000
TEC SUP      115000
TEC          115000
WOR BUS      280000
WOR OPE      270000
WOR SAL      490000
WOR SUP      435000
WOR         1475000
    BUS     1610000
    OPE     1320000
    SAL     4936000
    SUP     1015000
            8881000
```

Using the GROUPING() Function

The GROUPING() function accepts a column and returns 0 or 1. GROUPING() returns 1 when the column value is null and returns 0 when the column value is non-null. GROUPING() is used only in queries that use ROLLUP or CUBE. GROUPING() is useful when you want to display a value when a null would otherwise be returned.

Using GROUPING() with a Single Column in a ROLLUP

As you saw earlier in the section "Passing a Single Column to ROLLUP," the last row in the example's result set contained a total of the salaries:

```
SELECT division_id, SUM(salary)
FROM employees2
GROUP BY ROLLUP(division_id)
ORDER BY division_id;
```

```
DIV SUM(SALARY)
--- -----------
BUS    1610000
OPE    1320000
SAL    4936000
SUP    1015000
       8881000
```

The division_id column for the last row is null. You can use the GROUPING() function to determine whether this column is null, as shown in the following query; notice GROUPING() returns 0 for the rows that have non-null division_id values and returns 1 for the last row that has a null division_id:

```
SELECT GROUPING(division_id), division_id, SUM(salary)
FROM employees2
GROUP BY ROLLUP(division_id)
ORDER BY division_id;
```

```
GROUPING(DIVISION_ID) DIV SUM(SALARY)
--------------------- --- -----------
                    0 BUS    1610000
                    0 OPE    1320000
                    0 SAL    4936000
                    0 SUP    1015000
                    1          8881000
```

Using CASE to Convert the Returned Value from GROUPING()

You can use the CASE expression to convert the 1 in the previous example to a meaningful value. The following example uses CASE to convert 1 to the string 'All divisions':

```
SELECT
   CASE GROUPING(division_id)
     WHEN 1 THEN 'All divisions'
     ELSE division_id
   END AS div,
   SUM(salary)
```

```
FROM employees2
GROUP BY ROLLUP(division_id)
ORDER BY division_id;


DIV             SUM(SALARY)
-------------   -----------
BUS                 1610000
OPE                 1320000
SAL                 4936000
SUP                 1015000
All divisions       8881000
```

Using CASE and GROUPING() to Convert Multiple Column Values

The next example extends the idea of replacing null values to a ROLLUP containing multiple columns (division_id and job_id); notice that null division_id values are replaced with the string 'All divisions' and that null job_id values are replaced with 'All jobs':

```
SELECT
    CASE GROUPING(division_id)
      WHEN 1 THEN 'All divisions'
      ELSE division_id
    END AS div,
    CASE GROUPING(job_id)
      WHEN 1 THEN 'All jobs'
      ELSE job_id
    END AS job,
    SUM(salary)
FROM employees2
GROUP BY ROLLUP(division_id, job_id)
ORDER BY division_id, job_id;


DIV             JOB        SUM(SALARY)
-------------   --------   -----------
BUS             MGR             530000
BUS             PRE             800000
BUS             WOR             280000
BUS             All jobs       1610000
OPE             ENG             245000
OPE             MGR             805000
OPE             WOR             270000
OPE             All jobs       1320000
SAL             MGR            4446000
SAL             WOR             490000
SAL             All jobs       4936000
SUP             MGR             465000
SUP             TEC             115000
SUP             WOR             435000
SUP             All jobs       1015000
All divisions   All jobs       8881000
```

Using GROUPING() with CUBE

You can use the GROUPING() function with CUBE, as in this example:

```
SELECT
  CASE GROUPING(division_id)
    WHEN 1 THEN 'All divisions'
    ELSE division_id
  END AS div,
  CASE GROUPING(job_id)
    WHEN 1 THEN 'All jobs'
    ELSE job_id
  END AS job,
  SUM(salary)
FROM employees2
GROUP BY CUBE(division_id, job_id)
ORDER BY division_id, job_id;
```

```
DIV             JOB        SUM(SALARY)
--------------- --------   -----------
BUS             MGR             530000
BUS             PRE             800000
BUS             WOR             280000
BUS             All jobs       1610000
OPE             ENG             245000
OPE             MGR             805000
OPE             WOR             270000
OPE             All jobs       1320000
SAL             MGR            4446000
SAL             WOR             490000
SAL             All jobs       4936000
SUP             MGR             465000
SUP             TEC             115000
SUP             WOR             435000
SUP             All jobs       1015000
All divisions   ENG             245000
All divisions   MGR            6246000
All divisions   PRE             800000
All divisions   TEC             115000
All divisions   WOR            1475000
All divisions   All jobs       8881000
```

Using the GROUPING SETS Clause

You use the GROUPING SETS clause to get just the subtotal rows. The following example uses GROUPING SETS to get the subtotals for salaries by division_id and job_id:

```
SELECT division_id, job_id, SUM(salary)
FROM employees2
GROUP BY GROUPING SETS(division_id, job_id)
ORDER BY division_id, job_id;
```

```
DIV JOB SUM(SALARY)
--- --- -----------
BUS     1610000
OPE     1320000
```

```
SAL         4936000
SUP         1015000
     ENG     245000
     MGR    6246000
     PRE     800000
     TEC     115000
     WOR    1475000
```

Notice that only subtotals for the `division_id` and `job_id` columns are returned; the total for all salaries is not returned. You'll see how to get the total as well as the subtotals using the `GROUPING_ID()` function in the next section.

TIP
The `GROUPING SETS` *clause typically offers better performance than* `CUBE`. *Therefore, you should use* `GROUPING SETS` *rather than* `CUBE` *wherever possible.*

Using the GROUPING_ID() Function

You can use the `GROUPING_ID()` function to filter rows using a `HAVING` clause to exclude rows that don't contain a subtotal or total. The `GROUPING_ID()` function accepts one or more columns and returns the decimal equivalent of the `GROUPING` bit vector. The `GROUPING` bit vector is computed by combining the results of a call to the `GROUPING()` function for each column in order.

Computing the GROUPING Bit Vector

Earlier in the section "Using the GROUPING() Function," you saw that `GROUPING()` returns 1 when the column value is null and returns 0 when the column value is non-null; for example:

- If both `division_id` and `job_id` are non-null, `GROUPING()` returns 0 for both columns. The result for `division_id` is combined with the result for `job_id`, giving a bit vector of 00, whose decimal equivalent is 0. `GROUPING_ID()` therefore returns 0 when `division_id` and `job_id` are non-null.

- If `division_id` is non-null (the `GROUPING` bit is 0), but `job_id` is null (the `GROUPING` bit is 1), the resulting bit vector is 01 and `GROUPING_ID()` returns 1.

- If `division_id` is null (the `GROUPING` bit is 1), but `job_id` is non-null (the `GROUPING` bit is 0), the resulting bit vector is 10 and `GROUPING_ID()` returns 2.

- If both `division_id` and `job_id` are null (both `GROUPING` bits are 0), the bit vector is 11 and `GROUPING_ID()` returns 3.

The following table summarizes these results.

division_id	job_id	Bit Vector	GROUPING_ID() Return Value
non-null	non-null	00	0
non-null	null	01	1
null	non-null	10	2
null	null	11	3

An Example Query That Illustrates the Use of GROUPING_ID()

The following example passes `division_id` and `job_id` to `GROUPING_ID()`; notice that the output from the `GROUPING_ID()` function agrees with the expected returned values documented in the previous section:

```sql
SELECT
  division_id, job_id,
  GROUPING(division_id) AS DIV_GRP,
  GROUPING(job_id) AS JOB_GRP,
  GROUPING_ID(division_id, job_id) AS grp_id,
  SUM(salary)
FROM employees2
GROUP BY CUBE(division_id, job_id)
ORDER BY division_id, job_id;
```

DIV	JOB	DIV_GRP	JOB_GRP	GRP_ID	SUM(SALARY)
BUS	MGR	0	0	0	530000
BUS	PRE	0	0	0	800000
BUS	WOR	0	0	0	280000
BUS		0	1	1	1610000
OPE	ENG	0	0	0	245000
OPE	MGR	0	0	0	805000
OPE	WOR	0	0	0	270000
OPE		0	1	1	1320000
SAL	MGR	0	0	0	4446000
SAL	WOR	0	0	0	490000
SAL		0	1	1	4936000
SUP	MGR	0	0	0	465000
SUP	TEC	0	0	0	115000
SUP	WOR	0	0	0	435000
SUP		0	1	1	1015000
	ENG	1	0	2	245000
	MGR	1	0	2	6246000
	PRE	1	0	2	800000
	TEC	1	0	2	115000
	WOR	1	0	2	1475000
		1	1	3	8881000

A Useful Application of GROUPING_ID()

One useful application of `GROUPING_ID()` is to filter rows using a `HAVING` clause. The `HAVING` clause can exclude rows that don't contain a subtotal or total by simply checking if `GROUPING_ID()` returns a value greater than 0. For example:

```sql
SELECT
  division_id, job_id,
  GROUPING_ID(division_id, job_id) AS grp_id,
  SUM(salary)
FROM employees2
GROUP BY CUBE(division_id, job_id)
```

```
HAVING GROUPING_ID(division_id, job_id) > 0
ORDER BY division_id, job_id;
```

```
DIV JOB     GRP_ID SUM(SALARY)
--- ---  ---------- -----------
BUS             1     1610000
OPE             1     1320000
SAL             1     4936000
SUP             1     1015000
    ENG         2      245000
    MGR         2     6246000
    PRE         2      800000
    TEC         2      115000
    WOR         2     1475000
                3     8881000
```

Using a Column Multiple Times in a GROUP BY Clause

You can use a column many times in a GROUP BY clause. Doing this allows you to reorganize
your data or report on different groupings of data. For example, the following query contains a
GROUP BY clause that uses division_id twice, once to group by division_id and again
in a ROLLUP:

```
SELECT division_id, job_id, SUM(salary)
FROM employees2
GROUP BY division_id, ROLLUP(division_id, job_id);
```

```
DIV JOB SUM(SALARY)
--- --- -----------
BUS MGR    530000
BUS PRE    800000
BUS WOR    280000
OPE ENG    245000
OPE MGR    805000
OPE WOR    270000
SAL MGR   4446000
SAL WOR    490000
SUP MGR    465000
SUP TEC    115000
SUP WOR    435000
BUS       1610000
OPE       1320000
SAL       4936000
SUP       1015000
BUS       1610000
OPE       1320000
SAL       4936000
SUP       1015000
```

Notice, however, that the last four rows are duplicates of the previous four rows. You can
eliminate these duplicates using the GROUP_ID() function, which you'll learn about next.

Using the GROUP_ID() Function

You can use the GROUP_ID() function to remove duplicate rows returned by a GROUP BY clause. GROUP_ID() doesn't accept any parameters. If *n* duplicates exist for a particular grouping, GROUP_ID returns numbers in the range 0 to *n* – 1.

The following example rewrites the query shown in the previous section to include the output from GROUP_ID(); notice that GROUP_ID() returns 0 for all rows except the last four, which are duplicates of the previous four rows, and that GROUP_ID() returns 1:

```
SELECT division_id, job_id, GROUP_ID(), SUM(salary)
FROM employees2
GROUP BY division_id, ROLLUP(division_id, job_id);
```

```
DIV JOB GROUP_ID() SUM(SALARY)
--- --- ---------- -----------
BUS MGR          0      530000
BUS PRE          0      800000
BUS WOR          0      280000
OPE ENG          0      245000
OPE MGR          0      805000
OPE WOR          0      270000
SAL MGR          0     4446000
SAL WOR          0      490000
SUP MGR          0      465000
SUP TEC          0      115000
SUP WOR          0      435000
BUS              0     1610000
OPE              0     1320000
SAL              0     4936000
SUP              0     1015000
BUS              1     1610000
OPE              1     1320000
SAL              1     4936000
SUP              1     1015000
```

You can eliminate duplicate rows using a HAVING clause that allows only rows whose GROUP_ID() is 0; for example:

```
SELECT division_id, job_id, GROUP_ID(), SUM(salary)
FROM employees2
GROUP BY division_id, ROLLUP(division_id, job_id)
HAVING GROUP_ID() = 0;
```

```
DIV JOB GROUP_ID() SUM(SALARY)
--- --- ---------- -----------
BUS MGR          0      530000
BUS PRE          0      800000
BUS WOR          0      280000
OPE ENG          0      245000
OPE MGR          0      805000
OPE WOR          0      270000
```

```
SAL MGR          0      4446000
SAL WOR          0       490000
SUP MGR          0       465000
SUP TEC          0       115000
SUP WOR          0       435000
BUS              0      1610000
OPE              0      1320000
SAL              0      4936000
SUP              0      1015000
```

This concludes the discussion of the extended GROUP BY clauses.

Using the Analytic Functions

The database has many built-in analytic functions that enable you to perform complex calculations, such as finding the top-selling product type for each month, the top salespersons, and so on. The analytic functions are organized into the following categories:

- **Ranking functions** enable you to calculate ranks, percentiles, and *n*-tiles (tertiles, quartiles, and so on).

- **Inverse percentile functions** enable you to calculate the value that corresponds to a percentile.

- **Window functions** enable you to calculate cumulative and moving aggregates.

- **Reporting functions** enable you to calculate things like market share.

- **Lag and lead functions** enable you to get a value in a row where that row is a certain number of rows away from the current row.

- **First and last functions** enable you to get the first and last values in an ordered group.

- **Linear regression functions** enable you to fit an ordinary-least-squares regression line to a set of number pairs.

- **Hypothetical rank and distribution functions** enable you to calculate the rank and percentile that a new row would have if you inserted it into a table.

You'll learn about these functions shortly, but first let's examine the example table used next.

The Example Table

You'll see the use of the all_sales table in the following sections. The all_sales table stores the sum of all the sales by dollar amount for a particular year, month, product type, and employee. The all_sales table is created by the store_schema.sql script as follows:

```
CREATE TABLE all_sales (
  year INTEGER NOT NULL,
  month INTEGER NOT NULL,
  prd_type_id INTEGER
    CONSTRAINT all_sales_fk_product_types
    REFERENCES product_types(product_type_id),
  emp_id INTEGER
```

```
  CONSTRAINT all_sales_fk_employees2
  REFERENCES employees2(employee_id),
amount NUMBER(8, 2),
CONSTRAINT all_sales_pk PRIMARY KEY (
  year, month, prd_type_id, emp_id
)
);
```

As you can see, the `all_sales` table contains five columns, which are as follows:

- **YEAR** stores the year the sales took place.

- **MONTH** stores the month the sales took place (1 to 12).

- **PRD_TYPE_ID** stores the `product_type_id` of the product.

- **EMP_ID** stores the `employee_id` of the employee who handled the sales.

- **AMOUNT** stores the total dollar amount of the sales.

The following query retrieves the first 12 rows from the `all_sales` table:

```
SELECT *
FROM all_sales
WHERE ROWNUM <= 12;
```

```
    YEAR      MONTH PRD_TYPE_ID     EMP_ID      AMOUNT
---------- ---------- ----------- ---------- ----------
    2003          1           1         21    10034.84
    2003          2           1         21    15144.65
    2003          3           1         21    20137.83
    2003          4           1         21    25057.45
    2003          5           1         21    17214.56
    2003          6           1         21    15564.64
    2003          7           1         21    12654.84
    2003          8           1         21    17434.82
    2003          9           1         21    19854.57
    2003         10           1         21    21754.19
    2003         11           1         21    13029.73
    2003         12           1         21    10034.84
```

NOTE
The `all_sales` *table actually contains a lot more rows than this, but for space considerations I've omitted listing them all here.*

Let's examine the ranking functions next.

Using the Ranking Functions

You use the ranking functions to calculate ranks, percentiles, and *n*-tiles. The ranking functions are shown in Table 7-2.

Let's examine the `RANK()` and `DENSE_RANK()` functions first.

Function	Description
RANK()	Returns the rank of items in a group. RANK() leaves a gap in the sequence of rankings in the event of a tie.
DENSE_RANK()	Returns the rank of items in a group. DENSE_RANK() doesn't leave a gap in the sequence of rankings in the event of a tie.
CUME_DIST()	Returns the position of a specified value relative to a group of values. CUME_DIST() is short for cumulative distribution.
PERCENT_RANK()	Returns the percent rank of a value relative to a group of values.
NTILE()	Returns *n*-tiles: tertiles, quartiles, and so on.
ROW_NUMBER()	Returns a number with each row in a group.

TABLE 7-2   *The Ranking Functions*

Using the RANK() and DENSE_RANK() Functions

You use RANK() and DENSE_RANK() to rank items in a group. The difference between these two functions is in the way they handle items that tie: RANK() leaves a gap in the sequence when there is a tie, but DENSE_RANK() leaves no gaps. For example, if you were ranking sales by product type and two product types tie for first place, RANK() would put the two product types in first place, but the next product type would be in third place. DENSE_RANK() would also put the two product types in first place, but the next product type would be in second place.

The following query illustrates the use of RANK() and DENSE_RANK() to get the ranking of sales by product type for the year 2003; notice the use of the keyword OVER in the syntax when calling the RANK() and DENSE_RANK() functions:

```
SELECT
    prd_type_id, SUM(amount),
    RANK() OVER (ORDER BY SUM(amount) DESC) AS rank,
    DENSE_RANK() OVER (ORDER BY SUM(amount) DESC) AS dense_rank
FROM all_sales
WHERE year = 2003
AND amount IS NOT NULL
GROUP BY prd_type_id
ORDER BY prd_type_id;
```

```
PRD_TYPE_ID SUM(AMOUNT)      RANK DENSE_RANK
----------- -----------  ---------- ----------
          1   905081.84           1          1
          2   186381.22           4          4
          3   478270.91           2          2
          4   402751.16           3          3
```

Notice that sales for product type #1 are ranked first, sales for product type #2 are ranked fourth, and so on. Because there are no ties, RANK() and DENSE_RANK() return the same ranks.

The `all_sales` table actually contains nulls in the AMOUNT column for all rows whose PRD_TYPE_ID column is 5; the previous query omits these rows because of the inclusion of the line "AND amount IS NOT NULL" in the WHERE clause. The next example includes these rows by leaving out the AND line from the WHERE clause:

```
SELECT
  prd_type_id, SUM(amount),
  RANK() OVER (ORDER BY SUM(amount) DESC) AS rank,
  DENSE_RANK() OVER (ORDER BY SUM(amount) DESC) AS dense_rank
FROM all_sales
WHERE year = 2003
GROUP BY prd_type_id
ORDER BY prd_type_id;
```

PRD_TYPE_ID	SUM(AMOUNT)	RANK	DENSE_RANK
1	905081.84	2	2
2	186381.22	5	5
3	478270.91	3	3
4	402751.16	4	4
5		1	1

Notice that the last row contains null for the sum of the AMOUNT column and that RANK() and DENSE_RANK() return 1 for this row. This is because by default RANK() and DENSE_RANK() assign the highest rank of 1 to null values in descending rankings (that is, DESC is used in the OVER clause) and the lowest rank in ascending rankings (that is, ASC is used in the OVER clause).

Controlling Ranking of Null Values Using the NULLS FIRST and NULLS LAST Clauses   When using an analytic function, you can explicitly control whether nulls are the highest or lowest in a group using NULLS FIRST or NULLS LAST. The following example uses NULLS LAST to specify that nulls are the lowest:

```
SELECT
  prd_type_id, SUM(amount),
  RANK() OVER (ORDER BY SUM(amount) DESC NULLS LAST) AS rank,
  DENSE_RANK() OVER (ORDER BY SUM(amount) DESC NULLS LAST) AS dense_rank
FROM all_sales
WHERE year = 2003
GROUP BY prd_type_id
ORDER BY prd_type_id;
```

PRD_TYPE_ID	SUM(AMOUNT)	RANK	DENSE_RANK
1	905081.84	1	1
2	186381.22	4	4
3	478270.91	2	2
4	402751.16	3	3
5		5	5

Using the PARTITION BY Clause with Analytic Functions   You use the PARTITION BY clause with the analytic functions when you need to divide the groups into subgroups. For example, if you need to subdivide the sales amount by month, you can use PARTITION BY month, as shown in the following query:

```
SELECT
  prd_type_id, month, SUM(amount),
  RANK() OVER (PARTITION BY month ORDER BY SUM(amount) DESC) AS rank
FROM all_sales
WHERE year = 2003
AND amount IS NOT NULL
GROUP BY prd_type_id, month
ORDER BY prd_type_id, month;
```

PRD_TYPE_ID	MONTH	SUM(AMOUNT)	RANK
1	1	38909.04	1
1	2	70567.9	1
1	3	91826.98	1
1	4	120344.7	1
1	5	97287.36	1
1	6	57387.84	1
1	7	60929.04	2
1	8	75608.92	1
1	9	85027.42	1
1	10	105305.22	1
1	11	55678.38	1
1	12	46209.04	2
2	1	14309.04	4
2	2	13367.9	4
2	3	16826.98	4
2	4	15664.7	4
2	5	18287.36	4
2	6	14587.84	4
2	7	15689.04	3
2	8	16308.92	4
2	9	19127.42	4
2	10	13525.14	4
2	11	16177.84	4
2	12	12509.04	4
3	1	24909.04	2
3	2	15467.9	3
3	3	20626.98	3
3	4	23844.7	2
3	5	18687.36	3
3	6	19887.84	3
3	7	81589.04	1
3	8	62408.92	2
3	9	46127.42	3
3	10	70325.29	3
3	11	46187.38	2
3	12	48209.04	1

```
4        1      17398.43        3
4        2      17267.9         2
4        3      31026.98        2
4        4      16144.7         3
4        5      20087.36        2
4        6      33087.84        2
4        7      12089.04        4
4        8      58408.92        3
4        9      49327.42        2
4       10      75325.14        2
4       11      42178.38        3
4       12      30409.05        3
```

Using ROLLUP, CUBE, and GROUPING SETS Operators with Analytic Functions   You can use the
ROLLUP, CUBE, and GROUPING SETS operators with the analytic functions. The following query
uses ROLLUP and RANK() to get the sales rankings by product type ID:

```
SELECT
    prd_type_id, SUM(amount),
    RANK() OVER (ORDER BY SUM(amount) DESC) AS rank
FROM all_sales
WHERE year = 2003
GROUP BY ROLLUP(prd_type_id)
ORDER BY prd_type_id;
```

```
PRD_TYPE_ID SUM(AMOUNT)       RANK
----------- -----------  ----------
          1    905081.84          3
          2    186381.22          6
          3    478270.91          4
          4    402751.16          5
          5                       1
               1972485.13         2
```

The next query uses CUBE and RANK() to get all rankings of sales by product type ID and
employee ID:

```
SELECT
    prd_type_id, emp_id, SUM(amount),
    RANK() OVER (ORDER BY SUM(amount) DESC) AS rank
FROM all_sales
WHERE year = 2003
GROUP BY CUBE(prd_type_id, emp_id)
ORDER BY prd_type_id, emp_id;
```

```
PRD_TYPE_ID     EMP_ID SUM(AMOUNT)       RANK
----------- ----------  ----------- ----------
          1         21   197916.96          19
          1         22   214216.96          17
          1         23    98896.96          26
          1         24   207216.96          18
          1         25    93416.96          28
          1         26    93417.04          27
```

1		905081.84	9
2	21	20426.96	40
2	22	19826.96	41
2	23	19726.96	42
2	24	43866.96	34
2	25	32266.96	38
2	26	50266.42	31
2		186381.22	21
3	21	140326.96	22
3	22	116826.96	23
3	23	112026.96	24
3	24	34829.96	36
3	25	29129.96	39
3	26	45130.11	33
3		478270.91	10
4	21	108326.96	25
4	22	81426.96	30
4	23	92426.96	29
4	24	47456.96	32
4	25	33156.96	37
4	26	39956.36	35
4		402751.16	13
5	21		1
5	22		1
5	23		1
5	24		1
5	25		1
5	26		1
5			1
	21	466997.84	11
	22	432297.84	12
	23	323077.84	15
	24	333370.84	14
	25	187970.84	20
	26	228769.93	16
		1972485.13	8

The next query uses GROUPING SETS and RANK() to get just the sales amount subtotal rankings:

```
SELECT
    prd_type_id, emp_id, SUM(amount),
    RANK() OVER (ORDER BY SUM(amount) DESC) AS rank
FROM all_sales
WHERE year = 2003
GROUP BY GROUPING SETS(prd_type_id, emp_id)
ORDER BY prd_type_id, emp_id;
```

PRD_TYPE_ID	EMP_ID	SUM(AMOUNT)	RANK
1		905081.84	2
2		186381.22	11

3	478270.91	3
4	402751.16	6
5		1
21	466997.84	4
22	432297.84	5
23	323077.84	8
24	333370.84	7
25	187970.84	10
26	228769.93	9

Using the CUME_DIST() and PERCENT_RANK() Functions

You use CUME_DIST() to calculate the position of a specified value relative to a group of values; CUME_DIST() is short for cumulative distribution. You use PERCENT_RANK() to calculate the percent rank of a value relative to a group of values.

The following query illustrates the use of CUME_DIST() and PERCENT_RANK() to get the cumulative distribution and percent rank of sales:

```
SELECT
  prd_type_id, SUM(amount),
  CUME_DIST() OVER (ORDER BY SUM(amount) DESC) AS cume_dist,
  PERCENT_RANK() OVER (ORDER BY SUM(amount) DESC) AS percent_rank
FROM all_sales
WHERE year = 2003
GROUP BY prd_type_id
ORDER BY prd_type_id;
```

PRD_TYPE_ID	SUM(AMOUNT)	CUME_DIST	PERCENT_RANK
1	905081.84	.4	.25
2	186381.22	1	1
3	478270.91	.6	.5
4	402751.16	.8	.75
5		.2	0

Using the NTILE() Function

You use NTILE(*buckets*) to calculate *n*-tiles (tertiles, quartiles, and so on); *buckets* specifies the number of "buckets" into which groups of rows are placed. For example, NTILE(2) specifies two buckets and therefore divides the rows into two groups of rows; NTILE(4) divides the groups into four buckets and therefore divides the rows into four groups.

The following query illustrates the use of NTILE(); notice that 4 is passed to NTILE() to split the groups of rows into four buckets:

```
SELECT
  prd_type_id, SUM(amount),
  NTILE(4) OVER (ORDER BY SUM(amount) DESC) AS ntile
FROM all_sales
WHERE year = 2003
AND amount IS NOT NULL
GROUP BY prd_type_id
ORDER BY prd_type_id;
```

```
PRD_TYPE_ID SUM(AMOUNT)       NTILE
----------- ----------- ----------
          1   905081.84          1
          2   186381.22          4
          3   478270.91          2
          4   402751.16          3
```

Using the ROW_NUMBER() Function

You use ROW_NUMBER() to return a number with each row in a group, starting at 1. The following query illustrates the use of ROW_NUMBER():

```
SELECT
  prd_type_id, SUM(amount),
  ROW_NUMBER() OVER (ORDER BY SUM(amount) DESC) AS row_number
FROM all_sales
WHERE year = 2003
GROUP BY prd_type_id
ORDER BY prd_type_id;
```

```
PRD_TYPE_ID SUM(AMOUNT) ROW_NUMBER
----------- ----------- ----------
          1   905081.84          2
          2   186381.22          5
          3   478270.91          3
          4   402751.16          4
          5                      1
```

This concludes the discussion of ranking functions.

Using the Inverse Percentile Functions

In the section "Using the CUME_DIST() and PERCENT_RANK() Functions," you saw that CUME_DIST() is used to calculate the position of a specified value relative to a group of values. You also saw that PERCENT_RANK() is used to calculate the percent rank of a value relative to a group of values.

In this section, you'll see how to use the inverse percentile functions to get the value that corresponds to a percentile. There are two inverse percentile functions: PERCENTILE_DISC(x) and PERCENTILE_CONT(x). They operate in a manner the reverse of CUME_DIST() and PERCENT_RANK(). PERCENTILE_DISC(x) examines the cumulative distribution values in each group until it finds one that is greater than or equal to x. PERCENTILE_CONT(x) examines the percent rank values in each group until it finds one that is greater than or equal to x.

The following query illustrates the use of PERCENTILE_CONT() and PERCENTILE_DISC() to get the sum of the amount whose percentile is greater than or equal to 0.6:

```
SELECT
  PERCENTILE_CONT(0.6) WITHIN GROUP (ORDER BY SUM(amount) DESC)
    AS percentile_cont,
  PERCENTILE_DISC(0.6) WITHIN GROUP (ORDER BY SUM(amount) DESC)
    AS percentile_disc
FROM all_sales
WHERE year = 2003
GROUP BY prd_type_id;
```

```
PERCENTILE_CONT PERCENTILE_DISC
--------------- ---------------
      417855.11        402751.16
```

If you compare the sum of the amounts shown in these results with those shown in the earlier section "Using the CUME_DIST() and PERCENT_RANK() Functions," you'll see that the sums correspond to those whose cumulative distribution and percent rank are 0.6 and 0.75, respectively.

Using the Window Functions

You use the window functions to calculate things like cumulative sums and moving averages within a specified range of rows, a range of values, or an interval of time. As you know, a query returns a set of rows known as the result set. The term "window" is used to describe a subset of rows within the result set. The subset of rows "seen" through the window is then processed by the window functions, which return a value. You can define the start and end of the window.

You can use a window with the following functions: SUM(), AVG(), MAX(), MIN(), COUNT(), VARIANCE(), and STDDEV(); you saw these functions in Chapter 4. You can also use a window with FIRST_VALUE() and LAST_VALUE(), which return the first and last values in a window. (You'll learn more about the FIRST_VALUE() and LAST_VALUE() functions later in the section "Getting the First and Last Rows Using FIRST_VALUE() and LAST_VALUE().")

In the next section, you'll see how to perform a cumulative sum, a moving average, and a centered average.

Performing a Cumulative Sum

The following query performs a cumulative sum to compute the cumulative sales amount for 2003, starting with January and ending in December; notice that each monthly sales amount is added to the cumulative amount that grows after each month:

```
SELECT
   month, SUM(amount) AS month_amount,
   SUM(SUM(amount)) OVER
     (ORDER BY month ROWS BETWEEN UNBOUNDED PRECEDING AND CURRENT ROW)
     AS cumulative_amount
FROM all_sales
WHERE year = 2003
GROUP BY month
ORDER BY month;

     MONTH MONTH_AMOUNT CUMULATIVE_AMOUNT
---------- ------------ -----------------
         1     95525.55          95525.55
         2     116671.6         212197.15
         3    160307.92         372505.07
         4     175998.8         548503.87
         5    154349.44         702853.31
         6    124951.36         827804.67
         7    170296.16         998100.83
         8    212735.68        1210836.51
         9    199609.68        1410446.19
        10    264480.79        1674926.98
        11    160221.98        1835148.96
        12    137336.17        1972485.13
```

This query uses the following expression to compute the cumulative aggregate:

```
SUM(SUM(amount)) OVER
  (ORDER BY month ROWS BETWEEN UNBOUNDED PRECEDING AND CURRENT ROW)
  AS cumulative_amount
```

Let's break down this expression:

- `SUM(amount)` computes the sum of an amount. The outer `SUM()` computes the cumulative amount.

- `ORDER BY month` orders the rows read by the query by month.

- `ROWS BETWEEN UNBOUNDED PRECEDING AND CURRENT ROW` defines the start and end of the window. The start is set to `UNBOUNDED PRECEDING`, which means the start of the window is fixed at the first row in the result set returned by the query. The end of the window is set to `CURRENT ROW`; `CURRENT ROW` represents the current row in the result set being processed, and the end of the window slides down one row after the outer `SUM()` function computes and returns the current cumulative amount.

The entire query computes and returns the cumulative total of the sales amounts, starting at month 1, and then adding the sales amount for month 2, then month 3, and so on, up to and including month 12. The start of the window is fixed at month 1, but the bottom of the window moves down one row in the result set after each month's sales amounts are added to the cumulative total. This continues until the last row in the result set is processed by the window and the `SUM()` functions.

Don't confuse the end of the window with the end of the result set. In the previous example, the end of the window slides down one row in the result set as each row is processed (i.e., the sum of the sales amount for that month is added to the cumulative total). In the example, the end of the window starts at the first row, the sum sales amount for that month is added to the cumulative total, and then the end of the window moves down one row to the second row. At this point, the window sees two rows. The sum of the sales amount for that month is added to the cumulative total, and the end of the window moves down one row to the third row. At this point, the window sees three rows. This continues until the twelfth row is processed. At this point, the window sees twelve rows.

The following query uses a cumulative sum to compute the cumulative sales amount, starting with June of 2003 (month 6) and ending in December of 2003 (month 12):

```
SELECT
  month, SUM(amount) AS month_amount,
  SUM(SUM(amount)) OVER
    (ORDER BY month ROWS BETWEEN UNBOUNDED PRECEDING AND CURRENT ROW) AS
    cumulative_amount
FROM all_sales
WHERE year = 2003
AND month BETWEEN 6 AND 12
GROUP BY month
ORDER BY month;

     MONTH MONTH_AMOUNT CUMULATIVE_AMOUNT
---------- ------------ -----------------
         6    124951.36         124951.36
         7    170296.16         295247.52
```

8	212735.68	507983.2
9	199609.68	707592.88
10	264480.79	972073.67
11	160221.98	1132295.65
12	137336.17	1269631.82

Performing a Moving Average

The following query computes the moving average of the sales amount between the current month and the previous three months:

```
SELECT
  month, SUM(amount) AS month_amount,
  AVG(SUM(amount)) OVER
    (ORDER BY month ROWS BETWEEN 3 PRECEDING AND CURRENT ROW)
    AS moving_average
FROM all_sales
WHERE year = 2003
GROUP BY month
ORDER BY month;
```

MONTH	MONTH_AMOUNT	MOVING_AVERAGE
1	95525.55	95525.55
2	116671.6	106098.575
3	160307.92	124168.357
4	175998.8	137125.968
5	154349.44	151831.94
6	124951.36	153901.88
7	170296.16	156398.94
8	212735.68	165583.16
9	199609.68	176898.22
10	264480.79	211780.578
11	160221.98	209262.033
12	137336.17	190412.155

Notice that the query uses the following expression to compute the moving average:

```
AVG(SUM(amount)) OVER
  (ORDER BY month ROWS BETWEEN 3 PRECEDING AND CURRENT ROW)
  AS moving_average
```

Let's break down this expression:

- SUM(amount) computes the sum of an amount. The outer AVG() computes the average.

- ORDER BY month orders the rows read by the query by month.

- ROWS BETWEEN 3 PRECEDING AND CURRENT ROW defines the start of the window as including the three rows preceding the current row; the end of the window is the current row being processed.

So, the entire expression computes the moving average of the sales amount between the current month and the previous three months. Because for the first two months less than the full three months of data are available, the moving average is based on only the months available.

Both the start and the end of the window begin at row #1 read by the query. The end of the window moves down after each row is processed. The start of the window moves down only after row #4 has been processed, and subsequently moves down one row after each row is processed. This continues until the last row in the result set is read.

Performing a Centered Average

The following query computes the moving average of the sales amount centered between the previous and next month from the current month:

```
SELECT
    month, SUM(amount) AS month_amount,
    AVG(SUM(amount)) OVER
      (ORDER BY month ROWS BETWEEN 1 PRECEDING AND 1 FOLLOWING)
      AS moving_average
FROM all_sales
WHERE year = 2003
GROUP BY month
ORDER BY month;
```

```
    MONTH MONTH_AMOUNT MOVING_AVERAGE
---------- ------------ --------------
        1     95525.55     106098.575
        2     116671.6     124168.357
        3    160307.92     150992.773
        4     175998.8     163552.053
        5    154349.44     151766.533
        6    124951.36     149865.653
        7    170296.16     169327.733
        8    212735.68      194213.84
        9    199609.68     225608.717
       10    264480.79      208104.15
       11    160221.98     187346.313
       12    137336.17     148779.075
```

Notice that the query uses the following expression to compute the moving average:

```
AVG(SUM(amount)) OVER
  (ORDER BY month ROWS BETWEEN 1 PRECEDING AND 1 FOLLOWING)
  AS moving_average
```

Let's break down this expression:

- `SUM(amount)` computes the sum of an amount. The outer `AVG()` computes the average.

- `ORDER BY month` orders the rows read by the query by month.

- `ROWS BETWEEN 1 PRECEDING AND 1 FOLLOWING` defines the start of the window as including the row preceding the current row being processed. The end of the window is the row following the current row.

So, the entire expression computes the moving average of the sales amount between the current month and the previous month. Because for the first and last month less than the full three months of data are available, the moving average is based on only the months available.

The start of the window begins at row #1 read by the query. The end of the window begins at row #2 and moves down after each row is processed. The start of the window moves down only once row #2 has been processed. Processing continues until the last row read by the query is processed.

Getting the First and Last Rows Using FIRST_VALUE() and LAST_VALUE()

You use the FIRST_VALUE() and LAST_VALUE() functions to get the first and last rows in a window. The following query uses FIRST_VALUE() and LAST_VALUE() to get the previous and next month's sales amount:

```
SELECT
  month, SUM(amount) AS month_amount,
  FIRST_VALUE(SUM(amount)) OVER
    (ORDER BY month ROWS BETWEEN 1 PRECEDING AND 1 FOLLOWING)
    AS previous_month_amount,
  LAST_VALUE(SUM(amount)) OVER
    (ORDER BY month ROWS BETWEEN 1 PRECEDING AND 1 FOLLOWING)
    AS next_month_amount
FROM all_sales
WHERE year = 2003
GROUP BY month
ORDER BY month;
```

MONTH	MONTH_AMOUNT	PREVIOUS_MONTH_AMOUNT	NEXT_MONTH_AMOUNT
1	95525.55	95525.55	116671.6
2	116671.6	95525.55	160307.92
3	160307.92	116671.6	175998.8
4	175998.8	160307.92	154349.44
5	154349.44	175998.8	124951.36
6	124951.36	154349.44	170296.16
7	170296.16	124951.36	212735.68
8	212735.68	170296.16	199609.68
9	199609.68	212735.68	264480.79
10	264480.79	199609.68	160221.98
11	160221.98	264480.79	137336.17
12	137336.17	160221.98	137336.17

The next query divides the current month's sales amount by the previous month's sales amount (labeled as curr_div_prev) and also divides the current month's sales amount by the next month's sales amount (labeled as curr_div_next):

```
SELECT
  month, SUM(amount) AS month_amount,
  SUM(amount)/FIRST_VALUE(SUM(amount)) OVER
    (ORDER BY month ROWS BETWEEN 1 PRECEDING AND 1 FOLLOWING)
    AS curr_div_prev,
  SUM(amount)/LAST_VALUE(SUM(amount)) OVER
    (ORDER BY month ROWS BETWEEN 1 PRECEDING AND 1 FOLLOWING)
    AS curr_div_next
FROM all_sales
WHERE year = 2003
```

```
GROUP BY month
ORDER BY month;
```

```
    MONTH MONTH_AMOUNT CURR_DIV_PREV CURR_DIV_NEXT
---------- ------------ ------------- -------------
        1     95525.55             1    .818755807
        2     116671.6    1.22136538    .727796855
        3    160307.92    1.37400978    .910846665
        4     175998.8    1.09787963    1.14026199
        5    154349.44    .876991434    1.23527619
        6    124951.36    .809535558    .733729756
        7    170296.16    1.36289961    .800505867
        8    212735.68    1.24921008    1.06575833
        9    199609.68     .93829902    .754722791
       10    264480.79     1.3249898    1.65071478
       11    160221.98    .605798175    1.16664081
       12    137336.17    .857161858             1
```

This concludes the discussion of window functions.

Using the Reporting Functions

You use the reporting functions to perform calculations across groups and partitions within groups.

You can perform reporting with the following functions: SUM(), AVG(), MAX(), MIN(), COUNT(), VARIANCE(), and STDDEV(). You can also use the RATIO_TO_REPORT() function to compute the ratio of a value to the sum of a set of values.

In this section, you'll see how to perform a report on a sum and use the RATIO_TO_REPORT() function.

Reporting on a Sum

For the first three months of 2003, the following query reports

- The total sum of all sales for all three months (labeled as total_month_amount).

- The total sum of all sales for all product types (labeled as total_product_type_amount).

```sql
SELECT
  month, prd_type_id,
  SUM(SUM(amount)) OVER (PARTITION BY month)
    AS total_month_amount,
  SUM(SUM(amount)) OVER (PARTITION BY prd_type_id)
    AS total_product_type_amount
FROM all_sales
WHERE year = 2003
AND month <= 3
GROUP BY month, prd_type_id
ORDER BY month, prd_type_id;
```

```
    MONTH PRD_TYPE_ID TOTAL_MONTH_AMOUNT TOTAL_PRODUCT_TYPE_AMOUNT
---------- ----------- ------------------ -------------------------
        1           1           95525.55                 201303.92
        1           2           95525.55                  44503.92
```

1	3	95525.55	61003.92
1	4	95525.55	65693.31
1	5	95525.55	
2	1	116671.6	201303.92
2	2	116671.6	44503.92
2	3	116671.6	61003.92
2	4	116671.6	65693.31
2	5	116671.6	
3	1	160307.92	201303.92
3	2	160307.92	44503.92
3	3	160307.92	61003.92
3	4	160307.92	65693.31
3	5	160307.92	

Notice that the query uses the following expression to report the total sum of all sales for all months (labeled as `total_month_amount`):

```
SUM(SUM(amount)) OVER (PARTITION BY month)
  AS total_month_amount
```

Let's break down this expression:

- `SUM(amount)` computes the sum of an amount. The outer `SUM()` computes the total sum.

- `OVER (PARTITION BY month)` causes the outer `SUM()` to compute the sum for each month.

The previous query also uses the following expression to report the total sum of all sales for all product types (labeled as `total_product_type_amount`):

```
SUM(SUM(amount)) OVER (PARTITION BY prd_type_id)
  AS total_product_type_amount
```

Let's break down this expression:

- `SUM(amount)` computes the sum of an amount. The outer `SUM()` computes the total sum.

- `OVER (PARTITION BY prd_type_id)` causes the outer `SUM()` to compute the sum for each product type.

Using the RATIO_TO_REPORT() Function

You use the `RATIO_TO_REPORT()` function to compute the ratio of a value to the sum of a set of values.

For the first three months of 2003, the following query reports

- The sum of the sales amount by product type for each month (labeled as `prd_type_amount`).

- The ratio of the product type's sales amount to the entire month's sales (labeled as `prd_type_ratio`), which is computed using `RATIO_TO_REPORT()`.

```
SELECT
  month, prd_type_id,
  SUM(amount) AS prd_type_amount,
  RATIO_TO_REPORT(SUM(amount)) OVER (PARTITION BY month) AS prd_type_ratio
```

```
FROM all_sales
WHERE year = 2003
AND month <= 3
GROUP BY month, prd_type_id
ORDER BY month, prd_type_id;
```

```
     MONTH PRD_TYPE_ID PRD_TYPE_AMOUNT PRD_TYPE_RATIO
---------- ----------- --------------- --------------
         1           1        38909.04      .40731553
         1           2        14309.04     .149792804
         1           3        24909.04     .260757881
         1           4        17398.43     .182133785
         1           5
         2           1         70567.9     .604842138
         2           2         13367.9     .114577155
         2           3         15467.9     .132576394
         2           4         17267.9     .148004313
         2           5
         3           1        91826.98      .57281624
         3           2        16826.98     .104966617
         3           3        20626.98     .128670998
         3           4        31026.98     .193546145
         3           5
```

Notice that the query uses the following expression to compute the ratio (labeled as prd_type_ratio):

```
RATIO_TO_REPORT(SUM(amount)) OVER (PARTITION BY month) AS prd_type_ratio
```

Let's break down this expression:

- SUM(amount) computes the sum of the sales amount.

- OVER (PARTITION BY month) causes the outer SUM() to compute the sum of the sales amount for each month.

- The ratio is computed by dividing the sum of the sales amount for each product type by the sum of the entire month's sales amount.

This concludes the discussion of reporting functions.

Using the LAG() and LEAD() Functions

You use the LAG() and LEAD() functions to get a value in a row where that row is a certain number of rows away from the current row. The following query uses LAG() and LEAD() to get the previous and next month's sales amount:

```
SELECT
  month, SUM(amount) AS month_amount,
  LAG(SUM(amount), 1) OVER (ORDER BY month) AS previous_month_amount,
  LEAD(SUM(amount), 1) OVER (ORDER BY month) AS next_month_amount
FROM all_sales
WHERE year = 2003
```

```
GROUP BY month
ORDER BY month;
```

MONTH	MONTH_AMOUNT	PREVIOUS_MONTH_AMOUNT	NEXT_MONTH_AMOUNT
1	95525.55		116671.6
2	116671.6	95525.55	160307.92
3	160307.92	116671.6	175998.8
4	175998.8	160307.92	154349.44
5	154349.44	175998.8	124951.36
6	124951.36	154349.44	170296.16
7	170296.16	124951.36	212735.68
8	212735.68	170296.16	199609.68
9	199609.68	212735.68	264480.79
10	264480.79	199609.68	160221.98
11	160221.98	264480.79	137336.17
12	137336.17	160221.98	

Notice that the query uses the following expressions to get the previous and next month's sales:

```
LAG(SUM(amount), 1) OVER (ORDER BY month) AS previous_month_amount,
LEAD(SUM(amount), 1) OVER (ORDER BY month) AS next_month_amount
```

`LAG(SUM(amount), 1)` gets the previous row's sum of the amount. `LEAD(SUM(amount), 1)` gets the next row's sum of the amount.

Using the FIRST and LAST Functions

You use the `FIRST` and `LAST` functions to get the first and last values in an ordered group. You can use `FIRST` and `LAST` with the following functions: `MIN()`, `MAX()`, `COUNT()`, `SUM()`, `AVG()`, `STDDEV()`, and `VARIANCE()`.

The following query uses `FIRST` and `LAST` to get the months in 2003 that had the highest and lowest sales:

```
SELECT
  MIN(month) KEEP (DENSE_RANK FIRST ORDER BY SUM(amount))
    AS highest_sales_month,
  MIN(month) KEEP (DENSE_RANK LAST ORDER BY SUM(amount))
    AS lowest_sales_month
FROM all_sales
WHERE year = 2003
GROUP BY month
ORDER BY month;

HIGHEST_SALES_MONTH LOWEST_SALES_MONTH
------------------- ------------------
                  1                 10
```

Using the Linear Regression Functions

You use the linear regression functions to fit an ordinary-least-squares regression line to a set of number pairs. You can use the linear regression functions as aggregate, windowing, or reporting functions. The following table shows the linear regression functions. In the function syntax, y is interpreted by the functions as a variable that depends on x.

Function	Description
REGR_AVGX(*y*, *x*)	Returns the average of x after eliminating x and y pairs where either x or y is null
REGR_AVGY(*y*, *x*)	Returns the average of y after eliminating x and y pairs where either x or y is null
REGR_COUNT(*y*, *x*)	Returns the number of non-null number pairs that are used to fit the regression line
REGR_INTERCEPT(*y*, *x*)	Returns the intercept on the y-axis of the regression line
REGR_R2(*y*, *x*)	Returns the coefficient of determination (R-squared) of the regression line
REGR_SLOPE(*y*, *x*)	Returns the slope of the regression line
REGR_SXX(*y*, *x*)	Returns REG_COUNT (*y*, *x*) * VAR_POP(*x*)
REGR_SXY(*y*, *x*)	Returns REG_COUNT (*y*, *x*) * COVAR_POP(*y*, *x*)
REGR_SYY(*y*, *x*)	Returns REG_COUNT (*y*, *x*) * VAR_POP (*y*)

The following query shows the use of the linear regression functions:

```
SELECT
  prd_type_id,
  REGR_AVGX(amount, month) AS avgx,
  REGR_AVGY(amount, month) AS avgy,
  REGR_COUNT(amount, month) AS count,
  REGR_INTERCEPT(amount, month) AS inter,
  REGR_R2(amount, month) AS r2,
  REGR_SLOPE(amount, month) AS slope,
  REGR_SXX(amount, month) AS sxx,
  REGR_SXY(amount, month) AS sxy,
  REGR_SYY(amount, month) AS syy
FROM all_sales
WHERE year = 2003
GROUP BY prd_type_id;
```

```
PRD_TYPE_ID      AVGX        AVGY        COUNT       INTER         R2
-----------  ----------  ----------  ----------  ----------  ----------
     SLOPE       SXX         SXY         SYY
-----------  ----------  ----------  ----------

          1       6.5  12570.5811           72  13318.4543  .003746289
 -115.05741       858  -98719.26  3031902717

          2       6.5  2588.62806           72  2608.11268     .0000508
  -2.997634       858   -2571.97   151767392

          3       6.5  6642.65153           72  2154.23119  .126338815
```

```
690.526206            858 592471.485 3238253324

       4            6.5 5593.76611        72 2043.47164 .128930297
546.199149            858   468638.87 1985337488

       5                                   0
```

Using the Hypothetical Rank and Distribution Functions

You use the hypothetical rank and distribution functions to calculate the rank and percentile that a new row would have if you inserted it into a table. You can perform hypothetical calculations with the following functions: RANK(), DENSE_RANK(), PERCENT_RANK(), and CUME_DIST().

An example of a hypothetical function will be given after the following query, which uses RANK() and PERCENT_RANK() to get the rank and percent rank of sales by product type for 2003:

```
SELECT
  prd_type_id, SUM(amount),
  RANK() OVER (ORDER BY SUM(amount) DESC) AS rank,
  PERCENT_RANK() OVER (ORDER BY SUM(amount) DESC) AS percent_rank
FROM all_sales
WHERE year = 2003
AND amount IS NOT NULL
GROUP BY prd_type_id
ORDER BY prd_type_id;
```

```
PRD_TYPE_ID SUM(AMOUNT)       RANK PERCENT_RANK
----------- -----------  ---------- ------------
          1   905081.84           1            0
          2   186381.22           4            1
          3   478270.91           2  .333333333
          4   402751.16           3  .666666667
```

The next query shows the hypothetical rank and percent rank of a sales amount of $500,000:

```
SELECT
  RANK(500000) WITHIN GROUP (ORDER BY SUM(amount) DESC)
    AS rank,
  PERCENT_RANK(500000) WITHIN GROUP (ORDER BY SUM(amount) DESC)
    AS percent_rank
FROM all_sales
WHERE year = 2003
AND amount IS NOT NULL
GROUP BY prd_type_id
ORDER BY prd_type_id;
```

```
      RANK PERCENT_RANK
---------- ------------
         2         .25
```

As you can see, the hypothetical rank and percent rank of a sales amount of $500,000 are 2 and .25.

This concludes the discussion of hypothetical functions.

Using the MODEL Clause

The MODEL clause was introduced with Oracle Database 10*g* and enables you to perform inter-row calculations. The MODEL clause allows you to access a column in a row like a cell in an array. This gives you the ability to perform calculations in a similar manner to spreadsheet calculations. For example, the all_sales table contains sales information for the months in 2003. You can use the MODEL clause to calculate sales in future months based on sales in 2003.

An Example of the MODEL Clause

The easiest way to learn how to use the MODEL clause is to see an example. The following query retrieves the sales amount for each month in 2003 made by employee #21 for product types #1 and #2 and computes the predicted sales for January, February, and March of 2004 based on sales in 2003:

```
SELECT prd_type_id, year, month, sales_amount
FROM all_sales
WHERE prd_type_id BETWEEN 1 AND 2
AND emp_id = 21
MODEL
PARTITION BY (prd_type_id)
DIMENSION BY (month, year)
MEASURES (amount sales_amount) (
  sales_amount[1, 2004] = sales_amount[1, 2003],
  sales_amount[2, 2004] = sales_amount[2, 2003] + sales_amount[3, 2003],
  sales_amount[3, 2004] = ROUND(sales_amount[3, 2003] * 1.25, 2)
)
ORDER BY prd_type_id, year, month;
```

Let's break down this query:

- PARTITION BY (prd_type_id) specifies that the results are partitioned by prd_type_id.

- DIMENSION BY (month, year) specifies that the dimensions of the array are month and year. This means that a cell in the array is accessed by specifying a month and year.

- MEASURES (amount sales_amount) specifies that each cell in the array contains an amount and that the array name is sales_amount. To access the cell in the sales_amount array for January 2003, you use sales_amount[1, 2003], which returns the sales amount for that month and year.

- After MEASURES come three lines that compute the future sales for January, February, and March of 2004:

  - sales_amount[1, 2004] = sales_amount[1, 2003] sets the sales amount for January 2004 to the amount for January 2003.

  - sales_amount[2, 2004] = sales_amount[2, 2003] + sales_amount[3, 2003] sets the sales amount for February 2004 to the amount for February 2003 plus March 2003.

- `sales_amount[3, 2004] = ROUND(sales_amount[3, 2003] * 1.25,
2)` sets the sales amount for March 2004 to the rounded value of the sales amount for March 2003 multiplied by 1.25.

- `ORDER BY prd_type_id, year, month` simply orders the results returned by the entire query.

The output from the query is shown in the following listing; notice that the results contain the sales amounts for all months in 2003 for product types #1 and #2, plus the predicted sales amounts for the first three months in 2004 (which I've made bold to make them stand out):

PRD_TYPE_ID	YEAR	MONTH	SALES_AMOUNT
1	2003	1	10034.84
1	2003	2	15144.65
1	2003	3	20137.83
1	2003	4	25057.45
1	2003	5	17214.56
1	2003	6	15564.64
1	2003	7	12654.84
1	2003	8	17434.82
1	2003	9	19854.57
1	2003	10	21754.19
1	2003	11	13029.73
1	2003	12	10034.84
1	**2004**	**1**	**10034.84**
1	**2004**	**2**	**35282.48**
1	**2004**	**3**	**25172.29**
2	2003	1	1034.84
2	2003	2	1544.65
2	2003	3	2037.83
2	2003	4	2557.45
2	2003	5	1714.56
2	2003	6	1564.64
2	2003	7	1264.84
2	2003	8	1734.82
2	2003	9	1854.57
2	2003	10	2754.19
2	2003	11	1329.73
2	2003	12	1034.84
2	**2004**	**1**	**1034.84**
2	**2004**	**2**	**3582.48**
2	**2004**	**3**	**2547.29**

Using Positional and Symbolic Notation to Access Cells

In the previous example, you saw how to access a cell in an array using the following notation: `sales_amount[1, 2004]`, where 1 is the month and 2004 is the year. This is referred to as positional notation because the meaning of the dimensions is determined by their position: the first position contains the month and the second position contains the year.

You can also use symbolic notation to explicitly indicate the meaning of the dimensions, as in, for example, `sales_amount[month=1, year=2004]`. The following query rewrites the previous query to use symbolic notation:

```
SELECT prd_type_id, year, month, sales_amount
FROM all_sales
WHERE prd_type_id BETWEEN 1 AND 2
AND emp_id = 21
MODEL
PARTITION BY (prd_type_id)
DIMENSION BY (month, year)
MEASURES (amount sales_amount) (
  sales_amount[month=1, year=2004] = sales_amount[month=1, year=2003],
  sales_amount[month=2, year=2004] =
    sales_amount[month=2, year=2003] + sales_amount[month=3, year=2003],
  sales_amount[month=3, year=2004] =
    ROUND(sales_amount[month=3, year=2003] * 1.25, 2)
)
ORDER BY prd_type_id, year, month;
```

When using positional or symbolic notation, it is important to be aware of the different way they handle null values in the dimensions. For example, `sales_amount[null, 2003]` returns the amount whose month is null and year is 2003, but `sales_amount[month=null, year=2004]` won't access a valid cell because `null=null` always returns false.

Accessing a Range of Cells Using BETWEEN and AND

You can access a range of cells using the `BETWEEN` and `AND` keywords. For example, the following expression sets the sales amount for January 2004 to the rounded average of the sales between January and March of 2003:

```
sales_amount[1, 2004] =
  ROUND(AVG(sales_amount)[month BETWEEN 1 AND 3, 2003], 2)
```

The following query shows the use of this expression:

```
SELECT prd_type_id, year, month, sales_amount
FROM all_sales
WHERE prd_type_id BETWEEN 1 AND 2
AND emp_id = 21
MODEL
PARTITION BY (prd_type_id)
DIMENSION BY (month, year)
MEASURES (amount sales_amount) (
  sales_amount[1, 2004] =
    ROUND(AVG(sales_amount)[month BETWEEN 1 AND 3, 2003], 2)
)
ORDER BY prd_type_id, year, month;
```

Accessing All Cells Using ANY and IS ANY

You can access all cells in an array using the `ANY` and `IS ANY` predicates. You use `ANY` with positional notation and `IS ANY` with symbolic notation. For example, the following expression sets the sales amount for January 2004 to the rounded sum of the sales for all months and years:

```
sales_amount[1, 2004] =
    ROUND(SUM(sales_amount)[ANY, year IS ANY], 2)
```

The following query shows the use of this expression:

```
SELECT prd_type_id, year, month, sales_amount
FROM all_sales
WHERE prd_type_id BETWEEN 1 AND 2
AND emp_id = 21
MODEL
PARTITION BY (prd_type_id)
DIMENSION BY (month, year)
MEASURES (amount sales_amount) (
  sales_amount[1, 2004] =
    ROUND(SUM(sales_amount)[ANY, year IS ANY], 2)
)
ORDER BY prd_type_id, year, month;
```

Getting the Current Value of a Dimension Using CURRENTV()

You can get the current value of a dimension using the CURRENTV() function. For example, the following expression sets the sales amount for the first month of 2004 to 1.25 times the sales of the same month in 2003; notice the use of CURRENTV() to get the current month, which is 1:

```
sales_amount[1, 2004] =
    ROUND(sales_amount[CURRENTV(), 2003] * 1.25, 2)
```

The following query shows the use of this expression:

```
SELECT prd_type_id, year, month, sales_amount
FROM all_sales
WHERE prd_type_id BETWEEN 1 AND 2
AND emp_id = 21
MODEL
PARTITION BY (prd_type_id)
DIMENSION BY (month, year)
MEASURES (amount sales_amount) (
  sales_amount[1, 2004] =
    ROUND(sales_amount[CURRENTV(), 2003] * 1.25, 2)
)
ORDER BY prd_type_id, year, month;
```

The output from this query is as follows (I've highlighted the values for 2004 in bold):

```
PRD_TYPE_ID      YEAR      MONTH SALES_AMOUNT
----------- ---------- ---------- ------------
          1       2003          1     10034.84
          1       2003          2     15144.65
          1       2003          3     20137.83
          1       2003          4     25057.45
          1       2003          5     17214.56
          1       2003          6     15564.64
          1       2003          7     12654.84
```

1	2003	8	17434.82
1	2003	9	19854.57
1	2003	10	21754.19
1	2003	11	13029.73
1	2003	12	10034.84
1	**2004**	**1**	**12543.55**
2	2003	1	1034.84
2	2003	2	1544.65
2	2003	3	2037.83
2	2003	4	2557.45
2	2003	5	1714.56
2	2003	6	1564.64
2	2003	7	1264.84
2	2003	8	1734.82
2	2003	9	1854.57
2	2003	10	2754.19
2	2003	11	1329.73
2	2003	12	1034.84
2	**2004**	**1**	**1293.55**

Accessing Cells Using a FOR Loop

You can access cells using a FOR loop. For example, the following expression sets the sales amount for the first three months of 2004 to 1.25 times the sales of the same months in 2003; notice the use of the FOR loop and the INCREMENT keyword that specifies the amount to increment month by during each iteration of the loop:

```
sales_amount[FOR month FROM 1 TO 3 INCREMENT 1, 2004] =
  ROUND(sales_amount[CURRENTV(), 2003] * 1.25, 2)
```

The following query shows the use of this expression:

```
SELECT prd_type_id, year, month, sales_amount
FROM all_sales
WHERE prd_type_id BETWEEN 1 AND 2
AND emp_id = 21
MODEL
PARTITION BY (prd_type_id)
DIMENSION BY (month, year)
MEASURES (amount sales_amount) (
  sales_amount[FOR month FROM 1 TO 3 INCREMENT 1, 2004] =
    ROUND(sales_amount[CURRENTV(), 2003] * 1.25, 2)
)
ORDER BY prd_type_id, year, month;
```

The output from this query is as follows (I've highlighted the values for 2004 in bold):

PRD_TYPE_ID	YEAR	MONTH	SALES_AMOUNT
1	2003	1	10034.84
1	2003	2	15144.65
1	2003	3	20137.83
1	2003	4	25057.45

1	2003	5	17214.56
1	2003	6	15564.64
1	2003	7	12654.84
1	2003	8	17434.82
1	2003	9	19854.57
1	2003	10	21754.19
1	2003	11	13029.73
1	2003	12	10034.84
1	**2004**	**1**	**12543.55**
1	**2004**	**2**	**18930.81**
1	**2004**	**3**	**25172.29**
2	2003	1	1034.84
2	2003	2	1544.65
2	2003	3	2037.83
2	2003	4	2557.45
2	2003	5	1714.56
2	2003	6	1564.64
2	2003	7	1264.84
2	2003	8	1734.82
2	2003	9	1854.57
2	2003	10	2754.19
2	2003	11	1329.73
2	2003	12	1034.84
2	**2004**	**1**	**1293.55**
2	**2004**	**2**	**1930.81**
2	**2004**	**3**	**2547.29**

Handling Null and Missing Values

In this section, you'll learn how to handle null and missing values using the MODEL clause.

Using IS PRESENT

IS PRESENT returns true if the row specified by the cell reference existed prior to the execution of the MODEL clause. For example:

```
sales_amount[CURRENTV(), 2003] IS PRESENT
```

will return true if sales_amount[CURRENTV(), 2003] exists.

The following expression sets the sales amount for the first three months of 2004 to 1.25 multiplied by the sales of the same months in 2003:

```
sales_amount[FOR month FROM 1 TO 3 INCREMENT 1, 2004] =
  CASE WHEN sales_amount[CURRENTV(), 2003] IS PRESENT THEN
    ROUND(sales_amount[CURRENTV(), 2003] * 1.25, 2)
  ELSE
    0
  END
```

The following query shows the use of this expression:

```
SELECT prd_type_id, year, month, sales_amount
FROM all_sales
WHERE prd_type_id BETWEEN 1 AND 2
```

```
AND emp_id = 21
MODEL
PARTITION BY (prd_type_id)
DIMENSION BY (month, year)
MEASURES (amount sales_amount) (
  sales_amount[FOR month FROM 1 TO 3 INCREMENT 1, 2004] =
    CASE WHEN sales_amount[CURRENTV(), 2003] IS PRESENT THEN
      ROUND(sales_amount[CURRENTV(), 2003] * 1.25, 2)
    ELSE
      0
    END
)
ORDER BY prd_type_id, year, month;
```

The output of this query is the same as the example in the previous section.

Using PRESENTV()

PRESENTV(*cell*, *expr1*, *expr2*) returns the expression *expr1* if the row specified by the *cell* reference existed prior to the execution of the MODEL clause. If the row doesn't exist, the expression *expr2* is returned. For example:

```
PRESENTV(sales_amount[CURRENTV(), 2003],
  ROUND(sales_amount[CURRENTV(), 2003] * 1.25, 2), 0)
```

will return the rounded sales amount if sales_amount[CURRENTV(), 2003] exists; otherwise 0 will be returned.

The following query shows the use of this expression:

```
SELECT prd_type_id, year, month, sales_amount
FROM all_sales
WHERE prd_type_id BETWEEN 1 AND 2
AND emp_id = 21
MODEL
PARTITION BY (prd_type_id)
DIMENSION BY (month, year)
MEASURES (amount sales_amount) (
  sales_amount[FOR month FROM 1 TO 3 INCREMENT 1, 2004] =
    PRESENTV(sales_amount[CURRENTV(), 2003],
      ROUND(sales_amount[CURRENTV(), 2003] * 1.25, 2), 0)
)
ORDER BY prd_type_id, year, month;
```

Using PRESENTNNV()

PRESENTNNV(*cell*, *expr1*, *expr2*) returns the expression *expr1* if the row specified by the *cell* reference existed prior to the execution of the MODEL clause and the cell value is not null. If the row doesn't exist or the cell value is null, the expression *expr2* is returned. For example,

```
PRESENTNNV(sales_amount[CURRENTV(), 2003],
  ROUND(sales_amount[CURRENTV(), 2003] * 1.25, 2), 0)
```

will return the rounded sales amount if `sales_amount[CURRENTV(), 2003]` exists and is not null; otherwise 0 will be returned.

Using IGNORE NAV and KEEP NAV

`IGNORE NAV` returns

- 0 for null or missing numeric values.

- An empty string for null or missing string values.

- 01-JAN-2000 for null or missing date values.

- Null for all other database types.

`KEEP NAV` returns null for null or missing numeric values. Be aware that `KEEP NAV` is the default.

The following query shows the use of `IGNORE NAV`:

```
SELECT prd_type_id, year, month, sales_amount
FROM all_sales
WHERE prd_type_id BETWEEN 1 AND 2
AND emp_id = 21
MODEL IGNORE NAV
PARTITION BY (prd_type_id)
DIMENSION BY (month, year)
MEASURES (amount sales_amount) (
  sales_amount[FOR month FROM 1 TO 3 INCREMENT 1, 2004] =
    ROUND(sales_amount[CURRENTV(), 2003] * 1.25, 2)
)
ORDER BY prd_type_id, year, month;
```

Updating Existing Cells

By default, if the cell referenced on the left side of an expression exists, then it is updated. If the cell doesn't exist, then a new row in the array is created. You can change this default behavior using `RULES UPDATE`, which specifies that if the cell doesn't exist, a new row will not be created.

The following query shows the use of `RULES UPDATE`:

```
SELECT prd_type_id, year, month, sales_amount
FROM all_sales
WHERE prd_type_id BETWEEN 1 AND 2
AND emp_id = 21
MODEL
PARTITION BY (prd_type_id)
DIMENSION BY (month, year)
MEASURES (amount sales_amount)
RULES UPDATE (
  sales_amount[FOR month FROM 1 TO 3 INCREMENT 1, 2004] =
    ROUND(sales_amount[CURRENTV(), 2003] * 1.25, 2)
)
ORDER BY prd_type_id, year, month;
```

Because cells for 2004 don't exist and RULES UPDATE is used, no new rows are created in the array for 2004; therefore, the query doesn't return rows for 2004. The following listing shows the output for the query—notice there are no rows for 2004:

```
PRD_TYPE_ID       YEAR      MONTH SALES_AMOUNT
----------- ---------- ---------- ------------
          1       2003          1     10034.84
          1       2003          2     15144.65
          1       2003          3     20137.83
          1       2003          4     25057.45
          1       2003          5     17214.56
          1       2003          6     15564.64
          1       2003          7     12654.84
          1       2003          8     17434.82
          1       2003          9     19854.57
          1       2003         10     21754.19
          1       2003         11     13029.73
          1       2003         12     10034.84
          2       2003          1      1034.84
          2       2003          2      1544.65
          2       2003          3      2037.83
          2       2003          4      2557.45
          2       2003          5      1714.56
          2       2003          6      1564.64
          2       2003          7      1264.84
          2       2003          8      1734.82
          2       2003          9      1854.57
          2       2003         10      2754.19
          2       2003         11      1329.73
          2       2003         12      1034.84
```

Using the PIVOT and UNPIVOT Clauses

The PIVOT clause is new for Oracle Database 11*g* and enables you to rotate rows into columns in the output from a query, and, at the same time, to run an aggregation function on the data. Oracle Database 11*g* also has an UNPIVOT clause that rotates columns into rows in the output from a query.

PIVOT and UNPIVOT are useful to see overall trends in large amounts of data, such as trends in sales over a period of time. You'll see queries that show the use of PIVOT and UNPIVOT in the following sections.

A Simple Example of the PIVOT Clause

The easiest way to learn how to use the PIVOT clause is to see an example. The following query shows the total sales amount of product types #1, #2, and #3 for the first four months in 2003; notice that the cells in the query's output show the sum of the sales amounts for each product type in each month:

```
SELECT *
FROM (
  SELECT month, prd_type_id, amount
  FROM all_sales
  WHERE year = 2003
  AND prd_type_id IN (1, 2, 3)
)
PIVOT (
  SUM(amount) FOR month IN (1 AS JAN, 2 AS FEB, 3 AS MAR, 4 AS APR)
)
ORDER BY prd_type_id;

PRD_TYPE_ID        JAN         FEB         MAR         APR
----------- ----------- ----------- ----------- -----------
          1    38909.04     70567.9    91826.98   120344.7
          2    14309.04     13367.9    16826.98    15664.7
          3    24909.04     15467.9    20626.98    23844.7
```

Starting with the first line of output, you can see there was

- $38,909.04 of product type #1 sold in January.

- $70,567.90 of product type #1 sold in February.

- ...and so on for the rest of the first line.

The second line of output shows there was

- $14,309.04 of product type #2 sold in January.

- $13,367.90 of product type #2 sold in February.

- ...and so on for the rest of the output.

NOTE
PIVOT is a powerful tool that allows you to see trends in sales of types of products over a period of months. Based on such trends, a real store could use the information to alter their sales tactics and formulate new marketing campaigns.

The previous SELECT statement has the following structure:

```
SELECT *
FROM (
  inner_query
)
PIVOT (
  aggregate_function FOR pivot_column IN (list_of_values)
)
ORDER BY ...;
```

Let's break down the previous example into the structural elements:

- There is an inner and outer query. The inner query gets the month, product type, and amount from the `all_sales` table and passes the results to the outer query.

- `SUM(amount) FOR month IN (1 AS JAN, 2 AS FEB, 3 AS MAR, 4 AS APR)` is the line in the `PIVOT` clause.

  - The `SUM()` function adds up the sales amounts for the product types in the first four months (the months are listed in the `IN` part). Instead of returning the months as 1, 2, 3, and 4 in the output, the `AS` part renames the numbers to `JAN`, `FEB`, `MAR`, and `APR` to make the months more readable in the output.

  - The `month` column from the `all_sales` table is used as the pivot column. This means that the months appear as columns in the output. In effect, the rows are rotated—or *pivoted*—to view the months as columns.

- At the very end of the example, the `ORDER BY prd_type_id` line simply orders the results by the product type.

Pivoting on Multiple Columns

You can pivot on multiple columns by placing those columns in the `FOR` part of the `PIVOT`. The following example pivots on both the `month` and `prd_type_id` columns, which are referenced in the `FOR` part; notice that the list of values in the `IN` part of the `PIVOT` contains a value for the `month` and `prd_type_id` columns:

```
SELECT *
FROM (
  SELECT month, prd_type_id, amount
  FROM all_sales
  WHERE year = 2003
  AND prd_type_id IN (1, 2, 3)
)
PIVOT (
  SUM(amount) FOR (month, prd_type_id) IN (
    (1, 2) AS JAN_PRDTYPE2,
    (2, 3) AS FEB_PRDTYPE3,
    (3, 1) AS MAR_PRDTYPE1,
    (4, 2) AS APR_PRDTYPE2
  )
);


JAN_PRDTYPE2 FEB_PRDTYPE3 MAR_PRDTYPE1 APR_PRDTYPE2
------------ ------------ ------------ ------------
   14309.04      15467.9     91826.98      15664.7
```

The cells in the output show the sum of the sales amounts for each product type in the specified month (the product type and month to query are placed in the list of values in the `IN` part). As you can see from the query output, there were the following sales amounts:

- $14,309.04 of product type #2 in January

- $15,467.90 of product type #3 in February

- $91,826.98 of product type #1 in March

- $15,664.70 of product type #2 in April

You can put any values in the IN part to get the values of interest to you. In the following example, the values of the product types are shuffled in the IN part to get the sales for those product types in the specified months:

```
SELECT *
FROM (
  SELECT month, prd_type_id, amount
  FROM all_sales
  WHERE year = 2003
  AND prd_type_id IN (1, 2, 3)
)
PIVOT (
  SUM(amount) FOR (month, prd_type_id) IN (
    (1, 1) AS JAN_PRDTYPE1,
    (2, 2) AS FEB_PRDTYPE2,
    (3, 3) AS MAR_PRDTYPE3,
    (4, 1) AS APR_PRDTYPE1
  )
);
```

```
JAN_PRDTYPE1 FEB_PRDTYPE2 MAR_PRDTYPE3 APR_PRDTYPE1
------------ ------------ ------------ ------------
    38909.04      13367.9     20626.98     120344.7
```

As you can see from this output, there were the following sales amounts:

- $38,909.04 of product type #1 in January

- $13,367.90 of product type #2 in February

- $20,626.98 of product type #3 in March

- $120,344.70 of product type #1 in April

Using Multiple Aggregate Functions in a Pivot

You can use multiple aggregate functions in a pivot. For example, the following query uses SUM() to get the total sales for the product types in January and February and AVG() to get the averages of the sales:

```
SELECT *
FROM (
  SELECT month, prd_type_id, amount
  FROM all_sales
  WHERE year = 2003
  AND prd_type_id IN (1, 2, 3)
)
```

```
PIVOT (
  SUM(amount) AS sum_amount,
  AVG(amount) AS avg_amount
  FOR (month) IN (
    1 AS JAN, 2 AS FEB
  )
)
ORDER BY prd_type_id;
```

```
PRD_TYPE_ID JAN_SUM_AMOUNT JAN_AVG_AMOUNT FEB_SUM_AMOUNT FEB_AVG_AMOUNT
----------- -------------- -------------- -------------- --------------
          1       38909.04        6484.84        70567.9     11761.3167
          2       14309.04        2384.84        13367.9     2227.98333
          3       24909.04     4151.50667        15467.9     2577.98333
```

As you can see, the first line of output shows for product type #1:

- A total of $38,909.04 and an average of $6,484.84 sold in January

- A total of $70,567.90 and an average of $11,761.32 sold in February

The second line of output shows for product type #2:

- A total of $14,309.04 and an average of $2,384.84 sold in January

- A total of $13,367.90 and an average of $2,227.98 sold in February

...and so on for the rest of the output.

Using the UNPIVOT Clause

The UNPIVOT clause rotates columns into rows. The examples in this section use the following table named pivot_sales_data (created by the store_schema.sql script); pivot_sales_data is populated by a query that returns a pivoted version of the sales data:

```
CREATE TABLE pivot_sales_data AS
  SELECT *
  FROM (
   SELECT month, prd_type_id, amount
   FROM all_sales
   WHERE year = 2003
   AND prd_type_id IN (1, 2, 3)
  )
  PIVOT (
    SUM(amount) FOR month IN (1 AS JAN, 2 AS FEB, 3 AS MAR, 4 AS APR)
  )
  ORDER BY prd_type_id;
```

The following query returns the contents of the pivot_sales_data table:

```
SELECT *
FROM pivot_sales_data;
```

```
PRD_TYPE_ID       JAN        FEB        MAR        APR
----------- ---------- ---------- ---------- ----------
          1   38909.04    70567.9   91826.98   120344.7
          2   14309.04    13367.9   16826.98    15664.7
          3   24909.04    15467.9   20626.98    23844.7
```

The next query uses UNPIVOT to get the sales data in an unpivoted form:

```
SELECT *
FROM pivot_sales_data
UNPIVOT (
  amount FOR month IN (JAN, FEB, MAR, APR)
)
ORDER BY prd_type_id;

PRD_TYPE_ID MON     AMOUNT
----------- --- ----------
          1 JAN   38909.04
          1 FEB    70567.9
          1 MAR   91826.98
          1 APR   120344.7
          2 JAN   14309.04
          2 FEB    13367.9
          2 APR    15664.7
          2 MAR   16826.98
          3 JAN   24909.04
          3 MAR   20626.98
          3 FEB    15467.9
          3 APR    23844.7
```

Notice that the query rotates the pivoted data. For example, the monthly sales totals that appear in the horizontal rows of pivot_sales_data are shown in the vertical AMOUNT column.

TIP
Consider using UNPIVOT *when you have a query that returns rows with many columns and you want to view those columns as rows.*

Summary

In this chapter, you learned the following:

- The set operators (UNION ALL, UNION, INTERSECT, and MINUS) allow you to combine rows returned by two or more queries.

- TRANSLATE(*x*, *from_string*, *to_string*) translates characters in one string to characters in another string.

- DECODE(*value*, *search_value*, *result*, *default_value*) compares *value* with *search_value*. If the values are equal, DECODE() returns *search_value*; otherwise *default_value* is returned. DECODE() allows you to perform if-then-else logic in SQL.

- CASE is similar to DECODE (). You should use CASE because it is ANSI-compliant.

- Queries may be run against data that is organized into a hierarchy.

- ROLLUP extends the GROUP BY clause to return a row containing a subtotal for each group of rows, plus a row containing a grand total for all the groups.

- CUBE extends the GROUP BY clause to return rows containing a subtotal for all combinations of columns, plus a row containing the grand total.

- The database has many built-in analytic functions that enable you to perform complex calculations, such as finding the top-selling product type for each month, the top salespersons, and so on.

- The MODEL clause performs inter-row calculations and allows you to treat table data as an array. This gives you the ability to perform calculations in a similar manner to spreadsheet calculations.

- The Oracle Database 11*g* PIVOT and UNPIVOT clauses are useful for seeing overall trends in large amounts of data.

In the next chapter, you'll learn about changing the contents of a table.

CHAPTER
8

Changing Table Contents

n this chapter, you'll learn more about changing the contents of tables. Specifically, you'll learn the following:

- How to add, modify, and remove rows using the INSERT, UPDATE, and DELETE statements

- How database transactions may consist of multiple INSERT, UPDATE, and DELETE statements

- How to make the results of your transactions permanent using the COMMIT statement or undo their results entirely using the ROLLBACK statement

- How an Oracle database can process multiple transactions at the same time

- How to use query flashbacks to view rows as they originally were before you made changes to them

Adding Rows Using the INSERT Statement

You use the INSERT statement to add rows to a table. You can specify the following information in an INSERT statement:

- The table into which the row is to be inserted

- A list of columns for which you want to specify column values

- A list of values to store in the specified columns

When adding a row, you typically supply a value for the primary key and all other columns that are defined as NOT NULL. You don't have to specify values for NULL columns if you don't want to; by default they will be set to null.

You can find out which columns are defined as NOT NULL using the SQL*Plus DESCRIBE command. The following example describes the customers table:

```
DESCRIBE customers
Name                                      Null?    Type
----------------------------------------- -------- ------------
CUSTOMER_ID                               NOT NULL NUMBER(38)
FIRST_NAME                                NOT NULL VARCHAR2(10)
LAST_NAME                                 NOT NULL VARCHAR2(10)
DOB                                                DATE
PHONE                                              VARCHAR2(12)
```

As you can see, the customer_id, first_name, and last_name columns are NOT NULL, meaning that you must supply a value for these columns. The dob and phone columns don't require a value: If you omit these values when adding a row, the columns would be set to null.

The following INSERT statement adds a row to the customers table. Notice that the order of values in the VALUES clause matches the order in which the columns are specified in the column list. Also notice that the statement has three parts: the table name, the column list, and the values to be added:

```
INSERT INTO customers (
    customer_id, first_name, last_name, dob, phone
) VALUES (
    6, 'Fred', 'Brown', '01-JAN-1970', '800-555-1215'
);
```

```
1 row created.
```

SQL*Plus responds that one row has been created. You can verify this by performing the following SELECT statement:

```
SELECT *
FROM customers;
```

```
CUSTOMER_ID FIRST_NAME LAST_NAME  DOB       PHONE
----------- ---------- ---------- --------- ------------
          1 John       Brown      01-JAN-65 800-555-1211
          2 Cynthia    Green      05-FEB-68 800-555-1212
          3 Steve      White      16-MAR-71 800-555-1213
          4 Gail       Black                800-555-1214
          5 Doreen     Blue       20-MAY-70
          6 Fred       Brown      01-JAN-70 800-555-1215
```

Notice the new row appears in the results returned by the query.

Omitting the Column List

You may omit the column list when supplying values for every column, as in this example:

```
INSERT INTO customers
VALUES (7, 'Jane', 'Green', '01-JAN-1970', '800-555-1216');
```

When you omit the column list, the order of the values you supply must match the order of the columns as listed in the output from the DESCRIBE command.

Specifying a Null Value for a Column

You can specify a null value for a column using the NULL keyword. For example, the following INSERT specifies a null value for the dob and phone columns:

```
INSERT INTO customers
VALUES (8, 'Sophie', 'White', NULL, NULL);
```

When you view this row using a query, you won't see a value for the dob and phone columns, because they've been set to null values:

```
SELECT *
FROM customers
WHERE customer_id = 8;
```

```
CUSTOMER_ID FIRST_NAME LAST_NAME  DOB       PHONE
----------- ---------- ---------- --------- ------------
          8 Sophie     White
```

Notice the dob and phone column values are blank.

Including Single and Double Quotes in a Column Value

You can include a single and double quote in a column value. For example, the following INSERT specifies a last name of O'Malley for a new customer; notice the use of two single quotes in the last name after the letter O:

```
INSERT INTO customers
VALUES (9, 'Kyle', 'O''Malley', NULL, NULL);
```

The next example specifies the name The "Great" Gatsby for a new product:

```
INSERT INTO products (
    product_id, product_type_id, name, description, price
) VALUES (
    13, 1, 'The "Great" Gatsby', NULL, 12.99
);
```

Copying Rows from One Table to Another

You can copy rows from one table to another using a query in the place of the column values in the INSERT statement. The number of columns and the column types in the source and destination must match. The following example uses a SELECT to retrieve the first_name and last_name columns for customer #1 and supplies those columns to an INSERT statement:

```
INSERT INTO customers (customer_id, first_name, last_name)
SELECT 10, first_name, last_name
FROM customers
WHERE customer_id = 1;
```

Notice that the customer_id for the new row is set to 10.

NOTE
Oracle Database 9i introduced the MERGE *statement, which allows you to merge rows from one table to another.* MERGE *is much more flexible than combining an* INSERT *and a* SELECT *to copy rows from one table to another. You'll learn about* MERGE *later in the section "Merging Rows Using MERGE."*

Modifying Rows Using the UPDATE Statement

You use the UPDATE statement to modify rows in a table. When you use the UPDATE statement, you typically specify the following information:

- The table name

- A WHERE clause that specifies the rows to be changed

- A list of column names, along with their new values, specified using the SET clause

You can change one or more rows using the same UPDATE statement. If more than one row is specified, the same change will be implemented for all of those rows. For example, the following UPDATE statement sets the last_name column to Orange for the row whose customer_id is 2:

```
UPDATE customers
SET last_name = 'Orange'
WHERE customer_id = 2;
```

```
1 row updated.
```

SQL*Plus confirms that one row was updated. If the WHERE clause were omitted, then all the rows would be updated. The following query confirms the change was made:

```
SELECT *
FROM customers
WHERE customer_id = 2;
```

```
CUSTOMER_ID FIRST_NAME LAST_NAME  DOB       PHONE
----------- ---------- ---------- --------- ------------
          2 Cynthia    Orange     05-FEB-68 800-555-1212
```

You can change multiple rows and multiple columns in the same UPDATE statement. For example, the following UPDATE raises the price by 20 percent for all products whose current price is greater than or equal to $20. The UPDATE also changes those products' names to lowercase:

```
UPDATE products
SET
  price = price * 1.20,
  name = LOWER(name)
WHERE
  price >= 20;
```

```
3 rows updated.
```

As you can see, three rows are updated by this statement. The following query confirms the change:

```
SELECT product_id, name, price
FROM products
WHERE price >= (20 * 1.20);
```

```
ID NAME                             PRICE
-- ------------------------------   ----------
 2 chemistry                           36
 3 supernova                           31.19
 5 z-files                             59.99
```

NOTE
You can also use a subquery with an UPDATE statement. This is covered in Chapter 6 in the section "Writing an UPDATE Statement Containing a Subquery."

The RETURNING Clause

In Oracle Database 10g and above, you can use the RETURNING clause to return the value from an aggregate function such as AVG(). Aggregate functions were covered in Chapter 4.

The following tasks are performed by the next example:

- Declares a variable named `average_product_price`
- Decreases the `price` column of the rows in the `products` table and saves the average price in the `average_product_price` variable using the `RETURNING` clause
- Prints the value of the `average_product_price` variable

```
VARIABLE average_product_price NUMBER

UPDATE products
SET price =  price * 0.75
RETURNING AVG(price)  INTO :average_product_price;
12 rows updated.

PRINT average_product_price
AVERAGE_PRODUCT_PRICE
--------------------
           16.1216667
```

Removing Rows Using the DELETE Statement

You use the `DELETE` statement to remove rows from a table. Generally, you should specify a `WHERE` clause that limits the rows that you wish to delete; if you don't, *all* the rows will be deleted.

The following `DELETE` statement removes the row from the `customers` table whose `customer_id` is 10:

```
DELETE FROM customers
WHERE customer_id = 10;
```

```
1 row deleted.
```

SQL*Plus confirms that one row has been deleted.

You can also use a subquery with a `DELETE` statement. This is covered in Chapter 6 in the section "Writing a DELETE Statement Containing a Subquery."

NOTE

If you've been following along with the previous INSERT, UPDATE, *and* DELETE *statements, roll them back using* ROLLBACK *so that your results match those shown in the rest of this chapter. Don't worry if you've already disconnected from the database: simply rerun the* `store_schema.sql` *script to re-create everything.*

Database Integrity

When you execute a DML statement (an `INSERT`, `UPDATE`, or `DELETE`, for example), the database ensures that the rows in the tables maintain their integrity. This means that any changes made to the rows do not affect the primary key and foreign key relationships for the tables.

Enforcement of Primary Key Constraints

Let's examine some examples that show the enforcement of a primary key constraint. The
customers table's primary key is the customer_id column, which means that every value
stored in the customer_id column must be unique. If you try to insert a row with a duplicate
value for a primary key, the database returns the error ORA-00001, as in this example:

```
SQL> INSERT INTO customers (
  2    customer_id, first_name, last_name, dob, phone
  3  ) VALUES (
  4    1, 'Jason', 'Price', '01-JAN-60', '800-555-1211'
  5  );
INSERT INTO customers (
*
ERROR at line 1:
ORA-00001: unique constraint (STORE.CUSTOMERS_PK) violated
```

   If you attempt to update a primary key value to a value that already exists in the table, the
database returns the same error:

```
SQL> UPDATE customers
  2    SET customer_id = 1
  3    WHERE customer_id = 2;
UPDATE customers
*
ERROR at line 1:
ORA-00001: unique constraint (STORE.CUSTOMERS_PK) violated
```

Enforcement of Foreign Key Constraints

A foreign key relationship is one in which a column from one table is referenced in another. For
example, the product_type_id column in the products table references the product_
type_id column in the product_types table. The product_types table is known as the
parent table, and the products table is known as the *child* table, reflecting the dependence of
the product_type_id column in the products table on the product_type_id column
in the product_types table.

   If you try to insert a row into the products table with a nonexistent product_type_id,
the database will return the error ORA-02291. This error indicates the database couldn't find a
matching parent key value (the parent key is the product_type_id column of the product_
types table). In the following example, the error is returned because there is no row in the
product_types table whose product_type_id is 6:

```
SQL> INSERT INTO products (
  2    product_id, product_type_id, name, description, price
  3  ) VALUES (
  4    13, 6, 'Test', 'Test', NULL
  5  );
INSERT INTO products (
*
ERROR at line 1:
ORA-02291: integrity constraint (STORE.PRODUCTS_FK_PRODUCT_TYPES)
 violated - parent key not found
```

Similarly, if you attempt to update the `product_type_id` of a row in the `products` table to a nonexistent parent key value, the database returns the same error, as in this example:

```
SQL> UPDATE products
  2  SET product_type_id = 6
  3  WHERE product_id = 1;
UPDATE products
       *
ERROR at line 1:
ORA-02291: integrity constraint (STORE.PRODUCTS_FK_PRODUCT_TYPES)
 violated - parent key not found
```

Finally, if you attempt to delete a row in the parent table that has dependent child rows, the database returns error `ORA-02292`. For example, if you attempt to delete the row whose `product_type_id` is 1 from the `product_types` table, the database will return this error because the `products` table contains rows whose `product_type_id` is 1:

```
SQL> DELETE FROM product_types
  2  WHERE product_type_id = 1;
DELETE FROM product_types
            *
ERROR at line 1:
ORA-02292: integrity constraint (STORE.PRODUCTS_FK_PRODUCT_TYPES)
 violated - child record found
```

If the database were to allow this deletion, the child rows would be invalid because they wouldn't point to valid values in the parent table.

Using Default Values

Oracle Database 9*i* introduced a feature that allows you to define a default value for a column. For example, the following statement creates a table named `order_status`; the `status` column is defaulted to `'Order placed'` and the `last_modified` column is defaulted to the date and time returned by `SYSDATE`:

```
CREATE TABLE order_status (
  order_status_id INTEGER
    CONSTRAINT default_example_pk PRIMARY KEY,
  status VARCHAR2(20) DEFAULT 'Order placed' NOT NULL,
  last_modified DATE DEFAULT SYSDATE
);
```

NOTE
The `order_status` *table is created by the* `store_schema.sql` *script. This means you don't have to type in the previous* CREATE TABLE *statement yourself. Also, you don't have to type in the* INSERT *statements shown in this section.*

When you add a new row to the `order_status` table but don't specify the values for the `status` and `last_modified` columns, those columns are set to the default values. For example, the following INSERT statement omits values for the `status` and `last_modified` columns:

```
INSERT INTO order_status (order_status_id)
VALUES (1);
```

The `status` column is set to the default value of `'Order placed'`, and the `last_modified` column is set to the current date and time.

You can override the defaults by specifying a value for the columns, as shown in the following example:

```
INSERT INTO order_status (order_status_id, status, last_modified)
VALUES (2, 'Order shipped', '10-JUN-2004');
```

The following query retrieves the rows from `order_status`:

```
SELECT *
FROM order_status;
```

```
ORDER_STATUS_ID STATUS               LAST_MODI
--------------- -------------------- ---------
              1 Order placed         25-JUL-07
              2 Order shipped        10-JUN-04
```

You can set a column back to the default using the `DEFAULT` keyword in an `UPDATE` statement. For example, the following `UPDATE` sets the `status` column to the default:

```
UPDATE order_status
SET status = DEFAULT
WHERE order_status_id = 2;
```

The following query shows the change made by this `UPDATE` statement:

```
SELECT *
FROM order_status;
```

```
ORDER_STATUS_ID STATUS               LAST_MODI
--------------- -------------------- ---------
              1 Order placed         25-JUL-07
              2 Order placed         10-JUN-04
```

Merging Rows Using MERGE

Oracle Database 9*i* introduced the `MERGE` statement, which allows you to merge rows from one table into another. For example, you might want to merge changes to products listed in one table into the `products` table.

The `store` schema contains a table named `product_changes` that was created using the following `CREATE TABLE` statement in `store_schema.sql`:

```
CREATE TABLE product_changes (
  product_id INTEGER
    CONSTRAINT prod_changes_pk PRIMARY KEY,
  product_type_id INTEGER
    CONSTRAINT prod_changes_fk_product_types
    REFERENCES product_types(product_type_id),
  name VARCHAR2(30) NOT NULL,
```

```
  description VARCHAR2(50),
  price NUMBER(5, 2)
);
```

The following query retrieves the `product_id`, `product_type_id`, `name`, and `price` columns from this table:

```
SELECT product_id, product_type_id, name, price
FROM product_changes;
```

```
PRODUCT_ID PRODUCT_TYPE_ID NAME                                     PRICE
---------- --------------- ---------------------------- ----------
         1               1 Modern Science                              40
         2               1 New Chemistry                               35
         3               1 Supernova                                25.99
        13               2 Lunar Landing                            15.99
        14               2 Submarine                                15.99
        15               2 Airplane                                 15.99
```

Let's say you want to merge the rows from the `product_changes` table into the `products` table as follows:

- For rows with matching `product_id` values in the two tables, update the existing rows in `products` with the column values from `product_changes`. For example, product #1 has a different price in `product_changes` from the one in `products`; therefore, product #1's price must be updated in the `products` table. Similarly, product #2 has a different name and price, so both values must be updated in `products`. Finally, product #3 has a different `product_type_id`, and so this value must be updated in `products`.

- For new rows in `product_changes`, insert those new rows into the `products` table. Products #13, #14, and #15 are new in `product_changes` and must therefore be inserted into `products`.

The easiest way to learn how to use the MERGE statement is to see an example. The following example performs the merge as defined in the previous bullet points:

```
MERGE INTO products p
USING product_changes pc ON (
  p.product_id = pc.product_id
)
WHEN MATCHED THEN
  UPDATE
  SET
    p.product_type_id = pc.product_type_id,
    p.name = pc.name,
    p.description = pc.description,
    p.price = pc.price
WHEN NOT MATCHED THEN
  INSERT (
    p.product_id, p.product_type_id, p.name,
    p.description, p.price
  ) VALUES (
```

```
      pc.product_id, pc.product_type_id, pc.name,
      pc.description, pc.price
);
```

6 rows merged.

NOTE

You'll find a script named merge_example.sql *in the* SQL *directory. This script contains the previous* MERGE *statement.*

Notice the following points about the MERGE statement:

■ The MERGE INTO clause specifies the name of the table to merge the rows into. In the example, this is the products table, which is given an alias of p.

■ The USING ... ON clause specifies a table join. In the example, the join is made on the product_id columns in the products and product_changes tables. The product_changes table is also given an alias of pc.

■ The WHEN MATCHED THEN clause specifies the action to take when the USING ... ON clause is satisfied for a row. In the example, this action is an UPDATE statement that sets the product_type_id, name, description, and price columns of the existing row in the products table to the column values for the matching row in the product_ changes table.

■ The WHEN NOT MATCHED THEN clause specifies the action to take when the USING ... ON clause is *not* satisfied for a row. In the example, this action is an INSERT statement that adds a row to the products table, taking the column values from the row in the product_changes table.

If you run the previous MERGE statement, you'll see that it reports six rows are merged; these are the rows with product_id values of 1, 2, 3, 13, 14, and 15. The following query retrieves the six merged rows from the products table:

```
SELECT product_id, product_type_id, name, price
FROM products
WHERE product_id IN (1, 2, 3, 13, 14, 15);
```

```
PRODUCT_ID PRODUCT_TYPE_ID NAME                                   PRICE
---------- --------------- ------------------------------- ----------
         1               1 Modern Science                            40
         2               1 New Chemistry                             35
         3               1 Supernova                              25.99
        13               2 Lunar Landing                          15.99
        14               2 Submarine                              15.99
        15               2 Airplane                               15.99
```

The following changes were made to these rows:

■ Product #1 has a new price.

■ Product #2 has a new name and price.

■ Product #3 has a new product type ID.

■ Products #13, #14, and #15 are new.

Now that you've seen how to make changes to the contents of tables, let's move on to database transactions.

Database Transactions

A database *transaction* is a group of SQL statements that perform a *logical unit of work*. You can think of a transaction as an inseparable set of SQL statements whose results should be made permanent in the database as a whole (or undone as a whole).

An example of a database transaction is a transfer of money from one bank account to another. One UPDATE statement would subtract from the total amount of money from one account, and another UPDATE would add money to the other account. Both the subtraction and the addition must be permanently recorded in the database; otherwise, money will be lost. If there is a problem with the money transfer, then the subtraction and addition must both be undone. The simple example outlined in this paragraph uses only two UPDATE statements, but a transaction may consist of many INSERT, UPDATE, and DELETE statements.

Committing and Rolling Back a Transaction

To permanently record the results made by SQL statements in a transaction, you perform a *commit*, using the SQL COMMIT statement. If you need to undo the results, you perform a *rollback*, using the SQL ROLLBACK statement, which resets all the rows back to what they were originally.

The following example adds a row to the customers table and then makes the change permanent by performing a COMMIT:

```
INSERT INTO customers
VALUES (6, 'Fred', 'Green', '01-JAN-1970', '800-555-1215');

1 row created.

COMMIT;

Commit complete.
```

The following example updates customer #1 and then undoes the change by performing a ROLLBACK:

```
UPDATE customers
SET first_name = 'Edward'
WHERE customer_id = 1;

1 row updated.

ROLLBACK;

Rollback complete.
```

The following query shows the new row from the COMMIT statement:

```
SELECT *
FROM customers;
```

```
CUSTOMER_ID FIRST_NAME LAST_NAME  DOB       PHONE
----------- ---------- ---------- --------- ------------
          1 John       Brown      01-JAN-65 800-555-1211
          2 Cynthia    Green      05-FEB-68 800-555-1212
          3 Steve      White      16-MAR-71 800-555-1213
          4 Gail       Black                800-555-1214
          5 Doreen     Blue       20-MAY-70
          6 Fred       Green      01-JAN-70 800-555-1215
```

Notice that customer #6 has been made permanent by the COMMIT, but the change to customer #1's first name has been undone by the ROLLBACK.

Starting and Ending a Transaction

A transaction is a logical unit of work that enables you to split up your SQL statements. A transaction has a beginning and an end; it begins when one of the following events occurs:

- You connect to the database and perform a DML statement (an INSERT, UPDATE, or DELETE).

- A previous transaction ends and you enter another DML statement.

A transaction ends when one of the following events occurs:

- You perform a COMMIT or a ROLLBACK.

- You perform a DDL statement, such as a CREATE TABLE statement, in which case a COMMIT is automatically performed.

- You perform a DCL statement, such as a GRANT statement, in which case a COMMIT is automatically performed. You'll learn about GRANT in the next chapter.

- You disconnect from the database. If you exit SQL*Plus normally, by entering the EXIT command, a COMMIT is automatically performed for you. If SQL*Plus terminates abnormally—for example, if the computer on which SQL*Plus was running were to crash—a ROLLBACK is automatically performed. This applies to any program that accesses a database. For example, if you wrote a Java program that accessed a database and your program crashed, a ROLLBACK would be automatically performed.

- You perform a DML statement that fails, in which case a ROLLBACK is automatically performed for that individual DML statement.

TIP
It is poor practice not to explicitly commit or roll back your transactions, so perform a COMMIT or ROLLBACK at the end of your transactions.

Savepoints

You can also set a *savepoint* at any point within a transaction. These allow you to roll back changes to that savepoint. Savepoints can be useful to break up very long transactions, because, if you make a mistake after you've set a savepoint, you don't have to roll back the transaction all the way to the start. However, you should use savepoints sparingly: you might be better off restructuring your transaction into smaller transactions instead.

You'll see an example of a savepoint shortly, but first let's see the current price for products #4 and #5:

```
SELECT product_id, price
FROM products
WHERE product_id IN (4, 5);

PRODUCT_ID      PRICE
---------- ----------
         4      13.95
         5      49.99
```

The price for product #4 is $13.95, and the price for product #5 is $49.99. The following UPDATE increases the price of product #4 by 20 percent:

```
UPDATE products
SET price = price * 1.20
WHERE product_id = 4;

1 row updated.
```

The following statement sets a savepoint named save1:

```
SAVEPOINT save1;

Savepoint created.
```

Any DML statements run after this point can be rolled back to the savepoint, and the change made to product #4 will be kept.

The following UPDATE increases the price of product #5 by 30 percent:

```
UPDATE products
SET price = price * 1.30
WHERE product_id = 5;

1 row updated.
```

The following query gets the prices of the two products:

```
SELECT product_id, price
FROM products
WHERE product_id IN (4, 5);

PRODUCT_ID      PRICE
---------- ----------
         4      16.74
         5      64.99
```

Product #4's price is 20 percent greater, and product #5's price is 30 percent greater. The following statement rolls back the transaction to the savepoint established earlier:

```
ROLLBACK TO SAVEPOINT save1;
```

```
Rollback complete.
```

This has undone the price change for product #5, but left the price change for product #4 intact. The following query shows this:

```
SELECT product_id, price
FROM products
WHERE product_id IN (4, 5);
```

```
PRODUCT_ID     PRICE
---------- ----------
         4      16.74
         5      49.99
```

As expected, product #4 has kept its increased price, but product #5's price is back to the original. The following ROLLBACK undoes the entire transaction:

```
ROLLBACK;
```

```
Rollback complete.
```

This has undone the change made to product #4's price, as is shown by the following query:

```
SELECT product_id, price
FROM products
WHERE product_id IN (4, 5);
```

```
PRODUCT_ID     PRICE
---------- ----------
         4      13.95
         5      49.99
```

ACID Transaction Properties

Earlier, I defined a transaction as being a *logical unit of work*, that is, a group of related SQL statements that are either *committed* or *rolled back* as one unit. Database theory's more rigorous definition of a transaction states that a transaction has four fundamental properties, known as *ACID* properties (from the first letter of each property in the following list):

- **Atomic**   Transactions are atomic, meaning that the SQL statements contained in a transaction make up a single unit of work.

- **Consistent**   Transactions ensure that the database state remains consistent, meaning that the database is in a consistent state when a transaction begins and that it ends in another consistent state when the transaction finishes.

- **Isolated**   Separate transactions should not interfere with each other.

- **Durable**   Once a transaction has been committed, the database changes are preserved, even if the machine on which the database software is running crashes later.

The Oracle database software handles these ACID properties and has extensive recovery facilities for restoring databases after system crashes.

Concurrent Transactions

The Oracle database software supports many users interacting with a database, and each user can run their own transactions at the same time. These transactions are known as *concurrent* transactions.

If users are running transactions that affect the same table, the effects of those transactions are separated from each other until a COMMIT is performed. The following sequence of events, based on two transactions named T1 and T2 that access the customers table, illustrates the separation of transactions:

1. T1 and T2 perform a SELECT that retrieves all the rows from the customers table.
2. T1 performs an INSERT to add a row in the customers table, but T1 doesn't perform a COMMIT.
3. T2 performs another SELECT and retrieves the same rows as those in step 1. T2 doesn't "see" the new row added by T1 in step 2.
4. T1 finally performs a COMMIT to permanently record the new row added in step 2.
5. T2 performs another SELECT and finally "sees" the new row added by T1.

To summarize: T2 doesn't see the changes made by T1 until T1 commits its changes. This is the default level of isolation between transactions, but, as you'll learn later in the section "Transaction Isolation Levels," you can change the level of isolation.

Table 8-1 shows sample SQL statements that further illustrate how concurrent transactions work. The table shows the interleaved order in which the statements are performed by two transactions named T1 and T2. T1 retrieves rows, adds a row, and updates a row in the customers table. T2 retrieves rows from the customers table. T2 doesn't see the changes made by T1 until T1 commits its changes. You can enter the statements shown in Table 8-1 and see their results by starting two separate SQL*Plus sessions and connecting as the store user for both sessions; you enter the statements in the interleaved order shown in the table into the SQL*Plus sessions.

Transaction Locking

To support concurrent transactions, the Oracle database software must ensure that the data in the tables remains valid. It does this through the use of *locks*. Consider the following example in which two transactions named T1 and T2 attempt to modify customer #1 in the customers table:

1. T1 performs an UPDATE to modify customer #1, but T1 doesn't perform a COMMIT. T1 is said to have "locked" the row.
2. T2 also attempts to perform an UPDATE to modify customer #1, but since this row is already locked by T1, T2 is prevented from getting a lock on the row. T2's UPDATE statement has to wait until T1 ends and frees the lock on the row.
3. T1 ends by performing a COMMIT, thus freeing the lock on the row.
4. T2 gets the lock on the row and the UPDATE is performed. T2 holds the lock on the row until T2 ends.

To summarize: A transaction cannot get a lock on a row while another transaction already holds the lock on that row.

Transaction 1 T1	**Transaction 2 T2**
(1) `SELECT *` `FROM customers;`	(2) `SELECT *` `FROM customers;`

(3) `INSERT INTO customers (`
`  customer_id, first_name, last_name`
`) VALUES (`
`  7, 'Jason', 'Price'`
`);`	

(4) `UPDATE customers`
`SET last_name = 'Orange'`
`WHERE customer_id = 2;`	

(5) `SELECT *` `FROM customers;` The returned result set contains the new row and the update.	(6) `SELECT *` `FROM customers;` The returned result set doesn't contain the new row or the update made by T1. Instead, the result set contains the original rows retrieved in step 2.
(7) `COMMIT;` This commits the new row and the update.	
	(8) `SELECT *` `FROM customers;` The returned result set contains the new row and the update made by T1 in steps 3 and 4.

TABLE 8-1 *Concurrent Transactions*

NOTE
The easiest way to understand default locking is as follows: readers don't block readers, writers don't block readers, and writers only block writers when they attempt to modify the same row.

Transaction Isolation Levels

The *transaction isolation level* is the degree to which the changes made by one transaction are separated from other transactions running concurrently. Before you see the various transaction isolation levels available, you need to understand the types of problems that may occur when current transactions attempt to access the same rows in a table.

In the following list, you'll see examples of two concurrent transactions named T1 and T2 that are accessing the same rows; listed are the three types of potential transaction processing problems:

- ■ **Phantom reads** T1 reads a set of rows returned by a specified `WHERE` clause. T2 then inserts a new row, which also happens to satisfy the `WHERE` clause of the query previously used by T1. T1 then reads the rows again using the same query, but now sees the additional row just inserted by T2. This new row is known as a "phantom" because to T1 this row seems to have magically appeared.

- **Nonrepeatable reads** T1 reads a row, and T2 updates the same row just read by T1. T1 then reads the same row again and discovers that the row it read earlier is now different. This is known as a "nonrepeatable" read, because the row originally read by T1 has been changed.

- **Dirty reads** T1 updates a row, but doesn't commit the update. T2 then reads the updated row. T1 then performs a rollback, undoing the previous update. Now the row just read by T2 is no longer valid (it's "dirty") because the update made by T1 wasn't committed when the row was read by T2.

To deal with these potential problems, databases implement various levels of transaction isolation to prevent concurrent transactions from interfering with each other. The SQL standard defines the following transaction isolation levels, shown in order of increasing isolation:

- **READ UNCOMMITTED** Phantom reads, nonrepeatable reads, and dirty reads are permitted.

- **READ COMMITTED** Phantom reads and nonrepeatable reads are permitted, but dirty reads are not.

- **REPEATABLE READ** Phantom reads are permitted, but nonrepeatable and dirty reads are not.

- **SERIALIZABLE** Phantom reads, nonrepeatable reads, and dirty reads are not permitted.

The Oracle database software supports the READ COMMITTED and SERIALIZABLE transaction isolation levels. It doesn't support READ UNCOMMITTED or REPEATABLE READ levels.

The default transaction isolation level defined by the SQL standard is SERIALIZABLE, but the default used by the Oracle database is READ COMMITTED, which is acceptable for nearly all applications.

CAUTION
Although you can use SERIALIZABLE *with the Oracle database, it may increase the time your SQL statements take to complete. You should only use* SERIALIZABLE *if you absolutely have to.*

You set the transaction isolation level using the SET TRANSACTION statement. For example, the following statement sets the transaction isolation level to SERIALIZABLE:

```
SET TRANSACTION ISOLATION LEVEL SERIALIZABLE;
```

You'll see an example of a transaction that uses the isolation level of SERIALIZABLE next.

A SERIALIZABLE Transaction Example

In this section, you'll see an example that shows the effect of setting the transaction isolation level to SERIALIZABLE.

The example uses two transactions named T1 and T2. T1 has the default isolation level of READ COMMITTED; T2 has a transaction isolation level of SERIALIZABLE. T1 and T2 will read the rows in the customers table, and then T1 will insert a new row and update an existing row in the customers table. Because T2 is SERIALIZABLE, it doesn't see the inserted row or the update made to the existing row made by T1, even *after* T1 commits its changes. That's because reading the inserted row would be a phantom read, and reading the update would be a nonrepeatable read, which are not permitted by SERIALIZABLE transactions.

Table 8-2 shows the SQL statements that make up T1 and T2 in the interleaved order in which the statements are to be performed.

Transaction 1 T1 (READ COMMITTED)	Transaction 2 T2 (SERIALIZABLE)
	(1) `SET TRANSACTION ISOLATION LEVEL SERIALIZABLE;`
(3) `SELECT *` `FROM customers;`	(2) `SELECT *` `FROM customers;`

(4) `INSERT INTO customers (`
`  customer_id, first_name, last_name`
`) VALUES (`
`  8, 'Steve', 'Button'`
`);`	

(5) `UPDATE customers`
`SET last_name = 'Yellow'`
`WHERE customer_id = 3;`	

(6) `COMMIT;`	
(7) `SELECT *` `FROM customers;` The returned result set contains the new row and the update.	(8) `SELECT *` `FROM customers;` The returned result set *still* doesn't contain the new row or the update made by T1. That's because T2 is SERIALIZABLE.

TABLE 8-2 *SERIALIZABLE Transactions*

Query Flashbacks

If you mistakenly commit changes and you want to view rows as they originally were, you can use a query flashback. You can then use the results of a query flashback to manually change rows back to their original values if you need to.

Query flashbacks can be based on a datetime or system change number (SCN). The database uses SCNs to track changes made to data, and you can use them to flash back to a particular SCN in the database.

Granting the Privilege for Using Flashbacks

Flashbacks use the PL/SQL DBMS_FLASHBACK package, for which you must have the EXECUTE privilege to run. The following example connects as the sys user and grants the EXECUTE privilege on DBMS_FLASHBACK to the store user:

```
CONNECT sys/change_on_install AS sysdba
GRANT EXECUTE ON SYS.DBMS_FLASHBACK TO store;
```

> **NOTE**
> *Speak with your DBA if you are unable to perform these statements.*
> *You'll learn about privileges in the next chapter, and you'll learn about*
> *PL/SQL packages in Chapter 11.*

Time Query Flashbacks

The following example connects as store and retrieves the product_id, name, and price columns for the first five rows from the products table:

```
CONNECT store/store_password
SELECT product_id, name, price
FROM products
WHERE product_id <= 5;
```

```
PRODUCT_ID NAME                                        PRICE
---------- ------------------------------- ----------
         1 Modern Science                              19.95
         2 Chemistry                                      30
         3 Supernova                                   25.99
         4 Tank War                                    13.95
         5 Z Files                                     49.99
```

> **NOTE**
> *If you see different prices for any of these products, go ahead and*
> *rerun the* store_schema.sql *file.*

The next example reduces the price of these rows, commits the change, and retrieves the rows again so you can see the new prices:

```
UPDATE products
SET price = price * 0.75
WHERE product_id <= 5;
```

```
COMMIT;

SELECT product_id, name, price
FROM products
WHERE product_id <= 5;
```

```
PRODUCT_ID NAME                                     PRICE
---------- ------------------------------ ----------
         1 Modern Science                           14.96
         2 Chemistry                                 22.5
         3 Supernova                                19.49
         4 Tank War                                 10.46
         5 Z Files                                  37.49
```

The following statement executes the DBMS_FLASHBACK.ENABLE_AT_TIME() procedure, which enables you to perform a flashback to a particular datetime; notice the DBMS_FLASHBACK.ENABLE_AT_TIME() procedure accepts a datetime and the example passes SYSDATE - 10 / 1440 to the procedure (this expression evaluates to a datetime ten minutes in the past):

```
EXECUTE DBMS_FLASHBACK.ENABLE_AT_TIME(SYSDATE - 10 / 1440);
```

> **NOTE**
> *24 hours × 60 minutes per hour = 1440 minutes. Therefore* SYSDATE
> *- 10 / 1440 is a datetime ten minutes in the past.*

Any queries you execute now will display the rows as they were ten minutes ago. Assuming you performed the earlier UPDATE less than ten minutes ago, the following query will display the prices as they were before you updated them:

```
SELECT product_id, name, price
FROM products
WHERE product_id <= 5;
```

```
PRODUCT_ID NAME                                     PRICE
---------- ------------------------------ ----------
         1 Modern Science                           19.95
         2 Chemistry                                   30
         3 Supernova                                25.99
         4 Tank War                                 13.95
         5 Z Files                                  49.99
```

To disable a flashback, you execute DBMS_FLASHBACK.DISABLE(), as shown in the following example:

```
EXECUTE DBMS_FLASHBACK.DISABLE();
```

> **CAUTION**
> *You must disable a flashback before you can enable it again.*

Now when you perform queries, the rows as they currently exist will be retrieved, as shown here:

```
SELECT product_id, name, price
FROM products
WHERE product_id <= 5;
```

```
PRODUCT_ID NAME                                 PRICE
---------- ------------------------------- ----------
         1 Modern Science                       14.96
         2 Chemistry                             22.5
         3 Supernova                            19.49
         4 Tank War                             10.46
         5 Z Files                              37.49
```

System Change Number Query Flashbacks

Flashbacks based on system change numbers (SCNs) can be more precise than those based on a time, because the database uses SCNs to track changes made to data. To get the current SCN, you can execute DBMS_FLASHBACK.GET_SYSTEM_CHANGE_NUMBER(), as shown in the following example:

```
VARIABLE current_scn NUMBER

EXECUTE :current_scn := DBMS_FLASHBACK.GET_SYSTEM_CHANGE_NUMBER();

PRINT current_scn

CURRENT_SCN
-----------
     292111
```

The next example adds a row to the products table, commits the change, and retrieves the new row:

```
INSERT INTO products (
  product_id, product_type_id, name, description, price
) VALUES (
  15, 1, 'Physics', 'Textbook on physics', 39.95
);

COMMIT;

SELECT *
FROM products
WHERE product_id = 15;

PRODUCT_ID PRODUCT_TYPE_ID NAME
---------- --------------- -----------------------------
DESCRIPTION                                          PRICE
-------------------------------------------------- ----------
        15               1 Physics
Textbook on physics                                  39.95
```

The next example executes the following procedure, DBMS_FLASHBACK.ENABLE_AT_ SYSTEM_CHANGE_NUMBER(), which enables you to perform a flashback to an SCN; notice that this procedure accepts an SCN and that the example passes the current_scn variable to the procedure:

```
EXECUTE DBMS_FLASHBACK.ENABLE_AT_SYSTEM_CHANGE_NUMBER(:current_scn);
```

Any queries you execute now will display the rows as they were at the SCN stored in current_scn before you performed the INSERT. The following query attempts to get the row with a product_id of 15; it fails because that new row was added after the SCN stored in current_scn:

```
SELECT product_id
FROM products
WHERE product_id = 15;
```

```
no rows selected
```

To disable a flashback, you execute DBMS_FLASHBACK.DISABLE(), as shown in the following example:

```
EXECUTE DBMS_FLASHBACK.DISABLE();
```

If you perform the previous query again, you'll see the new row that was added by the INSERT.

NOTE
If you followed along with the examples, go ahead and rerun the store_schema.sql *script to recreate everything. That way, the results of your SQL statements will match mine as you progress through the rest of this book.*

Summary

In this chapter, you have learned the following:

- How to add rows using the INSERT statement.

- How to modify rows using the UPDATE statement.

- How to remove rows using the DELETE statement.

- How the database maintains referential integrity through the enforcement of constraints.

- How to use the DEFAULT keyword to specify default values for columns.

- How to merge rows using the MERGE statement.

- A database transaction is a group of SQL statements that comprise a logical unit of work.

- The Oracle database software can handle multiple concurrent transactions.

- How to use query flashbacks to view rows as they originally were before you made changes to them.

In the next chapter, you'll learn about users, privileges, and roles.

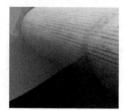

CHAPTER
9

Users, Privileges, and Roles

n this chapter, you will do the following:

- Learn more about users

- See how privileges are used to enable users to perform tasks in the database

- Explore the two types of privileges: system privileges and object privileges

- Learn how system privileges allow you to perform actions such as executing DDL statements

- See how object privileges allow you to perform actions such as executing DML statements

- Explore how to group privileges together into roles

- Learn how to audit the execution of SQL statements

NOTE
You'll need to type in the SQL statements shown in this chapter if you want to follow the examples: The statements are not contained in any script.

Users

In this section, you'll learn how to create a user, alter a user's password, and drop a user.

You will see the term "tablespace" used in this chapter. Tablespaces are used by the database to store separate objects, which can include tables, types, PL/SQL code, and so on. Typically, related objects are grouped together and stored in the same tablespace. For example, you might create an order entry application and store all the objects for that application in one tablespace, and you might create a supply chain application and store the objects for that application in a different tablespace. For more details on tablespaces, you should read the *Oracle Database Concepts* manual published by Oracle Corporation.

Creating a User

To create a user in the database, you use the CREATE USER statement. The simplified syntax for the CREATE USER statement is as follows:

```
CREATE USER user_name IDENTIFIED BY password
[DEFAULT TABLESPACE default_tablespace]
[TEMPORARY TABLESPACE temporary_tablespace];
```

where

- `user_name` is the name of the database user.

- `password` is the password for the database user.

- `default_tablespace` is the default tablespace where database objects are stored. If you omit a default tablespace, the default SYSTEM tablespace, which always exists in a database, is used.

■   `temporary_tablespace` is the default tablespace where temporary objects are stored. These objects include temporary tables that you'll learn about in the next chapter. If you omit a temporary tablespace, the default `SYSTEM` tablespace is used.

The following example connects as `system` and creates a user named `jason` with a password of `price`:

```
CONNECT system/manager
CREATE USER jason IDENTIFIED BY price;
```

NOTE
If you want to follow along with these examples you'll need to connect to the database as a privileged user. I used the `system` *user in the example, which has a password of* `manager` *in my database.*

The next example creates a user named `henry` and specifies a default and temporary tablespace:

```
CREATE USER henry IDENTIFIED BY hooray
DEFAULT TABLESPACE users
TEMPORARY TABLESPACE temp;
```

NOTE
If your database doesn't have tablespaces named `users` *and* `temp`*, you can skip this example. The* `henry` *user isn't used elsewhere in this book, and I included the example only so you can see how to specify tablespaces for a user. You can view all the tablespaces in a database by connecting as the* `system` *user and running the query* `SELECT tablespace_name FROM dba_tablespaces`*.*

If you want a user to be able to do things in the database, that user must be granted the necessary permissions to do those things. For example, to connect to the database a user must be granted the permission to create a session, which is the `CREATE SESSION` system privilege. Permissions are granted by a privileged user (`system`, for example) using the `GRANT` statement.
The following example grants the `CREATE SESSION` permission to `jason`:

```
GRANT CREATE SESSION TO jason;
```

The `jason` user will now be able to connect to the database.
The following example creates other users that are used in this chapter and grants the `CREATE SESSION` privilege to those users:

```
CREATE USER steve IDENTIFIED BY button;
CREATE USER gail IDENTIFIED BY seymour;
GRANT CREATE SESSION TO steve, gail;
```

Changing a User's Password
You can change a user's password using the `ALTER USER` statement. For example, the following statement changes the password for `jason` to `marcus`:

```
ALTER USER jason IDENTIFIED BY marcus;
```

You can also change the password for the user you're currently logged in as using the PASSWORD command. After you enter PASSWORD, SQL*Plus prompts you to enter the old password and the new password twice for confirmation. The following example connects as jason and executes PASSWORD; notice the password itself is masked using asterisks:

```
CONNECT jason/marcus
PASSWORD
Changing password for JASON
Old password: ******
New password: ******
Retype new password: ******
Password changed
```

Deleting a User

You delete a user using the DROP USER statement. The following example connects as system and uses DROP USER to delete jason:

```
CONNECT system/manager
DROP USER jason;
```

NOTE
You must add the keyword CASCADE *after the user's name in the* DROP USER *statement if that user's schema contains objects such as tables. However, you should ensure no other users need access to those objects before doing this.*

System Privileges

A *system privilege* allows a user to perform certain actions within the database, such as executing DDL statements. For example, CREATE TABLE allows a user to create a table in their schema. Some of the commonly used system privileges are shown in Table 9-1.

NOTE
You can get the full list of system privileges in the Oracle Database SQL Reference *manual published by Oracle Corporation.*

As you'll see later, privileges can be grouped together into *roles.* Two useful roles to grant to a user are CONNECT and RESOURCE; CONNECT allows a user to connect to the database; RESOURCE allows a user to create various database objects like tables, sequences, PL/SQL code, and so on.

Granting System Privileges to a User

You use GRANT to grant a system privilege to a user. The following example grants some system privileges to steve (assuming you're still connected to the database as system):

```
GRANT CREATE SESSION, CREATE USER, CREATE TABLE TO steve;
```

System Privilege	Allows You to...
CREATE SESSION	Connect to a database.
CREATE SEQUENCE	Create a sequence, which is a series of numbers that are typically used to automatically populate a primary key column. You'll learn about sequences in the next chapter.
CREATE SYNONYM	Create a synonym. A synonym allows you to reference a table in another schema. You'll learn about synonyms later in this chapter.
CREATE TABLE	Create a table in the user's schema.
CREATE ANY TABLE	Create a table in any schema.
DROP TABLE	Drop a table from the user's schema.
DROP ANY TABLE	Drop a table from any schema.
CREATE PROCEDURE	Create a stored procedure.
EXECUTE ANY PROCEDURE	Execute a procedure in any schema.
CREATE USER	Create a user.
DROP USER	Drop a user.
CREATE VIEW	Create a view. A view is a stored query that allows you to access multiple tables and columns. You may then query the view as you would a table. You'll learn about views in the next chapter.

TABLE 9-1 *Commonly Used System Privileges*

You can also use WITH ADMIN OPTION to allow a user to grant a privilege to another user. The following example grants the EXECUTE ANY PROCEDURE privilege with the ADMIN option to steve:

```
GRANT EXECUTE ANY PROCEDURE TO steve WITH ADMIN OPTION;
```

EXECUTE ANY PROCEDURE can then be granted to another user by steve. The following example connects as steve and grants EXECUTE ANY PROCEDURE to gail:

```
CONNECT steve/button
GRANT EXECUTE ANY PROCEDURE TO gail;
```

You can grant a privilege to all users by granting to PUBLIC. The following example connects as system and grants EXECUTE ANY PROCEDURE to PUBLIC:

```
CONNECT system/manager
GRANT EXECUTE ANY PROCEDURE TO PUBLIC;
```

Every user in the database now has the EXECUTE ANY PROCEDURE privilege.

Checking System Privileges Granted to a User

You can check which system privileges a user has by querying `user_sys_privs`. Table 9-2 describes some of the columns in `user_sys_privs`.

NOTE
`user_sys_privs` *forms part of the Oracle database's data dictionary. The data dictionary stores information about the database itself.*

The following example connects as `steve` and queries `user_sys_privs`:

```
CONNECT steve/button
SELECT *
FROM user_sys_privs
ORDER BY privilege;
```

```
USERNAME                        PRIVILEGE                                  ADM
------------------------------  -----------------------------------------  ---
STEVE                           CREATE SESSION                             NO
STEVE                           CREATE TABLE                               NO
STEVE                           CREATE USER                                NO
PUBLIC                          EXECUTE ANY PROCEDURE                      NO
STEVE                           EXECUTE ANY PROCEDURE                      YES
```

The next example connects as `gail` and queries `user_sys_privs`:

```
CONNECT gail/seymour
SELECT *
FROM user_sys_privs
ORDER BY privilege;
```

```
USERNAME            PRIVILEGE                          ADM
------------------  ---------------------------------  ---
GAIL                CREATE SESSION                     NO
GAIL                EXECUTE ANY PROCEDURE              NO
PUBLIC              EXECUTE ANY PROCEDURE              NO
```

Notice `gail` has the `EXECUTE ANY PROCEDURE` privilege that was granted earlier by `steve`.

Column	Type	Description
username	VARCHAR2(30)	Name of the current user
privilege	VARCHAR2(40)	The system privilege the user has
admin_option	VARCHAR2(3)	Whether the user is able to grant the privilege to another user

TABLE 9-2 *Some Columns in* `user_sys_privs`

Making Use of System Privileges

Once a user has been granted a system privilege, they can use it to perform the specified task. For example, `steve` has the `CREATE USER` privilege, so he is able to create a user:

```
CONNECT steve/button
CREATE USER roy IDENTIFIED BY williams;
```

If `steve` were to attempt to use a system privilege he doesn't have, the database will return the error `ORA-01031: insufficient privileges`. For example, `steve` doesn't have the `DROP USER` privilege, and in the following example `steve` attempts to drop `roy` and fails:

```
SQL> DROP USER roy;
DROP USER roy
*
ERROR at line 1:
ORA-01031: insufficient privileges
```

Revoking System Privileges from a User

You revoke system privileges from a user using `REVOKE`. The following example connects as `system` and revokes the `CREATE TABLE` privilege from `steve`:

```
CONNECT system/manager
REVOKE CREATE TABLE FROM steve;
```

The next example revokes `EXECUTE ANY PROCEDURE` from `steve`:

```
REVOKE EXECUTE ANY PROCEDURE FROM steve;
```

When you revoke `EXECUTE ANY PROCEDURE` from `steve`—who has already passed on this privilege to `gail`—then `gail` still keeps the privilege:

```
CONNECT gail/seymour
SELECT *
FROM user_sys_privs
ORDER BY privilege;
```

```
USERNAME             PRIVILEGE                        ADM
-------------------- -------------------------------- ---
GAIL                 CREATE SESSION                   NO
GAIL                 EXECUTE ANY PROCEDURE            NO
PUBLIC               EXECUTE ANY PROCEDURE            NO
```

Object Privileges

An *object privilege* allows a user to perform certain actions on database objects, such as executing DML statements on tables. For example, `INSERT ON store.products` allows a user to insert rows into the `products` table of the `store` schema. Some of the commonly used object privileges are shown in Table 9-3.

Object Privilege	Allows a User to...
SELECT	Perform a select.
INSERT	Perform an insert.
UPDATE	Perform an update.
DELETE	Perform a delete.
EXECUTE	Execute a stored procedure.

TABLE 9-3   *Commonly Used Object Privileges*

NOTE
You can get the full list of system privileges in the Oracle Database
SQL Reference *manual published by Oracle Corporation.*

Granting Object Privileges to a User

You use GRANT to grant an object privilege to a user. The following example connects as store
and grants the SELECT, INSERT, and UPDATE object privileges on the products table to
steve along with the SELECT privilege on the employees table:

```
CONNECT store/store_password
GRANT SELECT, INSERT, UPDATE ON store.products TO steve;
GRANT SELECT ON store.employees TO steve;
```

The next example grants the UPDATE privilege on the last_name and salary columns
to steve:

```
GRANT UPDATE (last_name, salary) ON store.employees TO steve;
```

You can also use the GRANT option to enable a user to grant a privilege to another user. The
following example grants the SELECT privilege on the customers table with the GRANT option
to steve:

```
GRANT SELECT ON store.customers TO steve WITH GRANT OPTION;
```

NOTE
You use the GRANT *option to allow a user to grant an* object privilege
to another user, and you use the ADMIN *option to allow a user to grant
a* system privilege *to another user.*

The SELECT ON store.customers privilege can then be granted to another user by steve.
The following example connects as steve and grants this privilege to gail:

```
CONNECT steve/button
GRANT SELECT ON store.customers TO gail;
```

Checking Object Privileges Made

You can check which table object privileges a user has made to other users by querying user_tab_privs_made. Table 9-4 documents the columns in user_tab_privs_made.

The following example connects as store and queries user_tab_privs_made. Because there are so many rows, I'll limit the retrieved rows to those where table_name is PRODUCTS:

```
CONNECT store/store_password
SELECT *
FROM user_tab_privs_made
WHERE table_name = 'PRODUCTS';

GRANTEE                    TABLE_NAME
-------------------------  ------------------------------
GRANTOR                    PRIVILEGE                       GRA HIE
-------------------------  ------------------------------  --- ---
STEVE                      PRODUCTS
STORE                      INSERT                          NO  NO

STEVE                      PRODUCTS
STORE                      SELECT                          NO  NO

STEVE                      PRODUCTS
STORE                      UPDATE                          NO  NO
```

You can check which column object privileges a user has made by querying user_col_privs_made. Table 9-5 documents the columns in user_col_privs_made.

Column	Type	Description
grantee	VARCHAR2(30)	User to whom the privilege was granted
table_name	VARCHAR2(30)	Name of the object (such as a table) on which the privilege was granted
grantor	VARCHAR2(30)	User who granted the privilege
privilege	VARCHAR2(40)	Privilege on the object
grantable	VARCHAR2(3)	Whether the grantee can grant the privilege to another (YES or NO)
hierarchy	VARCHAR2(3)	Whether the privilege forms part of a hierarchy (YES or NO)

TABLE 9-4   *Some Columns in* user_tab_privs_made

Column	Type	Description
grantee	VARCHAR2(30)	User to whom the privilege was granted
table_name	VARCHAR2(30)	Name of the object on which the privilege was granted
column_name	VARCHAR2(30)	Name of the object on which the privilege was granted
grantor	VARCHAR2(30)	User who granted the privilege
privilege	VARCHAR2(40)	Privilege on the object
grantable	VARCHAR2(3)	Whether the grantee can grant the privilege to another (YES or NO)

TABLE 9-5   *Some Columns in* user_col_privs_made

The following example queries user_col_privs_made:

```
SELECT *
FROM user_col_privs_made;

GRANTEE                          TABLE_NAME
-------------------------------- --------------
COLUMN_NAME                      GRANTOR
-------------------------------- --------------
PRIVILEGE                                  GRA
---------------------------------------- ---
STEVE                            EMPLOYEES
LAST_NAME                        STORE
UPDATE                                     NO

STEVE                            EMPLOYEES
SALARY                           STORE
UPDATE                                     NO
```

Checking Object Privileges Received

You can check which object privileges on a table a user has received by querying the user_tab_privs_recd table. Table 9-6 documents the columns in user_tab_privs_recd.

The next example connects as steve and queries user_tab_privs_recd:

Column	Type	Description
owner	VARCHAR2(30)	User who owns the object
table_name	VARCHAR2(30)	Name of the object on which the privilege was granted
grantor	VARCHAR2(30)	User who granted the privilege
privilege	VARCHAR2(40)	Privilege on the object
grantable	VARCHAR2(3)	Whether the grantee can grant the privilege to another (YES or NO)
hierarchy	VARCHAR2(3)	Whether the privilege forms part of a hierarchy (YES or NO)

TABLE 9-6   *Some Columns in user_tab_privs_recd*

```
CONNECT steve/button
SELECT *
FROM user_tab_privs_recd
ORDER BY privilege;

OWNER                            TABLE_NAME
-------------------------------- --------------------------------
GRANTOR                          PRIVILEGE                                GRA HIE
-------------------------------- ---------------------------------------- --- ---
STORE                            PRODUCTS
STORE                            INSERT                                   NO  NO

STORE                            CUSTOMERS
STORE                            SELECT                                   YES NO

STORE                            EMPLOYEES
STORE                            SELECT                                   NO  NO

STORE                            PRODUCTS
STORE                            SELECT                                   NO  NO

STORE                            PRODUCTS
STORE                            UPDATE                                   NO  NO
```

You can check which column object privileges a user has received by querying user_col_privs_recd. Table 9-7 documents the columns in user_col_privs_recd.

Column	Type	Description
owner	VARCHAR2(30)	User who owns the object
table_name	VARCHAR2(30)	Name of the table on which the privilege was granted
column_name	VARCHAR2(30)	Name of the column on which the privilege was granted
grantor	VARCHAR2(30)	User who granted the privilege
privilege	VARCHAR2(40)	Privilege on the object
grantable	VARCHAR2(3)	Whether the grantee can grant the privilege to another (YES or NO)

TABLE 9-7   *Some Columns in* user_col_privs_recd

The following example queries user_col_privs_recd:

```
SELECT *
FROM user_col_privs_recd;

OWNER                                  TABLE_NAME
-------------------------------------- --------------
COLUMN_NAME                            GRANTOR
-------------------------------------- --------------
PRIVILEGE                                       GRA
-------------------------------------- ---
STORE                                  EMPLOYEES
LAST_NAME                              STORE
UPDATE                                          NO

STORE                                  EMPLOYEES
SALARY                                 STORE
UPDATE                                          NO
```

Making Use of Object Privileges

Once a user has been granted an object privilege, they can use it to perform the specified task. For example, steve has the SELECT privilege on store.customers:

```
CONNECT steve/button
SELECT *
FROM store.customers;

CUSTOMER_ID FIRST_NAME LAST_NAME  DOB       PHONE
----------- ---------- ---------- --------- ------------
          1 John       Brown      01-JAN-65 800-555-1211
          2 Cynthia    Green      05-FEB-68 800-555-1212
          3 Steve      White      16-MAR-71 800-555-1213
          4 Gail       Black                800-555-1214
          5 Doreen     Blue       20-MAY-70
```

If `steve` were to attempt to retrieve from the `purchases` table—for which he doesn't have any permissions—the database will return the error `ORA-00942: table or view does not exist`:

```
SQL> SELECT *
  2  FROM store.purchases;
FROM store.purchases
         *
ERROR at line 2:
ORA-00942: table or view does not exist
```

Synonyms

In the examples in the previous section, you saw that you can access tables in another schema by specifying the schema name followed by the table. For example, when `steve` retrieved rows from the `customers` table in the `store` schema, he performed a query on `store.customers`. You can avoid having to enter the schema name by creating a *synonym* for a table, which you do by using the `CREATE SYNONYM` statement.

Let's take a look at an example. First, connect as `system` and grant the `CREATE SYNONYM` system privilege to `steve`:

```
CONNECT system/manager
GRANT CREATE SYNONYM TO steve;
```

Next, connect as `steve` and perform a `CREATE SYNONYM` statement to create a synonym for the `store.customers` table:

```
CONNECT steve/button
CREATE SYNONYM customers FOR store.customers;
```

To retrieve rows from `store.customers`, all `steve` has to do is to reference the `customers` synonym in the `FROM` clause of a `SELECT` statement. For example:

```
SELECT *
FROM customers;
```

```
CUSTOMER_ID FIRST_NAME LAST_NAME  DOB       PHONE
----------- ---------- ---------- --------- -----------
          1 John       Brown      01-JAN-65 800-555-1211
          2 Cynthia    Green      05-FEB-68 800-555-1212
          3 Steve      White      16-MAR-71 800-555-1213
          4 Gail       Black                800-555-1214
          5 Doreen     Blue       20-MAY-70
```

Public Synonyms

You can also create a *public* synonym for a table. When you do this, all users see the synonym. The following tasks

- Connect as `system`

- Grant the `CREATE PUBLIC SYNONYM` system privilege to `store`

- Connect as `store`

- Create a public synonym named `products` for `store.products`

are performed by the following statements:

```
CONNECT system/manager
GRANT CREATE PUBLIC SYNONYM TO store;
CONNECT store/store_password
CREATE PUBLIC SYNONYM products FOR store.products;
```

If you connect as `steve`, who has the SELECT privilege on `store.products`, you can now retrieve rows from `store.products` through the `products` public synonym:

```
CONNECT steve/button
SELECT *
FROM products;
```

Even though a public synonym has been created for `store.products`, a user still needs object privileges on that table to actually access the table. For example, `gail` can see the `products` public synonym, but `gail` doesn't have any object privileges on `store.products`. Therefore, if `gail` attempts to retrieve rows from `products`, the database returns the error `ORA-00942: table or view does not exist`:

```
SQL> CONNECT gail/seymour
Connected.
SQL> SELECT * FROM products;
SELECT * FROM products
              *
ERROR at line 1:
ORA-00942: table or view does not exist
```

If `gail` had the SELECT object privilege on the `store.products` table, the previous SELECT would succeed.

If a user has other object privileges, that user can exercise those object privileges through a synonym. For example, if `gail` had the INSERT object privilege on the `store.products` table, `gail` would be able to add a row to `store.products` through the `products` synonym.

Revoking Object Privileges

You revoke object privileges using REVOKE. The following example connects as `store` and revokes the INSERT privilege on the `products` table from `steve`:

```
CONNECT store/store_password
REVOKE INSERT ON products FROM steve;
```

The next example revokes the SELECT privilege on the `customers` table from `steve`:

```
REVOKE SELECT ON store.customers FROM steve;
```

When you revoke SELECT ON `store.customers` from `steve`—who has already passed on this privilege to `gail`—`gail` also loses the privilege.

Roles

A *role* is a group of privileges that you can assign to a user or to another role. The following points summarize the benefits and features of roles:

■ Rather than assigning privileges one at a time directly to a user, you can create a role, assign privileges to that role, and then grant that role to multiple users and roles.

■ When you add or delete a privilege from a role, all users and roles assigned that role automatically receive or lose that privilege.

■ You can assign multiple roles to a user or role.

■ You can assign a password to a role.

As you can see from these points, roles can help you manage multiple privileges assigned to multiple users.

Creating Roles

To create a role, you must have the CREATE ROLE system privilege. As you'll see in a later example, the store user also needs the ability to grant the CREATE USER system privilege with the ADMIN option. The following example connects as system and grants the required privileges to store:

```
CONNECT system/manager
GRANT CREATE ROLE TO store;
GRANT CREATE USER TO store WITH ADMIN OPTION;
```

Table 9-8 shows the roles you'll create shortly.

You create a role using the CREATE ROLE statement. The following statements connect as store and create the three roles shown in Table 9-8:

```
CONNECT store/store_password
CREATE ROLE product_manager;
CREATE ROLE hr_manager;
CREATE ROLE overall_manager IDENTIFIED by manager_password;
```

Notice overall_manager has a password of manager_password.

Role Name	Has Permissions to...
product_manager	Perform SELECT, INSERT, UPDATE, and DELETE operations on the product_types and products tables.
hr_manager	Perform SELECT, INSERT, UPDATE, and DELETE operations on the salary_grades and employees tables. Also, hr_manager is able to create users.
overall_manager	Perform SELECT, INSERT, UPDATE, and DELETE operations on all the tables shown in the previous roles; overall_manager will be granted the previous roles.

TABLE 9-8   *Roles to Be Created*

Granting Privileges to Roles

You grant privileges to a role using the GRANT statement. You can grant both system and object privileges to a role as well as grant another role to a role. The following example grants the required privileges to the `product_manager` and `hr_manager` roles and grants these two roles to `overall_manager`:

```
GRANT SELECT, INSERT, UPDATE, DELETE ON product_types TO product_manager;
GRANT SELECT, INSERT, UPDATE, DELETE ON products TO product_manager;
GRANT SELECT, INSERT, UPDATE, DELETE ON salary_grades TO hr_manager;
GRANT SELECT, INSERT, UPDATE, DELETE ON employees TO hr_manager;
GRANT CREATE USER TO hr_manager;
GRANT product_manager, hr_manager TO overall_manager;
```

Granting Roles to a User

You grant a role to a user using GRANT. The following example grants the `overall_manager` role to `steve`:

```
GRANT overall_manager TO steve;
```

Checking Roles Granted to a User

You can check which roles have been granted to a user by querying `user_role_privs`. Table 9-9 defines the columns in `user_role_privs`.
 The following example connects as `steve` and queries `user_role_privs`:

```
CONNECT steve/button
SELECT *
FROM user_role_privs;

USERNAME            GRANTED_ROLE               ADM DEF OS_
------------------  -------------------------  --- --- ---
STEVE               OVERALL_MANAGER            NO  YES NO
```

Column	Type	Description
username	VARCHAR2(30)	Name of the user to whom the role has been granted
granted_role	VARCHAR2(30)	Name of the role granted to the user
admin_option	VARCHAR2(3)	Whether the user is able to grant the role to another user or role (YES or NO)
default_role	VARCHAR2(3)	Whether the role is enabled by default when the user connects to the database (YES or NO)
os_granted	VARCHAR2(3)	Whether the role was granted by the operating system (YES or NO)

TABLE 9-9 *Some Columns in* `user_role_privs`

A user who creates a role is also granted that role by default. The following example connects as `store` and queries `user_role_privs`:

```
CONNECT store/store_password
SELECT *
FROM user_role_privs;
```

```
USERNAME              GRANTED_ROLE                ADM DEF OS_
--------------------  --------------------------  --- --- ---
STORE                 CONNECT                     NO  YES NO
STORE                 HR_MANAGER                  YES YES NO
STORE                 OVERALL_MANAGER             YES YES NO
STORE                 PRODUCT_MANAGER             YES YES NO
STORE                 RESOURCE                    NO  YES NO
```

Notice `store` has the roles `CONNECT` and `RESOURCE` in addition to the roles `store` created earlier.

NOTE
`CONNECT` and `RESOURCE` are built-in roles that were granted to `store` *when you ran the* `store_schema.sql` *script. As you'll see in the next section, the* `CONNECT` *and* `RESOURCE` *roles contain multiple privileges.*

Checking System Privileges Granted to a Role

You can check which system privileges have been granted to a role by querying `role_sys_privs`. Table 9-10 defines the columns in `role_sys_privs`.

The following example retrieves the rows from `role_sys_privs` (assuming you're still connected as `store`):

```
SELECT *
FROM role_sys_privs
ORDER BY privilege;
```

```
ROLE                            PRIVILEGE                                 ADM
------------------------------  ----------------------------------------  ---
RESOURCE                        CREATE CLUSTER                            NO
RESOURCE                        CREATE INDEXTYPE                          NO
RESOURCE                        CREATE OPERATOR                           NO
RESOURCE                        CREATE PROCEDURE                          NO
RESOURCE                        CREATE SEQUENCE                           NO
CONNECT                         CREATE SESSION                            NO
RESOURCE                        CREATE TABLE                              NO
RESOURCE                        CREATE TRIGGER                            NO
RESOURCE                        CREATE TYPE                               NO
HR_MANAGER                      CREATE USER                               NO
```

Notice that the `RESOURCE` role has many privileges assigned to it.

NOTE
The previous query was run using Oracle Database 11g. If you are using a different version of the database software, you may get slightly different results.

Column	Type	Description
role	VARCHAR2(30)	Name of the role
privilege	VARCHAR2(40)	System privilege granted to the role
admin_option	VARCHAR2(3)	Whether the privilege was granted with the ADMIN option (YES or NO)

TABLE 9-10 *Some Columns in* role_sys_privs

Checking Object Privileges Granted to a Role

You can check which object privileges have been granted to a role by querying role_tab_
privs. Table 9-11 defines the columns in role_tab_privs.

The following example queries role_tab_privs where role equals HR_MANAGER:

```
SELECT *
FROM role_tab_privs
WHERE role='HR_MANAGER'
ORDER BY table_name;
```

```
ROLE                                OWNER
----------------------------------  ----------------------------------
TABLE_NAME                          COLUMN_NAME
----------------------------------  ----------------------------------
PRIVILEGE                                           GRA
--------------------------------------------------  ---
HR_MANAGER                          STORE
EMPLOYEES
DELETE                                              NO

HR_MANAGER                          STORE
EMPLOYEES
INSERT                                              NO

HR_MANAGER                          STORE
EMPLOYEES
SELECT                                              NO

HR_MANAGER                          STORE
EMPLOYEES
UPDATE                                              NO

HR_MANAGER                          STORE
SALARY_GRADES
DELETE                                              NO

HR_MANAGER                          STORE
SALARY_GRADES
INSERT                                              NO
```

```
HR_MANAGER                      STORE
SALARY_GRADES
SELECT                                     NO

HR_MANAGER                      STORE
SALARY_GRADES
UPDATE                                     NO
```

Making Use of Privileges Granted to a Role

Once a user has been granted a privilege via a role, they can use that privilege to perform the authorized tasks. For example, steve has the overall_manager role. The overall_manager was granted the product_manager and hr_manager roles. The product_manager was granted the SELECT object privilege on the products and product_types tables. Therefore, steve is able to retrieve rows from these tables, as shown in the following example:

```
CONNECT steve/button
SELECT p.name, pt.name
FROM store.products p, store.product_types pt
WHERE p.product_type_id = pt.product_type_id;

NAME                              NAME
-------------------------------   ----------
Modern Science                    Book
Chemistry                         Book
Supernova                         Video
Tank War                          Video
Z Files                           Video
2412: The Return                  Video
Space Force 9                     DVD
From Another Planet               DVD
Classical Music                   CD
Pop 3                             CD
Creative Yell                     CD
```

Column	Type	Description
role	VARCHAR2(30)	User to whom the privilege was granted
owner	VARCHAR2(30)	User who owns the object
table_name	VARCHAR2(30)	Name of the object on which the privilege was granted
column_name	VARCHAR2(30)	Name of the column (if applicable)
privilege	VARCHAR2(40)	Privilege on the object
grantable	VARCHAR2(3)	Whether the privilege was granted with the GRANT option (YES or NO)

TABLE 9-11   *Some Columns in* role_tab_privs

Default Roles

By default, when a role is granted to a user, that role is enabled for that user. This means that when the user connects to the database, the role is automatically available to them. To enhance security, you can disable a role by default; when the user connects, they will have to enable the role themselves before they can use it. If the role has a password, the user must enter that password before the role is enabled. For example, the `overall_manager` role has a password of `manager_passsword`, and `overall_manager` is granted to `steve`. In the example you'll see next, you'll disable `overall_manager` so that `steve` has to enable this role and enter the password before he can use it. You do this by altering a role so that it is no longer a default role using the `ALTER ROLE` statement. The following example connects as `system` and alters `steve` so that `overall_manager` is no longer a default role:

```
CONNECT system/manager
ALTER USER steve DEFAULT ROLE ALL EXCEPT overall_manager;
```

When you connect as `steve`, you need to enable `overall_manager` using `SET ROLE`:

```
CONNECT steve/button
SET ROLE overall_manager IDENTIFIED BY manager_password;
```

Once you've set the role, you can use the privileges granted to that role. You can set your role to "none" (i.e. no role) using the following statement:

```
SET ROLE NONE;
```

You can also set your role to "all roles" except `overall_manager` using the following statement:

```
SET ROLE ALL EXCEPT overall_manager;
```

By assigning passwords to roles and setting roles to not be enabled by default for a user, you introduce an additional level of security.

Revoking a Role

You revoke a role using `REVOKE`. The following example connects as `store` and revokes the `overall_manager` role from `steve`:

```
CONNECT store/store_password
REVOKE overall_manager FROM steve;
```

Revoking Privileges from a Role

You revoke a privilege from a role using `REVOKE`. The following example connects as `store` and revokes all privileges on the `products` and `product_types` tables from `product_manager` (assuming you're still connected as `store`):

```
REVOKE ALL ON products FROM product_manager;
REVOKE ALL ON product_types FROM product_manager;
```

Dropping a Role

You drop a role using DROP ROLE. The following example drops the overall_manager, product_manager, and hr_manager roles (assuming you're still connected as store):

```
DROP ROLE overall_manager;
DROP ROLE product_manager;
DROP ROLE hr_manager;
```

Auditing

The Oracle database software contains auditing capabilities that enable you to keep track of database operations. Some operations may be audited at a high level, such as failed attempts to log into the database, while others may be audited at a detailed level, such as when a user retrieved rows from a specific table. Typically, your database administrator will be responsible for enabling auditing and monitoring the output for security violations. In this section, you will see some simple examples of auditing, which is performed using the AUDIT statement.

Privileges Required to Perform Auditing

Before a user can issue AUDIT statements, that user must have been granted certain privileges:

- For auditing high-level operations, the user must have the AUDIT SYSTEM privilege. An example of a high-level operation is the issuance of *any* SELECT statement, regardless of the table involved.

- For tracking operations on specific database objects, the user must either have the AUDIT ANY privilege or the database object must be in their schema. An example of specific database object operation is the issuance of a SELECT statement for a particular table.

The following example connects to the database as the system user and grants the AUDIT SYSTEM and AUDIT ANY privileges to the store user:

```
CONNECT system/manager
GRANT AUDIT SYSTEM TO store;
GRANT AUDIT ANY TO store;
```

Auditing Examples

The following example connects to the database as the store user and audits the issuance of CREATE TABLE statements:

```
CONNECT store/store_password
AUDIT CREATE TABLE;
```

As a result of this AUDIT statement, any CREATE TABLE statements issued will be audited; for example, the following statement creates a simple test table:

```
CREATE TABLE test (
  id INTEGER
);
```

You can view the audit trail of information for the user you are currently logged in as through the USER_AUDIT_TRAIL view. The following example shows the audit record generated by the previous CREATE TABLE statement:

```
SELECT username, extended_timestamp, audit_option
FROM user_audit_trail
WHERE audit_option='CREATE TABLE';

USERNAME
-----------------------------
EXTENDED_TIMESTAMP
----------------------------------
AUDIT_OPTION
----------------------------------
STORE
20-MAY-07 04.13.43.453000 PM -07:00
CREATE TABLE
```

You may also audit the issuance of statements by a particular user. The following example audits all SELECT statements issued by the store user:

```
AUDIT SELECT TABLE BY store;
```

The next example audits all INSERT, UPDATE, and DELETE statements made by the store and steve users:

```
AUDIT INSERT TABLE, UPDATE TABLE, DELETE TABLE BY store, steve;
```

You may also audit the issuance of statements made for a particular database object. The following example audits all SELECT statements issued for the products table:

```
AUDIT SELECT ON store.products;
```

The next example audits all statements issued for the employees table:

```
AUDIT ALL ON store.employees;
```

You may also use the WHENEVER SUCCESSFUL and WHENEVER NOT SUCCESSFUL options to indicate when auditing should be performed. WHENEVER SUCCESSFUL indicates auditing will be performed when the statement executed successfully. WHENEVER NOT SUCCESSFUL indicates auditing will be performed when the statement did not execute successfully. The default is to do both, that is, audit regardless of success. The following examples use the WHENEVER NOT SUCCESSFUL option:

```
AUDIT UPDATE TABLE BY steve WHENEVER NOT SUCCESSFUL;
AUDIT INSERT TABLE WHENEVER NOT SUCCESSFUL;
```

The next example uses the WHENEVER SUCCESSFUL option to audit the creation and deletion of a user:

```
AUDIT CREATE USER, DROP USER WHENEVER SUCCESSFUL;
```

The next example uses the WHENEVER SUCCESSFUL option to audit the creation and deletion of a user by the store user:

```
AUDIT CREATE USER, DROP USER BY store WHENEVER SUCCESSFUL;
```

You may also use the BY SESSION and BY ACCESS options. The BY SESSION option causes only one audit record to be logged when the same type of statement is issued during the same user database session; a database session starts when the user logs into the database and ends when the user logs out. The BY ACCESS option causes one audit record to be logged every time the same type of statement is issued, regardless of the user session. The following examples show the use of the BY SESSION and BY ACCESS options:

```
AUDIT SELECT ON store.products BY SESSION;
AUDIT DELETE ON store.employees BY ACCESS;
AUDIT INSERT, UPDATE ON store.employees BY ACCESS;
```

Audit Trail Views

Earlier, you saw the use of the USER_AUDIT_TRAIL view. This and the other audit trail views are outlined in the following list:

- **USER_AUDIT_OBJECT** displays the audit records for all objects accessible to the current user.

- **USER_AUDIT_SESSION** displays the audit records for connections and disconnections of the current user.

- **USER_AUDIT_STATEMENT** displays the audit records for GRANT, REVOKE, AUDIT, NOAUDIT, and ALTER SYSTEM statements issued by the current user.

- **USER_AUDIT_TRAIL** displays all audit trail entries related to the current user.

You may use these views to examine the contents of the audit trail. There are a number of similarly named views that the database administrator may use to examine the audit trail; these views are named DBA_AUDIT_OBJECT, DBA_AUDIT_SESSION, DBA_AUDIT_STATEMENT, DBA_AUDIT_TRAIL, plus others. These views allow the DBA to view audit records across all users. For more details on these views, you should consult the *Oracle Database Reference* manual published by Oracle Corporation.

Summary

In this chapter, you've learned the following:

- A user is created using the CREATE USER statement.

- System privileges allow you to perform certain actions within the database, such as executing DDL statements.

- Object privileges allow you to perform certain actions on database objects, such as executing DML statements on tables.

- You can avoid having to enter the schema name by creating a synonym for a table.

- A role is a group of privileges that you can assign to a user or another role.

- Auditing the execution of SQL statements can be performed using the `AUDIT` statement.

In the next chapter, you'll learn more about creating tables and see how to create indexes, sequences, and views.

CHAPTER
10

Creating Tables, Sequences, Indexes, and Views

n this chapter, you will do the following:

- Learn more about tables

- See how to create and use sequences, which generate a series of numbers

- Explore how to create and use indexes, which can improve the performance of queries

- Learn how to create and use views, which are predefined queries that allow you to hide complexity from users, among other benefits

- Examine flashback data archives, new for Oracle Database 11g, which store changes made to a table over a period of time

Let's plunge in and examine tables.

Tables

In this section, you'll learn more about creating a table. You'll see how to modify and drop a table as well as how to retrieve information about a table from the data dictionary. The data dictionary contains information about all the database items, such as tables, sequences, indexes, and so on.

Creating a Table

You use the CREATE TABLE statement to create a table. The simplified syntax for the CREATE TABLE statement is as follows:

```
CREATE [GLOBAL TEMPORARY] TABLE table_name (
  column_name type [CONSTRAINT constraint_def DEFAULT default_exp]
  [, column_name type [CONSTRAINT constraint_def DEFAULT default_exp] ...]
)
[ON COMMIT {DELETE | PRESERVE} ROWS]
TABLESPACE tab_space;
```

where

- GLOBAL TEMPORARY means the table's rows are temporary (these tables are known as temporary tables). The rows in a temporary table are specific to a user session, and how long the rows persist is set in the ON COMMIT clause.

- table_name is the name of the table.

- column_name is the name of a column.

- type is the type of a column.

- constraint_def is a constraint on a column.

- default_exp is an expression to assign a default value to a column.

- ON COMMIT controls the duration of the rows in a temporary table. DELETE means the rows are deleted at the end of a transaction. PRESERVE means the rows are kept until the end of a user session, at which point the rows are deleted. If you omit ON COMMIT for a temporary table, then the default DELETE is used.

- *tab_space* is the tablespace for the table. If you omit a tablespace, then the table is stored in the user's default tablespace.

NOTE
The full CREATE TABLE *syntax is far richer than that shown above. For full details, see the* Oracle Database SQL Reference *book published by Oracle Corporation.*

The following example connects as the store user and creates a table named order_status2:

```
CONNECT store/store_password
CREATE TABLE order_status2 (
  id INTEGER CONSTRAINT order_status2_pk PRIMARY KEY,
  status VARCHAR2(10),
  last_modified DATE DEFAULT SYSDATE
);
```

NOTE
*If you want to follow along with the examples in this chapter, you'll need to enter and run the SQL statements using SQL*Plus.*

The next example creates a temporary table named order_status_temp whose rows will be kept until the end of a user session (ON COMMIT PRESERVE ROWS):

```
CREATE GLOBAL TEMPORARY TABLE order_status_temp (
  id INTEGER,
  status VARCHAR2(10),
  last_modified DATE DEFAULT SYSDATE
)
ON COMMIT PRESERVE ROWS;
```

The next example performs the following:

- Adds a row to order_status_temp.

- Disconnects from the database to end the session, which causes the row in order_status_temp to be deleted.

- Reconnects as store and queries order_status_temp, which shows there are no rows in this table.

```
INSERT INTO order_status_temp (
  id, status
) VALUES (
  1, 'New'
);
```

```
1 row created.

DISCONNECT
CONNECT store/store_password
SELECT *
FROM order_status_temp;

no rows selected
```

Getting Information on Tables

You can get information about your tables by

- Performing a DESCRIBE command on the table. You've already seen examples that use the DESCRIBE command in earlier chapters.

- Querying the user_tables view, which forms part of the data dictionary.

Table 10-1 describes some of the columns in the user_tables view.

NOTE
You can retrieve information on all the tables you have access to by querying the all_tables *view.*

The following example retrieves some of the columns from user_tables where the table_name is order_status2 or order_status_temp:

```
SELECT table_name, tablespace_name, temporary
FROM user_tables
WHERE table_name IN ('ORDER_STATUS2', 'ORDER_STATUS_TEMP');

TABLE_NAME                     TABLESPACE_NAME                    T
------------------------------ ------------------------------ -
ORDER_STATUS2                  USERS                              N
ORDER_STATUS_TEMP                                                 Y
```

Notice the order_status_temp table is temporary, as indicated by the Y in the last column.

Column	Type	Description
table_name	VARCHAR2(30)	Name of the table.
tablespace_name	VARCHAR2(30)	Name of the tablespace in which the table is stored. A tablespace is an area used by the database to store objects such as tables.
temporary	VARCHAR2(1)	Whether the table is temporary. This is set to Y if temporary or N if not temporary.

TABLE 10-1 *Some Columns in the* user_tables *View*

Getting Information on Columns in Tables

You can retrieve information about the columns in your tables from the `user_tab_columns` view. Table 10-2 describes some of the columns in `user_tab_columns`.

NOTE
You can retrieve information on all the columns in tables you have access to by querying the `all_tab_columns` *view.*

The following example retrieves some of the columns from `user_tab_columns` for the `products` table:

```
COLUMN column_name FORMAT a15
COLUMN data_type FORMAT a10
SELECT column_name, data_type, data_length, data_precision, data_scale
FROM user_tab_columns
WHERE table_name = 'PRODUCTS';
```

```
COLUMN_NAME      DATA_TYPE  DATA_LENGTH DATA_PRECISION DATA_SCALE
---------------- ---------- ----------- -------------- ----------
PRODUCT_ID       NUMBER              22             38          0
PRODUCT_TYPE_ID  NUMBER              22             38          0
NAME             VARCHAR2            30
DESCRIPTION      VARCHAR2            50
PRICE            NUMBER              22              5          2
```

Altering a Table

You alter a table using the ALTER TABLE statement. You can use ALTER TABLE to perform tasks such as

- Adding, modifying, or dropping a column
- Adding or dropping a constraint
- Enabling or disabling a constraint

In the following sections, you'll learn how to use ALTER TABLE to perform each of these tasks.

Column	Type	Description
table_name	VARCHAR2(30)	Name of the table
column_name	VARCHAR2(30)	Name of the column
data_type	VARCHAR2(106)	Data type of the column
data_length	NUMBER	Length of the data
data_precision	NUMBER	Precision of a numeric column if a precision was specified for the column.
data_scale	NUMBER	Scale of a numeric column

TABLE 10-2 *Some Columns in the* `user_tab_columns` *View*

Adding a Column

The following example uses ALTER TABLE to add an INTEGER column named modified_by to the order_status2 table:

```
ALTER TABLE order_status2
ADD modified_by INTEGER;
```

The next example adds a column named initially_created to order_status2:

```
ALTER TABLE order_status2
ADD initially_created DATE DEFAULT SYSDATE NOT NULL;
```

You can verify the addition of the new column by executing a DESCRIBE command on order_status2:

```
DESCRIBE order_status2
Name                                      Null?    Type
----------------------------------------- -------- ------------
ID                                        NOT NULL NUMBER(38)
STATUS                                             VARCHAR2(10)
LAST_MODIFIED                                      DATE
MODIFIED_BY                                        NUMBER(38)
INITIALLY_CREATED                         NOT NULL DATE
```

Adding a Virtual Column

In Oracle Database 11*g*, you can add a virtual column, which is a column that refers only to other columns already in the table. For example, the following ALTER TABLE statement adds a virtual column named average_salary to the salary_grades table:

```
ALTER TABLE salary_grades
ADD (average_salary AS ((low_salary + high_salary)/2));
```

Notice average_salary is set to the average of the low_salary and high_salary values. The following DESCRIBE command confirms the addition of the average_salary column to the salary_grades table:

```
DESCRIBE salary_grades
Name                                      Null?    Type
----------------------------------------- -------- ----------
SALARY_GRADE_ID                           NOT NULL NUMBER(38)
LOW_SALARY                                         NUMBER(6)
HIGH_SALARY                                        NUMBER(6)
AVERAGE_SALARY                                     NUMBER
```

The following query retrieves the rows from the salary_grades table:

```
SELECT *
FROM salary_grades;

SALARY_GRADE_ID LOW_SALARY HIGH_SALARY AVERAGE_SALARY
--------------- ---------- ----------- --------------
              1          1      250000       125000.5
              2     250001      500000       375000.5
```

```
3       500001      750000      625000.5
4       750001      999999       875000
```

Modifying a Column
The following list shows some of the column aspects you can modify using ALTER TABLE:

- Change the size of a column (if the data type is one whose length may be changed, such as CHAR or VARCHAR2)

- Change the precision of a numeric column

- Change the data type of a column

- Change the default value of a column

You'll see examples of how to change these column aspects in the following sections.

Changing the Size of a Column
The following ALTER TABLE statement increases the maximum length of the order_status2 .status column to 15 characters:

```
ALTER TABLE order_status2
MODIFY status VARCHAR2(15);
```

CAUTION
You can only decrease *the length of a column if there are no rows in the table or all the rows contain null values for that column.*

Changing the Precision of a Numeric Column
The following ALTER TABLE statement changes the precision of the order_status2.id column to 5:

```
ALTER TABLE order_status2
MODIFY id NUMBER(5);
```

CAUTION
You can only decrease *the precision of a numeric column if there are no rows in the table or the column contains null values.*

Changing the Data Type of a Column
The following ALTER TABLE statement changes the data type of the order_status2.status column to CHAR:

```
ALTER TABLE order_status2
MODIFY status CHAR(15);
```

If the table is empty or the column contains null values, you can change the column to any data type (including a data type that is shorter); otherwise, you can change the data type of a column only to a compatible data type. For example, you can change a VARCHAR2 to CHAR (and vice versa) as long as you don't make the column shorter; you cannot change a DATE to a NUMBER.

Changing the Default Value of a Column

The following `ALTER TABLE` statement changes the default value for the `order_status2`
`.last_modified` column to `SYSDATE - 1`:

```
ALTER TABLE order_status2
MODIFY last_modified DEFAULT SYSDATE - 1;
```

The default value applies only to new rows added to the table. New rows will get their `last_modified` column set to the current date minus one day.

Dropping a Column

The following `ALTER TABLE` statement drops the `order_status2.initially_created` column:

```
ALTER TABLE order_status2
DROP COLUMN initially_created;
```

Adding a Constraint

In earlier chapters, you've seen examples of tables with `PRIMARY KEY`, `FOREIGN KEY`, and `NOT NULL` constraints. These constraints, along with the other types of constraints, are summarized in Table 10-3.

You'll see how to add some of the constraints shown in Table 10-3 in the following sections.

Constraint	Constraint Type	Meaning
CHECK	C	The value for a column, or group of columns, must satisfy a certain condition.
NOT NULL	C	The column cannot store a null value. This is actually enforced as a CHECK constraint.
PRIMARY KEY	P	The primary key of a table. A primary key is made up of one or more columns that uniquely identify each row in a table.
FOREIGN KEY	R	A foreign key for a table. A foreign key references a column in another table or a column in the same table (known as a self-reference).
UNIQUE	U	The column, or group of columns, can store only unique values.
CHECK OPTION	V	Changes to the table rows made through a view must pass a check first. (You'll learn about this later in the section "Views.")
READ ONLY	O	The view may only be read from. (You'll learn about this later in the section "Views.")

TABLE 10-3 *Constraints and Their Meaning*

Adding a CHECK Constraint

The following ALTER TABLE statement adds a CHECK constraint to the order_status2 table:

```
ALTER TABLE order_status2
ADD CONSTRAINT order_status2_status_ck
CHECK (status IN ('PLACED', 'PENDING', 'SHIPPED'));
```

This constraint ensures the status column is always set to PLACED, PENDING, or SHIPPED. The following INSERT adds a row to the order_status2 table (status is set to PENDING):

```
INSERT INTO order_status2 (
  id, status, last_modified, modified_by
) VALUES (
  1, 'PENDING', '01-JAN-2005', 1
);
```

If you attempt to add a row that doesn't satisfy the CHECK constraint, the database returns the error ORA-02290. For example, the following INSERT attempts to add a row whose status is not in the list:

```
INSERT INTO order_status2 (
  id, status, last_modified, modified_by
) VALUES (
  2, 'CLEARED', '01-JAN-2005', 2
);
INSERT INTO order_status2 (
*
ERROR at line 1:
ORA-02290: check constraint (STORE.ORDER_STATUS2_STATUS_CK) violated
```

Because the CHECK constraint is violated, the database rejects the new row.

You can use other comparison operators with a CHECK constraint. The next example adds a CHECK constraint that enforces that the id value is greater than zero:

```
ALTER TABLE order_status2
ADD CONSTRAINT order_status2_id_ck CHECK (id > 0);
```

When adding a constraint, the existing rows in the table must satisfy the constraint. For example, if the order_status2 table had rows in it, then the id column for the rows would need to be greater than zero.

NOTE
There are exceptions to the rule requiring that existing rows satisfy the constraint. You can disable a constraint when you initially add it, and you can set a constraint to apply only to new data, by specifying ENABLE NOVALIDATE. *You'll learn more about this later.*

Adding a NOT NULL Constraint

The following ALTER TABLE statement adds a NOT NULL constraint to the status column of the order_status2 table:

```
ALTER TABLE order_status2
MODIFY status CONSTRAINT order_status2_status_nn NOT NULL;
```

Notice that you use `MODIFY` to add a `NOT NULL` constraint rather than `ADD CONSTRAINT`. The next example adds a `NOT NULL` constraint to the `modified_by` column:

```
ALTER TABLE order_status2
MODIFY modified_by CONSTRAINT order_status2_modified_by_nn NOT NULL;
```

The following example adds a `NOT NULL` constraint to the `last_modified` column:

```
ALTER TABLE order_status2
MODIFY last_modified NOT NULL;
```

Notice that I didn't supply a name for this constraint. In this case, the database automatically assigns an unfriendly name to the constraint, like `SYS_C003381`.

TIP
Always specify a meaningful name to your constraints. That way, when a constraint error occurs, you can easily identify the problem.

Adding a FOREIGN KEY Constraint

Before you see an example of adding a `FOREIGN KEY` constraint, the following `ALTER TABLE` statement drops the `order_status2.modified_by` column:

```
ALTER TABLE order_status2
DROP COLUMN modified_by;
```

The next statement adds a `FOREIGN KEY` constraint that references the `employees.employee_id` column:

```
ALTER TABLE order_status2
ADD CONSTRAINT order_status2_modified_by_fk
modified_by REFERENCES employees(employee_id);
```

You use the `ON DELETE CASCADE` clause with a `FOREIGN KEY` constraint to specify that when a row in the parent table is deleted, any matching rows in the child table are also deleted. The following example drops the `modified_by` column and rewrites the previous example to include the `ON DELETE CASCADE` clause:

```
ALTER TABLE order_status2
DROP COLUMN modified_by;

ALTER TABLE order_status2
ADD CONSTRAINT order_status2_modified_by_fk
modified_by REFERENCES employees(employee_id) ON DELETE CASCADE;
```

When a row is deleted from the `employees` table, any matching rows in `order_status2` are also deleted.

You use the `ON DELETE SET NULL` clause with a `FOREIGN KEY` constraint to specify that when a row in the parent table is deleted, the foreign key column for the row (or rows) in the child table is set to null. The following example drops the `modified_by` column from `order_status2` and rewrites the previous example to include the `ON DELETE SET NULL` clause:

```
ALTER TABLE order_status2
DROP COLUMN modified_by;
```

```
ALTER TABLE order_status2
ADD CONSTRAINT order_status2_modified_by_fk
modified_by REFERENCES employees(employee_id) ON DELETE SET NULL;
```

When a row is deleted from the `employees` table, the `modified_by` column for any matching rows in `order_status2` is set to null.

To clean up before moving onto the next section, the following statement drops the `modified_by` column:

```
ALTER TABLE order_status2
DROP COLUMN modified_by;
```

Adding a UNIQUE Constraint

The following `ALTER TABLE` statement adds a `UNIQUE` constraint to the `order_status2`
`.status` column:

```
ALTER TABLE order_status2
ADD CONSTRAINT order_status2_status_uq UNIQUE (status);
```

Any existing or new rows must always have a unique value in the `status` column.

Dropping a Constraint

You drop a constraint using the `DROP CONSTRAINT` clause of `ALTER TABLE`. The following example drops the `order_status2_status_uq` constraint:

```
ALTER TABLE order_status2
DROP CONSTRAINT order_status2_status_uq;
```

Disabling a Constraint

By default, a constraint is enabled when you create it. You can initially disable a constraint by adding `DISABLE` to the end of the `CONSTRAINT` clause. The following example adds a constraint to `order_status2`, but also disables it:

```
ALTER TABLE order_status2
ADD CONSTRAINT order_status2_status_uq UNIQUE (status) DISABLE;
```

You can disable an existing constraint using the `DISABLE CONSTRAINT` clause of `ALTER TABLE`. The following example disables the `order_status2_status_nn` constraint:

```
ALTER TABLE order_status2
DISABLE CONSTRAINT order_status2_status_nn;
```

You can add `CASCADE` after `DISABLE CONSTRAINT` to disable all constraints that depend on the specified constraint. You use `CASCADE` when disabling a primary key or unique constraint that is part of a foreign key constraint of another table.

Enabling a Constraint

You can enable an existing constraint using the `ENABLE CONSTRAINT` clause of `ALTER TABLE`. The following example enables the `order_status2_status_uq` constraint:

```
ALTER TABLE order_status2
ENABLE CONSTRAINT order_status2_status_uq;
```

To enable a constraint, all the rows in the table must satisfy the constraint. For example, if the `order_status2` table contained rows, then the `status` column would have to contain unique values.

You can apply a constraint to new data only by specifying `ENABLE NOVALIDATE`; for example:

```
ALTER TABLE order_status2
ENABLE NOVALIDATE CONSTRAINT order_status2_status_uq;
```

> **NOTE**
> *The default is* `ENABLE VALIDATE`, *which means existing rows must pass the constraint check.*

Deferred Constraints

A deferred constraint is one that is enforced when a transaction is committed; you use the `DEFERRABLE` clause when you initially add the constraint. Once you've added a constraint, you cannot change it to `DEFERRABLE`; instead, you must drop and re-create the constraint.

When you add a `DEFERRABLE` constraint, you can mark it as `INITIALLY IMMEDIATE` or `INITIALLY DEFERRED`. Marking as `INITIALLY IMMEDIATE` means that the constraint is checked whenever you add, update, or delete rows from a table (this is the same as the default behavior of a constraint). `INITIALLY DEFERRED` means that the constraint is only checked when a transaction is committed. Let's take a look at an example.

The following statement drops the `order_status2_status_uq` constraint:

```
ALTER TABLE order_status2
DROP CONSTRAINT order_status2_status_uq;
```

The next example adds the `order_status2_status_uq` constraint, setting it to `DEFERRABLE INITIALLY DEFERRED`:

```
ALTER TABLE order_status2
ADD CONSTRAINT order_status2_status_uq UNIQUE (status)
DEFERRABLE INITIALLY DEFERRED;
```

If you add rows to `order_status2`, the `order_status2_status_uq` constraint isn't enforced until you perform a `commit`.

Getting Information on Constraints

You can retrieve information on your constraints by querying the `user_constraints` view. Table 10-4 describes some of the columns in `user_constraints`.

> **NOTE**
> *You can retrieve information on all the constraints you have access to by querying the* `all_constraints` *view.*

The following example retrieves some of the columns from `user_constraints` for the `order_status2` table:

```
SELECT constraint_name, constraint_type, status, deferrable, deferred
FROM user_constraints
WHERE table_name = 'ORDER_STATUS2';

CONSTRAINT_NAME                 C STATUS   DEFERRABLE     DEFERRED
------------------------------- - -------- -------------- ---------
ORDER_STATUS2_PK                P ENABLED  NOT DEFERRABLE IMMEDIATE
ORDER_STATUS2_STATUS_CK         C ENABLED  NOT DEFERRABLE IMMEDIATE
ORDER_STATUS2_ID_CK             C ENABLED  NOT DEFERRABLE IMMEDIATE
ORDER_STATUS2_STATUS_NN         C DISABLED NOT DEFERRABLE IMMEDIATE
ORDER_STATUS2_STATUS_UQ         U ENABLED  DEFERRABLE     DEFERRED
SYS_C004807                     C ENABLED  NOT DEFERRABLE IMMEDIATE
```

Notice that all the constraints except one have a helpful name. One constraint has the database-generated name of SYS_C004807 (this name is automatically generated, and it will be different in your database). This constraint is the one for which I omitted the name when creating it earlier.

TIP
Always add a descriptive name for your constraints.

Getting Information on the Constraints for a Column

You can retrieve information on the constraints for a column by querying the user_cons_columns view. Table 10-5 describes some of the columns in user_cons_columns.

NOTE
You can retrieve information on all the column constraints you have access to by querying the all_cons_columns *view.*

Column	Type	Description
owner	VARCHAR2(30)	Owner of the constraint.
constraint_name	VARCHAR2(30)	Name of the constraint.
constraint_type	VARCHAR2(1)	Constraint type (P, R, C, U, V, or O). See Table 10-3 for the constraint type meanings.
table_name	VARCHAR2(30)	Name of the table on which the constraint is defined.
status	VARCHAR2(8)	Constraint status (ENABLED or DISABLED).
deferrable	VARCHAR2(14)	Whether the constraint is deferrable (DEFERRABLE or NOT DEFERRABLE).
deferred	VARCHAR2(9)	Whether the constraint is enforced immediately or deferred (IMMEDIATE or DEFERRED).

TABLE 10-4 *Some Columns in the* user_constraints *View*

Column	Type	Description
owner	VARCHAR2(30)	Owner of the constraint
constraint_name	VARCHAR2(30)	Name of the constraint
table_name	VARCHAR2(30)	Name of the table on which the constraint is defined
column_name	VARCHAR2(4000)	Name of the column on which the constraint is defined

TABLE 10-5 *Some Columns in the* user_cons_columns *View*

The following example retrieves the constraint_name and column_name from user_cons_columns for the order_status2 table:

```
COLUMN column_name FORMAT a15
SELECT constraint_name, column_name
FROM user_cons_columns
WHERE table_name = 'ORDER_STATUS2'
ORDER BY constraint_name;
```

```
CONSTRAINT_NAME                  COLUMN_NAME
-------------------------------- ---------------
ORDER_STATUS2_ID_CK              ID
ORDER_STATUS2_PK                 ID
ORDER_STATUS2_STATUS_CK          STATUS
ORDER_STATUS2_STATUS_NN          STATUS
ORDER_STATUS2_STATUS_UQ          STATUS
SYS_C004807                      LAST_MODIFIED
```

The next query joins user_constraints and user_cons_columns to get the column_name, constraint_name, constraint_type, and status:

```
SELECT ucc.column_name, ucc.constraint_name, uc.constraint_type, uc.status
FROM user_constraints uc, user_cons_columns ucc
WHERE uc.table_name = ucc.table_name
AND uc.constraint_name = ucc.constraint_name
AND ucc.table_name = 'ORDER_STATUS2'
ORDER BY ucc.constraint_name;
```

```
COLUMN_NAME     CONSTRAINT_NAME                  C STATUS
--------------- -------------------------------- - --------
ID              ORDER_STATUS2_ID_CK              C ENABLED
ID              ORDER_STATUS2_PK                 P ENABLED
STATUS          ORDER_STATUS2_STATUS_CK          C ENABLED
STATUS          ORDER_STATUS2_STATUS_NN          C DISABLED
STATUS          ORDER_STATUS2_STATUS_UQ          U ENABLED
LAST_MODIFIED   SYS_C004807                      C ENABLED
```

Renaming a Table

You rename a table using the RENAME statement. The following example renames order_status2 to order_state:

```
RENAME order_status2 TO order_state;
```

NOTE
If you have used the table name in your constraint names, then you should change the names of your constraints.

The next example changes the table name back to the original:

```
RENAME order_state TO order_status2;
```

Adding a Comment to a Table

A comment can help you remember what the table or column is used for. You add a comment table or column using the COMMENT statement. The following example adds a comment to the order_status2 table:

```
COMMENT ON TABLE order_status2 IS
'order_status2 stores the state of an order';
```

The next example adds a comment to the order_status2.last_modified column:

```
COMMENT ON COLUMN order_status2.last_modified IS
'last_modified stores the date and time the order was modified last';
```

Retrieving Table Comments

You can retrieve the comments on your tables from the user_tab_comments view, as shown here:

```
SELECT *
FROM user_tab_comments
WHERE table_name = 'ORDER_STATUS2';

TABLE_NAME                      TABLE_TYPE
------------------------------- -----------
COMMENTS
----------------------------------------
ORDER_STATUS2                   TABLE
order_status2 stores the state of an order
```

Retrieving Column Comments

You can retrieve the comments on your columns from the user_col_comments view; for example:

```
SELECT *
FROM user_col_comments
WHERE table_name = 'ORDER_STATUS2';

TABLE_NAME                      COLUMN_NAME
------------------------------- ------------------------------
COMMENTS
------------------------------------------------------------
ORDER_STATUS2                   ID
```

```
ORDER_STATUS2                        STATUS

ORDER_STATUS2                        LAST_MODIFIED
last_modified stores the date and time the order was modified last
```

Truncating a Table

You truncate a table using the TRUNCATE statement. This removes *all* the rows from a table and resets the storage area for a table. The following example truncates order_status2:

 TRUNCATE TABLE order_status2;

TIP
If you need to remove all the rows from a table, you should use TRUNCATE *rather than* DELETE. *This is because* TRUNCATE *resets the storage area for a table ready to receive new rows. A* TRUNCATE *statement doesn't require any undo space in the database, and you don't have to run a* COMMIT *to make the delete permanent. Undo space is an area that the database software uses to record database changes.*

Dropping a Table

You drop a table using the DROP TABLE statement. The following example drops the order_status2 table:

DROP TABLE order_status2;

This concludes the discussion of tables. In the next section, you'll learn about sequences.

Sequences

A *sequence* is a database item that generates a sequence of integers. You typically use the integers generated by a sequence to populate a numeric primary key column. In this section, you'll learn how to

- Create a sequence.
- Retrieve information on a sequence from the data dictionary.
- Use a sequence.
- Modify a sequence.
- Drop a sequence.

Creating a Sequence

You create a sequence using the CREATE SEQUENCE statement, which has the following syntax:

```
CREATE SEQUENCE sequence_name
[START WITH start_num]
[INCREMENT BY increment_num]
[ { MAXVALUE maximum_num | NOMAXVALUE } ]
```

```
[ { MINVALUE minimum_num | NOMINVALUE } ]
[ { CYCLE | NOCYCLE } ]
[ { CACHE cache_num | NOCACHE } ]
[ { ORDER | NOORDER } ];
```

where

- *sequence_name* is the name of the sequence.

- *start_num* is the integer to start the sequence. The default start number is 1.

- *increment_num* is the integer to increment the sequence by. The default increment number is 1. The absolute value of *increment_num* must be less than the difference between *maximum_num* and *minimum_num*.

- *maximum_num* is the maximum integer of the sequence; *maximum_num* must be greater than or equal to *start_num*, and *maximum_num* must be greater than *minimum_num*.

- NOMAXVALUE specifies the maximum is 10^{27} for an ascending sequence or -1 for a descending sequence. NOMAXVALUE is the default.

- *minimum_num* is the minimum integer of the sequence; *minimum_num* must be less than or equal to *start_num*, and *minimum_num* must be less than *maximum_num*.

- NOMINVALUE specifies the minimum is 1 for an ascending sequence or -10^{26} for a descending sequence. NOMINVALUE is the default.

- CYCLE means the sequence generates integers even after reaching its maximum or minimum value. When an ascending sequence reaches its maximum value, the next value generated is the minimum. When a descending sequence reaches its minimum value, the next value generated is the maximum.

- NOCYCLE means the sequence cannot generate any more integers after reaching its maximum or minimum value. NOCYCLE is the default.

- *cache_num* is the number of integers to keep in memory. The default number of integers to cache is 20. The minimum number of integers that may be cached is 2. The maximum integers that may be cached is determined by the formula CEIL (*maximum_num* – *minimum_num*) /ABS (*increment_num*).

- NOCACHE means no caching. This stops the database from pre-allocating values for the sequence, which prevents numeric gaps in the sequence but reduces performance. Gaps occur because cached values are lost when the database is shut down. If you omit CACHE and NOCACHE, the database caches 20 sequence numbers by default.

- ORDER guarantees the integers are generated in the order of the request. You typically use ORDER when using Real Application Clusters, which are set up and managed by database administrators. Real Application Clusters are multiple database servers that share the same memory. Real Application Clusters can improve performance.

- NOORDER doesn't guarantee the integers are generated in the order of the request. NOORDER is the default.

The following example connects as the `store` user and creates a sequence named `s_test` (I always put `s_` at the beginning of sequences):

```
CONNECT store/store_password
CREATE SEQUENCE s_test;
```

Because this `CREATE SEQUENCE` statement omits the optional parameters, the default values are used. This means that *start_num* and *increment_num* are set to the default of 1.

The next example creates a sequence named `s_test2` and specifies values for the optional parameters:

```
CREATE SEQUENCE s_test2
START WITH 10 INCREMENT BY 5
MINVALUE 10 MAXVALUE 20
CYCLE CACHE 2 ORDER;
```

The final example creates a sequence named `s_test3` that starts at 10 and counts down to 1:

```
CREATE SEQUENCE s_test3
START WITH 10 INCREMENT BY -1
MINVALUE 1 MAXVALUE 10
CYCLE CACHE 5;
```

Retrieving Information on Sequences

You can retrieve information on your sequences from the `user_sequences` view. Table 10-6 describes the columns in `user_sequences`.

NOTE
You can retrieve information on all the sequences you have access to by querying the `all_sequences` *view.*

Column	Type	Description
sequence_name	VARCHAR2(30)	Name of the sequence
min_value	NUMBER	Minimum value
max_value	NUMBER	Maximum value
increment_by	NUMBER	Number to increment or decrement sequence by
cycle_flag	VARCHAR2(1)	Whether the sequence cycles (Y or N)
order_flag	VARCHAR2(1)	Whether the sequence is ordered (Y or N)
cache_size	NUMBER	Number of sequence values stored in memory
last_number	NUMBER	Last number that was generated or cached by the sequence

TABLE 10-6 *Some Columns in the* `user_sequences` *View*

The following example retrieves the details for the sequences from `user_sequences`:

```
COLUMN sequence_name FORMAT a13
SELECT * FROM user_sequences
ORDER BY sequence_name;
```

```
SEQUENCE_NAME  MIN_VALUE  MAX_VALUE INCREMENT_BY C O CACHE_SIZE LAST_NUMBER
------------- ---------- ---------- ------------ - - ---------- -----------
S_TEST                 1 1.0000E+27            1 N N         20           1
S_TEST2               10         20            5 Y Y          2          10
S_TEST3                1         10           -1 Y N          5          10
```

Using a Sequence

A sequence generates a series of numbers. A sequence contains two pseudo columns named `currval` and `nextval` that you use to get the current value and the next value from the sequence.

Before retrieving the current value, you must first initialize the sequence by retrieving the next value. When you select `s_test.nextval` the sequence is initialized to 1. For example, the following query retrieves `s_test.nextval`; notice that the `dual` table is used in the FROM clause:

```
SELECT s_test.nextval
FROM dual;
```

```
   NEXTVAL
----------
         1
```

The first value in the `s_test` sequence is 1. Once the sequence is initialized, you can get the current value from the sequence by retrieving `currval`. For example:

```
SELECT s_test.currval
FROM dual;
```

```
   CURRVAL
----------
         1
```

When you retrieve `currval`, `nextval` remains unchanged; `nextval` only changes when you retrieve `nextval` to get the next value. The following example retrieves `s_test.nextval` and `s_test.currval`; notice that these values are both 2:

```
SELECT s_test.nextval, s_test.currval
FROM dual;
```

```
   NEXTVAL    CURRVAL
---------- ----------
         2          2
```

Retrieving `s_test.nextval` gets the next value in the sequence, which is 2; `s_test`
`.currval` is also 2.

The next example initializes s_test2 by retrieving s_test2.nextval; notice that the first value in the sequence is 10:

```
SELECT s_test2.nextval
FROM dual;

  NEXTVAL
----------
       10
```

The maximum value for s_test2 is 20, and the sequence was created with the CYCLE option, meaning that the sequence will cycle back to 10 once it reaches the maximum of 20:

```
SELECT s_test2.nextval
FROM dual;

  NEXTVAL
----------
       15
```

```
SELECT s_test2.nextval
FROM dual;

  NEXTVAL
----------
       20
```

```
SELECT s_test2.nextval
FROM dual;

  NEXTVAL
----------
       10
```

The s_test3 sequence starts at 10 and counts down to 1:

```
SELECT s_test3.nextval
FROM dual;

  NEXTVAL
----------
       10
```

```
SELECT s_test3.nextval
FROM dual;

  NEXTVAL
----------
        9
```

```
SELECT s_test3.nextval
FROM dual;
```

```
NEXTVAL
----------
         8
```

Populating a Primary Key Using a Sequence

Sequences are useful for populating integer primary key column values. Let's take a look at an example. The following statement re-creates the `order_status2` table:

```
CREATE TABLE order_status2 (
  id INTEGER CONSTRAINT order_status2_pk PRIMARY KEY,
  status VARCHAR2(10),
  last_modified DATE DEFAULT SYSDATE
);
```

Next, the following statement creates a sequence named `s_order_status2` (this sequence will be used to populate the `order_status2.id` column shortly):

```
CREATE SEQUENCE s_order_status2 NOCACHE;
```

TIP

When using a sequence to populate a primary key column, you should typically use NOCACHE *to avoid gaps in the sequence of numbers (gaps occur because cached values are lost when the database is shut down). However, using* NOCACHE *reduces performance. If you are* absolutely sure *you can live with gaps in the primary key values, then consider using* CACHE.

The following INSERT statements add rows to `order_status2`; notice that the value for the id column is set using `s_order_status2.nextval` (returns 1 for the first INSERT and 2 for the second INSERT):

```
INSERT INTO order_status2 (
  id, status, last_modified
) VALUES (
  s_order_status2.nextval, 'PLACED', '01-JAN-2006'
);

INSERT INTO order_status2 (
  id, status, last_modified
) VALUES (
  s_order_status2.nextval, 'PENDING', '01-FEB-2006'
);
```

The following query retrieves the rows from `order_status2`; notice that the id column is set to the first two values (1 and 2) from the `s_order_status2` sequence:

```
SELECT *
FROM order_status2;

        ID STATUS     LAST_MODI
---------- ---------- ---------
         1 PLACED     01-JAN-06
         2 PENDING    01-FEB-06
```

Modifying a Sequence

You modify a sequence using the ALTER SEQUENCE statement. There are some limitations on what you can modify in a sequence:

- You cannot change the start value of a sequence.

- The minimum value cannot be more than the current value of the sequence.

- The maximum value cannot be less than the current value of the sequence.

The following example modifies s_test to increment the sequence of numbers by 2:

```
ALTER SEQUENCE s_test
INCREMENT BY 2;
```

When this is done, the new values generated by s_test will be incremented by 2. For example, if s_test.currval is 2, then s_test.nextval is 4. This is shown in the following example:

```
SELECT s_test.currval
FROM dual;

    CURRVAL
----------
          2

SELECT s_test.nextval
FROM dual;

    NEXTVAL
----------
          4
```

Dropping a Sequence

You drop a sequence using DROP SEQUENCE. The following example drops s_test3:

```
DROP SEQUENCE s_test3;
```

This concludes the discussion of sequences. In the next section, you'll learn about indexes.

Indexes

When looking for a particular topic in a book, you can either scan the whole book, or you can use the index to find the location. An index for a database table is similar in concept to a book index, except that database indexes are used to find specific rows in a table. The downside of indexes is that when a row is added to the table, additional time is required to update the index for the new row.

Generally, you should create an index on a column when you are retrieving a small number of rows from a table containing many rows. A good rule of thumb is

Create an index when a query retrieves <= 10 percent of the total rows in a table.

This means the column for the index should contain a wide range of values. These types of indexes are called "B-tree" indexes, a name which comes from a tree data structure used in computer science. A good candidate for B-tree indexing would be a column containing a unique value for each row (for example, a social security number). A poor candidate for B-tree indexing would be a column that contains only a small range of values (for example, N, S, E, W or 1, 2, 3, 4, 5, 6). An Oracle database automatically creates a B-tree index for the primary key of a table and for columns included in a unique constraint. For columns that contain a small range of values, you can use a "bitmap" index.

In this section, you'll learn how to

- Create a B-tree index.

- Create a function-based index.

- Retrieve information on an index from the data dictionary.

- Modify an index.

- Drop an index.

- Create a bitmap index.

Creating a B-tree Index

You create a B-tree index using CREATE INDEX, which has the following simplified syntax:

```
CREATE [UNIQUE] INDEX index_name ON
table_name(column_name[, column_name ...])
TABLESPACE tab_space;
```

where

- UNIQUE means that the values in the indexed columns must be unique.

- *index_name* is the name of the index.

- *table_name* is a database table.

- *column_name* is the indexed column. You can create an index on multiple columns (such an index is known as a *composite index*).

- *tab_space* is the tablespace for the index. If you don't provide a tablespace, the index is stored in the user's default tablespace.

TIP

For performance reasons, you should typically store indexes in a different tablespace from tables. For simplicity, the examples in this chapter use the default tablespace. In a production database, the database administrator should create separate tablespaces for the tables and indexes.

I'll now guide you through the thought processes you should follow when creating a B-tree index for the `customers.last_name` column. Assume that the `customers` table contains a large number of rows and that you regularly retrieve rows using the following type of query:

```
SELECT customer_id, first_name, last_name
FROM customers
WHERE last_name = 'Brown';
```

Also assume that the `last_name` column contains somewhat unique values, so that any query using the `last_name` column in a `WHERE` clause will return less than 10 percent of the total number of rows in the table. This means the `last_name` column is therefore a good candidate for indexing.

The following `CREATE INDEX` statement creates an index named `i_customers_last_name` on the `last_name` column of the `customers` table (I always put `i_` at the start of index names):

```
CREATE INDEX i_customers_last_name ON customers(last_name);
```

Once the index has been created, the previous query will take less time to complete.

You can enforce uniqueness of column values using a unique index. For example, the following statement creates a unique index named `i_customers_phone` on the `customers.phone` column:

```
CREATE UNIQUE INDEX i_customers_phone ON customers(phone);
```

You can also create a composite index on multiple columns. For example, the following statement creates a composite index named `i_employees_first_last_name` on the `first_name` and `last_name` columns of the `employees` table:

```
CREATE INDEX i_employees_first_last_name ON
employees(first_name, last_name);
```

Creating a Function-Based Index

In the previous section you saw the index `i_customers_last_name`. Let's say you run the following query:

```
SELECT first_name, last_name
FROM customers
WHERE last_name = UPPER('BROWN');
```

Because this query uses a function—`UPPER()`, in this case—the `i_customers_last_name` index isn't used. If you want an index to be based on the results of a function, you must create a function-based index, such as:

```
CREATE INDEX i_func_customers_last_name
ON customers(UPPER(last_name));
```

In addition, the database administrator must set the initialization parameter `QUERY_REWRITE_ENABLED` to `true` (the default is `false`) in order to take advantage of function-based indexes. The following example sets `QUERY_REWRITE_ENABLED` to `true`:

```
CONNECT system/manager
ALTER SYSTEM SET QUERY_REWRITE_ENABLED=TRUE;
```

Retrieving Information on Indexes

You can retrieve information on your indexes from the `user_indexes` view. Table 10-7 describes some of the columns in `user_indexes`.

NOTE
You can retrieve information on all the indexes you have access to by querying the `all_indexes` *view.*

The following example connects as the `store` user and retrieves some of the columns from `user_indexes` for the `customers` and `employees` tables; notice that the list of indexes includes `customers_pk`, which is a unique index automatically created by the database for the `customer_id` primary key column of the `customers` table:

```
CONNECT store/store_password
SELECT index_name, table_name, uniqueness, status
FROM user_indexes
WHERE table_name IN ('CUSTOMERS', 'EMPLOYEES')
ORDER BY index_name;

INDEX_NAME                        TABLE_NAME            UNIQUENES STATUS
--------------------------------  --------------------  --------- ------
CUSTOMERS_PK                      CUSTOMERS             UNIQUE    VALID
EMPLOYEES_PK                      EMPLOYEES             UNIQUE    VALID
I_CUSTOMERS_LAST_NAME             CUSTOMERS             NONUNIQUE VALID
I_CUSTOMERS_PHONE                 CUSTOMERS             UNIQUE    VALID
I_EMPLOYEES_FIRST_LAST_NAME       EMPLOYEES             NONUNIQUE VALID
I_FUNC_CUSTOMERS_LAST_NAME        CUSTOMERS             NONUNIQUE VALID
```

Retrieving Information on the Indexes on a Column

You can retrieve information on the indexes on a column by querying the `user_ind_columns` view. Table 10-8 describes some of the columns in `user_ind_columns`.

Column	Type	Description
index_name	VARCHAR2(30)	Name of the index
table_owner	VARCHAR2(30)	The user who owns the table
table_name	VARCHAR2(30)	The name of the table on which the index was created
uniqueness	VARCHAR2(9)	Indicates whether the index is unique (UNIQUE or NONUNIQUE)
status	VARCHAR2(8)	Indicates whether the index is valid (VALID or INVALID)

TABLE 10-7 *Some Columns in the* `user_indexes` *View*

Column	Type	Description
index_name	VARCHAR2(30)	Name of the index
table_name	VARCHAR2(30)	Name of the table
column_name	VARCHAR2(4000)	Name of the indexed column

TABLE 10-8   *Some Columns in the* `user_ind_columns` *View*

NOTE
You can retrieve information on all the indexes you have access to by querying the `all_ind_columns` *view.*

The following query retrieves some of the columns from `user_ind_columns` for the `customers` and `employees` tables:

```
COLUMN table_name FORMAT a15
COLUMN column_name FORMAT a15
SELECT index_name, table_name, column_name
FROM user_ind_columns
WHERE table_name IN ('CUSTOMERS', 'EMPLOYEES')
ORDER BY index_name;

INDEX_NAME                      TABLE_NAME        COLUMN_NAME
------------------------------- ----------------- ------------
CUSTOMERS_PK                    CUSTOMERS         CUSTOMER_ID
EMPLOYEES_PK                    EMPLOYEES         EMPLOYEE_ID
I_CUSTOMERS_LAST_NAME           CUSTOMERS         LAST_NAME
I_CUSTOMERS_PHONE               CUSTOMERS         PHONE
I_EMPLOYEES_FIRST_LAST_NAME     EMPLOYEES         LAST_NAME
I_EMPLOYEES_FIRST_LAST_NAME     EMPLOYEES         FIRST_NAME
I_FUNC_CUSTOMERS_LAST_NAME      CUSTOMERS         SYS_NC00006$
```

Modifying an Index

You modify an index using `ALTER INDEX`. The following example renames the `i_customers_phone` index to `i_customers_phone_number`:

```
ALTER INDEX i_customers_phone RENAME TO i_customers_phone_number;
```

Dropping an Index

You drop an index using the `DROP INDEX` statement. The following example drops the `i_customers_phone_number` index:

```
DROP INDEX i_customers_phone_number;
```

Creating a Bitmap Index

Bitmap indexes are typically used in *data warehouses*, which are databases containing very large amounts of data. The data in a data warehouse is typically read using many queries, but the data is not modified by many concurrent transactions. Data warehouses are typically used by organizations for business intelligence analysis, like monitoring sales trends.

A candidate for a bitmap index is a column that is referenced in many queries, but that contains only a small range of values; for example:

- N, S, E, W

- 1, 2, 3, 4, 5, 6

- "Order placed", "Order shipped"

An index basically contains a pointer to a row in a table that contains a given index key value; the key value is used to get the rowid for the row in the table. (As discussed in Chapter 2, a rowid is used internally by the database to store the physical location of the row.) In a B-tree index, a list of rowids is stored for each key corresponding to the rows with that key value. In a B-tree index, the database stores a list of key values with each rowid, which enables the database to locate an actual row in a table.

In a bitmap index, however, a bitmap is used for each key value; the bitmap enables the database to locate a row. Each bit in the bitmap corresponds to a possible rowid. If the bit is set, then it means that the row with the corresponding rowid contains the key value. A mapping function converts the bit position to an actual rowid.

Bitmap indexes are typically used in tables containing large amounts of data and whose contents are not modified very often. Also, a bitmap index should only be created on columns that contain a small number of distinct values. If the number of distinct values of a column is less than 1 percent of the number of rows in the table, or if the values in a column are repeated more than 100 times, then the column is a candidate for a bitmap index. For example, if you had a table with 1 million rows, a column with 10,000 distinct values or less is a good candidate for a bitmap index; also, updates to the rows in the table should be rare, and the column would need to be frequently used in the WHERE clause of queries.

The following statement creates a bitmap index on the `status` column of the `order_status` table:

```
CREATE BITMAP INDEX i_order_status ON order_status(status);
```

NOTE
Of course, this example is not a real-world example because the `order_status` *table does not contain enough rows.*

You can find more information on bitmap indexes in *Oracle Database Performance Tuning Guide* and *Oracle Database Concepts,* both books published by Oracle Corporation. These books also contain information about other exotic types of indexes you can use.

This concludes the discussion of indexes. In the next section, you'll learn about views.

Views

A view is a predefined query on one or more tables (known as *base tables*). Retrieving information from a view is done in the same manner as retrieving from a table: you simply include the view in the FROM clause of a query. With some views you can also perform DML operations on the base tables.

NOTE
Views don't store rows. Rows are always stored in tables.

You've already seen some examples of retrieving information from views when you selected rows from the data dictionary, which is accessed through views—for example, user_tables, user_sequences, and user_indexes are all views.

Views offer several benefits, such as the following:

- You can put a complex query into a view and grant users access to the view. This allows you to hide complexity from users.

- You can stop users from directly querying the base tables by granting them access only to the view.

- You can allow a view to access only certain rows in the base tables. This allows you to hide rows from an end user.

In this section, you'll learn how to

- Create and use a view.

- Get the details of a view from the data dictionary.

- Modify a view.

- Drop a view.

Creating and Using a View

You create a view using CREATE VIEW, which has the following simplified syntax:

```
CREATE [OR REPLACE] VIEW [{FORCE | NOFORCE}] VIEW view_name
[(alias_name[, alias_name ...])] AS subquery
[WITH {CHECK OPTION | READ ONLY} CONSTRAINT constraint_name];
```

where

- OR REPLACE means the view replaces an existing view.

- FORCE means the view is to be created even if the base tables don't exist.

- NOFORCE means the view is not created if the base tables don't exist. NOFORCE is the default.

- view_name is the name of the view.

- alias_name is the name of an alias for an expression in the subquery. There must be the same number of aliases as there are expressions in the subquery.

- subquery is the subquery that retrieves from the base tables. If you've supplied aliases, you can use those aliases in the list after the SELECT.

- WITH CHECK OPTION means that only the rows that would be retrieved by the subquery can be inserted, updated, or deleted. By default, the rows are not checked.

- *constraint_name* is the name of the WITH CHECK OPTION or WITH READ ONLY constraint.
- WITH READ ONLY means the rows may only read from the base tables.

There are two basic types of views:

- Simple views, which contain a subquery that retrieves from one base table
- Complex views, which contain a subquery that
  - Retrieves from multiple base tables
  - Groups rows using a GROUP BY or DISTINCT clause
  - Contains a function call

You'll learn how to create and use these types of views in the following sections.

Privilege for Views

In order to create a view, the user must have the CREATE VIEW privilege. The following example connects as the system user and grants the CREATE VIEW privilege to the store user:

```
CONNECT system/manager
GRANT CREATE VIEW TO store;
```

Creating and Using Simple Views

Simple views access one base table. The following example connects as the store user and creates a view named cheap_products_view whose subquery retrieves products only where the price is less than $15:

```
CONNECT store/store_password
CREATE VIEW cheap_products_view AS
SELECT *
FROM products
WHERE price < 15;
```

The next example creates a view named employees_view whose subquery retrieves all the columns from the employees table except salary:

```
CREATE VIEW employees_view AS
SELECT employee_id, manager_id, first_name, last_name, title
FROM employees;
```

Performing a Query on a View

Once you've created a view, you can use it to access the base table. The following query retrieves rows from cheap_products_view:

```
SELECT product_id, name, price
FROM cheap_products_view;
```

```
PRODUCT_ID NAME                                    PRICE
---------- ------------------------------ ----------
         4 Tank War                                13.95
         6 2412: The Return                        14.95
```

```
 7 Space Force 9                          13.49
 8 From Another Planet                    12.99
 9 Classical Music                        10.99
11 Creative Yell                          14.99
12 My Front Line                          13.49
```

The next example retrieves rows from `employees_view`:

```
SELECT *
FROM employees_view;
```

```
EMPLOYEE_ID MANAGER_ID FIRST_NAME LAST_NAME  TITLE
----------- ---------- ---------- ---------- -------------
          1            James      Smith      CEO
          2          1 Ron        Johnson    Sales Manager
          3          2 Fred       Hobbs      Salesperson
          4          2 Susan      Jones      Salesperson
```

Performing an INSERT Using a View

You can perform DML statements using `cheap_products_view`. The following example performs an `INSERT` using `cheap_products_view` and then retrieves the row:

```
INSERT INTO cheap_products_view (
  product_id, product_type_id, name, price
) VALUES (
  13, 1, 'Western Front', 13.50
);
```

```
1 row created.
```

```
SELECT product_id, name, price
FROM cheap_products_view
WHERE product_id = 13;
```

```
PRODUCT_ID NAME                                     PRICE
---------- -------------------------------- ----------
        13 Western Front                             13.5
```

NOTE
You can perform DML statements only with simple views. Complex views don't support DML.

Because `cheap_products_view` didn't use `WITH CHECK OPTION`, you can insert, update, and delete rows that aren't retrievable by the view. The following example inserts a row whose price is $16.50 (this is greater than $15 and therefore not retrievable by the view):

```
INSERT INTO cheap_products_view (
  product_id, product_type_id, name, price
) VALUES (
  14, 1, 'Eastern Front', 16.50
);
```

```
1 row created.
```

```
SELECT *
FROM cheap_products_view
WHERE product_id = 14;
```

```
no rows selected
```

The `employees_view` contains a subquery that selects every column from `employees` except `salary`. When you perform an `INSERT` using `employees_view`, the `salary` column in the `employees` base table will be set to null; for example:

```
INSERT INTO employees_view (
   employee_id, manager_id, first_name, last_name, title
) VALUES (
   5, 1, 'Jeff', 'Jones', 'CTO'
);
```

```
1 row created.
```

```
SELECT employee_id, first_name, last_name, salary
FROM employees
WHERE employee_id = 5;
```

```
EMPLOYEE_ID FIRST_NAME LAST_NAME    SALARY
----------- ---------- ---------- ---------
          5 Jeff       Jones
```

The `salary` column is null.

Creating a View with a CHECK OPTION Constraint

You can specify that DML statements on a view must satisfy the subquery using a `CHECK OPTION` constraint. For example, the following statement creates a view named `cheap_products_view2` that has a `CHECK OPTION` constraint:

```
CREATE VIEW cheap_products_view2 AS
SELECT *
FROM products
WHERE price < 15
WITH CHECK OPTION CONSTRAINT cheap_products_view2_price;
```

The next example attempts to insert a row using `cheap_products_view2` with a price of $19.50; notice that the database returns an error because the row isn't retrievable by the view:

```
INSERT INTO cheap_products_view2 (
   product_id, product_type_id, name, price
) VALUES (
   15, 1, 'Southern Front', 19.50
);
INSERT INTO cheap_products_view2 (
            *
ERROR at line 1:
ORA-01402: view WITH CHECK OPTION where-clause violation
```

Creating a View with a READ ONLY Constraint

You can make a view read-only by adding a READ ONLY constraint to the view. For example, the following statement creates a view named cheap_products_view3 that has a READ ONLY constraint:

```
CREATE VIEW cheap_products_view3 AS
SELECT *
FROM products
WHERE price < 15
WITH READ ONLY CONSTRAINT cheap_products_view3_read_only;
```

The following example attempts to insert a row using cheap_products_view3; notice that the database returns an error because the view is read-only and doesn't allow DML statements:

```
INSERT INTO cheap_products_view3 (
  product_id, product_type_id, name, price
) VALUES (
  16, 1, 'Northern Front', 19.50
);
  product_id, product_type_id, name, price
  *
ERROR at line 2:
ORA-42399: cannot perform a DML operation on a read-only view
```

Getting Information on View Definitions

You can retrieve information on view definitions using the DESCRIBE command. The following example uses DESCRIBE with cheap_products_view3:

```
DESCRIBE cheap_products_view3
 Name                                      Null?    Type
 ----------------------------------------- -------- ------------
 PRODUCT_ID                                NOT NULL NUMBER(38)
 PRODUCT_TYPE_ID                                    NUMBER(38)
 NAME                                      NOT NULL VARCHAR2(30)
 DESCRIPTION                                        VARCHAR2(50)
 PRICE                                              NUMBER(5,2)
```

You can also retrieve information about your views from the user_views view. Table 10-9 describes some of the columns in user_views.

Column	Type	Description
view_name	VARCHAR2(30)	Name of the view
text_length	NUMBER	Number of characters in the view's subquery
text	LONG	Text of the view's subquery

TABLE 10-9   *Some Columns in the* user_views *View*

NOTE
You can retrieve information on all the indexes you have access to by querying `all_views`.

To see the entire view definition stored in the `text` column, you use the SQL*Plus command `SET LONG`, which sets the number of characters displayed by SQL*Plus when retrieving `LONG` columns. For example, the following command sets `LONG` to 200:

```
SET LONG 200
```

The following query retrieves the `view_name`, `text_length`, and `text` columns from `user_views`:

```
SELECT view_name, text_length, text
FROM user_views
ORDER BY view_name;


VIEW_NAME                            TEXT_LENGTH
------------------------------ -----------
TEXT
-----------------------------------------------------------------
CHEAP_PRODUCTS_VIEW                       97
SELECT "PRODUCT_ID","PRODUCT_TYPE_ID","NAME","DESCRIPTION","PRICE"
FROM products
WHERE price < 15

CHEAP_PRODUCTS_VIEW2                      116
SELECT "PRODUCT_ID","PRODUCT_TYPE_ID","NAME","DESCRIPTION","PRICE"
FROM products
WHERE price < 15
WITH CHECK OPTION

CHEAP_PRODUCTS_VIEW3                      113
SELECT "PRODUCT_ID","PRODUCT_TYPE_ID","NAME","DESCRIPTION","PRICE"
FROM products
WHERE price < 15
WITH READ ONLY

EMPLOYEES_VIEW                            75
SELECT employee_id, manager_id, first_name, last_name, title
FROM employees
```

Retrieving Information on View Constraints

Earlier you saw that you can add CHECK OPTION and READ ONLY constraints to a view; `cheap_products_view2` contained a CHECK OPTION constraint to ensure the price was less than $15; `cheap_products_view3` contained a READ ONLY constraint to prevent modifications to the rows in the base table.

You retrieve information on view constraints from the `user_constraints` view; for example:

```
SELECT constraint_name, constraint_type, status, deferrable, deferred
FROM user_constraints
WHERE table_name IN ('CHEAP_PRODUCTS_VIEW2', 'CHEAP_PRODUCTS_VIEW3')
```

```
ORDER BY constraint_name;

CONSTRAINT_NAME                    C STATUS    DEFERRABLE     DEFERRED
--------------------------------   - --------  -------------- ---------
CHEAP_PRODUCTS_VIEW2_PRICE         V ENABLED   NOT DEFERRABLE IMMEDIATE
CHEAP_PRODUCTS_VIEW3_READ_ONLY     O ENABLED   NOT DEFERRABLE IMMEDIATE
```

The `constraint_type` for `CHEAP_PRODUCTS_VIEW2_PRICE` is V, which, as shown earlier in Table 10-3, corresponds to a `CHECK OPTION` constraint. The `constraint_type` for `CHEAP_PRODUCTS_VIEW3_READ_ONLY` is O, which corresponds to a `READ ONLY` constraint.

Creating and Using Complex Views

Complex views contain subqueries that

- Retrieve rows from multiple base tables.

- Group rows using a `GROUP BY` or `DISTINCT` clause.

- Contain a function call.

The following example creates a view named `products_and_types_view` whose subquery performs a full outer join on the `products` and `product_types` tables using the SQL/92 syntax:

```
CREATE VIEW products_and_types_view AS
SELECT p.product_id, p.name product_name, pt.name product_type_name, p.price
FROM products p FULL OUTER JOIN product_types pt
USING (product_type_id)
ORDER BY p.product_id;
```

The following example queries `products_and_types_view`:

```
SELECT *
FROM products_and_types_view;

PRODUCT_ID PRODUCT_NAME                    PRODUCT_TY     PRICE
---------- ------------------------------  ----------  ----------
         1 Modern Science                  Book           19.95
         2 Chemistry                       Book              30
         3 Supernova                       Video          25.99
         4 Tank War                        Video          13.95
         5 Z Files                         Video          49.99
         6 2412: The Return                Video          14.95
         7 Space Force 9                   DVD            13.49
         8 From Another Planet             DVD            12.99
         9 Classical Music                 CD             10.99
        10 Pop 3                           CD             15.99
        11 Creative Yell                   CD             14.99
        12 My Front Line                                  13.49
        13 Western Front                   Book            13.5
        14 Eastern Front                   Book            16.5
                                           Magazine
```

The next example creates a view named `employee_salary_grades_view` whose subquery uses an inner join to retrieve the salary grades for the employees:

```
CREATE VIEW employee_salary_grades_view AS
SELECT e.first_name, e.last_name, e.title, e.salary, sg.salary_grade_id
FROM employees e INNER JOIN salary_grades sg
ON e.salary BETWEEN sg.low_salary AND sg.high_salary
ORDER BY sg.salary_grade_id;
```

The following example queries `employee_salary_grades_view`:

```
SELECT *
FROM employee_salary_grades_view;

FIRST_NAME LAST_NAME  TITLE                    SALARY SALARY_GRADE_ID
---------- ---------- -------------------- ---------- ---------------
Fred       Hobbs      Salesperson              150000               1
Susan      Jones      Salesperson              500000               2
Ron        Johnson    Sales Manager            600000               3
James      Smith      CEO                      800000               4
```

The next example creates a view named `product_average_view` whose subquery uses

- A WHERE clause to filter the rows from the `products` table to those whose `price` is less than $15.

- A GROUP BY clause to group the remaining rows by the `product_type_id` column.

- A HAVING clause to filter the row groups to those whose average price is greater than $13.

```
CREATE VIEW product_average_view AS
SELECT product_type_id, AVG(price) average_price
FROM products
WHERE price < 15
GROUP BY product_type_id
HAVING AVG(price) > 13
ORDER BY product_type_id;
```

The following example queries `product_average_view`:

```
SELECT *
FROM product_average_view;

PRODUCT_TYPE_ID AVERAGE_PRICE
--------------- -------------
              1          13.5
              2         14.45
              3         13.24
                        13.49
```

Modifying a View

You can completely replace a view using CREATE OR REPLACE VIEW. The following example uses CREATE OR REPLACE VIEW to replace `product_average_view`:

```
CREATE OR REPLACE VIEW product_average_view AS
SELECT product_type_id, AVG(price) average_price
FROM products
```

```
WHERE price < 12
GROUP BY product_type_id
HAVING AVG(price) > 11
ORDER BY product_type_id;
```

You can alter the constraints on a view using ALTER VIEW. The following example uses ALTER VIEW to drop the cheap_products_view2_price constraint from cheap_products_view2:

```
ALTER VIEW cheap_products_view2
DROP CONSTRAINT cheap_products_view2_price;
```

Dropping a View

You drop a view using DROP VIEW. The following example drops cheap_products_view2:

```
DROP VIEW cheap_products_view2;
```

This concludes the discussion of views. In the next section, you'll learn about flashback data archives.

Flashback Data Archives

Flashback data archives, which are new for Oracle Database 11*g*, store changes made to a table over a period of time and provide you with a full audit trail. Once you've created a flashback archive and added a table to it you can do the following:

- View rows as they were at a specific timestamp

- View rows as they were between two timestamps

You create a flashback archive using the CREATE FLASHBACK ARCHIVE statement. The following example connects as the system user and creates a flashback archive named test_archive:

```
CONNECT system/manager
CREATE FLASHBACK ARCHIVE test_archive
TABLESPACE example
QUOTA 1 M
RETENTION 1 DAY;
```

Notice the following:

- The archive is created in the example tablespace; you can see the full list of tablespaces by running the query SELECT tablespace_name FROM dba_tablespaces.

- The test_archive has a quota of 1 megabyte, which means it can store up to 1 megabyte of data in the example tablespace.

- The data in test_archive is retained for 1 day, after which time the data is purged.

You may alter an existing table to store data in the archive; for example:

```
ALTER TABLE store.products FLASHBACK ARCHIVE test_archive;
```

Any subsequent changes made to the `store.products` table are now recorded in the archive. The following `INSERT` statement adds a row to the `store.products` table:

```
INSERT INTO store.products (
    product_id, product_type_id, name, description, price
) VALUES (
    15, 1, 'Using Linux', 'How to Use Linux', 39.99
);
```

The following query retrieves this row:

```
SELECT product_id, name, price
FROM store.products
WHERE product_id = 15;
```

```
PRODUCT_ID NAME                                 PRICE
---------- ------------------------------- ----------
        15 Using Linux                          39.99
```

You can view the rows as they were 5 minutes ago using the following query:

```
SELECT product_id, name, price
FROM store.products
AS OF TIMESTAMP
(SYSTIMESTAMP - INTERVAL '5' MINUTE);
```

```
PRODUCT_ID NAME                                 PRICE
---------- ------------------------------- ----------
         1 Modern Science                       19.95
         2 Chemistry                               30
         3 Supernova                            25.99
         4 Tank War                             13.95
         5 Z Files                              49.99
         6 2412: The Return                     14.95
         7 Space Force 9                        13.49
         8 From Another Planet                  12.99
         9 Classical Music                      10.99
        10 Pop 3                                15.99
        11 Creative Yell                        14.99
        12 My Front Line                        13.49
        13 Western Front                         13.5
        14 Eastern Front                         16.5
```

Notice that the new row is missing. This is because it was added to the table after the date and time specified in the query (assuming the previous `INSERT` was run less than 5 minutes ago).

You can also view the rows as they were at a specific timestamp using the following query (if you run this query, you need to change the timestamp to a date and time before you ran the `INSERT` statement earlier):

```
SELECT product_id, name, price
FROM store.products
AS OF TIMESTAMP
TO_TIMESTAMP('2007-08-12 13:05:00', 'YYYY-MM-DD HH24:MI:SS');
```

The new row will be missing from the results again, because it was added to the table after the date and time specified in the query.

You can view the rows as they were between two timestamps using the following query (you need to change the timestamps):

```
SELECT product_id, name, price
FROM store.products VERSIONS BETWEEN TIMESTAMP
TO_TIMESTAMP('2007-08-12 12:00:00', 'YYYY-MM-DD HH24:MI:SS')
AND TO_TIMESTAMP('2007-08-12 12:59:59', 'YYYY-MM-DD HH24:MI:SS');
```

You can view the rows as they were between one timestamp and the present time using the following query (you need to change the timestamp):

```
SELECT product_id, name, price
FROM store.products VERSIONS BETWEEN TIMESTAMP
TO_TIMESTAMP('2007-08-12 13:45:52', 'YYYY-MM-DD HH24:MI:SS')
AND MAXVALUE;
```

You can stop archiving of data for a table using ALTER TABLE; for example:

```
ALTER TABLE store.products NO FLASHBACK ARCHIVE;
```

When you create a table, you can specify a flashback archive for that table; for example:

```
CREATE TABLE store.test_table (
    id INTEGER,
    name VARCHAR2(10)
) FLASHBACK ARCHIVE test_archive;
```

You can view the details for an archive using the following views:

- user_flashback_archive and dba_flashback_archive, which display general information about the flashback archives

- user_flashback_archive_ts and dba_flashback_archive_ts, which display information about the tablespaces containing the flashback archives

- user_flashback_archive_tables and dba_flashback_archive_tables, which display information about the tables that are enabled for flashback archiving

You can alter a flashback archive; for example, the following statement changes the data retention period to 2 years:

```
ALTER FLASHBACK ARCHIVE test_archive
MODIFY RETENTION 2 YEAR;
```

You can purge the data from a flashback archive before a given timestamp; for example, the following statement purges data older than 1 day:

```
ALTER FLASHBACK ARCHIVE test_archive
PURGE BEFORE TIMESTAMP(SYSTIMESTAMP - INTERVAL '1' DAY);
```

You can purge all the data in a flashback archive; for example:

```
ALTER FLASHBACK ARCHIVE test_archive PURGE ALL;
```

You can drop a flashback archive; for example:

```
DROP FLASHBACK ARCHIVE test_archive;
```

NOTE
Go ahead and rerun store_schema.sql *to re-create the store tables so that your queries match mine in the rest of this book.*

Summary

In this chapter, you have learned the following:

- A table is created using the CREATE TABLE statement.

- A sequence generates a sequence of integers.

- A database index can speed up access to rows.

- A view is a predefined query on one or more base tables.

- A flashback data archive stores changes made to a table over a period of time.

In the next chapter, you'll learn about PL/SQL programming.

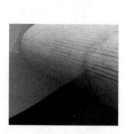

CHAPTER
11

Introducing PL/SQL
Programming

racle added a procedural programming language known as PL/SQL (Procedural Language/SQL) to Oracle Database 6. PL/SQL enables you to write programs that contain SQL statements. In this chapter, you'll learn about the following PL/SQL topics:

- Block structure

- Variables and types

- Conditional logic

- Loops

- Cursors, which allow PL/SQL to read the results returned by a query

- Procedures

- Functions

- Packages, which are used to group procedures and functions together in one unit

- Triggers, which are blocks of code that are run when a certain event occurs in the database

- Oracle Database 11*g* enhancements to PL/SQL

You can use PL/SQL to add business logic to a database application. This centralized business logic can be run by any program that can access the database, including SQL*Plus, Java programs, C# programs, and more.

NOTE
For full details on how to access a database through Java, see my book Oracle9*i* JDBC Programming *(Oracle Press, 2002). For details on how to access a database through C#, see my book* Mastering C# Database Programming *(Sybex, 2003).*

Block Structure

PL/SQL programs are divided up into structures known as *blocks*, with each block containing PL/SQL and SQL statements. A PL/SQL block has the following structure:

```
[DECLARE
  declaration_statements
]
BEGIN
  executable_statements
[EXCEPTION
  exception_handling_statements
]
END;
/
```

where

- *declaration_statements* declare the variables used in the rest of the PL/SQL block. DECLARE blocks are optional.

- *executable_statements* are the actual executable statements, which may include loops, conditional logic, and so on.

- *exception_handling_statements* are statements that handle any execution errors that might occur when the block is run. EXCEPTION blocks are optional.

Every statement is terminated by a semicolon (;), and a PL/SQL block is terminated using the forward slash (/) character. Before I get into the details of PL/SQL, you'll see a simple example to get a feel for the language. The following example (contained in the area_example.sql script in the SQL directory) calculates the width of a rectangle given its area and height:

```
SET SERVEROUTPUT ON

DECLARE
  v_width  INTEGER;
  v_height INTEGER := 2;
  v_area   INTEGER := 6;
BEGIN
  -- set the width equal to the area divided by the height
  v_width := v_area / v_height;
  DBMS_OUTPUT.PUT_LINE('v_width = ' || v_width);
EXCEPTION
  WHEN ZERO_DIVIDE THEN
    DBMS_OUTPUT.PUT_LINE('Division by zero');
END;
/
```

The SET SERVEROUTPUT ON command turns the server output on so you can see the lines produced by DBMS_OUTPUT.PUT_LINE() on the screen when you run the script in SQL*Plus. After this initial command comes the PL/SQL block itself, which is divided into the DECLARE, BEGIN, and EXCEPTION blocks.

The DECLARE block contains declarations for three INTEGER variables named v_width, v_height, and v_area (I always put v_ at the start of variable names). The v_height and v_area variables are initialized to 2 and 6 respectively.

Next comes the BEGIN block, which contains three lines. The first line is a comment that contains the text "set the width equal to the area divided by the height." The second line sets v_width to v_area divided by v_height; this means v_width is set to 3 (= 6 / 2). The third line calls DBMS_OUTPUT.PUT_LINE() to display the value of v_width on the screen. DBMS_OUTPUT is a built-in package of code that comes with the Oracle database; among other items, DBMS_OUTPUT contains procedures that allow you to output values to the screen.

Next, the EXCEPTION block handles any attempts to divide a number by zero. It does this by "catching" the ZERO_DIVIDE exception; in the example, no attempt is actually made to divide by zero, but if you change v_height to 0 and run the script you'll see the exception.

At the very end of the script, the forward slash character (/) marks the end of the PL/SQL block.

The following listing shows the execution of the `area_example.sql` script in SQL*Plus:

```
SQL> @ C:\SQL\area_example.sql
v_width = 3
```

> **NOTE**
> *If your* `area_example.sql` *script is in a directory other than* `C:\SQL`, *use your own directory in the previous command.*

Variables and Types

Variables are declared within a `DECLARE` block. As you saw in the previous example, a variable declaration has both a name and a type. For example, the `v_width` variable was declared as

```
v_width INTEGER;
```

> **NOTE**
> *The PL/SQL types are similar to the database column types. You can see all the types in the appendix.*

The following example shows more variable declarations (these variables could be used to store the column values from the `products` table):

```
v_product_id       INTEGER;
v_product_type_id  INTEGER;
v_name             VARCHAR2(30);
v_description       VARCHAR2(50);
v_price            NUMBER(5, 2);
```

You may also specify a variable's type using the `%TYPE` keyword, which tells PL/SQL to use the same type as a specified column in a table. The following example uses `%TYPE` to declare a variable of the same type as the `price` column of the `products` table, which is `NUMBER(5, 2)`:

```
v_product_price products.price%TYPE;
```

Conditional Logic

You use the `IF, THEN, ELSE, ELSIF,` and `END IF` keywords to perform conditional logic:

```
IF condition1 THEN
    statements1
ELSIF condition2 THEN
    statements2
ELSE
    statements3
END IF;
```

where

- `condition1` and `condition2` are Boolean expressions that evaluate to true or false.

- `statements1`, `statements2`, and `statements3` are PL/SQL statements.

The conditional logic flows as follows:

- If *condition1* is true, then *statements1* are executed.
- If *condition1* is false but *condition2* is true, then *statements2* are executed.
- If neither *condition1* nor *condition2* is true, then *statements3* are executed.

You can also embed an IF statement within another IF statement, as shown in the following example:

```
IF v_count > 0 THEN
  v_message := 'v_count is positive';
  IF v_area > 0 THEN
    v_message := 'v_count and v_area are positive';
  END IF
ELSIF v_count = 0 THEN
  v_message := 'v_count is zero';
ELSE
  v_message := 'v_count is negative';
END IF;
```

In this example, if v_count is greater than 0, then v_message is set to 'v_count is positive'. If v_count and v_area are greater than 0, then v_message is set to 'v_count and v_area are positive'. The rest of the logic is straightforward.

Loops

You use a loop to run statements zero or more times. There are three types of loops in PL/SQL:

- **Simple loops** run until you explicitly end the loop.
- **WHILE loops** run until a specified condition occurs.
- **FOR loops** run a predetermined number of times.

You'll learn about these loops in the following sections.

Simple Loops

A simple loop runs until you explicitly end the loop. The syntax for a simple loop is as follows:

```
LOOP
    statements
END LOOP;
```

To end the loop, you use either an EXIT or an EXIT WHEN statement. The EXIT statement ends a loop immediately; the EXIT WHEN statement ends a loop when a specified condition occurs.

The following example shows a simple loop. A variable named v_counter is initialized to 0 prior to the beginning of the loop. The loop adds 1 to v_counter and exits when v_counter is equal to 5 using an EXIT WHEN statement.

```
v_counter := 0;
LOOP
  v_counter := v_counter + 1;
  EXIT WHEN v_counter = 5;
END LOOP;
```

NOTE
The EXIT WHEN *statement can appear anywhere in the loop code.*

In Oracle Database 11*g* you can also end the current iteration of a loop using the CONTINUE or CONTINUE WHEN statement. The CONTINUE statement ends the current iteration of the loop unconditionally and continues with the next iteration; the CONTINUE WHEN statement ends the current iteration of the loop when a specified condition occurs and then continues with the next iteration. The following example shows the use of the CONTINUE statement:

```
v_counter := 0;
LOOP
  -- after the CONTINUE statement is executed, control returns here
  v_counter := v_counter + 1;
  IF v_counter = 3 THEN
    CONTINUE; -- end current iteration unconditionally
  END IF;
  EXIT WHEN v_counter = 5;
END LOOP;
```

The next example shows the use of the CONTINUE WHEN statement:

```
v_counter := 0;
LOOP
  -- after the CONTINUE WHEN statement is executed, control returns here
  v_counter := v_counter + 1;
  CONTINUE WHEN v_counter = 3; -- end current iteration when v_counter = 3
  EXIT WHEN v_counter = 5;
END LOOP;
```

NOTE
A CONTINUE *or* CONTINUE WHEN *statement cannot cross a procedure, function, or method boundary.*

WHILE Loops

A WHILE loop runs until a specified condition occurs. The syntax for a WHILE loop is as follows:

```
WHILE condition LOOP
  statements
END LOOP;
```

The following example shows a WHILE loop that executes while the v_counter variable is less than 6:

```
v_counter := 0;
WHILE v_counter < 6 LOOP
  v_counter := v_counter + 1;
END LOOP;
```

FOR Loops

A FOR loop runs a predetermined number of times; you determine the number of times the loop runs by specifying the *lower* and *upper bounds* for a loop variable. The loop variable is then incremented (or decremented) each time around the loop. The syntax for a FOR loop is as follows:

```
FOR loop_variable IN [REVERSE] lower_bound..upper_bound LOOP
   statements
END LOOP;
```

where

- *loop_variable* is the loop variable. You can use a variable that already exists as the loop variable, or you can just have the loop create a new variable for you (this occurs if the variable you specify doesn't exist). The loop variable value is increased (or decreased if you use the REVERSE keyword) by 1 each time through the loop.

- REVERSE means that the loop variable value is to be decremented each time through the loop. The loop variable is initialized to the upper boundary, and is decremented by 1 until the loop variable reaches the lower boundary. You must specify the lower boundary before the upper boundary.

- *lower_bound* is the loop's lower boundary. The loop variable is initialized to this lower boundary provided REVERSE is not used.

- *upper_bound* is the loop's upper boundary. If REVERSE is used, the loop variable is initialized to this upper boundary.

The following example shows a FOR loop. Notice that the variable v_counter2 isn't explicitly declared—so the FOR loop automatically creates a new INTEGER variable named v_counter2:

```
FOR v_counter2 IN 1..5 LOOP
   DBMS_OUTPUT.PUT_LINE(v_counter2);
END LOOP;
```

The following example uses REVERSE:

```
FOR v_counter2 IN REVERSE 1..5 LOOP
   DBMS_OUTPUT.PUT_LINE(v_counter2);
END LOOP;
```

In this example, v_counter2 starts at 5, is decremented by 1 each time through the loop, and ends at 1.

Cursors

You use a *cursor* to fetch rows returned by a query. You retrieve the rows into the cursor using a query and then fetch the rows one at a time from the cursor. You typically use the following five steps when using a cursor:

1. Declare variables to store the column values for a row.
2. Declare the cursor, which contains a query.
3. Open the cursor.
4. Fetch the rows from the cursor one at a time and store the column values in the variables declared in Step 1. You would then do something with those variables, such as display them on the screen, use them in a calculation, and so on.
5. Close the cursor.

You'll learn the details of these five steps in the following sections, and you'll see a simple example that gets the `product_id`, `name`, and `price` columns from the `products` table.

Step 1: Declare the Variables to Store the Column Values

The first step is to declare the variables that will be used to store the column values. These variables must be compatible with the column types.

TIP
Earlier you saw that `%TYPE` *may be used to get the type of a column. If you use* `%TYPE` *when declaring your variables, your variables will automatically be of the correct type.*

The following example declares three variables to store the `product_id`, `name`, and `price` columns from the `products` table; notice that `%TYPE` is used to automatically set the type of the variables to the same type as the columns:

```
DECLARE
  v_product_id products.product_id%TYPE;
  v_name       products.name%TYPE;
  v_price      products.price%TYPE;
```

Step 2: Declare the Cursor

Step 2 is to declare the cursor. A cursor declaration consists of a name that you assign to the cursor and the query you want to execute. The cursor declaration, like all other declarations, is placed in the declaration section. The syntax for declaring a cursor is as follows:

```
CURSOR cursor_name IS
  SELECT_statement;
```

where

- `cursor_name` is the name of the cursor.
- `SELECT_statement` is the query.

The following example declares a cursor named `v_product_cursor` whose query retrieves the `product_id`, `name`, and `price` columns from the `products` table:

```
CURSOR v_product_cursor IS
  SELECT product_id, name, price
  FROM products
  ORDER BY product_id;
```

The query isn't executed until you open the cursor.

Step 3: Open the Cursor

Step 3 is to open the cursor. You open a cursor using the OPEN statement, which must be placed in the executable section of the block.

The following example opens `v_product_cursor`, which executes the query:

```
OPEN v_product_cursor;
```

Step 4: Fetch the Rows from the Cursor

Step 4 is to fetch the rows from the cursor, which you do using the FETCH statement. The FETCH statement reads the column values into the variables declared in Step 1. FETCH uses the following syntax:

```
FETCH cursor_name
INTO variable[, variable ...];
```

where

- *cursor_name* is the name of the cursor.

- *variable* is the variable into which a column value from the cursor is stored. You need to provide matching variables for each column value.

The following FETCH example retrieves a row from v_product_cursor and stores the column values in the v_product_id, v_name, and v_price variables created earlier in Step 1:

```
FETCH v_product_cursor
INTO v_product_id, v_name, v_price;
```

Because a cursor may contain many rows, you need a loop to read them. To figure out when to end the loop, you can use the Boolean variable v_product_cursor%NOTFOUND. This variable is true when there are no more rows to read in v_product_cursor. The following example shows a loop:

```
LOOP
   -- fetch the rows from the cursor
   FETCH v_product_cursor
   INTO v_product_id, v_name, v_price;

   -- exit the loop when there are no more rows, as indicated by
   -- the Boolean variable v_product_cursor%NOTFOUND (= true when
   -- there are no more rows)
   EXIT WHEN v_product_cursor%NOTFOUND;

   -- use DBMS_OUTPUT.PUT_LINE() to display the variables
   DBMS_OUTPUT.PUT_LINE(
     'v_product_id = ' || v_product_id || ', v_name = ' || v_name ||
     ', v_price = ' || v_price
   );
END LOOP;
```

Notice that I've used DBMS_OUTPUT.PUT_LINE() to display the v_product_id, v_name, and v_price variables that were read for each row. In a real application, you might use v_price in a complex calculation.

Step 5: Close the Cursor

Step 5 is to close the cursor using the CLOSE statement. Closing a cursor frees up system resources. The following example closes v_product_cursor:

```
CLOSE v_product_cursor;
```

The following section shows a complete script that contains all five steps.

Complete Example: product_cursor.sql

The following `product_cursor.sql` script is contained in the `SQL` directory:

```
-- product_cursor.sql displays the product_id, name,
-- and price columns from the products table using a cursor

SET SERVEROUTPUT ON

DECLARE
  -- step 1: declare the variables
  v_product_id products.product_id%TYPE;
  v_name        products.name%TYPE;
  v_price       products.price%TYPE;

  -- step 2: declare the cursor
  CURSOR v_product_cursor IS
    SELECT product_id, name, price
    FROM products
    ORDER BY product_id;
BEGIN
  -- step 3: open the cursor
  OPEN v_product_cursor;

  LOOP
    -- step 4: fetch the rows from the cursor
    FETCH v_product_cursor
    INTO v_product_id, v_name, v_price;

    -- exit the loop when there are no more rows, as indicated by
    -- the Boolean variable v_product_cursor%NOTFOUND (= true when
    -- there are no more rows)
    EXIT WHEN v_product_cursor%NOTFOUND;

    -- use DBMS_OUTPUT.PUT_LINE() to display the variables
    DBMS_OUTPUT.PUT_LINE(
      'v_product_id = ' || v_product_id || ', v_name = ' || v_name ||
      ', v_price = ' || v_price
    );
  END LOOP;

  -- step 5: close the cursor
  CLOSE v_product_cursor;
END;
/
```

To run this script, follow these steps:

1. Connect to the database as `store` with the password `store_password`.

2. Run the `product_cursor.sql` script using SQL*Plus:

   ```
   SQL> @ C:\SQL\product_cursor.sql
   ```

NOTE
If your `product_cursor.sql` *script is in a different directory from*
`C:\SQL,` *use your own directory in the previous command.*

The output from `product_cursor.sql` is as follows:

```
v_product_id = 1, v_name = Modern Science, v_price = 19.95
v_product_id = 2, v_name = Chemistry, v_price = 30
v_product_id = 3, v_name = Supernova, v_price = 25.99
v_product_id = 4, v_name = Tank War, v_price = 13.95
v_product_id = 5, v_name = Z Files, v_price = 49.99
v_product_id = 6, v_name = 2412: The Return, v_price = 14.95
v_product_id = 7, v_name = Space Force 9, v_price = 13.49
v_product_id = 8, v_name = From Another Planet, v_price = 12.99
v_product_id = 9, v_name = Classical Music, v_price = 10.99
v_product_id = 10, v_name = Pop 3, v_price = 15.99
v_product_id = 11, v_name = Creative Yell, v_price = 14.99
v_product_id = 12, v_name = My Front Line, v_price = 13.49
```

Cursors and FOR Loops

You can use a FOR loop to access the rows in a cursor. When you do this, you don't have to explicitly open and close the cursor—the FOR loop does this automatically for you. The following `product_cursor2.sql` script uses a FOR loop to access the rows in v_product_cursor; notice that this script contains less code than `product_cursor.sql`:

```
-- product_cursor2.sql displays the product_id, name,
-- and price columns from the products table using a cursor
-- and a FOR loop

SET SERVEROUTPUT ON

DECLARE
  CURSOR v_product_cursor IS
    SELECT product_id, name, price
    FROM products
    ORDER BY product_id;
BEGIN
  FOR v_product IN v_product_cursor LOOP
    DBMS_OUTPUT.PUT_LINE(
      'product_id = ' || v_product.product_id ||
      ', name = ' || v_product.name ||
      ', price = ' || v_product.price
    );
  END LOOP;
END;
/
```

To run the `product_cursor2.sql` script, you issue a command similar to the following:

```
SQL> @ "C:\SQL\product_cursor2.sql"
```

The output from this script is as follows:

```
product_id = 1, name = Modern Science, price = 19.95
product_id = 2, name = Chemistry, price = 30
product_id = 3, name = Supernova, price = 25.99
product_id = 4, name = Tank War, price = 13.95
product_id = 5, name = Z Files, price = 49.99
product_id = 6, name = 2412: The Return, price = 14.95
product_id = 7, name = Space Force 9, price = 13.49
product_id = 8, name = From Another Planet, price = 12.99
product_id = 9, name = Classical Music, price = 10.99
product_id = 10, name = Pop 3, price = 15.99
product_id = 11, name = Creative Yell, price = 14.99
product_id = 12, name = My Front Line, price = 13.49
```

OPEN-FOR Statement

You may also use the OPEN-FOR statement with a cursor, which adds even more flexibility when processing cursors because you can assign the cursor to a different query. This is shown in the following product_cursor3.sql script:

```
-- product_cursor3.sql displays the product_id, name,
-- and price columns from the products table using a cursor
-- variable and the OPEN-FOR statement

SET SERVEROUTPUT ON

DECLARE
  -- declare a REF CURSOR type named t_product_cursor
  TYPE t_product_cursor IS
  REF CURSOR RETURN products%ROWTYPE;

  -- declare a t_product_cursor object named v_product_cursor
  v_product_cursor t_product_cursor;

  -- declare an object to store columns from the products table
  -- named v_product (of type products%ROWTYPE)
  v_product products%ROWTYPE;
BEGIN
  -- assign a query to v_product_cursor and open it using OPEN-FOR
  OPEN v_product_cursor FOR
  SELECT * FROM products WHERE product_id < 5;

  -- use a loop to fetch the rows from v_product_cursor into v_product
  LOOP
    FETCH v_product_cursor INTO v_product;
    EXIT WHEN v_product_cursor%NOTFOUND;
    DBMS_OUTPUT.PUT_LINE(
      'product_id = ' || v_product.product_id ||
      ', name = ' || v_product.name ||
      ', price = ' || v_product.price
    );
```

```
  END LOOP;

  -- close v_product_cursor
  CLOSE v_product_cursor;
END;
/
```

In the DECLARE block, the following statement declares a REF CURSOR type named t_product_cursor (I always put t_ at the start of type names):

```
TYPE t_product_cursor IS
REF CURSOR RETURN products%ROWTYPE;
```

A REF CURSOR is a pointer to a cursor, and is similar to a pointer in the C++ programming language. The previous statement declares a user-defined type named t_product_cursor, and returns a row containing the various columns of the products table (this is indicated using %ROWTYPE). This user-defined type may be used to declare an actual object, as shown in the following statement, which declares an object named v_product_cursor:

```
v_product_cursor t_product_cursor;
```

The following statement declares an object to store columns from the products table named v_product (of type products%ROWTYPE):

```
v_product products%ROWTYPE;
```

In the BEGIN block, v_product_cursor is assigned a query and opened by the following OPEN-FOR statement:

```
OPEN v_product_cursor FOR
SELECT * FROM products WHERE product_id < 5;
```

After this statement is executed, v_product_cursor will be loaded with the first four rows in the products table. The query assigned to v_product_cursor can be any valid SELECT statement; this means you can re-use the cursor and assign another query to the cursor later in the PL/SQL code.

Next, the following loop fetches the rows from v_product_cursor into v_product and displays the row details:

```
LOOP
  FETCH v_product_cursor INTO v_product;
  EXIT WHEN v_product_cursor%NOTFOUND;
  DBMS_OUTPUT.PUT_LINE(
    'product_id = ' || v_product.product_id ||
    ', name = ' || v_product.name ||
    ', price = ' || v_product.price
  );
END LOOP;
```

After the loop, v_product_cursor is closed using the following statement:

```
CLOSE v_product_cursor;
```

The output from this script is the same as the output from product_cursor2.sql.

Unconstrained Cursors

The cursors in the previous section all have a specific return type; these cursors are known as constrained cursors. The return type for a constrained cursor must match the columns in the query that is run by the cursor. An unconstrained cursor has no return type, and can therefore run any query.

The use of an unconstrained cursor is shown in the following `unconstrained_cursor` `.sql` script; notice `v_cursor` in the code is used to run two different queries:

```
-- This script shows the use of unconstrained cursors

SET SERVEROUTPUT ON

DECLARE
  -- declare a REF CURSOR type named t_cursor (this has no return
  -- type and can therefore run any query)
  TYPE t_cursor IS REF CURSOR;

  -- declare a t_cursor object named v_cursor
  v_cursor t_cursor;

  -- declare an object to store columns from the products table
  -- named v_product (of type products%ROWTYPE)
  v_product products%ROWTYPE;

  -- declare an object to store columns from the customers table
  -- named v_customer (of type customers%ROWTYPE)
  v_customer customers%ROWTYPE;
BEGIN
  -- assign a query to v_cursor and open it using OPEN-FOR
  OPEN v_cursor FOR
  SELECT * FROM products WHERE product_id < 5;

  -- use a loop to fetch the rows from v_cursor into v_product
  LOOP
    FETCH v_cursor INTO v_product;
    EXIT WHEN v_cursor%NOTFOUND;
    DBMS_OUTPUT.PUT_LINE(
      'product_id = ' || v_product.product_id ||
      ', name = ' || v_product.name ||
      ', price = ' || v_product.price
    );
  END LOOP;

  -- assign a new query to v_cursor and open it using OPEN-FOR
  OPEN v_cursor FOR
  SELECT * FROM customers WHERE customer_id < 3;

  -- use a loop to fetch the rows from v_cursor into v_product
  LOOP
    FETCH v_cursor INTO v_customer;
    EXIT WHEN v_cursor%NOTFOUND;
```

```
      DBMS_OUTPUT.PUT_LINE(
        'customer_id = ' || v_customer.customer_id ||
        ', first_name = ' || v_customer.first_name ||
        ', last_name = ' || v_customer.last_name
      );
    END LOOP;

    -- close v_cursor
    CLOSE v_cursor;
END;
/
```

To run the `unconstrained_cursor.sql` script, you issue a command similar to the following:

```
SQL> @ "C:\SQL\unconstrained_cursor.sql"
```

The output from this script is as follows:

```
product_id = 1, name = Modern Science, price = 19.95
product_id = 2, name = Chemistry, price = 30
product_id = 3, name = Supernova, price = 25.99
product_id = 4, name = Tank War, price = 13.95
customer_id = 1, first_name = John, last_name = Brown
customer_id = 2, first_name = Cynthia, last_name = Green
```

You'll learn more about `REF CURSOR` variables later in this chapter and more about user-defined types in the next chapter.

Exceptions

Exceptions are used to handle run-time errors in your PL/SQL code. Earlier, you saw the following PL/SQL example that contains an `EXCEPTION` block:

```
DECLARE
  v_width  INTEGER;
  v_height INTEGER := 2;
  v_area   INTEGER := 6;
BEGIN
  -- set the width equal to the area divided by the height
  v_width := v_area / v_height;
  DBMS_OUTPUT.PUT_LINE('v_width = ' || v_width);
EXCEPTION
  WHEN ZERO_DIVIDE THEN
    DBMS_OUTPUT.PUT_LINE('Division by zero');
END;
/
```

The `EXCEPTION` block in this example handles an attempt to divide a number by zero. In PL/SQL terminology, the `EXCEPTION` block *catches* a `ZERO_DIVIDE` exception that is *raised* in the `BEGIN` block (although in the example code, `ZERO_DIVIDE` is never actually raised). The `ZERO_DIVIDE` exception and the other common exceptions are shown in Table 11-1.

Exception	Error	Description
ACCESS_INTO_NULL	ORA-06530	An attempt was made to assign values to the attributes of an uninitialized object. (You'll learn about objects in Chapter 12.)
CASE_NOT_FOUND	ORA-06592	None of the WHEN clauses of a CASE statement was selected, and there is no default ELSE clause.
COLLECTION_IS_NULL	ORA-06531	An attempt was made to call a collection method (other than EXISTS) on an uninitialized nested table or varray, or an attempt was made to assign values to the elements of an uninitialized nested table or varray. (You'll learn about collections in Chapter 13.)
CURSOR_ALREADY_OPEN	ORA-06511	An attempt was made to open an already open cursor. The cursor must be closed before it can be reopened.
DUP_VAL_ON_INDEX	ORA-00001	An attempt was made to store duplicate values in a column that is constrained by a unique index.
INVALID_CURSOR	ORA-01001	An attempt was made to perform an illegal cursor operation, such as closing an unopened cursor.
INVALID_NUMBER	ORA-01722	An attempt to convert a character string into a number failed because the string does not represent a valid number. Note: In PL/SQL statements, VALUE_ERROR is raised instead of INVALID_NUMBER.
LOGIN_DENIED	ORA-01017	An attempt was made to connect to a database using an invalid user name or password.
NO_DATA_FOUND	ORA-01403	A SELECT INTO statement returned no rows, or an attempt was made to access a deleted element in a nested table or an uninitialized element in an "index by" table.
NOT_LOGGED_ON	ORA-01012	An attempt was made to access a database item without being connected to the database.
PROGRAM_ERROR	ORA-06501	PL/SQL had an internal problem.
ROWTYPE_MISMATCH	ORA-06504	The host cursor variable and the PL/SQL cursor variable involved in an assignment have incompatible return types. For example, when an open host cursor variable is passed to a stored procedure or function, the return types of the actual and formal parameters must be compatible.

TABLE 11-1   *Predefined Exceptions*

Exception	Error	Description
SELF_IS_NULL	ORA-30625	An attempt was made to call a MEMBER method on a null object. That is, the built-in parameter SELF (which is always the first parameter passed to a MEMBER method) is null.
STORAGE_ERROR	ORA-06500	The PL/SQL module ran out of memory or the memory has been corrupted.
SUBSCRIPT_BEYOND_COUNT	ORA-06533	An attempt was made to reference a nested table or varray element using an index number larger than the number of elements in the collection.
SUBSCRIPT_OUTSIDE_LIMIT	ORA-06532	An attempt was made to reference a nested table or varray element using an index number that is outside the legal range (–1 for example).
SYS_INVALID_ROWID	ORA-01410	The conversion of a character string to a universal rowid failed because the character string does not represent a valid rowid.
TIMEOUT_ON_RESOURCE	ORA-00051	A timeout occurred while the database was waiting for a resource.
TOO_MANY_ROWS	ORA-01422	A SELECT INTO statement returned more than one row.
VALUE_ERROR	ORA-06502	An arithmetic, conversion, truncation, or size-constraint error occurred. For example, when selecting a column value into a character variable, if the value is longer than the declared length of the variable, PL/SQL aborts the assignment and raises VALUE_ERROR. Note: In PL/SQL statements, VALUE_ERROR is raised if the conversion of a character string into a number fails. In SQL statements, INVALID_NUMBER is raised instead of VALUE_ERROR.
ZERO_DIVIDE	ORA-01476	An attempt was made to divide a number by zero.

TABLE 11-1 *Predefined Exceptions* (continued)

The following sections show examples that raise some of the exceptions shown in Table 11-1.

ZERO_DIVIDE Exception

The ZERO_DIVIDE exception is raised when an attempt is made to divide a number by zero. The following example attempts to divide 1 by 0 in the BEGIN block and therefore raises the ZERO_DIVIDE exception:

```
BEGIN
  DBMS_OUTPUT.PUT_LINE(1 / 0);
EXCEPTION
  WHEN ZERO_DIVIDE THEN
```

```
    DBMS_OUTPUT.PUT_LINE('Division by zero');
END;
/
```

Division by zero

When an exception is raised, program control passes to the EXCEPTION block and the WHEN clause is examined for a matching exception; the code inside the matching clause is then executed. In the previous example, the ZERO_DIVIDE exception is raised in the BEGIN block, and program control then passes to the EXCEPTION block; a matching exception is found in the WHEN clause, and the code inside the clause is executed.

If no matching exception is found, the exception is propagated to the enclosing block. For example, if the EXCEPTION block was omitted from the previous code, the exception is propagated up to SQL*Plus:

```
BEGIN
  DBMS_OUTPUT.PUT_LINE(1 / 0);
END;
BEGIN
*
ERROR at line 1:
ORA-01476: divisor is equal to zero
ORA-06512: at line 2
```

As you can see, SQL*Plus displays a default error that shows the line numbers, the Oracle error codes, and a simple description.

DUP_VAL_ON_INDEX Exception

The DUP_VAL_ON_INDEX exception is raised when an attempt is made to store duplicate values in a column that is constrained by a unique index. The following example attempts to insert a row in the customers table with a customer_id of 1; this causes DUP_VAL_ON_INDEX to be raised, because the customers table already contains a row with a customer_id of 1:

```
BEGIN
  INSERT INTO customers (
    customer_id, first_name, last_name
  ) VALUES (
    1, 'Greg', 'Green'
  );
EXCEPTION
  WHEN DUP_VAL_ON_INDEX THEN
    DBMS_OUTPUT.PUT_LINE('Duplicate value on an index');
END;
/
```

Duplicate value on an index

INVALID_NUMBER Exception

The INVALID_NUMBER exception is raised when an attempt is made to convert an invalid character string into a number. The following example attempts to convert the string 123X to a number that is used in an INSERT, which causes INVALID_NUMBER to be raised because 123X is not a valid number:

```
BEGIN
  INSERT INTO customers (
    customer_id, first_name, last_name
  ) VALUES (
    '123X', 'Greg', 'Green'
  );
EXCEPTION
  WHEN INVALID_NUMBER THEN
    DBMS_OUTPUT.PUT_LINE('Conversion of string to number failed');
END;
/
```

```
Conversion of string to number failed
```

OTHERS Exception

You can use the OTHERS exception to handle all exceptions, as shown here:

```
BEGIN
  DBMS_OUTPUT.PUT_LINE(1 / 0);
EXCEPTION
  WHEN OTHERS THEN
    DBMS_OUTPUT.PUT_LINE('An exception occurred');
END;
/
```

```
An exception occurred
```

Because OTHERS matches all exceptions, you must list it after any specific exceptions in your EXCEPTION block. If you attempt to list OTHERS elsewhere, the database returns the error PLS-00370; for example:

```
SQL> BEGIN
  2    DBMS_OUTPUT.PUT_LINE(1 / 0);
  3  EXCEPTION
  4    WHEN OTHERS THEN
  5      DBMS_OUTPUT.PUT_LINE('An exception occurred');
  6    WHEN ZERO_DIVIDE THEN
  7      DBMS_OUTPUT.PUT_LINE('Division by zero');
  8  END;
  9  /
  WHEN OTHERS THEN
  *
ERROR at line 4:
ORA-06550: line 4, column 3:
PLS-00370: OTHERS handler must be last among the exception
 handlers of a block
ORA-06550: line 0, column 0:
PL/SQL: Compilation unit analysis terminated
```

Procedures

A procedure contains a group of SQL and PL/SQL statements. Procedures allow you to centralize your business logic in the database and may be used by any program that accesses the database.

In this section, you'll learn how to

- Create a procedure.
- Call a procedure.
- Get information on procedures.
- Drop a procedure.
- View errors in a procedure.

Creating a Procedure

You create a procedure using the CREATE PROCEDURE statement. The simplified syntax for the CREATE PROCEDURE statement is as follows:

```
CREATE [OR REPLACE] PROCEDURE procedure_name
[(parameter_name [IN | OUT | IN OUT] type [, ...])]
{IS | AS}
BEGIN
  procedure_body
END procedure_name;
```

where

- OR REPLACE means the procedure is to replace an existing procedure.
- *procedure_name* is the name of the procedure.
- *parameter_name* is the name of a parameter that is passed to the procedure. You may pass multiple parameters to a procedure.
- IN | OUT | IN OUT is the *mode* of the parameter. You may pick one of the following modes for each parameter:
  - IN, which is the default mode for a parameter. An IN parameter must be set to a value when the procedure is run. The value of an IN parameter cannot be changed in the procedure body.
  - OUT, which means the parameter is set to a value in the procedure body.
  - IN OUT, which means the parameter can have a value when the procedure is run, and the value can be changed in the body.
- *type* is the type of the parameter.
- *procedure_body* contains the actual code for the procedure.

The following example creates a procedure named update_product_price()—this procedure, and the other PL/SQL code shown in the rest of this chapter, was created when you ran the `store_schema.sql` script. The `update_product_price()` procedure multiplies the price of a product by a factor; the product ID and the factor are passed as parameters to the procedure. If the product exists, the procedure multiplies the product price by the factor and commits the change.

```
CREATE PROCEDURE update_product_price(
    p_product_id IN products.product_id%TYPE,
    p_factor     IN NUMBER
) AS
    v_product_count INTEGER;
BEGIN
    -- count the number of products with the
    -- supplied product_id (will be 1 if the product exists)
    SELECT COUNT(*)
    INTO v_product_count
    FROM products
    WHERE product_id = p_product_id;

    -- if the product exists (v_product_count = 1) then
    -- update that product's price
    IF v_product_count = 1 THEN
      UPDATE products
      SET price = price * p_factor
      WHERE product_id = p_product_id;
      COMMIT;
    END IF;
EXCEPTION
  WHEN OTHERS THEN
    ROLLBACK;
END update_product_price;
/
```

The procedure accepts two parameters named `p_product_id` and `p_factor` (I always put `p_` at the start of parameter names). Both of these parameters use the `IN` mode, which means that their values must be set when the procedure is run and that the parameter values cannot be changed in the procedure body.

The declaration section contains an `INTEGER` variable named `v_product_count`:

```
v_product_count INTEGER;
```

The body of the procedure starts after `BEGIN`. The `SELECT` statement in the body gets the number of rows from the `products` table whose `product_id` is equal to `p_product_id`:

```
SELECT COUNT(*)
INTO v_product_count
FROM products
WHERE product_id = p_product_id;
```

NOTE
`COUNT(*)` *returns number of rows found.*

If the product is found, v_product_count will be set to 1; otherwise, v_product_count will be set to 0. If v_product_count is 1, the price column is multiplied by p_factor using the UPDATE statement, and the change is committed:

```
IF v_product_count = 1 THEN
   UPDATE products
   SET price = price * p_factor
   WHERE product_id = p_product_id;
   COMMIT;
END IF;
```

The EXCEPTION block performs a ROLLBACK if an exception is raised:

```
EXCEPTION
   WHEN OTHERS THEN
      ROLLBACK;
```

Finally, the END keyword is used to mark the end of the procedure:

```
END update_product_price;
/
```

> **NOTE**
> *The repetition of the procedure name after the END keyword is not required, but it is good programming practice to put it in.*

Calling a Procedure

You run (or *call*) a procedure using the CALL statement. The example you'll see in this section will multiply the price of product #1 by 1.5 using the procedure shown in the previous section. First, the following query retrieves the price of product #1 so you can compare it with the modified price later:

```
SELECT price
FROM products
WHERE product_id = 1;

   PRICE
----------
   19.95
```

The following statement calls update_product_price(), passing the parameter values 1 (the product_id) and 1.5 (the factor by which the product price is multiplied):

```
CALL update_product_price(1, 1.5);

Call completed.
```

This statement shows the use of *positional notation* to indicate the values to be passed to the procedure or function. In positional notation, the position of parameters is used to assign the values passed to the procedure. In the example, the first value in the call is 1, and this is passed to the first parameter in the procedure (p_product_id); the second value in the call is 1.5, and this is passed to the second parameter (p_factor). In Oracle Database 11*g*, you can also use named and mixed notation in addition to positional notation, and you'll learn about these types of notation shortly.

The next query retrieves the details for product #1 again; notice the price has been multiplied by 1.5:

```
SELECT price
FROM products
WHERE product_id = 1;

    PRICE
----------
    29.93
```

In Oracle Database 11*g* you can pass parameters using named and mixed notation. In *named notation*, you include the name of the parameter when calling a procedure. For example, the following statement calls `update_product_price()` using named notation; notice that the values for the `p_factor` and `p_product_id` parameters are indicated using =>:

```
CALL update_product_price(p_factor => 1.3, p_product_id => 2);
```

TIP
Named notation makes your code easier to read and maintain because the parameters are explicitly shown.

In *mixed notation*, you use both positional and named notation; you use positional notation for the first set of parameters and named notation for the last set of parameters. Mixed notation is useful when you have procedures and functions that have both required and optional parameters; you use positional notation for the required parameters, and named notation for the optional parameters. The following example uses mixed notation; notice that positional notation comes before named notation when specifying the parameter values:

```
CALL update_product_price(3, p_factor => 1.7);
```

Getting Information on Procedures

You can get information on your procedures from the `user_procedures` view. Table 11-2 describes some of the columns in `user_procedures`.

Column	Type	Description
OBJECT_NAME	VARCHAR2(30)	The object name, which may be a procedure, function, or package name
PROCEDURE_NAME	VARCHAR2(30)	The procedure name
AGGREGATE	VARCHAR2(3)	Whether the procedure is an aggregate function (YES or NO)
IMPLTYPEOWNER	VARCHAR2(30)	The owner of the type (if any)
IMPLTYPENAME	VARCHAR2(30)	The name of the type (if any)
PARALLEL	VARCHAR2(3)	Whether the procedure is enabled for parallel queries (YES or NO)

TABLE 11-2   *Some Columns in the* `user_procedures` *View*

NOTE
You can get information on all the procedures you have access to using all_procedures.

The following example retrieves the object_name, aggregate, and parallel columns from user_procedures for update_product_price():

```
SELECT object_name, aggregate, parallel
FROM user_procedures
WHERE object_name = 'UPDATE_PRODUCT_PRICE';

OBJECT_NAME                        AGG PAR
------------------------------     --- ---
UPDATE_PRODUCT_PRICE               NO  NO
```

Dropping a Procedure

You drop a procedure using DROP PROCEDURE. For example, the following statement drops update_product_price():

```
DROP PROCEDURE update_product_price;
```

Viewing Errors in a Procedure

If the database reports an error when you create a procedure, you can view the errors using the SHOW ERRORS command. For example, the following CREATE PROCEDURE statement attempts to create a procedure that has a syntax error at line 6 (the parameter should be p_dob, not p_dobs):

```
SQL> CREATE PROCEDURE update_customer_dob (
  2    p_customer_id INTEGER, p_dob DATE
  3  ) AS
  4  BEGIN
  5    UPDATE customers
  6    SET dob = p_dobs
  7    WHERE customer_id = p_customer_id;
  8  END update_customer_dob;
  9  /

Warning: Procedure created with compilation errors.
```

As you can see, there is a compilation error. To view the errors, you use SHOW ERRORS:

```
SQL> SHOW ERRORS
Errors for PROCEDURE UPDATE_CUSTOMER_DOB:

LINE/COL ERROR
-------- --------------------------------------------
5/3      PL/SQL: SQL Statement ignored
6/13     PL/SQL: ORA-00904: invalid column name
```

Line 5 was ignored because an invalid column name was referenced in line 6. You can fix the error by issuing an EDIT command to edit the CREATE PROCEDURE statement, changing p_dobs to p_dob, and rerunning the statement by entering /.

Functions

A *function* is similar to a procedure, except that a function must return a value. Together, stored procedures and functions are sometimes referred to as *stored subprograms* because they are small programs.

In this section, you'll learn how to

■ Create a function.

■ Call a function.

■ Get information on functions.

■ Drop a function.

Creating a Function

You create a function using the CREATE FUNCTION statement. The simplified syntax for the CREATE FUNCTION statement is as follows:

```
CREATE [OR REPLACE] FUNCTION function_name
[(parameter_name [IN | OUT | IN OUT] type [, ...])]
RETURN type
{IS | AS}
BEGIN
  function_body
END function_name;
```

where

■ OR REPLACE means the procedure is to replace an existing function.

■ *function_name* is the name of the function.

■ *parameter_name* is the name of a parameter that is passed to the function. You may pass multiple parameters to a function.

■ IN |OUT | IN OUT is the mode of the parameter.

■ *type* is the type of the parameter.

■ *function_body* contains actual code for the function. Unlike a procedure, the body of a function must return a value of the type specified in the RETURN clause.

The following example creates a function named circle_area(), which returns the area of a circle. The radius of the circle is passed as a parameter named p_radius to circle_area(); notice that circle_area() returns a NUMBER:

```
CREATE FUNCTION circle_area (
   p_radius IN NUMBER
) RETURN NUMBER AS
   v_pi   NUMBER := 3.1415926;
   v_area NUMBER;
BEGIN
   -- circle area is pi multiplied by the radius squared
```

```
  v_area := v_pi * POWER(p_radius, 2);
  RETURN v_area;
END circle_area;
/
```

The next example creates a function named `average_product_price()`, which returns the average price of products whose `product_type_id` equals the parameter value:

```
CREATE FUNCTION average_product_price (
  p_product_type_id IN INTEGER
) RETURN NUMBER AS
  v_average_product_price NUMBER;
BEGIN
  SELECT AVG(price)
  INTO v_average_product_price
  FROM products
  WHERE product_type_id = p_product_type_id;
  RETURN v_average_product_price;
END average_product_price;
/
```

Calling a Function

You call your own functions as you would call any of the built-in database functions; you saw how to call built-in functions in Chapter 4. (Just to refresh your memory, you can call a function using a SELECT statement that uses the dual table in the FROM clause.) The following example calls `circle_area()`, passing a radius of 2 meters to the function using positional notation:

```
SELECT circle_area(2)
FROM dual;

CIRCLE_AREA(2)
--------------
   12.5663704
```

In Oracle Database 11*g*, you can also use named and mixed notation when calling functions. For example, the following query uses named notation when calling `circle_area()`:

```
SELECT circle_area(p_radius => 4)
FROM dual;

CIRCLE_AREA(P_RADIUS=>4)
------------------------
             50.2654816
```

The next example calls `average_product_price()`, passing the parameter value 1 to the function to get the average price of products whose `product_type_id` is 1:

```
SELECT average_product_price(1)
FROM dual;

AVERAGE_PRODUCT_PRICE(1)
------------------------
                  29.965
```

Getting Information on Functions

You can get information on your functions from the `user_procedures` view; this view was covered earlier in the section "Getting Information on Procedures." The following example retrieves the `object_name`, `aggregate`, and `parallel` columns from `user_procedures` for `circle_area()` and `average_product_price()`:

```
SELECT object_name, aggregate, parallel
FROM user_procedures
WHERE object_name IN ('CIRCLE_AREA', 'AVERAGE_PRODUCT_PRICE');

OBJECT_NAME                      AGG PAR
------------------------------   --- ---
AVERAGE_PRODUCT_PRICE            NO  NO
CIRCLE_AREA                      NO  NO
```

Dropping a Function

You drop a function using `DROP FUNCTION`. For example, the following statement drops `circle_area()`:

```
DROP FUNCTION circle_area;
```

Packages

In this section, you'll learn how to group procedures and functions together into *packages*. Packages allow you to encapsulate related functionality into one self-contained unit. By modularizing your PL/SQL code through the use of packages, you build up your own libraries of code that other programmers can reuse. In fact, the Oracle database comes with a library of packages, which allow you to access external files, manage the database, generate HTML, and much more; to see all the packages, you should consult the *Oracle Database PL/SQL Packages and Types Reference* manual from Oracle Corporation.

Packages are typically made up of two components: a *specification* and a *body*. The package specification lists the available procedures, functions, types, and objects. You can make the items listed in the specification available to all database users, and I refer to these items as being *public* (although only users you have granted privileges to access your package can use it). The specification doesn't contain the code that makes up the procedures and functions; the code is contained in the package body.

Any items in the body that are not listed in the specification are *private* to the package. Private items can be used only inside the package body. By using a combination of public and private items, you can build up a package whose complexity is hidden from the outside world. This is one of the primary goals of all programming: hide complexity from your users.

Creating a Package Specification

You create a package specification using the `CREATE PACKAGE` statement. The simplified syntax for the `CREATE PACKAGE` statement is as follows:

```
CREATE [OR REPLACE] PACKAGE package_name
{IS | AS}
  package_specification
END package_name;
```

where

- *package_name* is the name of the package.

- *package_specification* lists the public procedures, functions, types, and objects available to your package's users.

The following example creates a specification for a package named `product_package`:

```
CREATE PACKAGE product_package AS
  TYPE t_ref_cursor IS REF CURSOR;
  FUNCTION get_products_ref_cursor RETURN t_ref_cursor;
  PROCEDURE update_product_price (
    p_product_id IN products.product_id%TYPE,
    p_factor     IN NUMBER
  );
END product_package;
/
```

The `t_ref_cursor` type is a PL/SQL `REF CURSOR` type. A `REF CURSOR` is similar to a pointer in the C++ programming language, and it points to a cursor; as you saw earlier, a cursor allows you to read the rows returned by a query. The `get_products_ref_cursor()` function returns a `t_ref_cursor`, and, as you'll see in the next section, it points to a cursor that contains the rows retrieved from the `products` table.

The `update_product_price()` procedure multiplies the price of a product and commits the change.

Creating a Package Body

You create a package body using the `CREATE PACKAGE BODY` statement. The simplified syntax for the `CREATE PACKAGE BODY` statement is as follows:

```
CREATE [OR REPLACE] PACKAGE BODY package_name
{IS | AS}
  package_body
END package_name;
```

where

- *package_name* is the name of the package, which must match the package name in the specification.

- *package_body* contains the code for the procedures and functions.

The following example creates the package body for `product_package`:

```
CREATE PACKAGE BODY product_package AS
  FUNCTION get_products_ref_cursor
  RETURN t_ref_cursor IS
    v_products_ref_cursor t_ref_cursor;
  BEGIN
    -- get the REF CURSOR
    OPEN v_products_ref_cursor FOR
      SELECT product_id, name, price
      FROM products;
```

```
    -- return the REF CURSOR
    RETURN v_products_ref_cursor;
  END get_products_ref_cursor;

  PROCEDURE update_product_price (
    p_product_id IN products.product_id%TYPE,
    p_factor     IN NUMBER
  ) AS
    v_product_count INTEGER;
  BEGIN
    -- count the number of products with the
    -- supplied product_id (will be 1 if the product exists)
    SELECT COUNT(*)
    INTO v_product_count
    FROM products
    WHERE product_id = p_product_id;

    -- if the product exists (v_product_count = 1) then
    -- update that product's price
    IF v_product_count = 1 THEN
      UPDATE products
      SET price = price * p_factor
      WHERE product_id = p_product_id;
      COMMIT;
    END IF;
  EXCEPTION
    WHEN OTHERS THEN
      ROLLBACK;
  END update_product_price;
END product_package;
/
```

The `get_products_ref_cursor()` function opens the cursor and retrieves the `product_id`, `name`, and `price` columns from the `products` table The reference to this cursor (the REF CURSOR) is stored in `v_products_ref_cursor` and returned by the function.

The `update_product_price()` procedure multiplies the price of a product and commits the change. This procedure is identical to the one shown earlier in the section "Creating a Procedure," so I won't go into the details on how it works again.

Calling Functions and Procedures in a Package

When calling functions and procedures in a package, you must include the package name in the call. The following example calls `product_package.get_products_ref_cursor()`, which returns a reference to a cursor containing the `product_id`, `name` and `price` for the products:

```
SELECT product_package.get_products_ref_cursor
FROM dual;

GET_PRODUCTS_REF_CUR
--------------------
CURSOR STATEMENT : 1

CURSOR STATEMENT : 1
```

```
PRODUCT_ID NAME                                    PRICE
---------- ------------------------------ ----------
         1 Modern Science                          19.95
         2 Chemistry                                  30
         3 Supernova                               25.99
         4 Tank War                                13.95
         5 Z Files                                 49.99
         6 2412: The Return                        14.95
         7 Space Force 9                           13.49
         8 From Another Planet                     12.99
         9 Classical Music                         10.99
        10 Pop 3                                   15.99
        11 Creative Yell                           14.99
        12 My Front Line                           13.49
```

The next example calls `product_package.update_product_price()` to multiply product #3's price by 1.25:

```
CALL product_package.update_product_price(3, 1.25);
```

The next query retrieves the details for product #3; notice that the price has increased:

```
SELECT price
FROM products
WHERE product_id = 3;
```

```
     PRICE
----------
     32.49
```

Getting Information on Functions and Procedures in a Package

You can get information on your functions and procedures in a package from the `user_procedures` view; this view was covered earlier in the section "Getting Information on Procedures." The following example retrieves the `object_name` and `procedure_name` columns from `user_procedures` for `product_package`:

```
SELECT object_name, procedure_name
FROM user_procedures
WHERE object_name = 'PRODUCT_PACKAGE';
```

```
OBJECT_NAME                      PROCEDURE_NAME
------------------------------   ------------------------------
PRODUCT_PACKAGE                  GET_PRODUCTS_REF_CURSOR
PRODUCT_PACKAGE                  UPDATE_PRODUCT_PRICE
```

Dropping a Package

You drop a package using `DROP PACKAGE`. For example, the following statement drops `product_package`:

```
DROP PACKAGE product_package;
```

Triggers

A *trigger* is a procedure that is run (or *fired*) automatically by the database when a specified DML statement (INSERT, UPDATE, or DELETE) is run against a certain database table. Triggers are useful for doing things like advanced auditing of changes made to column values in a table.

When a Trigger Fires

A trigger may fire before or after a DML statement runs. Also, because a DML statement can affect more than one row, the code for the trigger may be run once for every row affected (a *row-level trigger*), or just once for all the rows (a *statement-level trigger*). For example, if you create a row-level trigger that fires for an UPDATE on a table, and you run an UPDATE statement that modified ten rows of that table, then that trigger would run ten times. If, however, your trigger was a statement-level trigger, the trigger would fire once for the whole UPDATE statement, regardless of the number of rows affected.

There is another difference between a row-level trigger and a statement-level trigger: A row-level trigger has access to the old and new column values when the trigger fires as a result of an UPDATE statement on that column. The firing of a row-level trigger may also be limited using a trigger *condition*; for example, you could set a condition that limits the trigger to fire only when a column value is less than a specified value.

Set Up for the Example Trigger

As mentioned, triggers are useful for doing advanced auditing of changes made to column values. In the next section, you'll see a trigger that records when a product's price is lowered by more than 25 percent; when this occurs, the trigger will add a row to the product_price_audit table. The product_price_audit table is created by the following statement in the store_schema.sql script:

```
CREATE TABLE product_price_audit (
  product_id INTEGER
    CONSTRAINT price_audit_fk_products
    REFERENCES products(product_id),
  old_price  NUMBER(5, 2),
  new_price  NUMBER(5, 2)
);
```

As you can see, the product_id column of the product_price_audit table is a foreign key to the product_id column of the products table. The old_price column will be used to store the old price of a product prior to the change, and the new_price column will be used to store the new price after the change.

Creating a Trigger

You create a trigger using the CREATE TRIGGER statement. The simplified syntax for the CREATE TRIGGER statement is as follows:

```
CREATE [OR REPLACE] TRIGGER trigger_name
{BEFORE | AFTER | INSTEAD OF | FOR} trigger_event
ON table_name
[FOR EACH ROW]
[{FORWARD | REVERSE} CROSSEDITION]
```

```
[{FOLLOWS | PRECEDES} schema.other_trigger}
[{ENABLE | DISABLE}]
[WHEN trigger_condition]]
BEGIN
  trigger_body
END trigger_name;
```

where

- OR REPLACE means the trigger is to replace an existing trigger, if present.

- *trigger_name* is the name of the trigger.

- BEFORE means the trigger fires before the triggering event is performed. AFTER means the trigger fires after the triggering event is performed. INSTEAD OF means the trigger fires instead of performing the triggering event. FOR, which is new for Oracle Database 11*g*, allows you to create a compound trigger consisting of up to four sections in the trigger body.

- *trigger_event* is the event that causes the trigger to fire.

- *table_name* is the table that the trigger references.

- FOR EACH ROW means the trigger is a row-level trigger, that is, the code contained within *trigger_body* is run for each row when the trigger fires. If you omit FOR EACH ROW, the trigger is a statement-level trigger, which means the code within *trigger_body* is run once when the trigger fires.

- {FORWARD | REVERSE} CROSSEDITION is new for Oracle Database 11*g* and will typically be used by database administrators or application administrators. A FORWARD cross edition trigger is intended to fire when a DML statement makes a change in the database while an online application currently accessing the database *is being patched or upgraded* (FORWARD is the default); the code in the trigger body must be designed to handle the DML changes when the application patching or upgrade is complete. A REVERSE cross edition trigger is similar, except it is intended to fire and handle DML changes made *after the online application has been patched or upgraded.*

- {FOLLOWS | PRECEDES} *schema.other_trigger* is new for Oracle Database 11*g* and specifies whether the firing of the trigger follows or precedes the firing of another trigger specified in *schema.other_trigger*. You can create a series of triggers that fire in a specific order.

- {ENABLE | DISABLE} is new for Oracle Database 11*g* and indicates whether the trigger is initially enabled or disabled when it is created (the default is ENABLE). You enable a disabled trigger by using the ALTER TRIGGER *trigger_name* ENABLE statement or by enabling all triggers for a table using ALTER TABLE *table_name* ENABLE ALL TRIGGERS.

- *trigger_condition* is a Boolean condition that limits when a trigger actually runs its code.

- *trigger_body* contains the code for the trigger.

The example trigger you'll see in this section fires before an update of the price column in the products table; therefore, I'll name the trigger before_product_price_update. Also, because I want to use the price column values before and after an UPDATE statement modifies the price column's value, I must use a row-level trigger. Finally, I want to audit a price change when the new price is lowered by more than 25 percent of the old price; therefore, I'll need to specify a trigger condition to compare the new price with the old price. The following statement creates the before_product_price_update trigger:

```
CREATE TRIGGER before_product_price_update
BEFORE UPDATE OF price
ON products
FOR EACH ROW WHEN (new.price < old.price * 0.75)
BEGIN
  dbms_output.put_line('product_id = ' || :old.product_id);
  dbms_output.put_line('Old price = ' || :old.price);
  dbms_output.put_line('New price = ' || :new.price);
  dbms_output.put_line('The price reduction is more than 25%');

  -- insert row into the product_price_audit table
  INSERT INTO product_price_audit (
    product_id, old_price, new_price
  ) VALUES (
    :old.product_id, :old.price, :new.price
  );
END before_product_price_update;
/
```

There are five things you should notice about this statement:

- BEFORE UPDATE OF price means the trigger fires before an update of the price column.

- FOR EACH ROW means this as a row-level trigger, that is, the trigger code contained within the BEGIN and END keywords runs once for each row modified by the update.

- The trigger condition is (new.price < old.price * 0.75), which means the trigger fires only when the new price is less than 75 percent of the old price (that is, when the price is reduced by more than 25 percent).

- The new and old column values are accessed using the :old and :new aliases in the trigger.

- The trigger code displays the product_id, the old and new prices, and a message stating that the price reduction is more than 25 percent. The code then adds a row to the product_price_audit table containing the product_id and the old and new prices.

Firing a Trigger

To see the output from the trigger, you need to run the SET SERVEROUTPUT ON command:

```
SET SERVEROUTPUT ON
```

To fire the before_product_price_update trigger, you must reduce a product's price by more than 25 percent. Go ahead and perform the following UPDATE statement to reduce the price of products #5 and #10 by 30 percent (this is achieved by multiplying the `price` column by .7). The following `UPDATE` statement causes the `before_product_price_update` trigger to fire:

```
UPDATE products
SET price = price * .7
WHERE product_id IN (5, 10);

product_id = 10
Old price = 15.99
New price = 11.19
The price reduction is more than 25%
product_id = 5
Old price = 49.99
New price = 34.99
The price reduction is more than 25%

2 rows updated.
```

As you can see, the trigger fired for products #10 and #5. You can see that the trigger did indeed add the two required rows containing the `product_ids`, along with the old and new prices, to the `product_price_audit` table using the following query:

```
SELECT *
FROM product_price_audit
ORDER BY product_id;

PRODUCT_ID  OLD_PRICE  NEW_PRICE
----------  ---------  ---------
         5      49.99      34.99
        10      15.99      11.19
```

Getting Information on Triggers

You can get information on your triggers from the `user_triggers` view. Table 11-3 describes some of the columns in `user_triggers`.

Column	Type	Description
TRIGGER_NAME	VARCHAR2(30)	Name of the trigger.
TRIGGER_TYPE	VARCHAR2(16)	Type of the trigger.
TRIGGERING_EVENT	VARCHAR2(227)	Event that causes the trigger to fire.
TABLE_OWNER	VARCHAR2(30)	User who owns the table that the trigger references.
BASE_OBJECT_TYPE	VARCHAR2(16)	Type of the object referenced by the trigger.
TABLE_NAME	VARCHAR2(30)	Name of the table referenced by the trigger.
COLUMN_NAME	VARCHAR2(4000)	Name of the column referenced by the trigger.

TABLE 11-3 *Some Columns in the* `user_triggers` *View*

Column	Type	Description
REFERENCING_NAMES	VARCHAR2(128)	Name of the old and new aliases.
WHEN_CLAUSE	VARCHAR2(4000)	Trigger condition that limits when the trigger runs its code.
STATUS	VARCHAR2(8)	Whether the trigger is enabled or disabled (ENABLED or DISABLED).
DESCRIPTION	VARCHAR2(4000)	Description of the trigger.
ACTION_TYPE	VARCHAR2(11)	Action type of the trigger (CALL or PL/SQL).
TRIGGER_BODY	LONG	Code contained in the trigger body. (The LONG type allows storage of large amounts of text. You'll learn about the LONG type in Chapter 14.)

TABLE 11-3   *Some Columns in the* user_triggers *View* (continued)

NOTE
You can get information on all the triggers you have access to using
all_triggers.

The following example retrieves the details of the before_product_price_update trigger from user_triggers (the output is printed pretty for clarity):

```
SELECT trigger_name, trigger_type, triggering_event, table_owner
  base_object_type, table_name, referencing_names, when_clause, status,
  description, action_type, trigger_body
FROM user_triggers
WHERE trigger_name = 'BEFORE_PRODUCT_PRICE_UPDATE';

TRIGGER_NAME                        TRIGGER_TYPE
----------------------------------- ----------------
BEFORE_PRODUCT_PRICE_UPDATE         BEFORE EACH ROW

TRIGGERING_EVENT
----------------
UPDATE

TABLE_OWNER                         BASE_OBJECT_TYPE TABLE_NAME
----------------------------------- ---------------- -----------
STORE                               TABLE            PRODUCTS

REFERENCING_NAMES
----------------------------------------------------------------
REFERENCING NEW AS NEW OLD AS OLD

WHEN_CLAUSE
----------------------------------------------------------------
new.price < old.price * 0.75
```

```
STATUS
--------
ENABLED

DESCRIPTION
------------------------------------------------------------
before_product_price_update
BEFORE UPDATE OF
  price
ON
  products
FOR EACH ROW

ACTION_TYPE
-----------
PL/SQL

TRIGGER_BODY
------------------------------------------------------------
BEGIN
  dbms_output.put_line('product_id = ' || :old.product_id);
  dbms_output...
```

NOTE
You can see all the code for the trigger using the SQL*Plus SET LONG *command, for example,* SET LONG 1000.

Disabling and Enabling a Trigger

You can stop a trigger from firing by disabling it by using the ALTER TRIGGER statement. The following example disables the before_product_price_update trigger:

```
ALTER TRIGGER before_product_price_update DISABLE;
```

The next example enables the before_product_price_update trigger:

```
ALTER TRIGGER before_product_price_update ENABLE;
```

Dropping a Trigger

You drop a trigger using DROP TRIGGER. The following example drops the before_product_price_update trigger:

```
DROP TRIGGER before_product_price_update;
```

New Oracle Database 11*g* PL/SQL Features

In this section, you'll see some of the new PL/SQL features introduced in Oracle Database 11*g*. Specifically, the following will be discussed:

- The SIMPLE_INTEGER type
- Support for sequences in PL/SQL
- PL/SQL native machine code generation

SIMPLE_INTEGER Type

The SIMPLE_INTEGER type is a subtype of BINARY_INTEGER; the SIMPLE_INTEGER can store the same range as BINARY_INTEGER, except SIMPLE_INTEGER cannot store a NULL value. The range of values SIMPLE_INTEGER can store is -2^{31} ($-2,147,483,648$) to 2^{31} ($2,147,483,648$).

Arithmetic overflow is truncated when using SIMPLE_INTEGER values; therefore, calculations don't raise an error when overflow occurs. Because overflow errors are ignored, the values stored in a SIMPLE_INTEGER can wrap from positive to negative and from negative to positive, as, for example:

$$2^{30} + 2^{30} = 0x40000000 + 0x40000000 = 0x80000000 = -2^{31}$$
$$-2^{31} + -2^{31} = 0x80000000 + 0x80000000 = 0x00000000 = 0$$

In the first example, two positive values are added, and a negative total is produced. In the second example, two negative values are added, and zero is produced.

Because overflow is ignored and truncated when using SIMPLE_INTEGER values in calculations, SIMPLE_INTEGER offers much better performance than BINARY_INTEGER when the DBA configures the database to compile PL/SQL to native machine code. Because of this benefit, you should use SIMPLE_INTEGER in your PL/SQL code when you don't need to store a NULL and you don't care about overflow truncation occurring in your calculations; otherwise, you should use BINARY_INTEGER.

The following get_area() procedure shows the use of the SIMPLE_INTEGER type; get_area() calculates and displays the area of a rectangle:

```
CREATE PROCEDURE get_area
AS
  v_width  SIMPLE_INTEGER := 10;
  v_height SIMPLE_INTEGER := 2;
  v_area   SIMPLE_INTEGER := v_width * v_height;
BEGIN
  DBMS_OUTPUT.PUT_LINE('v_area = ' || v_area);
END get_area;
/
```

NOTE
You'll find this example, and the other examples in this section, in a script named plsql_11g_examples.sql *in the* SQL *directory. You may run this script if you are using Oracle Database 11g.*

The following example shows the execution of get_area():

```
SET SERVEROUTPUT ON
CALL get_area();
v_area = 20
```

As expected, the calculated area is 20.

Sequences in PL/SQL

In the previous chapter you saw how to create and use sequences of numbers in SQL. In Oracle Database 11g, you can also use sequences in PL/SQL code.

As a reminder, a sequence generates a series of numbers. When you create a sequence in SQL, you can specify its initial value and an increment for the series of subsequent numbers.

You use the `currval` pseudo column to get the current value in the sequence and `nextval` to generate the next number. Before you access `currval`, you must first use `nextval` to generate an initial number.

The following statement creates a table named `new_products`; this table will be used shortly:

```
CREATE TABLE new_products (
  product_id INTEGER CONSTRAINT new_products_pk PRIMARY KEY,
  name VARCHAR2(30) NOT NULL,
  price NUMBER(5, 2)
);
```

The next statement creates a sequence named `s_product_id`:

```
CREATE SEQUENCE s_product_id;
```

The following statement creates a procedure named `add_new_products`, which uses `s_product_id` to set the `product_id` column in a row added to the `new_products` table; notice the use of the `nextval` and `currval` pseudo columns in the PL/SQL code (this is new for Oracle Database 11*g*):

```
CREATE PROCEDURE add_new_products
AS
  v_product_id BINARY_INTEGER;
BEGIN
  -- use nextval to generate the initial sequence number
  v_product_id := s_product_id.nextval;
  DBMS_OUTPUT.PUT_LINE('v_product_id = ' || v_product_id);

  -- add a row to new_products
  INSERT INTO new_products
  VALUES (v_product_id, 'Plasma Physics book', 49.95);

  DBMS_OUTPUT.PUT_LINE('s_product_id.currval = ' || s_product_id.currval);

  -- use nextval to generate the next sequence number
  v_product_id := s_product_id.nextval;
  DBMS_OUTPUT.PUT_LINE('v_product_id = ' || v_product_id);

  -- add another row to new_products
  INSERT INTO new_products
  VALUES (v_product_id, 'Quantum Physics book', 69.95);

  DBMS_OUTPUT.PUT_LINE('s_product_id.currval = ' || s_product_id.currval);
END add_new_products;
/
```

The following example runs `add_new_products()` and shows the contents of the `new_products` table:

```
SET SERVEROUTPUT ON
CALL add_new_products();
v_product_id = 1
```

```
s_product_id.currval = 1
v_product_id = 2
s_product_id.currval = 2
```

```
SELECT * FROM new_products;
```
```
                                                 PRICE
PRODUCT_ID NAME
---------- ----------------------------- ----------
         1 Plasma Physics book               49.95
         2 Quantum Physics book              69.95
```

As expected, two rows were added to the table.

PL/SQL Native Machine Code Generation

By default, each PL/SQL program unit is compiled into intermediate form, machine-readable code. This machine-readable code is stored in the database and interpreted every time the code is run. With PL/SQL native compilation, the PL/SQL is turned into native code and stored in shared libraries. Native code runs much faster than intermediate code because native code doesn't have to be interpreted before it runs.

In certain versions of the database prior to Oracle Database 11*g*, you can compile PL/SQL code to C code, and then compile the C code into machine code; this is a very laborious and problematic process. In Oracle Database 11*g*, the PL/SQL complier can generate native machine code directly. Setting up the database to generate native machine code should be done only by an experienced DBA (as such, its coverage is beyond the scope of this book). You can read all about PL/SQL native machine code generation in the *PL/SQL User's Guide and Reference* manual from Oracle Corporation.

Summary

In this chapter, you learned the following:

- PL/SQL programs are divided up into blocks containing PL/SQL and SQL statements.

- A loop, such as a `WHILE` or `FOR` loop, runs statements multiple times.

- A cursor allows PL/SQL to read the rows returned by a query.

- Exceptions are used to handle run-time errors that occur in your PL/SQL code.

- A procedure contains a group of statements. Procedures allow you to centralize your business logic in the database and may be run by any program that accesses the database.

- A function is similar to a procedure except that a function must return a value.

- You can group procedures and functions together into packages, which encapsulate related functionality into one self-contained unit.

- A trigger is a procedure that is run automatically by the database when a specific `INSERT`, `UPDATE`, or `DELETE` statement is run. Triggers are useful for doing things like advanced auditing of changes made to column values in a table.

In the next chapter, you'll learn about database objects.

CHAPTER
12

Database Objects

n this chapter, you will do the following:

- Learn about objects in the database

- Learn how to create object types containing attributes and methods

- Use object types to define column objects and object tables

- Create and manipulate objects in SQL and PL/SQL

- Learn how a type may inherit from another type and create hierarchies of types

- Define your own constructors to set the attributes of an object

- See how to override a method in one type with a method from another type

Introducing Objects

Object-oriented programming languages such as Java, C++, and C# allow you to define classes, and these classes act as templates from which you can create objects. Classes define attributes and methods; attributes are used to store an object's state, and methods are used to model an object's behaviors.

With the release of Oracle Database 8, objects became available within the database, and object features have been improved upon in subsequent product releases. The availability of objects in the database was a major breakthrough because they enable you to define your own classes, known as *object types*, in the database. Like classes in Java and C#, database object types can contain attributes and methods. Object types are also sometimes known as user-defined types.

A simple example of an object type would be a type that represents a product. This object type could contain attributes for the product's name, description, price, and, in the case of a product that is perishable, the number of days the product can sit on the shelf before it must be thrown away. This product object type could also contain a method that returns the sell-by date of the product, based on the shelf life of the product and the current date. Another example of an object type is one that represents a person; this object type could store attributes for the person's first name, last name, date of birth, and address; the person's address could itself be represented by an object type, and it could store things like the street, city, state, and zip code. In this chapter you'll see examples of object types that represent a product, person, and address. You'll also see how to create tables from those object types, populate those tables with actual objects, and manipulate those objects in SQL and PL/SQL.

I've provided an SQL*Plus script named `object_schema.sql` in the `SQL` directory, which creates a user named `object_user` with a password of `object_password`. This script also creates the types and tables, performs the various `INSERT` statements, and creates the PL/SQL code shown in the first part of this chapter. You must run this script while logged in as a user with the required privileges to create a new user with the `CONNECT`, `RESOURCE`, and `CREATE PUBLIC SYNONYM` privileges; I log in as the `system` user on my database to run the scripts. After the script completes, you will be logged in as `object_user`.

Creating Object Types

You create an object type using the CREATE TYPE statement. The following example uses the CREATE TYPE statement to create an object type named t_address. This object type is used to represent an address and contains four attributes named street, city, state, and zip:

```
CREATE TYPE t_address AS OBJECT (
  street VARCHAR2(15),
  city   VARCHAR2(15),
  state  CHAR(2),
  zip    VARCHAR2(5)
);
/
```

The example shows that each attribute is defined using a database type. For example, street is defined as VARCHAR2(15). As you'll see shortly, the type of an attribute can itself be an object type.

The next example creates an object type named t_person; notice that t_person has an attribute named address, which is of type t_address:

```
CREATE TYPE t_person AS OBJECT (
  id         INTEGER,
  first_name VARCHAR2(10),
  last_name  VARCHAR2(10),
  dob        DATE,
  phone      VARCHAR2(12),
  address    t_address
);
/
```

The following example creates an object type named t_product that will be used to represent products; notice that this type declares a function named get_sell_by_date() using the MEMBER FUNCTION clause:

```
CREATE TYPE t_product AS OBJECT (
  id          INTEGER,
  name        VARCHAR2(15),
  description VARCHAR2(22),
  price       NUMBER(5, 2),
  days_valid  INTEGER,

  -- get_sell_by_date() returns the date by which the
  -- product must be sold
  MEMBER FUNCTION get_sell_by_date RETURN DATE
);
/
```

Because t_product contains a method declaration, a *body* for t_product must also be created. The body contains the actual code for the method, and the body is created using the CREATE TYPE BODY statement. The following example creates the body for t_product; notice the body contains the code for the get_sell_by_date() function.

```
CREATE TYPE BODY t_product AS
  -- get_sell_by_date() returns the date by which the
  -- product must be sold
  MEMBER FUNCTION get_sell_by_date RETURN DATE IS
    v_sell_by_date DATE;
  BEGIN
    -- calculate the sell by date by adding the days_valid attribute
    -- to the current date (SYSDATE)
    SELECT days_valid + SYSDATE
    INTO v_sell_by_date
    FROM dual;

    -- return the sell by date
    RETURN v_sell_by_date;
  END;
END;
/
```

As you can see, `get_sell_by_date()` calculates and returns the date by which the product must be sold; it does this by adding the `days_valid` attribute to the current date returned by the built-in database `SYSDATE()` function.

You can also create a public synonym for a type, which enables all users to see the type and use it to define columns in their own tables. The following example creates a public synonym named `t_pub_product` for `t_product`:

```
CREATE PUBLIC SYNONYM t_pub_product FOR t_product;
```

Using DESCRIBE to Get Information on Object Types

You can use the `DESCRIBE` command to get information on an object type. The following examples show the `t_address`, `t_person`, and `t_product` types:

```
DESCRIBE t_address
```

Name	Null?	Type
STREET		VARCHAR2(15)
CITY		VARCHAR2(15)
STATE		CHAR(2)
ZIP		VARCHAR2(5)

```
DESCRIBE t_person
```

Name	Null?	Type
ID		NUMBER(38)
FIRST_NAME		VARCHAR2(10)
LAST_NAME		VARCHAR2(10)
DOB		DATE
PHONE		VARCHAR2(12)
ADDRESS		T_ADDRESS

```
DESCRIBE t_product
Name                                      Null?    Type
---------------------------------------- -------- ------------
 ID                                                NUMBER(38)
 NAME                                              VARCHAR2(10)
 DESCRIPTION                                       VARCHAR2(22)
 PRICE                                             NUMBER(5,2)
 DAYS_VALID                                        INTEGER

METHOD
------
 MEMBER FUNCTION GET_SELL_BY_DATE RETURNS DATE
```

You can set the depth to which DESCRIBE will show information for embedded types using SET DESCRIBE DEPTH. The following example sets the depth to 2 and then describes t_person again; notice that the attributes of address are displayed, which is an embedded object of type t_address:

```
SET DESCRIBE DEPTH 2
DESCRIBE t_person
Name                                      Null?    Type
---------------------------------------- -------- ------------
 ID                                                NUMBER(38)
 FIRST_NAME                                        VARCHAR2(10)
 LAST_NAME                                         VARCHAR2(10)
 DOB                                               DATE
 PHONE                                             VARCHAR2(12)
 ADDRESS                                           T_ADDRESS
   STREET                                          VARCHAR2(15)
   CITY                                            VARCHAR2(15)
   STATE                                           CHAR(2)
   ZIP                                             VARCHAR2(5)
```

Using Object Types in Database Tables

Now that you've seen how to create object types, let's look at how you use these types in database tables. You can use an object type to define an individual column in a table, and the objects subsequently stored in that column are known as *column objects*. You can also use an object type to define an entire row in a table; the table is then known as an *object table*. Finally, you can use an *object reference* to access an individual row in an object table; an object reference is similar to a pointer in C++. You'll see examples of column objects, object tables, and object references in this section.

Column Objects

The following example creates a table named products that contains a column named product of type t_product; the table also contains a column named quantity_in_stock, which is used to store the number of those products currently in stock:

```
CREATE TABLE products (
  product           t_product,
  quantity_in_stock INTEGER
);
```

When adding a row to this table, you must use a *constructor* to supply the attribute values for the new t_product object; as a reminder, the t_product type was created using the following statement:

```
CREATE TYPE t_product AS OBJECT (
    id          INTEGER,
    name        VARCHAR2(10),
    description VARCHAR2(22),
    price       NUMBER(5, 2),
    days_valid  INTEGER,

    -- declare the get_sell_by_date() member function,
    -- get_sell_by_date() returns the date by which the
    -- product must be sold
    MEMBER FUNCTION get_sell_by_date RETURN DATE
);
/
```

A constructor is a built-in method for the object type, and it has the same name as the object type; the constructor accepts parameters that are used to set the attributes of the new object. The constructor for the t_product type is named t_product and accepts five parameters, one to set each of the attributes; for example, t_product(1, pasta, 20 oz bag of pasta, 3.95, 10) creates a new t_product object and sets its id to 1, name to pasta, description to 20 oz bag of pasta, price to 3.95, and days_valid to 10.

The following INSERT statements add two rows to the products table; notice the use of the t_product constructor to supply the attribute values for the product column objects:

```
INSERT INTO products (
    product,
    quantity_in_stock
) VALUES (
    t_product(1, 'pasta', '20 oz bag of pasta', 3.95, 10),
    50
);

INSERT INTO products (
    product,
    quantity_in_stock
) VALUES (
    t_product(2, 'sardines', '12 oz box of sardines', 2.99, 5),
    25
);
```

The following query retrieves these rows from the products table; notice that the product column objects' attributes are displayed within a constructor for t_product:

```
SELECT *
FROM products;
```

```
PRODUCT(ID, NAME, DESCRIPTION, PRICE, DAYS_VALID)
-----------------------------------------------------------
QUANTITY_IN_STOCK
-----------------
T_PRODUCT(1, 'pasta', '20 oz bag of pasta', 3.95, 10)
               50

T_PRODUCT(2, 'sardines', '12 oz box of sardines', 2.99, 5)
               25
```

You can also retrieve an individual column object from a table; to do this, you must supply a table alias through which you select the object. The following query retrieves product #1 from the products table; notice the use of the table alias p for the products table, through which the product object's id attribute is specified in the WHERE clause:

```
SELECT p.product
FROM products p
WHERE p.product.id = 1;
```

```
PRODUCT(ID, NAME, DESCRIPTION, PRICE, DAYS_VALID)
-------------------------------------------------------
T_PRODUCT(1, 'pasta', '20 oz bag of pasta', 3.95, 10)
```

The next query explicitly includes the product object's id, name, price, and days_valid attributes in the SELECT statement, plus the quantity_in_stock:

```
SELECT p.product.id, p.product.name,
  p.product.price, p.product.days_valid, p.quantity_in_stock
FROM products p
WHERE p.product.id = 1;
```

```
PRODUCT.ID PRODUCT.NA PRODUCT.PRICE PRODUCT.DAYS_VALID QUANTITY_IN_STOCK
---------- ---------- ------------- ------------------ -----------------
         1 pasta               3.95                 10                50
```

The t_product object type contains a function named get_sell_by_date(), which calculates and returns the date by which the product must be sold. The function does this by adding the days_valid attribute to the current date, which is obtained from the database using the SYSDATE() function. You can call the get_sell_by_date() function using a table alias, as shown in the following query that uses the table alias p for the products table:

```
SELECT p.product.get_sell_by_date()
FROM products p;
```

```
P.PRODUCT
---------
19-JUN-07
13-JUN-07
```

Of course, if you run this query your dates will be different, because they are calculated using SYSDATE(), which returns the current date and time.

The following UPDATE statement modifies the description of product #1; notice that the table alias p is used again:

```
UPDATE products p
SET p.product.description = '30 oz bag of pasta'
WHERE p.product.id = 1;
```

```
1 row updated.
```

The following DELETE statement removes product #2:

```
DELETE FROM products p
WHERE p.product.id = 2;
```

```
1 row deleted.
```

```
ROLLBACK;
```

NOTE
If you run these UPDATE *and* DELETE *statements, make sure you execute the* ROLLBACK *so that your example data matches that shown in the rest of this chapter.*

Object Tables

You can use an object type to define an entire table, and such a table is known as an object table. The following example creates an object table named object_products, which stores objects of type t_product; notice the use of the OF keyword to identify the table as an object table of type t_product:

```
CREATE TABLE object_products OF t_product;
```

When inserting a row into an object table, you can choose whether to use a constructor to supply attribute values or to supply the values in the same way that you would supply column values in a relational table. The following INSERT statement adds a row to the object_products table using the constructor for t_product:

```
INSERT INTO object_products VALUES (
    t_product(1, 'pasta', '20 oz bag of pasta', 3.95, 10)
);
```

The next INSERT statement omits the constructor for t_product; notice that the attribute values for t_product are supplied in the same way that columns would be in a relational table:

```
INSERT INTO object_products (
    id, name, description, price, days_valid
) VALUES (
    2, 'sardines', '12 oz box of sardines', 2.99, 5
);
```

The following query retrieves these rows from the object_products table:

```
SELECT *
FROM object_products;
```

```
        ID NAME        DESCRIPTION                   PRICE DAYS_VALID
---------- ---------- ---------------------- ---------- ----------
         1 pasta      20 oz bag of pasta          3.95         10
         2 sardines   12 oz box of sardines       2.99          5
```

You can also specify individual object attributes in a query; for example, by doing this:

```
SELECT id, name, price
FROM object_products op
WHERE id = 1;
```

```
        ID NAME            PRICE
---------- ---------- ----------
         1 pasta          3.95
```

or this:

```
SELECT op.id, op.name, op.price
FROM object_products op
WHERE op.id = 1;
```

```
        ID NAME            PRICE
---------- ---------- ----------
         1 pasta          3.95
```

You can use the built-in Oracle database VALUE() function to select a row from an object table. VALUE() treats the row as an actual object and returns the attributes for the object within a constructor for the object type. VALUE() accepts a parameter containing a table alias, as shown in the following query:

```
SELECT VALUE(op)
FROM object_products op;
```

```
VALUE(OP)(ID, NAME, DESCRIPTION, PRICE, DAYS_VALID)
----------------------------------------------------------
T_PRODUCT(1, 'pasta', '20 oz bag of pasta', 3.95, 10)
T_PRODUCT(2, 'sardines', '12 oz box of sardines', 2.99, 5)
```

You can also add an object attribute after VALUE():

```
SELECT VALUE(op).id, VALUE(op).name, VALUE(op).price
FROM object_products op;
```

```
VALUE(OP).ID VALUE(OP). VALUE(OP).PRICE
------------ ---------- ----------------
           1 pasta                  3.95
           2 sardines               2.99
```

The following UPDATE statement modifies the description of product #1:

```
UPDATE object_products
SET description = '25 oz bag of pasta'
WHERE id = 1;
```

```
1 row updated.
```

The following DELETE statement removes product #2:

```
DELETE FROM object_products
WHERE id = 2;
```

```
1 row deleted.
```

```
ROLLBACK;
```

Let's take a look at a more complex object table. The following CREATE TABLE statement creates an object table named object_customers, which stores objects of type t_person:

```
CREATE TABLE object_customers OF t_person;
```

The t_person type contains an embedded t_address object; t_person was created using the following statement:

```
CREATE TYPE t_person AS OBJECT (
    id          INTEGER,
    first_name VARCHAR2(10),
    last_name  VARCHAR2(10),
    dob         DATE,
    phone       VARCHAR2(12),
    address     t_address
);
/
```

The following INSERT statements add two rows into object_customers. The first INSERT uses constructors for t_person and t_address, while the second INSERT omits the t_person constructor:

```
INSERT INTO object_customers VALUES (
    t_person(1, 'John', 'Brown', '01-FEB-1955', '800-555-1211',
      t_address('2 State Street', 'Beantown', 'MA', '12345')
    )
);
```

```
INSERT INTO object_customers (
    id, first_name, last_name, dob, phone,
    address
) VALUES (
    2, 'Cynthia', 'Green', '05-FEB-1968', '800-555-1212',
    t_address('3 Free Street', 'Middle Town', 'CA', '12345')
);
```

The following query retrieves these rows from the object_customers table; notice that the attributes for the embedded address column object are displayed within the t_address constructor:

```
SELECT *
FROM object_customers;
```

```
        ID FIRST_NAME LAST_NAME  DOB       PHONE
---------- ---------- ---------- --------- ------------
ADDRESS(STREET, CITY, STATE, ZIP)
-------------------------------------------------------
         1 John       Brown      01-FEB-55 800-555-1211
T_ADDRESS('2 State Street', 'Beantown', 'MA', '12345')

         2 Cynthia    Green      05-FEB-68 800-555-1212
T_ADDRESS('3 Free Street', 'Middle Town', 'CA', '12345')
```

The next query retrieves customer #1 from `object_customers`; notice the use of the table alias `oc` through which the `id` attribute is specified in the `WHERE` clause:

```
SELECT *
FROM object_customers oc
WHERE oc.id = 1;
```

```
        ID FIRST_NAME LAST_NAME  DOB       PHONE
---------- ---------- ---------- --------- ------------
ADDRESS(STREET, CITY, STATE, ZIP)
-------------------------------------------------------
         1 John       Brown      01-FEB-55 800-555-1211
T_ADDRESS('2 State Street', 'Beantown', 'MA', '12345')
```

In the following query, a customer is retrieved based on the `state` attribute of the `address` column object:

```
SELECT *
FROM object_customers oc
WHERE oc.address.state = 'MA';
```

```
        ID FIRST_NAME LAST_NAME  DOB       PHONE
---------- ---------- ---------- --------- ------------
ADDRESS(STREET, CITY, STATE, ZIP)
-------------------------------------------------------
         1 John       Brown      01-FEB-55 800-555-1211
T_ADDRESS('2 State Street', 'Beantown', 'MA', '12345')
```

In the next query, the `id`, `first_name`, and `last_name` attributes of customer #1 are explicitly included in the `SELECT` statement, along with the attributes of the embedded `address` column object:

```
SELECT oc.id, oc.first_name, oc.last_name,
  oc.address.street, oc.address.city, oc.address.state, oc.address.zip
FROM object_customers oc
WHERE oc.id = 1;
```

```
        ID FIRST_NAME LAST_NAME  ADDRESS.STREET  ADDRESS.CITY    AD ADDRE
---------- ---------- ---------- --------------- --------------- -- -----
         1 John       Brown      2 State Street  Beantown        MA 12345
```

Object Identifiers and Object References

Each object in an object table has a unique *object identifier* (OID), and you can retrieve the OID for an object using the REF() function. For example, the following query retrieves the OID for customer #1 in the object_customers table:

```
SELECT REF(oc)
FROM object_customers oc
WHERE oc.id = 1;

REF(OC)
-------------------------------------------------------------------
0000280209D66AB93F991647649D78D08B267EE44858C7B9989D9D40689FB4DA92820
AFFE2010003280000
```

The long string of numbers and letters are the OID, which identifies the location of the object in the database. You can store an OID in an object reference and later access the object it refers to. An object reference, which is similar to a pointer in C++, points to an object stored in an object table using the OID. You may use object references to model relationships between object tables, and, as you'll see later, you can use object references in PL/SQL to access objects.

You use the REF type to define an object reference; the following statement creates a table named purchases that contains two object reference columns named customer_ref and product_ref:

```
CREATE TABLE purchases (
    id              INTEGER PRIMARY KEY,
    customer_ref REF t_person  SCOPE IS object_customers,
    product_ref  REF t_product SCOPE IS object_products
);
```

The SCOPE IS clause restricts an object reference to point to objects in a specific table. For example, the customer_ref column is restricted to point to objects in the object_customers table only; similarly, the product_ref column is restricted to point to objects in the object_products table only.

As I mentioned earlier, each object in an object table has a unique object identifier (OID) that you can store in an object reference; you can retrieve an OID using the REF() function and store it in an object reference. For example, the following INSERT statement adds a row to the purchases table; notice that the REF() function is used in the queries to get the object identifiers for customer #1 and product #1 from the object_customers and object_products tables:

```
INSERT INTO purchases (
    id,
    customer_ref,
    product_ref
) VALUES (
    1,
    (SELECT REF(oc) FROM object_customers oc WHERE oc.id = 1),
    (SELECT REF(op) FROM object_products  op WHERE op.id = 1)
);
```

This example records that customer #1 purchased product #1.

The following query selects the row from the `purchases` table; notice that the `customer_ref` and `product_ref` columns contain references to the objects in the `object_customers` and `object_products` tables:

```
SELECT *
FROM purchases;

        ID
----------
CUSTOMER_REF
-------------------------------------------------------------------
PRODUCT_REF
-------------------------------------------------------------------
        1
0000220208D66AB93F991647649D78D08B267EE44858C7B9989D9D40689FB4DA92820
AFFE2
0000220208662E2AB4256711D6A1B50010A4E7AE8A662E2AB2256711D6A1B50010A4E
7AE8A
```

You can retrieve the actual objects stored in an object reference using the `DEREF()` function, which accepts an object reference as a parameter and returns the actual object. For example, the following query uses `DEREF()` to retrieve customer #1 and product #1 through the `customer_ref` and `product_ref` columns of the `purchases` table:

```
SELECT DEREF(customer_ref), DEREF(product_ref)
FROM purchases;

DEREF(CUSTOMER_REF)(ID, FIRST_NAME, LAST_NAME, DOB, PHONE,
 ADDRESS(STREET, CITY,
-----------------------------------------------------------
DEREF(PRODUCT_REF)(ID, NAME, DESCRIPTION, PRICE, DAYS_VALID)
-----------------------------------------------------------
T_PERSON(1, 'John', 'Brown', '01-FEB-55', '800-555-1211',
 T_ADDRESS('2 State Street', 'Beantown', 'MA', '12345'))
T_PRODUCT(1, 'pasta', '20 oz bag of pasta', 3.95, 10)
```

The next query retrieves the customer's `first_name` and `address.street` attributes, plus the product's `name` attribute:

```
SELECT DEREF(customer_ref).first_name,
 DEREF(customer_ref).address.street, DEREF(product_ref).name
FROM purchases;

DEREF(CUST DEREF(CUSTOMER_ DEREF(PROD
---------- --------------- ----------
John       2 State Street  pasta
```

The following UPDATE statement modifies the `product_ref` column to point to product #2:

```
UPDATE purchases SET product_ref = (
   SELECT REF(op) FROM object_products op WHERE op.id = 2
) WHERE id = 1;

1 row updated.
```

The following query verifies this change:

```
SELECT DEREF(customer_ref), DEREF(product_ref)
FROM purchases;

DEREF(CUSTOMER_REF)(ID, FIRST_NAME, LAST_NAME, DOB, PHONE,
 ADDRESS(STREET, CITY,
-----------------------------------------------------------
DEREF(PRODUCT_REF)(ID, NAME, DESCRIPTION, PRICE, DAYS_VALID)
-----------------------------------------------------------
T_PERSON(1, 'John', 'Brown', '01-FEB-55', '800-555-1211',
 T_ADDRESS('2 State Street', 'Beantown', 'MA', '12345'))
T_PRODUCT(2, 'sardines', '12 oz box of sardines', 2.99, 5)
```

Comparing Object Values

You can compare the value of two objects in a WHERE clause of a query using the equality operator (=). For example, the following query retrieves customer #1 from the object_customers table:

```
SELECT oc.id, oc.first_name, oc.last_name, oc.dob
FROM object_customers oc
WHERE VALUE(oc) =
  t_person(1, 'John', 'Brown', '01-FEB-1955', '800-555-1211',
    t_address('2 State Street', 'Beantown', 'MA', '12345')
  );

        ID FIRST_NAME LAST_NAME  DOB
---------- ---------- ---------- ---------
         1 John       Brown      01-FEB-55
```

The next query retrieves product #1 from the object_products table:

```
SELECT op.id, op.name, op.price, op.days_valid
FROM object_products op
WHERE VALUE(op) = t_product(1, 'pasta', '20 oz bag of pasta', 3.95, 10);

        ID NAME       PRICE DAYS_VALID
---------- ---------- ---------- ----------
         1 pasta       3.95         10
```

You can also use the <> and IN operators in the WHERE clause:

```
SELECT oc.id, oc.first_name, oc.last_name, oc.dob
FROM object_customers oc
WHERE VALUE(oc) <>
  t_person(1, 'John', 'Brown', '01-FEB-1955', '800-555-1211',
    t_address('2 State Street', 'Beantown', 'MA', '12345')
  );

        ID FIRST_NAME LAST_NAME  DOB
---------- ---------- ---------- ---------
         2 Cynthia    Green      05-FEB-68
```

```
SELECT op.id, op.name, op.price, op.days_valid
FROM object_products op
WHERE VALUE(op) IN t_product(1, 'pasta', '20 oz bag of pasta', 3.95, 10);
```

```
       ID NAME          PRICE DAYS_VALID
---------- ---------- ---------- ----------
        1 pasta          3.95         10
```

If you want to use an operator like <, >, <=, >=, LIKE, or BETWEEN, you need to provide a map function for the type. A map function must return a single value of one of the built-in types that the database can then use to compare two objects. The value returned by the map function will be different for every object type, and you need to figure out what the best attribute, or concatenation of attributes, represents an object's value. For example, with the t_product type, I'd return the price attribute; with the t_person type, I'd return a concatenation of the last_ name and first_name attributes.

The following statements create a type named t_person2 that contains a map function named get_string(); notice that get_string() returns a VARCHAR2 string containing a concatenation of the last_name and first_name attributes:

```
CREATE TYPE t_person2 AS OBJECT (
  id          INTEGER,
  first_name VARCHAR2(10),
  last_name  VARCHAR2(10),
  dob         DATE,
  phone       VARCHAR2(12),
  address     t_address,

  -- declare the get_string() map function,
  -- which returns a VARCHAR2 string
  MAP MEMBER FUNCTION get_string RETURN VARCHAR2
);
/

CREATE TYPE BODY t_person2 AS
  -- define the get_string() map function
  MAP MEMBER FUNCTION get_string RETURN VARCHAR2 IS
  BEGIN
    -- return a concatenated string containing the
    -- last_name and first_name attributes
    RETURN last_name || ' ' || first_name;
  END get_string;
END;
/
```

As you'll see shortly, the database will automatically call get_string() when comparing t_person2 objects.

The following statements create a table named object_customers2 and add rows to it:

```
CREATE TABLE object_customers2 OF t_person2;

INSERT INTO object_customers2 VALUES (
```

```
    t_person2(1, 'John', 'Brown', '01-FEB-1955', '800-555-1211',
      t_address('2 State Street', 'Beantown', 'MA', '12345')
    )
);

INSERT INTO object_customers2 VALUES (
    t_person2(2, 'Cynthia', 'Green', '05-FEB-1968', '800-555-1212',
      t_address('3 Free Street', 'Middle Town', 'CA', '12345')
    )
);
```

The following query uses > in the WHERE clause:

```
SELECT oc2.id, oc2.first_name, oc2.last_name, oc2.dob
FROM object_customers2 oc2
WHERE VALUE(oc2) >
    t_person2(1, 'John', 'Brown', '01-FEB-1955', '800-555-1211',
      t_address('2 State Street', 'Beantown', 'MA', '12345')
    );
```

```
        ID FIRST_NAME LAST_NAME  DOB
---------- ---------- ---------- ---------
         2 Cynthia    Green      05-FEB-68
```

When the query is executed, the database automatically calls get_string() to compare the objects in the object_customers2 table to the object after the > in the WHERE clause. The get_string() function returns a concatenation of the last_name and first_name attributes of the objects, and because Green Cynthia is greater than Brown John, she is returned by the query.

Using Objects in PL/SQL

You can create and manipulate objects in PL/SQL. In this section, you'll see the use of a package named product_package, which is created when you run the object_schema.sql script; product_package contains the following methods:

- A function named get_products() that returns a REF CURSOR that points to the objects in the object_products table

- A procedure named display_product() that displays the attributes of a single object in the object_products table

- A procedure named insert_product() that adds an object to the object_products table

- A procedure named update_product_price() that updates the price attribute of an object in the object_products table

- A function named get_product() that returns a single object from the object_products table

- A procedure named update_product() that updates all the attributes of an object in the object_products table

■ A function named `get_product_ref()` that returns a reference to a single object from the `object_products` table

■ A procedure named `delete_product()` that deletes a single object from the `object_products` table

The `object_schema.sql` script contains the following package specification:

```
CREATE PACKAGE product_package AS
  TYPE t_ref_cursor IS REF CURSOR;
  FUNCTION get_products RETURN t_ref_cursor;
  PROCEDURE display_product(
    p_id IN object_products.id%TYPE
  );
  PROCEDURE insert_product(
    p_id          IN object_products.id%TYPE,
    p_name        IN object_products.name%TYPE,
    p_description IN object_products.description%TYPE,
    p_price       IN object_products.price%TYPE,
    p_days_valid  IN object_products.days_valid%TYPE
  );
  PROCEDURE update_product_price(
    p_id     IN object_products.id%TYPE,
    p_factor IN NUMBER
  );
  FUNCTION get_product(
    p_id IN object_products.id%TYPE
  ) RETURN t_product;
  PROCEDURE update_product(
    p_product t_product
  );
  FUNCTION get_product_ref(
    p_id IN object_products.id%TYPE
  ) RETURN REF t_product;
  PROCEDURE delete_product(
    p_id IN object_products.id%TYPE
  );
END product_package;
/
```

You'll see the methods in the body of `product_package` in the following sections.

The get_products() Function

The `get_products()` function returns a `REF CURSOR` that points to the objects in the `object_products` table; `get_products()` is defined as follows in the body of `product_package`:

```
FUNCTION get_products
RETURN t_ref_cursor IS
  -- declare a t_ref_cursor object
  v_products_ref_cursor t_ref_cursor;
BEGIN
```

```
  -- get the REF CURSOR
  OPEN v_products_ref_cursor FOR
    SELECT VALUE(op)
    FROM object_products op
    ORDER BY op.id;

  -- return the REF CURSOR
  RETURN v_products_ref_cursor;
END get_products;
```

The following query calls `product_package.get_products()` to retrieve the products from `object_products`:

```
SELECT product_package.get_products
FROM dual;

GET_PRODUCTS
-------------------
CURSOR STATEMENT : 1

CURSOR STATEMENT : 1

VALUE(OP)(ID, NAME, DESCRIPTION, PRICE, DAYS_VALID)
----------------------------------------------------------
T_PRODUCT(1, 'pasta', '20 oz bag of pasta', 3.95, 10)
T_PRODUCT(2, 'sardines', '12 oz box of sardines', 2.99, 5)
```

The display_product() Procedure

The `display_product()` procedure displays the attributes of a single object in the `object_products` table; `display_product()` is defined as follows in the body of `product_package`:

```
PROCEDURE display_product(
  p_id IN object_products.id%TYPE
) AS
  -- declare a t_product object named v_product
  v_product t_product;
BEGIN
  -- attempt to get the product and store it in v_product
  SELECT VALUE(op)
  INTO v_product
  FROM object_products op
  WHERE id = p_id;

  -- display the attributes of v_product
  DBMS_OUTPUT.PUT_LINE('v_product.id=' ||
    v_product.id);
  DBMS_OUTPUT.PUT_LINE('v_product.name=' ||
    v_product.name);
  DBMS_OUTPUT.PUT_LINE('v_product.description=' ||
    v_product.description);
  DBMS_OUTPUT.PUT_LINE('v_product.price=' ||
```

```
    v_product.price);
  DBMS_OUTPUT.PUT_LINE('v_product.days_valid=' ||
    v_product.days_valid);

  -- call v_product.get_sell_by_date() and display the date
  DBMS_OUTPUT.PUT_LINE('Sell by date=' ||
    v_product.get_sell_by_date());
END display_product;
```

The following example calls `product_package.display_product(1)` to retrieve product #1 from the `object_products` table:

```
SET SERVEROUTPUT ON
CALL product_package.display_product(1);
v_product.id=1
v_product.name=pasta
v_product.description=20 oz bag of pasta
v_product.price=3.95
v_product.days_valid=10
Sell by date=25-JUN-07
```

The insert_product() Procedure

The `insert_product()` procedure adds an object to the `object_products` table; `insert_product()` is defined as follows in the body of `product_package`:

```
PROCEDURE insert_product(
    p_id            IN object_products.id%TYPE,
    p_name          IN object_products.name%TYPE,
    p_description   IN object_products.description%TYPE,
    p_price         IN object_products.price%TYPE,
    p_days_valid    IN object_products.days_valid%TYPE
) AS
    -- create a t_product object named v_product
    v_product t_product :=
        t_product(
            p_id, p_name, p_description, p_price, p_days_valid
        );
BEGIN
    -- add v_product to the object_products table
    INSERT INTO object_products VALUES (v_product);
    COMMIT;
EXCEPTION
    WHEN OTHERS THEN
        ROLLBACK;
END insert_product;
```

The following example calls `product_package.insert_product()` to add a new object to the `object_products` table:

```
CALL product_package.insert_product(3, 'salsa',
  '15 oz jar of salsa', 1.50, 20);
```

The update_product_price() Procedure

The update_product_price() procedure updates the price attribute of an object in the object_products table; update_product_price() is defined as follows in the body of product_package:

```
PROCEDURE update_product_price(
  p_id     IN object_products.id%TYPE,
  p_factor IN NUMBER
) AS
  -- declare a t_product object named v_product
  v_product t_product;
BEGIN
  -- attempt to select the product for update and
  -- store the product in v_product
  SELECT VALUE(op)
  INTO v_product
  FROM object_products op
  WHERE id = p_id
  FOR UPDATE;

  -- display the current price of v_product
  DBMS_OUTPUT.PUT_LINE('v_product.price=' ||
    v_product.price);

  -- multiply v_product.price by p_factor
  v_product.price := v_product.price * p_factor;
  DBMS_OUTPUT.PUT_LINE('New v_product.price=' ||
    v_product.price);

  -- update the product in the object_products table
  UPDATE object_products op
  SET op = v_product
  WHERE id = p_id;
  COMMIT;
EXCEPTION
  WHEN OTHERS THEN
    ROLLBACK;
END update_product_price;
```

The following example calls product_package.update_product_price() to update the price of product #3 in the object_products table:

```
CALL product_package.update_product_price(3, 2.4);
v_product.price=1.5
New v_product.price=3.6
```

The get_product() Function

The get_product() function returns a single object from the object_products table; get_product() is defined as follows in the body of product_package:

```
FUNCTION get_product(
   p_id IN object_products.id%TYPE
)
RETURN t_product IS
  -- declare a t_product object named v_product
  v_product t_product;
BEGIN
  -- get the product and store it in v_product
  SELECT VALUE(op)
  INTO v_product
  FROM object_products op
  WHERE op.id = p_id;

  -- return v_product
  RETURN v_product;
END get_product;
```

The following query calls `product_package.get_product()` to get product #3 from the `object_products` table:

```
SELECT product_package.get_product(3)
FROM dual;

PRODUCT_PACKAGE.GET_PRODUCT(3)(ID, NAME, DESCRIPTION
----------------------------------------------------
T_PRODUCT(3, 'salsa', '15 oz jar of salsa', 3.6, 20)
```

The update_product() Procedure

The `update_product()` procedure updates all the attributes of an object in the `object_products` table; `update_product()` is defined as follows in the body of `product_package`:

```
PROCEDURE update_product(
   p_product IN t_product
) AS
BEGIN
  -- update the product in the object_products table
  UPDATE object_products op
  SET op = p_product
  WHERE id = p_product.id;
  COMMIT;
EXCEPTION
  WHEN OTHERS THEN
    ROLLBACK;
END update_product;
```

The following example calls `product_package.update_product()` to update product #3 in the `object_products` table:

```
CALL product_package.update_product(t_product(3, 'salsa',
  '25 oz jar of salsa', 2.70, 15));
```

The get_product_ref() Function

The `get_product_ref()` function returns a reference to a single object from the `object_products` table; `get_product_ref()` is defined as follows in the body of `product_package`:

```
FUNCTION get_product_ref(
  p_id IN object_products.id%TYPE
)
RETURN REF t_product IS
  -- declare a reference to a t_product
  v_product_ref REF t_product;
BEGIN
  -- get the REF for the product and
  -- store it in v_product_ref
  SELECT REF(op)
  INTO v_product_ref
  FROM object_products op
  WHERE op.id = p_id;

  -- return v_product_ref
  RETURN v_product_ref;
END get_product_ref;
```

The following query calls `product_package.get_product_ref()` to get the reference to product #3 from the `object_products` table:

```
SELECT product_package.get_product_ref(3)
FROM dual;

PRODUCT_PACKAGE.GET_PRODUCT_REF(3)
--------------------------------------------------------------------------------
000028020956DBE8BEFDEF4D5BA8C806A7B31B49DF916CDB2CAC1B46E9808BA181F9F2760F0100
033D0002
```

The next example calls `product_package.get_product_ref()` again, this time using `DEREF()` to get to the actual product:

```
SELECT DEREF(product_package.get_product_ref(3))
FROM dual;

DEREF(PRODUCT_PACKAGE.GET_PRODUCT_REF(3))(ID, NAME,
----------------------------------------------------
T_PRODUCT(3, 'salsa', '25 oz jar of salsa', 2.7, 15)
```

The delete_product() Procedure

The `delete_product()` procedure deletes a single object from the `object_products` table; `delete_product()` is defined as follows in the body of `product_package`:

```
PROCEDURE delete_product(
  p_id IN object_products.id%TYPE
) AS
BEGIN
```

```
   -- delete the product
   DELETE FROM object_products op
   WHERE op.id = p_id;
   COMMIT;
EXCEPTION
   WHEN OTHERS THEN
      ROLLBACK;
END delete_product;
```

The following example calls `product_package.delete_product()` to delete product #3 from the `object_products` table:

```
CALL product_package.delete_product(3);
```

Now that you've seen all the methods in `product_package`, it's time for you to see two procedures named `product_lifecycle()` and `product_lifecycle2()` that call the various methods in the package. Both procedures are created when you run the `object_schema.sql` script.

The product_lifecycle() Procedure

The `product_lifecycle()` procedure is defined as follows:

```
CREATE PROCEDURE product_lifecycle AS
   -- declare object
   v_product t_product;
BEGIN
   -- insert a new product
   product_package.insert_product(4, 'beef',
    '25 lb pack of beef', 32, 10);

   -- display the product
   product_package.display_product(4);

   -- get the new product and store it in v_product
   SELECT product_package.get_product(4)
   INTO v_product
   FROM dual;

   -- change some attributes of v_product
   v_product.description := '20 lb pack of beef';
   v_product.price := 36;
   v_product.days_valid := 8;

   -- update the product
   product_package.update_product(v_product);

   -- display the product
   product_package.display_product(4);

   -- delete the product
   product_package.delete_product(4);
END product_lifecycle;
/
```

The following example calls `product_lifecycle()`:

```
CALL product_lifecycle();
v_product.id=4
v_product.name=beef
v_product.description=25 lb pack of beef
v_product.price=32
v_product.days_valid=10
Sell by date=27-JUN-07
v_product.id=4
v_product.name=beef
v_product.description=20 lb pack of beef
v_product.price=36
v_product.days_valid=8
Sell by date=25-JUN-07
```

The product_lifecycle2() Procedure

The `product_lifecycle2()` procedure uses an object reference to access a product; `product_lifecycle2()` is defined as follows:

```
CREATE PROCEDURE product_lifecycle2 AS
   -- declare object
   v_product t_product;

   -- declare object reference
   v_product_ref REF t_product;
BEGIN
   -- insert a new product
   product_package.insert_product(4, 'beef',
    '25 lb pack of beef', 32, 10);

   -- display the product
   product_package.display_product(4);

   -- get the new product reference and store it in v_product_ref
   SELECT product_package.get_product_ref(4)
   INTO v_product_ref
   FROM dual;

   -- dereference v_product_ref using the following query
   SELECT DEREF(v_product_ref)
   INTO v_product
   FROM dual;

   -- change some attributes of v_product
   v_product.description := '20 lb pack of beef';
   v_product.price := 36;
   v_product.days_valid := 8;

   -- update the product
   product_package.update_product(v_product);
```

```
  -- display the product
  product_package.display_product(4);

  -- delete the product
  product_package.delete_product(4);
END product_lifecycle2;
/
```

One point to note in this procedure is that, in order to dereference `v_product_ref`, you have to use the following query:

```
SELECT DEREF(v_product_ref)
INTO v_product
FROM dual;
```

The reason you have to use this query is that you cannot use `DEREF()` directly in PL/SQL code. For example, the following statement won't compile in PL/SQL:

```
v_product := DEREF(v_product_ref);
```

The following example calls `product_lifecycle2()`:

```
CALL product_lifecycle2();
v_product.id=4
v_product.name=beef
v_product.description=25 lb pack of beef
v_product.price=32
v_product.days_valid=10
Sell by date=27-JUN-07
v_product.id=4
v_product.name=beef
v_product.description=20 lb pack of beef
v_product.price=36
v_product.days_valid=8
Sell by date=25-JUN-07
```

Type Inheritance

Oracle Database 9*i* introduced object type *inheritance*, which allows you to define hierarchies of object types. For example, you might want to define a business person object type and have that type inherit the existing attributes from `t_person`. The business person type could extend `t_person` with attributes to store the person's job title and the name of the company they work for. For `t_person` to be inherited from, the `t_person` definition must include the `NOT FINAL` clause:

```
CREATE TYPE t_person AS OBJECT (
    id          INTEGER,
    first_name  VARCHAR2(10),
    last_name   VARCHAR2(10),
    dob         DATE,
    phone       VARCHAR2(12),
    address     t_address,
    MEMBER FUNCTION display_details RETURN VARCHAR2
) NOT FINAL;
/
```

The NOT FINAL clause indicates that t_person can be inherited from when defining another type. (The default when defining types is FINAL, meaning that the object type cannot be inherited from.)

The following statement creates the body for t_person; notice that the display_details() function returns a VARCHAR2 containing the id and name of the person:

```
CREATE TYPE BODY t_person AS
  MEMBER FUNCTION display_details RETURN VARCHAR2 IS
  BEGIN
    RETURN 'id=' || id || ', name=' || first_name || ' ' || last_name;
  END;
END;
/
```

NOTE
I've provided an SQL*Plus script named object_schema2.sql, *which creates all the items shown in this and the following sections. You can run the script if you are using Oracle Database 9i or above. After the script completes, you will be logged in as* object_user2.

To have a new type inherit attributes and methods from an existing type, you use the UNDER keyword when defining your new type. Our business person type, which I'll name t_business_person, uses the UNDER keyword to inherit the attributes from t_person:

```
CREATE TYPE t_business_person UNDER t_person (
  title    VARCHAR2(20),
  company VARCHAR2(20)
);
/
```

In this example, t_person is known as the *supertype,* and t_business_person is known as the *subtype.* You can then use t_business_person when defining column objects or object tables. For example, the following statement creates an object table named object_business_customers:

```
CREATE TABLE object_business_customers OF t_business_person;
```

The following INSERT statement adds an object to object_business_customers; notice that the two additional title and company attributes are supplied at the end of the t_business_person constructor:

```
INSERT INTO object_business_customers VALUES (
  t_business_person(1, 'John', 'Brown', '01-FEB-1955', '800-555-1211',
    t_address('2 State Street', 'Beantown', 'MA', '12345'),
    'Manager', 'XYZ Corp'
  )
);
```

The following query retrieves this object:

```
SELECT *
FROM object_business_customers
WHERE id = 1;
```

```
        ID FIRST_NAME LAST_NAME  DOB        PHONE
---------- ---------- ---------- --------- ------------
ADDRESS(STREET, CITY, STATE, ZIP)
------------------------------------------------------
TITLE                COMPANY
-------------------- --------------------
         1 John      Brown       01-FEB-55 800-555-1211
T_ADDRESS('2 State Street', 'Beantown', 'MA', '12345')
Manager              XYZ Corp
```

The following query calls the `display_details()` function for this object:

```
SELECT o.display_details()
FROM object_business_customers o
WHERE id = 1;
```

```
O.DISPLAY_DETAILS()
--------------------
id=1, name=John Brown
```

When you call a method, the database searches for that method in the subtype first; if the method isn't found, the supertype is searched. If you have a hierarchy of types, the database will search for the method up the hierarchy; if the method cannot be found, the database will report an error.

Using a Subtype Object in Place of a Supertype Object

In this section you'll see how you can use a subtype object in place of a supertype object; doing this gives you great flexibility when storing and manipulating related types. In the examples, you'll see how you use a `t_business_person` object (a subtype object) in place of a `t_person` object (a supertype object).

SQL Examples

The following statement creates a table named `object_customers` of type `t_person`:

```
CREATE TABLE object_customers OF t_person;
```

The following `INSERT` statement adds a `t_person` object to this table (the name is Jason Bond):

```
INSERT INTO object_customers VALUES (
   t_person(1, 'Jason', 'Bond', '03-APR-1965', '800-555-1212',
     t_address('21 New Street', 'Anytown', 'CA', '12345')
   )
);
```

There's nothing unusual about the previous statement: The `INSERT` simply adds a `t_person` object to the `object_customers` table. Now, because the `object_customers` table stores objects of type `t_person`, and `t_person` is a supertype of `t_business_person`, you can store a t_business_person object in object_customers; the following INSERT shows this, adding a customer named Steve Edwards:

```
INSERT INTO object_customers VALUES (
  t_business_person(2, 'Steve', 'Edwards', '03-MAR-1955', '800-555-1212',
    t_address('1 Market Street', 'Anytown', 'VA', '12345'),
    'Manager', 'XYZ Corp'
  )
);
```

The object_customers table now contains two objects: the t_person object added earlier (Jason Bond) and the new t_business_person object (Steve Edwards). The following query retrieves these two objects; notice that the title and company attributes for Steve Edwards are missing from the output:

```
SELECT *
FROM object_customers o;

        ID FIRST_NAME LAST_NAME  DOB       PHONE
---------- ---------- ---------- --------- ------------
ADDRESS(STREET, CITY, STATE, ZIP)
----------------------------------------------------
         1 Jason      Bond       03-APR-65 800-555-1212
T_ADDRESS('21 New Street', 'Anytown', 'CA', '12345')

         2 Steve      Edwards    03-MAR-55 800-555-1212
T_ADDRESS('1 Market Street', 'Anytown', 'VA', '12345')
```

You can get the full set of attributes for Steve Edwards by using VALUE() in the query, as shown in the following example; notice the different types of the objects for Jason Bond (a t_person object) and Steve Edwards (a t_business_person object) and that the title and company attributes for Steve Edwards now appear in the output:

```
SELECT VALUE(o)
FROM object_customers o;

VALUE(O)(ID, FIRST_NAME, LAST_NAME, DOB, PHONE,
 ADDRESS(STREET, CITY, STATE, ZIP
-----------------------------------------------------------------
T_PERSON(1, 'Jason', 'Bond', '03-APR-65', '800-555-1212',
 T_ADDRESS('21 New Street', 'Anytown', 'CA', '12345'))

T_BUSINESS_PERSON(2, 'Steve', 'Edwards', '03-MAR-55', '800-555-1212',
 T_ADDRESS('1 Market Street', 'Anytown', 'VA', '12345'),
 'Manager', 'XYZ Corp')
```

PL/SQL Examples

You can also manipulate subtype and supertype objects in PL/SQL. For example, the following procedure named subtypes_and_supertypes() manipulates t_business_person and t_person objects:

```
CREATE PROCEDURE subtypes_and_supertypes AS
  -- create objects
```

```
  v_business_person t_business_person :=
    t_business_person(
      1, 'John', 'Brown',
      '01-FEB-1955', '800-555-1211',
      t_address('2 State Street', 'Beantown', 'MA', '12345'),
      'Manager', 'XYZ Corp'
    );
  v_person t_person :=
    t_person(1, 'John', 'Brown', '01-FEB-1955', '800-555-1211',
      t_address('2 State Street', 'Beantown', 'MA', '12345'));
  v_business_person2 t_business_person;
  v_person2 t_person;
BEGIN
  -- assign v_business_person to v_person2
  v_person2 := v_business_person;
  DBMS_OUTPUT.PUT_LINE('v_person2.id = ' || v_person2.id);
  DBMS_OUTPUT.PUT_LINE('v_person2.first_name = ' ||
    v_person2.first_name);
  DBMS_OUTPUT.PUT_LINE('v_person2.last_name = ' ||
    v_person2.last_name);

  -- the following lines will not compile because v_person2
  -- is of type t_person, and t_person does not know about the
  -- additional title and company attributes
  -- DBMS_OUTPUT.PUT_LINE('v_person2.title = ' ||
  --   v_person2.title);
  -- DBMS_OUTPUT.PUT_LINE('v_person2.company = ' ||
  --   v_person2.company);

  -- the following line will not compile because you cannot
  -- directly assign a t_person object to a t_business_person
  -- object
  -- v_business_person2 := v_person;
END subtypes_and_supertypes;
/
```

The following example shows the result of calling `subtypes_and_supertypes()`:

```
SET SERVEROUTPUT ON
CALL subtypes_and_supertypes();
v_person2.id = 1
v_person2.first_name = John
v_person2.last_name = Brown
```

NOT SUBSTITUTABLE Objects

If you want to prevent the use of a subtype object in place of a supertype object, you can mark an object table or object column as "not substitutable"; for example, the following statement creates a table named `object_customers2`:

```
CREATE TABLE object_customers_not_subs OF t_person
NOT SUBSTITUTABLE AT ALL LEVELS;
```

The NOT SUBSTITUTABLE AT ALL LEVELS clause indicates that no objects of a type other than t_person can be inserted into the table. If an attempt is made to add an object of type t_business_person to this table, an error is returned:

```
SQL> INSERT INTO object_customers_not_subs VALUES (
  2     t_business_person(1, 'Steve', 'Edwards', '03-MAR-1955', '800-555-1212',
  3       t_address('1 Market Street', 'Anytown', 'VA', '12345'),
  4       'Manager', 'XYZ Corp'
  5     )
  6   );
   t_business_person(1, 'Steve', 'Edwards', '03-MAR-1955', '800-555-1212',
   *
ERROR at line 2:
ORA-00932: inconsistent datatypes: expected OBJECT_USER2.T_PERSON got
OBJECT_USER2.T_BUSINESS_PERSON
```

You can also mark an object column as not substitutable; for example, the following statement creates a table with an object column named product that can store only objects of type t_product:

```
CREATE TABLE products (
  product          t_product,
  quantity_in_stock INTEGER
)
COLUMN product NOT SUBSTITUTABLE AT ALL LEVELS;
```

Any attempts to add an object not of type t_product to the product column will result in an error.

Other Useful Object Functions

In the earlier sections of this chapter you saw the use of the REF(), DEREF(), and VALUE() functions. In this section, you'll see the following additional functions that may be used with objects:

- IS OF() checks if an object is of a particular type or subtype.

- TREAT() does a run-time check to see if an object's type may be treated as a supertype.

- SYS_TYPEID() returns the ID of an object's type.

IS OF()

You use IS OF() to check whether an object is of a particular type or subtype. For example, the following query uses IS OF() to check whether the objects in the object_business_customers table are of type t_business_person—because they are, a row is returned by the query:

```
SELECT VALUE(o)
FROM object_business_customers o
WHERE VALUE(o) IS OF (t_business_person);

VALUE(O)(ID, FIRST_NAME, LAST_NAME, DOB, PHONE,
 ADDRESS(STREET, CITY, STATE, ZIP
------------------------------------------------------------------
```

```
T_BUSINESS_PERSON(1, 'John', 'Brown', '01-FEB-55', '800-555-1211',
 T_ADDRESS('2 State Street', 'Beantown', 'MA', '12345'),
 'Manager', 'XYZ Corp')
```

You can also use IS OF() to check whether an object is of a subtype of the specified type. For example, the objects in the object_business_customers table are of type t_business_person, which is a subtype of t_person; therefore, the following query returns the same result as that shown in the previous example:

```
SELECT VALUE(o)
FROM object_business_customers o
WHERE VALUE(o) IS OF (t_person);

VALUE(O)(ID, FIRST_NAME, LAST_NAME, DOB, PHONE,
 ADDRESS(STREET, CITY, STATE, ZIP
------------------------------------------------------------------
T_BUSINESS_PERSON(1, 'John', 'Brown', '01-FEB-55', '800-555-1211',
 T_ADDRESS('2 State Street', 'Beantown', 'MA', '12345'),
 'Manager', 'XYZ Corp')
```

You can include more than one type in IS OF(); for example:

```
SELECT VALUE(o)
FROM object_business_customers o
WHERE VALUE(o) IS OF (t_business_person, t_person);

VALUE(O)(ID, FIRST_NAME, LAST_NAME, DOB, PHONE,
 ADDRESS(STREET, CITY, STATE, ZIP
------------------------------------------------------------------
T_BUSINESS_PERSON(1, 'John', 'Brown', '01-FEB-55', '800-555-1211',
 T_ADDRESS('2 State Street', 'Beantown', 'MA', '12345'),
 'Manager', 'XYZ Corp')
```

In the earlier section entitled "Using a Subtype Object in Place of a Supertype Object," you saw the addition of a t_person object (Jason Bond) and t_business_person object (Steve Edwards) to the object_customers table. As a reminder, the following query shows these objects:

```
SELECT VALUE(o)
FROM object_customers o;

VALUE(O)(ID, FIRST_NAME, LAST_NAME, DOB, PHONE,
 ADDRESS(STREET, CITY, STATE, ZIP
------------------------------------------------------------------
T_PERSON(1, 'Jason', 'Bond', '03-APR-65', '800-555-1212',
 T_ADDRESS('21 New Street', 'Anytown', 'CA', '12345'))

T_BUSINESS_PERSON(2, 'Steve', 'Edwards', '03-MAR-55', '800-555-1212',
 T_ADDRESS('1 Market Street', 'Anytown', 'VA', '12345'),
 'Manager', 'XYZ Corp')
```

Because t_business_person type is a subtype of t_person, IS OF (t_person) returns true when a t_business_person object or a t_person object is checked; this is illustrated in the following query that retrieves both `Jason Bond` and `Steve Edwards` using `IS OF (t_person)`:

```
SELECT VALUE(o)
FROM object_customers o
WHERE VALUE(o) IS OF (t_person);

VALUE(O)(ID, FIRST_NAME, LAST_NAME, DOB, PHONE,
 ADDRESS(STREET, CITY, STATE, ZIP
-------------------------------------------------------------------
T_PERSON(1, 'Jason', 'Bond', '03-APR-65', '800-555-1212',
 T_ADDRESS('21 New Street', 'Anytown', 'CA', '12345'))

T_BUSINESS_PERSON(2, 'Steve', 'Edwards', '03-MAR-55', '800-555-1212',
 T_ADDRESS('1 Market Street', 'Anytown', 'VA', '12345'),
 'Manager', 'XYZ Corp')
```

You can also use the `ONLY` keyword in conjunction with `IS OF ()` to check for objects of a specific type only: `IS OF ()` returns `false` for objects of another type in the hierarchy. For example, `IS OF (ONLY t_person)` returns `true` for objects of type `t_person` only and returns `false` for objects of type `t_business_person`. In this way, you can use `IS OF (ONLY t_person)` to restrict the object returned by a query against the `object_customers` table to `Jason Bond`, as shown in the following example:

```
SELECT VALUE(o)
FROM object_customers o
WHERE VALUE(o) IS OF (ONLY t_person);

VALUE(O)(ID, FIRST_NAME, LAST_NAME, DOB, PHONE,
 ADDRESS(STREET, CITY, STATE, ZIP
-----------------------------------------------------------
T_PERSON(1, 'Jason', 'Bond', '03-APR-65', '800-555-1212',
 T_ADDRESS('21 New Street', 'Anytown', 'CA', '12345'))
```

Similarly, `IS OF(ONLY t_business_person)` returns `true` for objects of type `t_business_person` only, and returns `false` for objects of type `t_person`. For example, the following query retrieves the `t_business_person` object only and therefore `Steve Edwards` is returned:

```
SELECT VALUE(o)
FROM object_customers o
WHERE VALUE(o) IS OF (ONLY t_business_person);

VALUE(O)(ID, FIRST_NAME, LAST_NAME, DOB, PHONE,
 ADDRESS(STREET, CITY, STATE, ZIP
-----------------------------------------------------------
T_BUSINESS_PERSON(2, 'Steve', 'Edwards', '03-MAR-55', '800-555-1212',
 T_ADDRESS('1 Market Street', 'Anytown', 'VA', '12345'),
 'Manager', 'XYZ Corp')
```

You can include multiple types after `ONLY`. For example, `IS OF (ONLY t_person, t_business_person)` returns `true` for `t_person` and `t_business_person` objects only; the following query shows this by returning, as expected, both `Jason Bond` and `Steve Edwards`:

```
SELECT VALUE(o)
FROM object_customers o
WHERE VALUE(o) IS OF (ONLY t_person, t_business_person);

VALUE(O)(ID, FIRST_NAME, LAST_NAME, DOB, PHONE,
 ADDRESS(STREET, CITY, STATE, ZIP
-------------------------------------------------------------------
T_PERSON(1, 'Jason', 'Bond', '03-APR-65', '800-555-1212',
 T_ADDRESS('21 New Street', 'Anytown', 'CA', '12345'))

T_BUSINESS_PERSON(2, 'Steve', 'Edwards', '03-MAR-55', '800-555-1212',
 T_ADDRESS('1 Market Street', 'Anytown', 'VA', '12345'),
 'Manager', 'XYZ Corp')
```

You can also use IS OF() in PL/SQL. For example, the following procedure named check_
types() creates t_business_person and t_person objects, and it uses IS OF() to
check their types:

```
CREATE PROCEDURE check_types AS
  -- create objects
  v_business_person t_business_person :=
    t_business_person(
      1, 'John', 'Brown',
      '01-FEB-1955', '800-555-1211',
      t_address('2 State Street', 'Beantown', 'MA', '12345'),
      'Manager', 'XYZ Corp'
    );
  v_person t_person :=
    t_person(1, 'John', 'Brown', '01-FEB-1955', '800-555-1211',
      t_address('2 State Street', 'Beantown', 'MA', '12345'));
BEGIN
  -- check the types of the objects
  IF v_business_person IS OF (t_business_person) THEN
    DBMS_OUTPUT.PUT_LINE('v_business_person is of type ' ||
      't_business_person');
  END IF;
  IF v_person IS OF (t_person) THEN
    DBMS_OUTPUT.PUT_LINE('v_person is of type t_person');
  END IF;
  IF v_business_person IS OF (t_person) THEN
    DBMS_OUTPUT.PUT_LINE('v_business_person is of type t_person');
  END IF;
  IF v_business_person IS OF (t_business_person, t_person) THEN
    DBMS_OUTPUT.PUT_LINE('v_business_person is of ' ||
      'type t_business_person or t_person');
  END IF;
  IF v_business_person IS OF (ONLY t_business_person) THEN
    DBMS_OUTPUT.PUT_LINE('v_business_person is of only ' ||
      'type t_business_person');
  END IF;
  IF v_business_person IS OF (ONLY t_person) THEN
    DBMS_OUTPUT.PUT_LINE('v_business_person is of only ' ||
```

```
           'type t_person');
      ELSE
        DBMS_OUTPUT.PUT_LINE('v_business_person is not of only ' ||
           'type t_person');
      END IF;
END check_types;
/
```

The following example shows the result of calling `check_types()`:

```
SET SERVEROUTPUT ON
CALL check_types();
v_business_person is of type t_business_person
v_person is of type t_person
v_business_person is of type t_person
v_business_person is of type t_business_person or t_person
v_business_person is of only type t_business_person
v_business_person is not of only type t_person
```

TREAT()

You use TREAT() to do a run-time check to see whether an object of a subtype may be treated as an object of a supertype; if this is so, TREAT() returns an object, and if not so, TREAT() returns null. For example, because t_business_person is a subtype of t_person, a t_business_person object can be treated as a t_person object; you saw this earlier in the section entitled "Using a Subtype Object in Place of a Supertype Object," where a t_business_person object (Steve Edwards) was inserted into the object_customers table, which normally holds t_person objects. The following query uses TREAT() to check that Steve Edwards can be treated as a t_person object:

```
SELECT NVL2(TREAT(VALUE(o) AS t_person), 'yes', 'no')
FROM object_customers o
WHERE first_name = 'Steve' AND last_name = 'Edwards';

NVL
---
yes
```

NVL2() returns yes because TREAT(VALUE(o) AS t_person) returns an object (that is, not a null value). This means that Steve Edwards can be treated as a t_person object.

The next query checks whether Jason Bond (a t_person object) can be treated as a t_business_person object—he cannot, and, therefore, TREAT() returns null, and NVL2() returns no:

```
SELECT NVL2(TREAT(VALUE(o) AS t_business_person), 'yes', 'no')
FROM object_customers o
WHERE first_name = 'Jason' AND last_name = 'Bond';

NVL
---
no
```

Because TREAT() returns null for the whole object, all the individual attributes for the object are also null. For example, the following query attempts to access the first_name attribute through Jason Bond—null is returned (as expected):

```
SELECT
  NVL2(TREAT(VALUE(o) AS t_business_person).first_name, 'not null', 'null')
FROM object_customers o
WHERE first_name = 'Jason' AND last_name = 'Bond';

NVL2
----
null
```

The next query uses TREAT() to check whether Jason Bond can be treated as a t_person object—he *is* a t_person object and therefore yes is returned:

```
SELECT NVL2(TREAT(VALUE(o) AS t_person).first_name, 'yes', 'no')
FROM object_customers o
WHERE first_name = 'Jason' AND last_name = 'Bond';

NVL
---
yes
```

You can also retrieve an object through the use of TREAT(); for example, the following query retrieves Steve Edwards:

```
SELECT TREAT(VALUE(o) AS t_business_person)
FROM object_customers o
WHERE first_name = 'Steve' AND last_name = 'Edwards';

TREAT(VALUE(O)AST_BUSINESS_PERSON)(ID, FIRST_NAME, LAST_NAME, DOB, PHONE,
  ADDRESS
-----------------------------------------------------------------------
T_BUSINESS_PERSON(2, 'Steve', 'Edwards', '03-MAR-55', '800-555-1212',
  T_ADDRESS('1 Market Street', 'Anytown', 'VA', '12345'),
  'Manager', 'XYZ Corp')
```

If you try this query with Jason Bond, null is returned, as expected; therefore, nothing appears in the output of the following query:

```
SELECT TREAT(VALUE(o) AS t_business_person)
FROM object_customers o
WHERE first_name = 'Jason' AND last_name = 'Bond';

TREAT(VALUE(O)AST_BUSINESS_PERSON)(ID, FIRST_NAME, LAST_NAME, DOB, PHONE,
  ADDRESS
-----------------------------------------------------------------------
```

Let's take look at using TREAT() with the object_business_customers table, which contains the t_business_person object John Brown:

```
SELECT VALUE(o)
FROM object_business_customers o;
```

```
VALUE(O)(ID, FIRST_NAME, LAST_NAME, DOB, PHONE,
 ADDRESS(STREET, CITY, STATE, ZIP
--------------------------------------------------------------------
T_BUSINESS_PERSON(1, 'John', 'Brown', '01-FEB-55', '800-555-1211',
 T_ADDRESS('2 State Street', 'Beantown', 'MA', '12345'),
 'Manager', 'XYZ Corp')
```

The following query uses `TREAT()` to check whether `John Brown` can be treated as a `t_person` object—he can, because `t_business_person` is a subtype of `t_person`; therefore, `yes` is returned by the query:

```
SELECT NVL2(TREAT(VALUE(o) AS t_person), 'yes', 'no')
FROM object_business_customers o
WHERE first_name = 'John' AND last_name = 'Brown';

NVL
---
yes
```

The following example shows the object returned by `TREAT()` when querying the `object_business_customers` table; notice that you still get the `title` and `company` attributes for `John Brown`:

```
SELECT TREAT(VALUE(o) AS t_person)
FROM object_business_customers o;

TREAT(VALUE(O)AST_PERSON)(ID, FIRST_NAME, LAST_NAME, DOB, PHONE,
 ADDRESS(STREET,
--------------------------------------------------------------------
T_BUSINESS_PERSON(1, 'John', 'Brown', '01-FEB-55', '800-555-1211',
 T_ADDRESS('2 State Street', 'Beantown', 'MA', '12345'),
 'Manager', 'XYZ Corp')
```

You can also use `TREAT()` in PL/SQL. For example, the following procedure named `treat_example()` illustrates the use of `TREAT()` (you should study the comments in the code to understand how `TREAT()` works in PL/SQL):

```
CREATE PROCEDURE treat_example AS
  -- create objects
  v_business_person t_business_person :=
    t_business_person(
      1, 'John', 'Brown',
      '01-FEB-1955', '800-555-1211',
      t_address('2 State Street', 'Beantown', 'MA', '12345'),
      'Manager', 'XYZ Corp'
    );
  v_person t_person :=
    t_person(1, 'John', 'Brown', '01-FEB-1955', '800-555-1211',
      t_address('2 State Street', 'Beantown', 'MA', '12345'));
  v_business_person2 t_business_person;
  v_person2 t_person;
```

```
BEGIN
  -- assign v_business_person to v_person2
  v_person2 := v_business_person;
  DBMS_OUTPUT.PUT_LINE('v_person2.id = ' || v_person2.id);
  DBMS_OUTPUT.PUT_LINE('v_person2.first_name = ' ||
    v_person2.first_name);
  DBMS_OUTPUT.PUT_LINE('v_person2.last_name = ' ||
    v_person2.last_name);

  -- the following lines will not compile because v_person2
  -- is of type t_person, and t_person does not know about the
  -- additional title and company attributes
  -- DBMS_OUTPUT.PUT_LINE('v_person2.title = ' ||
  --    v_person2.title);
  -- DBMS_OUTPUT.PUT_LINE('v_person2.company = ' ||
  --    v_person2.company);

  -- use TREAT when assigning v_business_person to v_person2
  DBMS_OUTPUT.PUT_LINE('Using TREAT');
  v_person2 := TREAT(v_business_person AS t_person);
  DBMS_OUTPUT.PUT_LINE('v_person2.id = ' || v_person2.id);
  DBMS_OUTPUT.PUT_LINE('v_person2.first_name = ' ||
    v_person2.first_name);
  DBMS_OUTPUT.PUT_LINE('v_person2.last_name = ' ||
    v_person2.last_name);

  -- the following lines will still not compile because v_person2
  -- is of type t_person, and t_person does not know about the
  -- additional title and company attributes
  -- DBMS_OUTPUT.PUT_LINE('v_person2.title = ' ||
  --    v_person2.title);
  -- DBMS_OUTPUT.PUT_LINE('v_person2.company = ' ||
  --    v_person2.company);

  -- the following lines do compile because TREAT is used
  DBMS_OUTPUT.PUT_LINE('v_person2.title = ' ||
    TREAT(v_person2 AS t_business_person).title);
  DBMS_OUTPUT.PUT_LINE('v_person2.company = ' ||
    TREAT(v_person2 AS t_business_person).company);

  -- the following line will not compile because you cannot
  -- directly assign a t_person object to a t_business_person
  -- object
  -- v_business_person2 := v_person;

  -- the following line throws a runtime error because you cannot
  -- assign a supertype object (v_person) to a subtype object
  -- (v_business_person2)
  -- v_business_person2 := TREAT(v_person AS t_business_person);
END treat_example;
/
```

The following example shows the result of calling `treat_example()`:

```
SET SERVEROUTPUT ON
CALL treat_example();
v_person2.id = 1
v_person2.first_name = John
v_person2.last_name = Brown
Using TREAT
v_person2.id = 1
v_person2.first_name = John
v_person2.last_name = Brown
v_person2.title = Manager
v_person2.company = XYZ Corp
```

SYS_TYPEID()

You use `SYS_TYPEID()` to get the ID of an object's type. For example, the following query uses `SYS_TYPEID()` to get the ID of the object type in the `object_business_customers` table:

```
SELECT first_name, last_name, SYS_TYPEID(VALUE(o))
FROM object_business_customers o;

FIRST_NAME LAST_NAME  SY
---------- ---------- --
John       Brown      02
```

You can get details on the types defined by the user through the `user_types` view. The following query retrieves the details of the type with a `typeid` of `'02'` (the ID returned by `SYS_TYPEID()` earlier) and the `type_name` of `T_BUSINESS_PERSON`:

```
SELECT typecode, attributes, methods, supertype_name
FROM user_types
WHERE typeid = '02'
AND type_name = 'T_BUSINESS_PERSON';

TYPECODE ATTRIBUTES    METHODS SUPERTYPE_NAME
-------- ---------- ---------- --------------
OBJECT            8          1 T_PERSON
```

From the output of this query you can see that the supertype of `t_business_person` is `t_person`. Also, `t_business_person` has eight attributes and one method.

NOT INSTANTIABLE Object Types

You can mark an object type as `NOT INSTANTIABLE`, which prevents objects of that type from being created. You might want to mark an object type as `NOT INSTANTIABLE` when you use the type as an abstract supertype only and never create any objects of that type. For example, you could create a `t_vehicle` abstract type and use it as a supertype for a `t_car` subtype and a `t_motorcycle` subtype; you would then create actual `t_car` and `t_motorcycle` objects, but never `t_vehicle` objects.

The following statement creates a type named t_vehicle, which is marked as NOT INSTANTIABLE:

```
CREATE TYPE t_vehicle AS OBJECT (
  id    INTEGER,
  make  VARCHAR2(15),
  model VARCHAR2(15)
) NOT FINAL NOT INSTANTIABLE;
/
```

NOTE
The t_vehicle *type is also marked as* NOT FINAL, *because a* NOT INSTANTIABLE *type cannot be* FINAL. *If it were* FINAL, *you wouldn't be able to use it as a supertype, which is the whole point of creating it in the first place.*

The next example creates a subtype named t_car under the t_vehicle supertype; notice that t_car has an additional attribute named convertible, which will be used to record whether the car has a convertible roof (Y for yes, N for no):

```
CREATE TYPE t_car UNDER t_vehicle (
  convertible CHAR(1)
);
/
```

The following example creates a subtype named t_motorcycle under the t_vehicle supertype; notice that t_motorcycle has an additional attribute named sidecar, which will be used to record whether the motorcycle has a sidecar (Y for yes, N for no):

```
CREATE TYPE t_motorcycle UNDER t_vehicle (
  sidecar CHAR(1)
);
/
```

The next example creates tables named vehicles, cars, and motorcycles, which are object tables of the types t_vehicle, t_car, and t_motorcycle, respectively:

```
CREATE TABLE vehicles OF t_vehicle;
CREATE TABLE cars OF t_car;
CREATE TABLE motorcycles OF t_motorcycle;
```

Because t_vehicle is NOT INSTANTIABLE, you cannot add an object to the vehicles table. If you attempt to do so, the database returns an error:

```
SQL> INSERT INTO vehicles VALUES (
  2    t_vehicle(1, 'Toyota', 'MR2', '01-FEB-1955')
  3  );
  t_vehicle(1, 'Toyota', 'MR2', '01-FEB-1955')
  *
ERROR at line 2:
ORA-22826: cannot construct an instance of a non instantiable type
```

The following examples add objects to the `cars` and `motorcycles` tables:

```
INSERT INTO cars VALUES (
  t_car(1, 'Toyota', 'MR2', 'Y')
);

INSERT INTO motorcycles VALUES (
  t_motorcycle(1, 'Harley-Davidson', 'V-Rod', 'N')
);
```

The following queries retrieve the objects from the `cars` and `motorcycles` tables:

```
SELECT *
FROM cars;

        ID MAKE            MODEL           C
---------- --------------- --------------- -
         1 Toyota          MR2             Y

SELECT *
FROM motorcycles;

        ID MAKE            MODEL           S
---------- --------------- --------------- -
         1 Harley-Davidson V-Rod           N
```

User-Defined Constructors

As in other object-oriented languages like Java and C#, you can define your own constructors in PL/SQL to initialize a new object. You can define your own constructor to do such things as programmatically setting the attributes of a new object to default values.

The following example creates a type named `t_person2` that declares two constructor methods with differing numbers of parameters:

```
CREATE TYPE t_person2 AS OBJECT (
  id         INTEGER,
  first_name VARCHAR2(10),
  last_name  VARCHAR2(10),
  dob        DATE,
  phone      VARCHAR2(12),
  CONSTRUCTOR FUNCTION t_person2(
    p_id         INTEGER,
    p_first_name VARCHAR2,
    p_last_name  VARCHAR2
  ) RETURN SELF AS RESULT,
  CONSTRUCTOR FUNCTION t_person2(
    p_id         INTEGER,
    p_first_name VARCHAR2,
    p_last_name  VARCHAR2,
    p_dob        DATE
  ) RETURN SELF AS RESULT
);
/
```

Notice the following about the constructor declarations:

■ The CONSTRUCTOR FUNCTION keywords are used to identify the constructors.

■ The RETURN SELF AS RESULT keywords indicate the current object being processed
is returned by each constructor; SELF represents the current object being processed.
What this means is that the constructor returns the new object it creates.

■ The first constructor accepts three parameters (p_id, p_first_name, and p_last_
name), and the second constructor accepts four parameters (p_id, p_first_name,
p_last_name, and p_dob).

The constructor declarations don't contain the actual code definitions for the constructors; the
definitions are contained in the type body, which is created by the following statement:

```
CREATE TYPE BODY t_person2 AS
  CONSTRUCTOR FUNCTION t_person2(
    p_id          INTEGER,
    p_first_name  VARCHAR2,
    p_last_name   VARCHAR2
  ) RETURN SELF AS RESULT IS
  BEGIN
    SELF.id := p_id;
    SELF.first_name := p_first_name;
    SELF.last_name := p_last_name;
    SELF.dob := SYSDATE;
    SELF.phone := '555-1212';
    RETURN;
  END;
  CONSTRUCTOR FUNCTION t_person2(
    p_id          INTEGER,
    p_first_name  VARCHAR2,
    p_last_name   VARCHAR2,
    p_dob         DATE
  ) RETURN SELF AS RESULT IS
  BEGIN
    SELF.id := p_id;
    SELF.first_name := p_first_name;
    SELF.last_name := p_last_name;
    SELF.dob := p_dob;
    SELF.phone := '555-1213';
    RETURN;
  END;
END;
/
```

Notice the following:

■ The constructors use SELF to reference the new object being created. For example,
SELF.id := p_id sets the id attribute of the new object to the value of the p_id
parameter passed into the constructor.

- The first constructor sets the id, first_name, and last_name attributes to the p_id, p_first_name, and p_last_name parameter values passed into the constructor; the dob attribute is set to the current datetime returned by SYSDATE(), and the phone attribute is set to 555-1212.

- The second constructor sets the id, first_name, last_name, and dob attributes to the p_id, p_first_name, p_last_name, and p_dob parameter values passed into the constructor; the remaining phone attribute is set to 555-1213.

Although not shown, the database automatically provides a default constructor that accepts five parameters and sets each attribute to the appropriate parameter value passed into the constructor. You'll see an example of this shortly.

NOTE
The constructors show an example of method overloading, *whereby methods of the same name but different parameters are defined in the same type. A method may be overloaded by providing different* numbers *of parameters,* types *of parameters, or* ordering *of parameters.*

The following example describes t_person2; notice the constructor definitions in the output:

```
DESCRIBE t_person2
 Name                                          Null?    Type
 --------------------------------------------- -------- -------------------
 ID                                                     NUMBER(38)
 FIRST_NAME                                            VARCHAR2(10)
 LAST_NAME                                             VARCHAR2(10)
 DOB                                                   DATE
 PHONE                                                 VARCHAR2(12)


 METHOD
 ------
 FINAL CONSTRUCTOR FUNCTION T_PERSON2 RETURNS SELF AS RESULT
 Argument Name                     Type                    In/Out Default?
 --------------------------------- ----------------------- ------ --------
 P_ID                              NUMBER                  IN
 P_FIRST_NAME                      VARCHAR2                IN
 P_LAST_NAME                       VARCHAR2                IN

 METHOD
 ------
 FINAL CONSTRUCTOR FUNCTION T_PERSON2 RETURNS SELF AS RESULT
 Argument Name                     Type                    In/Out Default?
 --------------------------------- ----------------------- ------ --------
 P_ID                              NUMBER                  IN
 P_FIRST_NAME                      VARCHAR2                IN
 P_LAST_NAME                       VARCHAR2                IN
 P_DOB                             DATE                    IN
```

The following statement creates a table of type t_person2:

```
CREATE TABLE object_customers2 OF t_person2;
```

The following INSERT statement adds an object to the table; notice that three parameters are passed to the t_person2 constructor:

```
INSERT INTO object_customers2 VALUES (
  t_person2(1, 'Jeff', 'Jones')
);
```

Because three parameters are passed to t_person2, this INSERT statement exercises the first constructor. This constructor sets the id, first_name, and last_name attributes of the new object to 1, Jeff, and Jones; the remaining dob and phone attributes are set to the result returned by SYSDATE() and the literal 555-1212. The following query retrieves the new object:

```
SELECT *
FROM object_customers2
WHERE id = 1;
```

```
        ID FIRST_NAME LAST_NAME  DOB       PHONE
---------- ---------- ---------- --------- --------
         1 Jeff       Jones      17-JUN-07 555-1212
```

The next INSERT statement adds another object to the table; notice that four parameters are passed to the t_person2 constructor:

```
INSERT INTO object_customers2 VALUES (
  t_person2(2, 'Gregory', 'Smith', '03-APR-1965')
);
```

Because four parameters are passed to t_person2, this INSERT statement exercises the second constructor. This constructor sets the id, first_name, last_name, and dob attributes of the object to 2, Gregory, Smith, and 03-APR-1965, respectively; the remaining phone attribute is set to 555-1213. The following query retrieves the new object:

```
SELECT *
FROM object_customers2
WHERE id = 2;
```

```
        ID FIRST_NAME LAST_NAME  DOB       PHONE
---------- ---------- ---------- --------- --------
         2 Gregory    Smith      03-APR-65 555-1213
```

The next INSERT statement adds another object to the table; notice that five parameters are passed to the t_person2 constructor:

```
INSERT INTO object_customers2 VALUES (
  t_person2(3, 'Jeremy', 'Hill', '05-JUN-1975', '555-1214')
);
```

Because five parameters are passed to t_person2, this INSERT statement exercises the default constructor. This constructor sets the id, first_name, last_name, dob, and phone attributes to 3, Jeremy, Hill, 05-JUN-1975, and 555-1214, respectively. The following query retrieves the new object:

```
SELECT *
FROM object_customers2
WHERE id = 3;
```

```
        ID FIRST_NAME LAST_NAME  DOB       PHONE
---------- ---------- ---------- --------- --------
         3 Jeremy     Hill       05-JUN-75 555-1214
```

Overriding Methods

When you create a subtype under a supertype, you can override a method in the supertype with a method in the subtype. This gives you a very flexible way of defining methods in a hierarchy of types.

The following statements create a supertype named t_person3; notice that the display_details() function returns a VARCHAR2 containing the attribute values of the object:

```
CREATE TYPE t_person3 AS OBJECT (
  id         INTEGER,
  first_name VARCHAR2(10),
  last_name  VARCHAR2(10),
  MEMBER FUNCTION display_details RETURN VARCHAR2
) NOT FINAL;
/
CREATE TYPE BODY t_person3 AS
  MEMBER FUNCTION display_details RETURN VARCHAR2 IS
  BEGIN
    RETURN 'id=' || id ||
      ', name=' || first_name || ' ' || last_name;
  END;
END;
/
```

The next set of statements creates a subtype named t_business_person3 under t_person3; notice that the display_details() function is overridden using the OVERRIDING keyword and that the function returns a VARCHAR2 containing the original and extended attribute values of the object:

```
CREATE TYPE t_business_person3 UNDER t_person3 (
  title   VARCHAR2(20),
  company VARCHAR2(20),
  OVERRIDING MEMBER FUNCTION display_details RETURN VARCHAR2
);
/
CREATE TYPE BODY t_business_person3 AS
  OVERRIDING MEMBER FUNCTION display_details RETURN VARCHAR2 IS
  BEGIN
    RETURN 'id=' || id ||
      ', name=' || first_name || ' ' || last_name ||
      ', title=' || title || ', company=' || company;
```

```
   END;
END;
/
```

The use of the OVERRIDING keyword indicates that display_details() in t_business_
person3 overrides display_details() in t_person3; therefore, when display_details()
in t_business_person3 is called, it calls display_details() in t_business_person3, not
display_details() in t_person3.

NOTE
*In the next section of this chapter, you'll see how you can directly call
a method in a supertype from a subtype. This saves you from having
to recreate code in the subtype that is already in the supertype. You do
this direct calling by using a new feature called generalized invocation
in Oracle Database 11g.*

The following statements create a table named object_business_customers3 and add
an object to this table:

```
CREATE TABLE object_business_customers3 OF t_business_person3;

INSERT INTO object_business_customers3 VALUES (
  t_business_person3(1, 'John', 'Brown', 'Manager', 'XYZ Corp')
);
```

The following example calls display_details() using object_business_customers3:

```
SELECT o.display_details()
FROM object_business_customers3 o
WHERE id = 1;

O.DISPLAY_DETAILS()
-------------------------------------------------------
id=1, name=John Brown, title=Manager, company=XYZ Corp
```

Because the display_details() function as defined in t_business_person3 is called,
the VARCHAR2 returned by the function contains the id, first_name, and last_name attributes,
along with the title and company attributes.

Generalized Invocation

As you saw in the previous section, you can override a method in the supertype with a method in
the subtype. *Generalized invocation* is a new feature in Oracle Database 11g and allows you to
call a method in a supertype from a subtype. As you'll see, generalized invocation saves you from
having to recreate code in the subtype that is already in the supertype.

NOTE
*I've provided an SQL*Plus script named object_schema3.sql,
which creates all the items shown in the rest of this chapter. You can
run the object_schema3.sql script only if you are using Oracle
Database 11g. After the script completes, you will be logged in as
object_user3.*

The following statements create a supertype named `t_person`; notice that the `display_details()` function returns a VARCHAR2 containing the attribute values:

```
CREATE TYPE t_person AS OBJECT (
  id         INTEGER,
  first_name VARCHAR2(10),
  last_name  VARCHAR2(10),
  MEMBER FUNCTION display_details RETURN VARCHAR2
) NOT FINAL;
/

CREATE TYPE BODY t_person AS
  MEMBER FUNCTION display_details RETURN VARCHAR2 IS
  BEGIN
    RETURN 'id=' || id ||
      ', name=' || first_name || ' ' || last_name;
  END;
END;
/
```

The next set of statements creates a subtype named `t_business_person` under `t_person`; notice that the `display_details()` function is overridden using the OVERRIDING keyword:

```
CREATE TYPE t_business_person UNDER t_person (
  title   VARCHAR2(20),
  company VARCHAR2(20),
  OVERRIDING MEMBER FUNCTION display_details RETURN VARCHAR2
);
/

CREATE TYPE BODY t_business_person AS
  OVERRIDING MEMBER FUNCTION display_details RETURN VARCHAR2 IS
  BEGIN
    -- use generalized invocation to call display_details() in t_person
    RETURN (SELF AS t_person).display_details ||
      ', title=' || title || ', company=' || company;
  END;
END;
/
```

As you can see, `display_details()` in `t_business_person` overrides `display_details()` in `t_person`. The following line in `display_details()` uses generalized invocation to call a method in a supertype from a subtype:

```
RETURN (SELF AS t_person).display_details ||
  ', title=' || title || ', company=' || company;
```

What `(SELF AS t_person).display_details` does is to treat an object of the current type (which is `t_business_person`) as an object of type `t_person` and then to call `display_details()` in `t_person`. So, when `display_details()` in `t_business_person` is called, it first calls `display_details()` in `t_person` (which displays the id, first_name, and last_name attribute values), then displays the title and company attribute values. This meant I didn't have to re-create the code already in t_person.display_details() in t_business_person.display_details(), thereby saving some work. If you have more complex methods in your types, this feature can save a lot of work and make your code easier to maintain.

The following statements create a table named object_business_customers and add an object to this table:

```
CREATE TABLE object_business_customers OF t_business_person;

INSERT INTO object_business_customers VALUES (
  t_business_person(1, 'John', 'Brown', 'Manager', 'XYZ Corp')
);
```

The following query calls display_details() using object_business_customers:

```
SELECT o.display_details()
FROM object_business_customers o;

O.DISPLAY_DETAILS()
------------------------------------------------------------------
id=1, name=John Brown, dob=01-FEB-55, title=Manager, company=XYZ Corp
```

As you can see, the id, name, and date of birth (dob) are displayed (which come from display_details() in t_person), followed by the title and company (which come from display_details() in t_business_person).

Summary

In this chapter, you learned the following:

- The Oracle database allows you to create object types. An object type is like a class in Java, C++, and C#. An object type may contain attributes and methods; you create an object type using the CREATE TYPE statement.

- You can use an object type to define a column object or an object table.

- You can use an object reference to access an individual row in an object table. An object reference is similar to a pointer in C++.

- You can create and manipulate objects in SQL and PL/SQL.

- With the release of Oracle Database 9i, you can use object type inheritance. This allows you to define hierarchies of database types.

- You can use a subtype object in place of a supertype object, which gives you great flexibility when storing and manipulating related types. If you want to prevent the use of a subtype object in place of supertype object, you can mark an object table or object column as NOT SUBSTITUTABLE.

- You can use a number of useful functions with objects, such as REF(), DEREF(), VALUE(), IS OF(), SYS_TYPEID(), and TREAT().

■ You can mark an object type as NOT INSTANTIABLE, which prevents objects of that type from being created. You'll want to mark an object type as NOT INSTANTIABLE when you use that type as an abstract supertype and never actually create objects of that type.

■ You can define your own constructors to do things like programmatically setting a default for attributes of an object.

■ You can override a method in a supertype with a method in a subtype, giving you a very flexible way of defining methods in a hierarchy of types.

■ You can use the new Oracle Database 11*g* generalized invocation feature to call methods in supertype from a subtype. Doing this can save you a lot of work and make your code easier to maintain.

In the next chapter, you'll learn about collections.

CHAPTER
13

Collections

n this chapter, you will do the following:

- Learn about collections

- Learn how to create collection types

- Use collection types to define columns in tables

- Create and manipulate collection data in SQL and PL/SQL

- Learn how a collection may itself contain embedded collections (a "multilevel" collection)

- Examine the enhancements to collections that were introduced in Oracle Database 10*g*

Introducing Collections

Oracle Database 8 introduced two new database types, known as *collections*, that allow you to store sets of elements. Oracle Database 9*i* extended these features to include multilevel collections, which allow you to embed a collection within another collection. Oracle Database 10*g* further extended collections to include associative arrays and much more.

There are three types of collections:

- **Varrays**   A varray is similar to an array in Java, C++, and C#. A varray stores an ordered set of elements, and each element has an index that records its position in the array. Elements in a varray can be modified only as a whole, not individually; this means that even if you only want to modify one element, you must supply all the elements for the varray. A varray has a maximum size that you set when creating it, but you can change the size later.

- **Nested tables**   A nested table is a table that is embedded within another table. You can insert, update, and delete individual elements in a nested table; this makes them more flexible than a varray, whose elements can be modified only as a whole. A nested table doesn't have a maximum size, and you can store an arbitrary number of elements in a nested table.

- **Associative arrays (formerly known as index-by tables)**   An associative array is similar to a hash table in Java. Introduced in Oracle Database 10*g*, an associative array is a set of key and value pairs. You can get the value from the array using the key (which may be a string) or an integer that specifies the position of the value in the array. An associative array can be used only in PL/SQL and cannot be stored in the database.

You might be asking yourself why you would want to use collections in the first place. After all, using two tables with a foreign key already allows you to model relationships between data. The answer is that collections follow the object-oriented style of modern programming; in addition, the data stored in the collection may be accessed more rapidly by the database than if you were to use two relational tables to store the same data.

I've provided an SQL*Plus script named `collection_schema.sql` in the SQL directory. The script creates a user named `collection_user` with a password of `collection_password`, and creates the collection types, tables, and PL/SQL code used in the first part of this chapter. You must run this script while logged in as a user with the required privileges to create a new user with the `CONNECT` and `RESOURCE` privileges; I log in as the `system` user on my database to run the scripts. After the script completes, you will be logged in as `collection_user`.

Creating Collection Types

In this section, you'll see how to create a varray type and a nested table type.

Creating a Varray Type

A varray stores an ordered set of elements, all of the same type, and the type can be a built-in database type or a user-defined object type. Each element has an index that corresponds to its position in the array, and you can modify elements in the varray only as a whole.

You create a varray type using the `CREATE TYPE` statement, in which you specify the maximum size and the type of elements stored in the varray. The following example creates a type named `t_varray_address` that can store up to three `VARCHAR2` strings:

```
CREATE TYPE t_varray_address AS VARRAY(3) OF VARCHAR2(50);
/
```

Each `VARCHAR2` will be used to represent a different address for a customer of our example store.

In Oracle Database 10*g* and higher, you can change the maximum number of elements of a varray using the `ALTER TYPE` statement. For example, the following statement alters the maximum number of elements to ten:

```
ALTER TYPE t_varray_address MODIFY LIMIT 10 CASCADE;
```

The `CASCADE` option propagates the change to any dependent objects in the database.

Creating a Nested Table Type

A nested table stores an unordered set of any number of elements. You can insert, update, and delete individual elements in a nested table. A nested table doesn't have a maximum size, and you can store an arbitrary number of elements in a nested table.

In this section, you'll see a nested table type that stores `t_address` object types. You saw the use of `t_address` in the previous chapter; it is used to represent an address and is defined as follows:

```
CREATE TYPE t_address AS OBJECT (
   street VARCHAR2(15),
   city   VARCHAR2(15),
   state  CHAR(2),
   zip    VARCHAR2(5)
);
/
```

You create a nested table type using the `CREATE TYPE` statement, and the following example creates a type named `t_nested_table_address` that stores `t_address` objects:

```
CREATE TYPE t_nested_table_address AS TABLE OF t_address;
/
```

Notice that you don't specify the maximum size of a nested table. That's because a nested table can store any number of elements.

Using a Collection Type to Define a Column in a Table

Once you've created a collection type, you can use it to define a column in a table. You'll see how to use the varray type and nested table type created in the previous section to define a column in a table.

Using a Varray Type to Define a Column in a Table

The following statement creates a table named `customers_with_varray`, which uses `t_varray_address` to define a column named `addresses`:

```
CREATE TABLE customers_with_varray (
    id          INTEGER PRIMARY KEY,
    first_name  VARCHAR2(10),
    last_name   VARCHAR2(10),
    addresses   t_varray_address
);
```

The elements in a varray are stored directly inside the table when the size of the varray is 4KB or less; otherwise, the varray is stored outside of the table. When a varray is stored with the table, accessing its elements is faster than accessing elements in a nested table.

Using a Nested Table Type to Define a Column in a Table

The following statement creates a table named `customers_with_nested_table`, which uses `t_nested_table_address` to define a column named `addresses`:

```
CREATE TABLE customers_with_nested_table (
    id          INTEGER PRIMARY KEY,
    first_name  VARCHAR2(10),
    last_name   VARCHAR2(10),
    addresses   t_nested_table_address
)
NESTED TABLE
  addresses
STORE AS
  nested_addresses;
```

The `NESTED TABLE` clause identifies the name of the nested table column (`addresses` in the example), and the `STORE AS` clause specifies the name of the nested table (`nested_addresses` in the example) where the actual elements are stored. You cannot access the nested table independently of the table in which it is embedded.

Getting Information on Collections

As you'll see in this section, you can use the DESCRIBE command and a couple of user views to get information on your collections.

Getting Information on a Varray

The following example describes t_varray_address:

DESCRIBE t_varray_address
```
t_varray_address VARRAY(3) OF VARCHAR2(50)
```

The next example describes the customers_with_varray table, whose addresses column is of the t_varray_address type:

DESCRIBE customers_with_varray
```
Name                          Null?      Type
----------------------------- --------   ------------------
ID                            NOT NULL   NUMBER(38)
FIRST_NAME                               VARCHAR2(10)
LAST_NAME                                VARCHAR2(10)
ADDRESSES                                T_VARRAY_ADDRESS
```

You can also get information on your varrays from the user_varrays view. Table 13-1 describes the columns in user_varrays.

Column	Type	Description
parent_table_name	VARCHAR2(30)	Name of the table that contains the varray.
parent_table_column	VARCHAR2(4000)	Name of the column in the parent table containing the varray.
type_owner	VARCHAR2(30)	User who owns the varray type.
type_name	VARCHAR2(30)	Name of the varray type.
lob_name	VARCHAR2(30)	Name of the large object (LOB) when the varray is stored in an LOB. You'll learn about LOBs in the next chapter.
storage_spec	VARCHAR2(30)	Storage specification for the varray.
return_type	VARCHAR2(20)	Return type of the column.
element_ substitutable	VARCHAR2(25)	Whether or not (Y/N) the varray element is substitutable for a subtype.

TABLE 13-1 *Columns in the* user_varrays *View*

NOTE
You can get information on all the varrays you have access to using the `all_varrays` *view.*

The following example retrieves the details for `t_varray_address` from `user_varrays`:

```
SELECT parent_table_name, parent_table_column, type_name
FROM user_varrays
WHERE type_name = 'T_VARRAY_ADDRESS';

PARENT_TABLE_NAME
--------------------
PARENT_TABLE_COLUMN
--------------------
TYPE_NAME
--------------------
CUSTOMERS_WITH_VARRAY
ADDRESSES
T_VARRAY_ADDRESS
```

Getting Information on a Nested Table

You can also use `DESCRIBE` with a nested table, as shown in the following example that describes `t_nested_table_address`:

```
DESCRIBE t_nested_table_address
t_nested_table_address TABLE OF T_ADDRESS
 Name                                     Null?    Type
 ---------------------------------------- -------- ------------
 STREET                                            VARCHAR2(15)
 CITY                                              VARCHAR2(15)
 STATE                                             CHAR(2)
 ZIP                                               VARCHAR2(5)
```

The next example describes the `customers_with_nested_table` table, whose `addresses` column is of type `t_nested_table_address`:

```
DESCRIBE customers_with_nested_table
 Name                                     Null?    Type
 ---------------------------------------- -------- --------------------
 ID                                       NOT NULL NUMBER(38)
 FIRST_NAME                                        VARCHAR2(10)
 LAST_NAME                                         VARCHAR2(10)
 ADDRESSES                                         T_NESTED_TABLE_ADDRESS
```

If you set the depth to 2 and describe `customers_with_nested_table`, you can see the attributes that make up `t_nested_table_address`:

```
SET DESCRIBE DEPTH 2
DESCRIBE customers_with_nested_table
 Name                                     Null?    Type
 ---------------------------------------- -------- ------------
 ID                                       NOT NULL NUMBER(38)
 FIRST_NAME                                        VARCHAR2(10)
```

```
LAST_NAME                        VARCHAR2(10)
ADDRESSES                        T_NESTED_TABLE_ADDRESS
   STREET                        VARCHAR2(15)
   CITY                          VARCHAR2(15)
   STATE                         CHAR(2)
   ZIP                           VARCHAR2(5)
```

You can also get information on your nested tables from the `user_nested_tables` view. Table 13-2 describes the columns in `user_nested_tables`.

NOTE
You can get information on all the nested tables you have access to using the `all_nested_tables` *view.*

The following example retrieves the details for the `nested_addresses` table from `user_nested_tables`:

```
SELECT table_name, table_type_name, parent_table_name, parent_table_column
FROM user_nested_tables
WHERE table_name = 'NESTED_ADDRESSES';
```

```
TABLE_NAME                       TABLE_TYPE_NAME
------------------------------   ----------------------
PARENT_TABLE_NAME
----------------------------
PARENT_TABLE_COLUMN
-------------------------------------------------------
NESTED_ADDRESSES                 T_NESTED_TABLE_ADDRESS
CUSTOMERS_WITH_NESTED_TABLE
ADDRESSES
```

Column	Type	Description
table_name	VARCHAR2(30)	Name of the nested table
table_type_owner	VARCHAR2(30)	User who owns the nested table type
table_type_name	VARCHAR2(30)	Name of the nested table type
parent_table_name	VARCHAR2(30)	Name of the parent table that contains the nested table
parent_table_column	VARCHAR2(4000)	Name of the column in the parent table containing the nested table
storage_spec	VARCHAR2(30)	Storage specification for the nested table
return_type	VARCHAR2(20)	Return type of the column
element_substitutable	VARCHAR2(25)	Whether or not (Y/N) the nested table element is substitutable for a subtype.

TABLE 13-2 *Columns in the* `user_nested_tables` *View*

Populating a Collection with Elements

In this section, you'll see how to populate a varray and a nested table with elements using INSERT statements. You don't have to run the INSERT statements shown in this section: they are executed when you run the collection_schema.sql script.

Populating a Varray with Elements

The following INSERT statements add rows to the customers_with_varray table; notice the use of the t_varray_address constructor to specify the strings for the elements of the varray:

```
INSERT INTO customers_with_varray VALUES (
  1, 'Steve', 'Brown',
  t_varray_address(
    '2 State Street, Beantown, MA, 12345',
    '4 Hill Street, Lost Town, CA, 54321'
  )
);

INSERT INTO customers_with_varray VALUES (
  2, 'John', 'Smith',
  t_varray_address(
    '1 High Street, Newtown, CA, 12347',
    '3 New Street, Anytown, MI, 54323',
    '7 Market Street, Main Town, MA, 54323'
  )
);
```

As you can see, the first row has two addresses and the second has three. Any number of addresses up to the maximum limit for the varray can be stored.

Populating a Nested Table with Elements

The following INSERT statements add rows to customers_with_nested_table; notice the use of the t_nested_table_address and t_address constructors to specify the elements of the nested table:

```
INSERT INTO customers_with_nested_table VALUES (
  1, 'Steve', 'Brown',
  t_nested_table_address(
    t_address('2 State Street', 'Beantown', 'MA', '12345'),
    t_address('4 Hill Street', 'Lost Town', 'CA', '54321')
  )
);

INSERT INTO customers_with_nested_table VALUES (
  2, 'John', 'Smith',
  t_nested_table_address(
```

```
    t_address('1 High Street', 'Newtown', 'CA', '12347'),
    t_address('3 New Street', 'Anytown', 'MI', '54323'),
    t_address('7 Market Street', 'Main Town', 'MA', '54323')
  )
);
```

As you can see, the first row has two addresses and the second has three. Any number of addresses can be stored in a nested table.

Retrieving Elements from Collections

In this section, you'll see how to retrieve elements from a varray and a nested table using queries. The output from the queries has been formatted slightly to make the results more readable.

Retrieving Elements from a Varray

The following query retrieves customer #1 from the `customers_with_varray` table; one row is returned, and it contains the two addresses stored in the varray:

```
SELECT *
FROM customers_with_varray
WHERE id = 1;

        ID FIRST_NAME LAST_NAME
---------- ---------- ----------
ADDRESSES
-------------------------------------------------------
         1 Steve      Brown
T_VARRAY_ADDRESS('2 State Street, Beantown, MA, 12345',
 '4 Hill Street, Lost Town, CA, 54321')
```

The next query specifies the actual column names:

```
SELECT id, first_name, last_name, addresses
FROM customers_with_varray
WHERE id = 1;

        ID FIRST_NAME LAST_NAME
---------- ---------- ----------
ADDRESSES
-------------------------------------------------------
         1 Steve      Brown
T_VARRAY_ADDRESS('2 State Street, Beantown, MA, 12345',
 '4 Hill Street, Lost Town, CA, 54321')
```

These examples all return the addresses in the varray as a single row. Later, in the section "Using TABLE() to Treat a Collection as a Series of Rows," you'll see how you can treat the data stored in a collection as a series of rows.

Retrieving Elements from a Nested Table

The following query retrieves customer #1 from `customers_with_nested_table`; one row is returned, and it contains the two addresses stored in the nested table:

```
SELECT *
FROM customers_with_nested_table
WHERE id = 1;

        ID FIRST_NAME LAST_NAME
---------- ---------- ----------
ADDRESSES(STREET, CITY, STATE, ZIP)
----------------------------------------------------------
         1 Steve      Brown
T_NESTED_TABLE_ADDRESS(
 T_ADDRESS('2 State Street', 'Beantown', 'MA', '12345'),
 T_ADDRESS('4 Hill Street', 'Lost Town', 'CA', '54321'))
```

The next query specifies the actual column names:

```
SELECT id, first_name, last_name, addresses
FROM customers_with_nested_table
WHERE id = 1;

        ID FIRST_NAME LAST_NAME
---------- ---------- ----------
ADDRESSES(STREET, CITY, STATE, ZIP)
----------------------------------------------------------
         1 Steve      Brown
T_NESTED_TABLE_ADDRESS(
 T_ADDRESS('2 State Street', 'Beantown', 'MA', '12345'),
 T_ADDRESS('4 Hill Street', 'Lost Town', 'CA', '54321'))
```

The next query gets just the `addresses` nested table; as in the previous examples, one row is returned, and it contains the two addresses stored in the nested table:

```
SELECT addresses
FROM customers_with_nested_table
WHERE id = 1;

ADDRESSES(STREET, CITY, STATE, ZIP)
----------------------------------------------------------
T_NESTED_TABLE_ADDRESS(
 T_ADDRESS('2 State Street', 'Beantown', 'MA', '12345'),
 T_ADDRESS('4 Hill Street', 'Lost Town', 'CA', '54321'))
```

Using TABLE() to Treat a Collection as a Series of Rows

The previous queries you've seen in this chapter return the contents of a collection as a single row. Sometimes, you may wish to treat the data stored in a collection as a series of rows; for example, you might be working with a legacy application that can only use rows. To treat a collection as a series of rows, you use the TABLE() function. In this section, you'll see how to use TABLE() with a varray and a nested table.

Using TABLE() with a Varray

The following query uses TABLE() to retrieve customer #1's two addresses from the customers_with_varray table; two separate rows are returned:

```
SELECT a.*
FROM customers_with_varray c, TABLE(c.addresses) a
WHERE id = 1;

COLUMN_VALUE
-----------------------------------
2 State Street, Beantown, MA, 12345
4 Hill Street, Lost Town, CA, 54321
```

Notice how the Oracle database software automatically adds the column name of COLUMN_VALUE to the rows returned by the query. COLUMN_VALUE is a pseudo column alias, and it is automatically added when a collection contains data of one of the built-in data types, like VARCHAR2, CHAR, NUMBER, or DATE. Because the example varray contains VARCHAR2 data, the COLUMN_VALUE alias is added. If the varray had contained data of a user-defined object type, then TABLE() would return objects of that type and COLUMN_VALUE would not appear; you'll see an example of this in the next section.

You can also embed an entire SELECT statement inside TABLE(). For example, the following query rewrites the previous example, placing a SELECT inside TABLE():

```
SELECT *
FROM TABLE(
  -- get the addresses for customer #1
  SELECT addresses
  FROM customers_with_varray
  WHERE id = 1
);

COLUMN_VALUE
-----------------------------------
2 State Street, Beantown, MA, 12345
4 Hill Street, Lost Town, CA, 54321
```

The following query shows another example that uses TABLE() to get the addresses:

```
SELECT c.id, c.first_name, c.last_name, a.*
FROM customers_with_varray c, TABLE(c.addresses) a
WHERE id = 1;

        ID FIRST_NAME LAST_NAME
---------- ---------- ----------
COLUMN_VALUE
-----------------------------------
         1 Steve      Brown
```

```
2 State Street, Beantown, MA, 12345

        1 Steve        Brown
4 Hill Street, Lost Town, CA, 54321
```

Using TABLE() with a Nested Table

The following query uses TABLE() to retrieve customer #1's two addresses from customers_
with_nested_table; notice that two separate rows are returned:

```
SELECT a.*
FROM customers_with_nested_table c, TABLE(c.addresses) a
WHERE id = 1;

STREET            CITY              ST ZIP
---------------   ---------------   -- -----
2 State Street    Beantown          MA 12345
4 Hill Street     Lost Town         CA 54321
```

The next query gets the street and state attributes of the addresses:

```
SELECT a.street, a.state
FROM customers_with_nested_table c, TABLE(c.addresses) a
WHERE id = 1;

STREET            ST
---------------   --
2 State Street    MA
4 Hill Street     CA
```

The following query shows another example that uses TABLE() to get the addresses:

```
SELECT c.id, c.first_name, c.last_name, a.*
FROM customers_with_nested_table c, TABLE(c.addresses) a
WHERE c.id = 1;

   ID FIRST_NAME LAST_NAME  STREET            CITY              ST ZIP
------ ---------- ---------- ---------------   ---------------   -- -----
    1 Steve      Brown      2 State Street    Beantown          MA 12345
    1 Steve      Brown      4 Hill Street     Lost Town         CA 54321
```

You'll see an important use of TABLE() later in the section "Modifying Elements of a
Nested Table."

Modifying Elements of Collections

In this section, you'll see how to modify the elements in a varray and a nested table. You should
feel free to run the UPDATE, INSERT, and DELETE statements shown in this section.

Modifying Elements of a Varray

The elements in a varray can be modified only as a whole, which means that even if you only want
to modify one element, you must supply all the elements for the varray. The following UPDATE
statement modifies the addresses of customer #2 in the customers_with_varray table:

```
UPDATE customers_with_varray
SET addresses = t_varray_address(
  '6 Any Street, Lost Town, GA, 33347',
  '3 New Street, Anytown, MI, 54323',
  '7 Market Street, Main Town, MA, 54323'
)
WHERE id = 2;
```

```
1 row updated.
```

Modifying Elements of a Nested Table

Unlike in a varray, elements in a nested table can be modified individually. You can insert, update, and delete individual elements in a nested table; you'll see how to do all three of these modifications in this section.

The following INSERT statement adds an address to customer #2 in customer_with_ nested_table; notice that TABLE() is used to get the addresses as a series of rows:

```
INSERT INTO TABLE(
  -- get the addresses for customer #2
  SELECT addresses
  FROM customers_with_nested_table
  WHERE id = 2
) VALUES (
  t_address('5 Main Street', 'Uptown', 'NY', '55512')
);
```

```
1 row created.
```

The following UPDATE statement changes the '1 High Street' address of customer #2 to '9 Any Street'; notice the use of the alias addr in the VALUE clauses when specifying the addresses:

```
UPDATE TABLE(
  -- get the addresses for customer #2
  SELECT addresses
  FROM customers_with_nested_table
  WHERE id = 2
) addr
SET VALUE(addr) =
  t_address('9 Any Street', 'Lost Town', 'VA', '74321')
WHERE VALUE(addr) =
  t_address('1 High Street', 'Newtown', 'CA', '12347');
```

```
1 row updated.
```

The following DELETE statement removes the '3 New Street...' address from customer #2:

```
DELETE FROM TABLE(
  -- get the addresses for customer #2
  SELECT addresses
  FROM customers_with_nested_table
```

```
   WHERE id = 2
) addr
WHERE VALUE(addr) =
   t_address('3 New Street', 'Anytown', 'MI', '54323');
```

```
1 row deleted.
```

Using a Map Method to Compare the Contents of Nested Tables

You can compare the contents of one nested table with the contents of another. Two nested tables are equal only if

- They are of the same type.

- They have the same number of rows.

- All their elements contain the same values.

If the elements of the nested table are of a built-in database type, like NUMBER, VARCHAR2, and so on, then the database will automatically compare the contents of the nested tables for you. If, however, the elements are of a user-defined object type, then you will need to provide a map function that contains code to compare the objects (map functions were shown in the section "Comparing Object Values" of the previous chapter).

The following statements create a type named t_address2 that contains a map function named get_string(); notice that get_string() returns a VARCHAR2 containing the values for the zip, state, city, and street attributes:

```
CREATE TYPE t_address2 AS OBJECT (
    street VARCHAR2(15),
    city   VARCHAR2(15),
    state  CHAR(2),
    zip    VARCHAR2(5),

    -- declare the get_string() map function,
    -- which returns a VARCHAR2 string
    MAP MEMBER FUNCTION get_string RETURN VARCHAR2
);
/

CREATE TYPE BODY t_address2 AS
    -- define the get_string() map function
    MAP MEMBER FUNCTION get_string RETURN VARCHAR2 IS
    BEGIN
      -- return a concatenated string containing the
      -- zip, state, city, and street attributes
      RETURN zip || ' ' || state || ' ' || city || ' ' || street;
    END get_string;
END;
/
```

As you'll see shortly, the database will automatically call `get_string()` when comparing `t_address2` objects.

The following statements create a nested table type and a table, and add a row to the table:

```
CREATE TYPE t_nested_table_address2 AS TABLE OF t_address2;
/

CREATE TABLE customers_with_nested_table2 (
  id          INTEGER PRIMARY KEY,
  first_name  VARCHAR2(10),
  last_name   VARCHAR2(10),
  addresses   t_nested_table_address2
)
NESTED TABLE
  addresses
STORE AS
  nested_addresses2;

INSERT INTO customers_with_nested_table2 VALUES (
  1, 'Steve', 'Brown',
  t_nested_table_address2(
    t_address2('2 State Street', 'Beantown', 'MA', '12345'),
    t_address2('4 Hill Street', 'Lost Town', 'CA', '54321')
  )
);
```

The following query includes a nested table in the WHERE clause; notice that the addresses after the = in the WHERE clause are the same as those in the previous INSERT statement:

```
SELECT cn.id, cn.first_name, cn.last_name
FROM customers_with_nested_table2 cn
WHERE cn.addresses =
  t_nested_table_address2(
    t_address2('2 State Street', 'Beantown', 'MA', '12345'),
    t_address2('4 Hill Street', 'Lost Town', 'CA', '54321')
  );

        ID FIRST_NAME LAST_NAME
---------- ---------- ----------
         1 Steve      Brown
```

When the query is executed, the database automatically calls `get_string()` to compare the `t_address2` objects in `cn.addresses` to the `t_address2` objects after the = in the WHERE clause. The `get_string()` function returns a VARCHAR2 string containing the `zip`, `state`, `city`, and `street` attributes of the objects, and when the strings are equal for every object, the nested tables are also equal.

The next query returns no rows because the single address after the = in the WHERE clause matches only one of the addresses in `cn.addresses` (remember: two nested tables are equal only if they are of the same type, *have the same number of rows*, and their elements contain the same values):

```
SELECT cn.id, cn.first_name, cn.last_name
FROM customers_with_nested_table2 cn
```

```
WHERE cn.addresses =
  t_nested_table_address2(
    t_address2('4 Hill Street', 'Lost Town', 'CA', '54321')
  );
```

```
no rows selected
```

In Oracle Database 10*g* and higher, you can use the SUBMULTISET operator to check whether the contents of one nested table are a subset of another nested table. The following query rewrites the previous example and returns a row:

```
SELECT cn.id, cn.first_name, cn.last_name
FROM customers_with_nested_table2 cn
WHERE
  t_nested_table_address2(
    t_address2('4 Hill Street', 'Lost Town', 'CA', '54321')
  )
  SUBMULTISET OF cn.addresses;
```

```
        ID FIRST_NAME LAST_NAME
---------- ---------- ----------
         1 Steve      Brown
```

Because the address in the first part of the WHERE clause is a subset of the addresses in cn.addresses, a match is found and a row is returned.

The following query shows another example; this time the addresses in cn.addresses are a subset of the addresses after OF in the WHERE clause:

```
SELECT cn.id, cn.first_name, cn.last_name
FROM customers_with_nested_table2 cn
WHERE
  cn.addresses SUBMULTISET OF
  t_nested_table_address2(
    t_address2('2 State Street', 'Beantown', 'MA', '12345'),
    t_address2('4 Hill Street', 'Lost Town', 'CA', '54321'),
    t_address2('6 State Street', 'Beantown', 'MA', '12345')
  );
```

```
        ID FIRST_NAME LAST_NAME
---------- ---------- ----------
         1 Steve      Brown
```

You'll learn more about the SUBMULTISET operator later in this chapter in the section "SUBMULTISET Operator." Also, in the section "Equal and Not-Equal Operators," you'll see how to use the ANSI operators implemented in Oracle Database 10*g* to compare nested tables.

NOTE
There is no direct mechanism for comparing the contents of varrays.

Using CAST() to Convert Collections from One Type to Another

You may use CAST() to convert a collection of one type to another collection type. In this section, you'll see how to use CAST() to convert a varray to a nested table and vice versa.

Using CAST() to Convert a Varray to a Nested Table

The following statements create and populate a table named customers_with_varray2 that contains an addresses column of type t_varray_address2:

```
CREATE TYPE t_varray_address2 AS VARRAY(3) OF t_address;
/

CREATE TABLE customers_with_varray2 (
  id         INTEGER PRIMARY KEY,
  first_name VARCHAR2(10),
  last_name  VARCHAR2(10),
  addresses  t_varray_address2
);

INSERT INTO customers_with_varray2 VALUES (
  1, 'Jason', 'Bond',
  t_varray_address2(
    t_address('9 Newton Drive', 'Sometown', 'WY', '22123'),
    t_address('6 Spring Street', 'New City', 'CA', '77712')
  )
);
```

The following query uses CAST() to return the varray addresses for customer #1 as a nested table; notice that the addresses appear in a constructor for the T_NESTED_TABLE_ADDRESS type, indicating the conversion of the elements to this type:

```
SELECT CAST(cv.addresses AS t_nested_table_address)
FROM customers_with_varray2 cv
WHERE cv.id = 1;

CAST(CV.ADDRESSESAST_NESTED_TABLE_ADDRESS)(STREET, CITY, STATE, ZIP)
-------------------------------------------------------------------
T_NESTED_TABLE_ADDRESS(
  T_ADDRESS('9 Newton Drive', 'Sometown', 'WY', '22123'),
  T_ADDRESS('6 Spring Street', 'New City', 'CA', '77712'))
```

Using CAST() to Convert a Nested Table to a Varray

The following query uses CAST() to return the addresses for customer #1 in customers_with_nested_table as a varray; notice that the addresses appear in a constructor for T_VARRAY_ADDRESS2:

```
SELECT CAST(cn.addresses AS t_varray_address2)
FROM customers_with_nested_table cn
```

```
WHERE cn.id = 1;
```

```
CAST(CN.ADDRESSESAST_VARRAY_ADDRESS2)(STREET, CITY, STATE, ZIP)
-------------------------------------------------------------
T_VARRAY_ADDRESS2(
 T_ADDRESS('2 State Street', 'Beantown', 'MA', '12345'),
 T_ADDRESS('4 Hill Street', 'Lost Town', 'CA', '54321'))
```

Using Collections in PL/SQL

You can use collections in PL/SQL. In this section, you'll see how to perform the following tasks in PL/SQL:

- Manipulate a varray

- Manipulate a nested table

- Use the PL/SQL collection methods to access and manipulate collections

All the packages you'll see in this section are created when you run the collection_schema.sql script. If you performed any of the INSERT, UPDATE, or DELETE statements shown in the earlier sections of this chapter, go ahead and rerun the collection_schema.sql script so that your output matches mine in this section.

Manipulating a Varray

In this section, you'll see a package named varray_package; this package contains the following items:

- A REF CURSOR type named t_ref_cursor

- A function named get_customers(), which returns a t_ref_cursor object that points to the rows in the customers_with_varray table

- A procedure named insert_customer(), which adds a row to the customers_ with_varray table

The collection_schema.sql script contains the following package specification and body for varray_package:

```
CREATE PACKAGE varray_package AS
    TYPE t_ref_cursor IS REF CURSOR;
    FUNCTION get_customers RETURN t_ref_cursor;
    PROCEDURE insert_customer(
        p_id         IN customers_with_varray.id%TYPE,
        p_first_name IN customers_with_varray.first_name%TYPE,
        p_last_name  IN customers_with_varray.last_name%TYPE,
        p_addresses  IN customers_with_varray.addresses%TYPE
    );
END varray_package;
/
```

```
CREATE PACKAGE BODY varray_package AS
  -- get_customers() function returns a REF CURSOR
  -- that points to the rows in customers_with_varray
  FUNCTION get_customers
  RETURN t_ref_cursor IS
    --declare the REF CURSOR object
    v_customers_ref_cursor t_ref_cursor;
  BEGIN
    -- get the REF CURSOR
    OPEN v_customers_ref_cursor FOR
      SELECT *
      FROM customers_with_varray;
    -- return the REF CURSOR
    RETURN customers_ref_cursor;
  END get_customers;

  -- insert_customer() procedure adds a row to
  -- customers_with_varray
  PROCEDURE insert_customer(
    p_id        IN customers_with_varray.id%TYPE,
    p_first_name IN customers_with_varray.first_name%TYPE,
    p_last_name  IN customers_with_varray.last_name%TYPE,
    p_addresses  IN customers_with_varray.addresses%TYPE
  ) IS
  BEGIN
    INSERT INTO customers_with_varray
    VALUES (p_id, p_first_name, p_last_name, p_addresses);
    COMMIT;
  EXCEPTION
    WHEN OTHERS THEN
      ROLLBACK;
  END insert_customer;
END varray_package;
/
```

The following example calls insert_customer() to add a new row to the customers_with_varray table:

```
CALL varray_package.insert_customer(
  3, 'James', 'Red',
  t_varray_address(
    '10 Main Street, Green Town, CA, 22212',
    '20 State Street, Blue Town, FL, 22213'
  )
);
```

```
Call completed.
```

The next example calls get_products() to retrieve the rows from customers_with_varray:

```
SELECT varray_package.get_customers
FROM dual;

GET_CUSTOMERS
-------------------
CURSOR STATEMENT : 1

CURSOR STATEMENT : 1

        ID FIRST_NAME LAST_NAME
---------- ---------- ----------
ADDRESSES
-----------------------------------------------------------
         1 Steve      Brown
T_VARRAY_ADDRESS('2 State Street, Beantown, MA, 12345',
 '4 Hill Street, Lost Town, CA, 54321')


         2 John       Smith
T_VARRAY_ADDRESS('1 High Street, Newtown, CA, 12347',
 '3 New Street, Anytown, MI, 54323',
 '7 Market Street, Main Town, MA, 54323')


         3 James      Red
T_VARRAY_ADDRESS('10 Main Street, Green Town, CA, 22212',
 '20 State Street, Blue Town, FL, 22213')
```

Manipulating a Nested Table

In this section, you'll see a package named nested_table_package; this package contains the following items:

- A REF CURSOR type named t_ref_cursor

- A function named get_customers(), which returns a t_ref_cursor object that points to the rows in customers_with_nested_table

- A procedure named insert_customer(), which adds a row to customers_with_nested_table

The collection_schema.sql script contains the following package specification and body for nested_table_package:

```
CREATE PACKAGE nested_table_package AS
  TYPE t_ref_cursor IS REF CURSOR;
  FUNCTION get_customers RETURN t_ref_cursor;
  PROCEDURE insert_customer(
    p_id         IN customers_with_nested_table.id%TYPE,
    p_first_name IN customers_with_nested_table.first_name%TYPE,
    p_last_name  IN customers_with_nested_table.last_name%TYPE,
    p_addresses  IN customers_with_nested_table.addresses%TYPE
  );
```

```
END nested_table_package;
/

CREATE PACKAGE BODY nested_table_package AS
  -- get_customers() function returns a REF CURSOR
  -- that points to the rows in customers_with_nested_table
  FUNCTION get_customers
  RETURN t_ref_cursor IS
    -- declare the REF CURSOR object
    v_customers_ref_cursor t_ref_cursor;
  BEGIN
    -- get the REF CURSOR
    OPEN v_customers_ref_cursor FOR
      SELECT *
      FROM customers_with_nested_table;
    -- return the REF CURSOR
    RETURN customers_ref_cursor;
  END get_customers;

  -- insert_customer() procedure adds a row to
  -- customers_with_nested_table
  PROCEDURE insert_customer(
    p_id         IN customers_with_nested_table.id%TYPE,
    p_first_name IN customers_with_nested_table.first_name%TYPE,
    p_last_name  IN customers_with_nested_table.last_name%TYPE,
    p_addresses  IN customers_with_nested_table.addresses%TYPE
  ) IS
  BEGIN
    INSERT INTO customers_with_nested_table
    VALUES (p_id, p_first_name, p_last_name, p_addresses);
    COMMIT;
  EXCEPTION
    WHEN OTHERS THEN
      ROLLBACK;
  END insert_customer;
END nested_table_package;
/
```

The following example calls insert_customer() to add a new row to customers_ with_nested_table:

```
CALL nested_table_package.insert_customer(
  3, 'James', 'Red',
  t_nested_table_address(
    t_address('10 Main Street', 'Green Town', 'CA', '22212'),
    t_address('20 State Street', 'Blue Town', 'FL', '22213')
  )
);

Call completed.
```

The next example calls `get_customers()` to retrieve the rows from `customers_with_nested_table`:

```
SELECT nested_table_package.get_customers
FROM dual;

GET_CUSTOMERS
--------------------
CURSOR STATEMENT : 1

CURSOR STATEMENT : 1

        ID FIRST_NAME LAST_NAME
---------- ---------- ----------
ADDRESSES(STREET, CITY, STATE, ZIP)
------------------------------------------------------------
         1 Steve      Brown
T_NESTED_TABLE_ADDRESS(
 T_ADDRESS('2 State Street', 'Beantown', 'MA', '12345'),
 T_ADDRESS('4 Hill Street', 'Lost Town', 'CA', '54321'))

         2 John       Smith
T_NESTED_TABLE_ADDRESS(
 T_ADDRESS('1 High Street', 'Newtown', 'CA', '12347'),
 T_ADDRESS('3 New Street', 'Anytown', 'MI', '54323'),
 T_ADDRESS('7 Market Street', 'Main Town', 'MA', '54323'))

         3 James      Red
T_NESTED_TABLE_ADDRESS(
 T_ADDRESS('10 Main Street', 'Green Town', 'CA', '22212'),
 T_ADDRESS('20 State Street', 'Blue Town', 'FL', '22213'))
```

PL/SQL Collection Methods

In this section, you'll see the PL/SQL methods you can use with collections. Table 13-3 summarizes the collection methods. These methods can be used only in PL/SQL.

The following sections use a package named `collection_method_examples`; the examples illustrate the use of the methods shown in the previous table. The package is created by the `collection_schema.sql` script, and you'll see the individual methods defined in this package in the following sections.

COUNT()

`COUNT` returns the number of elements in a collection. Because a nested table can have individual elements that are empty, `COUNT` returns the number of non-empty elements in a nested table. For example, let's say you have a nested table named `v_nested_table` that has its elements set as shown in the following table.

Element Index	Empty/Not Empty
1	Empty
2	Not empty
3	Empty
4	Not empty

Method	Description
COUNT	Returns the number of elements in a collection. Because a nested table can have individual elements that are empty, COUNT returns the number of non-empty elements in a nested table.
DELETE DELETE(n) DELETE(n, m)	Removes elements from a collection. There are three forms of DELETE: ■ DELETE removes all elements. ■ DELETE(n) removes element n. ■ DELETE(n, m) removes elements n through m. Because varrays always have consecutive subscripts, you cannot delete individual elements from a varray (except from the end by using TRIM).
EXISTS(n)	Returns true if element n in a collection exists: EXISTS returns true for non-empty elements and false for empty elements of nested tables or elements beyond the range of a collection.
EXTEND EXTEND(n) EXTEND(n, m)	Adds elements to the end of a collection. There are three forms of EXTEND: ■ EXTEND adds one element, which is set to null. ■ EXTEND(n) adds n elements, which are set to null. ■ EXTEND(n, m) adds n elements, which are set to a copy of the m element.
FIRST	Returns the index of the first element in a collection. If the collection is completely empty, FIRST returns null. Because a nested table can have individual elements that are empty, FIRST returns the lowest index of a non-empty element in a nested table.
LAST	Returns the index of the last element in a collection. If the collection is completely empty, LAST returns null. Because a nested table can have individual elements that are empty, LAST returns the highest index of a non-empty element in a nested table.
LIMIT	For nested tables, which have no declared size, LIMIT returns null. For varrays, LIMIT returns the maximum number of elements that the varray can contain. You specify the limit in the type definition. The limit is changed when using TRIM and EXTEND, or when you use ALTER TYPE to change the limit.
NEXT(n)	Returns the index of the element after n. Because a nested table can have individual elements that are empty, NEXT returns the index of a non-empty element after n. If there are no elements after n, NEXT returns null.
PRIOR(n)	Returns the index of the element before n. Because a nested table can have individual elements that are empty, PRIOR returns the index of a non-empty element before n. If there are no elements before n, PRIOR returns null.
TRIM TRIM(n)	Removes elements from the end of a collection. There are two forms of TRIM: ■ TRIM removes one element from the end. ■ TRIM(n) removes n elements from the end.

TABLE 13-3 *PL/SQL Collection Methods*

Given this configuration, `v_nested_table.COUNT` returns 2, the number of non-empty elements.

`COUNT` is used in the `get_addresses()` and `display_addresses()` methods of the `collection_method_examples` package. The `get_addresses()` function returns the specified customer's addresses from `customers_with_nested_table`, whose id is passed to the function:

```
FUNCTION get_addresses(
  p_id customers_with_nested_table.id%TYPE
) RETURN t_nested_table_address IS
  -- declare object named v_addresses to store the
  -- nested table of addresses
  v_addresses t_nested_table_address;
BEGIN
  -- retrieve the nested table of addresses into v_addresses
  SELECT addresses
  INTO v_addresses
  FROM customers_with_nested_table
  WHERE id = p_id;

  -- display the number of addresses using v_addresses.COUNT
  DBMS_OUTPUT.PUT_LINE(
    'Number of addresses = '|| v_addresses.COUNT
  );

  -- return v_addresses
  RETURN v_addresses;
END get_addresses;
```

The following example sets the server output on and calls `get_addresses()` for customer #1:

```
SET SERVEROUTPUT ON
SELECT collection_method_examples.get_addresses(1) addresses
FROM dual;

ADDRESSES(STREET, CITY, STATE, ZIP)
---------------------------------------------------------
T_NESTED_TABLE_ADDRESS(
 T_ADDRESS('2 State Street', 'Beantown', 'MA', '12345'),
 T_ADDRESS('4 Hill Street', 'Lost Town', 'CA', '54321'))

Number of addresses = 2
```

The following `display_addresses()` procedure accepts a parameter named `p_addresses`, which contains a nested table of addresses; the procedure displays the number of addresses in `p_addresses` using `COUNT`, and then displays those addresses using a loop:

```
PROCEDURE display_addresses(
  p_addresses t_nested_table_address
) IS
  v_count INTEGER;
```

```
BEGIN
  -- display the number of addresses in p_addresses
  DBMS_OUTPUT.PUT_LINE(
    'Current number of addresses = '|| p_addresses.COUNT
  );

  -- display the addresses in p_addresses using a loop
  FOR v_count IN 1..p_addresses.COUNT LOOP
    DBMS_OUTPUT.PUT_LINE('Address #' || v_count || ':');
    DBMS_OUTPUT.PUT(p_addresses(v_count).street || ', ');
    DBMS_OUTPUT.PUT(p_addresses(v_count).city || ', ');
    DBMS_OUTPUT.PUT(p_addresses(v_count).state || ', ');
    DBMS_OUTPUT.PUT_LINE(p_addresses(v_count).zip);
  END LOOP;
END display_addresses;
```

You'll see the use of `display_addresses()` shortly.

DELETE()

DELETE removes elements from a collection. There are three forms of DELETE:

- DELETE removes all elements.

- DELETE(*n*) removes element *n*.

- DELETE(*n*, *m*) removes elements *n* through *m*.

For example, let's say you have a nested table named `v_nested_table` that has seven elements, then `v_nested_table.DELETE(2, 5)` removes elements 2 through 5.

The following `delete_address()` procedure gets the addresses for customer #1 and then uses DELETE to remove the address whose index is specified by the `p_address_num` parameter:

```
PROCEDURE delete_address(
  p_address_num INTEGER
) IS
  v_addresses t_nested_table_address;
BEGIN
  v_addresses := get_addresses(1);
  display_addresses(v_addresses);
  DBMS_OUTPUT.PUT_LINE('Deleting address #' || p_address_num);

  -- delete the address specified by p_address_num
  v_addresses.DELETE(p_address_num);

  display_addresses(v_addresses);
END delete_address;
```

The following example calls `delete_address(2)` to remove address #2 from customer #1:

```
CALL collection_method_examples.delete_address(2);
Number of addresses = 2
Current number of addresses = 2
```

```
Address #1:
2 State Street, Beantown, MA, 12345
Address #2:
4 Hill Street, Lost Town, CA, 54321
Deleting address #2
Current number of addresses = 1
Address #1:
2 State Street, Beantown, MA, 12345
```

EXISTS()

EXISTS(*n*) returns true if element *n* in a collection exists: EXISTS returns true for non-empty elements, and it returns false for empty elements of nested tables or elements beyond the range of a collection. For example, let's say you have a nested table named v_nested_table that has its elements set as shown in the following table.

Element Index	Empty/Not Empty
1	Empty
2	Not empty
3	Empty
4	Not empty

Given this configuration, v_nested_table.EXISTS(2) returns true (because element #2 is not empty), and v_nested_table.EXISTS(3) returns false (because element #3 is empty).

The following exist_addresses() procedure gets the addresses for customer #1, uses DELETE to remove address #1, and then uses EXISTS to check whether addresses #1 and #2 exist (#1 does not exist because it has been deleted, #2 does exist):

```
PROCEDURE exist_addresses IS
  v_addresses t_nested_table_address;
BEGIN
  v_addresses := get_addresses(1);
  DBMS_OUTPUT.PUT_LINE('Deleting address #1');
  v_addresses.DELETE(1);

  -- use EXISTS to check if the addresses exist
  IF v_addresses.EXISTS(1) THEN
    DBMS_OUTPUT.PUT_LINE('Address #1 does exist');
  ELSE
    DBMS_OUTPUT.PUT_LINE('Address #1 does not exist');
  END IF;
  IF v_addresses.EXISTS(2) THEN
    DBMS_OUTPUT.PUT_LINE('Address #2 does exist');
  END IF;
END exist_addresses;
```

The following example calls exist_addresses():

```
CALL collection_method_examples.exist_addresses();
Number of addresses = 2
```

```
Deleting address #1
Address #1 does not exist
Address #2 does exist
```

EXTEND()

EXTEND adds elements to the end of a collection. There are three forms of EXTEND:

- EXTEND adds one element, which is set to null.

- EXTEND(n) adds n elements, which are set to null.

- EXTEND(n, m) adds n elements, which are set to a copy of the m element.

For example, let's say you have a collection named v_nested_table that has seven elements, then v_nested_table.EXTEND(2, 5) adds element #5 twice to the end of the collection.

The following extend_addresses() procedure gets the addresses for customer #1 into v_addresses, then uses EXTEND to copy address #1 twice to the end of v_addresses:

```
PROCEDURE extend_addresses IS
  v_addresses t_nested_table_address;
BEGIN
  v_addresses := get_addresses(1);
  display_addresses(v_addresses);
  DBMS_OUTPUT.PUT_LINE('Extending addresses');

  -- copy address #1 twice to the end of v_addresses
  v_addresses.EXTEND(2, 1);

  display_addresses(v_addresses);
END extend_addresses;
```

The following example calls extend_addresses():

```
CALL collection_method_examples.extend_addresses();
Number of addresses = 2
Current number of addresses = 2
Address #1:
2 State Street, Beantown, MA, 12345
Address #2:
4 Hill Street, Lost Town, CA, 54321
Extending addresses
Current number of addresses = 4
Address #1:
2 State Street, Beantown, MA, 12345
Address #2:
4 Hill Street, Lost Town, CA, 54321
Address #3:
2 State Street, Beantown, MA, 12345
Address #4:
2 State Street, Beantown, MA, 12345
```

FIRST()

You use `FIRST` to get the index of the first element in a collection. If the collection is completely empty, `FIRST` returns null. Because a nested table can have individual elements that are empty, `FIRST` returns the lowest index of a non-empty element in a nested table. For example, let's say you have a nested table named `v_nested_table` that has its elements set as shown in the following table.

Element Index	Empty/Not Empty
1	Empty
2	Not empty
3	Empty
4	Not empty

Given this configuration, `v_nested_table.FIRST` returns 2, the lowest index containing a non-empty element.

The following `first_address()` procedure gets the addresses for customer #1 into `v_addresses` and then uses `FIRST` to display the index of the first address in `v_addresses`; the procedure then deletes address #1 using `DELETE` and displays the new index returned by `FIRST`:

```
PROCEDURE first_address IS
  v_addresses t_nested_table_address;
BEGIN
  v_addresses := get_addresses(1);

  -- display the FIRST address
  DBMS_OUTPUT.PUT_LINE('First address = ' || v_addresses.FIRST);
  DBMS_OUTPUT.PUT_LINE('Deleting address #1');
  v_addresses.DELETE(1);

  -- display the FIRST address again
  DBMS_OUTPUT.PUT_LINE('First address = ' || v_addresses.FIRST);
END first_address;
```

The following example calls `first_address()`:

```
CALL collection_method_examples.first_address();
Number of addresses = 2
First address = 1
Deleting address #1
First address = 2
```

LAST()

`LAST` returns the index of the last element in a collection. If the collection is completely empty, `LAST` returns null. Because a nested table can have individual elements that are empty, `LAST` returns the highest index of a non-empty element in a nested table. For example, let's say you have a nested table named `v_nested_table` that has its elements set as shown in the following table.

Element Index	Empty/Not Empty
1	Not empty
2	Empty
3	Empty
4	Not empty

Given this configuration, `v_nested_table.LAST` returns 4, the highest index containing a non-empty element.

The following `last_address()` procedure gets the addresses for customer #1 into `v_addresses` and then uses LAST to display the index of the last address in `v_addresses`; the procedure then deletes address #2 using DELETE and displays the new index returned by LAST:

```
PROCEDURE last_address IS
  v_addresses t_nested_table_address;
BEGIN
  v_addresses := get_addresses(1);

  -- display the LAST address
  DBMS_OUTPUT.PUT_LINE('Last address = ' || v_addresses.LAST);
  DBMS_OUTPUT.PUT_LINE('Deleting address #2');
  v_addresses.DELETE(2);

  -- display the LAST address again
  DBMS_OUTPUT.PUT_LINE('Last address = ' || v_addresses.LAST);
END last_address;
```

The following example calls `last_address()`:

```
CALL collection_method_examples.last_address();
Number of addresses = 2
Last address = 2
Deleting address #2
Last address = 1
```

NEXT()

NEXT (*n*) returns the index of the element after *n*. Because a nested table can have individual elements that are empty, NEXT returns the index of a non-empty element after *n*. If there are no elements after *n*, NEXT returns null. For example, let's say you have a nested table named `v_nested_table` that has its elements set as shown in the following table.

Element Index	Empty/Not Empty
1	Not empty
2	Empty
3	Empty
4	Not empty

Given this configuration, `v_nested_table.NEXT(1)` returns 4, the index containing the next non-empty element; `v_nested_table.NEXT(4)` returns null.

The following `next_address()` procedure gets the addresses for customer #1 into `v_addresses` and then uses `NEXT(1)` to get the index of the address after address #1 in `v_addresses`; the procedure then uses `NEXT(2)` to attempt to get the index of the address after address #2 (there isn't one, because customer #1 only has two addresses, so null is returned):

```
PROCEDURE next_address IS
  v_addresses t_nested_table_address;
BEGIN
  v_addresses := get_addresses(1);

  -- use NEXT(1) to get the index of the address
  -- after address #1
  DBMS_OUTPUT.PUT_LINE(
    'v_addresses.NEXT(1) = ' || v_addresses.NEXT(1)
  );

  -- use NEXT(2) to attempt to get the index of
  -- the address after address #2 (there isn't one,
  -- so null is returned)
  DBMS_OUTPUT.PUT_LINE(
    'v_addresses.NEXT(2) = ' || v_addresses.NEXT(2)
  );
END next_address;
```

The following example calls `next_address()`; `v_addresses.NEXT(2)` is null, and so no output is shown after the = for that element:

```
CALL collection_method_examples.next_address();
Number of addresses = 2
v_addresses.NEXT(1) = 2
v_addresses.NEXT(2) =
```

PRIOR()

`PRIOR(n)` returns the index of the element before *n*. Because a nested table can have individual elements that are empty, `PRIOR` returns the index of a non-empty element before *n*. If there are no elements before *n*, `PRIOR` returns null. For example, let's say you have a nested table named `v_nested_table` that has its elements set as shown in the following table.

Element Index	Empty/Not Empty
1	Not empty
2	Empty
3	Empty
4	Not empty

Given this configuration, `v_nested_table.PRIOR(4)` returns 1, the index containing the prior non-empty element; `v_nested_table.PRIOR(1)` returns null.

The following `prior_address()` procedure gets the addresses for customer #1 into `v_addresses` and then uses `PRIOR(2)` to get the index of the address before address #2 in `v_addresses`; the procedure then uses `PRIOR(1)` to attempt to get the index of the address before address #1 (there isn't one, so null is returned):

```
PROCEDURE prior_address IS
  v_addresses t_nested_table_address;
BEGIN
  v_addresses := get_addresses(1);

  -- use PRIOR(2) to get the index of the address
  -- before address #2
  DBMS_OUTPUT.PUT_LINE(
    'v_addresses.PRIOR(2) = ' || v_addresses.PRIOR(2)
  );

  -- use PRIOR(1) to attempt to get the index of
  -- the address before address #1 (there isn't one,
  -- so null is returned)
  DBMS_OUTPUT.PUT_LINE(
    'v_addresses.PRIOR(1) = ' || v_addresses.PRIOR(1)
  );
END prior_address;
```

The following example calls `prior_address()`; `v_addresses.PRIOR(1)` is null, and so no output is shown after the = for that element:

```
CALL collection_method_examples.prior_address();
Number of addresses = 2
v_addresses.PRIOR(2) = 1
v_addresses.PRIOR(1) =
```

TRIM()

`TRIM` removes elements from the end of a collection. There are two forms of `TRIM`:

- `TRIM` removes one element from the end.

- `TRIM(n)` removes n elements from the end.

For example, let's say you have a nested table named `v_nested_table`, then `v_nested_table.TRIM(2)` removes two elements from the end.

The following `trim_addresses()` procedure gets the addresses of customer #1, copies address #1 to the end of `v_addresses` three times using `EXTEND(3, 1)`, and then removes two addresses from the end of `v_addresses` using `TRIM(2)`:

```
PROCEDURE trim_addresses IS
  v_addresses t_nested_table_address;
BEGIN
  v_addresses := get_addresses(1);
  display_addresses(v_addresses);
  DBMS_OUTPUT.PUT_LINE('Extending addresses');
```

```
v_addresses.EXTEND(3, 1);
display_addresses(v_addresses);
DBMS_OUTPUT.PUT_LINE('Trimming 2 addresses from end');

-- remove 2 addresses from the end of v_addresses
-- using TRIM(2)
v_addresses.TRIM(2);

display_addresses(v_addresses);
END trim_addresses;
```

The following example calls `trim_addresses()`:

```
CALL collection_method_examples.trim_addresses();
Number of addresses = 2
Current number of addresses = 2
Address #1:
2 State Street, Beantown, MA, 12345
Address #2:
4 Hill Street, Lost Town, CA, 54321
Extending addresses
Current number of addresses = 5
Address #1:
2 State Street, Beantown, MA, 12345
Address #2:
4 Hill Street, Lost Town, CA, 54321
Address #3:
2 State Street, Beantown, MA, 12345
Address #4:
2 State Street, Beantown, MA, 12345
Address #5:
2 State Street, Beantown, MA, 12345
Trimming 2 addresses from end
Current number of addresses = 3
Address #1:
2 State Street, Beantown, MA, 12345
Address #2:
4 Hill Street, Lost Town, CA, 54321
Address #3:
2 State Street, Beantown, MA, 12345
```

Multilevel Collections

With the release of Oracle Database 9*i*, you can create a collection in the database whose elements are also a collection. These "collections of collections" are known as *multilevel collections*. The following list shows the valid multilevel collections:

- A nested table of nested tables
- A nested table of varrays
- A varray of varrays
- A varray of nested tables

I've provided an SQL*Plus script named `collection_schema2.sql` in the SQL directory. This script creates a user named `collection_user2`, with a password of `collection_password`, along with the types and the table shown in this section. You can run this script if you are using Oracle Database 9*i* or higher. After the script completes, you will be logged in as `collection_user2`.

Let's say you wanted to store a set of phone numbers for each address of a customer. The following example creates a varray type of three `VARCHAR2` strings named `t_varray_phone` to represent phone numbers:

```
CREATE TYPE t_varray_phone AS VARRAY(3) OF VARCHAR2(14);
/
```

Next, the following example creates an object type named `t_address` that contains an attribute named `phone_numbers`; this attribute is of type `t_varray_phone`:

```
CREATE TYPE t_address AS OBJECT (
  street          VARCHAR2(15),
  city            VARCHAR2(15),
  state           CHAR(2),
  zip             VARCHAR2(5),
  phone_numbers t_varray_phone
);
/
```

The next example creates a nested table type of `t_address` objects:

```
CREATE TYPE t_nested_table_address AS TABLE OF t_address;
/
```

The following example creates a table named `customers_with_nested_table`, which contains a column named `addresses` of type `t_nested_table_address`:

```
CREATE TABLE customers_with_nested_table (
  id          INTEGER PRIMARY KEY,
  first_name VARCHAR2(10),
  last_name  VARCHAR2(10),
  addresses   t_nested_table_address
)
NESTED TABLE
  addresses
STORE AS
  nested_addresses;
```

So, `customers_with_nested_table` contains a nested table whose elements contain an address with a varray of phone numbers.

The following `INSERT` statement adds a row to `customers_with_nested_table`; notice the structure and content of the `INSERT` statement, which contains elements for the nested table of addresses, each of which has an embedded varray of phone numbers:

```
INSERT INTO customers_with_nested_table VALUES (
  1, 'Steve', 'Brown',
  t_nested_table_address(
    t_address('2 State Street', 'Beantown', 'MA', '12345',
```

```
       t_varray_phone(
         '(800)-555-1211',
         '(800)-555-1212',
         '(800)-555-1213'
       )
     ),
     t_address('4 Hill Street', 'Lost Town', 'CA', '54321',
       t_varray_phone(
         '(800)-555-1211',
         '(800)-555-1212'
       )
     )
   )
);
```

You can see that the first address has three phone numbers, while the second address has two. The following query retrieves the row from `customers_with_nested_table`:

```
SELECT *
FROM customers_with_nested_table;

        ID FIRST_NAME LAST_NAME
---------- ---------- ----------
ADDRESSES(STREET, CITY, STATE, ZIP, PHONE_NUMBERS)
-----------------------------------------------------------------------
         1 Steve      Brown
T_NESTED_TABLE_ADDRESS(
 T_ADDRESS('2 State Street', 'Beantown', 'MA', '12345',
  T_VARRAY_PHONE('(800)-555-1211', '(800)-555-1212', '(800)-555-1213')),
 T_ADDRESS('4 Hill Street', 'Lost Town', 'CA', '54321',
  T_VARRAY_PHONE('(800)-555-1211', '(800)-555-1212')))
```

You can use `TABLE()` to treat the data stored in the collections as a series of rows, as shown in the following query:

```
SELECT cn.first_name, cn.last_name, a.street, a.city, a.state, p.*
FROM customers_with_nested_table cn,
 TABLE(cn.addresses) a, TABLE(a.phone_numbers) p;

FIRST_NAME LAST_NAME  STREET          CITY         ST COLUMN_VALUE
---------- ---------- --------------- ------------ -- --------------
Steve      Brown      2 State Street  Beantown     MA (800)-555-1211
Steve      Brown      2 State Street  Beantown     MA (800)-555-1212
Steve      Brown      2 State Street  Beantown     MA (800)-555-1213
Steve      Brown      4 Hill Street   Lost Town    CA (800)-555-1211
Steve      Brown      4 Hill Street   Lost Town    CA (800)-555-1212
```

The following `UPDATE` statement shows how to update the phone numbers for the `2 State Street` address; notice that `TABLE()` is used to get the addresses as a series of rows and that a varray containing the new phone numbers is supplied in the `SET` clause:

```
UPDATE TABLE(
  -- get the addresses for customer #1
  SELECT cn.addresses
  FROM customers_with_nested_table cn
  WHERE cn.id = 1
) addrs
SET addrs.phone_numbers =
  t_varray_phone(
    '(800)-555-1214',
    '(800)-555-1215'
  )
WHERE addrs.street = '2 State Street';
```

```
1 row updated.
```

The following query verifies the change:

```
SELECT cn.first_name, cn.last_name, a.street, a.city, a.state, p.*
FROM customers_with_nested_table cn,
 TABLE(cn.addresses) a, TABLE(a.phone_numbers) p;
```

```
FIRST_NAME LAST_NAME  STREET           CITY         ST COLUMN_VALUE
---------- ---------- ---------------  ------------ -- --------------
Steve      Brown      2 State Street   Beantown     MA (800)-555-1214
Steve      Brown      2 State Street   Beantown     MA (800)-555-1215
Steve      Brown      4 Hill Street    Lost Town    CA (800)-555-1211
Steve      Brown      4 Hill Street    Lost Town    CA (800)-555-1212
```

Support for multilevel collection types is a very powerful extension to the Oracle database software, and you might want to consider using them in any database designs you contribute to.

Oracle Database 10*g* Enhancements to Collections

In this section, you'll learn about the following enhancements made to collections in Oracle Database 10*g*:

- Support for associative arrays

- Ability to change the size or precision of an element type

- Ability to increase the number of elements in a varray

- Ability to use varray columns in temporary tables

- Ability to use a different tablespace for a nested table's storage table

- ANSI support for nested tables

The various statements that create the items shown in this section are contained in the `collection_schema3.sql` script. This script creates a user named `collection_user3` with a password of `collection_password` and creates the collection types, tables, and PL/SQL code. You can run this script if you are using Oracle Database 10*g* or higher. After the script completes, you will be logged in as `collection_user3`.

Associative Arrays

An associative array is a set of key and value pairs. You can get the value from the array using the key (which may be a string) or an integer that specifies the position of the value in the array. The following example procedure named `customers_associative_array()` illustrates the use of associative arrays:

```
CREATE PROCEDURE customers_associative_array AS
    -- define an associative array type named t_assoc_array;
    -- the value stored in each array element is a NUMBER,
    -- and the index key to access each element is a VARCHAR2
    TYPE t_assoc_array IS TABLE OF NUMBER INDEX BY VARCHAR2(15);

    -- declare an object named v_customer_array of type t_assoc_array;
    -- v_customer_array will be used to store the ages of customers
    v_customer_array t_assoc_array;
BEGIN
    -- assign the values to v_customer_array; the VARCHAR2 key is the
    -- customer name and the NUMBER value is the age of the customer
    v_customer_array('Jason') := 32;
    v_customer_array('Steve') := 28;
    v_customer_array('Fred') := 43;
    v_customer_array('Cynthia') := 27;

    -- display the values stored in v_customer_array
    DBMS_OUTPUT.PUT_LINE(
        'v_customer_array[''Jason''] = ' || v_customer_array('Jason')
    );
    DBMS_OUTPUT.PUT_LINE(
        'v_customer_array[''Steve''] = ' || v_customer_array('Steve')
    );
    DBMS_OUTPUT.PUT_LINE(
        'v_customer_array[''Fred''] = ' || v_customer_array('Fred')
    );
    DBMS_OUTPUT.PUT_LINE(
        'v_customer_array[''Cynthia''] = ' || v_customer_array('Cynthia')
    );
END customers_associative_array;
/
```

The following example sets the server output on and calls `customers_associative_array()`:

```
SET SERVEROUTPUT ON
CALL customers_associative_array();
v_customer_array['Jason'] = 32
v_customer_array['Steve'] = 28
v_customer_array['Fred'] = 43
v_customer_array['Cynthia'] = 27
```

Changing the Size of an Element Type

You can change the size of an element type in a collection when the element type is one of the character, numeric, or raw types (raw is used to store binary data— you'll learn about this in the next chapter). Earlier in this chapter, you saw the following statement that creates a varray type named t_varray_address:

```
CREATE TYPE t_varray_address AS VARRAY(2) OF VARCHAR2(50);
/
```

The following example changes the size of the VARCHAR2 elements in t_varray_address to 60:

```
ALTER TYPE t_varray_address
MODIFY ELEMENT TYPE VARCHAR2(60) CASCADE;
```

```
Type altered.
```

The CASCADE option propagates the change to any dependent objects in the database, which, in the example, is the customers_with_varray table that contains a column named addresses of type t_varray_address. You can also use the INVALIDATE option to invalidate any dependent objects and immediately recompile the PL/SQL code for the type.

Increasing the Number of Elements in a Varray

You can increase the number of elements in a varray. The following example increases the number of elements in t_varray_address to 5:

```
ALTER TYPE t_varray_address
MODIFY LIMIT 5 CASCADE;
```

```
Type altered.
```

Using Varrays in Temporary Tables

You can use varrays in temporary tables, which are tables whose rows are temporary and are specific to a user session (temporary tables were covered in the section "Creating a Table" in Chapter 10). The following example creates a temporary table named cust_with_varray_temp_table that contains a varray named addresses of type t_varray_address:

```
CREATE GLOBAL TEMPORARY TABLE cust_with_varray_temp_table (
    id          INTEGER PRIMARY KEY,
    first_name  VARCHAR2(10),
    last_name   VARCHAR2(10),
    addresses   t_varray_address
);
```

Using a Different Tablespace for a Nested Table's Storage Table

By default, a nested table's storage table is created in the same tablespace as the parent table (a tablespace is an area used by the database to store objects such as tables—see the section "Creating a Table" in Chapter 10 for details).

In Oracle Database 10*g* and higher, you can specify a different tablespace for a nested table's storage table. The following example creates a table named `cust_with_nested_table` that contains a nested table named `addresses` of type `t_nested_table_address`; notice that the tablespace for the `nested_addresses2` storage table is the `users` tablespace:

```
CREATE TABLE cust_with_nested_table (
    id            INTEGER PRIMARY KEY,
    first_name VARCHAR2(10),
    last_name  VARCHAR2(10),
    addresses  t_nested_table_address
)
NESTED TABLE
    addresses
STORE AS
    nested_addresses2 TABLESPACE users;
```

You must have a tablespace named `users` in order for this example to work, and for this reason I've commented out the example in the `collection_schema3.sql` script. You can see all the tablespaces you have access to by performing the following query:

```
SELECT tablespace_name
FROM user_tablespaces;

TABLESPACE_NAME
---------------
SYSTEM
SYSAUX
UNDOTBS1
TEMP
USERS
EXAMPLE
```

If you want to run the previous CREATE TABLE statement, you can edit the example in the `collection_schema3.sql` script to reference one of your tablespaces and then copy the statement into SQL*Plus and run it.

ANSI Support for Nested Tables

The American National Standards Institute (ANSI) specification includes a number of operators that may be used with nested tables. You'll learn about these operators in the following sections.

Equal and Not-Equal Operators

The equal (=) and not-equal (<>) operators compare two nested tables, which are considered equal when they satisfy all the following conditions:

- The tables are the same type.

- The tables are the same cardinality, that is, they contain the same number of elements.

- All the elements of the table have the same value.

The following `equal_example()` procedure illustrates the use of the equal and not-equal operators:

```
CREATE PROCEDURE equal_example AS
   -- declare a type named t_nested_table
   TYPE t_nested_table IS TABLE OF VARCHAR2(10);

   -- create t_nested_table objects named v_customer_nested_table1,
   -- v_customer_nested_table2, and v_customer_nested_table3
   -- these objects are used to store the names of customers
   v_customer_nested_table1 t_nested_table :=
     t_nested_table('Fred', 'George', 'Susan');
   v_customer_nested_table2 t_nested_table :=
     t_nested_table('Fred', 'George', 'Susan');
   v_customer_nested_table3 t_nested_table :=
     t_nested_table('John', 'George', 'Susan');

   v_result BOOLEAN;
BEGIN
   -- use = operator to compare v_customer_nested_table1 with
   -- v_customer_nested_table2 (they contain the same names, so
   -- v_result is set to true)
   v_result := v_customer_nested_table1 = v_customer_nested_table2;
   IF v_result THEN
     DBMS_OUTPUT.PUT_LINE(
       'v_customer_nested_table1 equal to v_customer_nested_table2'
     );
   END IF;

   -- use <> operator to compare v_customer_nested_table1 with
   -- v_customer_nested_table3 (they are not equal because the first
   -- names, 'Fred' and 'John', are different and v_result is set
   -- to true)
   v_result := v_customer_nested_table1 <> v_customer_nested_table3;
   IF v_result THEN
     DBMS_OUTPUT.PUT_LINE(
       'v_customer_nested_table1 not equal to v_customer_nested_table3'
     );
   END IF;
END equal_example;
/
```

The following example calls equal_example():

```
CALL equal_example();
v_customer_nested_table1 equal to v_customer_nested_table2
v_customer_nested_table1 not equal to v_customer_nested_table3
```

IN and NOT IN Operators

The IN operator checks if the elements of one nested table appear in another nested table. Similarly, NOT IN checks if the elements of one nested table do not appear in another nested table. The following in_example() procedure illustrates the use of IN and NOT IN:

```
CREATE PROCEDURE in_example AS
   TYPE t_nested_table IS TABLE OF VARCHAR2(10);
```

```
    v_customer_nested_table1 t_nested_table :=
      t_nested_table('Fred', 'George', 'Susan');
    v_customer_nested_table2 t_nested_table :=
      t_nested_table('John', 'George', 'Susan');
    v_customer_nested_table3 t_nested_table :=
      t_nested_table('Fred', 'George', 'Susan');
    v_result BOOLEAN;
BEGIN
    -- use IN operator to check if elements of v_customer_nested_table3
    -- are in v_customer_nested_table1 (they are, so v_result is
    -- set to true)
    v_result := v_customer_nested_table3 IN
      (v_customer_nested_table1);
    IF v_result THEN
      DBMS_OUTPUT.PUT_LINE(
        'v_customer_nested_table3 in v_customer_nested_table1'
      );
    END IF;

    -- use NOT IN operator to check if the elements of
    -- v_customer_nested_table3 are not in v_customer_nested_table2
    -- (they are not, so v_result is set to true)
    v_result := v_customer_nested_table3 NOT IN
      (v_customer_nested_table2);
    IF v_result THEN
      DBMS_OUTPUT.PUT_LINE(
        'v_customer_nested_table3 not in v_customer_nested_table2'
      );
    END IF;
END in_example;
/
```

The following example calls in_example():

```
CALL in_example();
v_customer_nested_table3 in v_customer_nested_table1
v_customer_nested_table3 not in v_customer_nested_table2
```

SUBMULTISET Operator

The SUBMULTISET operator checks whether the elements of one nested table are a subset of another nested table. The following submultiset_example() procedure illustrates the use of SUBMULTISET:

```
CREATE PROCEDURE submultiset_example AS
    TYPE t_nested_table IS TABLE OF VARCHAR2(10);
    v_customer_nested_table1 t_nested_table :=
      t_nested_table('Fred', 'George', 'Susan');
    v_customer_nested_table2 t_nested_table :=
      t_nested_table('George', 'Fred', 'Susan', 'John', 'Steve');
    v_result BOOLEAN;
BEGIN
```

```
-- use SUBMULTISET operator to check if elements of
-- v_customer_nested_table1 are a subset of v_customer_nested_table2
-- (they are, so v_result is set to true)
v_result :=
  v_customer_nested_table1 SUBMULTISET OF v_customer_nested_table2;
IF v_result THEN
  DBMS_OUTPUT.PUT_LINE(
    'v_customer_nested_table1 subset of v_customer_nested_table2'
  );
END IF;
END submultiset_example;
/
```

The following example calls `submultiset_example()`:

```
CALL submultiset_example();
customer_nested_table1 subset of customer_nested_table2
```

MULTISET Operator

The `MULTISET` operator returns a nested table whose elements are set to certain combinations of elements from two supplied nested tables. There are three `MULTISET` operators:

- **MULTISET UNION** returns a nested table whose elements are set to the sum of the elements from two supplied nested tables.

- **MULTISET INTERSECT** returns a nested table whose elements are set to the elements that are common to two supplied nested tables.

- **MULTISET EXCEPT** returns a nested table whose elements are in the first supplied nested table but not in the second.

You may also use one of the following options with `MULTISET`:

- **ALL** indicates that all the applicable elements are in the returned nested table. `ALL` is the default. For example, `MULTISET UNION ALL` returns a nested table whose elements are set to the sum of elements from two supplied nested tables, and all elements, including duplicates, are in the returned nested table.

- **DISTINCT** indicates that only the non-duplicate (that is, distinct) elements are in the returned nested table. For example, `MULTISET UNION DISTINCT` returns a nested table whose elements are set to the sum of elements from two supplied nested tables, but duplicates are removed from the returned nested table.

The following `multiset_example()` procedure illustrates the use of `MULTISET`:

```
CREATE PROCEDURE multiset_example AS
  TYPE t_nested_table IS TABLE OF VARCHAR2(10);
  v_customer_nested_table1 t_nested_table :=
    t_nested_table('Fred', 'George', 'Susan');
  v_customer_nested_table2 t_nested_table :=
    t_nested_table('George', 'Steve', 'Rob');
  v_customer_nested_table3 t_nested_table;
```

```
   v_count INTEGER;
BEGIN
   -- use MULTISET UNION (returns a nested table whose elements
   -- are set to the sum of the two supplied nested tables)
   v_customer_nested_table3 :=
     v_customer_nested_table1 MULTISET UNION
        v_customer_nested_table2;
   DBMS_OUTPUT.PUT('UNION: ');
   FOR v_count IN 1..v_customer_nested_table3.COUNT LOOP
     DBMS_OUTPUT.PUT(v_customer_nested_table3(v_count) || ' ');
   END LOOP;
   DBMS_OUTPUT.PUT_LINE(' ');

   -- use MULTISET UNION DISTINCT (DISTINCT indicates that only
   -- the non-duplicate elements of the two supplied nested tables
   -- are set in the returned nested table)
   v_customer_nested_table3 :=
     v_customer_nested_table1 MULTISET UNION DISTINCT
        v_customer_nested_table2;
   DBMS_OUTPUT.PUT('UNION DISTINCT: ');
   FOR v_count IN 1..v_customer_nested_table3.COUNT LOOP
     DBMS_OUTPUT.PUT(v_customer_nested_table3(v_count) || ' ');
   END LOOP;
   DBMS_OUTPUT.PUT_LINE(' ');

   -- use MULTISET INTERSECT (returns a nested table whose elements
   -- are set to the elements that are common to the two supplied
   -- nested tables)
   v_customer_nested_table3 :=
     v_customer_nested_table1 MULTISET INTERSECT
        v_customer_nested_table2;
   DBMS_OUTPUT.PUT('INTERSECT: ');
   FOR v_count IN 1..v_customer_nested_table3.COUNT LOOP
     DBMS_OUTPUT.PUT(v_customer_nested_table3(v_count) || ' ');
   END LOOP;
   DBMS_OUTPUT.PUT_LINE(' ');

   -- use MULTISET EXCEPT (returns a nested table whose
   -- elements are in the first nested table but not in
   -- the second)
   v_customer_nested_table3 :=
     v_customer_nested_table1 MULTISET EXCEPT
        v_customer_nested_table2;
   DBMS_OUTPUT.PUT_LINE('EXCEPT: ');
   FOR v_count IN 1..v_customer_nested_table3.COUNT LOOP
     DBMS_OUTPUT.PUT(v_customer_nested_table3(v_count) || ' ');
   END LOOP;
END multiset_example;
/
```

The following example calls `multiset_example()`:

```
CALL multiset_example();
UNION: Fred George Susan George Steve Rob
UNION DISTINCT: Fred George Susan Steve Rob
INTERSECT: George
EXCEPT:
```

CARDINALITY() Function

The `CARDINALITY()` function returns the number of elements in a collection. The following `cardinality_example()` procedure illustrates the use of `CARDINALITY()`:

```
CREATE PROCEDURE cardinality_example AS
  TYPE t_nested_table IS TABLE OF VARCHAR2(10);
  v_customer_nested_table1 t_nested_table :=
    t_nested_table('Fred', 'George', 'Susan');
  v_cardinality INTEGER;
BEGIN
  -- call CARDINALITY() to get the number of elements in
  -- v_customer_nested_table1
  v_cardinality := CARDINALITY(v_customer_nested_table1);
  DBMS_OUTPUT.PUT_LINE('v_cardinality = ' || v_cardinality);
END cardinality_example;
/
```

The following example calls `cardinality_example()`:

```
CALL cardinality_example();
v_cardinality = 3
```

MEMBER OF Operator

The `MEMBER OF` operator checks whether an element is in a nested table. The following `member_of_example()` procedure illustrates the use of `MEMBER OF`:

```
CREATE PROCEDURE member_of_example AS
  TYPE t_nested_table IS TABLE OF VARCHAR2(10);
  v_customer_nested_table1 t_nested_table :=
    t_nested_table('Fred', 'George', 'Susan');
  v_result BOOLEAN;
BEGIN
  -- use MEMBER OF to check if 'George' is in
  -- v_customer_nested_table1 (he is, so v_result is set
  -- to true)
  v_result := 'George' MEMBER OF v_customer_nested_table1;
  IF v_result THEN
    DBMS_OUTPUT.PUT_LINE('''George'' is a member');
  END IF;
END member_of_example;
/
```

The following example calls `member_of_example()`:

```
CALL member_of_example();
'George' is a member
```

SET() Function

The `SET()` function first converts a nested table into a set, then removes duplicate elements from the set, and finally returns the set as a nested table. The following `set_example()` procedure illustrates the use of `SET()`:

```
CREATE PROCEDURE set_example AS
  TYPE t_nested_table IS TABLE OF VARCHAR2(10);
  v_customer_nested_table1 t_nested_table :=
    t_nested_table('Fred', 'George', 'Susan', 'George');
  v_customer_nested_table2 t_nested_table;
  v_count INTEGER;
BEGIN
  -- call SET() to convert a nested table into a set,
  -- remove duplicate elements from the set, and get the set
  -- as a nested table
  v_customer_nested_table2 := SET(v_customer_nested_table1);
  DBMS_OUTPUT.PUT('v_customer_nested_table2: ');
  FOR v_count IN 1..v_customer_nested_table2.COUNT LOOP
    DBMS_OUTPUT.PUT(v_customer_nested_table2(v_count) || ' ');
  END LOOP;
  DBMS_OUTPUT.PUT_LINE(' ');
END set_example;
/
```

The following example calls `set_example()`:

```
CALL set_example();
v_customer_nested_table2: Fred George Susan
```

IS A SET Operator

The `IS A SET` operator checks if the elements in a nested table are distinct. The following `is_a_set_example()` procedure illustrates the use of `IS A SET`:

```
CREATE PROCEDURE is_a_set_example AS
  TYPE t_nested_table IS TABLE OF VARCHAR2(10);
  v_customer_nested_table1 t_nested_table :=
    t_nested_table('Fred', 'George', 'Susan', 'George');
  v_result BOOLEAN;
BEGIN
  -- use IS A SET operator to check if the elements in
  -- v_customer_nested_table1 are distinct (they are not, so
  -- v_result is set to false)
  v_result := v_customer_nested_table1 IS A SET;
  IF v_result THEN
    DBMS_OUTPUT.PUT_LINE('Elements are all unique');
  ELSE
    DBMS_OUTPUT.PUT_LINE('Elements contain duplicates');
  END IF;
```

```
END is_a_set_example;
/
```

The following example calls `is_a_set_example()`:

```
CALL is_a_set_example();
Elements contain duplicates
```

IS EMPTY Operator

The IS EMPTY operator checks if a nested table doesn't contain elements. The following is_empty_example() procedure illustrates the use of IS EMPTY:

```
CREATE PROCEDURE is_empty_example AS
  TYPE t_nested_table IS TABLE OF VARCHAR2(10);
  v_customer_nested_table1 t_nested_table :=
    t_nested_table('Fred', 'George', 'Susan');
  v_result BOOLEAN;
BEGIN
  -- use IS EMPTY operator to check if
  -- v_customer_nested_table1 is empty (it is not, so
  -- v_result is set to false)
  v_result := v_customer_nested_table1 IS EMPTY;
  IF v_result THEN
    DBMS_OUTPUT.PUT_LINE('Nested table is empty');
  ELSE
    DBMS_OUTPUT.PUT_LINE('Nested table contains elements');
  END IF;
END is_empty_example;
/
```

The following example calls `is_empty_example()`:

```
CALL is_empty_example();
Nested table contains elements
```

COLLECT() Function

The COLLECT() function returns a nested table from a set of elements. The following query illustrates the use of COLLECT():

```
SELECT COLLECT(first_name)
FROM customers_with_varray;

COLLECT(FIRST_NAME)
---------------------------------------------
SYSTPfrFhAg+WRJGwW7ma9zy1KA==('Steve', 'John')
```

You can use CAST() to convert the elements returned by COLLECT() to a specific type, as shown in the following query:

```
SELECT CAST(COLLECT(first_name) AS t_table)
FROM customers_with_varray;

CAST(COLLECT(FIRST_NAME)AST_TABLE)
----------------------------------
T_TABLE('Steve', 'John')
```

For your reference, the `t_table` type used in the previous example is created by the following statement in the `collection_schema3.sql` script:

```
CREATE TYPE t_table AS TABLE OF VARCHAR2(10);
/
```

POWERMULTISET() Function

The `POWERMULTISET()` function returns all combinations of elements in a given nested table, as shown in the following query:

```
SELECT *
FROM TABLE(
  POWERMULTISET(t_table('This', 'is', 'a', 'test'))
);
```

```
COLUMN_VALUE
---------------------------------
T_TABLE('This')
T_TABLE('is')
T_TABLE('This', 'is')
T_TABLE('a')
T_TABLE('This', 'a')
T_TABLE('is', 'a')
T_TABLE('This', 'is', 'a')
T_TABLE('test')
T_TABLE('This', 'test')
T_TABLE('is', 'test')
T_TABLE('This', 'is', 'test')
T_TABLE('a', 'test')
T_TABLE('This', 'a', 'test')
T_TABLE('is', 'a', 'test')
T_TABLE('This', 'is', 'a', 'test')
```

POWERMULTISET_BY_CARDINALITY() Function

The `POWERMULTISET_BY_CARDINALITY()` function returns the combinations of elements in a given nested table that have a specified number of elements (or "cardinality"). The following query illustrates the use of `POWERMULTISET_BY_CARDINALITY()`, specifying a cardinality of 3:

```
SELECT *
FROM TABLE(
  POWERMULTISET_BY_CARDINALITY(
    t_table('This', 'is', 'a', 'test'), 3
  )
);
```

```
COLUMN_VALUE
---------------------------
T_TABLE('This', 'is', 'a')
T_TABLE('This', 'is', 'test')
T_TABLE('This', 'a', 'test')
T_TABLE('is', 'a', 'test')
```

Summary

In this chapter, you have learned the following:

- Collections allow you to store sets of elements.

- There are three types of collections: varrays, nested tables, and associative arrays.

- A varray is similar to an array in Java; you can use a varray to store an ordered set of elements with each element having an index associated with it. The elements in a varray are of the same type, and a varray has one dimension. A varray has a maximum size that you set when creating it, but you can change the size later.

- A nested table is a table that is embedded within another table, and you can insert, update, and delete individual elements in a nested table. Because you can modify individual elements in a nested table, they are more flexible than a varray—a varray can be modified only as a whole. A nested table doesn't have a maximum size, and you can store an arbitrary number of elements in a nested table.

- An associative array is a set of key and value pairs. You can get the value from the array using the key (which may be a string) or an integer that specifies the position of the value in the array. An associative array is similar to a hash table in programming languages such as Java.

- A collection may itself contain embedded collections. Such a collection is known as a multilevel collection.

In the next chapter, you'll learn about large objects.

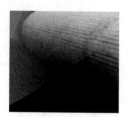

CHAPTER
14

Large Objects

n this chapter, you will do the following:

- Learn about large objects (LOBs)

- See files whose content will be used to populate example LOBs

- Examine the differences between the different types of LOBs

- Create tables containing LOBs

- Use LOBs in SQL and PL/SQL

- Examine the LONG and LONG RAW types

- See the Oracle Database 10*g* and 11*g* enhancements to LOBs

Introducing Large Objects (LOBs)

Today's websites demand more than just the storage and retrieval of text and numbers: they also require multimedia. Consequently, databases are now being called upon to store items like music and video. Prior to the release of Oracle Database 8, you had to store large blocks of character data using the LONG database type, and large blocks of binary data had to be stored using either the LONG RAW type or the shorter RAW type.

With the release Oracle Database 8, a new class of database types known as *large objects*, or LOBs for short, was introduced. LOBs may be used to store binary data, character data, and references to files. The binary data can contain images, music, video, documents, executables, and so on. LOBs can store up to 128 terabytes of data, depending on the database configuration.

The Example Files

You'll see the use of the following two files in this chapter:

- **textContent.txt**   A text file

- **binaryContent.doc**   A Microsoft Word file

NOTE
These files are contained in the sample_files *directory, which is created when you extract the Zip file for this book. If you want to follow along with the examples, you should copy the* sample_files *directory to the C partition on your database server. If you're using Linux or Unix, you can copy the directory to one of your partitions.*

The file `textContent.txt` contains an extract from Shakespeare's play *Macbeth*. The following text is the speech made by Macbeth shortly before he is killed:

To-morrow, and to-morrow, and to-morrow,
Creeps in this petty pace from day to day,
To the last syllable of recorded time;
And all our yesterdays have lighted fools
The way to a dusty death. Out, out, brief candle!
Life's but a walking shadow; a poor player,
That struts and frets his hour upon the stage,
And then is heard no more: it is a tale
Told by an idiot, full of sound and fury,
Signifying nothing.

The `binaryContent.doc` file is a Word document that contains the same text as `textContent.txt`. (A Word document is a binary file.) Although a Word document is used in the examples, you can use any binary file, for example, MP3, DivX, JPEG, MPEG, PDF, or EXE. I have tested the examples with all these types of files.

Large Object Types

There are four LOB types:

- **CLOB** The character LOB type, which is used to store character data.

- **NCLOB** The National Character Set LOB type, which is used to store multiple byte character data (typically used for non-English characters). You can learn all about non-English character sets in the *Oracle Database Globalization Support Guide* published by Oracle Corporation.

- **BLOB** The binary LOB type, which is used to store binary data.

- **BFILE** The binary FILE type, which is used to store a pointer to a file. The file can be on a hard disk, CD, DVD, Blu-Ray disk, HD-DVD, or any other device that is accessible through the database server's file system. The file itself is never stored in the database, only a pointer to the file.

Prior to Oracle Database 8 your only choice for storing large amounts of data was to use the `LONG` and `LONG RAW` types (you could also use the `RAW` type for storing binary data of less than 4 kilobytes in size). The LOB types have three advantages over these older types:

- A LOB can store up to 128 terabytes of data. This is far more data than you can store in a `LONG` and `LONG RAW` column, which may only store up to 2 gigabytes of data.

- A table can have multiple LOB columns, but a table can only have one `LONG` or `LONG RAW` column.

- LOB data can be accessed in random order; `LONG` and `LONG RAW` data can be accessed only in sequential order.

A LOB consists of two parts:

■ **The LOB locator** A pointer that specifies the location of the LOB data

■ **The LOB data** The actual character or byte data stored in the LOB

Depending on the amount of data stored in a CLOB, NCLOB or BLOB column, the data will be stored either inside or outside of the table. If the data is less than 4 kilobytes, the data is stored in the same table; otherwise, the data is stored outside the table. With a BFILE column, only the locator is stored in the table—and the locator points to an external file stored in the file system.

Creating Tables Containing Large Objects

You'll see the use of the following three tables in this section:

■ The clob_content table, which contains a CLOB column named clob_column

■ The blob_content table, which contains a BLOB column named blob_column

■ The bfile_content table, which contains a BFILE column named bfile_column

I've provided an SQL*Plus script named lob_schema.sql in the SQL directory. This script may be run using Oracle Database 8 and higher. The script creates a user named lob_user with a password of lob_password, and it creates the tables and PL/SQL code used in the first part of this chapter. After the script completes, you will be logged in as lob_user.

The three tables are created using the following statements in the script:

```
CREATE TABLE clob_content (
  id            INTEGER PRIMARY KEY,
  clob_column CLOB NOT NULL
);

CREATE TABLE blob_content (
  id            INTEGER PRIMARY KEY,
  blob_column BLOB NOT NULL
);

CREATE TABLE bfile_content (
  id             INTEGER PRIMARY KEY,
  bfile_column BFILE NOT NULL
);
```

Using Large Objects in SQL

In this section, you'll learn how to use SQL to manipulate large objects. You'll start by examining CLOB and BLOB objects and then move on to BFILE objects.

Using CLOBs and BLOBs

The following sections show how to populate CLOB and BLOB objects with data, retrieve the data, and then modify the data.

Populating CLOBs and BLOBs with Data

The following INSERT statements add two rows to the clob_content table; notice the use of the TO_CLOB() function to convert the text to a CLOB:

```
INSERT INTO clob_content (
  id, clob_column
) VALUES (
  1, TO_CLOB('Creeps in this petty pace')
);

INSERT INTO clob_content (
  id, clob_column
) VALUES (
  2, TO_CLOB(' from day to day')
);
```

The following INSERT statements add two rows to the blob_content table; notice the use of the TO_BLOB() function to convert the numbers to a BLOB (the first statement contains a binary number, and the second contains a hexadecimal number):

```
INSERT INTO blob_content (
  id, blob_column
) VALUES (
  1, TO_BLOB('1001110101011111')
);

INSERT INTO blob_content (
  id, blob_column
) VALUES (
  2, TO_BLOB('A0FFB71CF90DE')
);
```

Retrieving Data from CLOBs

The following query retrieves the rows from the clob_content table:

```
SELECT *
FROM clob_content;

        ID
----------
CLOB_COLUMN
------------------------
         1
Creeps in this petty pace

         2
 from day to day
```

The next query attempts to retrieve the row from the blob_content table and fails:

```
SELECT *
FROM blob_content;
SP2-0678: Column or attribute type can not be displayed by SQL*Plus
```

This example fails because SQL*Plus cannot display the binary data in a BLOB. You'll learn how to retrieve the data from a BLOB later in the section "Using Large Objects in PL/SQL."

You can, however, get the non-BLOB columns from the table:

```
SELECT id
FROM blob_content;

        ID
----------
         1
         2
```

Modifying the Data in CLOBs and BLOBs

You should feel free to run the UPDATE and INSERT statements shown in this section. The following UPDATE statements show how you modify the contents of a CLOB and a BLOB:

```
UPDATE clob_content
SET clob_column = TO_CLOB('What light through yonder window breaks')
WHERE id = 1;

UPDATE blob_content
SET blob_column = TO_BLOB('1110011010101011111')
WHERE id = 1;
```

You can also initialize the LOB locator, but not store actual data in the LOB. You do this using the EMPTY_CLOB() function to store an empty CLOB, and EMPTY_BLOB() to store an empty BLOB:

```
INSERT INTO clob_content(
  id, clob_column
) VALUES (
  3, EMPTY_CLOB()
);

INSERT INTO blob_content(
  id, blob_column
) VALUES (
  3, EMPTY_BLOB()
);
```

These statements initialize the LOB locator, but set the LOB data to empty.

You can also use EMPTY_CLOB() and EMPTY_BLOB() in UPDATE statements when you want to empty out the LOB data. For example:

```
UPDATE clob_content
SET clob_column = EMPTY_CLOB()
WHERE id = 1;

UPDATE blob_content
SET blob_column = EMPTY_BLOB()
WHERE id = 1;
```

If you ran any of the INSERT and UPDATE statements shown in this section, go ahead and roll back the changes so that your output matches mine in the rest of this chapter:

```
ROLLBACK;
```

Using BFILEs

A BFILE stores a pointer to a file that is accessible through the database server's file system. The important point to remember is that these files are stored outside of the database. A BFILE can point to files located on any media: a hard disk, CD, DVD, Blu-Ray, HD-DVD, and so on.

NOTE
A BFILE *contains a pointer to an external file. The actual file itself is never stored in the database, only a pointer to that file is stored. The file must be accessible through the database server's file system.*

Creating a Directory Object

Before you can store a pointer to a file in a BFILE, you must first create a directory object in the database. The directory object stores the directory in the file system where the files are located. You create a directory object using the CREATE DIRECTORY statement, and to run this statement you must have the CREATE ANY DIRECTORY database privilege.

The following example (contained in lob_schema.sql) creates a directory object named SAMPLE_FILES_DIR for the file system directory C:\sample_files:

```
CREATE DIRECTORY SAMPLE_FILES_DIR AS 'C:\sample_files';
```

NOTE
Windows uses the backslash character (\) in directories, while Linux and Unix use the forward slash character (/). Also, if your sample_files *directory is not stored in the C partition, then you need to specify the appropriate path in the previous example.*

When you create a directory object you must ensure that

- The actual directory exists in the file system.

- The user account in the operating system that was used to install the Oracle software has read permission on the directory and on any files that are to be pointed to by a BFILE in the database.

If you're using Windows, you shouldn't need to worry about the second point. The Oracle database software should have been installed using a user account that has administrator privileges, and such a user account has read permission on everything in the file system. If you're using Linux or Unix, you'll need to grant read access to the appropriate Oracle user account that owns the database (you do this using the chmod command).

Populating a BFILE Column with a Pointer to a File

Because a BFILE is just a pointer to an external file, populating a BFILE column is very simple. All you have to do is to use the Oracle database's BFILENAME() function to populate a BFILE with a pointer to your external file. The BFILENAME() function accepts two parameters: the directory object's name and the name of the file.

For example, the following INSERT adds a row to the bfile_content table; notice that the BFILENAME() function is used to populate bfile_column with a pointer to the textContent.txt file:

```
INSERT INTO bfile_content (
    id, bfile_column
) VALUES (
    1, BFILENAME('SAMPLE_FILES_DIR', 'textContent.txt')
);
```

The next INSERT adds a row to the bfile_content table; notice that the BFILENAME() function is used to populate bfile_column with a pointer to the binaryContent.doc file:

```
INSERT INTO bfile_content (
    id, bfile_column
) VALUES (
    2, BFILENAME('SAMPLE_FILES_DIR', 'binaryContent.doc')
);
```

The following query attempts to retrieve the rows from bfile_content and fails because SQL*Plus cannot display the content in a BFILE:

```
SELECT *
FROM bfile_content;
SP2-0678: Column or attribute type can not be displayed by SQL*Plus
```

You may use PL/SQL to access the content in a BFILE or a BLOB, and you'll learn how to do that next.

Using Large Objects in PL/SQL

In this section, you'll learn how to use LOBs in PL/SQL. You'll start off by examining the methods in the DBMS_LOB package, which comes with the database. Later, you'll see plenty of PL/SQL programs that show how to use the DBMS_LOB methods to read data in a LOB, copy data from one LOB to another, search data in a LOB, copy data from a file to a LOB, copy data from a LOB to a file, and much more.

Table 14-1 summarizes the most commonly used methods in the DBMS_LOB package.

In the following sections, you'll see the details of some of the methods shown in the previous table. You can see all the DBMS_LOB methods in the *Oracle Database PL/SQL Packages and Types Reference* manual published by Oracle Corporation.

Method	Description
APPEND(*dest_lob*, src_lob)	Adds the data read from *src_lob* to the end of *dest_lob*.
CLOSE(*lob*)	Closes a previously opened LOB.
COMPARE(*lob1*, *lob2*, *amount*, *offset1*, *offset2*)	Compares the data stored in *lob1* and *lob2*, starting at *offset1* in *lob1* and *offset2* in *lob2*. Offsets always start at 1, which is the position of the first character or byte in the data. The data in the LOBs are compared over a maximum number of characters or bytes (the maximum is specified in *amount*).
CONVERTTOBLOB(*dest_blob*, *src_clob*, *amount*, *dest_offset*, *src_offset*, *blob_csid*, *lang_context*, *warning*)	Converts the character data read from *src_clob* into binary data written to *dest_blob*. The read begins at *src_offset* in *src_clob*, and the write begins at *dest_offset* in *dest_blob*. *blob_csid* is the desired character set for the converted data written to *dest_blob*. You should typically use DBMS_LOB.DEFAULT_CSID, which is the default character set for the database. *lang_context* is the language context to use when converting the characters read from *src_clob*. You should typically use DBMS_LOB.DEFAULT_LANG_CTX, which is the default language context for the database. *warning* is set to DBMS_LOB.WARN_INCONVERTIBLE_CHAR if there was a character that could not be converted.
CONVERTTOCLOB(*dest_clob*, *src_blob*, *amount*, *dest_offset*, *src_offset*, *blob_csid*, *lang_context*, *warning*)	Converts the binary data read from *src_blob* into character data written to *dest_clob*. *blob_csid* is the character set for the data read from *dest_blob*. You should typically use DBMS_LOB.DEFAULT_CSID. *lang_context* is the language context to use when writing the converted characters to *dest_clob*. You should typically use DBMS_LOB.DEFAULT_LANG_CTX. *warning* is set to DBMS_LOB.WARN_INCONVERTIBLE_CHAR if there was a character that could not be converted.
COPY(*dest_lob*, *src_lob*, *amount*, *dest_offset*, *src_offset*)	Copies data from *src_lob* to *dest_lob*, starting at the offsets for a total amount of characters or bytes.
CREATETEMPORARY(*lob*, *cache*, duration)	Creates a temporary LOB in the user's default temporary tablespace.
ERASE(*lob*, *amount*, *offset*)	Erases data from a LOB, starting at the offset for a total amount of characters or bytes.
FILECLOSE(*bfile*)	Closes *bfile*. You should use the newer CLOSE() method instead of FILECLOSE().
FILECLOSEALL()	Closes all previously opened BFILEs.
FILEEXISTS(*bfile*)	Checks if the external file pointed to by *bfile* actually exists.
FILEGETNAME(*bfile*, *directory*, *filename*)	Returns the directory and filename of the external file pointed to by *bfile*.
FILEISOPEN(*bfile*)	Checks if *bfile* is currently open. You should use the newer ISOPEN() method instead of FILEISOPEN().
FILEOPEN(*bfile*, *open_mode*)	Opens *bfile* in the indicated mode, which can be set only to DBMS_LOB.FILE_READONLY, which indicates the file may only be read from (and never written to). You should use the newer OPEN() method instead of FILEOPEN().

TABLE 14-1   *DBMS_LOB Methods*

Method	Description
FREETEMPORARY(*lob*)	Frees a temporary LOB.
GETCHUNKSIZE(*lob*)	Returns the chunk size used when reading and writing the data stored in the LOB. A chunk is a unit of data.
GET_STORAGE_LIMIT()	Returns the maximum allowable size for a LOB.
GETLENGTH(*lob*)	Gets the length of the data stored in the LOB.
INSTR(*lob, pattern, offset, n*)	Returns the starting position of characters or bytes that match the *nth* occurrence of a pattern in the LOB data. The data is read from the LOB starting at the offset.
ISOPEN(*lob*)	Checks if the LOB was already opened.
ISTEMPORARY(*lob*)	Checks if the LOB is a temporary LOB.
LOADFROMFILE(*dest_lob, src_bfile, amount, dest_offset, src_offset*)	Loads the data retrieved via *src_bfile* to *dest_lob*, starting at the offsets for a total amount of characters or bytes; *src_bfile* is a BFILE that points to an external file. LOADFROMFILE() is old, and you should use the higher-performance LOADBLOBFROMFILE() or LOADCLOBFROMFILE() methods.
LOADBLOBFROMFILE(*dest_blob, src_bfile, amount, dest_offset, src_offset*)	Loads the data retrieved via *src_bfile* to *dest_blob*, starting at the offsets for a total amount of bytes; *src_bfile* is a BFILE that points to an external file. LOADBLOBFROMFILE() offers improved performance over LOADFROMFILE() when using a BLOB.
LOADCLOBFROMFILE(*dest_clob, src_bfile, amount, dest_offset, src_offset, src_csid, lang_context, warning*)	Loads the data retrieved via *src_bfile* to *dest_clob*, starting at the offsets for a total amount of characters; *src_bfile* is a BFILE that points to an external file. LOADCLOBFROMFILE() offers improved performance over LOADFROMFILE() when using a CLOB/NCLOB.
LOBMAXSIZE	Returns the maximum size for a LOB in bytes (currently 2^{64}).
OPEN(*lob, open_mode*)	Opens the LOB in the indicated mode, which may be set to ■ DBMS_LOB.FILE_READONLY, which indicates the LOB may only be read from ■ DBMS_LOB.FILE_READWRITE, which indicates the LOB may read from and written to
READ(*lob, amount, offset, buffer*)	Reads the data from the LOB and stores them in the *buffer* variable, starting at the offset in the LOB for a total amount of characters or bytes.
SUBSTR(*lob, amount, offset*)	Returns part of the LOB data, starting at the offset in the LOB for a total amount of characters or bytes.
TRIM(*lob, newlen*)	Trims the LOB data to the specified shorter length.
WRITE(*lob, amount, offset, buffer*)	Writes the data from the *buffer* variable to the LOB, starting at the offset in the LOB for a total amount of characters or bytes.
WRITEAPPEND(*lob, amount, buffer*)	Writes the data from the *buffer* variable to the end of the LOB, starting at the offset in the LOB for a total amount of characters or bytes.

TABLE 14-1   *DBMS_LOB Methods* (continued)

APPEND()

APPEND() adds the data in a source LOB to the end of a destination LOB. There are two versions of APPEND():

```
DBMS_LOB.APPEND(
    dest_lob IN OUT NOCOPY BLOB,
    src_lob  IN             BLOB
);

DBMS_LOB.APPEND(
    dest_lob IN OUT NOCOPY CLOB/NCLOB CHARACTER SET ANY_CS,
    src_lob  IN             CLOB/NCLOB CHARACTER SET dest_lob%CHARSET
);
```

where

- *dest_lob* is the destination LOB to which the data is appended.

- *src_lob* is the source LOB from which the data is read.

- CHARACTER SET ANY_CS means the data in *dest_lob* can be any character set.

- CHARACTER SET *dest_lob*%CHARSET is the character set of dest_lob.

The following table shows the exception thrown by APPEND().

Exception	Thrown When
VALUE_ERROR	Either *dest_lob* or *src_lob* is null.

CLOSE()

CLOSE() closes a previously opened LOB. There are three versions of CLOSE():

```
DBMS_LOB.CLOSE(
    lob IN OUT NOCOPY BLOB
);

DBMS_LOB.CLOSE(
    lob IN OUT NOCOPY CLOB/NCLOB CHARACTER SET ANY_CS
);

DBMS_LOB.CLOSE(
    lob IN OUT NOCOPY BFILE
);
```

where lob is the LOB to be closed.

COMPARE()

COMPARE() compares the data stored in two LOBs, starting at the offsets over a total amount of characters or bytes. There are three versions of COMPARE():

```
DBMS_LOB.COMPARE(
    lob1    IN BLOB,
    lob2    IN BLOB,
    amount  IN INTEGER := 4294967295,
    offset1 IN INTEGER := 1,
    offset2 IN INTEGER := 1
) RETURN INTEGER;

DBMS_LOB.COMPARE(
    lob1    IN CLOB/NCLOB  CHARACTER SET ANY_CS,
    lob2    IN CLOB/NCLOB  CHARACTER SET lob_1%CHARSET,
    amount  IN INTEGER := 4294967295,
    offset1 IN INTEGER := 1,
    offset2 IN INTEGER := 1
) RETURN INTEGER;

DBMS_LOB.COMPARE(
    lob1    IN BFILE,
    lob2    IN BFILE,
    amount  IN INTEGER,
    offset1 IN INTEGER := 1,
    offset2 IN INTEGER := 1
) RETURN INTEGER;
```

where

- *lob1* and *lob2* are the LOBs to compare.

- *amount* is the maximum number of characters to read from a CLOB/NCLOB, or the maximum number of bytes to read from a BLOB/BFILE.

- *offset1* and *offset2* are the offsets in characters or bytes in *lob1* and *lob2* to start the comparison (the offsets start at 1).

COMPARE() returns

- 0 if the LOBs are identical.

- 1 if the LOBs aren't identical.

- Null if

  - *amount* < 1

  - *amount* > LOBMAXSIZE (Note: LOBMAXSIZE is the maximum size of the LOB)

  - *offset1* or *offset2* < 1

  - *offset1* or *offset2* > LOBMAXSIZE

The following table shows the exceptions thrown by COMPARE().

Exception	Thrown When
UNOPENED_FILE	The file hasn't been opened yet.
NOEXIST_DIRECTORY	The directory doesn't exist.
NOPRIV_DIRECTORY	You don't have privileges to access the directory.
INVALID_DIRECTORY	The directory is invalid.
INVALID_OPERATION	The file exists, but you don't have privileges to access the file.

COPY()

COPY() copies data from a source LOB to a destination LOB, starting at the offsets for a total amount of characters or bytes. There are two versions of COPY():

```
DBMS_LOB.COPY(
    dest_lob    IN OUT NOCOPY BLOB,
    src_lob     IN            BLOB,
    amount      IN            INTEGER,
    dest_offset IN            INTEGER := 1,
    src_offset  IN            INTEGER := 1
);

DBMS_LOB.COPY(
    dest_lob    IN OUT NOCOPY CLOB/NCLOB CHARACTER SET ANY_CS,
    src_lob     IN            CLOB/NCLOB CHARACTER SET dest_lob%CHARSET,
    amount      IN            INTEGER,
    dest_offset IN            INTEGER := 1,
    src_offset  IN            INTEGER := 1
);
```

where

- *dest_lob* and *src_lob* are the LOBs to write to and read from, respectively.

- *amount* is the maximum number of characters to read from a CLOB/NCLOB, or the maximum number of bytes to read from a BLOB/BFILE.

- *dest_offset* and *src_offset* are the offsets in characters or bytes in *dest_lob* and *src_lob* to start the copy (the offsets start at 1).

The following table shows the exceptions thrown by COPY().

Exception	Thrown When
VALUE_ERROR	Any of the parameters are null.
INVALID_ARGVAL	Either: ■ *src_offset* < 1 ■ *dest_offset* < 1 ■ *src_offset* > LOBMAXSIZE ■ *dest_offset* > LOBMAXSIZE ■ *amount* < 1 ■ *amount* > LOBMAXSIZE

CREATETEMPORARY()

CREATETEMPORARY() creates a temporary LOB in the user's default temporary tablespace. There are two versions of CREATETEMPORARY():

```
DBMS_LOB.CREATETEMPORARY(
    lob      IN OUT NOCOPY BLOB,
    cache    IN            BOOLEAN,
    duration IN            PLS_INTEGER := 10
);

DBMS_LOB.CREATETEMPORARY (
    lob      IN OUT NOCOPY CLOB/NCLOB CHARACTER SET ANY_CS,
    cache    IN            BOOLEAN,
    duration IN            PLS_INTEGER := 10
);
```

where

- *lob* is the temporary LOB to create.

- *cache* indicates whether the LOB should be read into the buffer cache (true for yes, false for no).

- *duration* is a hint (can be set to SESSION, TRANSACTION, or CALL) as to whether the temporary LOB is removed at the end of the session, transaction, or call (the default is SESSION).

The following table shows the exception thrown by CREATETEMPORARY().

Exception	Thrown When
VALUE_ERROR	The *lob* parameter is null.

ERASE()

ERASE() removes data from a LOB, starting at the offset for a total amount of characters or bytes. There are two versions of ERASE():

```
DBMS_LOB.ERASE(
    lob    IN OUT NOCOPY BLOB,
    amount IN OUT NOCOPY INTEGER,
    offset IN            INTEGER := 1
);

DBMS_LOB.ERASE(
    lob    IN OUT NOCOPY CLOB/NCLOB CHARACTER SET ANY_CS,
    amount IN OUT NOCOPY INTEGER,
    offset IN            INTEGER := 1
);
```

where

- *lob* is the LOB to erase.

- *amount* is the maximum number of characters to read from a CLOB/NCLOB, or the number of bytes to read from a BLOB.

- *offset* is the offset in characters or bytes in *lob* to start the erasure (the offset starts at 1).

The following table shows the exceptions thrown by ERASE().

Exception	Thrown When
VALUE_ERROR	Any of the parameters are null.
INVALID_ARGVAL	Either: ■ *amount* < 1 ■ *amount* > LOBMAXSIZE ■ *offset* < 1 ■ *offset* > LOBMAXSIZE

FILECLOSE()

FILECLOSE() closes a BFILE. You should use the newer CLOSE() procedure, as Oracle Corporation does not plan to extend the older FILECLOSE() procedure. I'm only including coverage of FILECLOSE() here so you can understand older programs.

```
DBMS_LOB.FILECLOSE(
   bfile IN OUT NOCOPY BFILE
);
```

where bfile is the BFILE to close.
The following table shows the exceptions thrown by FILECLOSE().

Exception	Thrown When
VALUE_ERROR	The *bfile* parameter is null.
UNOPENED_FILE	The file hasn't been opened yet.
NOEXIST_DIRECTORY	The directory doesn't exist.
NOPRIV_DIRECTORY	You don't have privileges to access the directory.
INVALID_DIRECTORY	The directory is invalid.
INVALID_OPERATION	The file exists, but you don't have privileges to access the file.

FILECLOSEALL()

FILECLOSEALL() closes all BFILE objects.

```
DBMS_LOB.FILECLOSEALL;
```

The following table shows the exception thrown by FILECLOSEALL().

Exception	Thrown When
UNOPENED_FILE	No files have been opened in the session.

FILEEXISTS()

FILEEXISTS() checks if a file exists.

```
DBMS_LOB.FILEEXISTS(
    bfile IN BFILE
) RETURN INTEGER;
```

where bfile is a BFILE that points to an external file.
FILEEXISTS() returns

- 0 if the file doesn't exist.

- 1 if the file exists.

The following table shows the exceptions thrown by FILEEXISTS().

Exception	Thrown When
VALUE_ERROR	The *bfile* parameter is null.
NOEXIST_DIRECTORY	The directory doesn't exist.
NOPRIV_DIRECTORY	You don't have privileges to access the directory.
INVALID_DIRECTORY	The directory is invalid.

FILEGETNAME()

FILEGETNAME() returns the directory and filename from a BFILE.

```
DBMS_LOB.FILEGETNAME(
    bfile      IN  BFILE,
    directory OUT VARCHAR2,
    filename  OUT VARCHAR2
);
```

where

- *bfile* is the pointer to the file.

- *directory* is the directory where the file is stored.

- *filename* is the name of the file.

The following table shows the exceptions thrown by FILEGETNAME().

Exception	Thrown When
VALUE_ERROR	Any of the input parameters are null or invalid.
INVALID_ARGVAL	The *directory* or *filename* parameters are null.

FILEISOPEN()

FILEISOPEN() checks if a file is open. You should use the newer ISOPEN() procedure to check if a file is open in your own programs, as Oracle Corporation does not plan to extend the older FILEISOPEN() method. I'm including coverage of FILEISOPEN() here only so you can understand older programs.

```
DBMS_LOB.FILEISOPEN(
    bfile IN BFILE
) RETURN INTEGER;
```

where *bfile* is the pointer to the file.
  FILEISOPEN() returns

- 0 if the file isn't open.

- 1 if the file is open.

The following table shows the exceptions thrown by FILEISOPEN().

Exception	Thrown When
NOEXIST_DIRECTORY	The directory doesn't exist.
NOPRIV_DIRECTORY	You don't have privileges to access the directory.
INVALID_DIRECTORY	The directory is invalid.
INVALID_OPERATION	The file doesn't exist or you don't have privileges to access the file.

FILEOPEN()

FILEOPEN() opens a file. You should use the newer OPEN() procedure to open a file in your own programs, as Oracle Corporation does not plan to extend the older FILEOPEN() procedure. I'm including coverage of FILEOPEN() here only so you can understand older programs.

```
DBMS_LOB.FILEOPEN(
    bfile       IN OUT NOCOPY BFILE,
    open_mode IN              BINARY_INTEGER := DBMS_LOB.FILE_READONLY
);
```

where

- *bfile* is the pointer to the file.

- *open_mode* indicates the open mode; the only open mode is DBMS_LOB.FILE_READONLY, which indicates the file may be read from.

The following table shows the exceptions thrown by FILEOPEN().

Exception	Thrown When
VALUE_ERROR	Any of the input parameters are null or invalid.
INVALID_ARGVAL	The *open_mode* is not set to DBMS_LOB.FILE_READONLY.
OPEN_TOOMANY	An attempt was made to open more than SESSION_MAX_OPEN_FILES files, where SESSION_MAX_OPEN_FILES is a database initialization parameter set by a database administrator.
NOEXIST_DIRECTORY	The directory doesn't exist.
INVALID_DIRECTORY	The directory is invalid.
INVALID_OPERATION	The file exists, but you don't have privileges to access the file.

FREETEMPORARY()

FREETEMPORARY() frees a temporary LOB from the default temporary tablespace of the user. There are two versions of FREETEMPORARY():

```
DBMS_LOB.FREETEMPORARY (
    lob IN OUT NOCOPY BLOB
);

DBMS_LOB.FREETEMPORARY (
    lob IN OUT NOCOPY CLOB/NCLOB CHARACTER SET ANY_CS
);
```

where *lob* is the lob to be freed.

The following table shows the exception thrown by FREETEMPORARY().

Exception	Thrown When
VALUE_ERROR	Any of the input parameters are null or invalid.

GETCHUNKSIZE()

GETCHUNKSIZE() returns the chunk size when reading and writing LOB data (a chunk is a unit of data). There are two versions of GETCHUNKSIZE():

```
DBMS_LOB.GETCHUNKSIZE(
    lob IN BLOB
) RETURN INTEGER;

DBMS_LOB.GETCHUNKSIZE(
    lob IN CLOB/NCLOB CHARACTER SET ANY_CS
) RETURN INTEGER;
```

where lob is the LOB to get the chunk size for.

GETCHUNKSIZE() returns

- The chunk size in bytes for a BLOB

- The chunk size in characters for a CLOB/NCLOB

The following table shows the exception thrown by GETCHUNKSIZE().

Exception	Thrown When
VALUE_ERROR	The *lob* parameter is null.

GET_STORAGE_LIMIT()

GET_STORAGE_LIMIT() returns the maximum allowable size for a LOB.

```
DBMS_LOB.GET_STORAGE_LIMIT()
RETURN INTEGER;
```

GETLENGTH()

GETLENGTH() returns the length of the LOB data. There are three versions of GETLENGTH():

```
DBMS_LOB.GETLENGTH(
    lob IN BLOB
) RETURN INTEGER;

DBMS_LOB.GETLENGTH(
    lob IN CLOB/NCLOB CHARACTER SET ANY_CS
) RETURN INTEGER;

DBMS_LOB.GETLENGTH(
    bfile IN BFILE
) RETURN INTEGER;
```

where

- *lob* is the BLOB, CLOB, or NCLOB data to get the length of.

- *bfile* is the BFILE data to get the length of.

GETLENGTH() returns

- The length in bytes for a BLOB or BFILE

- The length in characters for a CLOB or NCLOB

The following table shows the exception thrown by GETLENGTH().

Exception	Thrown When
VALUE_ERROR	The *lob* or *bfile* parameter is null.

INSTR()

INSTR() returns the starting position of characters that match the *nth* occurrence of a pattern in the LOB data, starting at an offset. There are three versions of INSTR():

```
DBMS_LOB.INSTR(
    lob     IN BLOB,
    pattern IN RAW,
    offset  IN INTEGER := 1,
    n       IN INTEGER := 1
) RETURN INTEGER;

DBMS_LOB.INSTR(
    lob     IN CLOB/NCLOB CHARACTER SET ANY_CS,
    pattern IN VARCHAR2 CHARACTER SET lob%CHARSET,
    offset  IN INTEGER := 1,
    n       IN INTEGER := 1
) RETURN INTEGER;
```

```
DBMS_LOB.INSTR(
  bfile    IN BFILE,
  pattern  IN RAW,
  offset   IN INTEGER := 1,
  n        IN INTEGER := 1
) RETURN INTEGER;
```

where

- *lob* is the BLOB, CLOB, or NCLOB to read from.

- *bfile* is the BFILE to read from.

- *pattern* is the pattern to search for in the LOB data; the pattern is a group of RAW bytes for a BLOB or BFILE, and a VARCHAR2 character string for a CLOB; the maximum size of the pattern is 16,383 bytes.

- *offset* is the offset to start reading data from the LOB (the offset starts at 1).

- *n* is the occurrence of the pattern to search the data for.

INSTR() returns

- The offset of the start of the pattern (if found)

- Zero if the pattern isn't found

- Null if

  - Any of the IN parameters are null or invalid

  - *offset* < 1 or *offset* > LOBMAXSIZE

  - *n* < 1 or *n* > LOBMAXSIZE

The following table shows the exceptions thrown by INSTR().

Exception	Thrown When
VALUE_ERROR	Any of the input parameters are null or invalid.
UNOPENED_FILE	The BFILE isn't open.
NOEXIST_DIRECTORY	The directory doesn't exist.
NOPRIV_DIRECTORY	The directory exists, but you don't have privileges to access the directory.
INVALID_DIRECTORY	The directory is invalid.
INVALID_OPERATION	The file exists, but you don't have privileges to access the file.

ISOPEN()

ISOPEN() checks if the LOB was already opened. There are three versions of ISOPEN():

```
DBMS_LOB.ISOPEN(
   lob IN BLOB
) RETURN INTEGER;

DBMS_LOB.ISOPEN(
   lob IN CLOB/NCLOB CHARACTER SET ANY_CS
) RETURN INTEGER;

DBMS_LOB.ISOPEN(
   bfile IN BFILE
) RETURN INTEGER;
```

where

- *lob* is the BLOB, CLOB, or NCLOB to check.

- *bfile* is the BFILE to check.

ISOPEN() returns

- 0 if the LOB isn't open.

- 1 if the LOB is open.

The following table shows the exception thrown by ISOPEN().

Exception	Thrown When
VALUE_ERROR	The *lob* or *bfile* parameter is null or invalid.

ISTEMPORARY()

ISTEMPORARY() checks if the LOB is a temporary LOB. There are two versions of ISTEMPORARY():

```
DBMS_LOB.ISTEMPORARY(
   lob IN BLOB
) RETURN INTEGER;

DBMS_LOB.ISTEMPORARY (
   lob IN CLOB/NCLOB CHARACTER SET ANY_CS
) RETURN INTEGER;
```

where

- *lob* is the LOB to check.

ISTEMPORARY() returns

- 0 if the LOB isn't temporary.

- 1 if the LOB is temporary.

The following table shows the exception thrown by `ISTEMPORARY()`.

Exception	Thrown When
VALUE_ERROR	The *lob* parameter is null or invalid.

LOADFROMFILE()

`LOADFROMFILE()` loads data retrieved via a `BFILE` into a `CLOB`, `NCLOB`, or `BLOB`, starting at the offsets for a total amount of characters or bytes. You should use the higher-performance `LOADCLOBFROMFILE()` or `LOADBLOBFROMFILE()` procedures in your own programs, and I'm including coverage of `LOADFROMFILE()` here only so you can understand older programs.

There are two versions of `LOADFROMFILE()`:

```
DBMS_LOB.LOADFROMFILE(
   dest_lob     IN OUT NOCOPY BLOB,
   src_bfile    IN            BFILE,
   amount       IN            INTEGER,
   dest_offset  IN            INTEGER  := 1,
   src_offset   IN            INTEGER  := 1
);

DBMS_LOB.LOADFROMFILE(
   dest_lob     IN OUT NOCOPY CLOB/NCLOB CHARACTER SET ANY_CS,
   src_bfile    IN            BFILE,
   amount       IN            INTEGER,
   dest_offset  IN            INTEGER := 1,
   src_offset   IN            INTEGER := 1
);
```

where

- *dest_lob* is the LOB into which the data is to be written.

- *src_bfile* is the pointer to the file from which the data is to be read.

- *amount* is the maximum number of bytes or characters to read from `src_bfile`.

- *dest_offset* is the offset in bytes or characters in *dest_lob* to start writing data (the offset starts at 1).

- *src_offset* is the offset in bytes in *src_bfile* to start reading data (the offset starts at 1).

The following table shows the exceptions thrown by `LOADFROMFILE()`.

Exception	Thrown When
VALUE_ERROR	Any of the input parameters are null or invalid.
INVALID_ARGVAL	Either: ■ *src_offset* < 1 ■ *dest_offset* < 1 ■ *src_offset* > LOBMAXSIZE ■ *dest_offset* > LOBMAXSIZE ■ *amount* < 1 ■ *amount* > LOBMAXSIZE

LOADBLOBFROMFILE()

LOADBLOBFROMFILE() loads data retrieved via a BFILE into a BLOB. LOADBLOBFROMFILE() offers improved performance over the LOADFROMFILE() method when using a BLOB.

```
DBMS_LOB.LOADBLOBFROMFILE(
    dest_blob   IN OUT NOCOPY BLOB,
    src_bfile   IN            BFILE,
    amount      IN            INTEGER,
    dest_offset IN OUT        INTEGER := 1,
    src_offset  IN OUT        INTEGER := 1
);
```

where

- *dest_blob* is the BLOB into which the data is to be written.

- *src_bfile* is the pointer to the file from which the data is to be read.

- *amount* is the maximum number of bytes to read from src_bfile.

- *dest_offset* is the offset in bytes in *dest_lob* to start writing data (the offset starts at 1).

- *src_offset* is the offset in bytes in *src_bfile* to start reading data (the offset starts at 1).

The following table shows the exceptions thrown by LOADBLOBFROMFILE().

Exception	Thrown When
VALUE_ERROR	Any of the input parameters are null or invalid.
INVALID_ARGVAL	Either: ■ *src_offset* < 1 ■ *dest_offset* < 1 ■ *src_offset* > LOBMAXSIZE ■ *dest_offset* > LOBMAXSIZE ■ *amount* < 1 ■ *amount* > LOBMAXSIZE

LOADCLOBFROMFILE()

LOADCLOBFROMFILE() loads data retrieved via a BFILE into a CLOB/NCLOB. LOADCLOBFROMFILE() offers improved performance over the LOADFROMFILE() method when using a CLOB/NCLOB. LOADCLOBFROMFILE() also automatically converts binary data to character data.

```
DBMS_LOB.LOADCLOBFROMFILE(
    dest_clob   IN OUT NOCOPY CLOB/NCLOB,
    src_bfile   IN            BFILE,
    amount      IN            INTEGER,
    dest_offset IN OUT        INTEGER,
    src_offset  IN OUT        INTEGER,
    src_csid    IN            NUMBER,
```

```
    lang_context IN OUT        INTEGER,
    warning      OUT           INTEGER
);
```

where

- *dest_blob* is the CLOB/NCLOB into which the data is to be written.

- *src_bfile* is the pointer to the file from which the data is to be read.

- *amount* is the maximum number of characters to read from *src_bfile*.

- *dest_offset* is the offset in characters in *dest_lob* to start writing data (the offset starts at 1).

- *src_offset* is the offset in characters in *src_bfile* to start reading data (the offset starts at 1).

- *src_csid* is the character set of *src_bfile* (you should typically use DBMS_LOB .DEFAULT_CSID, which is the default character set for the database).

- *lang_context* is the language context to use for the load (you should typically use DBMS_LOB.DEFAULT_LANG_CTX, which is the default language context for the database).

- *warning* is a warning message that contains information if there was a problem with the load; a common problem is that a character in *src_bfile* cannot be converted to a character in *dest_lob* (in which case, *warning* is set to DBMS_LOB.WARN_ INCONVERTIBLE_CHAR).

NOTE
You can learn all about character sets, contexts, and how to convert characters from one language to another in the Oracle Database Globalization Support Guide *published by Oracle Corporation.*

The following table shows the exceptions thrown by LOADCLOBFROMFILE().

Exception	Thrown When
VALUE_ERROR	Any of the input parameters are null or invalid.
INVALID_ARGVAL	Either: ■ *src_offset* < 1 ■ *dest_offset* < 1 ■ *src_offset* > LOBMAXSIZE ■ *dest_offset* > LOBMAXSIZE ■ *amount* < 1 ■ *amount* > LOBMAXSIZE

OPEN()

OPEN() opens a LOB. There are three versions of OPEN():

```
DBMS_LOB.OPEN(
  lob      IN OUT NOCOPY BLOB,
  open_mode IN           BINARY_INTEGER
);

DBMS_LOB.OPEN(
  lob      IN OUT NOCOPY CLOB/NCLOB CHARACTER SET ANY_CS,
  open_mode IN           BINARY_INTEGER
);

DBMS_LOB.OPEN(
  bfile    IN OUT NOCOPY BFILE,
  open_mode IN           BINARY_INTEGER := DBMS_LOB.FILE_READONLY
);
```

where

- *lob* is the LOB to open.

- *bfile* is the pointer to the file to open.

- *open_mode* indicates the open mode; the default is DBMS_LOB.FILE_READONLY, which indicates the LOB may only be read from; DBMS_LOB.FILE_READWRITE indicates the LOB may be read from and written to.

The following table shows the exception thrown by OPEN().

Exception	Thrown When
VALUE_ERROR	Any of the input parameters are null or invalid.

READ()

READ() reads data into a buffer from a LOB. There are three versions of READ():

```
DBMS_LOB.READ(
  lob    IN           BLOB,
  amount IN OUT NOCOPY BINARY_INTEGER,
  offset IN           INTEGER,
  buffer OUT          RAW
);

DBMS_LOB.READ(
  lob    IN           CLOB/NCLOB CHARACTER SET ANY_CS,
  amount IN OUT NOCOPY BINARY_INTEGER,
  offset IN           INTEGER,
  buffer OUT          VARCHAR2 CHARACTER SET lob%CHARSET
);

DBMS_LOB.READ(
  bfile  IN           BFILE,
  amount IN OUT NOCOPY BINARY_INTEGER,
```

```
   offset IN               INTEGER,
   buffer OUT              RAW
);
```

where

- *lob* is the CLOB, NCLOB, or BLOB to read from.

- *bfile* is the BFILE to read from.

- *amount* is the maximum number of characters to read from a CLOB/NCLOB, or the maximum number of bytes to read from a BLOB/BFILE.

- *offset* is the offset to start reading (the offset starts at 1).

- *buffer* is the variable where the data read from the LOB is to be stored.

The following table shows the exceptions thrown by READ().

Exception	Thrown When
VALUE_ERROR	Any of the input parameters are null.
INVALID_ARGVAL	Either: ■ *amount* < 1 ■ *amount* > MAXBUFSIZE ■ *amount* > capacity of buffer in bytes or characters ■ *offset* < 1 ■ *offset* > LOBMAXSIZE
NO_DATA_FOUND	The end of the LOB was reached and there are no more bytes or characters to read from the LOB.

SUBSTR()

SUBSTR() returns part of the LOB data, starting at the offset for a total amount of characters or bytes. There are three versions of SUBSTR():

```
DBMS_LOB.SUBSTR(
   lob    IN BLOB,
   amount IN INTEGER := 32767,
   offset IN INTEGER := 1
) RETURN RAW;

DBMS_LOB.SUBSTR (
   lob    IN CLOB/NCLOB CHARACTER SET ANY_CS,
   amount IN INTEGER := 32767,
   offset IN INTEGER := 1
) RETURN VARCHAR2 CHARACTER SET lob%CHARSET;

DBMS_LOB.SUBSTR (
   bfile  IN BFILE,
   amount IN INTEGER := 32767,
   offset IN INTEGER := 1
) RETURN RAW;
```

where

- *lob* is the BLOB, CLOB, or NCLOB to read from.

- *bfile* is the pointer to the file to read from.

- *amount* is the maximum number of characters read from a CLOB/NCLOB, or the maximum number of bytes to read from a BLOB/BFILE.

- *offset* is the offset to start reading data from the LOB (the offset starts at 1).

SUBSTR() returns

- RAW data when reading from a BLOB/BFILE.

- VARCHAR2 data when reading from a CLOB/NCLOB.

- Null if

  - *amount* < 1

  - *amount* > 32767

  - *offset* < 1

  - *offset* > LOBMAXSIZE

The following table shows the exceptions thrown by SUBSTR().

Exception	Thrown When
VALUE_ERROR	Any of the input parameters are null or invalid.
UNOPENED_FILE	The BFILE isn't open.
NOEXIST_DIRECTORY	The directory doesn't exist.
NOPRIV_DIRECTORY	You don't have privileges on the directory.
INVALID_DIRECTORY	The directory is invalid.
INVALID_OPERATION	The file exists, but you don't have privileges to access the file.

TRIM()

TRIM() trims the LOB data to the specified shorter length. There are two versions of TRIM():

```
DBMS_LOB.TRIM(
    lob     IN OUT NOCOPY BLOB,
    newlen IN            INTEGER
);

DBMS_LOB.TRIM(
    lob     IN OUT NOCOPY CLOB/NCLOB CHARACTER SET ANY_CS,
    newlen IN            INTEGER
);
```

where

- *lob* is the BLOB, CLOB, or NCLOB to trim.
- *newlen* is the new length (in bytes for a BLOB, or characters for a CLOB/NCLOB).

The following table shows the exceptions thrown by TRIM().

Exception	Thrown When
VALUE_ERROR	The lob parameter is null.
INVALID_ARGVAL	Either: ■ *newlen* < 0 ■ *newlen* > LOBMAXSIZE

WRITE()

WRITE() writes data from a buffer to a LOB. There are two versions of WRITE():

```
DBMS_LOB.WRITE(
    lob    IN OUT NOCOPY BLOB,
    amount IN            BINARY_INTEGER,
    offset IN            INTEGER,
    buffer IN            RAW
);

DBMS_LOB.WRITE(
    lob    IN OUT NOCOPY CLOB/NCLOB CHARACTER SET ANY_CS,
    amount IN            BINARY_INTEGER,
    offset IN            INTEGER,
    buffer IN            VARCHAR2 CHARACTER SET lob%CHARSET
);
```

where

- *lob* is the LOB to write to.
- *amount* is the maximum number of characters to write to a CLOB/NCLOB, or the maximum number of bytes to write to a BLOB.
- *offset* is the offset to start writing data to the LOB (the offset starts at 1).
- *buffer* is the variable that contains the data to be written to the LOB.

The following table shows the exceptions thrown by WRITE().

Exception	Thrown When
VALUE_ERROR	Any of the input parameters are null or invalid.
INVALID_ARGVAL	Either: ■ *amount* < 1 ■ *amount* > MAXBUFSIZE ■ *offset* < 1 ■ *offset* > LOBMAXSIZE

WRITEAPPEND()

WRITEAPPEND() writes data from the buffer to the end of a LOB, starting at the offset for a total amount of characters or bytes. There are two versions of WRITEAPPEND():

```
DBMS_LOB.WRITEAPPEND(
   lob     IN OUT NOCOPY BLOB,
   amount IN             BINARY_INTEGER,
   buffer IN             RAW
);

DBMS_LOB.WRITEAPPEND(
   lob     IN OUT NOCOPY CLOB/NCLOB CHARACTER SET ANY_CS,
   amount IN             BINARY_INTEGER,
   buffer IN             VARCHAR2 CHARACTER SET lob%CHARSET
);
```

where

- *lob* is the BLOB, CLOB, or NCLOB to write to.

- *amount* is the maximum number of characters to write to a CLOB/NCLOB, or the maximum number of bytes to write to a BLOB.

- *buffer* is the variable that contains the data to be written to the LOB.

The following table shows the exceptions thrown by WRITEAPPEND().

Exception	Thrown When
VALUE_ERROR	Any of the input parameters are null or invalid.
INVALID_ARGVAL	Either: ■ *amount* < 1 ■ *amount* > MAXBUFSIZE

Example PL/SQL Procedures

In this section, you'll see example PL/SQL procedures that use the various methods described in the previous sections. The example procedures are created when you run the lob_schema.sql script.

Retrieving a LOB Locator

The following get_clob_locator() procedure gets a LOB locator from the clob_content table; get_clob_locator() performs the following tasks:

- Accepts an IN OUT parameter named p_clob of type CLOB; p_clob is set to a LOB locator inside the procedure. Because p_clob is IN OUT, the value is passed out of the procedure.

- Accepts an IN parameter named p_id of type INTEGER, which specifies the id of a row to retrieve from the clob_content table.

- Selects clob_column from the clob_content table into p_clob; this stores the LOB locator of clob_column in p_clob.

```
CREATE PROCEDURE get_clob_locator(
    p_clob IN OUT CLOB,
    p_id   IN INTEGER
) AS
BEGIN
    -- get the LOB locator and store it in p_clob
    SELECT clob_column
    INTO p_clob
    FROM clob_content
    WHERE id = p_id;
END get_clob_locator;
/
```

The following get_blob_locator() procedure does the same thing as the previous procedure, except it gets the locator for a BLOB from the blob_content table:

```
CREATE PROCEDURE get_blob_locator(
    p_blob IN OUT BLOB,
    p_id   IN INTEGER
) AS
BEGIN
    -- get the LOB locator and store it in p_blob
    SELECT blob_column
    INTO p_blob
    FROM blob_content
    WHERE id = p_id;
END get_blob_locator;
/
```

These two procedures are used in the code shown in the following sections.

Reading Data from CLOBs and BLOBs

The following read_clob_example() procedure reads the data from a CLOB and displays the data on the screen; read_clob_example() performs the following tasks:

- Calls get_clob_locator() to get a locator and stores it in v_clob

- Uses READ() to read the contents of v_clob into a VARCHAR2 variable named v_char_buffer

- Displays the contents of v_char_buffer on the screen

```
CREATE PROCEDURE read_clob_example(
    p_id IN INTEGER
) AS
    v_clob CLOB;
    v_offset INTEGER := 1;
    v_amount INTEGER := 50;
    v_char_buffer VARCHAR2(50);
BEGIN
    -- get the LOB locator and store it in v_clob
    get_clob_locator(v_clob, p_id);
```

```
-- read the contents of v_clob into v_char_buffer, starting at
-- the v_offset position and read a total of v_amount characters
DBMS_LOB.READ(v_clob, v_amount, v_offset, v_char_buffer);

-- display the contents of v_char_buffer
DBMS_OUTPUT.PUT_LINE('v_char_buffer = ' || v_char_buffer);
DBMS_OUTPUT.PUT_LINE('v_amount = ' || v_amount);
END read_clob_example;
/
```

The following example turns the server output on and calls `read_clob_example()`:

```
SET SERVEROUTPUT ON
CALL read_clob_example(1);
v_char_buffer = Creeps in this petty pace
v_amount = 25
```

The following `read_blob_example()` procedure reads the data from a BLOB; read_blob_example() performs the following tasks:

- Calls `get_blob_locator()` to get the locator and stores it in `v_blob`

- Calls `READ()` to read the contents of `v_blob` into a RAW variable named `v_binary_buffer`

- Displays the contents of `v_binary_buffer` on the screen

```
CREATE PROCEDURE read_blob_example(
    p_id IN INTEGER
) AS
  v_blob BLOB;
  v_offset INTEGER := 1;
  v_amount INTEGER := 25;
  v_binary_buffer RAW(25);
BEGIN
  -- get the LOB locator and store it in v_blob
  get_blob_locator(v_blob, p_id);

  -- read the contents of v_blob into v_binary_buffer, starting at
  -- the v_offset position and read a total of v_amount bytes
  DBMS_LOB.READ(v_blob, v_amount, v_offset, v_binary_buffer);

  -- display the contents of v_binary_buffer
  DBMS_OUTPUT.PUT_LINE('v_binary_buffer = ' || v_binary_buffer);
  DBMS_OUTPUT.PUT_LINE('v_amount = ' || v_amount);
END read_blob_example;
/
```

The following example calls `read_blob_example()`:

```
CALL read_blob_example(1);
v_binary_buffer = 100111010101011111
v_amount = 9
```

Writing to a CLOB

The following `write_example()` procedure writes a string in `v_char_buffer` to `v_clob` using `WRITE()`; notice that the `SELECT` statement in the procedure uses the `FOR UPDATE` clause, which is used because the `CLOB` is written to using `WRITE()`:

```
CREATE PROCEDURE write_example(
  p_id IN INTEGER
) AS
  v_clob CLOB;
  v_offset INTEGER := 7;
  v_amount INTEGER := 6;
  v_char_buffer VARCHAR2(10) := 'pretty';
BEGIN
  -- get the LOB locator into v_clob for update (for update
  -- because the LOB is written to using WRITE() later)
  SELECT clob_column
  INTO v_clob
  FROM clob_content
  WHERE id = p_id
  FOR UPDATE;

  -- read and display the contents of the CLOB
  read_clob_example(p_id);

  -- write the characters in v_char_buffer to v_clob, starting
  -- at the v_offset position and write a total of v_amount characters
  DBMS_LOB.WRITE(v_clob, v_amount, v_offset, v_char_buffer);

  -- read and display the contents of the CLOB
  -- and then rollback the write
  read_clob_example(p_id);
  ROLLBACK;
END write_example;
/
```

The following example calls `write_example()`:

```
CALL write_example(1);
v_char_buffer = Creeps in this petty pace
v_amount = 25
v_char_buffer = Creepsprettyis petty pace
v_amount = 25
```

Appending Data to a CLOB

The following `append_example()` procedure uses `APPEND()` to copy the data from `v_src_clob` to the end of `v_dest_clob`:

```
CREATE PROCEDURE append_example AS
  v_src_clob CLOB;
  v_dest_clob CLOB;
BEGIN
  -- get the LOB locator for the CLOB in row #2 of
```

```
    -- the clob_content table into v_src_clob
    get_clob_locator(v_src_clob, 2);

    -- get the LOB locator for the CLOB in row #1 of
    -- the clob_content table into v_dest_clob for update
    -- (for update because the CLOB will be added to using
    -- APPEND() later)
    SELECT clob_column
    INTO v_dest_clob
    FROM clob_content
    WHERE id = 1
    FOR UPDATE;

    -- read and display the contents of CLOB #1
    read_clob_example(1);

    -- use APPEND() to copy the contents of v_src_clob to v_dest_clob
    DBMS_LOB.APPEND(v_dest_clob, v_src_clob);

    -- read and display the contents of CLOB #1
    -- and then rollback the change
    read_clob_example(1);
    ROLLBACK;
END append_example;
/
```

The following example calls `append_example()`:

```
CALL append_example();
v_char_buffer = Creeps in this petty pace
v_amount = 25
v_char_buffer = Creeps in this petty pace from day to day
v_amount = 41
```

Comparing the Data in Two CLOBs

The following `compare_example()` procedure compares the data in `v_clob1` and `v_clob2` using `COMPARE()`:

```
CREATE PROCEDURE compare_example AS
    v_clob1 CLOB;
    v_clob2 CLOB;
    v_return INTEGER;
BEGIN
    -- get the LOB locators
    get_clob_locator(v_clob1, 1);
    get_clob_locator(v_clob2, 2);

    -- compare v_clob1 with v_clob2 (COMPARE() returns 1
    -- because the contents of v_clob1 and v_clob2 are different)
    DBMS_OUTPUT.PUT_LINE('Comparing v_clob1 with v_clob2');
    v_return := DBMS_LOB.COMPARE(v_clob1, v_clob2);
    DBMS_OUTPUT.PUT_LINE('v_return = ' || v_return);
```

```
   -- compare v_clob1 with v_clob1 (COMPARE() returns 0
   -- because the contents are the same)
   DBMS_OUTPUT.PUT_LINE('Comparing v_clob1 with v_clob1');
   v_return := DBMS_LOB.COMPARE(v_clob1, v_clob1);
   DBMS_OUTPUT.PUT_LINE('v_return = ' || v_return);
END compare_example;
/
```

The following example calls compare_example():

```
CALL compare_example();
Comparing v_clob1 with v_clob2
v_return = 1
Comparing v_clob1 with v_clob1
v_return = 0
```

Notice that v_return is 1 when comparing v_clob1 with v_clob2, which indicates the LOB data is different; v_return is 0 when comparing v_clob1 with v_clob1, which indicates the LOB data is the same.

Copying Data from One CLOB to Another

The following copy_example() procedure copies some characters from v_src_clob to v_dest_clob using COPY():

```
CREATE PROCEDURE copy_example AS
    v_src_clob CLOB;
    v_dest_clob CLOB;
    v_src_offset INTEGER := 1;
    v_dest_offset INTEGER := 7;
    v_amount INTEGER := 5;
BEGIN
    -- get the LOB locator for the CLOB in row #2 of
    -- the clob_content table into v_dest_clob
    get_clob_locator(v_src_clob, 2);

    -- get the LOB locator for the CLOB in row #1 of
    -- the clob_content table into v_dest_clob for update
    -- (for update because the CLOB will be added to using
    -- COPY() later)
    SELECT clob_column
    INTO v_dest_clob
    FROM clob_content
    WHERE id = 1
    FOR UPDATE;

    -- read and display the contents of CLOB #1
    read_clob_example(1);

    -- copy characters to v_dest_clob from v_src_clob using COPY(),
    -- starting at the offsets specified by v_dest_offset and
    -- v_src_offset for a total of v_amount characters
```

```
  DBMS_LOB.COPY(
    v_dest_clob, v_src_clob,
    v_amount, v_dest_offset, v_src_offset
  );

  -- read and display the contents of CLOB #1
  -- and then rollback the change
  read_clob_example(1);
  ROLLBACK;
END copy_example;
/
```

The following example calls `copy_example()`:

```
CALL copy_example();
v_char_buffer = Creeps in this petty pace
v_amount = 25
v_char_buffer = Creeps fromhis petty pace
v_amount = 25
```

Using Temporary CLOBs

The following `temporary_lob_example()` procedure illustrates the use of a temporary CLOB:

```
CREATE PROCEDURE temporary_lob_example AS
  v_clob CLOB;
  v_amount INTEGER;
  v_offset INTEGER := 1;
  v_char_buffer VARCHAR2(17) := 'Juliet is the sun';
BEGIN
  -- use CREATETEMPORARY() to create a temporary CLOB named v_clob
  DBMS_LOB.CREATETEMPORARY(v_clob, TRUE);

  -- use WRITE() to write the contents of v_char_buffer to v_clob
  v_amount := LENGTH(v_char_buffer);
  DBMS_LOB.WRITE(v_clob, v_amount, v_offset, v_char_buffer);

  -- use ISTEMPORARY() to check if v_clob is temporary
  IF (DBMS_LOB.ISTEMPORARY(v_clob) = 1) THEN
    DBMS_OUTPUT.PUT_LINE('v_clob is temporary');
  END IF;

  -- use READ() to read the contents of v_clob into v_char_buffer
  DBMS_LOB.READ(
    v_clob, v_amount, v_offset, v_char_buffer
  );
  DBMS_OUTPUT.PUT_LINE('v_char_buffer = ' || v_char_buffer);

  -- use FREETEMPORARY() to free v_clob
  DBMS_LOB.FREETEMPORARY(v_clob);
END temporary_lob_example;
/
```

The following example calls `temporary_lob_example()`:

```
CALL temporary_lob_example();
v_clob is temporary
v_char_buffer = Juliet is the sun
```

Erasing Data from a CLOB

The following `erase_example()` procedure erases part of a CLOB using `ERASE()`:

```
CREATE PROCEDURE erase_example IS
  v_clob CLOB;
  v_offset INTEGER := 2;
  v_amount INTEGER := 5;
BEGIN
  -- get the LOB locator for the CLOB in row #1 of
  -- the clob_content table into v_dest_clob for update
  -- (for update because the CLOB will be erased using
  -- ERASE() later)
  SELECT clob_column
  INTO v_clob
  FROM clob_content
  WHERE id = 1
  FOR UPDATE;

  -- read and display the contents of CLOB #1
  read_clob_example(1);

  -- use ERASE() to erase a total of v_amount characters
  -- from v_clob, starting at v_offset
  DBMS_LOB.ERASE(v_clob, v_amount, v_offset);

  -- read and display the contents of CLOB #1
  -- and then rollback the change
  read_clob_example(1);
  ROLLBACK;
END erase_example;
/
```

The following example calls `erase_example()`:

```
CALL erase_example();
v_char_buffer = Creeps in this petty pace
v_amount = 25
v_char_buffer = C      in this petty pace
v_amount = 25
```

Searching the Data in a CLOB

The following `instr_example()` procedure uses `INSTR()` to search the character data stored in a CLOB:

```
CREATE PROCEDURE instr_example AS
    v_clob CLOB;
    v_char_buffer VARCHAR2(50) := 'It is the east and Juliet is the sun';
    v_pattern VARCHAR2(5);
    v_offset INTEGER := 1;
    v_amount INTEGER;
    v_occurrence INTEGER;
    v_return INTEGER;
BEGIN
    -- use CREATETEMPORARY() to create a temporary CLOB named v_clob
    DBMS_LOB.CREATETEMPORARY(v_clob, TRUE);

    -- use WRITE() to write the contents of v_char_buffer to v_clob
    v_amount := LENGTH(v_char_buffer);
    DBMS_LOB.WRITE(v_clob, v_amount, v_offset, v_char_buffer);

    -- use READ() to read the contents of v_clob into v_char_buffer
    DBMS_LOB.READ(v_clob, v_amount, v_offset, v_char_buffer);
    DBMS_OUTPUT.PUT_LINE('v_char_buffer = ' || v_char_buffer);

    -- use INSTR() to search v_clob for the second occurrence of is,
    -- and INSTR() returns 27
    DBMS_OUTPUT.PUT_LINE('Searching for second ''is''');
    v_pattern := 'is';
    v_occurrence := 2;
    v_return := DBMS_LOB.INSTR(v_clob, v_pattern, v_offset, v_occurrence);
    DBMS_OUTPUT.PUT_LINE('v_return = ' || v_return);

    -- use INSTR() to search v_clob for the first occurrence of Moon,
    -- and INSTR() returns 0 because Moon doesn't appear in v_clob
    DBMS_OUTPUT.PUT_LINE('Searching for ''Moon''');
    v_pattern := 'Moon';
    v_occurrence := 1;
    v_return := DBMS_LOB.INSTR(v_clob, v_pattern, v_offset, v_occurrence);
    DBMS_OUTPUT.PUT_LINE('v_return = ' || v_return);

    -- use FREETEMPORARY() to free v_clob
    DBMS_LOB.FREETEMPORARY(v_clob);
END instr_example;
/
```

The following example calls instr_example():

```
CALL instr_example();
v_char_buffer = It is the east and Juliet is the sun
Searching for second 'is'
v_return = 27
Searching for 'Moon'
v_return = 0
```

Copying Data from a File into a CLOB and a BLOB

The following `copy_file_data_to_clob()` procedure shows how to read text from a file and store it in a CLOB:

```
CREATE PROCEDURE copy_file_data_to_clob(
  p_clob_id INTEGER,
  p_directory VARCHAR2,
  p_file_name VARCHAR2
) AS
  v_file UTL_FILE.FILE_TYPE;
  v_chars_read INTEGER;
  v_dest_clob CLOB;
  v_amount INTEGER := 32767;
  v_char_buffer VARCHAR2(32767);
BEGIN
  -- insert an empty CLOB
  INSERT INTO clob_content(
    id, clob_column
  ) VALUES (
    p_clob_id, EMPTY_CLOB()
  );

  -- get the LOB locator of the CLOB
  SELECT clob_column
  INTO v_dest_clob
  FROM clob_content
  WHERE id = p_clob_id
  FOR UPDATE;

  -- open the file for reading of text (up to v_amount characters per line)
  v_file := UTL_FILE.FOPEN(p_directory, p_file_name, 'r', v_amount);

  -- copy the data from the file into v_dest_clob one line at a time
  LOOP
    BEGIN
      -- read a line from the file into v_char_buffer;
      -- GET_LINE() does not copy the newline character into
      -- v_char_buffer
      UTL_FILE.GET_LINE(v_file, v_char_buffer);
      v_chars_read := LENGTH(v_char_buffer);

      -- append the line to v_dest_clob
      DBMS_LOB.WRITEAPPEND(v_dest_clob, v_chars_read, v_char_buffer);

      -- append a newline to v_dest_clob because v_char_buffer;
      -- the ASCII value for newline is 10, so CHR(10) returns newline
      DBMS_LOB.WRITEAPPEND(v_dest_clob, 1, CHR(10));
    EXCEPTION
      -- when there is no more data in the file then exit
```

```
        WHEN NO_DATA_FOUND THEN
            EXIT;
      END;
  END LOOP;

  -- close the file
  UTL_FILE.FCLOSE(v_file);

  DBMS_OUTPUT.PUT_LINE('Copy successfully completed.');
END copy_file_data_to_clob;
/
```

There are a number of things to note about this procedure:

- UTL_FILE is a package included with the database and contains methods and types that enable you to read and write files. For example, UTL_FILE.FILE_TYPE is an object type used to represent a file.

- The v_amount variable is set to 32767, which is the maximum number of characters that can be read from a file during each read operation.

- The v_char_buffer variable is used to store the results read from the file before they are appended to v_dest_clob. The maximum length of v_char_buffer is set to 32767; this length is large enough to store the maximum number of characters read from the file during each read operation.

- UTL_FILE.FOPEN(*directory*, *file_name*, *open_mode*, *amount*) opens a file; *open_mode* can be set to one of the following modes:

  - r to read text

  - w to write text

  - a to append text

  - rb to read bytes

  - wb to write bytes

  - ab to append bytes

- UTL_FILE.GET_LINE(v_file, v_char_buffer) gets a line of text from v_file into v_char_buffer. GET_LINE() does not add the newline to v_char_buffer; because I want the newline, I add it using DBMS_LOB.WRITEAPPEND(v_dest_clob, 1, CHR(10)).

The following example calls copy_file_data_to_clob() to copy the contents of the file textContent.txt to a new CLOB with an id of 3:

```
CALL copy_file_data_to_clob(3, 'SAMPLE_FILES_DIR', 'textContent.txt');
Copy successfully completed.
```

The following `copy_file_data_to_blob()` procedure shows how to read binary data from a file and store it in a BLOB; notice that a RAW array is used to store the binary data read from the file:

```
CREATE PROCEDURE copy_file_data_to_blob(
  p_blob_id INTEGER,
  p_directory VARCHAR2,
  p_file_name VARCHAR2
) AS
  v_file UTL_FILE.FILE_TYPE;
  v_bytes_read INTEGER;
  v_dest_blob BLOB;
  v_amount INTEGER := 32767;
  v_binary_buffer RAW(32767);
BEGIN
  -- insert an empty BLOB
  INSERT INTO blob_content(
    id, blob_column
  ) VALUES (
    p_blob_id, EMPTY_BLOB()
  );

  -- get the LOB locator of the BLOB
  SELECT blob_column
  INTO v_dest_blob
  FROM blob_content
  WHERE id = p_blob_id
  FOR UPDATE;

  -- open the file for reading of bytes (up to v_amount bytes at a time)
  v_file := UTL_FILE.FOPEN(p_directory, p_file_name, 'rb', v_amount);

  -- copy the data from the file into v_dest_blob
  LOOP
    BEGIN
      -- read binary data from the file into v_binary_buffer
      UTL_FILE.GET_RAW(v_file, v_binary_buffer, v_amount);
      v_bytes_read := LENGTH(v_binary_buffer);

      -- append v_binary_buffer to v_dest_blob
      DBMS_LOB.WRITEAPPEND(v_dest_blob, v_bytes_read/2,
        v_binary_buffer);
    EXCEPTION
      -- when there is no more data in the file then exit
      WHEN NO_DATA_FOUND THEN
        EXIT;
    END;
  END LOOP;

  -- close the file
  UTL_FILE.FCLOSE(v_file);
```

```
    DBMS_OUTPUT.PUT_LINE('Copy successfully completed.');
END copy_file_data_to_blob;
/
```

The following example calls `copy_file_data_to_blob()` to copy the contents of the file `binaryContent.doc` to a new `BLOB` with an `id` of 3:

```
CALL copy_file_data_to_blob(3, 'SAMPLE_FILES_DIR', 'binaryContent.doc');
Copy successfully completed.
```

Of course, `copy_file_data_to_blob()` can be used to write any binary data contained in a file to a `BLOB`. The binary data can contain music, video, images, executables, and so on. Go ahead and try this using your own files.

TIP
*You can also bulk-load data into a LOB using the Oracle SQL*Loader and Data Pump utilities; see the* Oracle Database Large Objects Developer's Guide *published by Oracle Corporation for details.*

Copying Data from a CLOB and a BLOB to a File

The following `copy_clob_data_to_file()` procedure shows how to read text from a `CLOB` and save it to a file:

```
CREATE PROCEDURE copy_clob_data_to_file(
  p_clob_id INTEGER,
  p_directory VARCHAR2,
  p_file_name VARCHAR2
) AS
  v_src_clob CLOB;
  v_file UTL_FILE.FILE_TYPE;
  v_offset INTEGER := 1;
  v_amount INTEGER := 32767;
  v_char_buffer VARCHAR2(32767);
BEGIN
  -- get the LOB locator of the CLOB
  SELECT clob_column
  INTO v_src_clob
  FROM clob_content
  WHERE id = p_clob_id;

  -- open the file for writing of text (up to v_amount characters at a time)
  v_file := UTL_FILE.FOPEN(p_directory, p_file_name, 'w', v_amount);

  -- copy the data from v_src_clob to the file
  LOOP
    BEGIN
      -- read characters from v_src_clob into v_char_buffer
      DBMS_LOB.READ(v_src_clob, v_amount, v_offset, v_char_buffer);

      -- copy the characters from v_char_buffer to the file
      UTL_FILE.PUT(v_file, v_char_buffer);
```

```
      -- add v_amount to v_offset
      v_offset := v_offset + v_amount;
    EXCEPTION
      -- when there is no more data in the file then exit
      WHEN NO_DATA_FOUND THEN
        EXIT;
    END;
  END LOOP;

  -- flush any remaining data to the file
  UTL_FILE.FFLUSH(v_file);

  -- close the file
  UTL_FILE.FCLOSE(v_file);

  DBMS_OUTPUT.PUT_LINE('Copy successfully completed.');
END copy_clob_data_to_file;
/
```

The following example calls copy_clob_data_to_file() to copy the contents of CLOB #3 to a new file named textContent2.txt:

```
CALL copy_clob_data_to_file(3, 'SAMPLE_FILES_DIR', 'textContent2.txt');
Copy successfully completed.
```

If you look in the C:\sample_files directory, you will find the new textContent2.txt file. This file contains identical text to textContent.txt.

The following copy_blob_data_to_file() procedure shows how to read binary data from a BLOB and save it to a file:

```
CREATE PROCEDURE copy_blob_data_to_file(
    p_blob_id INTEGER,
    p_directory VARCHAR2,
    p_file_name VARCHAR2
) AS
    v_src_blob BLOB;
    v_file UTL_FILE.FILE_TYPE;
    v_offset INTEGER := 1;
    v_amount INTEGER := 32767;
    v_binary_buffer RAW(32767);
BEGIN
    -- get the LOB locator of the BLOB
    SELECT blob_column
    INTO v_src_blob
    FROM blob_content
    WHERE id = p_blob_id;

    -- open the file for writing of bytes (up to v_amount bytes at a time)
    v_file := UTL_FILE.FOPEN(p_directory, p_file_name, 'wb', v_amount);

    -- copy the data from v_src_blob to the file
```

```
    LOOP
      BEGIN
        -- read characters from v_src_blob into v_binary_buffer
        DBMS_LOB.READ(v_src_blob, v_amount, v_offset, v_binary_buffer);

        -- copy the binary data from v_binary_buffer to the file
        UTL_FILE.PUT_RAW(v_file, v_binary_buffer);

        -- add v_amount to v_offset
        v_offset := v_offset + v_amount;
      EXCEPTION
        -- when there is no more data in the file then exit
        WHEN NO_DATA_FOUND THEN
          EXIT;
      END;
    END LOOP;

    -- flush any remaining data to the file
    UTL_FILE.FFLUSH(v_file);

    -- close the file
    UTL_FILE.FCLOSE(v_file);

    DBMS_OUTPUT.PUT_LINE('Copy successfully completed.');
END copy_blob_data_to_file;
/
```

The following example calls `copy_blob_data_to_file()` to copy the contents of BLOB #3 to a new file named `binaryContent2.doc`:

```
CALL copy_blob_data_to_file(3, 'SAMPLE_FILES_DIR', 'binaryContent2.doc');
Copy successfully completed.
```

If you look in the `C:\sample_files` directory, you will find the new `binaryContent2.doc` file. This file contains identical text to `binaryContent.doc`.

Of course, `copy_blob_data_to_file()` can be used to write any binary data contained in a BLOB to a file. The binary data can contain music, video, images, executables, and so on.

Copying Data from a BFILE to a CLOB and a BLOB

The following `copy_bfile_data_to_clob()` procedure shows how to read text from a BFILE and save it to a CLOB:

```
CREATE PROCEDURE copy_bfile_data_to_clob(
    p_bfile_id INTEGER,
    p_clob_id INTEGER
) AS
    v_src_bfile BFILE;
    v_directory VARCHAR2(200);
    v_filename VARCHAR2(200);
    v_length INTEGER;
    v_dest_clob CLOB;
```

```
  v_amount INTEGER := DBMS_LOB.LOBMAXSIZE;
  v_dest_offset INTEGER := 1;
  v_src_offset INTEGER := 1;
  v_src_csid INTEGER := DBMS_LOB.DEFAULT_CSID;
  v_lang_context INTEGER := DBMS_LOB.DEFAULT_LANG_CTX;
  v_warning INTEGER;
BEGIN
  -- get the locator of the BFILE
  SELECT bfile_column
  INTO v_src_bfile
  FROM bfile_content
  WHERE id = p_bfile_id;

  -- use FILEEXISTS() to check if the file exists
  -- (FILEEXISTS() returns 1 if the file exists)
  IF (DBMS_LOB.FILEEXISTS(v_src_bfile) = 1) THEN
    -- use OPEN() to open the file
    DBMS_LOB.OPEN(v_src_bfile);

    -- use FILEGETNAME() to get the name of the file and the directory
    DBMS_LOB.FILEGETNAME(v_src_bfile, v_directory, v_filename);
    DBMS_OUTPUT.PUT_LINE('Directory = ' || v_directory);
    DBMS_OUTPUT.PUT_LINE('Filename = ' || v_filename);

    -- insert an empty CLOB
    INSERT INTO clob_content(
      id, clob_column
    ) VALUES (
      p_clob_id, EMPTY_CLOB()
    );

    -- get the LOB locator of the CLOB (for update)
    SELECT clob_column
    INTO v_dest_clob
    FROM clob_content
    WHERE id = p_clob_id
    FOR UPDATE;

    -- use LOADCLOBFROMFILE() to get up to v_amount characters
    -- from v_src_bfile and store them in v_dest_clob, starting
    -- at offset 1 in v_src_bfile and v_dest_clob
    DBMS_LOB.LOADCLOBFROMFILE(
      v_dest_clob, v_src_bfile,
      v_amount, v_dest_offset, v_src_offset,
      v_src_csid, v_lang_context, v_warning
    );

    -- check v_warning for an inconvertible character
    IF (v_warning = DBMS_LOB.WARN_INCONVERTIBLE_CHAR) THEN
      DBMS_OUTPUT.PUT_LINE('Warning! Inconvertible character.');
    END IF;
```

```
      -- use CLOSE() to close v_src_bfile
      DBMS_LOB.CLOSE(v_src_bfile);
      DBMS_OUTPUT.PUT_LINE('Copy successfully completed.');
    ELSE
      DBMS_OUTPUT.PUT_LINE('File does not exist');
    END IF;
END copy_bfile_data_to_clob;
/
```

The following example calls `copy_bfile_data_to_clob()` to copy the contents of BFILE #1 to a new CLOB with an id of 4:

```
CALL copy_bfile_data_to_clob(1, 4);
Copy successfully completed.
```

The next example calls `copy_clob_data_to_file()` to copy the contents of CLOB #4 to a new file named `textContent3.txt`:

```
CALL copy_clob_data_to_file(4, 'SAMPLE_FILES_DIR', 'textContent3.txt');
Copy successfully completed.
```

If you look in the `C:\sample_files` directory, you will find the new `textContent3.txt` file. This file contains identical text to `textContent.txt`.

The following `copy_bfile_data_to_blob()` procedure shows how to read binary data from a BFILE and save it to a BLOB:

```
CREATE PROCEDURE copy_bfile_data_to_blob(
  p_bfile_id INTEGER,
  p_blob_id INTEGER
) AS
  v_src_bfile BFILE;
  v_directory VARCHAR2(200);
  v_filename VARCHAR2(200);
  v_length INTEGER;
  v_dest_blob BLOB;
  v_amount INTEGER := DBMS_LOB.LOBMAXSIZE;
  v_dest_offset INTEGER := 1;
  v_src_offset INTEGER := 1;
BEGIN
  -- get the locator of the BFILE
  SELECT bfile_column
  INTO v_src_bfile
  FROM bfile_content
  WHERE id = p_bfile_id;

  -- use FILEEXISTS() to check if the file exists
  -- (FILEEXISTS() returns 1 if the file exists)
  IF (DBMS_LOB.FILEEXISTS(v_src_bfile) = 1) THEN
    -- use OPEN() to open the file
    DBMS_LOB.OPEN(v_src_bfile);

    -- use FILEGETNAME() to get the name of the file and
```

```
    -- the directory
    DBMS_LOB.FILEGETNAME(v_src_bfile, v_directory, v_filename);
    DBMS_OUTPUT.PUT_LINE('Directory = ' || v_directory);
    DBMS_OUTPUT.PUT_LINE('Filename = ' || v_filename);

    -- insert an empty BLOB
    INSERT INTO blob_content(
      id, blob_column
    ) VALUES (
      p_blob_id, EMPTY_BLOB()
    );

    -- get the LOB locator of the BLOB (for update)
    SELECT blob_column
    INTO v_dest_blob
    FROM blob_content
    WHERE id = p_blob_id
    FOR UPDATE;

    -- use LOADBLOBFROMFILE() to get up to v_amount bytes
    -- from v_src_bfile and store them in v_dest_blob, starting
    -- at offset 1 in v_src_bfile and v_dest_blob
    DBMS_LOB.LOADBLOBFROMFILE(
      v_dest_blob, v_src_bfile,
      v_amount, v_dest_offset, v_src_offset
    );

    -- use CLOSE() to close v_src_bfile
    DBMS_LOB.CLOSE(v_src_bfile);
    DBMS_OUTPUT.PUT_LINE('Copy successfully completed.');
  ELSE
    DBMS_OUTPUT.PUT_LINE('File does not exist');
  END IF;
END copy_bfile_data_to_blob;
/
```

The following example calls copy_bfile_data_to_blob() to copy the contents of BFILE #2 to a new BLOB with an id of 4:

```
CALL copy_bfile_data_to_blob(2, 4);
Copy successfully completed.
```

The next example calls copy_blob_data_to_file() to copy the contents of BLOB #4 to a new file named binaryContent3.doc:

```
CALL copy_blob_data_to_file(4, 'SAMPLE_FILES_DIR', 'binaryContent3.doc');
Copy successfully completed.
```

If you look in the C:\sample_files directory, you will find the new binaryContent3 .doc file. This file contains identical text to binaryContent.doc.

This is the end of the coverage on large objects. In the next section, you'll learn about the LONG and LONG RAW types.

LONG and LONG RAW Types

I mentioned at the start of this chapter that LOBs are the preferred storage type for large blocks of data, but you may encounter databases that still use the following types:

- **LONG** Used to store up to 2 gigabytes of character data

- **LONG RAW** Used to store up to 2 gigabytes of binary data

- **RAW** Used to store up to 4 kilobytes of binary data

In this section, you'll learn how to use LONG and LONG RAW types. RAW is used in the same way as a LONG RAW, so I've omitted coverage of RAW.

The Example Tables

In this section, you'll see the use of the following two tables:

- **long_content** Contains a LONG column named long_column

- **long_raw_content** Contains a LONG RAW column named long_raw_column

These two tables are created by the lob_schema.sql script using the following statements:

```
CREATE TABLE long_content (
  id           INTEGER PRIMARY KEY,
  long_column LONG NOT NULL
);

CREATE TABLE long_raw_content (
  id              INTEGER PRIMARY KEY,
  long_raw_column LONG RAW NOT NULL
);
```

Adding Data to LONG and LONG RAW Columns

The following INSERT statements add rows to the long_content table:

```
INSERT INTO long_content (
  id, long_column
) VALUES (
  1, 'Creeps in this petty pace'
);

INSERT INTO long_content (
  id, long_column
) VALUES (
  2, ' from day to day'
);
```

The following INSERT statements add rows to the long_raw_content table (the first INSERT contains a binary number, the second a hexadecimal number):

```
INSERT INTO long_raw_content (
  id, long_raw_column
```

```
) VALUES (
  1, '100111010101011111'
);

INSERT INTO long_raw_content (
  id, long_raw_column
) VALUES (
  2, 'A0FFB71CF90DE'
);
```

In the next section, you'll see how to convert LONG and LONG RAW columns to LOBs.

Converting LONG and LONG RAW Columns to LOBs

You can convert a LONG to a CLOB using the TO_LOB() function. For example, the following statement converts long_column to a CLOB using TO_LOB() and stores the results in the clob_content table:

```
INSERT INTO clob_content
SELECT 10 + id, TO_LOB(long_column)
FROM long_content;
```

```
2 rows created.
```

You can convert a LONG RAW to a BLOB using the TO_LOB() function. For example, the following statement converts long_raw_column to a BLOB using TO_LOB() and stores the results in the blob_content table:

```
INSERT INTO blob_content
SELECT 10 + id, TO_LOB(long_raw_column)
FROM long_raw_content;
```

```
2 rows created.
```

You can also use the ALTER TABLE statement to convert LONG and LONG RAW columns directly. For example, the following statement converts long_column to a CLOB:

```
ALTER TABLE long_content MODIFY (long_column CLOB);
```

The next example converts long_raw_column to a BLOB:

```
ALTER TABLE long_raw_content MODIFY (long_raw_column BLOB);
```

CAUTION
You should not modify tables that are currently used in a production application.

Once a LONG or LONG RAW column is converted to a LOB, you can use the rich PL/SQL methods described earlier to access the LOB.

Oracle Database 10*g* Enhancements to Large Objects

In this section, you'll learn about the following enhancements made to large objects in Oracle Database 10*g*:

- Implicit conversion between CLOB and NCLOB objects

- Use of the :new attribute when using LOBs in a trigger

I've provided an SQL*Plus script named lob_schema2.sql in the SQL directory. This script can be run using Oracle Database 10*g* and higher. The script creates a user named lob_user2 with a password of lob_password and creates the tables and PL/SQL code used in this section. After the script completes, you will be logged in as lob_user2.

Implicit Conversion Between CLOB and NCLOB Objects

In today's global business environment, you might have to deal with conversions between Unicode and a national language character set. Unicode is a universal character set that enables you to store text that can be converted into any language; it does this by providing a unique code for every character, regardless of the language. A national character set stores text in a specific language.

In versions of the database below Oracle Database 10*g*, you have to explicitly convert between Unicode text and the national character set text using the TO_CLOB() and TO_NCLOB() functions. TO_CLOB() allows you to convert text stored in a VARCHAR2, NVARCHAR2, or NCLOB to a CLOB. Similarly, TO_NCLOB() allows you to convert text stored in a VARCHAR2, NVARCHAR2, or CLOB to an NCLOB.

Oracle Database 10*g* and higher implicitly converts Unicode text and national character set text in CLOB and NCLOB objects, which saves you from using TO_CLOB() and TO_NCLOB(). You can use this implicit conversion for IN and OUT variables in queries and DML statements as well as for PL/SQL method parameters and variable assignments.

Let's take a look at an example. The following statement creates a table named nclob_content that contains an NCLOB column named nclob_column:

```
CREATE TABLE nclob_content (
   id INTEGER PRIMARY KEY,
   nclob_column NCLOB
);
```

The following nclob_example() procedure shows the implicit conversion of a CLOB to an NCLOB, and vice versa:

```
CREATE PROCEDURE nclob_example
AS
   v_clob CLOB := 'It is the east and Juliet is the sun';
   v_nclob NCLOB;
BEGIN
```

```
-- insert v_clob into nclob_column; this implicitly
-- converts the CLOB v_clob to an NCLOB, storing
-- the contents of v_clob in the nclob_content table
INSERT INTO nclob_content (
  id, nclob_column
) VALUES (
  1, v_clob
);

-- select nclob_column into v_clob; this implicitly
-- converts the NCLOB stored in nclob_column to a
-- CLOB, retrieving the contents of nclob_column
-- into v_clob
SELECT nclob_column
INTO v_clob
FROM nclob_content
WHERE id = 1;

-- display the contents of v_clob
DBMS_OUTPUT.PUT_LINE('v_clob = ' || v_clob);
END nclob_example;
/
```

The following example turns the server output on and calls `nclob_example()`:

```
SET SERVEROUTPUT ON
CALL nclob_example();
v_clob = It is the east and Juliet is the sun
```

Use of the :new Attribute When Using LOBs in a Trigger

In Oracle Database 10*g* and higher, you can use the `:new` attribute when referencing LOBs in a `BEFORE UPDATE` or `BEFORE INSERT` row level trigger. The following example creates a trigger named `before_clob_content_update`; the trigger fires when the `clob_content` table is updated and displays the length of the new data in `clob_column`; notice that `:new` is used to access the new data in `clob_column`:

```
CREATE TRIGGER before_clob_content_update
BEFORE UPDATE
ON clob_content
FOR EACH ROW
BEGIN
  DBMS_OUTPUT.PUT_LINE('clob_content changed');
  DBMS_OUTPUT.PUT_LINE(
    'Length = ' || DBMS_LOB.GETLENGTH(:new.clob_column)
  );
END before_clob_content_update;
/
```

The following example updates the `clob_content` table, causing the trigger to be fired:

```
UPDATE clob_content
SET clob_column = 'Creeps in this petty pace'
WHERE id = 1;
clob_content changed
Length = 25
```

Oracle Database 11*g* Enhancements to Large Objects

In this section, you'll learn about the following enhancements made to large objects in Oracle Database 11*g*:

- Encryption of BLOB, CLOB, and NCLOB data, which prevents unauthorized viewing and modification of the data

- Compression to squeeze BLOB, CLOB, and NCLOB data

- De-duplication of BLOB, CLOB, and NCLOB data to automatically detect and remove repeated data

Encrypting LOB Data

You can disguise your data using encryption so that unauthorized users cannot view or modify it. You should encrypt sensitive data such as credit card numbers, social security numbers, and so on.

Before you can encrypt data, either you or a database administrator needs to set up a "wallet" to store security details. The data in a wallet includes a private key for encrypting and decrypting data. In this section, you'll see how to create a wallet, encrypt LOB data, and encrypt regular column data.

Creating a Wallet

To create a wallet, you must first create a directory called wallet in the directory $ORACLE_BASE\admin\$ORACLE_SID, where ORACLE_BASE is the base directory where the Oracle database software is installed, and ORACLE_SID is the system identifier for the database in which the wallet is to be created. For example, on my computer running Windows XP and Oracle Database 11*g*, I created my wallet directory in C:\oracle_11g\admin\orcl.

Once the wallet directory is created, you need to run SQL*Plus, connect to the database using a privileged user account (for example, system), and run an ALTER SYSTEM command to set the password for the wallet encryption key, as shown here:

```
SQL> CONNECT system/manager
SQL> ALTER SYSTEM SET ENCRYPTION KEY IDENTIFIED BY "testpassword123";
System altered.
```

Once this is done, a file called ewallet.p12 appears in the wallet directory, and the database automatically opens the wallet. The encryption key password is stored in the wallet, and is used to encrypt and decrypt data behind the scenes.

I've provided an SQL*Plus script named `lob_schema3.sql` in the `SQL` directory. This script may be run using Oracle Database 11*g*. The script creates a user named `lob_user3` with a password of `lob_password`, and it also creates the tables used later in this section. After the script completes, you will be logged in as `lob_user3`.

Encrypting LOB Data

You can encrypt the data stored in a `BLOB`, `CLOB`, or `NCLOB` to prevent unauthorized access to that data; you cannot encrypt a `BFILE`, because the file itself is stored outside the database.

You can use the following algorithms to encrypt data:

- **3DES168** The Triple-DES (Data Encryption Standard) algorithm with a key length of 168 bits.

- **AES128** The Advanced Encryption Standard algorithm with a key length of 128 bits. The AES algorithms were developed to replace the older algorithms based on DES.

- **AES192** The Advanced Encryption Standard algorithm with a key length of 192 bits.

- **AES256** The Advanced Encryption Standard algorithm with a key length of 256 bits. This is the most secure encryption algorithm supported by the Oracle database.

The following statement creates a table with a `CLOB` whose contents are to be encrypted using the AES128 algorithm; notice the use of the `ENCRYPT` and `SECUREFILE` keywords, which are required when encrypting data:

```
CREATE TABLE clob_content (
  id INTEGER PRIMARY KEY,
  clob_column CLOB ENCRYPT USING 'AES128'
) LOB(clob_column) STORE AS SECUREFILE (
  CACHE
);
```

As you can see, the contents of `clob_column` will be encrypted using the AES128 algorithm. If you omit the `USING` keyword and the algorithm, then the default AES192 algorithm is used.

The `CACHE` keyword in the `CREATE TABLE` statement indicates that the database places data from the LOB into the buffer cache for faster access. The options you can use for buffer caching are as follows:

- **CACHE READS** Use when the LOB data will be frequently read, but written only once or occasionally.

- **CACHE** Use when the LOB data will be frequently read and frequently written.

- **NOCACHE** Use when the LOB data will be read once or occasionally and written once or occasionally. This is the default option.

The following `INSERT` statements add two rows to the `clob_content` table:

```
INSERT INTO clob_content (
  id, clob_column
) VALUES (
  1, TO_CLOB('Creeps in this petty pace')
```

```
);

INSERT INTO clob_content (
  id, clob_column
) VALUES (
  2, TO_CLOB(' from day to day')
);
```

The data supplied to `clob_column` in these statements are automatically encrypted behind the scenes by the database.

The following query retrieves the rows from the `clob_content` table:

SELECT *
FROM clob_content;

```
        ID
----------
CLOB_COLUMN
------------------------
         1
Creeps in this petty pace

         2
 from day to day
```

When the data is retrieved, it is automatically decrypted by the database and then returned to SQL*Plus.

As long as the wallet is open, you can store and retrieve encrypted data; when the wallet is closed, you cannot. Let's see what happens when the wallet is closed; the following statements connect as the `system` user and close the wallet:

CONNECT system/manager
ALTER SYSTEM SET WALLET CLOSE;

If you now attempt to connect as `lob_user3` and retrieve `clob_column` from the `clob_content` table, you get the error `ORA-28365: wallet is not open`:

CONNECT lob_user3/lob_password
SELECT clob_column
FROM clob_content;
ORA-28365: wallet is not open

You can still retrieve and modify the contents of unencrypted columns; for example, the following query retrieves the `id` column from the `clob_content` table:

SELECT id
FROM clob_content;

```
        ID
----------
         1
         2
```

The following statements connect as the `system` user and re-open the wallet:

```
CONNECT system/manager
ALTER SYSTEM SET WALLET OPEN IDENTIFIED BY "testpassword123";
```

Once this is done, you can retrieve and modify the contents of `clob_column` from the `clob_content` table.

Encrypting Column Data

You can also encrypt regular column data. This feature was introduced in Oracle Database 10*g* Release 2. For example, the following statement creates a table named `credit_cards` with an encrypted column named `card_number`:

```
CREATE TABLE credit_cards (
  card_number NUMBER(16, 0) ENCRYPT,
  first_name  VARCHAR2(10),
  last_name   VARCHAR2(10),
  expiration  DATE
);
```

You can use the same algorithms to encrypt a column as for a LOB: 3DES168, AES128, AES192 (the default), and AES256. Because I didn't specify an algorithm after the `ENCRYPT` keyword for the `card_number` column, the default AES192 algorithm is used.

The following `INSERT` statements add two rows to the `credit_cards` table:

```
INSERT INTO credit_cards (
  card_number, first_name, last_name, expiration
) VALUES (
  1234, 'Jason', 'Bond', '03-FEB-2008'
);

INSERT INTO credit_cards (
  card_number, first_name, last_name, expiration
) VALUES (
  5768, 'Steve', 'Edwards', '07-MAR-2009'
);
```

As long as the wallet is open, you can retrieve and modify the contents of the `card_number` column. If the wallet is closed, you get the error `ORA-28365: wallet is not open`. You saw examples that illustrate these concepts in the previous section, so I won't repeat similar examples here.

Accessing data in an encrypted column introduces additional overhead. The overhead for encrypting or decrypting a column is estimated by Oracle Corporation to be about 5 percent; this means a `SELECT` or an `INSERT` takes about 5 percent more time to complete. The total overhead depends on the number of encrypted columns and their frequency of access; therefore, you should only encrypt columns that contain sensitive data.

NOTE
If you are interested in learning more about wallets and database security generally, you should read the Advanced Security Administrator's Guide *published by Oracle Corporation.*

Compressing LOB Data

You can compress the data stored in a BLOB, CLOB, or NCLOB to reduce storage space. For example, the following statement creates a table with a CLOB whose contents are to be compressed; notice the use of the COMPRESS keyword:

```
CREATE TABLE clob_content3 (
   id            INTEGER PRIMARY KEY,
   clob_column CLOB
) LOB(clob_column) STORE AS SECUREFILE (
   COMPRESS
   CACHE
);
```

> **NOTE**
> *Even though the table does not contain encrypted data, the* SECUREFILE *clause must be used.*

When you add data to the LOB, it will be automatically compressed by the database; similarly, when you read data from a LOB, it will be automatically decompressed. You can use COMPRESS HIGH for maximum data compression; the default is COMPRESS MEDIUM, and the MEDIUM keyword is optional. The higher the compression, the higher the overhead when reading and writing LOB data.

Removing Duplicate LOB Data

You can configure a BLOB, CLOB, or NCLOB so that any duplicate data supplied to it is automatically removed; this process is known as de-duplicating data and can save storage space. For example, the following statement creates a table with a CLOB whose contents are to be de-duplicated; notice the use of the DEDUPLICATE LOB keywords:

```
CREATE TABLE clob_content2 (
   id            INTEGER PRIMARY KEY,
   clob_column CLOB
) LOB(clob_column) STORE AS SECUREFILE (
   DEDUPLICATE LOB
   CACHE
);
```

Any duplicate data added to the LOB will be automatically removed by the database. The database uses the SHA1 secure hash algorithm to detect duplicate data.

You can learn even more about large objects in the *Oracle Database Large Objects Developer's Guide* published by Oracle Corporation.

Summary

In this chapter, you have learned the following:

■ LOBs may be used to store binary data, character data, and references to external files. LOBs can store up to 128 terabytes of data.

- There are four LOB types: CLOB, NCLOB, BLOB, and BFILE.

- A CLOB stores character data.

- An NCLOB stores multiple byte character data.

- A BLOB stores binary data.

- A BFILE stores a pointer to a file located in the file system.

- A LOB consists of two parts: a locator, which specifies the location of the LOB data, and the data itself.

- The DBMS_LOB PL/SQL package contains methods for accessing LOBs.

In the next chapter, you'll learn how to run SQL statements from a Java program.

CHAPTER
15

Running SQL Using Java

n this chapter, you will do the following:

- Learn how to run SQL from Java programs using the Java Database Connectivity (JDBC) Application Programming Interface (API)

- Examine the various Oracle JDBC drivers that may be used to connect to an Oracle database

- Perform queries and SQL DML statements to access database tables

- Use the various Java types to get and set column values in the database

- Examine how to perform transaction control statements and SQL DDL statements

- Handle database exceptions that may occur when a Java program runs

- Examine the Oracle database software extensions to JDBC

- See complete Java programs that illustrate the use of JDBC

NOTE
This chapter gives an introduction to JDBC. For full details on using JDBC with an Oracle database, you should read my book Oracle9i JDBC Programming *(McGraw-Hill/Osborne, 2002).*

Getting Started

Prior to running the examples in this chapter, you'll need to install a version of Sun's Java Software Development Kit (SDK). You can download the SDK and view full installation instructions from Sun's Java website at java.sun.com.

NOTE
I used Java 1.6.0 when writing this chapter, which is installed with Java EE 5 SDK Update 2.

The directory where you installed the Oracle software on your machine is called the ORACLE_HOME directory. On my Windows computer, this directory is E:\oracle_11g\ product\11.1.0\db1. Inside ORACLE_HOME are many subdirectories, one of which is the jdbc directory. The jdbc directory contains the following:

- A text file named Readme.txt. You should open and read this file, as it contains important items such as release information and the latest installation instructions.

- A directory named lib, which contains a number of Java Archive (JAR) files.

Configuring Your Computer

Once you've downloaded and installed the required software, your next step is to configure your computer to develop and run Java programs containing JDBC statements. You must set four environment variables on your machine:

- `ORACLE_HOME`

- `JAVA_HOME`

- `PATH`

- `CLASSPATH`

If you're using Unix or Linux, you'll also need to set the additional `LD_LIBRARY_PATH` environment variable. You'll learn how to set these environment variables in the following sections.

CAUTION
The information in this section was correct at time of writing. You need to read the Readme.txt file in the ORACLE_HOME\jdbc directory to check the latest release notes and installation instructions.

Setting the ORACLE_HOME Environment Variable

The ORACLE_HOME subdirectory is located in the directory where you installed the Oracle software. You'll need to set an environment variable named `ORACLE_HOME` on your machine that specifies this directory.

Setting an Environment Variable in Windows XP

To set an environment variable in Windows XP, you perform the following steps:

1. Open the Control Panel.
2. Double-click System. This displays the System Properties dialog box.
3. Select the Advanced tab.
4. Click the Environment Variables button. This displays the Environment Variables dialog box.
5. Click the New button in the System Variables area (the lower pane of the dialog box).
6. Set the variable name to `ORACLE_HOME` and set the value to your ORACLE_HOME directory. (On my Windows XP machine, I have `ORACLE_HOME` set to E:\oracle_11g\product\11.1.0\db1.)

Setting an Environment Variable with Unix or Linux

To set an environment variable in Unix or Linux, you need to add lines to a special file; the file you need to modify depends on which shell you're using. If you're using the Bourne, Korn, or Bash shell, then you add lines similar to the following ones to your .profile (when using Bourne or Korn shell) or your .bash_profile (Bash shell):

```
ORACLE_HOME=/u01/app/oracle/product/11.1.0/db_1
export ORACLE_HOME
```

NOTE
You'll need to replace the directory shown in the previous example with the correct ORACLE_HOME for your setup.

If you're using the C shell, you add the following line to your .login file:

```
setenv ORACLE_HOME /u01/app/oracle/product/11.1.0/db_1
```

Setting the JAVA_HOME Environment Variable

The JAVA_HOME environment variable specifies the directory where you installed the Java SDK. For example, if you installed the Java SDK in the E:\java\jdk directory, you create a JAVA_HOME system variable and set it to E:\java\jdk. To do this, you can use similar steps to those shown in the previous section.

Setting the PATH Environment Variable

The PATH environment variable contains a list of directories. When you enter a command using the operating system command line, the computer searches the directories in the PATH for the executable you are trying to run. You need to add the following two directories to your existing PATH:

- The bin subdirectory where you installed the Java SDK
- The BIN subdirectory of ORACLE_HOME

For example, if you installed the Java SDK in the E:\java\jdk directory, and your ORACLE_HOME is E:\oracle_11g\product\11.1.0\db1, then you add E:\java\jdk\bin; E:\oracle_11g\product\11.1.0\db1 to your PATH (notice a semicolon separates the two directories). To add the directories to the PATH in Windows XP, you can use steps similar to those shown earlier.

To add to an existing PATH in Unix or Linux, you need to modify the appropriate file for your shell. For example, if you're using the Bash shell with Linux, then you add lines to the .bash_profile file that are similar to the following:

```
PATH=$PATH:$JAVA_HOME/bin:$ORACLE_HOME/BIN
export PATH
```

Notice that a colon (:) separates the directories.

Setting the CLASSPATH Environment Variable

The CLASSPATH environment variable contains a list of locations where Java class packages are found. A location can be a directory name or the name of a Zip file or JAR file containing classes. The ORACLE_HOME\jdbc\lib directory contains a number of JAR files; which ones you add to your CLASSPATH depends on what Java SDK you're using.

At time of writing, the following was correct for setting a CLASSPATH:

- If you're using JDK 1.6 (or higher), add ORACLE_HOME\jdbc\lib\ojdbc6.jar to your CLASSPATH.
- If you're using JDK 1.5, add ORACLE_HOME\jdbc\lib\ojdbc5.jar to your CLASSPATH.
- If you need National Language support, add ORACLE_HOME\jlib\orai18n.jar to your CLASSPATH.

- If you need the JTA and JNDI features, add ORACLE_HOME\jlib\jta.jar and ORACLE_HOME\jlib\jndi.jar to your `CLASSPATH`. JNDI is the *Java Naming and Directory Interface*. JTA is the *Java Transaction API*.

- You also need to add the current directory to your `CLASSPATH`. You do this by adding a period (`.`) to your `CLASSPATH`. That way, the classes in your current directory will be found by Java when you run your programs.

When Java 1.6 is used and the ORACLE_HOME is E:\oracle_11g\product\11.1.0\db1, an example `CLASSPATH` for Windows XP is as follows:

```
.;E:\oracle_11g\product\11.1.0\db1\jdbc\lib\ojdbc6.jar;
E:\oracle_11g\product\11.1.0\db1\jlib\orai18n.jar
```

If you're using Windows XP, you use the steps described earlier to create a system environment variable called `CLASSPATH`. If you're using Linux and Java 1.6, you should add the following lines to your .bash_profile:

```
CLASSPATH=$CLASSPATH:.:$ORACLE_HOME/jdbc/lib/ojdbc6.jar:
$ORACLE_HOME/jlib/orai18n.jar
export CLASSPATH
```

Setting the LD_LIBRARY_PATH Environment Variable

If you're using Unix or Linux, you'll also need to set the `LD_LIBRARY_PATH` environment variable to $ORACLE_HOME/jdbc/lib. This directory contains shared libraries that are used by the JDBC OCI driver. You add `LD_LIBRARY_PATH` to the appropriate file; for example:

```
LD_LIBRARY_PATH=$ORACLE_HOME/jdbc/lib
export CLASSPATH
```

That concludes configuring your computer. You'll learn about the Oracle JDBC drivers next.

The Oracle JDBC Drivers

In this section, you'll learn about the various Oracle JDBC drivers. These drivers enable the JDBC statements in a Java program to access an Oracle database. There are four Oracle JDBC drivers:

- Thin driver

- OCI driver

- Server-side internal driver

- Server-side Thin driver

The following sections describe each of these drivers.

The Thin Driver

The Thin driver has the smallest footprint of all the drivers, meaning that it requires the least amount of system resources to run. The Thin driver is written entirely in Java. If you are writing a Java applet, you should use the Thin driver. The Thin driver may also be used in stand-alone Java applications and may be used to access all versions of the Oracle database. The Thin driver works only with TCP/IP and requires that Oracle Net be up and running. For details on Oracle Net, you can read the *Oracle Database Net Services Administrator's Guide* published by Oracle Corporation.

NOTE
You don't have to install anything on the client computer to use the Thin driver, and therefore you can use it for applets.

The OCI Driver

The OCI driver requires more resources than the Thin driver, but it generally has better performance. The OCI driver is suitable for programs deployed on the middle tier—a web server, for example.

NOTE
The OCI driver requires that you install it on the client computer and is therefore not suitable for applets.

The OCI driver has a number of performance enhancing features, including the ability to pool database connections and prefetch rows from the database. The OCI driver works with all versions of the database and all of the supported Oracle Net protocols.

The Server-Side Internal Driver

The server-side internal driver provides direct access to the database, and it is used by the Oracle JVM to communicate with that database The Oracle JVM is a Java Virtual Machine that is integrated with the database. You can load a Java class into the database, then publish and run methods contained in that class using the Oracle JVM; the Java code runs on the database server and can access data from a single Oracle session.

The Server-Side Thin Driver

The server-side Thin driver is also used by the Oracle JVM and provides access to remote databases. Like the Thin driver, this driver is also written entirely in Java. Java code that uses the server-side Thin driver can access another session on the same database server or a remote server.

Importing the JDBC Packages

In order for your programs to use JDBC, you must import the required JDBC packages into your Java programs. There are two sets of JDBC packages:

- Standard JDBC packages from Sun Microsystems
- Extension packages from Oracle Corporation

The standard JDBC packages enable your Java programs to access the basic features of most databases, including the Oracle database, SQL Server, DB2, and MySQL. The Oracle extensions to JDBC enable your programs to access all of the Oracle-specific features as well as the Oracle-specific performance extensions. You'll learn about some of the Oracle-specific features later in this chapter.

To use JDBC in your programs you should import the standard `java.sql.*` packages, as shown in the following `import` statement:

```
import java.sql.*;
```

Of course, importing `java.sql.*` imports *all* of the standard JDBC packages. As you become proficient in JDBC, you'll find that you don't always need to import all the classes: you can just import those packages that your program actually uses.

Registering the Oracle JDBC Drivers

Before you can open a database connection, you must first register the Oracle JDBC drivers with your Java program. As mentioned earlier, the JDBC drivers enable your JDBC statements to access the database.

There are two ways to register the Oracle JDBC drivers:

- Use the `forName()` method of the class `java.lang.Class`

- Use the `registerDriver()` method of the JDBC `DriverManager` class

The following example illustrates the use of the `forName()` method:

```
Class.forName("oracle.jdbc.OracleDriver");
```

The second way to register the Oracle JDBC drivers is to use the `registerDriver()` method of the `java.sql.DriverManager` class, as shown in the following example:

```
DriverManager.registerDriver(new oracle.jdbc.OracleDriver());
```

Once you have registered the Oracle JDBC drivers, you can open a connection to a database.

Opening a Database Connection

Before you can issue SQL statements in your Java programs, you must open a database connection. There are two main ways to open a database connection:

- Use the `getConnection()` method of the `DriverManager` class

- Use an Oracle data source object, which must first be created and then connected to. This method uses a standardized way of setting database connection details, and an Oracle data source object may be used with the Java Naming and Directory Interface (JNDI).

I'll describe both of these ways to open a database connection in the following sections, starting with the `getConnection()` method of the `DriverManager` class.

Connecting to the Database Using getConnection()

The `getConnection()` method returns a JDBC `Connection` object, which should be stored in your program so it can be referenced later. The syntax of a call to the `getConnection()` method is as follows:

```
DriverManager.getConnection(URL, username, password);
```

where

- *URL* is the database that your program connects to, along with the JDBC driver you want to use. (See the following section, "The Database URL," for details on the URL.)

- *username* is the name of the database user that your program connects as.

- *password* is the password for the username.

The following example shows the getConnection() method being used to connect to a database:

```
Connection myConnection = DriverManager.getConnection(
    "jdbc:oracle:thin:@localhost:1521:ORCL",
    "store",
    "store_password"
);
```

In this example, the connection is made to a database running on the machine identified as localhost with an Oracle System Identifier (SID) of ORCL; the Oracle JDBC Thin driver is used. The connection is made with the username store and the password store_password. The Connection object returned by the call to getConnection() is stored in myConnection. The connection to a database is made through Oracle Net, which should be up and running when the program line is run.

The Database URL

The database URL specifies the location of the database. The structure of the database URL is dependent on the vendor who provides the JDBC drivers. In the case of Oracle's JDBC drivers, the database URL structure is as follows:

```
driver_name:@driver_information
```

where

- *driver_name* is the name of the Oracle JDBC driver that your program uses. This may be set to one of the following:

  - **jdbc:oracle:thin** The Oracle JDBC Thin driver

  - **jdbc:oracle:oci** The Oracle JDBC OCI driver

- *driver_information* The driver-specific information required to connect to the database. This is dependent on the driver being used. In the case of the Oracle JDBC Thin driver, the driver-specific information may be specified in the following format:

  - **host_name:port:database_SID** Where host_name is the name of the computer, port is the port to access the database, and database_SID is the database SID

For all the Oracle JDBC drivers, including the Thin driver and the various OCI drivers, the driver-specific information may also be specified using Oracle Net keyword-value pairs, which may be specified in the following format:

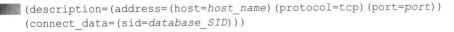

```
(description=(address=(host=host_name)(protocol=tcp)(port=port))
(connect_data=(sid=database_SID)))
```

where

- *host_name* is the name of the computer on which the database is running.

- *port* is the port number on which the Oracle Net database listener waits for requests; 1521 is the default port number. Your DBA can provide the port number.

- *database_SID* is the Oracle SID of the database instance to which you want to connect. Your DBA can provide the database SID.

The following example shows the `getConnection()` method being used to connect to a database using the Oracle OCI driver, with the driver-specific information specified using Oracle Net keyword-value pairs:

```
Connection myConnection = DriverManager.getConnection(
    "jdbc:oracle:oci:@(description=(address=(host=localhost)" +
    "(protocol=tcp)(port=1521))(connect_data=(sid=ORCL)))",
    "store",
    "store_password"
);
```

As you can see, in this example a connection is made to a database running on the machine identified as `localhost`, with an Oracle SID of `ORCL`, using the Oracle OCI driver. The connection to the database is made with the username `store` and with a password of `store_password`. The `Connection` object returned by the call to `getConnection()` is stored in `myConnection`.

> **NOTE**
> *For the Oracle OCI driver, you may also use an Oracle Net TNSNAMES string. For more information on this, speak with your DBA or consult the* Oracle Database Net Services Administrator's Guide *published by Oracle Corporation.*

Connecting to the Database Using an Oracle Data Source

You can also use an Oracle *data source* to connect to a database. An Oracle data source uses a more standardized way of supplying the various parameters to connect to a database than the previous method, which used `DriverManager.getConnection()`. In addition, an Oracle data source may also be registered with JNDI. Using JNDI with JDBC is very useful, because it allows you to register, or *bind*, data sources, and then *look up* those data sources in your program without having to provide the exact database connection details. Thus, if the database connection details change, only the JNDI object must be changed.

> **NOTE**
> *You can learn about JNDI in my book* Oracle9i JDBC Programming *(McGraw-Hill/Osborne, 2002).*

There are three steps that must be performed to use an Oracle data source:

1. Create an Oracle data source object of the `oracle.jdbc.pool.OracleDataSource` class.

2. Set the Oracle data source object attributes using the `set` methods, which are defined in the class.

3. Connect to the database via the Oracle data source object using the `getConnection()` method.

The following sections describe these three steps.

Step 1: Create an Oracle Data Source Object

The first step is to create an Oracle data source object of the `oracle.jdbc.pool` `.OracleDataSource` class. The following example creates an `OracleDataSource` object named myDataSource (you may assume that the `oracle.jdbc.pool.OracleDataSource` class has been imported):

```
OracleDataSource myDataSource = new OracleDataSource();
```

Once you have your `OracleDataSource` object, the second step is to set that object's attributes using the `set` methods.

Step 2: Set the Oracle Data Source Object Attributes

Before you can use your `OracleDataSource` object to connect to a database, you must set a number of attributes in that object to indicate the connection details, using various `set` methods defined in the class. These details include items like the database name, the JDBC driver to use, and so on; each of these details has a corresponding attribute in an `OracleDataSource` object.

The `oracle.jdbc.pool.OracleDataSource` class actually implements the `javax` `.sql.DataSource` interface provided with JDBC. The `javax.sql.DataSource` interface defines a number of attributes, which are listed in Table 15-1. This table shows the name, description, and type of each attribute.

The `oracle.jdbc.pool.OracleDataSource` class provides an additional set of attributes, which are listed in Table 15-2.

You may use a number of methods to read from and write to each of the attributes listed in Tables 15-1 and 15-2. The methods that read from the attributes are known as *get* methods, and the methods that write to the attributes are known as *set* methods.

The `set` and `get` method names are easy to remember: you take the attribute name, convert the first letter to uppercase, and add the word "set" or "get" to the beginning. For example, to set the database name (stored in the `databaseName` attribute), you use the `setDatabaseName()` method; to get the name of the database currently set, you use the `getDatabaseName()` method. There is one exception to this: there is no `getPassword()` method (this is for security reasons—you don't want someone to be able to get your password programmatically).

Most of the attributes are Java `String` objects, so most of the `set` methods accept a single `String` parameter, and most of the `get` methods return a `String`. The exception to this is the `portNumber` attribute, which is an `int`. Therefore, its `set method setPortNumber()` accepts an `int`, and its `get method getPortNumber()` returns an `int`.

Attribute Name	Attribute Description	Attribute Type
databaseName	The database name (Oracle SID).	String
dataSourceName	The name of the underlying data source class.	String
description	Description of the data source.	String
networkProtocol	The network protocol to use to communicate with the database. This applies only to the Oracle JDBC OCI drivers, and defaults to tcp. For further details, read the *Oracle Database Net Services Administrator's Guide* published by Oracle Corporation.	String
password	The password for the supplied username.	String
portNumber	The port on which the Oracle Net listener waits for database connection requests. The default is 1521.	int
serverName	The database server machine name (TCP/IP address or DNS alias).	String
user	The database username.	String

TABLE 15-1　*DataSource Attributes*

Attribute Name	Attribute Description	Attribute Type
driverType	The JDBC driver to use. If you are using the server-side internal driver, this is set to kprb, and the other settings for the attributes are ignored.	String
url	May be used to specify an Oracle database URL, which can be used as an alternative to setting the database location. See the section earlier on database URLs for details.	String
tnsEntryName	May be used to specify an Oracle Net TNSNAMES string, which can also be used to specify the database location when using the OCI drivers.	String

TABLE 15-2　*OracleDataSource Attributes*

The following examples illustrate the use of the `set` methods to write to the attributes of the `OracleDataSource` object `myDataSource` that was created earlier in Step 1:

```
myDataSource.setServerName("localhost");
myDataSource.setDatabaseName("ORCL");
myDataSource.setDriverType("oci");
myDataSource.setNetworkProtocol("tcp");
myDataSource.setPortNumber(1521);
myDataSource.setUser("scott");
myDataSource.setPassword("tiger");
```

The next examples illustrate the use of some of the `get` methods to read the attributes previously set in `myDataSource`:

```
String serverName = myDataSource.getServerName();
String databaseName = myDataSource.getDatabaseName();
String driverType = myDataSource.getDriverType();
String networkProtocol = myDataSource.getNetworkProtocol();
int portNumber = myDataSource.getPortNumber();
```

Once you've set your `OracleDataSource` object attributes, you can use it to connect to the database.

Step 3: Connect to the Database via the Oracle Data Source Object

The third step is to connect to the database via the `OracleDataSource` object. You do this by calling the `getConnection()` method of your `OracleDataSource` object. The `getConnection()` method returns a JDBC `Connection` object, which must be stored.

The following example shows how to call the `getConnection()` method using the `myDataSource` object populated in the previous step:

```
Connection myConnection = myDataSource.getConnection();
```

The `Connection` object returned by `getConnection()` is stored in `myConnection`. You can also pass a username and password as parameters to the `getConnection()` method, as shown in the following example:

```
Connection myConnection = myDataSource.getConnection(
  "store", "store_password"
);
```

In this example, the username and password will override the username and password previously set in `myDataSource`. Therefore, the connection to the database will be made using the username of `store` with a password of `store_password`, rather than `scott` and `tiger`, which were set in `myDataSource` in the previous section.

Once you have your `Connection` object, you can use it to create a JDBC `Statement` object.

Creating a JDBC Statement Object

Next, you need to create a JDBC `Statement` object of the class `java.sql.Statement`. A `Statement` object is used to represent an SQL statement, such as a query, a DML statement (`INSERT`, `UPDATE`, or `DELETE`), or a DDL statement (such as `CREATE TABLE`). You'll learn how to issue queries, DML, and DDL statements later in this chapter.

To create a `Statement` object, you use the `createStatement()` method of a `Connection` object. In the following example, a `Statement` object named `myStatement` is created using the `createStatement()` method of the `myConnection` object created in the previous section:

```
Statement myStatement = myConnection.createStatement();
```

The method used in the `Statement` class to run the SQL statement will depend on the SQL statement you want to perform. If you want to perform a query, you use the `executeQuery()` method. If you want to perform an `INSERT`, `UPDATE`, or `DELETE` statement, you use the `executeUpdate()` method. If you don't know ahead of time which type of SQL statement is to be performed, you can use the `execute()` method, which may be used to perform any SQL statement.

There is another JDBC class that may be used to represent an SQL statement: the `PreparedStatement` class. This offers more advanced functionality than the `Statement` class; I will discuss the `PreparedStatement` class after I have explained the use of the `Statement` class.

Once you have a `Statement` object, you're ready to issue SQL statements using JDBC.

Retrieving Rows from the Database

To perform a query using JDBC, you use the `executeQuery()` method of the `Statement` object, which accepts a Java `String` containing the text for the query.

Because a query may return more than one row, the `executeQuery()` method returns an object that stores the row(s) returned by your query. This object is known as a JDBC *result set* and is of the `java.sql.ResultSet` class. When using a `ResultSet` object to read rows from the database, there are three steps you follow:

1. Create a `ResultSet` object and populate it with the results returned by a query.

2. Read the column values from the `ResultSet` object using `get` methods.

3. Close the `ResultSet` object.

I will now walk you through an example that uses a `ResultSet` object to retrieve the rows from the `customers` table.

Step 1: Create and Populate a ResultSet Object

You first create a `ResultSet` object and populate it with the results returned by a query. The following example creates a `ResultSet` object named `customerResultSet` and populates it with the `customer_id`, `first_name`, `last_name`, `dob`, and `phone` columns from the `customers` table:

```
ResultSet customerResultSet = myStatement.executeQuery(
  "SELECT customer_id, first_name, last_name, dob, phone " +
  "FROM customers"
);
```

After this statement is executed, the `ResultSet` object will contain the column values for the rows retrieved by the query. The `ResultSet` object may then be used to access the column values for the retrieved rows. In the example, `customerResultSet` will contain the five rows retrieved from the `customers` table.

Because the execute() method accepts a Java String, you can build up your SQL statements when your program actually runs. This means that you can do some fairly powerful things in JDBC. For example, you could have the user of your program type in a string containing a WHERE clause for a query when they run the program—or even enter the whole query. The following example shows a WHERE clause string:

```
String whereClause = "WHERE customer_id = 1";
ResultSet customerResultSet2 = myStatement.executeQuery(
  "SELECT customer_id, first_name, last_name, dob, phone " +
  "FROM customers " +
  whereClause
);
```

You're not limited to queries in using this dynamic build-up method: you can build up other SQL statements in a similar manner.

Step 2: Read the Column Values from the ResultSet Object

To read the column values for the rows stored in a ResultSet object, the ResultSet class provides a series of get methods. Before I get into the details of these get methods, you need to understand how the data types used to represent values in Oracle may be mapped to compatible Java data types.

Oracle and Java Types

A Java program uses a different set of types from the Oracle database types to represent values. Fortunately, the types used by Oracle are compatible with certain Java types. This allows Java and Oracle to interchange data stored in their respective types. Table 15-3 shows one set of compatible type mappings.

From this table, you can see that an Oracle INTEGER is compatible with a Java int. (I'll talk about the other numeric types later in this chapter in the section "Handling Numbers.") This means that the customer_id column of the customers table (which is defined as an Oracle INTEGER)

Oracle Type	Java Type
CHAR	String
VARCHAR2	String
DATE	java.sql.Date
	java.sql.Time
	java.sql.Timestamp
INTEGER	short
	int
	long
NUMBER	float
	double
	java.math.BigDecimal

TABLE 15-3 *Compatible Type Mappings*

may be stored in a Java `int` variable. Similarly, the `first_name`, `last_name`, and `phone` column values (`VARCHAR2s`) may be stored in Java `String` variables.

The Oracle `DATE` type stores a year, month, day, hour, minute, and second. You may use a `java.sql.Date` object to store the date part of the `dob` column value and a `java.sql.Time` variable to store the time part. You may also use a `java.sql.Timestamp` object to store both the date and time parts of the `dob` column. Later in this chapter, I'll discuss the `oracle.sql.DATE` type, which is an Oracle extension to the JDBC standard and provides a superior way of storing dates and times.

Getting back to the example, the `customer_id`, `first_name`, `last_name`, `dob`, and `phone` columns are retrieved by the query in the previous section, and the following examples declare Java variables and objects that are compatible with those columns:

```
int customerId = 0;
String firstName = null;
String lastName = null;
java.sql.Date dob = null;
String phone = null;
```

The `int` and `String` types are part of the core Java language, while `java.sql.Date` is part of JDBC and is an extension of the core Java language. JDBC provides a number of such types that allow Java and a relational database to exchange data. However, JDBC doesn't have types to handle all of the types used by Oracle; one example is the `ROWID` type—you must use the `oracle.sql.ROWID` type to store an Oracle `ROWID`.

To handle all of the Oracle types, Oracle provides a number of additional types, which are defined in the `oracle.sql` package. Also, Oracle has a number of types that may be used as an alternative to the core Java and JDBC types, and in some cases these alternatives offer more functionality and better performance than the core Java and JDBC types. I'll talk more about the Oracle types defined in the `oracle.sql` package later in this chapter.

Now that you understand a little bit about compatible Java and Oracle types, let's continue with the example and see how to use the `get` methods to read column values.

Using the Get Methods to Read Column Values

The `get` methods are used to read values stored in a `ResultSet` object. The name of each `get` method is simple to understand: take the name of the Java type you want the column value to be returned as and add the word "get" to the beginning. For example, use `getInt()` to read a column value as a Java `int`, and use `getString()` to read a column value as a Java `String`. To read the value as a `java.sql.Date`, you would use `getDate()`. Each `get` method accepts one parameter: either an `int` representing the position of the column in the original query or a `String` containing the name of the column. Let's examine some examples based on the earlier example that retrieved the columns from the `customers` table in the `customerResultSet` object.

To get the value of the `customer_id` column, which was the first column specified in the query, you use `getInt(1)`. You can also use the name of the column in the `get` method, so you could also use `getInt("customer_id")` to get the same value.

TIP
Using the column name rather than the column position number in a get method makes your code easier to read.

To get the value of the `first_name` column, which was the second column specified in the query, you use `getString(2)` or `getString("first_name")`. You use similar method calls to get the `last_name` and `phone` column values because those columns are also text strings. To get the value of the `dob` column, you could use `getDate(4)` or `getDate("dob")`. To actually read the values stored in a `ResultSet` object, you must call the `get` methods using that `ResultSet` object.

Because a `ResultSet` object may contain more than one row, JDBC provides a method named `next()` that allows you to step through each row stored in a `ResultSet` object. You must call the `next()` method to access the first row in the `ResultSet` object, and each successive call to `next()` steps to the next row. When there are no more rows in the `ResultSet` object to read, the `next()` method returns the Boolean `false` value.

Okay, let's get back to our example: we have a `ResultSet` object named `customerResultSet` that has five rows containing the column values retrieved from the `customer_id, first_name, last_name, dob,` and `phone` columns in the `customers` table. The following example shows a `while` loop that reads the column values from `customerResultSet` into the `customerId, firstName, lastName, dob,` and `phone` objects created earlier:

```
while (customerResultSet.next()) {
    customerId = customerResultSet.getInt("customer_id");
    firstName = customerResultSet.getString("first_name");
    lastName = customerResultSet.getString("last_name");
    dob = customerResultSet.getDate("dob");
    phone = customerResultSet.getString("phone");

    System.out.println("customerId = " + customerId);
    System.out.println("firstName = " + firstName);
    System.out.println("lastName = " + lastName);
    System.out.println("dob = " + dob);
    System.out.println("phone = " + phone);
} // end of while loop
```

When there are no more rows to read from `customerResultSet`, the `next()` method returns `false` and the loop terminates. You'll notice that the example passes the name of the column to be read, rather than numeric positions, to the `get` methods. Also, I've copied the column values into Java variables and objects; for example, the value returned from `customerResultSet.getInt("customer_id")` is copied to `customerId`. You don't have to do that copy: you could simply use the `get` method call whenever you need the value. However, it is generally better if you copy it to a Java variable or object, because it will save time if you use that value more than once (the time is saved because you don't have to call the `get` method again).

Step 3: Close the ResultSet Object

Once you've finished with your `ResultSet` object, you must close that `ResultSet` object using the `close()` method. The following example closes `customerResultSet`:

```
customerResultSet.close();
```

NOTE
It is important that you remember to close your `ResultSet` *object once you've finished with it. Doing so ensures that the object is scheduled for garbage collection.*

Now that you've seen how to retrieve rows, I'll show you how to add rows to a database table using JDBC.

Adding Rows to the Database

You use the SQL INSERT statement to add rows to a table. There are two main ways you can perform an INSERT statement using JDBC:

- Use the `executeUpdate()` method defined in the `Statement` class.

- Use the `execute()` method defined in the `PreparedStatement` class. (I will discuss this class later in this chapter.)

The examples in this section illustrate how to add a row to the `customers` table. The `customer_id`, `first_name`, `last_name`, `dob`, and `phone` columns for this new row will be set to 6; Jason; Price; February 22, 1969; and 800-555-1216, respectively.

To add this new row, I'll use the same `Statement` object declared earlier (`myStatement`), along with the same variables and objects that were used to retrieve the rows from the `customers` table in the previous section. First off, I'll set those variables and objects to the values that I want to set the database columns to in the `customers` table:

```
customerId = 6;
firstName = "Jason";
lastName = "Red";
dob = java.sql.Date.valueOf("1969-02-22");
phone = "800-555-1216";
```

NOTE
The `java.sql.Date` *class stores dates using the format* `YYYY-MM-DD`, *where* `YYYY` *is the year,* `MM` *is the month number, and* `DD` *is the day number. You can also use the* `java.sql.Time` *and* `java.sql` `.Timestamp` *classes to represent times and dates containing times, respectively.*

When you attempt to specify a date in an SQL statement, you first convert it to a format that the database can understand by using the TO_DATE() built-in database function. TO_DATE() accepts a string containing a date, along with the format for that date. You'll see the use of the TO_DATE() function shortly in the INSERT statement example. Later in this chapter, I'll discuss the Oracle JDBC extensions, and you'll see a superior way of representing Oracle-specific dates using the `oracle.sql.DATE` type.

We're ready to perform an INSERT to add the new row to the `customers` table. The `myStatement` object is used to perform the INSERT statement, setting the `customer_id`, first_name, last_name, dob, and phone column values equal to the values previously set in the customerId, firstName, lastName, dob, and phone variables.

```
myStatement.executeUpdate(
  "INSERT INTO customers " +
  "(customer_id, first_name, last_name, dob, phone) VALUES (" +
    customerId + ", '" + firstName + "', '" + lastName + "', " +
  "TO_DATE('" + dob + "', 'YYYY, MM, DD'), '" + phone + "')"
);
```

Notice the use of the TO_DATE() function to convert the contents of the dob object to an acceptable Oracle database date. Once this statement has completed, the customers table will contain the new row.

Modifying Rows in the Database

You use the SQL UPDATE statement to modify existing rows in a table. Just as with performing an INSERT statement with JDBC, you can use the executeUpdate() method defined in the Statement class or the execute() method defined in the PreparedStatement class. Use of the PreparedStatement class is covered later in this chapter.

The following example illustrates how to modify the row where the customer_id column is equal to 1:

```
first_name = "Jean";
myStatement.executeUpdate(
  "UPDATE customers " +
  "SET first_name = '" + firstName + "' " +
  "WHERE customer_id = 1"
);
```

After this statement runs, customer #1's first name will be set to "Jean".

Deleting Rows from the Database

You use the SQL DELETE statement to delete existing rows from a table. You can use the executeUpdate() method defined in the Statement class or the execute() method defined in the PreparedStatement class.

The following example illustrates how to delete customer #5 from the customers table:

```
myStatement.executeUpdate(
  "DELETE FROM customers " +
  "WHERE customer_id = 5"
);
```

After this statement runs, the row for customer #5 will have been removed from the customers table.

Handling Numbers

This section describes the issues associated with storing numbers in your Java programs. An Oracle database is capable of storing numbers with a precision of up to 38 digits. In the context of number representation, precision refers to the accuracy with which a floating-point number may be represented in a digital computer's memory. The 38 digits level of precision offered by the database allows you to store very large numbers.

That precision capability is fine when working with numbers in the database, but Java uses its own set of types to represent numbers. This means you must be careful when selecting the Java type that will be used to represent numbers in your programs, especially if those numbers are going to be stored in a database.

To store integers in your Java program, you can use the `short`, `int`, `long`, or `java.math` `.BigInteger` types, depending on how big the integer you want to store is. Table 15-4 shows the number of bits used to store `short`, `int`, and `long` types, along with the low and high values supported by each type.

To store floating-point numbers in your Java programs, you can use the `float`, `double`, or `java.math.BigDecimal` types. Table 15-5 shows the same columns as Table 15-4 for the `float` and `double` types, along with the precision supported by each of these types.

As you can see, a `float` may be used to store floating-point numbers with a precision of up to 6 digits, and a `double` may be used for floating-point numbers with a precision of up to 15 digits. If you have a floating-point number that requires more than 15 digits of precision for storage in your Java program, you can use the `java.math.BigDecimal` type, which can store an arbitrarily long floating-point number.

In addition to these types, there is one of the Oracle JDBC extension types you can use to store your integers or floating-point numbers. This type is `oracle.sql.NUMBER`, and it allows you to store numbers with up to 38 digits of precision. You'll learn more about the `oracle.sql` `.NUMBER` type later in this chapter. In Oracle Database 10g and above, you can use the `oracle` `.sql.BINARY_FLOAT` and `oracle.sql.BINARY_DOUBLE` types. These types allow you to store the `BINARY_FLOAT` and `BINARY_DOUBLE` numbers.

Let's take a look at some examples of using these integer and floating-point types to store the `product_id` and `price` column values for a row retrieved from the `products` table. Assume that a `ResultSet` object named `productResultSet` has been populated with the `product_id` and `price` columns for a row from the `products` table. The `product_id` column is defined

Type	Bits	Low Value	High Value
short	16	–32768	32767
int	32	–2147483648	2147483647
long	64	–9223372036854775808	9223372036854775807

TABLE 15-4 *The short, int, and long Types*

Type	Bits	Low Value	High Value	Precision
float	32	−3.4E+38	3.4E+38	6 digits
double	64	−1.7E+308	1.7E+308	15 digits

TABLE 15-5 *The float and double Types*

as a database INTEGER, and the price column is defined as a database NUMBER. The following example creates variables of the various integer and floating-point types and retrieves the product_id and price column values into those variables:

```
short productIdShort = productResultSet.getShort("product_id");
int productIdInt = productResultSet.getInt("product_id");
long productIdLong = productResultSet.getLong("product_id");
float priceFloat = productResultSet.getFloat("price");
double priceDouble = productResultSet.getDouble("price");
java.math.BigDecimal priceBigDec = productResultSet.getBigDecimal("price");
```

Notice the use of the different get methods to retrieve the column values as the different types, the output of which is then stored in a Java variable of the appropriate type.

Handling Database Null Values

A column in a database table may be defined as being NULL or NOT NULL. NULL indicates that the column may store a NULL value; NOT NULL indicates that the column may not contain a NULL value. A NULL value means that the value is unknown. When a table is created in the database and you don't specify that a column is NULL or NOT NULL, the database assumes you mean NULL.

The Java object types, such as String, may be used to store database NULL values. When a query is used to retrieve a column that contains a NULL value into a Java String, that String will contain a Java null value. For example, the phone column (a VARCHAR2) for customer #5 is NULL, and the following statement uses the getString() method to read that value into a String named phone:

```
phone = customerResultSet.getString("phone");
```

Once the statement is run, the phone Java String will contain the Java null value.

That method's fine for NULL values being stored in Java objects, but what about the Java numeric, logical, and bit type types? If you retrieve a NULL value into a Java numeric, logical, or bit variable—int, float, boolean, or byte, for example—that variable will contain the value zero. To the database, zero and NULL are different values: zero is a definite value; NULL means the value is unknown. This causes a problem if you want to differentiate between zero and NULL in your Java program.

There are two ways to get around this problem:

■ You can use the wasNull() method in the ResultSet. The wasNull() method returns true if the value retrieved from the database was NULL; otherwise, the method returns false.

■ You can use a Java *wrapper class*. A wrapper class is a Java class that allows you to define a *wrapper object*, which can then be used to store the column value returned from the database. A wrapper object stores database NULL values as Java null values, and non-NULL values are stored as regular values.

Let's take a look at an example that illustrates the use of first technique, using product #12 from the products table. This row has a NULL value in the product_type_id column, and this column is defined as a database INTEGER. Also, assume that a ResultSet object named productResultSet has been populated with the product_id and product_type_id columns for product #12 from the products table. The following example uses the wasNull() method to check if the value read for the product_type_id column was NULL:

```
System.out.println("product_type_id = " +
  productResultSet.getInt("product_type_id"));
if (productResultSet.wasNull()) {
  System.out.println("Last value read was NULL");
}
```

Because the product_type_id column contains a NULL value, wasNull() will return true, and so the string "Last value read was NULL" would be displayed.

Before you see an example of the second method that uses the Java wrapper classes, I need to explain what these wrapper classes actually are. The wrapper classes are defined in the java.lang package, with the following seven wrapper classes being defined in that package:

■ java.lang.Short

■ java.lang.Integer

■ java.lang.Long

■ java.lang.Float

■ java.lang.Double

■ java.lang.Boolean

■ java.lang.Byte

Objects declared using these wrapper classes can be used to represent database NULL values for the various types of numbers as well as for the Boolean type. When a database NULL is retrieved into such an object, it will contain the Java null value. The following example declares a java.lang.Integer named productTypeId:

```
java.lang.Integer productTypeId;
```

A database NULL may then be stored in productTypeId using a call to the getObject() method, as shown in the following example:

```
productTypeId =
  (java.lang.Integer) productResultSet.getObject("product_type_id");
```

The getObject() method returns an instance of the java.lang.Object class and must be cast into an appropriate type, in this case, to a java.lang.Integer. Assuming this example reads the same row from `productResultSet` as the previous example, `getObject()` will return a Java `null` value, and this value will be copied into `productTypeId`. Of course, if the value retrieved from the database had a value other than `NULL`, `productTypeId` would contain that value. For example, if the value retrieved from the database was 1, `productTypeId` would contain the value 1.

You can also use a wrapper object in a JDBC statement that performs an `INSERT` or `UPDATE` to set a column to a regular value or a `NULL` value. If you want to set a column value to `NULL` using a wrapper object, you would set that wrapper object to `null` and use it in an `INSERT` or `UPDATE` statement to set the database column to `NULL`. The following example sets the `price` column for product #12 to `NULL` using a `java.lang.Double` object that is set to `null`:

```
java.lang.Double price = null;
myStatement.executeUpdate(
  "UPDATE products " +
  "SET price = " + price + " " +
  "WHERE product_id = 12"
);
```

Controlling Database Transactions

In Chapter 8 you learned about database transactions and how to use the SQL `COMMIT` statement to permanently record changes you make to the contents of tables. You also saw how to use the `ROLLBACK` statement to undo changes in a database transaction. The same concepts apply to SQL statements executed using JDBC statements within your Java programs.

By default, the results of your `INSERT`, `UPDATE`, and `DELETE` statements executed using JDBC are immediately committed. This is known as *auto-commit* mode. Generally, using auto-commit mode is *not* the preferred way of committing changes, because it is counter to the idea of considering transactions as logical units of work. With auto-commit mode, all statements are considered as individual transactions, and this assumption is usually incorrect. Also, auto-commit mode may cause your SQL statements to take longer to complete, due to the fact that each statement is always committed.

Fortunately, you can enable or disable auto-commit mode using the `setAutoCommit()` method of the `Connection` class, passing it a Boolean `true` or `false` value. The following example disables auto-commit mode for the `Connection` object named `myConnection`:

```
myConnection.setAutoCommit(false);
```

TIP
You should disable auto-commit mode. Doing this will usually make your programs run faster.

Once auto-commit has been disabled, you can commit your transaction changes using the `commit()` method of the `Connection` class, or you can roll back your changes using the `rollback()` method. In the following example, the `commit()` method is used to commit changes made to the database using the `myConnection` object:

```
myConnection.commit();
```

In the next example, the `rollback()` method is used to roll back changes made to the database:

```
myConnection.rollback();
```

If auto-commit has been disabled and you close your `Connection` object, an implicit commit is performed. Therefore, any DML statements you have performed up to that point and haven't already committed will be committed automatically.

Performing Data Definition Language Statements

The SQL Data Definition Language (DDL) statements are used to create database users, tables, and many other types of database structures that make up a database. DDL consists of statements such as CREATE, ALTER, DROP, TRUNCATE, and RENAME. DDL statements may be performed in JDBC using the `execute()` method of the `Statement` class. In the following example, the CREATE TABLE statement is used to create a table named addresses, which may be used to store customer addresses:

```
myStatement.execute(
  "CREATE TABLE addresses (" +
  "   address_id INTEGER CONSTRAINT addresses_pk PRIMARY KEY," +
  "   customer_id INTEGER CONSTRAINT addresses_fk_customers " +
  "     REFERENCES customers(customer_id)," +
  "   street VARCHAR2(20) NOT NULL," +
  "   city VARCHAR2(20) NOT NULL," +
  "   state CHAR(2) NOT NULL" +
  ")"
);
```

NOTE
Performing a DDL statement results in an implicit commit being issued. Therefore, if you've performed uncommitted DML statements prior to issuing a DDL statement, those DML statements will also be committed.

Handling Exceptions

When an error occurs in either the database or the JDBC driver, a `java.sql.SQLException` will be raised. The `java.sql.SQLException` class is a subclass of the `java.lang.Exception` class. For this reason, you must place all your JDBC statements within a `try`/`catch` statement in order for your code not to throw a `java.sql.SQLException`. When such an exception occurs, Java attempts to locate the appropriate handler to process the exception.

If you include a handler for a `java.sql.SQLException` in a `catch` clause, when an error occurs in either the database or the JDBC driver, Java will move to that handler and run the appropriate code that you've included in that `catch` clause. In the handler code, you can do things like display the error code and error message, which will help you determine what happened.

The following `try`/`catch` statement contains a handler for exceptions of type `java.sql.SQLException` that may occur in the `try` statement:

```
try {
  ...
} catch (SQLException e) {
  ...
}
```

NOTE
I'm assuming java.sql.* *has been imported, so I can simply use*
SQLException *in the catch, rather than having to reference* java
.sql.SQLException.

The try statement will contain your JDBC statements that may cause an SQLException to be thrown, and the catch clause will contain your error handling code.

The SQLException class defines four methods that are useful for finding out what caused the exception to occur:

- **getErrorCode()**   In the case of errors that occur in the database or the JDBC driver, this method returns the Oracle error code, which is a five-digit number.

- **getMessage()**   In the case of errors that occur in the database, this method returns the error message along with the five-digit Oracle error code. In the case of errors that occur in the JDBC driver, this method returns just the error message.

- **getSQLState()**   In the case of errors that occur in the database, this method returns a five-digit code containing the SQL state. In the case of errors that occur in the JDBC driver, this method doesn't return anything of interest.

- **printStackTrace()**   This method displays the contents of the stack when the exception occurred. This information may further assist you in finding out what went wrong.

The following try/catch statement illustrates the use of these four methods:

```
try {
  ...
} catch (SQLException e) {
  System.out.println("Error code = " + e.getErrorCode());
  System.out.println("Error message = " + e.getMessage());
  System.out.println("SQL state = " + e.getSQLState());
  e.printStackTrace();
}
```

If your code throws an SQLException rather than handling it locally as just shown, Java will search for an appropriate handler in the calling procedure or function until one is found. If none is found, the exception will be handled by the default exception handler, which displays the Oracle error code, the error message, and the stack trace.

Closing Your JDBC Objects

In the examples shown in this chapter, I've created a number of JDBC objects: a Connection object named myConnection, a Statement object named myStatement, and two ResultSet objects named customerResultSet and productResultSet. ResultSet objects should be closed when they are no longer needed using the close() method. Similarly, you should also close the Statement and Connection objects when those objects are no longer needed.

In the following example, the myStatement and myConnection objects are closed using the close() method:

```
myStatement.close();
myConnection.close();
```

You should typically close your `Statement` and `Connection` objects in a `finally` clause. Any code contained in a `finally` clause is guaranteed to be run, no matter how control leaves the `try` statement. If you want to add a `finally` clause to close your `Statement` and `Connection` objects, those objects should be declared before the first `try`/`catch` statement used to trap exceptions. The following example shows how to structure the `main()` method so that the `Statement` and `Connection` objects may be closed in a `finally` clause:

```java
public static void main (String args []) {
  // declare Connection and Statement objects
  Connection myConnection = null;
  Statement myStatement = null;

  try {
    // register the Oracle JDBC drivers
    DriverManager.registerDriver(
      new oracle.jdbc.driver.OracleDriver()
    );

    // connect to the database as store
    // using the Oracle JDBC Thin driver
    myConnection = DriverManager.getConnection(
      "jdbc:oracle:thin:@localhost:1521:ORCL",
      "store",
      "store_password"
    );

    // create a Statement object
    myStatement = myConnection.createStatement();

    // more of your code goes here
    ...
  } catch (SQLException e) {
    e.printStackTrace();
  } finally {
    try {
      // close the Statement object using the close() method
      if (myStatement != null) {
        myStatement.close();
      }

      // close the Connection object using the close() method
      if (myConnection != null) {
        myConnection.close();
      }
    } catch (SQLException e) {
      e.printStackTrace();
    }
  }
} // end of main()
```

Notice that the code in the `finally` clause checks to see if the `Statement` and `Connection` objects are not equal to `null` before closing them using the `close()` method. If they are equal to `null`, there is no need to close them. Because the code in the `finally` clause is the last thing to be run and is guaranteed to be run, the `Statement` and `Connection` objects are always closed, regardless of what else happens in your program. For the sake of brevity, only the first program featured in this chapter uses a `finally` clause to close the `Statement` and `Connection` objects.

You have now seen how to write JDBC statements that connect to a database, run DML and DDL statements, control transactions, handle exceptions, and close JDBC objects. The following section contains a complete program that illustrates the use of JDBC.

Example Program: BasicExample1.java

The `BasicExample1.java` program illustrates the concepts covered in this chapter so far. This program and the other programs featured in this chapter may be found in the `Java` folder where you extracted this book's Zip file. All the programs contain detailed comments that you should study.

```
/*
  BasicExample1.java shows how to:
  - import the JDBC packages
  - load the Oracle JDBC drivers
  - connect to a database
  - perform DML statements
  - control transactions
  - use ResultSet objects to retrieve rows
  - use the get methods
  - perform DDL statements
*/

// import the JDBC packages
import java.sql.*;

public class BasicExample1 {
  public static void main (String args []) {
    // declare Connection and Statement objects
    Connection myConnection = null;
    Statement myStatement = null;

    try {
      // register the Oracle JDBC drivers
      DriverManager.registerDriver(
        new oracle.jdbc.OracleDriver()
      );

      // EDIT AS NECESSARY TO CONNECT TO YOUR DATABASE
      // create a Connection object, and connect to the database
      // as the store user using the Oracle JDBC Thin driver
      myConnection = DriverManager.getConnection(
        "jdbc:oracle:thin:@localhost:1521:ORCL",
        "store",
```

```
  "store_password"
);

// disable auto-commit mode
myConnection.setAutoCommit(false);

// create a Statement object
myStatement = myConnection.createStatement();

// create variables and objects used to represent
// column values
int customerId = 6;
String firstName = "Jason";
String lastName = "Red";
java.sql.Date dob = java.sql.Date.valueOf("1969-02-22");
java.sql.Time dobTime;
java.sql.Timestamp dobTimestamp;
String phone = "800-555-1216";

// perform SQL INSERT statement to add a new row to the
// customers table using the values set in the previous
// step - the executeUpdate() method of the Statement
// object is used to perform the INSERT
myStatement.executeUpdate(
  "INSERT INTO customers " +
  "(customer_id, first_name, last_name, dob, phone) VALUES (" +
    customerId + ", '" + firstName + "', '" + lastName + "', " +
  "TO_DATE('" + dob + "', 'YYYY, MM, DD'), '" + phone + "')"
);
System.out.println("Added row to customers table");

// perform SQL UPDATE statement to modify the first_name
// column of customer #1
firstName = "Jean";
myStatement.executeUpdate(
  "UPDATE customers " +
  "SET first_name = '" + firstName + "' " +
  "WHERE customer_id = 1"
);
System.out.println("Updated row in customers table");

// perform SQL DELETE statement to remove customer #5
myStatement.executeUpdate(
  "DELETE FROM customers " +
  "WHERE customer_id = 5"
);
System.out.println("Deleted row from customers table");

// create a ResultSet object, and populate it with the
// result of a SELECT statement that retrieves the
// customer_id, first_name, last_name, dob, and phone columns
```

```
// for all the rows from the customers table  - the
// executeQuery() method of the Statement object is used
// to perform the SELECT
ResultSet customerResultSet = myStatement.executeQuery(
  "SELECT customer_id, first_name, last_name, dob, phone " +
  "FROM customers"
);
System.out.println("Retrieved rows from customers table");

// loop through the rows in the ResultSet object using the
// next() method, and use the get methods to read the values
// retrieved from the database columns
while (customerResultSet.next()) {
  customerId = customerResultSet.getInt("customer_id");
  firstName = customerResultSet.getString("first_name");
  lastName = customerResultSet.getString("last_name");
  dob = customerResultSet.getDate("dob");
  dobTime = customerResultSet.getTime("dob");
  dobTimestamp = customerResultSet.getTimestamp("dob");
  phone = customerResultSet.getString("phone");

  System.out.println("customerId = " + customerId);
  System.out.println("firstName = " + firstName);
  System.out.println("lastName = " + lastName);
  System.out.println("dob = " + dob);
  System.out.println("dobTime = " + dobTime);
  System.out.println("dobTimestamp = " + dobTimestamp);
  System.out.println("phone = " + phone);
} // end of while loop

// close the ResultSet object using the close() method
customerResultSet.close();

// roll back the changes made to the database
myConnection.rollback();

// create numeric variables to store the product_id and price columns
short productIdShort;
int productIdInt;
long productIdLong;
float priceFloat;
double priceDouble;
java.math.BigDecimal priceBigDec;

// create another ResultSet object and retrieve the
// product_id, product_type_id, and price columns for product #12
// (this row has a NULL value in the product_type_id column)
ResultSet productResultSet = myStatement.executeQuery(
  "SELECT product_id, product_type_id, price " +
  "FROM products " +
  "WHERE product_id = 12"
);
```

```java
System.out.println("Retrieved row from products table");

while (productResultSet.next()) {
  System.out.println("product_id = " +
    productResultSet.getInt("product_id"));
  System.out.println("product_type_id = " +
    productResultSet.getInt("product_type_id"));

  // check if the value just read by the get method was NULL
  if (productResultSet.wasNull()) {
    System.out.println("Last value read was NULL");
  }

  // use the getObject() method to read the value, and convert it
  // to a wrapper object - this converts a database NULL value to a
  // Java null value
  java.lang.Integer productTypeId =
    (java.lang.Integer) productResultSet.getObject("product_type_id");
  System.out.println("productTypeId = " + productTypeId);

  // retrieve the product_id and price column values into
  // the various numeric variables created earlier
  productIdShort = productResultSet.getShort("product_id");
  productIdInt = productResultSet.getInt("product_id");
  productIdLong = productResultSet.getLong("product_id");
  priceFloat = productResultSet.getFloat("price");
  priceDouble = productResultSet.getDouble("price");
  priceBigDec = productResultSet.getBigDecimal("price");
  System.out.println("productIdShort = " + productIdShort);
  System.out.println("productIdInt = " + productIdInt);
  System.out.println("productIdLong = " + productIdLong);
  System.out.println("priceFloat = " + priceFloat);
  System.out.println("priceDouble = " + priceDouble);
  System.out.println("priceBigDec = " + priceBigDec);
} // end of while loop

// close the ResultSet object
productResultSet.close();

// perform SQL DDL CREATE TABLE statement to create a new table
// that may be used to store customer addresses
myStatement.execute(
  "CREATE TABLE addresses (" +
  "  address_id INTEGER CONSTRAINT addresses_pk PRIMARY KEY," +
  "  customer_id INTEGER CONSTRAINT addresses_fk_customers " +
  "    REFERENCES customers(customer_id)," +
  "  street VARCHAR2(20) NOT NULL," +
  "  city VARCHAR2(20) NOT NULL," +
  "  state CHAR(2) NOT NULL" +
  ")"
);
System.out.println("Created addresses table");
```

```
            // drop this table using the SQL DDL DROP TABLE statement
            myStatement.execute("DROP TABLE addresses");
            System.out.println("Dropped addresses table");
        } catch (SQLException e) {
            System.out.println("Error code = " + e.getErrorCode());
            System.out.println("Error message = " + e.getMessage());
            System.out.println("SQL state = " + e.getSQLState());
            e.printStackTrace();
        } finally {
            try {
                // close the Statement object using the close() method
                if (myStatement != null) {
                    myStatement.close();
                }

                // close the Connection object using the close() method
                if (myConnection != null) {
                    myConnection.close();
                }
            } catch (SQLException e) {
                e.printStackTrace();
            }
        }
    } // end of main()
}
```

NOTE
You may need to edit the line labeled with the text EDIT AS
NECESSARY... *with the correct settings to access your database.*

Compile BasicExample1

To compile `BasicExample1.java`, you type the following command using your operating
system command prompt:

```
javac BasicExample1.java
```

If you haven't set the CLASSPATH environment variable properly, you'll get the following
error message when trying to compile the `FirstExample.java` program:

```
FirstExample.java:22: cannot resolve symbol
symbol  : class OracleDriver
location: package jdbc
        new oracle.jdbc.OracleDriver()
                   ^
1 error
```

You should check the setting for your CLASSPATH environment variable—it's likely your
CLASSPATH is missing the Oracle JDBC classes file (`ojdbc6.jar`, for example). Refer to the
earlier section "Setting the CLASSPATH Environment Variable."

TIP
You can enter javac -help *to get help on the Java compiler.*

Run BasicExample1

Once `BasicExample1.java` is compiled, you can run the resulting executable class file
(named `BasicExample1.class`) by entering the following command:

```
java BasicExample1
```

CAUTION
Java is case-sensitive, so make sure you enter `BasicExample1` *with
uppercase B and E characters.*

If the program fails with the following error code and message, it means the `store` user with
a password of `store_password` doesn't exist in your database:

```
Error code = 1017
Error message = ORA-01017: invalid username/password; logon denied
```

If you get this error, check that the `store` user is in the database.

The program may also be unable to find your database, in which case you'll get the following
error:

```
Error code = 17002
Error message = Io exception: The Network Adapter could not establish
 the connection
```

Typically, there are two reasons why you might get this error:

■ There is no database running on your `localhost` machine with the Oracle SID of `ORCL`.

■ Oracle Net is not running or is not listening for connections on port 1521.

You should ensure that you have the right connection string in the program and also that the
database and Oracle Net are running.

Assuming the program runs, you should get the following output:

```
Added row to customers table
Updated row in customers table
Deleted row from customers table
Retrieved rows from customers table
customerId = 1
firstName = Jean
lastName = Brown
dob = 1965-01-01
dobTime = 00:00:00
dobTimestamp = 1965-01-01 00:00:00.0
phone = 800-555-1211
customerId = 2
firstName = Cynthia
lastName = Green
dob = 1968-02-05
dobTime = 00:00:00
dobTimestamp = 1968-02-05 00:00:00.0
phone = 800-555-1212
```

```
customerId = 3
firstName = Steve
lastName = White
dob = 1971-03-16
dobTime = 00:00:00
dobTimestamp = 1971-03-16 00:00:00.0
phone = 800-555-1213
customerId = 4
firstName = Gail
lastName = Black
dob = null
dobTime = null
dobTimestamp = null
phone = 800-555-1214
customerId = 6
firstName = Jason
lastName = Red
dob = 1969-02-22
dobTime = 00:00:00
dobTimestamp = 1969-02-22 00:00:00.0
phone = 800-555-1216
Retrieved row from products table
product_id = 12
product_type_id = 0
Last value read was NULL
productTypeId = null
productIdShort = 12
productIdInt = 12
productIdLong = 12
priceFloat = 13.49
priceDouble = 13.49
priceBigDec = 13.49
Created addresses table
Dropped addresses table
```

Prepared SQL Statements

When you send an SQL statement to the database, the database software reads the SQL statement and verifies that it is correct. This is known as *parsing* the SQL statement. The database software then builds a plan, known as the *execution plan*, to actually run the statement. So far, all the SQL statements sent to the database through JDBC have required a new execution plan to be built. This is because each SQL statement sent to the database has been different.

Suppose you had a Java application that was performing the same INSERT statement repeatedly; an example is loading many new products to our example store, a process that would require adding lots of rows to the products table using INSERT statements. Let's see Java statements that would actually do this. Assume that a class named Product has been defined as follows:

```
class Product {
    int productId;
    int productTypeId;
    String name;
```

```
  String description;
  double price;
}
```

The following code creates an array of five `Product` objects. Because the `products` table already contains rows with `product_id` values from 1 to 12, the `productId` attributes for the new `Product` objects start at 13:

```
Product [] productArray = new Product[5];
for (int counter = 0; counter < productArray.length; counter ++) {
  productArray[counter] = new Product();
  productArray[counter].productId = counter + 13; //start at 13
  productArray[counter].productTypeId = 1;
  productArray[counter].name = "Test product";
  productArray[counter].description = "Test product";
  productArray[counter].price = 19.95;
} // end of for loop
```

To add the rows to the `products` table, I'll use a `for` loop that contains a JDBC statement to perform an `INSERT` statement, and the column values will come from `productArray`:

```
Statement myStatement = myConnection.createStatement();
for (int counter = 0; counter < productArray.length; counter ++) {
  myStatement.executeUpdate(
    "INSERT INTO products " +
    "(product_id, product_type_id, name, description, price) VALUES (" +
    productArray[counter]. productId + ", " +
    productArray[counter]. productTypeId + ", '" +
    productArray[counter].name + "', '" +
    productArray[counter].description + "', " +
    productArray[counter].price + ")"
  );
} // end of for loop
```

Each iteration through the loop results in an `INSERT` statement being sent to the database. Because the string representing each `INSERT` statement contains different values, the actual `INSERT` sent to the database is slightly different each time. This means that the database creates a different execution plan for every `INSERT` statement—very inefficient.

You'll be glad to know that JDBC provides a better way to run such SQL statements. Instead of using a JDBC `Statement` object to run your SQL statements, you can use a JDBC `PreparedStatement` object. A `PreparedStatement` object allows you to perform the same SQL statement but supply different values for actual execution of that statement. This is more efficient because the same execution plan is used by the database when the SQL statement is run. The following example creates a `PreparedStatement` object containing an `INSERT` statement similar to the one used in the previous loop:

```
PreparedStatement myPrepStatement = myConnection.prepareStatement(
    "INSERT INTO products " +
    "(product_id, product_type_id, name, description, price) VALUES (" +
    "?, ?, ?, ?, ?"
    ")"
);
```

There are two things you should notice about this example:

■ The `prepareStatement()` method is used to specify the SQL statement.

■ Question mark characters (?) are used to indicate the positions where you will later provide variables to be used when the SQL statement is actually run.

The positions of the question marks are important: they are referenced according to their position, with the first question mark being referenced using number 1, the second as number 2, and so on.

The process of supplying Java variables to a prepared statement is known as *binding* the variables to the statement, and the variables themselves are known as *bind variables*. To actually supply variables to the prepared SQL statement, you must use `set` methods. These methods are similar to the `get` methods discussed earlier, except that `set` methods are used to supply variable values, rather than read them.

For example, to bind a Java `int` variable named `intVar` to the `product_id` column in the `PreparedStatement` object, you use `setInt(1, intVar)`. The first parameter indicates the numeric position of the question mark (?) in the string previously specified in the `prepareStatement()` method call. For this example, the value 1 corresponds to the first question mark, which supplies a value to the `product_id` column in the `INSERT` statement. Similarly, to bind a Java `String` variable named `stringVar` to the `name` column, you use `setString(3, stringVar)`, because the third question mark corresponds to the `name` column. Other methods you can call in a `PreparedStatement` object include `setFloat()` and `setDouble()`, which are used for setting single-precision floating-point and double-precision floating-point numbers.

The following example features a loop that shows the use of `set` methods to bind the attributes of the `Product` objects in `productArray` to the `PreparedStatement` object; notice the `execute()` method is used to actually run the SQL statement:

```
for (int counter = 0; counter < productArray.length; counter ++) {
    myPrepStatement.setInt(1, productArray[counter]. productId);
    myPrepStatement.setInt(2, productArray[counter]. productTypeId);
    myPrepStatement.setString(3, productArray[counter].name);
    myPrepStatement.setString(4, productArray[counter].description);
    myPrepStatement.setDouble(5, productArray[counter].price);
    myPrepStatement.execute();
} // end of for loop
```

After this code is executed, the `products` table will contain five new rows.

To set a database column to `NULL` using a `PreparedStatement` object, you may use the `setNull()` method. For example, the following statement sets the `description` column to `NULL`:

```
myPrepStatement.setNull(4, java.sql.Types.VARCHAR);
```

The first parameter in the call to `setNull()` is the numeric position of the column you want to set to `NULL`. The second parameter is an `int` that corresponds to the database type of the column that is to be set to `NULL`. This second parameter should be specified using one of the constants defined in the `java.sql.Types` class. For a `VARCHAR2` column (the `description` column is a `VARCHAR2`), you should use `java.sql.Types.VARCHAR`.

Example Program: BasicExample2.java

The following `BasicExample2.java` program contains the statements shown in the previous sections.

```
/*
  BasicExample2.java shows how to use prepared SQL statements
*/

// import the JDBC packages
import java.sql.*;

class Product {
  int productId;
  int productTypeId;
  String name;
  String description;
  double price;
}

public class BasicExample2 {
  public static void main (String args []) {
    try {
      // register the Oracle JDBC drivers
      DriverManager.registerDriver(
        new oracle.jdbc.OracleDriver()
      );

      // EDIT AS NECESSARY TO CONNECT TO YOUR DATABASE
      // create a Connection object, and connect to the database
      // as the store user using the Oracle JDBC Thin driver
      Connection myConnection = DriverManager.getConnection(
        "jdbc:oracle:thin:@localhost:1521:ORCL",
        "store",
        "store_password"
      );

      // disable auto-commit mode
      myConnection.setAutoCommit(false);

      Product [] productArray = new Product[5];
      for (int counter = 0; counter < productArray.length; counter ++) {
        productArray[counter] = new Product();
        productArray[counter].productId = counter + 13;
        productArray[counter].productTypeId = 1;
        productArray[counter].name = "Test product";
        productArray[counter].description = "Test product";
        productArray[counter].price = 19.95;
      } // end of for loop

      // create a PreparedStatement object
```

```
PreparedStatement myPrepStatement = myConnection.prepareStatement(
  "INSERT INTO products " +
  "(product_id, product_type_id, name, description, price) VALUES (" +
  "?, ?, ?, ?, ?" +
  ")"
);

// initialize the values for the new rows using the
// appropriate set methods
for (int counter = 0; counter < productArray.length; counter ++) {
  myPrepStatement.setInt(1, productArray[counter].productId);
  myPrepStatement.setInt(2, productArray[counter].productTypeId);
  myPrepStatement.setString(3, productArray[counter].name);
  myPrepStatement.setString(4, productArray[counter].description);
  myPrepStatement.setDouble(5, productArray[counter].price);
  myPrepStatement.execute();
} // end of for loop

// close the PreparedStatement object
myPrepStatement.close();

// retrieve the product_id, product_type_id, name, description, and
// price columns for these new rows using a ResultSet object
Statement myStatement = myConnection.createStatement();
ResultSet productResultSet = myStatement.executeQuery(
  "SELECT product_id, product_type_id, " +
  "  name, description, price " +
  "FROM products " +
  "WHERE product_id > 12"
);

// display the column values
while (productResultSet.next()) {
  System.out.println("product_id = " +
    productResultSet.getInt("product_id"));
  System.out.println("product_type_id = " +
    productResultSet.getInt("product_type_id"));
  System.out.println("name = " +
    productResultSet.getString("name"));
  System.out.println("description = " +
    productResultSet.getString("description"));
  System.out.println("price = " +
    productResultSet.getDouble("price"));
} // end of while loop

// close the ResultSet object using the close() method
productResultSet.close();

// roll back the changes made to the database
myConnection.rollback();

// close the other JDBC objects
```

```
      myStatement.close();
      myConnection.close();

   } catch (SQLException e) {
      System.out.println("Error code = " + e.getErrorCode());
      System.out.println("Error message = " + e.getMessage());
      System.out.println("SQL state = " + e.getSQLState());
      e.printStackTrace();
   }
 } // end of main()
}
```

The output from this program is as follows:

```
product_id = 13
product_type_id = 1
name = Test product
description = Test product
price = 19.95
product_id = 14
product_type_id = 1
name = Test product
description = Test product
price = 19.95
product_id = 15
product_type_id = 1
name = Test product
description = Test product
price = 19.95
product_id = 16
product_type_id = 1
name = Test product
description = Test product
price = 19.95
product_id = 17
product_type_id = 1
name = Test product
description = Test product
price = 19.95
```

The Oracle JDBC Extensions

The Oracle extensions to JDBC enable you to access all of the data types provided by Oracle, along with Oracle-specific performance extensions. You'll learn about handling of strings, numbers, dates, and row identifiers in this section. You may read my book *Oracle9i JDBC Programming* for all of the Oracle types and performance enhancements.

There are two JDBC extension packages supplied by Oracle Corporation:

- **oracle.sql** contains the classes that support all the Oracle database types.

- **oracle.jdbc** contains the interfaces that support access to an Oracle database.

To import the Oracle JDBC packages into your Java programs, you add the following `import` statements to your program:

```
import oracle.sql.*;
import oracle.jdbc.*;
```

Of course, you don't have to import all the packages—you could just import the classes and interfaces you actually use in your program. In the following sections, you'll learn the key features of the `oracle.sql` and `oracle.jdbc` packages.

The oracle.sql Package

The `oracle.sql` package contains the classes that support all of the Oracle database types. Using objects of the classes defined in this package to store database values is more efficient than using regular Java objects. This is because the database values don't need to be converted to an appropriate base Java type first. Also, using a Java `float` or `double` to represent a floating-point number may result in a loss of precision for that number. If you use an `oracle.sql.NUMBER` object, your numbers never lose precision.

TIP
If you are writing a program that moves a lot of data around in the database, you should use the `oracle.sql.*` classes.

The `oracle.sql` classes extend the `oracle.sql.Datum` class, which contains the functionality that is common to all the classes. Table 15-6 shows a subset of the `oracle.sql` classes, along with the mapping to the compatible Oracle database types.

From Table 15-6, you can see that an `oracle.sql.NUMBER` object is compatible with a database `INTEGER` or `NUMBER` type. An `oracle.sql.CHAR` object is compatible with a database `CHAR`, `VARCHAR2`, `NCHAR`, and `NVARCHAR2` (`NCHAR` and `NVARCHAR2` are typically used to store non-English characters).

Class	Compatible Database Type
`oracle.sql.NUMBER`	`INTEGER`
	`NUMBER`
`oracle.sql.CHAR`	`CHAR`
	`VARCHAR2`
	`NCHAR`
	`NVARCHAR2`
`oracle.sql.DATE`	`DATE`
`oracle.sql.BINARY_FLOAT`	`BINARY_FLOAT`
`oracle.sql.BINARY_DOUBLE`	`BINARY_DOUBLE`
`oracle.sql.ROWID`	`ROWID`

TABLE 15-6 *Classes and Compatible Oracle Database Types*

Objects declared using the `oracle.sql` classes store data as byte arrays—also known as *SQL format*—and don't reformat the data retrieved from the database. This means that no information is lost when converting between an SQL format object and a value stored in the database.

Each `oracle.sql` object has a `getBytes()` method that returns the binary data stored in the object. Each object also has a `toJdbc()` method that returns the binary data as a compatible Java type (an exception to this is the `oracle.sql.ROWID`, where `toJdbc()` always returns an `oracle.sql.ROWID`).

Each `oracle.sql` class also provides methods to convert their SQL format binary data to a core Java type. For example, `stringValue()` returns the value as Java `String`, `intValue()` returns a Java `int`, `floatValue()` returns a `float`, `doubleValue()` returns a `double`, `bigDecimalValue()` returns a `java.math.BigDecimal`, `dateValue()` returns a `java.sql.Date`, and so on. You use these methods when you want to store the SQL format data in a core Java type or to display the SQL data on the screen. Each `oracle.sql` class also contains a constructor that accepts a Java variable, object, or byte array as input.

As you will see later, the `oracle.jdbc.OraclePreparedStatement` class contains a number of `set` methods that you use to specify values for `oracle.sql` objects. The `OracleResultSet` class defines a number of `get` methods that you use to read values from `oracle.sql` objects.

The following sections describe the main `oracle.sql` classes.

The oracle.sql.NUMBER Class

The `oracle.sql.NUMBER` class is compatible with the database `INTEGER` and `NUMBER` types. The `oracle.sql.NUMBER` class may be used to represent a number with up to 38 digits of precision. The following example creates an `oracle.sql.NUMBER` object named `customerId`, which is set to the value 6 using the constructor:

```
oracle.sql.NUMBER customerId = new oracle.sql.NUMBER(6);
```

You can read the value stored in `customerId` using the `intValue()` method, which returns the value as a Java `int`. For example:

```
int customerIdInt = customerId.intValue();
```

You can also set an `oracle.sql.NUMBER` object to a floating-point number. The next example passes the value 19.95 to the constructor of an object named `price`:

```
oracle.sql.NUMBER price = new oracle.sql.NUMBER(19.95);
```

You can read the floating-point number stored in `price` using the `floatValue()`, `doubleValue()`, and `bigDecimalValue()` methods, which return a Java `float`, `double`, and `bigDecimal` respectively. You can also get a floating-point number truncated to an `int` using `intValue()` (for example, 19.95 would be returned as 19). The following examples show the use of these methods:

```
float priceFloat = price.floatValue();
double priceDouble = price.doubleValue();
java.math.BigDecimal priceBigDec = price.bigDecimalValue();
int priceInt = price.intValue();
```

The stringValue() method returns the value as a Java String:

```
String priceString = price.stringValue();
```

The oracle.sql.CHAR Class

The oracle.sql.CHAR class is compatible with the database CHAR, VARCHAR2, NCHAR, and NVARCHAR2 types. Both the Oracle database and the oracle.sql.CHAR class contain globalization support for many different languages. For full details of the various languages supported by Oracle, see the *Oracle Database Globalization Support Guide* published by Oracle Corporation.

When you retrieve character data from the database into an oracle.sql.CHAR object, the Oracle JDBC driver returns that object using either the database character set (the default), the WE8ISO8859P1 character set (ISO 8859-1 West European), or the UTF8 character set (Unicode 3.0 UTF-8 Universal).

When passing an oracle.sql.CHAR object to the database, there are restrictions on the character set for the object. The character set depends on the database column type that the object will be stored in. If you are storing the oracle.sql.CHAR object in a CHAR or VARCHAR2 column, you must use US7ASCII (ASCII 7-bit American), WE8ISO8859P1 (ISO 8859-1 West European), or UTF8 (Unicode 3.0 UTF-8 Universal). If you are storing the oracle.sql.CHAR object in an NCHAR or NVARCHAR2 column, you must use the character set used by the database.

When creating your own oracle.sql.CHAR object, there are two steps you must follow:

1. Create an oracle.sql.CharacterSet object with the character set you wish to use.

2. Create an oracle.sql.CHAR object through the oracle.sql.CharacterSet object.

The following sections cover these steps.

Step 1: Create an oracle.sql.CharacterSet Object   The following example creates an oracle .sql.CharacterSet object named myCharSet:

```
oracle.sql.CharacterSet myCharSet =
    CharacterSet.make(CharacterSet.US7ASCII_CHARSET);
```

The make() method accepts an int that specifies the character set. In the example, the constant US7ASCII_CHARSET (defined in the oracle.sql.CharacterSet class) specifies the US7ASCII character set. Other int values include UTF8_CHARSET (for UTF8) and DEFAULT_CHARSET (for the character set used by the database).

Step 2: Create an oracle.sql.CHAR Object   The next example creates an oracle.sql.CHAR object named firstName, using the myCharSet object created in the previous step:

```
oracle.sql.CHAR firstName = new oracle.sql.CHAR("Jason", myCharSet);
```

The firstName object is populated with the string Jason. You can read this string using the stringValue() method; for example:

```
String firstNameString = firstName.stringValue();
System.out.println("firstNameString = " + firstNameString);
```

This will display `firstNameString = Jason`.

Similarly, the following example creates another `oracle.sql.CHAR` object named `lastName`:

```
oracle.sql.CHAR lastName = new oracle.sql.CHAR("Price", myCharSet);
```

You can also display the value in an `oracle.sql.CHAR` object directly, as shown in the following example:

```
System.out.println("lastName = " + lastName);
```

This statement displays the following:

```
lastName = Price
```

The oracle.sql.DATE Class

The `oracle.sql.DATE` class is compatible with the database `DATE` type. The following example creates an `oracle.sql.DATE` object named `dob`:

```
oracle.sql.DATE dob = new oracle.sql.DATE("1969-02-22 13:54:12");
```

Notice that the constructor may accept a string in the format `YYYY-MM-DD HH:MI:SS`, where `YYYY` is the year, `MM` is the month, `DD` is the day, `HH` is the hour, `MI` is the minute, and `SS` is the second. You can read the value stored in `dob` as a Java `String` using the `stringValue()` method, as shown in the following example:

```
String dobString = dob.stringValue();
```

In this example, `dobString` will contain `2/22/1969 13:54:12` (the format changes to `MM/DD/YYYY HH:MI:SS` when using a Java `String`).

You can also pass a `java.sql.Date` object to the `oracle.sql.DATE` constructor, as shown in the following example:

```
oracle.sql.DATE anotherDob =
    new oracle.sql.DATE(java.sql.Date.valueOf("1969-02-22"));
```

In this example, `anotherDob` will contain the `oracle.sql.DATE 1969-02-22 00:00:00`.

The oracle.sql.ROWID Class

The `oracle.sql.ROWID` class is compatible with the database `ROWID` type. The `ROWID` contains the physical address of a row in the database. The following example creates an `oracle.sql.ROWID` object named `rowid`:

```
oracle.sql.ROWID rowid;
```

The oracle.jdbc Package

The classes and interfaces of the `oracle.jdbc` package allow you to read and write column values in the database via `oracle.sql` objects. The `oracle.jdbc` package also contains a number of performance enhancements. In this section, you'll learn about the contents of the `oracle.jdbc` package and see how to create a row in the `customers` table. Then you'll learn how to read that row using `oracle.sql` objects.

The Classes and Interfaces of the oracle.jdbc Package

Table 15-7 shows the classes and interfaces of the `oracle.jdbc` package.

Using an OraclePreparedStatement Object

The `OraclePreparedStatement` interface implements `java.sql.PreparedStatement`. This interface supports the various `set` methods for binding `oracle.sql` objects.

In the previous section, you saw the following `oracle.sql` objects:

- An `oracle.sql.NUMBER` object named `customerId`, which was set to 6

- An `oracle.sql.CHAR` object named `firstName`, which was set to `Jason`

- Another `oracle.sql.CHAR` object named `lastName`, which was set to `Price`

- An `oracle.sql.DATE` object named `dob`, which was set to `1969-02-22 13:54:12`

To use these objects in an SQL DML statement, you must use an `OraclePreparedStatement` object, which contains `set` methods to handle `oracle.sql` objects. The following example creates an `OraclePreparedStatement` named `myPrepStatement`, which will be used later to add a row to the `customers` table:

```
OraclePreparedStatement myPrepStatement =
  (OraclePreparedStatement) myConnection.prepareStatement(
    "INSERT INTO customers " +
    "(customer_id, first_name, last_name, dob, phone) VALUES (" +
    "?, ?, ?, ?, ?" +
    ")"
);
```

Notice that the `PreparedStatement` object returned by the `prepareStatement()` method is cast to an `OraclePreparedStatement` object and is stored in `myPrepStatement`.

The next step is to bind the `oracle.sql` objects to `myPrepStatement` using the `set` methods. This involves assigning values to the placeholders marked by question mark (?) characters in `myPrepStatement`. Just as you use `set` methods like `setInt()`, `setFloat()`, `setString()`, and `setDate()` to bind Java variables to a `PreparedStatement` object, you also use `set` methods to bind `oracle.sql` objects to an `OraclePreparedStatement` object (these `set` methods include `setNUMBER()`, `setCHAR()`, `setDATE()`, and so on).

The following example illustrate how to bind the `customerId`, `firstName`, `lastName`, and `dob` objects to `myPrepStatement` using the appropriate `set` methods:

```
myPrepStatement.setNUMBER(1, customerId);
myPrepStatement.setCHAR(2, firstName);
myPrepStatement.setCHAR(3, lastName);
myPrepStatement.setDATE(4, dob);
```

The next example sets the fifth question mark (?) in `myPrepStatement` to `NULL` (the fifth question mark (?) corresponds to the `phone` column in the `customers` table):

```
myPrepStatement.setNull(5, OracleTypes.CHAR);
```

Name	Class or Interface	Description
OracleDriver	Class	Implements `java.sql.Driver`. You input an object of this class when registering the Oracle JDBC drivers using the `registerDriver()` method of the `java.sql.DriverManager` class.
OracleConnection	Interface	Implements `java.sql.Connection`. This interface extends the standard JDBC connection functionality to use `OracleStatement` objects. It also improves performance over the standard JDBC functions.
OracleStatement	Interface	Implements `java.sql.Statement` and is the superclass of the `OraclePreparedStatement` and `OracleCallableStatement` classes.
OraclePreparedStatement	Interface	Implements `java.sql.PreparedStatement`, and is the superclass of `OracleCallableStatement`. This interface supports the various `set` methods for binding `oracle.sql` objects.
OracleCallableStatement	Interface	Implements `java.sql.CallableStatement`. This interface contains various `get` and `set` methods for binding `oracle.sql` objects.
OracleResultSet	Interface	Implements `java.sql.ResultSet`. This interface contains various `get` methods for binding `oracle.sql` objects.
OracleResultSetMetaData	Interface	Implements `java.sql.ResultSetMetaData`. This interface contains methods for retrieving meta data about Oracle result sets (such as column names and their types).
OracleDatabaseMetaData	Class	Implements `java.sql.DatabaseMetaData`. This class contains methods for retrieving meta data about the Oracle database (such as the database software version).
OracleTypes	Class	Defines integer constants for the database types. This class duplicates the standard `java.sql.Types` class and contains additional integer constants for all of the Oracle types.

TABLE 15-7   *Classes and Interfaces of the* `oracle.jdbc` *Package*

The `int` constant `OracleTypes.CHAR` specifies that the database type is compatible with the `oracle.sql.CHAR` type; `OracleTypes.CHAR` is used because the `phone` column is a `VARCHAR2`.

The only thing left to do is to run the `INSERT` statement using the `execute()` method:

```
myPrepStatement.execute();
```

Doing this adds the row to the `customers` table.

Using an OracleResultSet Object

The `OracleResultSet` interface implements `java.sql.ResultSet` and contains `get` methods to handle `oracle.sql` objects. In this section, you'll see how to use an `OracleResultSet` object to retrieve the row previously added to the `customers` table.

The first thing needed is a JDBC `Statement` object through which an SQL statement may be run:

```
Statement myStatement = myConnection.createStatement();
```

Next, the following example creates an `OracleResultSet` object named `customerResultSet`, which is populated with the `ROWID`, `customer_id`, `first_name`, `last_dob`, and `phone` columns retrieved from customer #6:

```
OracleResultSet customerResultSet =
  (OracleResultSet) myStatement.executeQuery(
    "SELECT ROWID, customer_id, first_name, last_name, dob, phone " +
    "FROM customers " +
    "WHERE customer_id = 6"
  );
```

I defined the following `oracle.sql` objects earlier: `rowid`, `customerId`, `firstName`, `lastName`, and `dob`. These may be used to hold the first five column values. In order to store the value for the `phone` column, an `oracle.sql.CHAR` object is needed:

```
oracle.sql.CHAR phone = new oracle.sql.CHAR("", myCharSet);
```

An `OracleResultSet` object contains `get` methods that return `oracle.sql` objects. You use `getCHAR()` to get an `oracle.sql.CHAR`, `getNUMBER()` to get an `oracle.sql.NUMBER`, `getDATE()` to get an `oracle.sql.DATE`, and so on.

The following `while` loop contains calls to the appropriate `get` methods to copy the values from `customerResultSet` to `rowid`, `customerId`, `firstName`, `lastName`, `dob`, and `phone`:

```
while (customerResultSet.next()) {
  rowid = customerResultSet.getROWID("ROWID");
  customerId = customerResultSet.getNUMBER("customer_id");
  firstName = customerResultSet.getCHAR("first_name");
  lastName = customerResultSet.getCHAR("last_name");
  dob = customerResultSet.getDATE("dob");
  phone = customerResultSet.getCHAR("phone");

  System.out.println("rowid = " + rowid.stringValue());
  System.out.println("customerId = " + customerId.stringValue());
  System.out.println("firstName = " + firstName);
  System.out.println("lastName = " + lastName);
  System.out.println("dob = " + dob.stringValue());
```

```
    System.out.println("phone = " + phone);
} // end of while loop
```

To display the values, the example uses calls to the `stringValue()` method to convert the `rowid`, `customerId`, and `dob` objects to Java `String` values. For the `firstName`, `lastName`, and `phone` objects, the example simply uses these objects directly in the `System.out` `.println()` calls.

The following section shows a complete program containing the statements shown in the previous sections.

Example Program: BasicExample3.java

The following `BasicExample3.java` program contains the statements shown in the previous sections:

```
/*
  BasicExample3.java shows how to use the Oracle JDBC extensions
  to add a row to the customers table, and then retrieve that row
*/

// import the JDBC packages
import java.sql.*;

// import the Oracle JDBC extension packages
import oracle.sql.*;
import oracle.jdbc.*;

public class BasicExample3 {
  public static void main (String args []) {
    try {
      // register the Oracle JDBC drivers
      DriverManager.registerDriver(
        new oracle.jdbc.OracleDriver()
      );

      // EDIT AS NECESSARY TO CONNECT TO YOUR DATABASE
      // create a Connection object, and connect to the database
      // as the store user using the Oracle JDBC Thin driver
      Connection myConnection = DriverManager.getConnection(
        "jdbc:oracle:thin:@localhost:1521:ORCL",
        "store",
        "store_password"
      );

      // disable auto-commit mode
      myConnection.setAutoCommit(false);

      // create an oracle.sql.NUMBER object
      oracle.sql.NUMBER customerId = new oracle.sql.NUMBER(6);
      int customerIdInt = customerId.intValue();
      System.out.println("customerIdInt = " + customerIdInt);

      // create two oracle.sql.CHAR objects
```

```
oracle.sql.CharacterSet myCharSet =
  CharacterSet.make(CharacterSet.US7ASCII_CHARSET);
oracle.sql.CHAR firstName = new oracle.sql.CHAR("Jason", myCharSet);
String firstNameString = firstName.stringValue();
System.out.println("firstNameString = " + firstNameString);
oracle.sql.CHAR lastName = new oracle.sql.CHAR("Price", myCharSet);
System.out.println("lastName = " + lastName);

// create an oracle.sql.DATE object
oracle.sql.DATE dob = new oracle.sql.DATE("1969-02-22 13:54:12");
String dobString = dob.stringValue();
System.out.println("dobString = " + dobString);

// create an OraclePreparedStatement object
OraclePreparedStatement myPrepStatement =
  (OraclePreparedStatement) myConnection.prepareStatement(
    "INSERT INTO customers " +
    "(customer_id, first_name, last_name, dob, phone) VALUES (" +
    "?, ?, ?, ?, ?" +
    ")"
  );

// bind the objects to the OraclePreparedStatement using the
// appropriate set methods
myPrepStatement.setNUMBER(1, customerId);
myPrepStatement.setCHAR(2, firstName);
myPrepStatement.setCHAR(3, lastName);
myPrepStatement.setDATE(4, dob);

// set the phone column to NULL
myPrepStatement.setNull(5, OracleTypes.CHAR);

// run the PreparedStatement
myPrepStatement.execute();
System.out.println("Added row to customers table");

// retrieve the ROWID, customer_id, first_name, last_name, dob, and
// phone columns for this new row using an OracleResultSet
// object
Statement myStatement = myConnection.createStatement();
OracleResultSet customerResultSet =
  (OracleResultSet) myStatement.executeQuery(
    "SELECT ROWID, customer_id, first_name, last_name, dob, phone " +
    "FROM customers " +
    "WHERE customer_id = 6"
  );
System.out.println("Retrieved row from customers table");

// declare an oracle.sql.ROWID object to store the ROWID, and
// an oracle.sql.CHAR object to store the phone column
oracle.sql.ROWID rowid;
oracle.sql.CHAR phone = new oracle.sql.CHAR("", myCharSet);
```

```
        // display the column values for row using the
        // get methods to read the values
        while (customerResultSet.next()) {
          rowid = customerResultSet.getROWID("ROWID");
          customerId = customerResultSet.getNUMBER("customer_id");
          firstName = customerResultSet.getCHAR("first_name");
          lastName = customerResultSet.getCHAR("last_name");
          dob = customerResultSet.getDATE("dob");
          phone = customerResultSet.getCHAR("phone");

          System.out.println("rowid = " + rowid.stringValue());
          System.out.println("customerId = " + customerId.stringValue());
          System.out.println("firstName = " + firstName);
          System.out.println("lastName = " + lastName);
          System.out.println("dob = " + dob.stringValue());
          System.out.println("phone = " + phone);
        } // end of while loop

        // close the OracleResultSet object using the close() method
        customerResultSet.close();

        // roll back the changes made to the database
        myConnection.rollback();

        // close the other JDBC objects
        myPrepStatement.close();
        myConnection.close();

      } catch (SQLException e) {
        System.out.println("Error code = " + e.getErrorCode());
        System.out.println("Error message = " + e.getMessage());
        System.out.println("SQL state = " + e.getSQLState());
        e.printStackTrace();
      }
    } // end of main()
}
```

The output from this program is as follows:

```
customerIdInt = 6
firstNameString = Jason
lastName = Price
dobString = 2/22/1969 13:54:12
Added row to customers table
Retrieved row from customers table
rowid = AAARk5AAEAAAAGPAAF
customerId = 6
firstName = Jason
lastName = Price
dob = 2/22/1969 13:54:12
phone = null
dobString2 = 2/22/1969 0:0:0
```

Summary

In this chapter, you have learned the following:

- The JDBC API enables a Java program to access a database.

- The Oracle JDBC drivers are used to connect to an Oracle database.

- SQL statements may be executed using JDBC.

- Oracle has developed a number of extensions to standard JDBC that allow you to gain access to all of the Oracle database types.

In the next chapter, you'll learn how to tune your SQL statements for maximum performance.

CHAPTER
16

SQL Tuning

n this chapter, you will do the following:

- Learn about SQL tuning

- See SQL tuning tips that you can use to shorten the length of time your queries take to execute

- Learn about the Oracle optimizer

- See how to compare the cost of performing queries

- Examine optimizer hints

- Learn about some additional tuning tools

Introducing SQL Tuning

One of the main strengths of SQL is that you don't have to tell the database exactly how to obtain the data requested. You simply run a query specifying the information you want, and the database software figures out the best way to get it. Sometimes, you can improve the performance of your SQL statements by "tuning" them. In the following sections, you'll see tuning tips that can make your queries run faster; later, you'll see more advanced tuning techniques.

Use a WHERE Clause to Filter Rows

Many novices retrieve all the rows from a table when they only want one row (or a few rows). This is very wasteful. A better approach is to add a WHERE clause to a query. That way, you restrict the rows retrieved to just those actually needed.

For example, say you want the details for customer #1 and #2. The following query retrieves all the rows from the customers table in the store schema (wasteful):

```
-- BAD (retrieves all rows from the customers table)
SELECT *
FROM customers;

CUSTOMER_ID FIRST_NAME LAST_NAME  DOB       PHONE
----------- ---------- ---------- --------- ------------
          1 John       Brown      01-JAN-65 800-555-1211
          2 Cynthia    Green      05-FEB-68 800-555-1212
          3 Steve      White      16-MAR-71 800-555-1213
          4 Gail       Black                800-555-1214
          5 Doreen     Blue       20-MAY-70
```

The next query adds a WHERE clause to the previous example to just get customer #1 and #2:

```
-- GOOD (uses a WHERE clause to limit the rows retrieved)
SELECT *
FROM customers
WHERE customer_id IN (1, 2);
```

```
CUSTOMER_ID FIRST_NAME LAST_NAME  DOB       PHONE
----------- ---------- ---------- --------- ------------
          1 John       Brown      01-JAN-65 800-555-1211
          2 Cynthia    Green      05-FEB-68 800-555-1212
```

You should avoid using functions in the WHERE clause, as that increases execution time.

Use Table Joins Rather than Multiple Queries

If you need information from multiple related tables, you should use join conditions rather than multiple queries. In the following bad example, two queries are used to get the product name and the product type name for product #1 (using two queries is wasteful). The first query gets the name and product_type_id column values from the products table for product #1. The second query then uses that product_type_id to get the name column from the product_types table.

```
-- BAD (two separate queries when one would work)
SELECT name, product_type_id
FROM products
WHERE product_id = 1;

NAME                            PRODUCT_TYPE_ID
------------------------------- ---------------
Modern Science                                1


SELECT name
FROM product_types
WHERE product_type_id = 1;

NAME
----------
Book
```

Instead of using the two queries, you should write one query that uses a join between the products and product_types tables. The following good query shows this:

```
-- GOOD (one query with a join)
SELECT p.name, pt.name
FROM products p, product_types pt
WHERE p.product_type_id = pt.product_type_id
AND p.product_id = 1;

NAME                            NAME
------------------------------- ----------
Modern Science                  Book
```

This query results in the same product name and product type name being retrieved as in the first example, but the results are obtained using one query. One query is generally more efficient than two.

You should choose the join order in your query so that you join fewer rows to tables later in the join order. For example, say you were joining three related tables named tab1, tab2, and tab3. Assume tab1 contains 1,000 rows, tab2 100 rows, and tab3 10 rows. You should join tab1 with tab2 first, followed by tab2 and tab3.

Also, avoid joining complex views in your queries, because doing so causes the queries for the views to be run first, followed by your actual query. Instead, write your query using the tables rather than the views.

Use Fully Qualified Column References When Performing Joins

Always include table aliases in your queries and use the alias for each column in your query (this is known as "fully qualifying" your column references). That way, the database doesn't have to search for each column in the tables used in your query.

The following bad example uses the aliases p and pt for the products and product_types tables, respectively, but the query doesn't fully qualify the description and price columns:

```
-- BAD (description and price columns not fully qualified)
SELECT p.name, pt.name, description, price
FROM products p, product_types pt
WHERE p.product_type_id = pt.product_type_id
AND p.product_id = 1;
```

```
NAME                              NAME
-----------------------------     ----------
DESCRIPTION                                            PRICE
--------------------------------------------------    ----------
Modern Science                    Book
A description of modern science                        19.95
```

This example works, but the database has to search both the products and product_types tables for the description and price columns; that's because there's no alias that tells the database which table those columns are in. The extra time spent by the database having to do the search is wasted time.

The following good example includes the table alias p to fully qualify the description and price columns:

```
-- GOOD (all columns are fully qualified)
SELECT p.name, pt.name, p.description, p.price
FROM products p, product_types pt
WHERE p.product_type_id = pt.product_type_id
AND p.product_id = 1;
```

```
NAME                              NAME
-----------------------------     ----------
DESCRIPTION                                            PRICE
--------------------------------------------------    ----------
Modern Science                    Book
A description of modern science                        19.95
```

Because all references to columns include a table alias, the database doesn't have to waste time searching the tables for the columns, and execution time is reduced.

Use CASE Expressions Rather than Multiple Queries

Use CASE expressions rather than multiple queries when you need to perform many calculations on the same rows in a table. The following bad example uses multiple queries to count the number of products within various price ranges:

```
-- BAD (three separate queries when one CASE statement would work)
SELECT COUNT(*)
FROM products
WHERE price < 13;

   COUNT(*)
----------
         2

SELECT COUNT(*)
FROM products
WHERE price BETWEEN 13 AND 15;

   COUNT(*)
----------
         5

SELECT COUNT(*)
FROM products
WHERE price > 15;

   COUNT(*)
----------
         5
```

Rather than using three queries, you should write one query that uses CASE expressions. This is shown in the following good example:

```
-- GOOD (one query with a CASE expression)
SELECT
 COUNT(CASE WHEN price < 13 THEN 1 ELSE null END) low,
 COUNT(CASE WHEN price BETWEEN 13 AND 15 THEN 1 ELSE null END) med,
 COUNT(CASE WHEN price > 15 THEN 1 ELSE null END) high
FROM products;

       LOW        MED       HIGH
---------- ---------- ----------
         2          5          5
```

Notice that the counts of the products with prices less than $13 are labeled as low, products between $13 and $15 are labeled med, and products greater than $15 are labeled high.

NOTE
You can, of course, use overlapping ranges and different functions in your CASE expressions.

Add Indexes to Tables

When looking for a particular topic in a book, you can either scan the whole book or use the index to find the location. An index for a database table is similar in concept to a book index, except that database indexes are used to find specific rows in a table. The downside of indexes is that when a row is added to the table, additional time is required to update the index for the new row.

Generally, you should create an index on a column when you are retrieving a small number of rows from a table containing many rows. A good rule of thumb is

Create an index when a query retrieves <= 10 percent of the total rows in a table.

This means the column for the index should contain a wide range of values. A good candidate for indexing would be a column containing a unique value for each row (for example, a social security number). A poor candidate for indexing would be a column that contains only a small range of values (for example, N, S, E, W or 1, 2, 3, 4, 5, 6). An Oracle database automatically creates an index for the primary key of a table and for columns included in a unique constraint.

In addition, if your database is accessed using a lot of hierarchical queries (that is, a query containing a CONNECT BY), you should add indexes to the columns referenced in the START WITH and CONNECT BY clauses (see Chapter 7 for details on hierarchical queries).

Finally, for a column that contains a small range of values and is frequently used in the WHERE clause of queries, you should consider adding a bitmap index to that column. Bitmap indexes are typically used in data warehouses, which are databases containing very large amounts of data. The data in a data warehouse is typically read using many queries, but the data is not modified by many concurrent transactions.

Normally, a database administrator is responsible for creating indexes. However, as an application developer, you'll be able to provide the DBA with feedback on which columns are good candidates for indexing, because you may know more about the application than the DBA. Chapter 10 covers indexes in depth, and you should re-read the section on indexes if necessary.

Use WHERE Rather than HAVING

You use the WHERE clause to filter rows; you use the HAVING clause to filter groups of rows. Because the HAVING clause filters groups of rows *after* they have been grouped together (which takes some time to do), you should first filter rows using a WHERE clause whenever possible. That way, you avoid the time taken to group the filtered rows together in the first place.

The following bad query retrieves the product_type_id and average price for products whose product_type_id is 1 or 2. To do this, the query performs the following:

- It uses the GROUP BY clause to group rows into blocks with the same product_type_id.

- It uses the HAVING clause to filter the returned results to those groups that have a product_type_id in 1 or 2 (this is bad, because a WHERE clause would work).

```
-- BAD (uses HAVING rather than WHERE)
SELECT product_type_id, AVG(price)
FROM products
GROUP BY product_type_id
HAVING product_type_id IN (1, 2);
```

```
PRODUCT_TYPE_ID AVG(PRICE)
--------------- ----------
              1     24.975
              2      26.22
```

The following good query rewrites the previous example to use WHERE rather than HAVING to first filter the rows to those whose product_type_id is 1 or 2:

```
-- GOOD (uses WHERE rather than HAVING)
SELECT product_type_id, AVG(price)
FROM products
WHERE product_type_id IN (1, 2)
GROUP BY product_type_id;
```

```
PRODUCT_TYPE_ID AVG(PRICE)
--------------- ----------
              1     24.975
              2      26.22
```

Use UNION ALL Rather than UNION

You use UNION ALL to get all the rows retrieved by two queries, including duplicate rows; you use UNION to get all non-duplicate rows retrieved by the queries. Because UNION removes duplicate rows (which takes some time to do), you should use UNION ALL whenever possible.

The following bad query uses UNION (bad because UNION ALL would work) to get the rows from the products and more_products tables; notice that all non-duplicate rows from products and more_products are retrieved:

```
-- BAD (uses UNION rather than UNION ALL)
SELECT product_id, product_type_id, name
FROM products
UNION
SELECT prd_id, prd_type_id, name
FROM more_products;
```

```
PRODUCT_ID PRODUCT_TYPE_ID NAME
---------- --------------- --------------------
         1               1 Modern Science
         2               1 Chemistry
         3               2 Supernova
         3                 Supernova
         4               2 Lunar Landing
         4               2 Tank War
         5               2 Submarine
         5               2 Z Files
         6               2 2412: The Return
         7               3 Space Force 9
         8               3 From Another Planet
         9               4 Classical Music
        10               4 Pop 3
        11               4 Creative Yell
        12                 My Front Line
```

The following good query rewrites the previous example to use UNION ALL; notice that all the rows from products and more_products are retrieved, including duplicates:

```
-- GOOD (uses UNION ALL rather than UNION)
SELECT product_id, product_type_id, name
FROM products
UNION ALL
SELECT prd_id, prd_type_id, name
FROM more_products;

PRODUCT_ID PRODUCT_TYPE_ID NAME
---------- --------------- ---------------------------------
         1               1 Modern Science
         2               1 Chemistry
         3               2 Supernova
         4               2 Tank War
         5               2 Z Files
         6               2 2412: The Return
         7               3 Space Force 9
         8               3 From Another Planet
         9               4 Classical Music
        10               4 Pop 3
        11               4 Creative Yell
        12                 My Front Line
         1               1 Modern Science
         2               1 Chemistry
         3                 Supernova
         4               2 Lunar Landing
         5               2 Submarine
```

Use EXISTS Rather than IN

You use IN to check if a value is contained in a list. You use EXISTS to check for the existence of rows returned by a subquery. EXISTS is different from IN: EXISTS just checks for the existence of rows, whereas IN checks actual values. EXISTS typically offers better performance than IN with subqueries. Therefore, you should use EXISTS rather than IN whenever possible.

You should refer back to the section entitled "Using EXISTS and NOT EXISTS with a Correlated Subquery" in Chapter 6 for full details on when you should use EXISTS with a correlated subquery (an important point to remember is that correlated subqueries can resolve null values).

The following bad query uses IN (bad because EXISTS would work) to retrieve products that have been purchased:

```
-- BAD (uses IN rather than EXISTS)
SELECT product_id, name
FROM products
WHERE product_id IN
  (SELECT product_id
   FROM purchases);

PRODUCT_ID NAME
---------- ----------------------------
         1 Modern Science
```

```
                2 Chemistry
                3 Supernova
```

The following good query rewrites the previous example to use `EXISTS`:

```
-- GOOD (uses EXISTS rather than IN)
SELECT product_id, name
FROM products outer
WHERE EXISTS
   (SELECT 1
    FROM purchases inner
    WHERE inner.product_id = outer.product_id);


PRODUCT_ID NAME
---------- ------------------------------
         1 Modern Science
         2 Chemistry
         3 Supernova
```

Use EXISTS Rather than DISTINCT

You can suppress the display of duplicate rows using `DISTINCT`. You use `EXISTS` to check for the existence of rows returned by a subquery. Whenever possible, you should use `EXISTS` rather than `DISTINCT`, because `DISTINCT` sorts the retrieved rows before suppressing the duplicate rows.

The following bad query uses `DISTINCT` (bad because `EXISTS` would work) to retrieve products that have been purchased:

```
-- BAD (uses DISTINCT when EXISTS would work)
SELECT DISTINCT pr.product_id, pr.name
FROM products pr, purchases pu
WHERE pr.product_id = pu.product_id;


PRODUCT_ID NAME
---------- ------------------------------
         1 Modern Science
         2 Chemistry
         3 Supernova
```

The following good query rewrites the previous example to use `EXISTS` rather than `DISTINCT`:

```
-- GOOD (uses EXISTS rather than DISTINCT)
SELECT product_id, name
FROM products outer
WHERE EXISTS
   (SELECT 1
    FROM purchases inner
    WHERE inner.product_id = outer.product_id);

PRODUCT_ID NAME
---------- ------------------------------
         1 Modern Science
         2 Chemistry
         3 Supernova
```

Use GROUPING SETS Rather than CUBE

The GROUPING SETS clause typically offers better performance than CUBE. Therefore, you should use GROUPING SETS rather than CUBE wherever possible. This is fully covered in the section entitled "Using the GROUPING SETS Clause" in Chapter 7.

Use Bind Variables

The Oracle database software caches SQL statements; a cached SQL statement is reused if an identical statement is submitted to the database. When an SQL statement is reused, the execution time is reduced. However, the SQL statement must be *absolutely identical* in order for it to be reused. This means that

- All characters in the SQL statement must be the same.

- All letters in the SQL statement must be in the same case.

- All spaces in the SQL statement must be the same.

If you need to supply different column values in a statement, you can use bind variables instead of literal column values. You'll see examples that clarify these ideas next.

Non-Identical SQL Statements

In this section, you'll see some non-identical SQL statements. The following non-identical queries retrieve products #1 and #2:

```
SELECT * FROM products WHERE product_id = 1;
SELECT * FROM products WHERE product_id = 2;
```

These queries are not identical, because the value 1 is used in the first statement, but the value 2 is used in the second.

The following non-identical queries have spaces in different positions:

```
SELECT * FROM  products  WHERE  product_id = 1;
SELECT * FROM products WHERE product_id = 1;
```

The following non-identical queries use a different case for some of the characters:

```
select * from products where product_id = 1;
SELECT * FROM products WHERE product_id = 1;
```

Now that you've seen some non-identical statements, let's take a look at identical SQL statements that use bind variables.

Identical SQL Statements That Use Bind Variables

You can ensure that a statement is identical by using bind variables to represent column values. You create a bind variable using the SQL*Plus VARIABLE command. For example, the following command creates a variable named v_product_id of type NUMBER:

```
VARIABLE v_product_id NUMBER
```

NOTE
You can use the types shown in Table A-1 of the appendix to define the type of a bind variable.

You reference a bind variable in an SQL or PL/SQL statement using a colon followed by the variable name (such as `:v_product_id`). For example, the following PL/SQL block sets `v_product_id` to 1:

```
BEGIN
  :v_product_id := 1;
END;
/
```

The following query uses `v_product_id` to set the `product_id` column value in the WHERE clause; because `v_product_id` was set to 1 in the previous PL/SQL block, the query retrieves the details of product #1:

```
SELECT * FROM products WHERE product_id = :v_product_id;

PRODUCT_ID PRODUCT_TYPE_ID NAME
---------- --------------- ------------------------------
DESCRIPTION                                            PRICE
-------------------------------------------------- ----------
         1               1 Modern Science
A description of modern science                       19.95
```

The next example sets `v_product_id` to 2 and repeats the query:

```
BEGIN
  :v_product_id := 2;
END;
/
SELECT * FROM products WHERE product_id = :v_product_id;

PRODUCT_ID PRODUCT_TYPE_ID NAME
---------- --------------- ------------------------------
DESCRIPTION                                            PRICE
-------------------------------------------------- ----------
         2               1 Chemistry
Introduction to Chemistry                                30
```

Because the query used in this example is identical to the previous query, the cached query is reused and there's an improvement in performance.

TIP
You should typically use bind variables if you're performing the same query many times. Also, in the example, the bind variables are session specific and need to be reset if the session is lost.

Listing and Printing Bind Variables

You list bind variables in SQL*Plus using the VARIABLE command. For example:

```
VARIABLE
variable    v_product_id
datatype    NUMBER
```

You display the value of a bind variable in SQL*Plus using the PRINT command. For example:

```
PRINT v_product_id
V_PRODUCT_ID
-------------
            2
```

Using a Bind Variable to Store a Value Returned by a PL/SQL Function

You can also use a bind variable to store returned values from a PL/SQL function. The following example creates a bind variable named v_average_product_price and stores the result returned by the function average_product_price() (this function was described in Chapter 11 and calculates the average product price for the supplied product_type_id):

```
VARIABLE v_average_product_price NUMBER
BEGIN
  :v_average_product_price := average_product_price(1);
END;
/
PRINT v_average_product_price

V_AVERAGE_PRODUCT_PRICE
-----------------------
                 24.975
```

Using a Bind Variable to Store Rows from a REFCURSOR

You can also use a bind variable to store returned values from a REFCURSOR (a REFCURSOR is a pointer to a list of rows). The following example creates a bind variable named v_products_refcursor and stores the result returned by the function product_package.get_products_ref_cursor() (this function was introduced in Chapter 11; it returns a pointer to the rows in the products table):

```
VARIABLE v_products_refcursor REFCURSOR
BEGIN
  :v_products_refcursor := product_package.get_products_ref_cursor();
END;
/
PRINT v_products_refcursor

PRODUCT_ID NAME                                   PRICE
---------- ------------------------------- ----------
         1 Modern Science                         19.95
         2 Chemistry                                 30
```

```
 3 Supernova                                    25.99
 4 Tank War                                     13.95
 5 Z Files                                      49.99
 6 2412: The Return                             14.95
 7 Space Force 9                                13.49
 8 From Another Planet                          12.99
 9 Classical Music                              10.99
10 Pop 3                                        15.99
11 Creative Yell                                14.99

PRODUCT_ID NAME                                  PRICE
---------- ------------------------------ ----------
12 My Front Line                                13.49
```

Comparing the Cost of Performing Queries

The Oracle database software uses a subsystem known as the *optimizer* to generate the most
efficient path to access the data stored in the tables. The path generated by the optimizer is
known as an *execution plan*. Oracle Database 10*g* and above automatically gathers statistics
about the data in your tables and indexes in order to generate the best execution plan (this is
known as *cost-based* optimization).

Comparing the execution plans generated by the optimizer allows you to judge the relative
cost of one SQL statement versus another. You can use the results to improve your SQL statements.
In this section, you'll learn how to view and interpret a couple of example execution plans.

NOTE
*Database versions prior to Oracle Database 10g don't automatically
gather statistics, and the optimizer automatically defaults to rule-based
optimization. Rule-based optimization uses syntactic rules to generate
the execution plan. Cost-based optimization is typically better than
rule-based optimization because the former uses actual information
gathered from the data in the tables and indexes. If you're using
Oracle Database 9i or below, you can gather statistics yourself (you'll
learn how to do that later in the section "Gathering Table Statistics").*

Examining Execution Plans

The optimizer generates an execution plan for an SQL statement. You can examine the execution
plan using the SQL*Plus EXPLAIN PLAN command. The EXPLAIN PLAN command populates
a table named plan_table with the SQL statement's execution plan (plan_table is often
referred to as the "plan table"). You may then examine that execution plan by querying the plan
table. The first thing you must do is check if the plan table currently exists in the database.

Checking if the Plan Table Currently Exists in the Database

To check if the plan table currently exists in the database, you should connect to the database as
the store user and run the following DESCRIBE command:

```
SQL> DESCRIBE plan_table
```

```
Name                                      Null?     Type
----------------------------------------- -------- --------------
STATEMENT_ID                                        VARCHAR2(30)
```

```
PLAN_ID                        NUMBER
TIMESTAMP                      DATE
REMARKS                        VARCHAR2(4000)
OPERATION                      VARCHAR2(30)
OPTIONS                        VARCHAR2(255)
OBJECT_NODE                    VARCHAR2(128)
OBJECT_OWNER                   VARCHAR2(30)
OBJECT_NAME                    VARCHAR2(30)
OBJECT_ALIAS                   VARCHAR2(65)
OBJECT_INSTANCE                NUMBER(38)
OBJECT_TYPE                    VARCHAR2(30)
OPTIMIZER                      VARCHAR2(255)
SEARCH_COLUMNS                 NUMBER
ID                             NUMBER(38)
PARENT_ID                      NUMBER(38)
DEPTH                          NUMBER(38)
POSITION                       NUMBER(38)
COST                           NUMBER(38)
CARDINALITY                    NUMBER(38)
BYTES                          NUMBER(38)
OTHER_TAG                      VARCHAR2(255)
PARTITION_START                VARCHAR2(255)
PARTITION_STOP                 VARCHAR2(255)
PARTITION_ID                   NUMBER(38)
OTHER                          LONG
OTHER_XML                      CLOB
DISTRIBUTION                   VARCHAR2(30)
CPU_COST                       NUMBER(38)
IO_COST                        NUMBER(38)
TEMP_SPACE                     NUMBER(38)
ACCESS_PREDICATES              VARCHAR2(4000)
FILTER_PREDICATES              VARCHAR2(4000)
PROJECTION                     VARCHAR2(4000)
TIME                           NUMBER(38)
QBLOCK_NAME                    VARCHAR2(30)
```

If you get a table description similar to these results, you have the plan table already. If you get an error, then you need to create the plan table.

Creating the Plan Table

If you don't have the plan table, you must create it. To do this, you run the SQL*Plus script utlxplan.sql (on my Windows computer, the script is located in the directory E:\oracle_ 11g\product\11.1.0\db_1\RDBMS\ADMIN). The following example shows the command to run the utlxplan.sql script:

```
SQL> @ E:\oracle_11g\product\11.1.0\db_1\RDBMS\ADMIN\utlxplan.sql
```

NOTE
You'll need to replace the directory path with the path for your environment.

The most important columns in the plan table are shown in Table 16-1.

Creating a Central Plan Table

If necessary, a database administrator can create one central plan table. That way, individual users don't have to create their own plan tables. To do this, a database administrator performs the following steps:

1. Creates the plan table in a schema of their choice by running the `utlxplan.sql` script
2. Creates a public synonym for the plan table
3. Grants access on the plan table to the public role

Here is an example of these steps:

```
@ E:\oracle_11g\product\11.1.0\db_1\RDBMS\ADMIN\utlxplan.sql
CREATE PUBLIC SYNONYM plan_table FOR plan_table;
GRANT SELECT, INSERT, UPDATE, DELETE ON plan_table TO PUBLIC;
```

Column	Description
statement_id	Name you assign to the execution plan.
operation	Database operation performed, which can be ■ Scanning a table ■ Scanning an index ■ Accessing rows from a table by using an index ■ Joining two tables together ■ Sorting a row set For example, the operation for accessing a table is TABLE ACCESS.
options	Name of the option used in the operation. For example, the option for a complete scan is FULL.
object_name	Name of the database object referenced in the operation.
object_type	Attribute of object. For example, a unique index has the attribute of UNIQUE.
id	Number assigned to this operation in the execution plan.
parent_id	Parent number for the current step in the execution plan. The parent_id value relates to an id value from a parent step.
position	Processing order for steps that have the same parent_id.
cost	Estimate of units of work for operation. Cost-based optimization uses disk I/O, CPU usage, and memory usage as units of work. Therefore, the cost is an estimate of the number of disk I/Os and the amount of CPU and memory used in performing an operation.

TABLE 16-1   *Plan Table Columns*

Generating an Execution Plan

Once you have a plan table, you can use the EXPLAIN PLAN command to generate an execution plan for an SQL statement. The syntax for the EXPLAIN PLAN command is as follows:

```
EXPLAIN PLAN SET STATEMENT_ID = statement_id FOR sql_statement;
```

where

- *statement_id* is the name you want to call the execution plan. This can be any alphanumeric text.

- *sql_statement* is the SQL statement you want to generate an execution plan for.

The following example generates the execution plan for a query that retrieves all rows from the customers table (notice that the statement_id is set to 'CUSTOMERS'):

```
EXPLAIN PLAN SET STATEMENT_ID = 'CUSTOMERS' FOR
SELECT customer_id, first_name, last_name FROM customers;
Explained
```

After the command completes, you may examine the execution plan stored in the plan table. You'll see how to do that next.

NOTE
The query in the EXPLAIN PLAN *statement doesn't return rows from the* customers *table. The* EXPLAIN PLAN *statement simply generates the execution plan that would be used if the query was run.*

Querying the Plan Table

For querying the plan table, I have provided an SQL*Plus script named explain_plan.sql in the SQL directory. The script prompts you for the statement_id and then displays the execution plan for that statement.

The explain_plan.sql script is as follows:

```
-- Displays the execution plan for the specified statement_id

UNDEFINE v_statement_id;

SELECT
  id ||
  DECODE(id, 0, '', LPAD(' ', 2*(level - 1))) || ' ' ||
  operation || ' ' ||
  options || ' ' ||
  object_name || ' ' ||
  object_type || ' ' ||
  DECODE(cost, NULL, '', 'Cost = ' || position)
AS execution_plan
FROM plan_table
CONNECT BY PRIOR id = parent_id
AND statement_id = '&&v_statement_id'
START WITH id = 0
AND statement_id = '&v_statement_id';
```

An execution plan is organized into a hierarchy of database operations similar to a tree; the details of these operations are stored in the plan table. The operation with an `id` of 0 is the root of the hierarchy, and all the other operations in the plan stem from this root. The query in the script retrieves the details of the operations, starting with the root operation and then navigating the tree from the root.

The following example shows how to run the `explain_plan.sql` script to retrieve the `'CUSTOMERS'` plan created earlier:

```
SQL> @ c:\sql_book\sql\explain_plan.sql
Enter value for v_statement_id: CUSTOMERS
old  12:    statement_id = '&&v_statement_id'
new  12:    statement_id = 'CUSTOMERS'
old  14:    statement_id = '&v_statement_id'
new  14:    statement_id = 'CUSTOMERS'


EXECUTION_PLAN
---------------------------------------------
0 SELECT STATEMENT    Cost = 3
1    TABLE ACCESS FULL CUSTOMERS TABLE Cost = 1
```

The operations shown in the `EXECUTION_PLAN` column are executed in the following order:

- The rightmost indented operation is executed first, followed by any parent operations above it.

- For operations with the same indentation, the topmost operation is executed first, followed by any parent operations above it.

Each operation feeds its results back up the chain to its immediate parent operation, and the parent operation is then executed. In the `EXECUTION_PLAN` column, the operation ID is shown on the far left. In the example execution plan, operation 1 is run first, with the results of that operation being passed to operation 0. The following example illustrates the ordering for a more complex example:

```
0 SELECT STATEMENT    Cost = 6
1    MERGE JOIN    Cost = 1
2       TABLE ACCESS BY INDEX ROWID PRODUCT_TYPES TABLE Cost = 1
3          INDEX FULL SCAN PRODUCT_TYPES_PK INDEX (UNIQUE) Cost = 1
4       SORT JOIN    Cost = 2
5          TABLE ACCESS FULL PRODUCTS TABLE Cost = 1
```

The order in which the operations are executed in this example is 3, 2, 5, 4, 1, and 0.

Now that you've seen the order in which operations are executed, it's time to move onto what the operations actually do. The execution plan for the `'CUSTOMERS'` query was

```
0 SELECT STATEMENT    Cost = 3
1    TABLE ACCESS FULL CUSTOMERS TABLE Cost = 1
```

Operation 1 is run first, with the results of that operation being passed to operation 0. Operation 1 involves a full table scan—indicated by the string `TABLE ACCESS FULL`—on the `customers` table. Here's the original command used to generate the `'CUSTOMERS'` query:

```
EXPLAIN PLAN SET STATEMENT_ID = 'CUSTOMERS' FOR
SELECT customer_id, first_name, last_name FROM customers;
```

A full table scan is performed because the `SELECT` statement specifies that all the rows from the `customers` table are to be retrieved.

The total cost of the query is three work units, as indicated in the cost part shown to the right of operation 0 in the execution plan (`0 SELECT STATEMENT Cost = 3`). A work unit is the amount of processing the software has to do to perform a given operation. The higher the cost, the more work the database software has to do to complete the SQL statement.

NOTE
If you're using a version of the database prior to Oracle Database 10g, then the output for the overall statement cost may be blank. That's because earlier database versions don't automatically collect table statistics. In order to gather statistics, you have to use the ANALYZE command. You'll learn how to do that later in the section "Gathering Table Statistics."

Execution Plans Involving Table Joins

Execution plans for queries with table joins are more complex. The following example generates the execution plan for a query that joins the `products` and `product_types` tables:

```
EXPLAIN PLAN SET STATEMENT_ID = 'PRODUCTS' FOR
SELECT p.name, pt.name
FROM products p, product_types pt
WHERE p.product_type_id = pt.product_type_id;
```

The execution plan for this query is shown in the following example:

```
@ c:\sql_book\sql\explain_plan.sql
Enter value for v_statement_id: PRODUCTS

EXECUTION_PLAN
----------------------------------------------------------------
0 SELECT STATEMENT    Cost = 6
1   MERGE JOIN    Cost = 1
2     TABLE ACCESS BY INDEX ROWID PRODUCT_TYPES TABLE Cost = 1
3       INDEX FULL SCAN PRODUCT_TYPES_PK INDEX (UNIQUE) Cost = 1
4     SORT JOIN    Cost = 2
5       TABLE ACCESS FULL PRODUCTS TABLE Cost = 1
```

NOTE
If you run the example, you may get a slightly different execution plan depending on the version of the database you are using and on the settings of the parameters in the database's init.ora configuration file.

The previous execution plan is more complex, and you can see the hierarchical relationships between the various operations. The execution order of the operations is 3, 2, 5, 4, 1, and 0. Table 16-2 describes each operation in the order they are performed.

Operation ID	Description
3	Full scan of the index product_types_pk (which is a unique index) to obtain the addresses of the rows in the product_types table. The addresses are in the form of ROWID values, which are passed to operation 2.
2	Access the rows in the product_types table using the list of ROWID values passed from operation 3. The rows are passed to operation 1.
5	Access the rows in the products table. The rows are passed to operation 4.
4	Sort the rows passed from operation 5. The sorted rows are passed to operation 1.
1	Merge the rows passed from operations 2 and 5. The merged rows are passed to operation 0.
0	Return the rows from operation 1 to the user. The total cost of the query is 6 work units.

TABLE 16-2 *Execution Plan Operations*

Gathering Table Statistics

If you're using a version of the database prior to Oracle Database 10g (such as 9i), then you'll have to gather table statistics yourself using the ANALYZE command. By default, if no statistics are available then rule-based optimization is used. Rule-based optimization isn't usually as good as cost-based optimization.

The following examples use the ANALYZE command to gather statistics for the products and product_types tables:

```
ANALYZE TABLE products COMPUTE STATISTICS;
ANALYZE TABLE product_types COMPUTE STATISTICS;
```

Once the statistics have been gathered, cost-based optimization will be used rather than rule-based optimization.

Comparing Execution Plans

By comparing the total cost shown in the execution plan for different SQL statements, you can determine the value of tuning your SQL. In this section, you'll see how to compare two execution plans and see the benefit of using EXISTS rather than DISTINCT (a tip I gave earlier). The following example generates an execution plan for a query that uses EXISTS:

```
EXPLAIN PLAN SET STATEMENT_ID = 'EXISTS_QUERY' FOR
SELECT product_id, name
FROM products outer
WHERE EXISTS
  (SELECT 1
   FROM purchases inner
   WHERE inner.product_id = outer.product_id);
```

The execution plan for this query is shown in the following example:

```
@ c:\sql_book\sql\explain_plan.sql
Enter value for v_statement_id: EXISTS_QUERY

EXECUTION_PLAN
------------------------------------------------------------
0 SELECT STATEMENT Cost = 4
1   MERGE JOIN SEMI Cost = 1
2     TABLE ACCESS BY INDEX ROWID PRODUCTS TABLE Cost = 1
3       INDEX FULL SCAN PRODUCTS_PK INDEX (UNIQUE) Cost = 1
4     SORT UNIQUE Cost = 2
5       INDEX FULL SCAN PURCHASES_PK INDEX (UNIQUE) Cost = 1
```

As you can see, the total cost of the query is 4 work units. The next example generates an execution plan for a query that uses DISTINCT:

```
EXPLAIN PLAN SET STATEMENT_ID = 'DISTINCT_QUERY' FOR
SELECT DISTINCT pr.product_id, pr.name
FROM products pr, purchases pu
WHERE pr.product_id = pu.product_id;
```

The execution plan for this query is shown in the following example:

```
@ c:\sql_book\sql\explain_plan.sql
Enter value for v_statement_id: DISTINCT_QUERY

EXECUTION_PLAN
------------------------------------------------------------
0 SELECT STATEMENT Cost = 5
1   HASH UNIQUE Cost = 1
2     MERGE JOIN Cost = 1
3       TABLE ACCESS BY INDEX ROWID PRODUCTS TABLE Cost = 1
4         INDEX FULL SCAN PRODUCTS_PK INDEX (UNIQUE) Cost = 1
5       SORT JOIN    Cost = 2
6         INDEX FULL SCAN PURCHASES_PK INDEX (UNIQUE) Cost = 1
```

The cost for the query is 5 work units. This query is more costly than the earlier query that used EXISTS (that query had a cost of only 4 work units). These results prove it is better to use EXISTS than DISTINCT.

Passing Hints to the Optimizer

You can pass hints to the optimizer. A hint is an optimizer directive that influences the optimizer's choice of execution plan. The correct hint may improve the performance of an SQL statement. You can check the effectiveness of a hint by comparing the cost in the execution plan of an SQL statement with and without the hint.

In this section, you'll see an example query that uses one of the more useful hints: the FIRST_ROWS(n) hint. The FIRST_ROWS(n) hint tells the optimizer to generate an execution plan that will minimize the time taken to return the first n rows in a query. This hint can be useful when you don't want to wait around too long before getting *some* rows back from your query, but you still want to see all the rows.

The following example generates an execution plan for a query that uses `FIRST_ROWS(2)`; notice that the hint is placed within the strings `/*+` and `*/`:

```
EXPLAIN PLAN SET STATEMENT_ID = 'HINT' FOR
SELECT /*+ FIRST_ROWS(2) */ p.name, pt.name
FROM products p, product_types pt
WHERE p.product_type_id = pt. product_type_id;
```

CAUTION
Your hint must use the exact *syntax shown—otherwise, the hint will be ignored. The syntax is: `/*+` followed by one space, the hint, followed by one space, and `*/`.*

The execution plan for this query is shown in the following example; notice that the cost is 4 work units:

```
@ c:\sql_book\sql\explain_plan.sql
Enter value for v_statement_id: HINT


EXECUTION_PLAN
----------------------------------------------------------------
0 SELECT STATEMENT      Cost = 4
1   NESTED LOOPS
2     NESTED LOOPS      Cost = 1
3       TABLE ACCESS FULL PRODUCTS TABLE Cost = 1
4       INDEX UNIQUE SCAN PRODUCT_TYPES_PK INDEX (UNIQUE) Cost = 2
5     TABLE ACCESS BY INDEX ROWID PRODUCT_TYPES TABLE Cost = 2
```

The next example generates an execution plan for the same query without the hint:

```
EXPLAIN PLAN SET STATEMENT_ID = 'NO_HINT' FOR
SELECT p.name, pt.name
FROM products p, product_types pt
WHERE p.product_type_id = pt. product_type_id;
```

The execution plan for the query is shown in the following example; notice the cost is 6 work units (higher than the query with the hint):

```
@ c:\sql_book\sql\explain_plan.sql
Enter value for v_statement_id: NO_HINT


EXECUTION_PLAN
----------------------------------------------------------------
0 SELECT STATEMENT      Cost = 6
1   MERGE JOIN      Cost = 1
2     TABLE ACCESS BY INDEX ROWID PRODUCT_TYPES TABLE Cost = 1
3       INDEX FULL SCAN PRODUCT_TYPES_PK INDEX (UNIQUE) Cost = 1
4     SORT JOIN      Cost = 2
5       TABLE ACCESS FULL PRODUCTS TABLE Cost = 1
```

These results show that the inclusion of the hint reduces the cost of running the query by 2 work units.

There are many hints that you can use, and this section has merely given you a taste of the subject.

Additional Tuning Tools

In this final section, I'll mention some other tuning tools. Full coverage of these tools is beyond the scope of this book. You can read the *Oracle Database Performance Tuning Guide,* published by Oracle Corporation, for full details of the tools mentioned in this section and for a comprehensive list of hints.

Oracle Enterprise Manager Diagnostics Pack

The Oracle Enterprise Manager Diagnostics Pack captures operating system, middle tier, and application performance data, as well as database performance data. The Diagnostics Pack analyzes this performance data and displays the results graphically. A database administrator can also configure the Diagnostics Pack to alert them immediately of performance problems via e-mail or page. Oracle Enterprise Manager also includes software guides to help resolve performance problems.

Automatic Database Diagnostic Monitor

The Automatic Database Diagnostic Monitor (ADDM) is a self-diagnostic module built into the Oracle database software. ADDM enables a database administrator to monitor the database for performance problems by analyzing system performance over a long period of time. The database administrator can view the performance information generated by ADDM in Oracle Enterprise Manager. When ADDM finds performance problems, it will suggest solutions for corrective action. Some example ADDM suggestions include

- Hardware changes—for example, adding CPUs to the database server

- Database configuration—for example, changing the database initialization parameter settings

- Application changes—for example, using the cache option for sequences or using bind variables

- Use other advisors—for example, running the SQL Tuning Advisor and SQL Access Advisor on SQL statements that are consuming the most database resources to execute

You'll learn about the SQL Tuning Advisor and SQL Access Advisor next.

SQL Tuning Advisor

The SQL Tuning Advisor allows a developer or database administrator to tune an SQL statement using the following items:

- The text of the SQL statement

- The SQL identifier of the statement (obtained from the V$SQL_PLAN view, which is one of the views available to a database administrator)

- The range of snapshot identifiers

- The SQL Tuning Set name

An SQL Tuning Set is a set of SQL statements with their associated execution plan and execution statistics. SQL Tuning Sets are analyzed to generate SQL Profiles that help the optimizer to choose the optimal execution plan. SQL Profiles contain collections of information that enable optimization of the execution plan.

SQL Access Advisor

The SQL Access Advisor provides a developer or database administrator with performance advice on materialized views, indexes, and materialized view logs. The SQL Access Advisor examines space usage and query performance and recommends the most cost-effective configuration of new and existing materialized views and indexes.

Summary

In this chapter, you have learned the following:

- Tuning is the process of making your SQL statements run faster.

- The optimizer is a subsystem of the Oracle database software that generates an execution plan, which is a set of operations used to perform a particular SQL statement.

- Hints may be passed to the optimizer to influence the generated execution plan for an SQL statement.

- There are a number of additional software tools a database administrator can use to tune the database.

In the next chapter, you'll learn about XML.

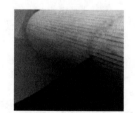

CHAPTER
17

XML and the Oracle Database

n this chapter, you will do the following:

■ Become introduced to XML

■ See how to generate XML from relational data

■ Examine how to save XML in the database

Introducing XML

The Extensible Markup Language (XML) is a general-purpose markup language. XML enables you to share structured data across the Internet, and can be used to encode data and other documents. Some advantages of XML include the following:

■ XML can be read by humans and computers, and is stored as plain text.

■ XML is platform independent.

■ XML supports Unicode, which means it can store information written in many human languages.

■ XML uses a self-documenting format that contains the document structure, element names, and element values.

Because of these advantages, XML is widely used for document storage and processing, and it is used by many organizations to send data between their computer systems. For example, many suppliers allow their customers to send purchase orders as XML files over the Internet.

Oracle Database 9*i* introduced the ability to store XML in the database, along with extensive functionality for manipulating and processing XML. Oracle Database 10*g* Release 2 added additional XML-generating functions, and Oracle Database 11*g* adds capabilities like Java and C processing of binary XML (binary XML provides more efficient storage and manipulation of XML in the database). This chapter focuses on a useful subset of the XML capabilities in the Oracle database.

If you are new to XML, you will find a wealth of information at the following websites:

■ http://www.w3.org/XML

■ http://www.wikipedia.org/wiki/XML

Generating XML from Relational Data

The Oracle database contains a number of SQL functions you can use for generating XML, and in this section you'll see how to generate XML from relational data using some of these functions.

XMLELEMENT()

You use the XMLELEMENT() function to generate XML elements from relational data. You supply a name for the element, plus the column you wish to retrieve to XMLELEMENT(), and it returns the elements as XMLType objects. The XMLType is a built-in Oracle database type that is used to represent XML data. By default, an XMLType object stores the XML data as text in a CLOB (character large object).

The following example connects as the store user and gets the customer_id column values as XMLType objects:

```
CONNECT store/store_password
SELECT XMLELEMENT("customer_id", customer_id)
AS xml_customers
FROM customers;


XML_CUSTOMERS
-------------------------
<customer_id>1</customer_id>
<customer_id>2</customer_id>
<customer_id>3</customer_id>
<customer_id>4</customer_id>
<customer_id>5</customer_id>
```

As you can see from these results, XMLELEMENT("customer_id", customer_id) returns the customer_id values within a customer_id tag. You can use whatever tag name you want, as shown in the following example which uses the tag "cust_id":

```
SELECT XMLELEMENT("cust_id", customer_id)
AS xml_customers
FROM customers;


XML_CUSTOMERS
-------------------
<cust_id>1</cust_id>
<cust_id>2</cust_id>
<cust_id>3</cust_id>
<cust_id>4</cust_id>
<cust_id>5</cust_id>
```

The next example gets the first_name and dob values for customer #2:

```
SELECT XMLELEMENT("first_name", first_name) || XMLELEMENT("dob", dob)
AS xml_customer
FROM customers
WHERE customer_id = 2;


XML_CUSTOMER
----------------------------------------------------
<first_name>Cynthia</first_name><dob>1968-02-05</dob>
```

The following example uses the TO_CHAR() function to change the date format for the dob value:

```
SELECT XMLELEMENT("dob", TO_CHAR(dob, 'MM/DD/YYYY'))
AS xml_dob
FROM customers
WHERE customer_id = 2;

XML_DOB
--------------------
<dob>02/05/1968</dob>
```

The next example embeds two calls to XMLELEMENT() within an outer call to XMLELEMENT(); notice that the returned customer_id and name elements are contained within an outer customer element:

```
SELECT XMLELEMENT(
    "customer",
    XMLELEMENT("customer_id", customer_id),
    XMLELEMENT("name", first_name || ' ' || last_name)
)
AS xml_customers
FROM customers
WHERE customer_id IN (1, 2);

XML_CUSTOMERS
------------------------------
<customer>
  <customer_id>1</customer_id>
  <name>John Brown</name>
</customer>

<customer>
  <customer_id>2</customer_id>
  <name>Cynthia Green</name>
</customer>
```

NOTE
I've added some line breaks and spaces in the XML returned by this query to make the XML easier to read. I've done the same thing in some of the other examples in this chapter.

You can retrieve regular relational data as well as XML, as shown in the following example, which retrieves the customer_id column as a regular relational result and the first_name and last_name columns concatenated together as XML elements:

```
SELECT customer_id,
    XMLELEMENT("customer", first_name || ' ' || last_name) AS xml_customer
FROM customers;
```

```
CUSTOMER_ID XML_CUSTOMER
----------- -----------------------------------
          1 <customer>John Brown</customer>
          2 <customer>Cynthia Green</customer>
          3 <customer>Steve White</customer>
          4 <customer>Gail Black</customer>
          5 <customer>Doreen Blue</customer>
```

You can generate XML for database objects, as shown in the next example which connects as `object_user` and gets the `id` and `address` columns for customer #1 in the `object_customers` table (the `address` column stores an object of type `t_address`):

```
CONNECT object_user/object_password
SELECT XMLELEMENT("id", id) || XMLELEMENT("address", address)
AS xml_object_customer
FROM object_customers
WHERE id = 1;

XML_OBJECT_CUSTOMER
-----------------------------------
<id>1</id>
<address>
  <T_ADDRESS>
    <STREET>2 State Street</STREET>
    <CITY>Beantown</CITY>
    <STATE>MA</STATE>
    <ZIP>12345</ZIP>
  </T_ADDRESS>
</address>
```

You can generate XML for collections, as shown in the next example, which connects as `collection_user` and gets the `id` and `addresses` columns for customer #1 stored in `customers_with_nested_table` (the `addresses` column stores an object of type `t_nested_table_address`, which is a nested table of `t_address` objects):

```
CONNECT collection_user/collection_password
SELECT XMLELEMENT("id", id) || XMLELEMENT("addresses", addresses)
AS xml_customer
FROM customers_with_nested_table
WHERE id = 1;

XML_CUSTOMER
----------------------------------------------------
<id>1</id>
<addresses>
  <T_NESTED_TABLE_ADDRESS>
    <T_ADDRESS>
      <STREET>2 State Street</STREET><CITY>Beantown</CITY>
      <STATE>MA</STATE><ZIP>12345</ZIP>
    </T_ADDRESS>
```

```
    <T_ADDRESS>
      <STREET>4 Hill Street</STREET>
      <CITY>Lost Town</CITY>
      <STATE>CA</STATE>
      <ZIP>54321</ZIP>
    </T_ADDRESS>
  </T_NESTED_TABLE_ADDRESS>
</addresses>
```

XMLATTRIBUTES()

You use XMLATTRIBUTES() in conjunction with XMLELEMENT() to specify the attributes for the XML elements retrieved by XMLELEMENT(). The following example connects as the store user and uses XMLATTRIBUTES() to set attribute names for the customer_id, first_name, last_name, and dob elements:

```
CONNECT store/store_password
SELECT XMLELEMENT(
  "customer",
  XMLATTRIBUTES(
    customer_id AS "id",
    first_name || ' ' || last_name AS "name",
    TO_CHAR(dob, 'MM/DD/YYYY') AS "dob"
  )
)
AS xml_customers
FROM customers
WHERE customer_id IN (1, 2);

XML_CUSTOMERS
-----------------------------------------------------------------
<customer id="1" name="John Brown" dob="01/01/1965"></customer>
<customer id="2" name="Cynthia Green" dob="02/05/1968"></customer>
```

Notice that the id, name, and dob attributes are returned inside customer.

XMLFOREST()

You use XMLFOREST() to generate a "forest" of XML elements. XMLFOREST() concatenates XML elements together without you having to use the concatenation operator || with multiple calls to XMLELEMENT(). The following example uses XMLFOREST() to get the customer_id, phone, and dob for customers #1 and #2:

```
SELECT XMLELEMENT(
  "customer",
  XMLFOREST(
    customer_id AS "id",
    phone AS "phone",
    TO_CHAR(dob, 'MM/DD/YYYY') AS "dob"
  )
)
AS xml_customers
```

```
FROM customers
WHERE customer_id IN (1, 2);

XML_CUSTOMERS
----------------------------
<customer>
  <id>1</id>
  <phone>800-555-1211</phone>
  <dob>01/01/1965</dob>
</customer>

<customer>
  <id>2</id>
  <phone>800-555-1212</phone>
  <dob>02/05/1968</dob>
</customer>
```

The following command sets the SQL*Plus LONG parameter to 500, so you can see all the XML returned by the subsequent queries (LONG controls the maximum length of text data displayed by SQL*Plus):

```
SET LONG 500
```

The following query places the customer name inside the customer element tag using XMLATTRIBUTES():

```
SELECT XMLELEMENT(
  "customer",
  XMLATTRIBUTES(first_name || ' ' || last_name AS "name"),
  XMLFOREST(phone AS "phone", TO_CHAR(dob, 'MM/DD/YYYY') AS "dob")
)
AS xml_customers
FROM customers
WHERE customer_id IN (1, 2);

XML_CUSTOMERS
-------------------------------
<customer name="John Brown">
  <phone>800-555-1211</phone>
  <dob>01/01/1965</dob>
</customer>

<customer name="Cynthia Green">
  <phone>800-555-1212</phone>
  <dob>02/05/1968</dob>
</customer>
```

XMLAGG()

You use XMLAGG() to generate a forest of XML elements from a collection of XML elements. XMLAGG() is typically used for grouping XML together into a common list of items underneath one parent or for retrieving data from collections. You can use the GROUP BY clause of a query to group the retuned set of rows into multiple groups, and you can use an ORDER BY clause of XMLAGG() to sort the rows.

By default, ORDER BY sorts the results in ascending order, but you can add DESC after the list of columns to sort the rows in descending order. You can add ASC to explicitly indicate an ascending sort. You can also add NULLS LAST to put any null values at the end of the results.

The following example retrieves the customer first_name and last_name values and returns them in a list named customer_list; notice that ORDER BY is used with XMLAGG() to sort the results by the first_name column. I've added ASC to explicitly indicate an ascending sort:

```
SELECT XMLELEMENT(
  "customer_list",
  XMLAGG(
    XMLELEMENT("customer", first_name || ' ' || last_name)
    ORDER BY first_name ASC
  )
)
AS xml_customers
FROM customers
WHERE customer_id IN (1, 2);

XML_CUSTOMERS
-----------------------------------
<customer_list>
  <customer>Cynthia Green</customer>
  <customer>John Brown</customer>
</customer_list>
```

The next example retrieves the product_type_id and average price for each group of products; notice that the products are grouped by product_type_id using the GROUP BY clause of the query, and NULLS LAST is used in the ORDER BY clause of XMLAGG() to place the row with the null product_type_id at the end of the returned results:

```
SELECT XMLELEMENT(
  "product_list",
  XMLAGG(
    XMLELEMENT(
      "product_type_and_avg", product_type_id || ' ' || AVG(price)
    )
    ORDER BY product_type_id NULLS LAST
  )
)
AS xml_products
FROM products
GROUP BY product_type_id;

XML_PRODUCTS
-------------------------------------------------------
<product_list>
  <product_type_and_avg>1 24.975</product_type_and_avg>
  <product_type_and_avg>2 26.22</product_type_and_avg>
  <product_type_and_avg>3 13.24</product_type_and_avg>
```

```
  <product_type_and_avg>4 13.99</product_type_and_avg>
  <product_type_and_avg> 13.49</product_type_and_avg>
</product_list>
```

NOTE
You can also place the null row first by specifying NULLS FIRST *in the* ORDER BY *clause of* XMLAGG().

The next example retrieves the product_type_id and name for the products with product_type_id values of 1 and 2, and the products are grouped by product_type_id:

```
SELECT XMLELEMENT(
  "products_in_group",
  XMLATTRIBUTES(product_type_id AS "prd_type_id"),
  XMLAGG(
    XMLELEMENT("name", name)
  )
)
AS xml_products
FROM products
WHERE product_type_id IN (1, 2)
GROUP BY product_type_id;

XML_PRODUCTS
-----------------------------------
<products_in_group prd_type_id="1">
  <name>Modern Science</name>
  <name>Chemistry</name>
</products_in_group>

<products_in_group prd_type_id="2">
  <name>Supernova</name>
  <name>2412: The Return</name>
</products_in_group>
```

The next example connects as collection_user and retrieves the addresses for customer #1 from customers_with_nested_table:

```
CONNECT collection_user/collection_password
SELECT XMLELEMENT("customer",
  XMLAGG(
    XMLELEMENT("addresses", addresses)
  )
)
AS xml_customer
FROM customers_with_nested_table
WHERE id = 1;

XML_CUSTOMER
-------------------------------------
<customer>
  <addresses>
```

```
    <T_NESTED_TABLE_ADDRESS>
      <T_ADDRESS>
        <STREET>2 State Street</STREET>
        <CITY>Beantown</CITY>
        <STATE>MA</STATE>
        <ZIP>21345</ZIP>
      </T_ADDRESS>
      <T_ADDRESS>
        <STREET>4 Hill Street</STREET>
        <CITY>Lost Town</CITY>
        <STATE>CA</STATE>
        <ZIP>54321</ZIP>
      </T_ADDRESS>
    </T_NESTED_TABLE_ADDRESS>
  </addresses>
</customer>
```

XMLCOLATTVAL()

You use XMLCOLATTVAL() to create an XML fragment and then expand the resulting XML. Each XML fragment has the name column with the attribute name. You can use the AS clause to change the attribute name.

The following example connects as the store user retrieves the customer_id, dob, and phone values for customers #1 and #2:

```
CONNECT store/store_password
SELECT XMLELEMENT(
  "customer",
  XMLCOLATTVAL(
    customer_id AS "id",
    dob AS "dob",
    phone AS "phone"
  )
)
AS xml_customers
FROM customers
WHERE customer_id IN (1, 2);

XML_CUSTOMERS
--------------------------------------------
<customer>
  <column name = "id">1</column>
  <column name = "dob">1965-01-01</column>
  <column name = "phone">800-555-1211</column>
</customer>

<customer>
  <column name = "id">2</column>
  <column name = "dob">1968-02-05</column>
  <column name = "phone">800-555-1212</column>
</customer>
```

XMLCONCAT()

You use XMLCONCAT() to concatenate a series of elements for each row. The following example concatenates the XML elements for first_name, last_name, and phone values for customers #1 and #2:

```
SELECT XMLCONCAT(
  XMLELEMENT("first name", first_name),
  XMLELEMENT("last name", last_name),
  XMLELEMENT("phone", phone)
)
AS xml_customers
FROM customers
WHERE customer_id IN (1, 2);

XML_CUSTOMERS
--------------------------------
<first name>John</first name>
<last name>Brown</last name>
<phone>800-555-1211</phone>

<first name>Cynthia</first name>
<last name>Green</last name>
<phone>800-555-1212</phone>
```

XMLPARSE()

You use XMLPARSE() to parse and generate XML from the evaluated result of an expression. The expression must resolve to a string; if the expression resolves to null, then XMLPARSE() returns null. You must specify one of the following items before the expression:

- CONTENT, which means the expression must resolve to a valid XML value
- DOCUMENT, which means the expression must resolve to a singly rooted XML document

You can also add WELLFORMED after the expression, which means you are guaranteeing that your expression resolves to a well-formed XML document. This also means that the database will not perform validity checks on your expression.

The following example parses an expression containing the details for a customer:

```
SELECT XMLPARSE(
  CONTENT
  '<customer><customer_id>1</customer_id><name>John Brown</name></customer>'
  WELLFORMED
)
AS xml_customer
FROM dual;

XML_CUSTOMER
-----------------------------
<customer>
  <customer_id>1</customer_id>
  <name>John Brown</name>
</customer>
```

NOTE
You can read more about well-formed XML documents and values at
http://www.w3.org/TR/REC-xml.

XMLPI()

You use XMLPI() to generate an XML processing instruction. You typically use a processing instruction to provide an application with information that is associated with XML data; the application can then use the processing instruction to determine how to process the XML data.

The following example generates a processing instruction for an order status:

```
SELECT XMLPI(
  NAME "order_status",
  'PLACED, PENDING, SHIPPED'
)
AS xml_order_status_pi
FROM dual;

XML_ORDER_STATUS_PI
-----------------------------------------
<?order_status PLACED, PENDING, SHIPPED?>
```

The next example generates a processing instruction to display an XML document using a cascading stylesheet file named example.css:

```
SELECT XMLPI(
  NAME "xml-stylesheet",
  'type="text/css" href="example.css"'
)
AS xml_stylesheet_pi
FROM dual;

XML_STYLESHEET_PI
-----------------------------------------------------
<?xml-stylesheet type="text/css" href="example.css"?>
```

XMLCOMMENT()

You use XMLCOMMENT() to generate an XML comment, which is a text string placed within <!-- and -->. For example:

```
SELECT XMLCOMMENT(
  'An example XML Comment'
)
AS xml_comment
FROM dual;

XML_COMMENT
-----------------------------
<!--An example XML Comment-->
```

XMLSEQUENCE()

You use XMLSEQUENCE() to generate an XMLSequenceType object, which is a varray of XMLType objects. Because XMLSEQUENCE() returns a varray, you can use it in the FROM clause of a query. For example:

```
SELECT VALUE(list_of_values).GETSTRINGVAL() order_values
FROM TABLE(
  XMLSEQUENCE(
    EXTRACT(
      XMLType('<A><B>PLACED</B><B>PENDING</B><B>SHIPPED</B></A>'),
      '/A/B'
    )
  )
) list_of_values;

ORDER_VALUES
--------------
<B>PLACED</B>
<B>PENDING</B>
<B>SHIPPED</B>
```

Let's break down this example. The call to XMLType() is

```
XMLType('<A><B>PLACED</B><B>PENDING</B><B>SHIPPED</B></A>')
```

This creates an XMLType object containing the XML

```
<A><B>PLACED</B><B>PENDING</B><B>SHIPPED</B></A>.
```

The call to the EXTRACT() function is

```
EXTRACT(
  XMLType('<A><B>PLACED</B><B>PENDING</B><B>SHIPPED</B></A>'),
  '/A/B'
)
```

EXTRACT() extracts the XML data from the XMLType object returned by the call to XMLType(). The second parameter to EXTRACT() is an XPath string. XPath is a language that allows you access specific elements in XML data. For example, in the previous call to EXTRACT(), '/A/B' returns all the B elements that are children of the A elements; therefore, the EXTRACT() function returns the following:

```
<B>PLACED</B>
<B>PENDING</B>
<B>SHIPPED</B>
```

The call to XMLSEQUENCE() in the example simply returns a varray containing the elements returned by EXTRACT(). TABLE() converts the varray into a table of rows and applies the alias list_of_values to the table. The SELECT statement retrieves the string value of the rows in the table using GETSTRINGVAL().

You'll see more examples of EXTRACT() and XPath later in this chapter.

XMLSERIALIZE()

You use XMLSERIALIZE() to generate a string or LOB (large object) representation of XML data from the evaluated result of an expression. You must specify one of the following items before the expression:

- CONTENT, which means the expression must resolve to a valid XML value

- DOCUMENT, which means the expression must resolve to a singly rooted XML document

The following example uses XMLSERIALIZE() with CONTENT to generate an XML value:

```
SELECT XMLSERIALIZE(
  CONTENT XMLType('<order_status>SHIPPED</order_status>')
)
AS xml_order_status
FROM DUAL;

XML_ORDER_STATUS
-----------------------------------
<order_status>SHIPPED</order_status>
```

The next example uses XMLSERIALIZE() with DOCUMENT to generate an XML document, with the document returned in a CLOB (character large object):

```
SELECT XMLSERIALIZE(
  DOCUMENT XMLType('<description>Description of a product</description>')
  AS CLOB
)
AS xml_product_description
FROM DUAL;

XML_PRODUCT_DESCRIPTION
---------------------------------------------------
<description>Description of a product</description>
```

A PL/SQL Example That Writes XML Data to a File

In this section, you'll see a complete PL/SQL example that writes customer names to an XML file. First, you need to connect as a privileged user (for example, the system user) and grant the CREATE ANY DIRECTORY privilege to the store user:

```
CONNECT system/manager;
GRANT CREATE ANY DIRECTORY TO store;
```

Next, you need to connect as the store user and create a directory object:

```
CONNECT store/store_password;
CREATE DIRECTORY TEMP_FILES_DIR AS 'C:\temp_files';
```

You'll also need to create a directory named temp_files in the C partition. (If you're using Linux or Unix, you can create the directory on one of your partitions and use an appropriate CREATE DIRECTORY command with the correct path. Also, make sure you grant write permissions on the directory to the Oracle user account you used to install the database software.)

Next, you need to run the `xml_examples.sql` script located in the `SQL` directory, as shown here:

```
@ "E:\Oracle SQL book\sql_book\SQL\xml_examples.sql"
```

CAUTION
Run only the `xml_examples.sql` *script at this point. You may notice there is a script named* `xml_schema.sql` *in the* `SQL` *directory. Do not run* `xml_schema.sql` *yet.*

The `xml_examples.sql` script creates two procedures; the one you'll see in this section is named `write_xml_data_to_file()`, which retrieves the customer names and writes them to an XML file. The `write_xml_data_to_file()` procedure is defined as follows:

```
CREATE PROCEDURE write_xml_data_to_file(
  p_directory VARCHAR2,
  p_file_name VARCHAR2
) AS
  v_file UTL_FILE.FILE_TYPE;
  v_amount INTEGER := 32767;
  v_xml_data XMLType;
  v_char_buffer VARCHAR2(32767);
BEGIN
  -- open the file for writing of text (up to v_amount
  -- characters at a time)
  v_file := UTL_FILE.FOPEN(p_directory, p_file_name, 'w', v_amount);

  -- write the starting line to v_file
  UTL_FILE.PUT_LINE(v_file, '<?xml version="1.0"?>');

  -- retrieve the customers and store them in v_xml_data
  SELECT
    EXTRACT(
      XMLELEMENT(
        "customer_list",
        XMLAGG(
          XMLELEMENT("customer", first_name || ' ' || last_name)
          ORDER BY last_name
        )
      ),
      '/customer_list'
    )
  AS xml_customers
  INTO v_xml_data
  FROM customers;

  -- get the string value from v_xml_data and store it in v_char_buffer
  v_char_buffer := v_xml_data.GETSTRINGVAL();

  -- copy the characters from v_char_buffer to the file
  UTL_FILE.PUT(v_file, v_char_buffer);
```

```
-- flush any remaining data to the file
UTL_FILE.FFLUSH(v_file);

-- close the file
UTL_FILE.FCLOSE(v_file);
END write_xml_data_to_file;
/
```

The following statement calls `write_xml_data_to_file()`:

```
CALL write_xml_data_to_file('TEMP_FILES_DIR', 'customers.xml');
```

After you run this statement, you'll find a file named `customers.xml` in `C:\temp_files`, or whichever directory you used when using the `CREATE DIRECTORY` command earlier. The contents of the `customers.xml` file is as follows:

```
<?xml version="1.0"?>
<customer_list><customer>Gail Black</customer><customer>Doreen Blue
</customer><customer>John Brown</customer><customer>Cynthia Green
</customer><customer>Steve White</customer></customer_list>
```

You can modify the `write_xml_data_to_file()` procedure to retrieve any relational data from the database and write it out to an XML file.

XMLQUERY()

You use `XMLQUERY()` to construct XML or query XML. You pass an XQuery expression to `XMLQUERY()`. XQuery is a query language that allows you to construct and query XML. `XMLQUERY()` returns the result of evaluating the XQuery expression.

The following simple example illustrates the use of `XMLQUERY()`:

```
SELECT XMLQUERY(
  '(1, 2 + 5, "d", 155 to 161, <A>text</A>)'
  RETURNING CONTENT
)
AS xml_output
FROM DUAL;

XML_OUTPUT
-------------------------------------------
1 7 d 155 156 157 158 159 160 161<A>text</A>
```

Here are some notes for the example:

- The string passed to `XMLQUERY()` is the XQuery expression, that is, the XQuery expression is (1, 2 + 5, "d", 155 to 161, <A>text</A>). 1 is an integer literal, 2 + 5 is an arithmetic expression, d is a string literal, 155 to 161 is a sequence of integers, and <A>text</A> is an XML element.

- Each of the items in the XQuery is evaluated in turn. For example, 2 + 5 is evaluated, and 7 is returned. Similarly, 155 to 161 is evaluated and 155 156 157 158 159 160 161 is returned.

■ RETURNING CONTENT means an XML fragment is returned. This XML fragment is a
single XML element with any number of "children," which can themselves be of any XML
element type, including text elements. The XML fragment also conforms to the extended
Infoset data model. Infoset is a specification describing an abstract data model of an XML
document. You can learn more about Infoset at http://www.w3.org/TR/xml-infoset.

Let's explore a more complex example. The following statement (contained in the xml_
examples.sql script) creates a procedure named create_xml_resources(); this
procedure creates XML strings for products and product types. It uses methods in the PL/SQL
DBMS_XDB package to delete and create XML resource files in the Oracle XML DB Repository
(the XML DB Repository is a storage area for XML data within the database):

```
CREATE PROCEDURE create_xml_resources AS
  v_result BOOLEAN;

  -- create string containing XML for products
  v_products VARCHAR2(300):=
    '<?xml version="1.0"?>' ||
    '<products>' ||
      '<product product_id="1" product_type_id="1" name="Modern Science"'
      || ' price="19.95"/>' ||
      '<product product_id="2" product_type_id="1" name="Chemistry"' ||
      ' price="30"/>' ||
      '<product product_id="3" product_type_id="2" name="Supernova"' ||
      ' price="25.99"/>' ||
    '</products>';

  -- create string containing XML for product types
  v_product_types VARCHAR2(300):=
    '<?xml version="1.0"?>' ||
    '<product_types>' ||
      '<product_type product_type_id="1" name="Book"/>' ||
      '<product_type product_type_id="2" name="Video"/>' ||
    '</product_types>';
BEGIN
  -- delete any existing resource for products
  DBMS_XDB.DELETERESOURCE('/public/products.xml',
    DBMS_XDB.DELETE_RECURSIVE_FORCE);

  -- create resource for products
  v_result := DBMS_XDB.CREATERESOURCE('/public/products.xml',
    v_products);

  -- delete any existing resource for product types
  DBMS_XDB.DELETERESOURCE('/public/product_types.xml',
    DBMS_XDB.DELETE_RECURSIVE_FORCE);

  -- create resource for product types
  v_result := DBMS_XDB.CREATERESOURCE('/public/product_types.xml',
    v_product_types);
END create_xml_resources;
/
```

Here are some notes for `create_xml_resources()`:

- The `DBMS_XDB.DELETERESOURCE()` procedure deletes an XML resource from the database. This procedure is called by `create_xml_resources()` so that you don't have to manually remove the resources if you run `create_xml_resources()` more than once.

- The `DBMS_XDB.DELETE_RECURSIVE_FORCE` constant forces the deletion of the resource, including any child objects.

- The `DBMS_XDB.CREATERESOURCE()` function creates an XML resource in the database and returns a Boolean `true`/`false` value indicating whether the operation was successful. The two calls to this function create resources for the products and product types in `/public`, which is the absolute path to store the resources.

The following statement calls `create_xml_resources()`:

```
CALL create_xml_resources();
```

The following query uses `XMLQUERY()` to retrieve the products from the `/public/products.xml` resource:

```
SELECT XMLQUERY(
  'for $product in doc("/public/products.xml")/products/product
  return <product name="{$product/@name}"/>'
  RETURNING CONTENT
)
AS xml_products
FROM DUAL;

XML_PRODUCTS
----------------------------------------
<product name="Modern Science"></product>
<product name="Chemistry"></product>
<product name="Supernova"></product>
```

The XQuery expression inside `XMLQUERY()` in the previous example is

```
for $product in doc("/public/products.xml")/products/product
return <product name="{$product/@name}"/>
```

Let's break down this XQuery expression:

- The `for` loop iterates over the products in `/public/products.xml`.

- `$product` is a binding variable that is bound to the sequence of products returned by `doc("/public/products.xml")/products/product`; `doc("/public/products.xml")` returns the `products.xml` document stored in `/public`. With each iteration of the loop, `$product` is set to each product in `products.xml`, one after another.

- The `return` part of the expression returns the product name in `$product`.

The next query retrieves the product types from the `/public/product_types.xml` resource:

```
SELECT XMLQUERY(
  'for $product_type in
  doc("/public/product_types.xml")/product_types/product_type
  return <product_type name="{$product_type/@name}"/>'
  RETURNING CONTENT
)
AS xml_product_types
FROM DUAL;

XML_PRODUCT_TYPES
-----------------------------------------
<product_type name="Book"></product_type>
<product_type name="Video"></product_type>
```

The following query retrieves the products whose price is greater than 20, along with their product type:

```
SELECT XMLQUERY(
  'for $product in doc("/public/products.xml")/products/product
  let $product_type :=
    doc("/public/product_types.xml")//product_type[@product_type_id =
      $product/@product_type_id]/@name
  where $product/@price > 20
  order by $product/@product_id
  return <product name="{$product/@name}"
    product_type="{$product_type}"/>'
  RETURNING CONTENT
)
AS xml_query_results
FROM DUAL;

XML_QUERY_RESULTS
------------------------------------------------------------
<product name="Chemistry" product_type="Book"></product>
<product name="Supernova" product_type="Video"></product>
```

Let's break down the XQuery expression in this example:

- Two binding variables are used: $product and $product_type. These variables are used to store the products and product types.

- The let part of the expression sets $product_type to the product type retrieved from $product. The expression on the right-hand side of the := performs a join using the product_type_id value stored in $product_type and $product. The // means retrieve all elements.

- The where part retrieves only products whose price is greater than 20.

- The order by part orders the results by the product ID (in ascending order by default).

The next example shows the use of the following XQuery functions:

- `count()`, which counts the number of objects passed to it.

- `avg()`, which calculates the average of the numbers passed to it.

- `integer()`, which truncates a number and returns the integer. The `integer()` function is in the `xs` namespace. (The `count()` and `avg()` functions are in the `fn` namespace, which is automatically referenced by the database, thereby allowing you to omit this namespace when calling these functions.)

The following example returns the product type name, the number of products in each product type, and the average price of the products in each product type (truncated to an integer):

```
SELECT XMLQUERY(
    'for $product_type in
    doc("/public/product_types.xml")/product_types/product_type
    let $product :=
      doc("/public/products.xml")//product[@product_type_id =
        $product_type/@product_type_id]
    return
      <product_type name="{$product_type/@name}"
       num_products="{count($product)}"
       average_price="{xs:integer(avg($product/@price))}"
      />'
  RETURNING CONTENT
)
AS xml_query_results
FROM DUAL;

XML_QUERY_RESULTS
--------------------------------------------------------------
<product_type name="Book" num_products="2" average_price="24">
</product_type>

<product_type name="Video" num_products="1" average_price="25">
</product_type>
```

As you can see from the results, there are two books and one video.

NOTE
You can read more about functions at http://www.w3.org/TR/xquery-operators. You can find more information on XMLQUERY() *at http://www.sqlx.org.*

Saving XML in the Database

In this section, you'll see how to store an XML document in the database and retrieve information from the stored XML.

The Example XML File

You'll see the use of a file named `purchase_order.xml`, which is an XML file that contains a purchase order. This file is contained in the `xml_files` directory, which is created when you extracted the Zip file for this book. If you want to follow along with the examples, you should copy the `xml_files` directory to the C partition on your database server (if you're using Linux or Unix, you can copy the directory to one of your partitions).

NOTE
If you copy the `xml_files` *directory to a location different from* C, *then you'll need to edit the* `xml_schema.sql` *script (you'll see this script shortly).*

The contents of the `purchase_order.xml` file is as follows:

```
<?xml version="1.0"?>
<purchase_order>
  <customer_order_id>176</customer_order_id>
  <order_date>2007-05-17</order_date>
  <customer_name>Best Products 456 Inc.</customer_name>
  <street>10 Any Street</street>
  <city>Any City</city>
  <state>CA</state>
  <zip>94440</zip>
  <phone_number>555-121-1234</phone_number>
  <products>
    <product>
      <product_id>1</product_id>
      <name>Supernova video</name>
      <quantity>5</quantity>
    </product>
    <product>
      <product_id>2</product_id>
      <name>Oracle SQL book</name>
      <quantity>4</quantity>
    </product>
  </products>
</purchase_order>
```

In the following sections, you'll see how to store this XML file in the database.

In a real-world example, the purchase order could be sent via the Internet to an online store, which would then dispatch the requested items to the customer.

Creating the Example XML Schema

I've provided an SQL*Plus script named `xml_schema.sql` in the SQL directory. The script creates a user named `xml_user` with a password of `xml_password`, and it creates the items used in the rest of this chapter. Don't run this script yet.

The script contains the following statements that create an object type named `t_product` (used to represent products), a nested table type named `t_nested_table_product` (used to represent a nested table of products), and a table named `purchase_order`:

```
CREATE TYPE t_product AS OBJECT (
  product_id INTEGER,
  name VARCHAR2(15),
  quantity INTEGER
);
/

CREATE TYPE t_nested_table_product AS TABLE OF t_product;
/

CREATE TABLE purchase_order (
  purchase_order_id INTEGER CONSTRAINT purchase_order_pk PRIMARY KEY,
  customer_order_id INTEGER,
  order_date DATE,
  customer_name VARCHAR2(25),
  street VARCHAR2(15),
  city VARCHAR2(15),
  state VARCHAR2(2),
  zip VARCHAR2(5),
  phone_number VARCHAR2(12),
  products t_nested_table_product,
  xml_purchase_order XMLType
)
NESTED TABLE products
STORE AS nested_products;
```

Notice that the `xml_purchase_order` column is of type `XMLType`, which is a built-in Oracle database type that allows you to store XML data. By default, an `XMLType` column stores the XML data as text in a CLOB (character large object).

The `xml_schema.sql` script also contains the following statement that creates a directory object named `XML_FILES_DIR`:

```
CREATE OR REPLACE DIRECTORY XML_FILES_DIR AS 'C:\xml_files';
```

You'll need to modify this line if you copied the `xml_files` directory to a location different from `C`. If you need to modify this line, go ahead and do it now and then save the script.

The following `INSERT` statement (also contained in the script) adds a row to the `purchase_order` table:

```
INSERT INTO purchase_order (
  purchase_order_id,
  xml_purchase_order
) VALUES (
  1,
  XMLType(
    BFILENAME('XML_FILES_DIR', 'purchase_order.xml'),
    NLS_CHARSET_ID('AL32UTF8')
  )
);
```

As you can see, the `XMLType()` constructor accepts two parameters. The first parameter is a `BFILE`, which is a pointer to an external file. The second parameter is the character set for the XML text in the external file. In the previous `INSERT`, the `BFILE` points to the `purchase_order.xml` file, and the character set is AL32UTF8, which is standard UTF-8 encoding. When the `INSERT` is run, the XML from the `purchase_order.xml` file is read and then stored in the database as CLOB text in the `xml_purchase_order` column.

NOTE
When you are working with XML files written in English, you should typically use the AL32UTF8 character set. You can find more information about different character sets in the Oracle Database Globalization Support Guide *published by Oracle Corporation.*

You may have noticed the `customer_order_id`, `order_date`, `customer_name`, `street`, `city`, `state`, `zip`, `phone_number`, and `products` columns in the `purchase_order` table are empty. The data for these columns can be extracted from the XML stored in the `xml_purchase_order` column. Later in this chapter, you'll see a PL/SQL procedure that reads the XML and sets the other columns accordingly.

Go ahead and run the `xml_schema.sql` script as a privileged user (such as the `system` user):

```
CONNECT system/manager
@ "E:\Oracle SQL book\sql_book\SQL\xml_schema.sql"
```

After the script completes, you will be logged in as `xml_user`.

Retrieving Information from the Example XML Schema

In this section, you'll see how to retrieve information from the `xml_user` schema.

The following example retrieves the row from the `purchase_order` table:

```
SET LONG 1000
SET PAGESIZE 500
SELECT purchase_order_id, xml_purchase_order
FROM purchase_order;


PURCHASE_ORDER_ID
-----------------
XML_PURCHASE_ORDER
----------------------------------------------------------
                1
<?xml version="1.0"?>
<purchase_order>
  <customer_order_id>176</customer_order_id>
  <order_date>2007-05-17</order_date>
  <customer_name>Best Products 456 Inc.</customer_name>
  <street>10 Any Street</street>
  <city>Any City</city>
  <state>CA</state>
  <zip>94440</zip>
  <phone_number>555-121-1234</phone_number>
  <products>
```

```
    <product>
      <product_id>1</product_id>
      <name>Supernova video</name>
      <quantity>5</quantity>
    </product>
    <product>
      <product_id>2</product_id>
      <name>Oracle SQL book</name>
      <quantity>4</quantity>
    </product>
  </products>
</purchase_order>
```

The next query extracts the customer_order_id, order_date, customer_name, and phone_number from the XML stored in the xml_purchase_order column using the EXTRACT() function:

```
SELECT
  EXTRACT(xml_purchase_order,
    '/purchase_order/customer_order_id') cust_order_id,
  EXTRACT(xml_purchase_order, '/purchase_order/order_date') order_date,
  EXTRACT(xml_purchase_order, '/purchase_order/customer_name') cust_name,
  EXTRACT(xml_purchase_order, '/purchase_order/phone_number') phone_number
FROM purchase_order
WHERE purchase_order_id = 1;

CUST_ORDER_ID
-----------------------------------------
ORDER_DATE
-----------------------------------
CUST_NAME
-------------------------------------------------
PHONE_NUMBER
-----------------------------------------
<customer_order_id>176</customer_order_id>
<order_date>2007-05-17</order_date>
<customer_name>Best Products 456 Inc.</customer_name>
<phone_number>555-121-1234</phone_number>
```

The EXTRACT() function returns the values as XMLType objects.

You can use the EXTRACTVALUE() function to get the values as strings. For example, the following query extracts the same values as strings using the EXTRACTVALUE() function:

```
SELECT
  EXTRACTVALUE(xml_purchase_order,
    '/purchase_order/customer_order_id') cust_order_id,
  EXTRACTVALUE(xml_purchase_order,
    '/purchase_order/order_date') order_date,
  EXTRACTVALUE(xml_purchase_order,
    '/purchase_order/customer_name') cust_name,
  EXTRACTVALUE(xml_purchase_order,
```

```
      '/purchase_order/phone_number') phone_number
FROM purchase_order
WHERE purchase_order_id = 1;


CUST_ORDER_ID
--------------------
ORDER_DATE
--------------------
CUST_NAME
--------------------
PHONE_NUMBER
--------------------
176
2007-05-17
Best Products 456 Inc.
555-121-1234
```

The next query extracts and converts order_date to a DATE using the TO_DATE()
function; notice that the format for the date as stored in the XML is supplied using the second
parameter to TO_DATE() and that TO_DATE() returns the date in the default date format used
by the database (DD-MON-YY):

```
SELECT
  TO_DATE(
    EXTRACTVALUE(xml_purchase_order, '/purchase_order/order_date'),
    'YYYY-MM-DD'
  ) AS ord_date
FROM purchase_order
WHERE purchase_order_id = 1;


ORD_DATE
---------
17-MAY-07
```

The following query retrieves all the products from xml_purchase_order as XML using
EXTRACT(); notice the use of // to get all the products:

```
SELECT
  EXTRACT(xml_purchase_order, '/purchase_order//products') xml_products
FROM purchase_order
WHERE purchase_order_id = 1;


XML_PRODUCTS
--------------------------------
<products>
  <product>
    <product_id>1</product_id>
    <name>Supernova video</name>
    <quantity>5</quantity>
  </product>
  <product>
```

```
    <product_id>2</product_id>
    <name>Oracle SQL book</name>
    <quantity>4</quantity>
  </product>
</products>
```

The next query retrieves product #2 from `xml_purchase_order`; notice `product[2]` returns product #2:

```
SELECT
  EXTRACT(
    xml_purchase_order,
    '/purchase_order/products/product[2]'
  ) xml_product
FROM purchase_order
WHERE purchase_order_id = 1;

XML_PRODUCT
---------------------------------
<product>
  <product_id>2</product_id>
  <product>Oracle SQL book</name>
  <quantity>4</quantity>
</product>
```

The following query retrieves the "Supernova video" product from `xml_purchase_order`; notice that the name of the product to retrieve is placed inside square brackets:

```
SELECT
  EXTRACT(
    xml_purchase_order,
    '/purchase_order/products/product[name="Supernova video"]'
  ) xml_product
FROM purchase_order
WHERE purchase_order_id = 1;

XML_PRODUCT
-----------------------------
<product>
  <product_id>1</product_id>
  <name>Supernova video</name>
  <quantity>5</quantity>
</product>
```

You use the `EXISTSNODE()` function to check if an XML element exists. `EXISTSNODE()` returns 1 if the element exists; otherwise, it returns 0. For example, the following query returns the string `'Exists'` because product #1 exists:

```
SELECT 'Exists' AS "EXISTS"
FROM purchase_order
WHERE purchase_order_id = 1
AND EXISTSNODE(
```

```
  xml_purchase_order,
  '/purchase_order/products/product[product_id=1]'
) = 1;

EXISTS
------
Exists
```

The next query returns no rows because product #3 does not exist:

```
SELECT 'Exists'
FROM purchase_order
WHERE purchase_order_id = 1
AND EXISTSNODE(
  xml_purchase_order,
  '/purchase_order/products/product[product_id=3]'
) = 1;

no rows selected
```

The following query retrieves the products as a varray of XMLType objects using the XMLSEQUENCE() function; notice the use of product.* to retrieve all the products and their XML elements:

```
SELECT product.*
FROM TABLE(
  SELECT
    XMLSEQUENCE(EXTRACT(xml_purchase_order, '/purchase_order//product'))
  FROM purchase_order
  WHERE purchase_order_id = 1
) product;

COLUMN_VALUE
-----------------------------
<product>
  <product_id>1</product_id>
  <name>Supernova video</name>
  <quantity>5</quantity>
</product>

<product>
  <product_id>2</product_id>
  <name>Oracle SQL book</name>
  <quantity>4</quantity>
</product>
```

The next query retrieves the product_id, name, and quantity for the products as strings using the EXTRACTVALUE() function:

```
SELECT
  EXTRACTVALUE(product.COLUMN_VALUE, '/product/product_id') AS product_id,
  EXTRACTVALUE(product.COLUMN_VALUE, '/product/name') AS name,
```

```
  EXTRACTVALUE(product.COLUMN_VALUE, '/product/quantity') AS quantity
FROM TABLE(
  SELECT
    XMLSEQUENCE(EXTRACT(xml_purchase_order, '/purchase_order//product'))
  FROM purchase_order
  WHERE purchase_order_id = 1
) product;


PRODUCT_ID
--------------
PRODUCT
--------------
QUANTITY
--------------
1
Supernova video
5

2
Oracle SQL book
4
```

Updating Information in the Example XML Schema

The `customer_order_id`, `order_date`, `customer_name`, `street`, `city`, `state`, `zip`, `phone_number`, and `products` columns in the `purchase_order` table are empty. The data for these columns can be extracted from the XML stored in the `xml_purchase_order` column. In this section, you'll a PL/SQL procedure named `update_purchase_order()` that reads the XML and sets the other columns accordingly.

The most complex aspect of `update_purchase_order()` is the process of reading the products from the XML and storing them in the `products` nested table column of the `purchase_order` table. In this procedure, a cursor is used to read the products from the XML, then the XML is converted to strings using `EXTRACTVALUE()`, and the strings are stored in a nested table.

The following statement (contained in the `xml_schema.sql` script) creates the `update_purchase_order()` procedure:

```
CREATE PROCEDURE update_purchase_order(
  p_purchase_order_id IN purchase_order.purchase_order_id%TYPE
) AS
  v_count INTEGER := 1;

  -- declare a nested table to store products
  v_nested_table_products t_nested_table_product :=
    t_nested_table_product();

  -- declare a type to represent a product record
  TYPE t_product_record IS RECORD (
    product_id INTEGER,
    name VARCHAR2(15),
    quantity INTEGER
  );
```

```
  -- declare a REF CURSOR type to point to product records
  TYPE t_product_cursor IS REF CURSOR RETURN t_product_record;

  -- declare a cursor
  v_product_cursor t_product_cursor;

  -- declare a variable to store a product record
  v_product t_product_record;
BEGIN
  -- open v_product_cursor to read the product_id, name, and quantity for
  -- each product stored in the XML of the xml_purchase_order column
  -- in the purchase_order table
  OPEN v_product_cursor FOR
  SELECT
    EXTRACTVALUE(product.COLUMN_VALUE, '/product/product_id')
      AS product_id,
    EXTRACTVALUE(product.COLUMN_VALUE, '/product/name') AS name,
    EXTRACTVALUE(product.COLUMN_VALUE, '/product/quantity') AS quantity
  FROM TABLE(
    SELECT
      XMLSEQUENCE(EXTRACT(xml_purchase_order, '/purchase_order//product'))
    FROM purchase_order
    WHERE purchase_order_id = p_purchase_order_id
  ) product;

  -- loop over the contents of v_product_cursor
  LOOP
    -- fetch the product records from v_product_cursor and exit when there
    -- are no more records found
    FETCH v_product_cursor INTO v_product;
    EXIT WHEN v_product_cursor%NOTFOUND;

    -- extend v_nested_table_products so that a product can be stored in it
    v_nested_table_products.EXTEND;

    -- create a new product and store it in v_nested_table_products
    v_nested_table_products(v_count) :=
      t_product(v_product.product_id, v_product.name, v_product.quantity);

    -- display the new product stored in v_nested_table_products
    DBMS_OUTPUT.PUT_LINE('product_id = ' ||
      v_nested_table_products(v_count).product_id);
    DBMS_OUTPUT.PUT_LINE('name = ' ||
      v_nested_table_products(v_count).name);
    DBMS_OUTPUT.PUT_LINE('quantity = ' ||
      v_nested_table_products(v_count).quantity);

    -- increment v_count ready for the next iteration of the loop
    v_count := v_count + 1;
  END LOOP;

  -- close v_product_cursor
```

```
    CLOSE v_product_cursor;

    -- update the purchase_order table using the values extracted from the
    -- XML stored in the xml_purchase_order column (the products nested
    -- table is set to v_nested_table_products already populated by the
    -- previous loop)
    UPDATE purchase_order
    SET
      customer_order_id =
        EXTRACTVALUE(xml_purchase_order,
          '/purchase_order/customer_order_id'),
      order_date =
        TO_DATE(EXTRACTVALUE(xml_purchase_order,
          '/purchase_order/order_date'), 'YYYY-MM-DD'),
      customer_name =
        EXTRACTVALUE(xml_purchase_order, '/purchase_order/customer_name'),
      street =
        EXTRACTVALUE(xml_purchase_order, '/purchase_order/street'),
      city =
        EXTRACTVALUE(xml_purchase_order, '/purchase_order/city'),
      state =
        EXTRACTVALUE(xml_purchase_order, '/purchase_order/state'),
      zip =
        EXTRACTVALUE(xml_purchase_order, '/purchase_order/zip'),
      phone_number =
        EXTRACTVALUE(xml_purchase_order, '/purchase_order/phone_number'),
      products = v_nested_table_products
    WHERE purchase_order_id = p_purchase_order_id;

    -- commit the transaction
    COMMIT;
END update_purchase_order;
/
```

The following example sets the server output on and calls update_purchase_order() to update purchase order #1:

```
SET SERVEROUTPUT ON
CALL update_purchase_order(1);
product_id = 1
name = Supernova video
quantity = 5
product_id = 2
name = Oracle SQL book
quantity = 4
```

The following query retrieves the columns from purchase order #1:

```
SELECT purchase_order_id, customer_order_id, order_date, customer_name,
  street, city, state, zip, phone_number, products
FROM purchase_order
```

```
WHERE purchase_order_id = 1;

PURCHASE_ORDER_ID CUSTOMER_ORDER_ID  ORDER_DAT  CUSTOMER_NAME
----------------- -----------------  ---------  ----------------------
STREET          CITY            ST  ZIP    PHONE_NUMBER
--------------- --------------- --  -----  ------------
PRODUCTS(PRODUCT_ID, NAME, QUANTITY)
------------------------------------
                1                  176  17-MAY-07  Best Products 456 Inc.
10 Any Street   Any City        CA  94440  555-121-1234
T_NESTED_TABLE_PRODUCT(
 T_PRODUCT(1, 'Supernova video', 5),
 T_PRODUCT(2, 'Oracle SQL book', 4)
)
```

The `products` nested table contains the same data as stored in the XML product elements in the `xml_purchase_order` column. I've added some line breaks to separate the products in the example's results to make them easier to see.

Summary

In this chapter, you have learned

- How to generate XML from relational data.

- How to save XML in the database and subsequently read that XML to update relational columns.

This short chapter has barely scratched the surface of the rich XML functionality available in the Oracle database. You can find more information in the *Oracle XML Developer's Kit* and the *Oracle XML DB Developer's Guide*, both published by Oracle Corporation.

Apart from the final appendix, this is the end of this book. I hope you've found the book informative and useful, and that I've held your interest!

APPENDIX

Oracle Data Types

his appendix contains two tables documenting the data types that are available in Oracle SQL and that may be used to define columns in a table, along with the additional types supported by Oracle PL/SQL.

Oracle SQL Types

Table A-1 shows the Oracle SQL types.

Type	Description
CHAR[(*length* [BYTE | CHAR])][1]	Fixed-length character data of *length* bytes or characters and padded with trailing spaces. Maximum length is 2,000 bytes.
VARCHAR2(*length* [BYTE | CHAR])[1]	Variable-length character data of up to *length* bytes or characters. Maximum length is 4,000 bytes.
NCHAR[(*length*)]	Fixed-length Unicode character data of *length* characters. Number of bytes stored is 2 multiplied by *length* for AL16UTF16 encoding and 3 multiplied by *length* for UTF8 encoding. Maximum length is 2,000 bytes.
NVARCHAR2(*length*)	Variable-length Unicode character data of *length* characters. Number of bytes stored is 2 multiplied by *length* for AL16UTF16 encoding and 3 multiplied by *length* for UTF8 encoding. Maximum length is 4,000 bytes.
BINARY_FLOAT	Introduced in Oracle Database 10*g*, stores a single-precision 32-bit floating-point number. Operations involving BINARY_FLOAT are typically performed faster than operations using NUMBER values. BINARY_FLOAT requires 5 bytes of storage space.
BINARY_DOUBLE	Introduced in Oracle Database 10*g*, stores a double-precision 64-bit floating-point number. Operations involving BINARY_DOUBLE are typically performed faster than operations using NUMBER values. BINARY_DOUBLE requires 9 bytes of storage space.
NUMBER(*precision*, *scale*) and NUMERIC(*precision*, *scale*)	Variable-length number; *precision* is the maximum number of digits (left and right of a decimal point, if used) that may be used for the number. The maximum precision supported is 38; *scale* is the maximum number of digits to the right of a decimal point (if used). If neither *precision* nor *scale* is specified, then a number with up to a precision and scale of 38 digits may be supplied (meaning you can supply a number with up to 38 digits, and any of those 38 digits may be right or left of the decimal point).
DEC and DECIMAL	Subtype of NUMBER. A fixed-point decimal number with up to 38 digits of decimal precision.
DOUBLE PRECISION and FLOAT	Subtype of NUMBER. A floating-point number with up to 38 digits of precision.
REAL	Subtype of NUMBER. A floating-point number with up to 18 digits of precision.
INT, INTEGER, and SMALLINT	Subtype of NUMBER. An integer with up to 38 digits of decimal precision.
DATE	Date and time with the century; all four digits of year, month, day, hour (in 24-hour format), minute, and second. May be used to store a date and time between January 1, 4712 B.C. and December 31, 4712 A.D. Default format is specified by the NLS_DATE_FORMAT database parameter (for example: DD-MON-RR).
INTERVAL YEAR[(*years_precision*)] TO MONTH	Time interval measured in years and months; *years_precision* specifies the precision for the years, which may be an integer from 0 to 9 (default is 2). Can be used to represent a positive or negative time interval.

TABLE A-1   *Oracle SQL Types*

Type	Description
INTERVAL DAY[(*days_precision*)] TO SECOND[(*seconds_precision*)]	Time interval measured in days and seconds; *days_precision* specifies the precision for the days, which is an integer from 0 to 9 (default is 2); *seconds_precision* specifies the precision for the fractional part of the seconds, which is an integer from 0 to 9 (default is 6). Can be used to represent a positive or negative time interval.
TIMESTAMP[(*seconds_precision*)]	Date and time with the century; all four digits of year, month, day, hour (in 24-hour format), minute, and second; *seconds_precision* specifies the number of digits for the fractional part of the seconds, which can be an integer from 0 to 9 (default is 6). Default format is specified by the NLS_TIMESTAMP_FORMAT database parameter.
TIMESTAMP[(*seconds_precision*)] WITH TIME ZONE	Extends TIMESTAMP to store a time zone. The time zone can be an offset from UTC, such as -8:0, or a region name, such as US/Pacific or PST. Default format is specified by the NLS_TIMESTAMP_TZ_FORMAT database parameter.
TIMESTAMP[(*seconds_precision*)] WITH LOCAL TIME ZONE	Extends TIMESTAMP to convert a supplied datetime to the local time zone set for the database. The process of conversion is known as *normalizing* the datetime. Default format is specified by the NLS_TIMESTAMP_FORMAT database parameter.
CLOB	Variable-length single-byte character data of up to 128 terabytes.
NCLOB	Variable-length Unicode national character set data of up to 128 terabytes.
BLOB	Variable-length binary data of up to 128 terabytes.
BFILE	Pointer to an external file. The external file is not stored in the database.
LONG	Variable-length character data of up to 2 gigabytes. Superseded by the CLOB and NCLOB types, but supported for backwards compatibility.
RAW(*length*)	Variable-length binary data of up to *length* bytes. Maximum length is 2,000 bytes. Superseded by the BLOB type, but supported for backwards compatibility.
LONG RAW	Variable-length binary data of up to 2 gigabytes. Superseded by the BLOB type but supported for backwards compatibility.
ROWID	Hexadecimal string used to represent a row address.
UROWID[(*length*)]	Hexadecimal string representing the logical address of a row of an index-organized table; *length* specifies the number of bytes. Maximum length is 4,000 bytes (also the default length if none is specified).
REF object_type	Reference to an object type. Similar to a pointer in the C++ programming language.
VARRAY	Variable-length array. This is a composite type and stores an ordered set of elements.
NESTED TABLE	Nested table. This is a composite type and stores an unordered set of elements.
XMLType	Stores XML data.
User defined object type	You can define your own object type and create objects of that type. See Chapter 12 for details.

[1]The BYTE and CHAR keywords work only with Oracle Database 9*i* and above. If neither BYTE nor CHAR is specified, the default is BYTE.

TABLE A-1 *Oracle SQL Types* (continued)

Oracle PL/SQL Types

Oracle PL/SQL supports all the types previously shown in Table A-1, plus the following additional Oracle PL/SQL specific types shown in Table A-2.

Type	Description
BOOLEAN	Boolean value (TRUE, FALSE, or NULL).
BINARY_INTEGER	Integer between -2^{31} (–2,147,483,648) and 2^{31} (2,147,483,648).
NATURAL	Subtype of BINARY_INTEGER. A non-negative integer.
NATURALN	Subtype of BINARY_INTEGER. A non-negative integer (cannot be NULL).
POSITIVE	Subtype of BINARY_INTEGER. A positive integer.
POSITIVEN	Subtype of BINARY_INTEGER. A positive integer (cannot be NULL).
SIGNTYPE	Subtype of BINARY_INTEGER. An integer set to –1, 0, or 1.
PLS_INTEGER	Integer between -2^{31} (–2,147,483,648) and 2^{31} (2,147,483,648). Identical to BINARY_INTEGER.
SIMPLE_INTEGER	New for Oracle Database 11*g*, SIMPLE_INTEGER is a subtype of BINARY_INTEGER. SIMPLE_INTEGER can store the same range of values as BINARY_INTEGER, except for NULL values, which cannot be stored in a SIMPLE_INTEGER. Also, arithmetic overflow does not cause an error when using SIMPLE_INTEGER values; instead, the result is simply truncated.
STRING	Same as VARCHAR2.
RECORD	Composite of a group of other types. Similar to a structure in the C++ programming language.
REF CURSOR	Pointer to a set of rows.

TABLE A-2 *Oracle PL/SQL Types*

Index

GET YOUR **FREE SUBSCRIPTION**
TO ORACLE MAGAZINE

Oracle Magazine is essential gear for today's information technology professionals. Stay informed and increase your productivity with every issue of *Oracle Magazine*. Inside each free bimonthly issue you'll get:

IF THERE ARE OTHER ORACLE USERS AT YOUR LOCATION WHO WOULD LIKE TO RECEIVE THEIR OWN SUB-SCRIPTION TO ORACLE MAGAZINE, PLEASE PHOTOCOPY THIS FORM AND PASS IT ALONG.

ORACLE
M A G A Z I N E

- Up-to-date information on Oracle Database, Oracle Application Server, Web development, enterprise grid computing, database technology, and business trends

- Third-party vendor news and announcements

- Technical articles on Oracle and partner products, technologies, and operating environments

- Development and administration tips

- Real-world customer stories

Three easy ways to subscribe:

① Web
Visit our Web site at otn.oracle.com/oraclemagazine.
You'll find a subscription form there, plus much more!

② Fax
Complete the questionnaire on the back of this card
and fax the questionnaire side only to +1.847.763.9638.

③ Mail
Complete the questionnaire on the back of this card
and mail it to P.O. Box 1263, Skokie, IL 60076-8263

FREE SUBSCRIPTION

○ **Yes, please send me a FREE subscription to *Oracle Magazine*.**   ○ **NO**

To receive a free subscription to *Oracle Magazine*, you must fill out the entire card, sign it, and date it (incomplete cards cannot be processed or acknowledged). You can also fax your application to +1.847.763.9638.
Or subscribe at our Web site at otn.oracle.com/oraclemagazine

○ From time to time, Oracle Publishing allows our partners exclusive access to our e-mail addresses for special promotions and announcements. To be included in this program, please check this circle.

○ Oracle Publishing allows sharing of our mailing list with selected third parties. If you prefer your mailing address not to be included in this program, please check here. If at any time you would like to be removed from this mailing list, please contact Customer Service at +1.847.647.9630 or send an e-mail to oracle@halldata.com.

signature (required)   date

X

name   title

company   e-mail address

street/p.o. box

city/state/zip or postal code   telephone

country   fax

YOU MUST ANSWER ALL TEN QUESTIONS BELOW.

① WHAT IS THE PRIMARY BUSINESS ACTIVITY OF YOUR FIRM AT THIS LOCATION? (check one only)
- ☐ 01 Aerospace and Defense Manufacturing
- ☐ 02 Application Service Provider
- ☐ 03 Automotive Manufacturing
- ☐ 04 Chemicals, Oil and Gas
- ☐ 05 Communications and Media
- ☐ 06 Construction/Engineering
- ☐ 07 Consumer Sector/Consumer Packaged Goods
- ☐ 08 Education
- ☐ 09 Financial Services/Insurance
- ☐ 10 Government (civil)
- ☐ 11 Government (military)
- ☐ 12 Healthcare
- ☐ 13 High Technology Manufacturing, OEM
- ☐ 14 Integrated Software Vendor
- ☐ 15 Life Sciences (Biotech, Pharmaceuticals)
- ☐ 16 Mining
- ☐ 17 Retail/Wholesale/Distribution
- ☐ 18 Systems Integrator, VAR/VAD
- ☐ 19 Telecommunications
- ☐ 20 Travel and Transportation
- ☐ 21 Utilities (electric, gas, sanitation, water)
- ☐ 98 Other Business and Services

② WHICH OF THE FOLLOWING BEST DESCRIBES YOUR PRIMARY JOB FUNCTION? (check one only)
Corporate Management/Staff
- ☐ 01 Executive Management (President, Chair, CEO, CFO, Owner, Partner, Principal)
- ☐ 02 Finance/Administrative Management (VP/Director/ Manager/Controller, Purchasing, Administration)
- ☐ 03 Sales/Marketing Management (VP/Director/Manager)
- ☐ 04 Computer Systems/Operations Management (CIO/VP/Director/ Manager MIS, Operations)
IS/IT Staff
- ☐ 05 Systems Development/ Programming Management
- ☐ 06 Systems Development/ Programming Staff
- ☐ 07 Consulting
- ☐ 08 DBA/Systems Administrator
- ☐ 09 Education/Training
- ☐ 10 Technical Support Director/Manager
- ☐ 11 Other Technical Management/Staff
- ☐ 98 Other

③ WHAT IS YOUR CURRENT PRIMARY OPERATING PLATFORM? (select all that apply)
- ☐ 01 Digital Equipment UNIX
- ☐ 02 Digital Equipment VAX VMS
- ☐ 03 HP UNIX

- ☐ 04 IBM AIX
- ☐ 05 IBM UNIX
- ☐ 06 Java
- ☐ 07 Linux
- ☐ 08 Macintosh
- ☐ 09 MS-DOS
- ☐ 10 MVS
- ☐ 11 NetWare
- ☐ 12 Network Computing
- ☐ 13 OpenVMS
- ☐ 14 SCO UNIX
- ☐ 15 Sequent DYNIX/ptx
- ☐ 16 Sun Solaris/SunOS
- ☐ 17 SVR4
- ☐ 18 UnixWare
- ☐ 19 Windows
- ☐ 20 Windows NT
- ☐ 21 Other UNIX
- ☐ 98 Other
- 99 ☐ None of the above

④ DO YOU EVALUATE, SPECIFY, RECOMMEND, OR AUTHORIZE THE PURCHASE OF ANY OF THE FOLLOWING? (check all that apply)
- ☐ 01 Hardware
- ☐ 02 Software
- ☐ 03 Application Development Tools
- ☐ 04 Database Products
- ☐ 05 Internet or Intranet Products
- 99 ☐ None of the above

⑤ IN YOUR JOB, DO YOU USE OR PLAN TO PURCHASE ANY OF THE FOLLOWING PRODUCTS? (check all that apply)
Software
- ☐ 01 Business Graphics
- ☐ 02 CAD/CAE/CAM
- ☐ 03 CASE
- ☐ 04 Communications
- ☐ 05 Database Management
- ☐ 06 File Management
- ☐ 07 Finance
- ☐ 08 Java
- ☐ 09 Materials Resource Planning
- ☐ 10 Multimedia Authoring
- ☐ 11 Networking
- ☐ 12 Office Automation
- ☐ 13 Order Entry/Inventory Control
- ☐ 14 Programming
- ☐ 15 Project Management
- ☐ 16 Scientific and Engineering
- ☐ 17 Spreadsheets
- ☐ 18 Systems Management
- ☐ 19 Workflow

Hardware
- ☐ 20 Macintosh
- ☐ 21 Mainframe
- ☐ 22 Massively Parallel Processing
- ☐ 23 Minicomputer
- ☐ 24 PC
- ☐ 25 Network Computer
- ☐ 26 Symmetric Multiprocessing
- ☐ 27 Workstation
Peripherals
- ☐ 28 Bridges/Routers/Hubs/Gateways
- ☐ 29 CD-ROM Drives
- ☐ 30 Disk Drives/Subsystems
- ☐ 31 Modems
- ☐ 32 Tape Drives/Subsystems
- ☐ 33 Video Boards/Multimedia
Services
- ☐ 34 Application Service Provider
- ☐ 35 Consulting
- ☐ 36 Education/Training
- ☐ 37 Maintenance
- ☐ 38 Online Database Services
- ☐ 39 Support
- ☐ 40 Technology-Based Training
- ☐ 98 Other
- 99 ☐ None of the above

⑥ WHAT ORACLE PRODUCTS ARE IN USE AT YOUR SITE? (check all that apply)
Oracle E-Business Suite
- ☐ 01 Oracle Marketing
- ☐ 02 Oracle Sales
- ☐ 03 Oracle Order Fulfillment
- ☐ 04 Oracle Supply Chain Management
- ☐ 05 Oracle Procurement
- ☐ 06 Oracle Manufacturing
- ☐ 07 Oracle Maintenance Management
- ☐ 08 Oracle Service
- ☐ 09 Oracle Contracts
- ☐ 10 Oracle Projects
- ☐ 11 Oracle Financials
- ☐ 12 Oracle Human Resources
- ☐ 13 Oracle Interaction Center
- ☐ 14 Oracle Communications/Utilities (modules)
- ☐ 15 Oracle Public Sector/University (modules)
- ☐ 16 Oracle Financial Services (modules)
Server/Software
- ☐ 17 Oracle9i
- ☐ 18 Oracle9i Lite
- ☐ 19 Oracle8i
- ☐ 20 Other Oracle database
- ☐ 21 Oracle9i Application Server
- ☐ 22 Oracle9i Application Server Wireless
- ☐ 23 Oracle Small Business Suite

Tools
- ☐ 24 Oracle Developer Suite
- ☐ 25 Oracle Discoverer
- ☐ 26 Oracle JDeveloper
- ☐ 27 Oracle Migration Workbench
- ☐ 28 Oracle9i AS Portal
- ☐ 29 Oracle Warehouse Builder
Oracle Services
- ☐ 30 Oracle Outsourcing
- ☐ 31 Oracle Consulting
- ☐ 32 Oracle Education
- ☐ 33 Oracle Support
- ☐ 98 Other
- 99 ☐ None of the above

⑦ WHAT OTHER DATABASE PRODUCTS ARE IN USE AT YOUR SITE? (check all that apply)
- ☐ 01 Access
- ☐ 02 Baan
- ☐ 03 dbase
- ☐ 04 Gupta
- ☐ 05 IBM DB2
- ☐ 06 Informix
- ☐ 07 Ingres
- ☐ 98 Other
- 99 ☐ None of the above
- ☐ 08 Microsoft Access
- ☐ 09 Microsoft SQL Server
- ☐ 10 PeopleSoft
- ☐ 11 Progress
- ☐ 12 SAP
- ☐ 13 Sybase
- ☐ 14 VSAM

⑧ WHAT OTHER APPLICATION SERVER PRODUCTS ARE IN USE AT YOUR SITE? (check all that apply)
- ☐ 01 BEA
- ☐ 02 IBM
- ☐ 03 Sybase
- ☐ 04 Sun
- ☐ 05 Other

⑨ DURING THE NEXT 12 MONTHS, HOW MUCH DO YOU ANTICIPATE YOUR ORGANIZATION WILL SPEND ON COMPUTER HARDWARE, SOFTWARE, PERIPHERALS, AND SERVICES FOR YOUR LOCATION? (check only one)
- ☐ 01 Less than $10,000
- ☐ 02 $10,000 to $49,999
- ☐ 03 $50,000 to $99,999
- ☐ 04 $100,000 to $499,999
- ☐ 05 $500,000 to $999,999
- ☐ 06 $1,000,000 and over

⑩ WHAT IS YOUR COMPANY'S YEARLY SALES REVENUE? (please choose one)
- ☐ 01 $500, 000, 000 and above
- ☐ 02 $100, 000, 000 to $500, 000, 000
- ☐ 03 $50, 000, 000 to $100, 000, 000
- ☐ 04 $5, 000, 000 to $50, 000, 000
- ☐ 05 $1, 000, 000 to $5, 000, 000

100103